THE CENTURY PSYCHOLOGY SERIES

Richard M. Elliott, *Editor*

Developmental
PSYCHOLOGY

THE CENTURY PSYCHOLOGY SERIES

Edited by
RICHARD M. ELLIOTT, Ph.D., *University of Minnesota*

Developmental
PSYCHOLOGY

AN INTRODUCTION TO THE
STUDY OF HUMAN BEHAVIOR

by

Florence L. Goodenough

Professor, Institute of Child Welfare
University of Minnesota

SECOND EDITION

D. APPLETON-CENTURY COMPANY
Incorporated

NEW YORK   LONDON

Growth may be conceived as the creative function of the nervous system, not only with regard to the form of the behavior pattern but also with regard to its control. The creative component of thought, upon this hypothesis, is growth.

Man is more than the sum of his reflexes, instincts, and immediate reactions of all sorts. He is all these, plus his creative potential for the future.... The real measure of the individual, accordingly, whether lower animal or man, must include the element of growth as a creative power. Man is indeed a mechanism, but he is a mechanism which, within his limitations of life, sensitivity, and growth, is creating and operating himself.—From G. E. COGHILL, *Anatomy and the Problems of Behavior* (Cambridge: The University Press, 1929).

Preface to the Second Edition

For many years I have felt that no sound understanding of human or animal behavior can be had without reference to its beginnings, its course of development, and the factors by which that course is influenced. Man does not come into the world full grown. His talents do not originate in the psychological laboratory, even though they may there be first reduced to quotients and deciles. Behavior is quite as much a matter of growth as is stature. Its qualitative variants and their permutations and combinations are beyond human reckoning; yet their organization and patterning is at all times unitary and coherent. But because of these multiple aspects, it is easy to lose sight of the individual in our concern with his reactions. We reify man's "traits," and in so doing we forget the man. The cordial reception given to the first edition of this book has encouraged me to think that the concept of psychology as the study of the growing and changing reactions of human beings throughout the life span provides a framework within which the established principles of human behavior can be presented in a dynamic and meaningful way. Because the ghost of faculty psychology is hard to exorcise, it becomes essential for students to realize from the start that the fundamental behaviorial unit is not a depersonalized trait but a living individual.

Like the first edition, the present volume is intended as a basic text for the first course in psychology. The content has been thoroughly revised, and a number of new features have been added. Although the organization is in terms of a developmental sequence, examination of the *Index of Subjects* will show that most, if not all, of the major topics of the conventional elementary course in psychology have been included, in spite of the different arrangement. In addition, a number of subjects not usually taken up in the elementary course but of practical import for everyday living are discussed in the belief that students will gain most value from their first contact with psychology if they are enabled to see how the knowledge thus gained may be applied to the

vii

real world of human affairs. For this reason the possibility of utilizing psychological principles for the furtherance of happier and more effective living has been stressed throughout the book.

Attention may perhaps be called to two special features of this volume that differ from the usual plan of the conventional text-book. The first is the list of questions placed at the beginning of each chapter rather than in the more usual position at the end of the chapter. This was done as a means of orienting the student in his reading. The questions are designed to stimulate an attitude of intelligent inquiry, even though the topic is unfamiliar. Students should be advised to go over the questions carefully before beginning each chapter and to keep them in mind as they read. Although not designed as tests of the student's knowledge, the questions will also be useful guides in reviewing the field.

In place of the usual list of selected references, at the end of each chapter will be found a brief description of a single book or a fairly complete outline of a class experiment dealing with one of the topics covered in the chapter. It has been my experience that undergraduate students make little use of the long lists of references so painfully collated by the authors of college text-books. The bare citation of titles has an uninviting appearance, and the very length of these lists is likely to defeat its own purpose, since, in the manifest impossibility of reading all, the problem of choice becomes both baffling and discouraging to the novice. It is hoped that the present plan of naming only a single book on each topic and recommending that with more vigor than is expended in merely mentioning its title may encourage students to do at least a moderate amount of collateral reading in addition to the text-book. Instructors will find it desirable to request the college library to see that copies of these books are made available to students. If there is a separate departmental library, a special shelf may well be allotted to that purpose.

In conclusion, I should like to express my gratitude to my many friends and colleagues whose comments and suggestions regarding the first edition have been of much help in preparing the revision. My thanks also go to the authors and publishers who have kindly permitted the reproduction of figures or the quotation of selected excerpts from their works.

F. L. G.

Contents

PART I

Principles and Methods of Modern Psychology

Chapter I. PSYCHOLOGY: THE STUDY OF HUMAN DEVELOPMENT

Why do people differ?—Growth is more than an increase in size—The relationship of experience to growth—What is meant by "environment"?—The growth of meaning—Psychology, the study of the development of human behavior .   3

Chapter II. PROBLEMS AND METHODS OF MODERN PSYCHOLOGY

The field of psychology—Changing points of view—How psychology secures its facts—Methods of improving the accuracy of psychological observation and of reducing the likelihood of error in interpreting the subject's responses .   20

PART II

The Child's Equipment for Living

Chapter III. OUR HEREDITARY BACKGROUND

How does human life begin?—What is given by heredity?—The physical basis of heredity—The determination of sex—Sex-linked traits—The protective effect of biparental heredity—Mutation: the mechanism by which new traits appear—

Chapter IV. PRENATAL DEVELOPMENT

Chapter V. THE CHILD AT BIRTH

Chapter VI. HOW ACTIVITY IS AROUSED

Chapter VII. HOW ACTIVITY IS PATTERNED

PART III

The Normal Course of Human Development

Chapter VIII. THE PERIOD BEFORE SPEECH: I. BASIC DRIVES AND EMOTIONAL REACTIONS

Chapter XVIII. ADOLESCENCE

Chapter XIX. THE COLLEGE YEARS

Chapter XX. MATURITY

Chapter XXI. THE INDIVIDUAL AT WORK

Chapter XXII. THE MATURATION AND DECLINE OF ABILITIES

Chapter XXIII. OLD AGE

PART IV

Personality Deviations

PART V

The Mental Hygiene of Development

Chapter XXIX. INCREASING HAPPINESS AND EFFICIENCY
IN THE ADULT

Chapter XXX. A BACKWARD LOOK WITH THOUGHTS
FOR THE FUTURE

List of Figures

List of Tables

PART I
Principles and Methods of Modern Psychology

Chapter I

PSYCHOLOGY: THE STUDY OF HUMAN DEVELOPMENT

Why do different people behave so differently under the same conditions?

How does age affect behavior?

In the same situation, why do not all persons have the same or similar experiences?

How do objects or situations take on meaning for us?

With what is the study of psychology chiefly concerned?

WHY DO PEOPLE DIFFER?

Modern psychology is founded on experiment. The psychologist of a century ago hoped to learn how the human mind worked by sitting quietly in his arm-chair and, as an irreverent student once put it, "listening to hear himself tick." But the introspective method, which is the scientific name for the study of mental activity by means of self-observation, is no longer looked upon with much favor. Nowadays when we wish to learn how human beings think and act, we set them a problem to do and then record what happens. So your introduction to this fascinating subject of human behavior will be made by way of an experiment. Get a pencil and sheet of paper. Are you ready? Then turn to Figure 1 on page 5.

Here you have a series of six ink blots. Most people find that each of these blots reminds them of something—an animal, perhaps, or a person doing something, or it may be a bird or a flower or something quite different from any of these. Look at each blot and write down the first thing it suggests to you. Work quickly and be sure to put down your *first* association for each blot.

Now show the page to some of your acquaintances and have them write their impressions. How many of them agree with yours?

Look at the blots again, more carefully this time. See how many different things you can see in each. Turn the page to different positions so as to get as many different associations as possible. Have your friends do the same and once more compare results.

This simple experiment affords a nice illustration of the fact that every one lives in a perceptual world of his own that is to some extent different from all other worlds. No two people interpret what they see in exactly the same way. Yet the external facts remain the same; the differences, evidently, are in the people who deal with these facts. Because people differ from each other, they regard the world from different points of view, and so the same facts take on different meanings for them. It is not surprising, then, that under the same external situations they often behave very differently.

The next time you go to the theater or to the movies, notice how the other members of the audience act. A joke is told. Most of the people laugh, some merely smile, others look bored; a few, perhaps, make audible comments of a disparaging nature. Observe their postures. Unless the play is unusually thrilling, most people assume an attitude of easy attention, sitting well back in their chairs with muscles partially relaxed in a position calculated to combine an unobstructed view of the stage with a maximum of bodily comfort. If it is impossible to get a good view and at the same time sit comfortably, some content themselves with such glimpses as they can easily get while others continually twist and wriggle about in their efforts to see more. Some, regardless of the location of their seats, lean forward with set faces and tensed muscles; others loll back with half-closed eyes and seem hardly aware of what is going on. A parcel is dropped with a loud thud. Several persons start visibly, others crane their necks to see what happened, still others continue to watch the stage with no outward sign of distraction.

But these, you say, are only trifles. Turn, then, to matters of greater importance. Here are five men, each forty years old. As

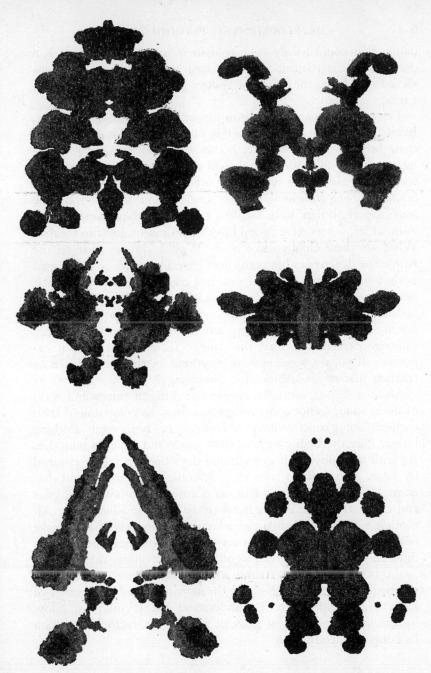

FIG. 1.—WHAT DO THESE BLOTS MAKE YOU THINK OF?

babies you could hardly have told them apart. To-day one is a distinguished statesman, another a farm laborer, the third a convicted murderer, the fourth a college professor, and the fifth a garbage collector.

Try to recall the children you played with at the age of eight. Even then, as you will recollect if your memory is fairly good, their behavior was not alike. Some were quick in their movements, others slow; some were fond of companionship and active sports, others were always slipping off by themselves with a book. Some did well in school, others poorly; some usually took the lead in play, others were satisfied to follow; some were always in mischief, others were "good boys" who rarely got into trouble. What are these children like now? Would you say that on the whole the differences between them have increased or diminished as they have grown older? If you had tried to predict from their behavior at the age of eight what they would be like at the present time, in how many cases would your guess have been approximately right? Are there any who have turned out very differently from the way that might formerly have been expected? If so, do you know of anything in their experience or training that might account for the change?

Abilities, habits, attitudes, ways of looking at things and ways of doing them do not come full-grown into the possession of their owners like garments bought from a ready-to-wear clothing house. Like the bodily organs, they grow and develop with age. As with the body, their growth and development are determined by laws. As yet these laws are not completely understood, but enough is known to show that, as is true of the laws of physics and chemistry, their action is relatively fixed and inevitable. Although we cannot change these laws, we can nevertheless make use of them if we learn what they are and how they operate. The differences, little and great, significant and trifling, that you see in the behavior of your friends and in yourself are not the result of chance but have come about through the combined action of growth and experience. To understand them you must know something of the laws of growth and of the factors by which its course in determined.

GROWTH IS MORE THAN AN INCREASE IN SIZE

All living beings grow. With this growth come changes, not only in size and appearance but in behavior. The baby does not look like a grown-up and he does not act like a grown-up.

He is different. We sometimes say of an acquaintance, "What a babyish face he has!" We do not mean that his face is small; it may even be larger than the average. But the contour of his features reminds us of a baby. Likewise, when we say that some adult is "acting like a baby" we do not necessarily mean that his behavior is simpler, more naïve, less elaborately organized than that of other adults. It is not simply a matter of doing less than we expect, but of doing something different.

Growth, whether physical or mental, is something more than a mere increase in size or an added ability to do things. The adult is not just a big baby, either in body or in mind. He has grown bigger, it is true, and his mental powers have improved. But he has also changed in many other ways that have nothing to do with size or with amount of ability. His bodily proportions have changed. His arms and legs make up a greater part of his body than they did in infancy; his head is smaller in proportion to his trunk. The composition of his bodily tissues has changed. His bones are becoming more brittle, his muscles less resilient. His features have become more clear-cut; the chin and lower jaw have increased in size and firmness. As age advances, the layer of fat directly underneath the skin gradually disappears, and wrinkles result.

Mental growth, like the growth of the body, is more than a gain in quantity. It is not just a matter of being able to do more things or of being able to do them better. It also involves changes in the way we think and act, in the emotions, interests, and desires that influence all our conduct. These changes are just as truly a part of mental growth as are gains in the ability to memorize, to form correct judgments, or to see relationships, and they merit quite a careful study.

THE RELATIONSHIP OF EXPERIENCE TO GROWTH

Picture to yourself a person reared from birth under conditions controlled by clockwork in such a way that all events in his world occur in a fixed order and nothing new ever takes place. Under these circumstances, would his experiences change from day to day and from year to year or would they be completely controlled by the revolutions of the clockwork?

Before trying to answer this question, think of another and a somewhat similar case. Suppose that a man, after having been totally blind and deaf from birth, were gradually to gain the power to hear and see. Every day, as his senses improved, he would be receiving new impressions, trying out new activities, forming new habits, acquiring new interests, gaining new experiences. Although to every one else his surroundings might remain exactly the same as they were before, to him they would be new and different each day. In like manner, the child reared under conditions of clocklike regularity would nevertheless be constantly finding out new things, having new experiences, as his developing abilities enabled him to respond to an increasing number of different factors or aspects of his environment in an ever greater number of different ways. It is hard to think of two sets of purely external conditions that could bring about differences in the behavior of two adults that can at all compare with the contrast between the behavior of a normal adult and a normal infant two weeks old in the same surroundings. Although we have no way of knowing just how the world "seems" to the baby, since he is unable to tell us about it, it would be a great mistake to suppose that objects look the same to him as they do to us, that sounds have the same meaning for him, or in short, that a given set of external conditions constitutes the same "environment" for the infant as for the adult.

The kind of thinking that ascribes to animals or children the same kind of mental processes, attitudes, motives, or desires that we as adults experience is known as *anthropomorphism*,[1] and it

---

[1] From the Greek *anthropos* ("man") and *morphe* ("form"); hence ascribing the form or characteristics of man to anything not human.

Strictly speaking, of course, children do not come under this category. Nevertheless, our interpretation of the behavior of infants who have not

has been responsible for many errors in psychological theory and practice. It is an error to which we are all particularly liable, just because we know ourselves so much more thoroughly than we know any one else. Our most common way of attempting to understand others is to "put ourselves in their place." Such a feat of legerdemain is difficult at best, and it may lead to the grossest of errors unless the abilities and limitations as well as the past experiences of the person in question are known and the effect of these abilities, limitations, and experiences upon the way the environment "seems" to him and upon his consequent reactions to it are understood. We have seen that even to grown people of very similar general background, the same ink-blots "look" very different. How much greater, then, must be the difference between the world of childhood and the world as it is known by adults! Yet every adult was once a child who lived in a child's world and behaved as a child does. The changes in his world did not occur all at once, nor without a reason. They took place gradually, and like a rear-view mirror they reflected the experiences through which he passed.

WHAT IS MEANT BY "ENVIRONMENT"?

So far we have been talking about the "environment" rather loosely. It is time now to attempt to get a clear idea of what environment really is, or perhaps we had better say, of the meaning that we shall attach to it in this book. By the environment of any person we mean whatever objects and events (whether they be material objects, happenings, relationships, actions of other people or what not) are present in his immediate neighborhood and to which *he is capable of responding in some way*. When looked at in this manner, it will be seen at once that environment cannot be thought of as something distinct and apart from the individual but rather as something highly dependent upon the individual, his interests, abilities, and past ex-

---

yet learned to speak is based upon almost exactly the same kind of evidence as is our interpretation of animal behavior. The hazards of ascribing to the infant or young child the same kind of motives, attitudes, and feelings as those with which we are familiar as adults are so great that the use of the term *anthropomorphic* in this connection is perhaps justified.

periences. A color-blind person has not the same enviroment as one with normal color vision, even though they share the same room. To the infant who has not yet learned to speak or to understand language it makes little difference whether the family spends its evenings reading Shakespeare aloud or in listening to the latest comic program over the radio. When the understanding is limited, the environment is also limited. As the mind grows, the environment broadens. The relationship is not perfect, because it is possible to rear a very able mind in a very limited environment or to provide an undeveloped mind with many or few situations to which it is able to respond. Nevertheless the association exists, and we cannot afford to ignore it.

A few of the modern psychologists, especially those who belong to what is known as the Gestalt school (a system of psychological theories about which we shall have more to say later on) go even further than this. They prefer not to speak of "environment" in an unqualified way at all. Instead they differentiate between two kinds of environment; the "physical environment" and the "psychological environment." The first is static. It is made up of all those features of the outside world about which there is well-nigh universal agreement. It includes houses, considered simply as buildings of certain shapes, sizes, and colors. It includes people, dogs, the wind, and the rain. It includes everything external to the person, whether he pays attention to it or not.

The psychological environment is very different. It includes only that portion of one's surroundings to which he is responding and its psychological character is inextricably bound up with his response; the one defines the other. The physical house is just a house, but the psychological house is, let us say, the house where I used to live and had many good times. That little tree at its side is the one my brother planted. Up there is the window of my old room. Surely no one can deny that this house is psychologically *not the same house* for me as it is for you who have never seen it before. You see in it many deficiencies that I overlook; I find beauties to which you are blind.

That it is the psychological, rather than the physical environment which is of real importance to the individual, I think we shall all agree. But since the difference between the two actually resides in the person who projects his own attitudes outward and ascribes them to the things of the outside world, we shall avoid some confusion of thought if, in place of the term *psychological environment* we make use of the simpler word, *meaning*. The physical features of the house of which we just spoke are much the same to both of us, but the house has a meaning for me that it does not have for you.

THE GROWTH OF MEANING

With added experience the environment takes on enriched meaning. Let us return to our hypothetical child reared by clockwork. At times he is fed, and certain events always immediately precede the feeding. It will not be long before these events, whatever they may be, come to stand apart from the rest of the series as something very special. No longer are they simply "a bright object before my eyes," "a warm touch on my cheek," but rather "the signs that my dinner is coming." Under the more variable conditions in which most children are reared, associations are formed somewhat more slowly than it is probable would be the case in such a constant situation as we have described; nevertheless there is enough similarity in the relationships between events from day to day to cause many associations to be formed at a very early age. Marquis [2] has shown that as early as the first week of life, infants whose feeding-time has always been preceded by the sound of an electric buzzer will show a decrease in general activity and will frequently open the mouth and make suckling movements when the buzzer is sounded. (See Figure 2.) By the age of a few weeks, most babies will stop crying momentarily when the mother approaches the crib, or even at the sound of the mother's voice or footsteps. Later on, sounds linked together in certain ways become such perfect symbols of the objects or events we have learned to associate with them that they are actually used as convenient substitutes for the things themselves. When these sounds are uttered by human beings, we speak of them as "language." As far as our understanding of them is concerned, however, many other sounds have a language function

[2] D. P. Marquis, "Can Conditioned Responses Be Established in the Newborn Infant?" *J. Genet, Psychol.*, 1931, 39: 479-492.

for us. A whistle in the distance tells me that a train is passing; a series of caterwaulings under my window tells me that a cat-fight is in progress. These associations or "meanings" are built up in exactly the same way as the more simple forms by which the baby learns to connect certain events with his feeding-time. Nothing else in human experience, however, approaches human speech in the range and flexibility of the meanings that come to be associated with it.

It is to meanings and not to the simple sensory qualities which underlie them that we respond in our everyday behavior. That pattern of lights and shades I see over there, which I have learned to call a chair, is very much more than a visual pattern. It is a thing to be sat upon when I am tired, a thing to avoid when it gets in my way, a thing to be climbed upon when I wish to secure something beyond my reach. In a dim light I mistake it for a person, or for a large dog, and I greet it cheerfully or pat it on what I take to be its head. I smile at it when it recalls an absent friend; it brings tears to my eyes when I know that the friend who formerly sat there can never return. Is it the chair, con-sidered simply as a material object, that calls forth all these varied reactions on my part? Not at all. The chair remains the same, but its meaning varies, and it is the meaning that determines my be-havior. Like other aspects of mental life, meanings, too, grow and change with advancing age.

PSYCHOLOGY, THE STUDY OF THE DEVELOPMENT OF HUMAN BEHAVIOR

Psychology is sometimes defined as the study of mental activity and conduct. Modern psychology, however, is not content with the separate description of single activities, for events, however important in themselves, lose much of their meaning if considered apart from their normal surroundings and out of their natural sequence. Psychologists to-day are asking not only what a given form of behavior is like but how it came to be so and into what it is likely to develop later on. *Psychology is largely concerned with the study of the processes by which early potentialities interact with later experience to form new patterns of behavior, new ways of doing things.*

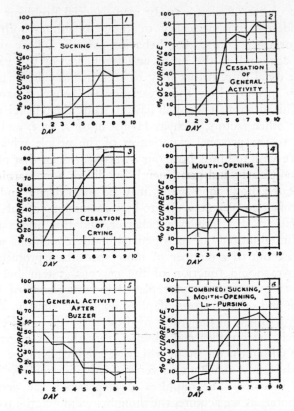

FIG. 2.—THE ESTABLISHMENT OF CONDITIONED RESPONSES IN
NEW-BORN INFANTS

This figure shows the day to day changes in response to the buzzer (p. 11)
in terms of the percentages of the total number of occasions that the behavior in question was observed. For example, the first curve shows that
while the sound of the buzzer did not arouse sucking movements on the
first day, an occasional instance of this response was seen on the second
and third days. After the third day, sucking in response to the buzzer occurred more and more frequently until by the seventh day the sound of
the buzzer elicited sucking movements on 45 per cent of all occasions. The
remaining curves are to be read in the same way. For a more complete discussion of the process of conditioning see Chapters VI-VII.

(From D. P. Marquis, "Can Conditioned Responses Be Established in the
Newborn Infant?" *J. Genet. Psychol.*, 1931, 39: 479-492. Courtesy of Clark
University Press.)

In the course of such a study many special problems have to be considered. It is necessary to know something both of the normal or usual course that behavior patterns follow with advancing age, and of the exent and frequency of the variations from the usual pattern that may be seen in individual cases. We need also to know how these variations in behavior have come about. This means that we shall have to study them in relationship to many other factors, such as family history, race, and sex, in addition to the personal experiences of the people who exhibit them. We wish to know how our own behavior or that of others can be most easily and permanently modified, how learning may be facilitated, how good habits may be formed and undesirable habits broken up. We need also to know something of the physiological factors that influence behavior, and this brings us to a consideration not only of such general bodily conditions as health and disease but to a number of more specialized problems such as the growth and function of the nervous system and of the various sense-organs, the part played by the glands of internal secretion, and other matters of physiological chemistry. And we should not forget, in the study of these relatively concrete matters which the outsider can observe, that there is a great deal going on within the organism which we are unable to see directly and for the study of which no very effective instruments have so far been invented. The impulses we experience, the desires we feel, the interests we acquire, the thoughts we think, the meanings that we ascribe to what goes on about us are just as integral parts of our lives and actions as the movements of our muscles. Probably if all were known we should find that every observable action has as its starting point some intra-organic change. To these changes we give the name of "mental activities"; sometimes for convenience we refer to them collectively as "mind." There is no sharp distinction between the mental and physical activity of a living organism. The mental activity, the change within the organism, is merely the first stage in a single event which may or may not terminate in an external movement that other people can see. We know a little more about our own mental activities than about those of other people, but it is a mistake to think that we know all there is to be known, even about our own. Of the physiological processes involved in these intra-organic changes we get no inkling either from trying to analyze our own thoughts and feelings or from observing the actions of other people. We know a little about *what* we think, but not much about *how* we think. We often misjudge our own motives. We do many things without knowing why. In reality, while it is true that every person knows a little more about his own mental activities than anybody else can know merely from watching how he moves his arms and legs and the other parts of his body, most of us flatter ourselves into thinking that we know our own minds a great deal better than we actually do.

At this stage we might easily become tangled up in a great deal of metaphysical discussion about the distinction between the mind and the body, but such a discussion would profit us little. The point of view we shall adopt here is that the organism acts as a whole,[3] but that it is sometimes desirable to study certain features of its behavior separately, just as we may examine the spark-plugs of an engine without paying much attention to the

[3] Of course this does not mean that every part of the organism is *overtly* concerned with the activity of every other part. I move my hands while my feet are quiet; my heart beats, and various other physiological processes go on while my body lies quiet in sleep. Nevertheless, these acts are not isolated from the rest of the body, though their relation is not always apparent. The movement of my hand uses up a small but measurable amount of the bodily store of nutriment which was available for any part that needed it, and the common reserve is thereby lessened by just that amount. On the psychological side, relationships between the active and passive parts of the body likewise exist, though they are not always easy to detect. During the early stages of healthy digestion when the smooth muscles of the stomach are active, the external muscles tend to become relaxed below their usual state of tension, and if the meal has been unusually hearty one may even find it difficult to avoid falling asleep. Those who doubt the psychological interdependence of the various parts of the organism may find it enlightening to try the old schoolboy trick of patting the head with one hand while rubbing the stomach with the other. Of course this can be learned, but the effort involved in learning it is testimony to the fact that human action is never truly part-action but always involves the total organism, even though nature or habit may have so freed an act from those connections that would interfere with the individual's effectiveness that it seems to be independent. We shall see later that one of the most important aspects of maturation consists in the growing independence of the actions of the various parts of the body from each other. But the independence is never complete. Always it is the organism and not merely one of its parts that initiates and controls behavior.

rest, although we know that the spark-plugs are not the whole of the engine. So, when we contrast mental activity with physical activity, we mean only that some of the changes which take place in the relationship of the organism to its environment can be observed by everybody, while others are known only to the organism within which they occur. Characteristically, these changes known only to the organism—the intra-organic changes— are the first stages in a given activity which, in many cases, though not always, is continued to a point at which it can be observed by others as well.

I find myself in need of a pencil. This involves some kind of an inner change from a state of indifference with reference to pencils to one of dissatisfaction [4] and tension. So far, no one except myself knows that anything has occurred, and even I do not know just what has happened in any physiological sense. All that I really know is that some kind of mildly disturbing change has taken place in me that experience has taught me can be relieved by going to get a pencil. Now if the activity spreads outward to include the muscles, if I get out of my chair where I have been sitting quietly all this time and go for the pencil, we call this final part of the activity a physical reaction because it is observable to others as well as to the subject himself. But the two are not really distinct; they are only earlier and later stages in a single act.

Note further that the mental part of the act might have occurred without the subsequent physical action. I might have felt a desire for the pencil without going to get it, in which case the desire would have been just as real (though perhaps we may raise a question as to its strength), but no one would have known about it except myself. Or the physical act might have taken a different form. Instead of going for the pencil myself, I might have asked some one to bring it to me. Again, the physical action may have had as its starting point something quite different from a desire to get the pencil. Getting the pencil may have been only an excuse. My real motive may have been to escape from a

---

[4] We do not know in what this change consists, but there is a good deal of evidence pointing to the conclusion that its major features occur somewhere within the outer gray portion or *cortex* of the two great lobes making up the upper forward portion of the brain which are called the *cerebral hemispheres* or, taken together, the *cerebrum*.

difficult social situation, or to secure a minute's respite from study. We cannot get a complete picture of an activity without knowing both the motive, which is its starting point, and the later stages, which may take the form of muscular action. Both are necessary for a complete psychological description.

As age advances and experience increases, both the internal and the external phases of activity are constantly changing. It is the aim of psychology to learn how these changes take place, how to predict them, and how, when possible, to control them. To do this we must begin early, for actions are not independent of each other but form a continuous series, the completion of one giving rise to the next. Nor are they independent of the growth of the organism, for acts that would be impossible at one stage emerge at later stages and exert new effects upon subsequent behavior. *The study of psychology may therefore be defined as the study of the development of activity, including both its internal and its external phases.*

TRY THESE EXPERIMENTS

Prepare a series of ink-blots like those shown in Figure 1. You can make these by putting a drop of ink on a sheet of ordinary typewriting paper, folding the paper across the drop, and rubbing the outside to spread the ink. Then unfold the paper and you will find that you have a symmetrical blot like those in Figure 1. Make from six to ten of these blots and mount each one on a separate card.[5] In showing the cards, give each subject two or three minutes' time in which to respond; show each card in each of the four possible orientations (each side successively becomes the bottom). Show the cards, one at a time, to a number of men and women of about the same age and educational training, taking each person individually so that his responses will not be heard by the others. Ask each one to name everything he sees in each blot. Record the responses and the time required for the subject to respond on a prepared form something like the one shown on page 18 in which the four orientations of each card are indicated as A, B, C, and D.

[5] As an alternative, the blots shown in Figure 1 may be used, though because of their small size they are somewhat less suitable. If used, they should be cut apart and mounted on separate cards, or else a cardboard screen should be prepared of such a size and shape that all the blots except the one to which the subject is responding can be concealed from view.

Subject's name.............. Age.... Sex....... Education............

Card # and orientation	Time required in minutes	Responses given
1 A		
1 B		
1 C		
1 D		
etc.		

1. Differences among individuals

    a. What is the largest number of different responses given by any one person? The smallest?

    b. Is there any single response given to a particular card by all of the subjects?

    c. Are there any consistent differences in the type of response given by the different subjects? (Consider here such things as the proportion of the total number of responses in which there was mention of animals, people, etc.)

2. Differences between the sexes

    a. Are there consistent differences between the sexes in the number of responses given?

    b. Are there differences in the kind of response? Can you think of any possible reasons for such differences?

3. Age differences. Obtain the same data for a group of children all of whom are of about the same age.

    a. Are there differences in the number of responses of children and adults of the same sex?

    b. Are there differences in the type of response given by children and adults of the same sex?

4. Age-sex differences. Determine the pattern of sex differences in the responses given by children. Is this the same pattern as that shown by the adults? If not, how is it different?

5. A series of ink-blots similar to these has been widely used as a measure of the "total personality." The method of scoring is very elaborate and much special training is needed in order to learn it. It is worth noting, however, particularly in view of what has been said about the "wholeness" of an organism's responses, that even from so apparently trivial a form of behavior as the kind of objects suggested by the shapes accidentally taken by a blot of ink dropped on paper, much can be inferred about a person by one who has learned to understand the signs.

Without this specialized training, any inferences you may be inclined to draw about the characteristics of the persons participating in your experiment must be made with extreme caution.

But it may be worth your while to look for any well-marked special tendencies, different from those given by the majority, that set off certain members of your group from the others, and to see whether anything that you may know about the personality or experiences of these persons seems likely to account for the differences noted.

Chapter II

PROBLEMS AND METHODS OF MODERN PSYCHOLOGY

With what kind of facts is psychology concerned?

How does it obtain these facts?

What are the advantages of experimentation in psychology?

What is meant by the "personal equation" in scientific work?

Why is a knowledge of this factor important?

THE FIELD OF PSYCHOLOGY

In the early stages of any science, a great deal of spadework has to be done in the way of describing, arranging, and classifying the material with which it deals. During this time there is likely to be some friendly wrangling among the workers about what kinds of material should be included, what names should be given it, whether this or that bit of data is significant or worthless.

Since psychology is so young a science, it is not surprising that up to the present time there has been much discussion among psychologists about what kind of facts should be regarded as suitable material for the psychologists to handle. The group of German psychologists led by Wundt were at first very insistent that the field of psychology stopped with the study of sensations and their attributes. They also held that the aim of psychology was to discover general principles and trends only, that it had no concern with the individual person as such, nor with questions about how differences between persons were brought about. In spite of Wundt's lack of sympathy with the problem, however, Cattell, who was one of the pioneers among American psychologists, began his work on individual differences while he was an assistant in Wundt's laboratory, and it is in large measure due to his efforts that the study of differences in the abilities and personality of individuals has become such an important part of psychology to-day.

But the rising interest in differences between people has in no way lessened the significance of knowing what principles hold good for people in general, and while it is true that there are many respects in which people differ, it is also true that there are many psychological laws that hold good for practically all normal persons. The following are just a few of them: To persons with normal color vision, red colors look darker and blues look lighter when seen in twilight than when viewed under full day light. Children become able to draw a circle from copy before they can make a square, and the square can be copied at a considerably earlier age than they can copy a diamond. Straight lines terminating in obtuse angles are judged to be longer than lines of the same length that terminate in acute angles. (See Figure 3.)

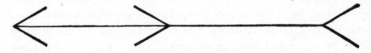

FIG. 3.—THE MÜLLER-LYER ILLUSION

The horizontal line on the left is the same length as the one on the right. If you don't believe it, measure them.

Psychology, therefore, is concerned with two kinds of knowledge: that which tells us *how people in general react to different kinds of stimulating conditions*, and that which has to do with *differences in the responses of individual persons when the external conditions remain the same.* Only a very narrow-minded person could insist that one of these is more important than the other. Both kinds of information are needed for the understanding of human behavior. Indeed, if you will turn back to pages 9-12 and read again what was said there about the nature of environment and its relationship to the characteristics of the individual, it should be clear that the differences between the two types of problem are often more apparent than real.

The following examples show how the two kinds of informa-

tion supplement each other. You will note that all have to do with
the same general topic and make use of the same experimental
set-up. The difference lies in the kind of problem that each is
designed to solve.

The ability to react quickly and correctly when a stimulus is
given is a matter of rather obvious practical import, and it has a
number of theoretical implications as well. Common observation
tells us that some people are quick to respond, whereas others
are slower, and it is reasonable to suppose that certain kinds of
stimuli are likely to evoke more rapid responses than others.
But these statements are too indefinite to be serviceable. Specifically, we need to know just what conditions make for speedy
reactions and what significance may be attached to individual
speed of response. Casual observation is not exact enough to answer these questions, but the laboratory has provided us with
information about some of them. For example, psychologists interested mainly in questions of the first type have conducted
experiments to find out whether people react more quickly to a
visual stimulus or to an auditory stimulus. The usual method of
conducting the experiment is to have the subject seated comfortably at a table with his finger resting on a telegraph key
which is connected with an electrical timer that records time in
small fractions of a second. In the experiments on visual reaction
time he is told to watch for a light that will appear at a specified
point and to press the key the instant he sees the light. In the
experiments on auditory reaction, the instructions are the same
except that he is told to listen for a specified sound. Both the
giving of the stimulus and the recording of the response are
mechanically controlled.

This experiment has been tried many times by different investigators and always with the same result: the response to the
auditory stimulus will be decidedly more prompt than that to the
visual stimulus. The time required for response to a touch on
the skin is about the same or perhaps a trifle slower than that
required for an auditory stimulus, and the responses to taste and
smell are the slowest of all.

Whatever the sense-organs stimulated, there is a direct relationship between the intensity of the stimulus and the speed of the

response. A loud sound or a bright light will induce a quicker response than will a faint sound or a dim light.[1]

There are other changes in the conditions of experiment that affect the speed of reaction. A Danish psychologist, Lange, about whom we shall have more to say later on, is credited with having been the first one to point out (in 1888) that if the instructions are given to the subject in such a way as to lead him to direct his efforts chiefly upon watching for the stimulus, his responses will be slower than if he fixes his attention upon the part of his body that is to make the response. The first is usually spoken of as the *sensorial reaction* because the attention is fixed upon the stimulus that affects the sense organ; the second is known as the *muscular reaction.*

Other psychologists have studied the question of reaction time from a different point of view. Their interest has centered around the reacting individuals, rather than the conditions of reaction. Some people, they found, were consistently slow in their reactions, others quick, and still others were variable, reacting now quickly, now slowly, and never seeming to settle down to a reasonably uniform rate. What, they asked, do these differences signify? Is quick reaction a sign of superior intelligence, of a particular type of personality, or is it a kind of special ability that is mainly important for success in certain skilled acts, such as driving an automobile? Does speed of reaction vary with sex? How does it change with age?

These and other similar questions have also been put to experimental test by many investigators, and while the findings have not always shown complete agreement, the general trend may be summed up about as follows: On the average, persons of superior intelligence react to a stimulus more quickly than do those of less ability, but the difference is so small and there are so many individual exceptions to the general rule that it is unsafe to judge the intelligence of any person on the basis of his speed of reaction. Measures of reaction time have also been included as parts of standard tests for predicting ability to learn certain trades or special skills such as automobile driving. The results indicate

[1] This is true only within limits. A stimulus that is so intense as to be disorganizing may block the response instead of accelerating it.

that while the "simple reaction time" described in an earlier paragraph has not much value in predicting these abilities, "discrimination time" in which a number of different stimuli are presented in irregular order and the subject is told to press the key only when a certain one—say, a *red* light—appears, may be more meaningful. The problem is sometimes made still more complicated by providing the subject with two keys and telling him to press the left-hand key in response to one kind of stimulus, the right-hand key for another. This is known as the "choice reaction."

Some of the reaction time experiments used in tests for automobile drivers have been made very realistic by placing the subject in a stationary apparatus like the driver's seat of an automobile with steering wheel, pedals and gear shift all connected to a recording device so as to give a graphic record of all his responses, thus making it possible to know just what he does and how quickly he does it. Before his eyes is a screen on which a moving picture is projected of the "highway" along which he is supposed to be driving. Various emergencies occur at unexpected intervals. Traffic signals change, a dog leaps suddenly out of a ditch, a child runs from behind a parked car. These tests have distinct value in showing what a prospective driver can do when he puts his mind to it; they do not, unfortunately, guarantee that he will be equally careful when on the road!

Most investigators have found a very slight superiority of males over females in average speed of reaction, but this, too, is a rule that has many exceptions. The reactions of children are slower and much more variable than those of adults, and in old age the pattern of childhood gradually returns with a slow decrease in speed and a more rapid increase in variability.

For many years, a special kind of reaction time, often referred to as "association time" has been used by clinical psychologists to uncover emotional "sore spots" in persons coming to them for help. A prepared list of words [2] is read to the subject, one at a time, and he is instructed to respond to each one with the *first*

[2] Sometimes a standard list is used, but if the psychologist has any inkling about the probable nature of the difficulty, a special list is often made out in which words that are likely to have special associations for the subject are interspersed at irregular intervals with other words that are not likely to have particular emotional significance.

word that comes to his mind. The time required for each response is noted. It has been found that words having a strong emotional connotation require a longer time for response than do words of indifferent meaning. Thus, by noting where the long delays occur, a clue to the patient's difficulties may often be obtained.

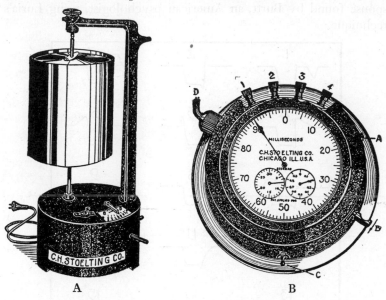

A   B

FIG. 4.—A KYMOGRAPH (*A*) AND AN ELECTRICAL TIMER (*B*)

A. A kymograph. The cylindrical drum covered with smoked paper is rotated at a constant slow speed by a spring motor which is concealed in the base. By means of a tambour with writing attachment which responds to small changes in air pressure, records of breathing, pulse beat, and other bodily movements are obtained.

B. An electrical timer. The large dial shows time intervals to 1/1000 of a second; the two smaller dials record tenths of a second and full seconds. By reading all three dials, time intervals ranging from 1/1000 of a second to ½ minute can be measured. For intervals longer than this, other instruments such as stop watches are commonly employed.

(Courtesy C. H. Stoelting Co.)

Recently Luria, a Russian psychologist, has shown that not only the time required to make the response but also the pattern of motor movement involved in making it has diagnostic significance. A tambour with writing attachment is connected with the telegraph key in such a way that when the key is pressed, air is forced out of the tambour and a record of the resultant movement of the writing attachment is made on a kymograph. (See Figure 4.) The subject is told to press the key at the same time that he responds verbally with his word association.[3]

Figure 5 shows some of the different patterns of the motor response found by Burtt, an American psychologist, using Luria's technique.

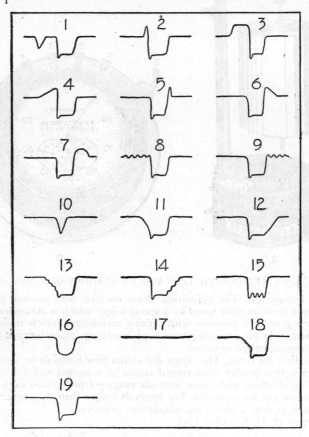

FIG. 5—DIAGNOSTIC SIGNS IN THE MOTOR RESPONSE TO WORDS HAVING
EMOTIONAL SIGNIFICANCE FOR THE SUBJECT

(*For description of this figure see opposite page.*)

[3] This is but one of many similar methods employed by Luria and others who have adopted his procedures.

It would be possible to devote many more pages to the description of reaction time experiments, but the examples that have been given are probably sufficient to show how incomplete and one-sided our knowledge of any field of behavior would be if we failed to take into account both the characteristics of the stimulus by which a response is evoked and the characteristics of the subject who responds to the stimulus. We study each by experimental comparison when one (and only one) feature is changed at a time. This means that if we wish to compare the responses to two different kinds of stimuli we must keep the subjects the same; [4] if we are interested in comparing the behavior of one person with another we must keep the stimulating conditions the same.

Figure 5 (description)

In this experiment the subjects were given a series of stimulus words and instructed to respond to each with the first word that occurred to them and at the same time to press a telegraph key on which the finger was resting. The pressure forced air from a bellows into a tambour and thus made a graphic record on a kymograph.

The usual form of the motor response was approximately like that shown in No. 19 above. A sharp initial pressure is followed by a slight relaxation while the response is given, after which the finger is lifted and the key returns to its normal position. With some subjects, however, the finger was lifted from the key so sharply at the end of the response that there was a slight rebound, as shown in No. 5. It was found that each subject had his own characteristic pattern of motor response. Deviations from that pattern were frequently found to indicate some form of emotional disturbance. For example, Nos. 8, 9, 13, 14, and 15 show distinct hand tremors at some stage in the response. In No. 1 the subject "jumped the gun," partially depressing the key before the main response was given. This suggests the possibility that the first response that occurred to him was rejected in favor of another that may have been less revealing. A rather hesitant type of response is illustrated by No. 11, while in No. 10 the subject released the key before it had been completely depressed. In No. 17 the subject went still further and failed to press the key at all. While too much confidence must not be placed in evidence of this kind since many factors such as temporary distraction of the attention may operate to produce changes in the form of the motor response, the method nevertheless has definite possibilities for uncovering emotional "sore spots" in the individual. (After H. E. Burtt, "Motor Concomitants of the Association Reaction," *J. Exper. Psychol.*, 1936, 19: 51-63.)

[4] Or at least closely similar.

CHANGING POINTS OF VIEW

For a time psychologists were much occupied with the study of so-called mental faculties, such as memory, imagination, and attention. These, they believed, were distinct and special powers of the individual, to be observed and studied independently. They were accordingly regarded as the central facts under which psychological material should be classified. Since then we have grown to realize that factors such as these are not distinct from each other, that one cannot, for example, "reason" without at the same time remembering, imagining, and paying attention. We can take the same behavior and classify or describe it in a dozen different ways, depending upon which of its many aspects we choose to observe. We may notice the movements of our subject's arms and hands and describe or classify these movements according to their speed, their accuracy, their force, their gracefulness. Or we may ignore the arm movements and center our attention upon those of his legs and feet, or upon his facial expression, or upon his speech, and here we may give attention either to what he says or to how he says it. Speed, accuracy, grace, memory, persistence, and so on are nothing more than descriptive terms that we sometimes find useful in classifying behavior as it is shown at any particular time. A complete picture of psychology as it is to-day cannot be given in these terms any more than we can take the qualities they are supposed to represent and by putting them together like the pieces of a jig-saw puzzle turn out a real likeness of a human being.

Many other important questions have arisen in the course of psychology's attempts to define its field of interest. One of the most significant of these is the question whether or not verbal reports about such private and unverifiable data as feelings, sensations, or thought processes have any real scientific value or whether the psychologist might not better confine his attention to the later stages of activity, the external features that are open to general observation. This battle between the "behaviorists" and the "introspectionists" was hard fought for a number of years, but most psychologists now seem committed to a middle ground where data of both kinds are accepted if they seem likely to be useful. If, for example, we are interested in studying food preferences among a group of intelligent adults, it would be unsafe to generalize very far from their behavior, because Smith may be very fond of griddle-cakes but consistently refrain from eating them because they give him indigestion, while Brown may manfully swallow his portion of the rice pudding he detests in order not to disappoint his hostess. If we want to know what foods our subjects like best, we should select a suitable time and place and ask them. But if we are interested in finding out what they eat, the way to do it is to observe them and keep a record. Observation of behavior gives us one set of facts; verbal reports by the subjects themselves give us another. Sometimes one method is to be preferred, sometimes the other. It depends on what we want to find out.

More recently still another school of thought has arisen, which, as was the case with "behaviorism," may be looked upon as a reaction against an extreme and restricted point of view. This new psychology is known as the psychology of Gestalt (from the German word, Gestalt which means *form* or *shape*). Just as the advocates of behaviorism criticised those who put too much trust in the data obtained by intro-

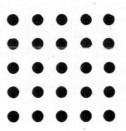

FIG. 6.—DOTS ILLUSTRATING THE TENDENCY TO PERCEIVE FORMS OR FIGURES

Look intently at these dots for a moment or two. What organized arrangements or figures do you see?

spection, so the supporters of Gestalt theory criticize the behaviorists for concerning themselves only with fractional bits of behavior which lose their essential character when viewed out of their natural setting. A musical tone, they point out, is one thing when heard by itself; it is quite a different thing when it is part of a melody. If you arrange sixteen dots to form a square as in Figure 6, and then look at the square intently for a minute or two, you will find that some of the dots appear to stand out from the others to form patterns and that these patterns shift themselves about from time to time but always maintain some kind of internal organization. They are patterns, figures, and not just haphazard arrangements. So with things in general. We respond, not to simple isolated features of the world around us but to patterns, to groups of objects or conditions that stand out from moment to moment as unified wholes, as *gestalts* [5] that cannot be divided further without destroying their essential character. And these patterns or gestalts are individual matters. They do not depend entirely upon the external conditions surrounding the person, nor are they merely the constructs of his own fancy. Rather they represent the special ways in which every person organizes the objects and events of his life as he lives it. Both the individual and his physical surroundings play a part in determining the pattern of an experience, and it is the pattern, the design, rather than the parts of which it is composed that determines his behavior. The error of those who carried behaviorism to an extreme, so say the Gestalt psychologists, was that they looked upon behavior and the conditions that stimulate it as something on the order of a physical, additive compound like hash, whereas it is more nearly analogous to a chemical compound like water.

These and other points of controversy that have arisen in the past have served a useful purpose, not only in defining more exactly what psychology is and does, but in suggesting new ways of attacking psychological problems and in correcting extreme and restricted points of view. As time passes and our knowledge increases, other questions will doubtless arise and be debated as hotly as their predecessors have been. The student who finds that the authorities in his subject sometimes hold conflicting views should neither be disappointed nor alarmed. A reasonable amount of controversy is a sign of health. It is only in death that scientists never disagree.

---

[5] The German plural is, of course, *Gestalten* but now that the term *Gestalt* is rapidly becoming a part of the psychological vocabulary of English-speaking people, the Anglicized plural is frequently used.

HOW PSYCHOLOGY SECURES ITS FACTS

Before psychology can give an organized account of mental activity and of the effect of growth and experience upon the manner in which human beings respond to their environment, it must first of all gather a great many facts. We have already seen how the exact study of such an apparently simple form of behavior as reaction time can yield significant information about a wide variety of different problems. But these problems do not by any means indicate the scope of modern psychological interest, which extends into every realm of human conduct. Psychology to-day is concerned not only with the classical problems of sensation, perception, memory, and the like but with the morals and manners of individuals and of social groups, with their talents and defects, their beliefs, conflicts and goals. We want to know how learning takes place and what are the conditions under which people learn fastest and retain longest. We want to know what causes the mind to become diseased, what makes the alcoholic patient see snakes where there are none, and why some insane persons think they hear the voices of angels or of devils urging them to great deeds. Why do perfectly normal people see and do such fantastic things in dreams? Whence come our motives, our interests and desires, and why are people so different in their interests? Why does John like books and school, while Jerry who is in the same class plays truant on every possible occasion? Why is Mary so popular while her sister is shunned and disliked?

The answers to questions such as these cannot be obtained by means of arm-chair theorizing. The modern psychologist is as dependent upon the laboratory for the data with which he works as is the chemist or physicist. His laboratory, however, is not confined to the big room you have seen at the university, with its array of queer-looking instruments and its shelves piled with record forms, although many psychological investigations are carried out there. Because the psychologist of to-day is interested in finding out how people behave in everyday life as well as how they react to the kind of precisely controlled conditions that can be set up in the formal laboratory, he must extend his observations to the home, the street, the classroom, the factory. The condemned criminal in his cell, the commuter on the 5:15,

the new-born baby in the hospital, the genius and the idiot, the
butcher, the baker and the candle-stick maker, all furnish their
grist for the psychological mill. Armed with a stop-watch and
a mechanical counter, the psychologist to-day studies the attention value of various window displays as indicated by the number
of people who stop to look at each and the length of time they
stay. To-morrow we find him in the school-room conducting
experiments in learning or giving psychological tests to discover
the special aptitudes and weaknesses of the children in order that
their training may be more wisely directed. On other occasions
he may observe and record the social reactions of children or
adults toward each other, or, back in his laboratory, he may busy
himself with photographing the eye-movements of good and
poor readers, or with studying changes in heart rate or in the
electrical resistance of the skin during strong emotion. Whether
they are collected in the seclusion of the formal laboratory or
under the more flexible conditions of everyday life, the data of
modern psychology are the observed and recorded facts of actual
behavior. The psychology of to-day bears slight resemblance
to the philosophy from which it sprang.

METHODS OF IMPROVING THE ACCURACY OF
PSYCHOLOGICAL OBSERVATION AND OF RE-
DUCING THE LIKELIHOOD OF ERROR IN IN-
TERPRETING THE SUBJECT'S RESPONSES

Every one, no matter how carefully he tries to observe, is likely
to make mistakes. He may overlook important features of the
behavior he is studying, or be led by suggestion to record events
that never occurred. He may make errors in counting, in timing,
in measuring. Even more common are the errors of interpretation
due to failure to recognize what it is to which his subject is giving
attention or to what stimulus he is responding. A mother was
greatly impressed by the rapt attention with which her small
son listened to the sermon at church. He sat motionless with eyes
fixed on the minister, apparently drinking in every word. As
they left the church, however, he inquired earnestly, "Mother,
did you know that Dr. Brown's back teeth are made of gold?
Every time he opened his mouth I could see them shine!"

Whenever a number of different stimuli are presented at the same time, there is danger that an observer may not be able to tell which one is determining the subject's behavior. If the small boy just mentioned had been listening to the same sermon given on a phonograph concealed from his sight by a screen, it would have been easier to judge from his behavior whether or not the sermon itself interested him. One of the main advantages of the formal laboratory experiment as compared to casual observation lies in the possibility of safeguarding interpretation by reducing the number of stimulating conditions to a minimum.

It is interesting to know that experiments in psychology had their beginning in the important discovery that no human being can observe and record with absolute accuracy. In 1796, Maskelyne, an astronomer at Greenwich, found that Kinnebrook, his assistant, was observing and recording the time of stellar transits almost a second later, on the average, than Maskelyne himself did. This was a very serious error indeed, since upon these observations depended the calibration of the clock by which the world's time was regulated, as well as all astronomical calculations about time and space. Although Kinnebrook strove to correct the error after his attention was called to it, he was unable to do so. If anything it grew worse. Maskelyne therefore decided that Kinnebrook could not be following the accepted method of observation but must have "fallen into some irregular and confused method of his own." Kinnebrook was accordingly dismissed.

Several years later, Bessel, the astronomer at Königsberg, became interested in the matter and decided to find out whether the Maskelyne-Kinnebrook affair was a unique case or whether other astronomers might not also disagree in their observations if put to the test. In 1820, he found an opportunity to compare his own observations with those of Walbeck. It was found that Bessel always observed a transit earlier than Walbeck and that the average difference between their observations was even greater than that found between Maskelyne and Kinnebrook. This discovery led to a number of further investigations from which it became evident that the time required to observe and report any external event will differ from person to person, even when the utmost efforts to secure accuracy are made. This difference came to be known as the "personal equation," and while it was at first considered a problem of interest chiefly to astronomers, its wider significance soon became recognized, and many important investigations aimed at determining its physiological and psychological attributes were undertaken.

Since that time, psychologists have been devoting much time to the question of errors of observation, and many important discoveries about the peculiarities of human nature have had their origin in attempts to account for the prevalence of certain kinds of mistakes. Early psychological experimentation was largely concerned with questions of sensation and its attributes. Careful investigations were made of the extent and manner in which color qualities as perceived by us are dependent upon such matters as lighting, position with reference to other colors (contrast), and whether the colors are seen in direct or marginal vision. As a result of these and many other investigations in the field of the senses, it became evident that small changes in the surrounding conditions may bring about large differences in the appearance of any external object, and that accordingly, unless the external conditions are carefully controlled, the difficulty of interpreting behavior is vastly increased. More recently we have come to see that the internal state of the subject himself, his emotional and physical condition, his level of mental development and his past experiences also exert a great influence upon the way the world looks to him. Although matters such as these are not easy to deal with, their importance at least is recognized and attempts to control them are being made.

In psychological investigation, although ideal conditions of experiment are never reached, research workers are continually trying to find ways by which the conditions under which experiments are carried on can be kept under better control and to develop instruments for refining observation and for making records in a more uniform and exact fashion. In the psychological laboratory are to be found chronoscopes for measuring time in units as small as the thousandth part of a second, photographic apparatus of many kinds for making permanent records of behavior that would otherwise be over before it could fairly be seen, galvanometers for measuring electrical changes in the skin, and apparatus for studying other bodily functions such as heart rate, blood-pressure, and changes in the distribution of blood. There are special arrangements for controlling lighting and sound-proof rooms to prevent distraction from outside noises. There are machines for presenting the stimuli to which the subject is supposed to respond, so arranged that such factors as the intensity of the stimulus, its duration, and the intervals between successive trials are kept exactly the same from one trial to another. There are other instruments for recording the responses made by the subject, thus keeping the results free from the effects of unconscious bias or imperfect observation on the part of the experimenter.

Even when the psychologist leaves his laboratory and sallies forth into the outside world to learn what he can of behavior as it is shown there, he cannot afford to ignore the question of scientific technique. He may not be able to control conditions as he does in his laboratory, but he can and does select from the wide variety of circumstances open to him certain ones in which the conditions that have a bearing on his particular field of investigation are sufficiently uniform for his purpose. Stopwatches, moving-picture cameras, and the like can be carried with him and used where he happens to be, and other pieces of apparatus can often be set up temporarily in the home, the school, the factory, or other places as they are needed. Psychological equipment, moreover, is not confined to pieces of mechanical apparatus but includes also printed blanks for various kinds of tests, questionnaires, rating scales, and standardized interview forms. Even the humble pad and pencil in the hands of one who knows what to observe and how to record his observations in a systematic fashion may yield information of greater scientific value than the most elaborate apparatus will furnish to those unskilled in its use.

There are many important aspects of behavior that cannot be studied by means of any mechanical devices now known to us but must be observed and recorded as they naturally occur in everyday life. Social behavior is an example. We cannot weigh it or measure it. Yet social behavior can be studied, though not as easily as other forms of behavior that are more amenable to control. By making repeated observations under different circumstances, comparing the results, and checking the facts for accuracy in as many different ways as possible, even behavior that at first thought appears to be so fluctuating and uncertain as to fall completely outside the field of possible experiment can often be reduced to some form of order by means of a carefully organized system of records. When this is done, it is often found that behavior that appears irrational and unpredictable is consistent enough, once we have got hold of the right key for understanding it.

Even from the very incomplete account given in this chapter, you can see how great is the variety of problems that the psychologist of to-day is attempting to solve, and how absurd it would be for him to confine himself to any one method for studying them. Methods and techniques do not spring up in a vacuum; they are the tools we construct as we feel the need for them. We find out their inaccuracies and inadequacies by using them, not by letting them lie idle in the hope that by some miracle they will perfect themselves. The method is always the outgrowth of the problems that it is designed to solve. It is the aim of every science to perfect its techniques, but no science would progress far if it refused to use imperfect tools when no others were available.

A BOOK YOU WILL ENJOY READING

Henry E. Garrett, *Great Experiments in Psychology*, Revised and Enlarged Edition (New York, D. Appleton-Century Co., 1941), pp. xxi + 452.

This book gives an account of fifteen experiments that have made psychological history. It tells how the idea of measuring intelligence originated and what intelligence tests are like. It describes the many different ways by which psychologists have tried to find out how people and animals learn, and tells you what modern science has discovered about many practical questions in the field of learning. For example, is it true, as many people think, that learning one thing "strengthens" the mind so that it then becomes easier to learn something else? Do animals think or reason in solving problems or learning tricks? Is there any advantage in going over a lesson again after it has once been thoroughly learned?

The book also includes a fascinating chapter on methods of studying personality and another that describes the changes that take place in the body during strong emotion. It shows how experiments on animals and young children have helped us to understand the behavior of human adults and why people differ from each other. An account of one of the earliest experiments in reaction time will interest you, as well as the story of how Weber and Fechner discovered the mathematical relation between a change in the physical magnitude of an object and our perception of that change, a law that is perhaps the most famous in all psychology. A number of other topics of equal interest are discussed.

The book is easy to read and contains many helpful illustrations. Your college library probably has a copy.

PART II

The Child's Equipment for Living

Chapter III

OUR HEREDITARY BACKGROUND

What do we mean by heredity?

Why are children sometimes like one parent, sometimes like the other, and sometimes like neither?

Why do some plants and animals not breed true to type?

How and when is sex determined?

Why are men more likely than women to be color-blind?

What are the biological advantages of having two parents instead of one?

Will a hereditary trait always show itself in any environment?

Do we inherit habits formed by our parents?

If a mother is badly frightened during pregnancy, is the baby likely to be affected?

What can be said about the relative importance of heredity and environment in bringing about the mental differences we see in our friends?

HOW DOES HUMAN LIFE BEGIN?

When people speak of the beginning of life, they usually refer to the time of birth. But the life of any person goes back further than birth. In one sense it may be said to begin with the fertilization of the egg-cell, but even this is not strictly its beginning. Life is continuous from one generation to another. The egg-cell at the time it is fertilized is a living bit of tissue that is changing and developing according to its own laws of growth. The sperm by which it is fertilized is also alive. Each was originally part of a living body, one of the vast numbers of cells of which that body was composed. However, these germ-cells, as they are often called, differ from the other body cells in several important ways, one of which is their ability to detach themselves from the tissue in which they have grown and to live an independent life within the body for a short period of time. But this period of independent life is limited unless something happens to change the course of development and to give to the individual germ-cell a new impetus for growth. If a male germ-cell or spermatozoön meets and fuses with a female cell or ovum, the single cell that results from the fusion takes on a new lease of life. Had they remained apart, both ovum and sperm must soon have died; combined they live and in time develop into a new individual who in his turn will pass on to others the life that has been given him.

In all the higher animals and plants, sexual reproduction is the rule. Even among the lower forms of life that commonly reproduce by simple division of a mature cell to form two new individuals, occasional reproduction by the fusion of two parent cells is seen in the greater number of species. In these cases, the generations immediately following the sexual reproduction commonly exhibit greater vigor than those that preceded it. An increase in vitality thus seems to result from the conjunction of the parent cells even in those organisms that are able to reproduce themselves independently for many generations.

Sexual reproduction has other advantages. Since each new individual represents the convergence of two lines of ancestry, greater possibility of variation is afforded than would be the case if reproduction took place by the division of a single parent cell. As we shall see later, the number of "traits" (by which we mean tendencies to grow and develop in certain ways rather than in others) handed down by each parent is very great, and these may be recombined in the offspring in a vast number of different ways. The likelihood that any two persons will receive exactly the same combination is very small unless the parents, to begin with, are exactly alike, and in the human race this is never true. Biparental ancestry thus makes for differences between the individual members of the species, and as a result of these differences a complex form of social organization develops. People with special abilities perform certain tasks for which they are particularly fitted, and are repaid by having other kinds of work done for them by persons whose abilities excel along those lines. Modern civilization has in large measure been built up by utilizing the differences between people in the formation of coöperative social groups.

WHAT IS GIVEN BY HEREDITY?

Many people think of heredity as some kind of vague "force" or "influence" that the parent in some unknown way exerts upon the child. This is just as inexact as it would be to think of the reaction that occurs when two chemicals combine to form a new substance as some mysterious force acting upon the chemicals from without. The laws of heredity are simply the rules to which the behavior of the physical substances contained in the germ-cells conforms. Although these laws are not as yet completely understood, much is known concerning them, and the way to further study has been cleared. Just as a chemical reaction consists of the breaking up of the original molecules into the atoms of which they are composed and the recombination of these atoms into new molecules with different atomic arrangement and composition, so when two germ-cells meet and fuse certain physical substances called *genes*, half of which were originally contained in the sperm and half in the ovum, combine to form a new cell with a *genetic composition* different from either of the parent cells.

We cannot say as yet whether the process is essentially the same as that of the ordinary chemical reaction or whether it belongs in a separate class, but at any rate the two reactions have many points of similarity. One important difference, however, is found in the fact that whereas the chemical reaction is "touched off" as it were, when the two original substances meet, the genetic reaction begins before the union of the cells. At the proper stage in its development, something in the growth process provides the initial stimulus that causes the dormant cell to grow and change, to reorganize its internal structure and finally to separate itself from the glandular tissue in which it originated and start out on an independent career where it may find the mate without which it must soon die.

THE PHYSICAL BASIS OF HEREDITY

In each sex the germ-cells originate in paired organs known as the *gonads*. The male gonads are called the *testes*, the male germ-cells the *spermatozoa;* the female gonads are called the *ovaries*, the female germ-cells the *ova*. The ovum or egg-cell differs greatly from the sperm-cell in form and size. In its free state, that is, after it has been extruded from the ovary, the human ovum is a sphere about one tenth of a millimeter in diameter, just visible to the naked eye under favorable conditions. It has no means of locomotion within itself. Its movements are determined solely by the contraction of the tissues by which it is surrounded. The greater part of its bulk is composed of a protoplasmic material known as the *cytoplasm*. The cytoplasm provides the material—for convenience we may call it nutriment, though it is really more than that—by which the first stages of development are made possible. Within the cytoplasm is a denser part known as the *nucleus*, which is made up almost entirely of strings or bundles of the genes to which we have already referred.

The spermatozoa, on the other hand, are fashioned for free locomotion under their own motive power. They are microscopic in size, since they contain very little cytoplasm, and in form are not unlike the tadpoles that you have seen wriggling about in warm, stagnant water in the early summer. There is an ovate head, consisting chiefly of the nucleus which, like the nucleus of the ovum, is composed mainly of bundles of genes. Back of the head is an elongated portion called the body, to which is attached a fine hairlike "whip" or *cilium* that lashes back and forth and so enables the sperm to swim forward through the milky fluid or semen in which they are released.

If the developing germ-cell, either sperm or ovum, is viewed under a microscope, certain very interesting changes can be observed. In the early stages of development the nucleus is seen as a kind of network within which are long-drawn-out chains of minute particles of material like tangled strings of beads. It is important to remember that the genes in each string are arranged in a definite linear order that is always the same from one cell to another within a given species.

Later the strings contract and fold into thick bundles of definite size and form. These bundles are known as *chromosomes*. Examination of the chromosomes shows that they are always arranged in pairs. The two members of each pair are exactly alike in size and appearance. Each one contains the same number of genes, arranged in the same order, so that if the bundles were to be unfolded and the two sets of strings laid out side by side, the genes of each pair would correspond exactly in number and position. Moreover, any two corresponding genes affect the same part of the body or its function, but they do not always affect it in the same way.

The reason for this is very simple. It is known that every cell is the product of two parents. One of the two chromosomes in each pair was received from the father, one from the mother. Throughout all the complicated process of growth and development, throughout the countless number of cell divisions and multiplications, the basic substances received from the two par-

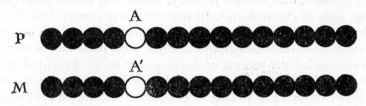

FIG. 7.—DIAGRAM ILLUSTRATING LINEAR ARRANGEMENT OF GENES

ents have maintained their separate identity in the cell. Now that the time has come when they, in their turn, are ready to play a part in the production of a new individual, they are still distinct. Each individual chromosome passes on as a whole.

Examine Figure 7. Here we have represented diagrammatically two chromosomes belonging to the same pair. The upper chromosome came from the father, the lower one from the mother. The genes are shown as beadlike structures joined in a string

Let us assume that the fifth gene from the left (A—A′) affects eye-color.[1] The upper chromosome (P) of the pair belonging to

---

[1] The student should not get the idea that any one gene or pair of genes *produces* a given trait in the developing individual. Even for the production of such a simple characteristic as eye-color in the fruit-fly it is known that the combined action of fifty or more genes is necessary. But since a *change*

this cell came from a brown-eyed father and carries within it something, we do not know exactly what, that has power of producing brown eyes in the child of which this cell may be the starting point. The lower chromosome (M) came from a blue-eyed mother and carries the power of transmitting blue eyes to the offspring. Although, for reasons that will be made clear later on, the man in whose germ-cells this pair of chromosomes is found will probably have brown eyes himself, his children may have either brown eyes or blue eyes, depending upon circumstances.[2]

If the cell in its present condition with its full complement of paired chromosomes were to mate with another in the same state, it is evident that the offspring would have double the number of chromosomes possessed by either of its parents. We know, however, that the number of chromosomes is always the same for a given species, although it varies from one species to another. For example, the common fruit-fly, *Drosophila melanogaster*, has four pairs of chromosomes. In man there are twenty-four pairs. This constant number is maintained without increase by a process known as the *reduction division*, which takes place before fertilization, during the process of development in the individual cell. At a certain stage of development the chromosomes separate, one member of each pair passing to one side of the nucleus, the other to the opposite side. As far as we know, chance alone determines

---

in any one gene brings about a change in the character or quality of the trait with which all are concerned, we may, for the sake of simplifying our thinking, forget about the large number that interact in the production of the trait itself and speak only in terms of the *changes* that result from an alteration in the total complex. These changes frequently involve only a single gene. The fruit-fly could have no eye-color at all—indeed it could have no eyes—were it not for the action of all the fifty-odd pairs of genes that affect the color of the eyes. But when, for example, an alteration occurs in the single gene that is located at a point 52.5 units from one end of the second chromosome, the normal red color of the eye is changed to purple. Any trait owes its existence to the combined action of many genes, but a change in any single gene or in a small group of the genes that go to make up the total, brings about some change in the trait which all combine to produce.

[2] One cannot always tell from the characteristics of the parents what the inherited characteristics of the children will be like. Heredity does not start with the generation immediately preceding. It may go back to the grandparents, the great-grandparents, or for any number of generations.

the nature of the division. One of the resulting groups may be made up entirely of paternal, the other of maternal, chromosomes, or each group may contain half of each kind or any other combination.

After the chromosomes have separated, the cell divides in such a way that each one of the new cells formed from the division has one member (and only one) of each pair of chromosomes. Each of these single chromosomes now divides lengthwise so that half of each of the "beads" or genes is contained in each part. The halves then move to opposite sides of the cells and the cells again divide as before. From these divisions there result in the case of the spermatozoa four cells where but one was previously, but the new cells differ from the parent cell in having but half the original number of chromosomes. (See Figure 8.) In the ovum a similar process of reduction takes place but with this difference, that at each division most of the cytoplasm remains with one of the newly formed cells while the other half of the divided nucleus with its freight of chromosomes passes off as a microscopic bit of protoplasm known as a *polar body*. The polar bodies are soon absorbed or excreted. In the ovum, therefore, only one functional cell results from the reduction division, and this cell, like the newly formed sperm-cells, contains only one member of each of the original pairs of chromosomes.

Fertilization consists in the penetration of the outer membrane of the ovum by one of the spermatozoa, which then passes directly to the nucleus, where the chromosomes range themselves with the half-set remaining in the ovum so that the cell again has its full complement of genes.

What are the consequences of the reduction division? In each new generation, some of the genes that the parents received from the preceding generation are lost when the cell divides. Let us return to our earlier illustration of the father who received from one of his parents a gene making for brown eyes and from the other parent one making for blue eyes. After the reduction division has taken place, each of his spermatozoa will contain one of these genes but not both. If it so happens that the ovum is fertilized by a sperm containing the gene for blue eyes, then, for all practical purposes, the paternal ancestry of the resultant offspring is as free from the tendency to produce brown eyes as if the family tree for countless generations had produced nothing but blonds.

But the paternal ancestry is only half the story. The sperm containing the gene for blue eyes has now mated with an ovum, and in the ovum there is a corresponding chromosome that also contains a gene for eye-color. If it chances that this gene also makes for blue eyes, there is no question as to what will happen. The child into which the fertilized cell develops will also have blue eyes, and moreover, since both its genes are alike, it can transmit only blue eyes, no matter how its chromosomes happen to divide in the next generation.

What happens when the genes are unlike? Suppose that the

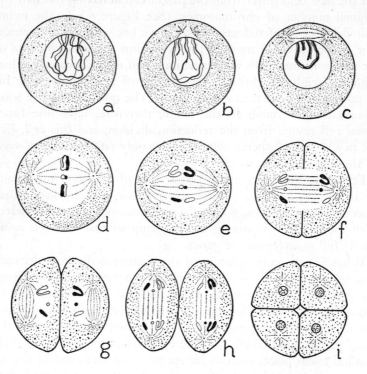

FIG. 8.—DIAGRAMMATIC REPRESENTATION OF THE TWO TYPES OF CELL DIVISION IN THE MATURATION OF A SPERM CELL

(*For description of this figure see opposite page.*)

sperm, with its gene for blue eyes, had chanced to mate with an ovum containing a gene making for brown eyes. What color will the child's eyes be?

One might think, perhaps, that in such cases each gene would have a partial effect, and that the result would be a child with eyes of an intermediate shade. In eye-color, however, as in many other characteristics, blending of this kind does not seem to occur. What does happen is that the offspring resulting from a union of unlike genes will resemble one of its parents in the trait affected by that gene and in this particular trait the gene from the other parent appears to exert no effect. The gene that determines the trait in the offspring is known as the "dominant" gene; that which exerts no apparent effect is called the "recessive" gene. In most cases a single gene is thus sufficient to determine any

---

Figure 8 (description)

The three drawings in the top line show the chromosomes coming together in pairs. The heavy black lines represent the paternal set, the light lines the maternal set. In *a* the cell is shown at an early stage of maturation with the two sets of chromosomes spread out more or less irregularly within the nucleus. In *b* the corresponding members of each pair have come together and lie alongside each other. In *c* the long strings have folded into compact bundles, and the two members of each pair are so closely associated with each other that they can hardly be distinguished.

The second line of drawings shows the reduction division. The line of separation between the cytoplasm and the nucleus has now largely broken down; a spindle has formed within the cell; and the chromosomes have moved to the center of the spindle and separated, one member of each pair lying just to one side of the central division, the other on the other side. In *e* they are beginning to move farther away from each other. In *f* this movement has continued still farther, and a fissure can be seen indicating the point at which the cell will later divide. Each of the new cells, it will be noted, contains only one member of each pair of chromosomes; either a paternal or a maternal representative, but not both.

The second division is illustrated in the third line of drawings. A new spindle forms within each of the two cells formed by the reduction division, whereupon each chromosome splits lengthwise and the two halves of each new pair move to opposite sides as before. New fissures then appear by which each part divides in half again as shown at *i*. Later the four cells thus formed separate completely from each other and increase in bulk until they are the same size as the original cell.

(Adapted from Figure 3 in "The Mechanism and Laws of Heredity," by T. H. Morgan, Chapter I in *The Foundations of Experimental Psychology,* Carl Murchison, ed., Clark University Press.)

single characteristic in a child,[3] but the presence of two genes for each trait still operates to the advantage of the individual.[4]

Let us return to our hypothetical mating of the sperm containing a gene for blue eyes with an ovum whose corresponding gene produces brown eyes. Since the gene for brown eyes is dominant over the gene for blue eyes, the child resulting from this mating would itself have brown eyes, and since in this case the dominance is nearly complete, the child's eyes would usually be just as brown as if there had been no blue eyes at all in its ancestry. The inheritance is determined entirely by the single dominant gene acquired from the mother. But although there may be nothing in the child's outward appearance to tell us of the fact, deep in his body, in the chromosomes contained in his own germ-cells, the gene for blue eyes that he received from his father still exists unchanged. Paired with it is the gene for brown eyes that came from his mother and determined his own eye-color, but when his time for mating comes, and the chromosomes separate for the reduction division of the cell, the gene making for blue eyes is just as likely to be the one that takes part in the fertilization of a new ovum as is the one for brown eyes. If this occurs and the ovum also carries a gene for blue eyes, the offspring will have blue eyes, because whenever both genes are recessive (and only when both are recessive) the offspring will show the recessive trait.

If, then, we have to do with some one who shows a trait that is known to be dependent upon a recessive gene, we know that both his genes for that trait must be recessive, and that no matter how the chromosomes separate at the time of the reduction division, his own contribution to the determination of that trait in his offspring will always be a recessive gene. If he mates with some one bearing only dominant genes, then the children will all receive one dominant and one recessive gene, and will consequently show only the dominant trait. But the children's chromo-

[3] That is, sufficient to determine a change in that characteristic. (See footnote on page 45-46.) An apparent exception to this rule occurs in the case of a few characteristics for which the combined action of several genes is necessary to produce the change. But here, too, only one member of each of the contributing pairs of genes is needed; and as these may all come from the same parent, no real exception is involved.

[4] See pp. 58-59.

somes carry a recessive gene, and when their turn comes to mate, the recessive trait may again appear if they happen to choose as a mate either some one who, like themselves, carries an unrecognized recessive gene of the same kind or one who has two recessive genes and therefore actually displays the trait.

Consider the following possibilities, each of which is represented graphically in Figure 9:

1. If either two pure dominants or two pure recessives (i.e., persons who carry two genes of the same kind) mate, all their offspring will be of the pure type and can transmit only dominance or recessiveness as the case may be.

2. If a pure dominant mates with a pure recessive, all the offspring will show the dominant trait and all will carry in their chromosomes one dominant and one recessive gene for that trait, with an equal probability that either of these genes may be transmitted to any of their children.

3. If a pure dominant mates with a person showing the dominant trait but

Case I

DD DD or RR RR

Case 2   Case 3

DD RR   DD DR

Case 4   Case 5

DR RR   DR DR

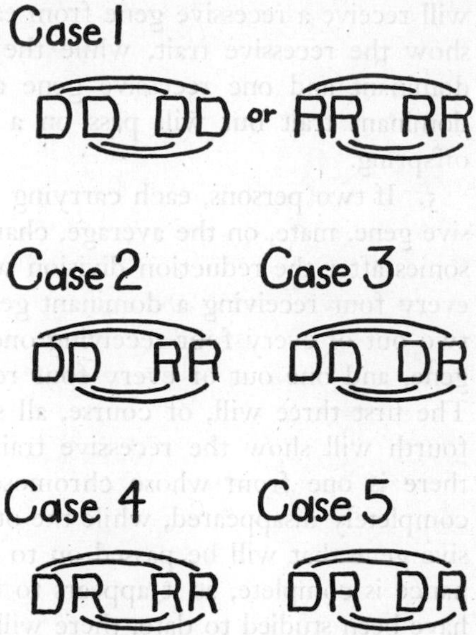

FIG. 9.—POSSIBLE COMBINATIONS OF DOMINANT (D) AND RECESSIVE (R) GENES

Each mature cell, before the reduction division, contains two genes for each trait and each of these genes may be either dominant or recessive. Chance segregation at the time of the reduction division and recombination after fertilization means that all possible pairings of two characters may occur. In this diagram a simple device for determining what proportions of dominant and recessive genes will occur in the offspring from any given type of mating is illustrated.

carrying one recessive gene, all the offspring will show the dominant trait, but half of them will receive a recessive gene from one parent which may be passed on to their offspring. Their genetic constitution will be identical with that of the second generation described under 2.

4. If a pure recessive mates with a person showing the dominant trait but carrying one recessive gene, then half the offspring will receive a recessive gene from each parent and will therefore show the recessive trait, while the other half will receive one dominant and one recessive gene and will therefore show the dominant trait but will pass on a recessive gene to half their offspring.

5. If two persons, each carrying one dominant and one recessive gene, mate, on the average, chance matching of the chromosomes after the reduction division will result in one child out of every four receiving a dominant gene from each of his parents, two out of every four receiving one dominant and one recessive gene, and one out of every four receiving two recessive genes. The first three will, of course, all show the dominant trait; the fourth will show the recessive trait. But among the first three there is one from whose chromosomes the recessive gene has completely disappeared, while the other two still carry one recessive gene that will be passed on to half their offspring. If dominance is complete, as it appears to be in many of the traits that have been studied to date, there will be no way of distinguishing the pure dominant from his brothers and sisters who carry the recessive gene. As generations succeed one another, sooner or later it may happen that a mating will occur in which this hidden gene meets another like itself, and then the recessive trait will again appear. On the other hand, it is entirely possible that none of the cells bearing the recessive gene may chance to produce offspring. They may all be lost in the passing-off of the polar bodies from the ovum, or among the millions of spermatozoa that never take part in reproduction. Among some of the lower animals that reproduce frequently and in vast numbers, breeding records will soon enable one to infer with a high degree of probability which of the two possibilities has occurred; but in the human race, where children are few and the interval between generations is long, a recessive gene may be unknowingly passed on for many generations until a mating occurs that brings it into combination with another of its kind, when the recessive trait will again appear. This is the explanation of the oft-observed fact

that physical or mental traits frequently skip one or more generations and reappear in children who thus resemble some remote ancestor far more closely than they resemble their parents.

The three-to-one ratio described at the beginning of the last paragraph, which occurs whenever the offspring from the crossing of a pure dominant with a pure recessive are interbred, is often called the Mendelian ratio because of the fact that it was first discovered by an Austrian monk named Gregor Mendel, who became interested in the question of heredity about the middle of the nineteenth century and conducted a number of experiments on the breeding of peas. Mendel's report of his experiments was published in 1865 in an obscure journal where it attracted little attention and was soon forgotten. In 1900 the paper was discovered by botanists working along similar lines, and Mendel, long since dead, was acclaimed as the father of modern genetics.

Since that time thousands of breeding experiments have been conducted, as a result of which our knowledge of heredity has been greatly extended. We have learned, for example, that while many traits show complete dominance and while, when complete dominance exists, an individual bearing a single recessive gene is indistinguishable from the pure dominant, cases of partial dominance also occur in which the individual with one recessive gene is unlike either the pure recessive or the pure dominant. An example is found in one of the four-o'clocks in which the first generation resulting from the crossing of a pure-bred white variety with a pure-bred red variety bears pink flowers. Another example is seen in a kind of domestic fowl known as the "blue Andalusian" that comes from the crossing of a certain breed of white fowls splashed with blue or black with another breed of black ones, from which poultry breeders long sought to develop a fowl that would breed true to type. But whenever a "blue Andalusian" was crossed with a mate of the same kind, one fourth of the chicks would be splashed white and another fourth black like the original stock, and only half would resemble their parents. No matter how often the poultrymen tried, they could not produce a stock that would breed true. We now know that they failed because they were dealing with a case of partial dominance, and that the fowl with which they were working could never be made to yield a uniform type of offspring because its existence depended upon the presence of two genes of different kinds, neither of which was completely dominant over the other. A stock pure with respect to a particular character can be produced only when both genes for that character are alike.

Incomplete dominance is only one of many special conditions that make the study of heredity a much more complicated matter than it was thought to be a quarter of a century ago. Sometimes a change in several genes is necessary to produce a given characteristic in the offspring; in others a change in any one of several different genes may produce the same apparent effect. The student should bear in mind, therefore, that the principles of heredity are much more complex than many of the present-day dabblers in the field would lead us to suppose. Particularly when it comes to the question of human inheritance, our ignorance still greatly exceeds our knowledge.

THE DETERMINATION OF SEX

"Is it a boy or a girl?" is likely to be the first question when a new baby is announced. This is not surprising, for few things are more important than sex in shaping the later career of any person. When and how is the sex of the developing ovum determined?

Shortly after the discovery of the paired arrangement of the chromosomes, an important exception to the general rule that every chromosome has its mate was noticed. In every species in which sexual reproduction is the rule, one sex has been found to have one of its pairs of chromosomes represented only by a single member or, in some species, the unmatched chromosome has a partner in the shape of a very small and rudimentary chromosome that, so far as can be determined, serves no useful function. In most species, including man, the unmatched chromosome occurs in the male, while the female has all her pairs fully represented. It was reasonable to suppose, therefore, that the odd chromosome might have something to do with the determination of sex, and later investigation has shown this to be the case. When the chromosomes are segregated at the time of the reduction division, the odd chromosome in the male (often called the

X chromosome) ranges itself by chance, sometimes with one set, sometimes with the other. When the cell divides, therefore, half the spermatozoa thus produced will contain an X chromosome, half will not. The ovum, however, has a complete pair of X chromosomes, one of which will always remain in the cell after the polar bodies have been extruded. Now if the ovum chances to be fertilized by a sperm in which the X chromosome has remained, the fusion will result in a cell with a complete sex of X chromosomes and the child will be a female. If, on the other hand, the ovum is fertilized by a sperm from which the X chromosome is missing, the result will be a cell that has only the single X chromosome provided by the mother and the child will develop into a male. Since there are as many sperm without X chromosomes as there are with them, it follows that on the average about as many of one sex as of the other will be born.[5]

SEX-LINKED TRAITS

Recessive traits that develop from genes carried in the X (or sex-determining) chromosome show a pattern of transmission that differs from the ordinary Mendelian heredity in certain ways. The principle involved is exactly the same, but the fact that one sex has only a single X chromosome causes the principle to work out differently. In man, a number of sex-linked hereditary characteristics are known, and two have been studied rather extensively. There is a hereditary defect known as hemophilia in which the mechanism that causes the blood to coagulate when exposed to the air is so defective that the affected person is likely to bleed to death from a very slight wound. There is another condition in which the mechanism in the eye for perceiving certain colors is defective. Persons having this defect are said to be color-blind. Color-blindness is of several types and occurs in various degrees

---

[5] The actual sex ratio at birth is about 105 males to 100 females. Studies of the sex of fetuses that have miscarried show that at the time of conception the excess of males must be even greater. Other evidence, however, shows that the primary explanation for the determination of sex lies in the division of the chromosomes as described above, and that the departure from the expected 50-50 ratio is the result of some disturbing factor that does not affect the general principle. For discussion of this point the student is referred to any recent textbook of genetics.

ranging ail the way from "color-weakness," in which there is greater than normal difficulty in distinguishing certain colors, to very rare cases of complete color-blindness when all colors are seen merely as differing shades of gray as they appear in an ordinary photograph. The most common form is red-green blindness, in which red cannot be told from green. This was not a very great handicap a century ago, but it is one that may have serious results under modern conditions of traffic regulation.[6] Both hemophilia and color-blindness are carried by genes in the X chromosome and are completely or almost completely recessive to the normal gene that accompanies them in the female. Their pattern of inheritance will be easily understood if it is remembered that the male has only a single X chromosome and that this chromosome always comes from the mother, for if the father had also supplied an X chromosome, the child would not have been a male.

Let us start with a man in whose X chromosome the gene for hemophilia, or "bleeding" as it is popularly called, is present. In such cases, the man will himself be a "bleeder" because he had no extra gene to protect him, and so the single gene that he received from his mother exercised its full effect. Suppose that this man mates with a woman who has two normal genes with respect to this trait. None of their children will be bleeders because the sons will get their only X chromosomes from their mother who is normal, and although the daughters will each receive a defective gene from their father, the protective influence of the dominant normal gene that comes from the mother will keep the defective gene from exercising any effect upon them. But the defective gene is there, biding its time. If the daughter of such a mating marries a normal man, half her sons,

[6] In order to lessen the hazards from this source, a test for color vision is usually made a part of the examination for drivers' licenses required in most states. Moreover, the actual color of the standard traffic lights is such that a color-blind person can distinguish them, since the red will appear darker to him than does the green. But because the difference in the lights is far less apparent to him than it is to the person with normal color vision, it is of great importance that every color-blind driver shall be made aware of his defect and of the need to compensate for it by greater attention to the traffic signals. Surprisingly enough, many partially color-blind persons reach maturity without ever finding out that their vision differs from that of other people.

on the average, will receive from her an X chromosome carrying the defective gene and will therefore be bleeders. The other half will receive the normal chromosome that came from their mother's mother and will therefore be normal. In the case of sex-linked traits, a man who is himself normal need have no fear of transmitting the defect to his offspring, no matter how often it may have appeared in his own ancestry. Any such trait that is carried in his germ-plasm will appear in his own person; if it does not, he may be satisfied that he is free from the taint. But this is not true of the woman in a family where a sex-linked defect is present. Because her sex depends on the presence of two X chromosomes, a single one of which, if normal, is sufficient to protect her from the appearance of the defect, a normal woman with one defective gene will on the average transmit this gene to half her offspring, regardless of their sex. But the males will exhibit the defect; the females will not unless their father is also defective. Since in the general population the normal genes for most of these traits occur far more often than the defective ones, it is much more probable that a normal woman who carries a defective gene will marry a normal man than that she will marry a defective one. If the latter event should occur, however, half her sons will receive from her a defective gene and will accordingly show the defect. She will also transmit a defective gene to half her daughters, and since all her daughters receive a defective gene from their father, half of them will likewise show the trait. This is the explanation for the curious fact that sex-linked traits appear among males far more often than they do among females, but their inheritance in males comes from the female ancestry alone.

Two other possibilities remain. The woman who receives a defective gene from both parents and who accordingly shows the defect may marry either a normal man or one who carries the same defect. In the first case, all the sons will receive a defective gene from their mother and will consequently show the defect. All the daughters, however, will receive a normal gene from their father as well as the defective gene from their mother and will accordingly be normal themselves but will transmit a defective gene to half their offspring. If a woman with two defective genes marries a man who has the same defect, all the offspring, regardless of their sex, will be defective.

THE PROTECTIVE EFFECT OF BIPARENTAL HEREDITY

As I was writing this, my small niece, whose proclivity for accidents is the despair of her family, came into my study to explain to me that although her mother had forbidden her to go swimming until she had mended her bathing suit, it would be quite all right for her to go because she had found another suit of nearly the same color that she could wear outside the torn one. Although both suits were somewhat the worse for wear, no two holes chanced to coincide in position, and therefore, in her opinion, the combination was entirely adequate for all requirements.

Most of us carry in our germ-plasm a fairly large number of defective genes of one kind or another. Some of the defects that would result from these genes might be fairly serious if they were allowed to come into being. But so long as a defective gene is balanced by a normal gene received from the other parent, the individual is protected in the great majority of cases, since the normal characteristic usually dominates over the defective one. As with the child and her bathing suits, it is only when the defects from both lines of ancestry coincide that harm results. This protection, to be sure, extends only to the individual himself. His children will receive the defective genes unchanged, ready to show themselves for what they are as soon as the protective effect of the normal gene is removed through mating with another who carries the same defect. It is not within our province here to debate whether or not this all-determining effect of the dominant gene, which protects the individual from the influence of a recessive defect but in so doing conceals its presence without affecting its likelihood of being transmitted to further generations, is in the long run desirable for the race. We can say confidently, however, that because of the protection afforded by having two genes provided for each trait when one would be sufficient, defects of all kinds occur much less frequently than would be the case if we had but one parent instead of two. The latter condition is well exemplified in the cases already described of hereditary defects that are carried in the X chromosome. So far as these traits are concerned, males may be said to have only one parent, for their only X chromosome comes from the mother. If any of the genes in this chromosome are defective, nothing can protect the sons from the consequences. They will always exhibit the defect. But the daughters may receive the same defective genes and yet be normal if the corresponding genes in the second X chromosome that comes to them from the father are normal. Only when both lines of descent are defective will the daughters be affected, while a defect in the maternal line alone is sufficient to bring about the defective condition in the sons.

MUTATION: THE MECHANISM BY WHICH NEW TRAITS APPEAR

In animals and plants that have been bred under controlled conditions for many generations and whose ancestry is therefore well known, it occasionally happens that a change of unknown nature occurs in one of the chromosomes by which a new gene, affecting some part of the body or its functions in a way not previously observed, comes into existence. In the fruit-fly a number of such changes in genetic constitution are on record. They affect such factors as eye-color, length and form of wing, and abdominal bands. These changes are called *mutations*. Once they occur, they are inherited in exactly the same way as other traits. Most of the mutations on record have proved to be recessive, but a few dominant genes have also appeared in this way.

Mutations probably occur in the human race as well as in the lower animals, but unless their frequency in terms of generations born is far greater than has been found for organisms such as the fruit-fly, they take place only at exceedingly long intervals. The fruit-fly produces a new generation every ten or twelve days. Counting three generations to a century, it will take more than a thousand years to trace the ancestry of a human family as far as that of a fruit fly can be followed in the course of a single year. When further allowance is made for the enormous difference in the number of offspring produced by each individual in the human race as compared to the fruit-fly, the absence of authentic records of the occurrence of genuine mutations in human beings is not surprising. If we had any laboratory records of human heredity equaling those available for the fruit-fly in length and accuracy, much that is now uncertain about the inheritance of specific traits in man would be made clear.

HEREDITY IN RELATION TO ENVIRONMENT

The question is often asked whether a particular characteristic is due to heredity or to environment. The answer must always •be that it is due to both. It is not a matter of heredity *or* environment, but of heredity *and* environment, for neither can operate without the other. From the beginning, growth and development proceed by interaction between the hereditary substances —the genes—that the individual receives from his ancestors, and the new environment in which these genes find themselves. Different genes react in diverse ways to the same environment; the same genes will grow and develop differently if the external conditions under which they develop are changed. In our old friend the fruit-fly there is a gene known as "abnormal abdomen" the effect of which is to cause the abdominal segments to be irregularly shaped, not sharply marked off from each other. This is a recessive gene found in the X chromosome and therefore shows sex-linked inheritance. It appears in males whose mothers carry the defective gene whenever the flies are reared under adequate conditions of food and moisture. But if the food becomes dry and scanty the trait no longer appears, even in males known to carry the defective gene. The production of the abnormal abdomen is therefore dependent both on the presence of the defective gene and on the supply of food and moisture. As Jennings [7] puts it, "When grown in a moist environment, the difference between normal and abnormal individuals is due to a gene difference, or, as it is usually put, to heredity. If the defective gene is present in all the individuals compared, the difference between normal and abnormal individuals is due to an environmental diversity; to moisture or dryness. The same difference that is produced in some cases by diversity of genes is produced in others by alteration of the environment."

A number of similar cases have been noted in the study of the fruit-fly. There is a gene that produces reduplicated legs which

[7] H. S. Jennings, *The Biological Basis of Human Nature* (New York, W. W. Norton and Co., 1930).

exerts its effect if flies carrying the gene are reared in a cold atmosphere but not otherwise. There is another that causes the number of facets in the eye to be reduced, making the eye imperfect. This condition is also dependent upon temperature as well as upon the presence of the defective gene, but in this case the colder temperatures favor normal development. As the temperature under which the flies develop is increased, the number of perfect facets in the eye decreases.

Two principles of major importance may be inferred from these examples. An inherited defect is not always the inevitable, inescapable thing that some people imagine. What is inherited is not the defect itself but a tendency, a constitution that under certain conditions will produce the defect but may not do so if the conditions are changed. Secondly, we cannot tell by any *a priori* process of reasoning what conditions will favor normal development in individuals with defective genes. Take the examples just cited for the fruit-fly. In the case of flies bearing the gene that makes for abnormal abdomen, normal development is favored by the very conditions that a modern social worker among flies would probably try to change, i.e., by a scanty supply of food and moisture. Flies having an inherited tendency to reduplicated legs are more likely to be normal if they are reared in warm temperatures, but those with a tendency to imperfect eyes are more likely to escape when reared in the cold. Experimental breeding has proved these things to be true, but we do not know the reason for them, and they do not tell us how the environment should be modified to prevent other defective genes from exercising their effect.

CAN ACQUIRED CHARACTERISTICS BE INHERITED?

Few questions in the field of genetics have aroused more heated controversy than the one just stated. To put it concretely, if parents for many generations are trained to perform a given act, will their children be able to learn it more easily because of the skill acquired by the parents? After their ancestors have lived for centuries under the rays of a tropical sun, will the babies born to fair-skinned Northern races have swarthier complexions than their progenitors if there is no intermarriage with dark-skinned races during that time?

Many experiments have been conducted in an attempt to answer this question, with results that have upon the whole been negative. Often it has seemed for a time that the results pointed to some effect of parental experience upon the abilities or physical characteristics of the offspring, but in all cases that have been investigated so far, it has later been shown that the effects could be explained in terms of selective breeding or other factors making for imperfect control. Social custom has also provided us with many experiments of this kind, and here too the results seem to be negative. The feet of Chinese women have been bound for centuries, but neither the size nor the shape of the feet of Chinese babies has been altered thereby. Generations of fox-terriers have had their tails cut short, but the length of the puppies' tails has not lessened by an inch. Babies whose ancestors for many generations have spoken only German nevertheless have no special predisposition toward speaking German rather than any other language. If adopted at birth into English-speaking homes, they learn English as readily as they would have learned German and speak it without an accent. If they attempt to learn German later on, say in high school or college, the knowledge acquired by their forebears does not give them an hour's advantage over their classmates of English or American stock.

A special phase of this question that has given concern to many expectant mothers is the matter of "prenatal influence." Even intelligent women sometimes believe the popular superstition that it is possible for an unborn child to be "marked" by some terrifying experience of the mother's, or that its abilities and character can be influenced by the mother's physical and mental regimen during pregnancy. Without going into details, it may be said that the tales reported in this connection are usually just nonsense. Dozens of them have been investigated and found to have no basis in fact or to be easily explainable in terms of other well-known factors, such as physical injury or a genetic defect that has skipped one or more generations, without resort to any question of maternal influence. Furthermore, since there is no nerve-connection between mother and child, the mechanism for transmitting a mental experience of the mother to the child is lacking.

THE INHERITANCE OF BEHAVIOR

Until recently, most of our knowledge concerning the possibility of the transmission of behavior-tendencies from parent to offspring was inferential rather than scientifically proved. True, stock breeders have for many years succeeded in producing strains of fast-trotting horses, but these animals usually differ from the generality of horses in build as well as in performance on the race-track. And fond mothers, for countless generations, have assured each other that all Johnnie's naughtiness was inherited from his father! (Their hearers have not always agreed!) The fact that certain special talents such as musical ability or special defects like feeble-mindedness often seem to "run in families" does not always provide incontrovertible evidence that heredity is the cause, since the children from musical families are likely to be reared in a musical environment and to receive special training in music, and the children of feeble-minded parents typically come from homes where there is little intellectual stimulation. Is there, then, any clear evidence that behavior-tendencies as well as differences in bodily form may be passed on as a biological inheritance from parent to offspring?

At the University of Minnesota, psychologists have applied the principles of selective breeding in the development of two strains of rats, one characterized by great physical activity, the other by lethargy. The method employed was to measure the activity of each rat in each successive generation by placing him in a special cage to which a recording device for registering movement within the cage was attached. From the records so obtained the most active rats were selected for breeding Strain A and those showing least activity for breeding Strain B. This was repeated in each new generation with the results shown in Figure 10.

A similar experiment has been carried out at the University of California by Tryon. In this case, however, the separation was made on the basis of a special manifestation of rat "intelligence" as shown by the animals' ability to learn the pattern of a complicated maze so that they could run through it quickly from entrance to food compartment without entering any of the blind alleys that were set to confuse them. Animals who showed unusual aptitude for learning the mazes were selected for breeding the superior strain; those who learned only with difficulty or were unable to learn at all became the parents of the inferior strain. As in the case of the Minnesota experiment, the two groups be-

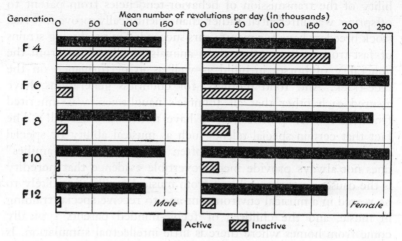

FIG. 10.—THE EFFECT OF SELECTIVE BREEDING FOR ACTIVITY IN THE WHITE RAT

Because of the greater activity of the female rats, the sexes have been kept separate in the tabulation of results. For the first three generations (not shown here) the selection of active and inactive rats for breeding purposes was made from the entire group without reference to the degree of activity in the ancestors of the selected rats. Only a very slight difference in the activity of the offspring was brought about in that way. Beginning with the fourth generation (F_4) the two strains were kept separate. Active rats for breeding were selected only from the active strain; inactive rats from the inactive strain. The rapid differentiation of the two groups after this plan was followed is a neat illustration of the fact that heredity goes back for many generations and does not depend only upon the immediate parents.

Rundquist points out that the results shown above suggest that activity is a dominant trait and that inactivity is recessive to it. The discussion on pages 49-54 of this book give you the basis for his thinking. Application of these principles to the data of Figure 10 provides a good test of your understanding of the basic theory involved. (The data for this figure are taken from "Inheritance of Spontaneous Activity in Rats," by E. A. Rundquist, *J. Comp. Psychol.*, 1933, 16: 415-438.)

came increasingly different with each successive generation until eventually a race of rat "geniuses" had been evolved from the first strain in contrast with a group of "mental defectives" from the other. (See Figure 11.)

These results show that the differences in the nervous system that lie at the base of differences in behavior are subject to the same laws of heredity as differences in external strucure and form. They do not show, as the careless reader might perhaps think, that acquired tendencies may be inherited, but only that superior stock tends to reproduce its kind and inferior stock does likewise. By continually selecting the most able members of a group for purposes of breeding, advantage is taken of all favorable variations whether they result from mutation in the desired direction, from elimination of undesirable genes from the stock, or from unusually favorable recombination of the genes already present.

Many years ago, Darwin pointed out the effect of "natural selection" in changing the characteristics of man and animal. But natural selection works slowly because the selective process is so uncertain. When man steps in to control the selection, the number of generations necessary to effect a major change is vastly reduced. And this man has done, to the great improvement of many breeds of plants and animals. He alone remains untouched. Do we hear a whisper, *Physician, heal thyself?*

MENTAL INHERITANCE IN MAN

The fruit-fly of the biological laboratory, reared in bottles under conditions that can be kept the same from generation to generation or varied at the will of the experimenter, with its thirty or more generations a year and every mating carefully controlled and recorded, affords possibilities for the study of inheritance that in man can hardly be approximated. Yet the close agreement of the facts of human heredity, as far as they have been learned, with those obtained by the experimental breeding of plants and animals leaves little doubt that the fundamental principles are the same for both. Specific facts, however, such as the question of which of two companion genes is dominant over the other, which genes are carried in the same chromosome and therefore tend to be inherited together, and how environment operates to modify inherited tendencies, must be determined separately for each individual trait in man and animal alike. Few of these facts are known with certainty as yet; nevertheless the problem of heredity is one of the most important in the entire field of human behavior. We cannot ignore it, for it underlies every reaction shown by the individual in later life. But we must not be dogmatic in asserting either its powers or its limitations

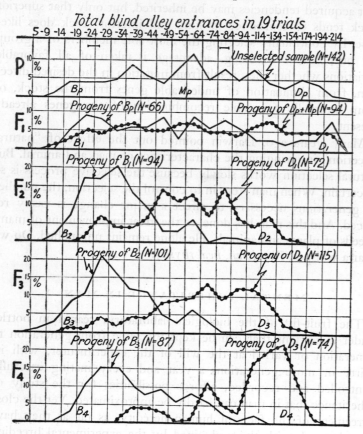

FIG. 11.—THE EFFECT OF SELECTIVE BREEDING ON MAZE LEARNING
IN THE WHITE RAT

The first curve (P) shows the distribution of errors (blind-alley entrances) made by an unselected sample of laboratory-reared white rats in learning to find their way through a maze to a food-box at the end. You will notice that the rats differed greatly in their ability to learn. Some smart (or lucky) animals made fewer than 10 errors in 19 trials; others made as many as 200.

From this parental (P) generation, the brightest (B) and the dullest (D) animals were chosen for breeding. In the first filial (F_1) generation, not

in any given instance. The same genes in different environments may produce very different effects; under the same environment different genes may develop in diverse ways. If this is true of the physical characteristics of the fruit-fly, how much more

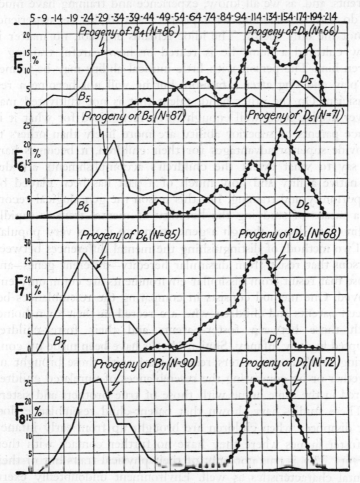

much difference between the bright and the dull strains can be noted, but by the second (F_2) generation the separation begins to be clearly apparent. By the eighth (F_8) generation, two distinct strains have been developed in which the smartest rat of the dull strain does only a little better than the most stupid rat of the bright strain. (Reproduced by courtesy of the author and the publisher from "Individual Differences," by Robert C. Tryon, Chapter 13 in *Comparative Psychology*, F. A. Moss, ed., Prentice-Hall, Inc.)

likely it is to be true of the mental traits of man in the development of which learning plays so important a part.

The difficulty of studying mental inheritance in man is greatly increased by the fact that most children are reared by their own parents, and, as we all know, experience and training have much to do with determining what people learn to do. Yet experience is not the only factor. The idiot remains an idiot, no matter in how cultured a home he is reared or how careful training is given him. The person with little musical ability may be trained to play and sing after a fashion, but he will not become a real musician. On the other hand, talent that is not cultivated may never display itself well enough to be recognized for what it is. Since parents of superior ability are more likely than others to provide superior advantages for their children, it becomes hard to say to what extent the children's accomplishments are due to native ability and how much of a part has been played by opportunity and training. For this reason the genealogical record as a means of studying the heredity of mental traits is rapidly falling into disuse, though a generation ago it was very popular.

Two methods of distinguishing the mental differences between persons that result from dissimilar heredity—different genes—and those that result from dissimilar environments are commonly employed. One method consists in comparing the resemblances between parents and children who are reared in their own homes with those between foster-parents and their foster-children adopted in early infancy. Similar checks have been made by comparing brothers and sisters reared apart with those brought up together or by comparing the resemblances of unrelated children reared in the same home with those of true brothers and sisters.

These studies have shown that parent-child resemblance does not disappear when children are brought up from early infancy in foster homes where they have no further contact with their parents. This is true not only of their physical traits but of their mental characteristics as well. Environment undoubtedly exerts some effect, but just how great this effect is likely to be is still a matter of controversy. It is reasonable to suppose that some characteristics can more easily be changed by environmental factors than others, and this seems to be the case. It is unlikely that the color of a child's eyes or hair will be affected by taking him away from his family at birth and rearing him among strangers. Probably his mental abilities will not be greatly changed, though of this we are less certain. But his conduct, the use that he makes of whatever abilities he may possess, is likely to depend very largely upon the conditions under which he has been reared and the particular kind of training he has received. One person of exceptional mental powers may become a great scientist; another, equally gifted, may become a master criminal. Equal ability in no way ensures similar accomplishment.

Another method often used for studying the relative effectiveness of heredity and environment in producing mental differences among individuals is by means of a comparison of the resemblances of identical and fraternal twins. It is now generally conceded that there are two kinds of twins. Among human beings, as a rule, only one ovum matures at a time, and consequently there is only one child at a birth. Sometimes, however, two or more ova may develop simultaneously and both be fertilized at the same time. When the chromosomes of each ovum separate for the reduction division, it is unlikely that the grouping will be the same. One ovum may receive a preponderance of chromosomes that came from the maternal grandfather of the child-to-be; in the other the grandmother's chromosomes may be in the majority. In like manner the sperm-cells by which they are fertilized will in most cases carry different assortments of chromosomes as a result of dissimilar grouping at the time of the reduction division. The children who develop from these fertilized ova will then, as a rule, carry genes of which some are alike (because by chance it is likely that some of the chromosomes will be the same for each) and others unlike. They will resemble each other in those hereditary traits that develop from similar genes, but may be very unlike each other in traits that arise from unlike genes. This is exactly what happens in the case of ordinary brothers and sisters. We have all noticed that some brothers and sisters are much more alike than others. This is quite to be expected, because it will sometimes happen that the chromosomes divide in much the same fashion on the two occasions, so that both receive about the same assortment of genes, while in the other cases the division may take a very different pattern.

Twins that result from the simultaneous fertilization of two different ova are therefore no more closely related than are ordinary brothers and sisters. They may be of either the same or of different sex. Their heredity may be fairly similar or very different; in rare cases it may be completely different. Because they are only brothers or sisters born at the same time, they are commonly known as *fraternal twins*. (See Figure 12.)

Twins sometimes originate in another way. After the usual single ovum has been fertilized by a single sperm, it begins to develop by a process of cell-division. Normally, however, the new cells formed by this division do not separate but remain attached to each other, and in this way the body of the new child is formed. At each cell-division every chromosome divides itself lengthwise, so that every new cell receives a portion of each gene. Now it occasionally happens that at the time of the first division, when the newly fertilized ovum divides to form two, these new cells do not remain together; they separate, and each part develops into a complete individual. Twins formed in this way are known as *identical twins* because they have exactly the same assortment of genes and therefore resemble each other very closely in all their hereditary traits. Identical twins are always of the same sex. (See Figure 13.)

By comparing a large number of such minute physical characteristics as palm and sole prints, form of ear, color and texture of hair, and so on, it is possible to distinguish between identical and fraternal twins with considerable accuracy. Now by noting the mental resemblances found in each group, we can measure roughly the extent to which identical heredity plus very similar environment [8] can increase resemblances between individuals be-

8 Even in the matter of environmental similarity, however, the two types of twins differ to some extent. Just because they are more likely to differ in ability, fraternal twins are the more likely to make unequal progress through the school grades, and because they are then in different classes they are less likely to have the same playmates. Differences in size and strength may lead them to prefer different games; differences in special talents make for differences in interests that lead to differential choice of surroundings and playmates. Here we have one more illustration of the close interaction between heredity and environment; a change in one almost inevitably means a change in the other. Even in childhood the relationship appears, and as with advancing age the individual becomes more free to choose his own environment and more dependent upon his own abilities in making a place for himself in the world, the association, at first slight, becomes increasingly stronger and more apparent.

FIG. 12.—THREE PAIRS OF FRATERNAL TWINS

The oldest pair are much alike in coloring but differ markedly in height. The second pair also differ somewhat in height, and one of them is obliged to wear glasses, while the other has normal vision. This is also the case with the youngest pair, who, in addition to the difference in visual acuity, are of opposite sex and very different in coloring. The boy is a typical blonde, the girl a brunette. (Courtesy of John E. Anderson.)

yond that which results when the environment is similar but the heredity is only partially similar.

A number of studies of this kind have been made, with results that upon the whole agree very closely. In most tests of mental ability, identical twins reared together resemble each other about

FIG. 13.—TWO PAIRS OF IDENTICAL TWINS

The older pair were eighty-three years of age, the babies four months old at the time this photograph was taken. In spite of the slight difference in facial expression at the moment, the resemblance of the old men is very striking. Note the similarity in the shape of the ears, nose, and chin and the distribution of wrinkles and veins. (Acme photograph.)

as closely as two tests of the same person on different occasions, while the resemblance of fraternal twins is about the same as that of ordinary brothers and sisters. In social and emotional characteristics, temperament, and such personality traits as persistence, effort, energy, and so on, the difference between the two groups is usually less marked, a fact which suggests that traits such as these are more strongly influenced by experience and training than is mental ability. However, in every trait studied, identical twins usually resemble each other somewhat more closely than fraternal twins.

An important study of twin resemblances recently reported from the University of Chicago [9] includes one section that is of special interest because it combines the two techniques we have mentioned—the study of twins and the study of foster children. This study gives a very detailed report of the later resemblances of nineteen pairs of identical twins who were separated in infancy and brought up under different surroundings. Although in four of these pairs, for whom the environmental differences were very marked, the differences in intelligence and personality were somewhat greater than was true of the other members of the group, in the remaining fifteen cases the resemblances in mental ability were almost (though not quite) as close as has usually been reported for identical twins reared together. In such matters as temperament and personality, greater divergences appeared. Upon the whole, however, the resemblances were decidedly closer than is usually found for brothers and sisters reared in the same household. We may separate a child from his family after he has been born but we cannot separate him from the genes with which he was born.

What shall we conclude from all this? Is our destiny packed up in our germ-cells, fixed and inevitable from the time of our birth? Will heredity alone make from this infant a genius, from that one a criminal? Or, on the other hand, are all men created equal, with similar talents, similar potentialities, equal ability to learn by experience, to persist in spite of difficulties, to foresee consequences and stand fast in the face of temptation?

Neither the one nor the other. No one above the rank of imbecility need be a helpless victim of his hereditary defects, if he has any, nor can he depend on his native gifts to take him on his way unaided by his own efforts or without recourse to the advantages offered by education and training. But people are not alike, and those who wish to make the most of themselves will recognize the fact frankly and try to plan their lives in such

[9] H. H. Newman, F. N. Freeman, and K. J. Holzinger, *Twins: A Study of Heredity and Environment* (Chicago, University of Chicago Press, 1937), p. 369.

a way that their natural abilities will be given the fullest opportunity for expression and the defects or weaknesses from which no one is entirely free will be as little of a handicap as possible. We no longer insist that the man with weak lungs shall try to brave the rigors of a New England winter; we send him to a climate that he can stand. We do not try to make an opera singer from the girl who cannot distinguish one note from another, but instead we try to find out where her talents lie and to direct her training along lines where it seems likely to be most effective. No one need be discouraged because he has weaknesses, nor should he hesitate to look his weak points squarely in the face. Whether they have a hereditary basis or not, they can often be improved if it seems worth while to do so; if they cannot, the thing to do is to adjust one's mode of living so that they will interfere with it as little as possible. We cannot change our genes, but to a great extent we can determine for ourselves which of them shall be the governing forces in our lives.

DO YOU KNOW ANY TWINS?

If so, you will find it interesting to try to decide to which of the two types described in this chapter they belong. To be sure, your decision will sometimes be wrong, for the distinction is one that depends upon more precise measurements than you are likely to be able to make, and even experts will disagree in their classification in a small number of the most difficult cases. But if you will give careful attention to the rules given below, you should be able to form a correct decision in the greater number of cases. Moreover, because of modern interest in the subject, many twins or their parents will already have taken the trouble to ascertain their type, and in those cases you can check your judgment afterward by inquiry.

1. If the twins are not of the same sex, no further inquiry is needed. Such twins are always fraternal.
2. Identical twins always have a single placenta to which both umbilical cords are attached * and they are enclosed within a single membraneous sac. Fraternal twins have separate placentas, and each is in its own sac. If an examination of the membranes was made by a competent person at the time of birth, this is probably the most dependable single criterion of identity or fraternity that can be had; but it is not infallible, since fusion at an early prenatal period sometimes occurs and

---

* See Chapter IV.

gives the appearance of a single set of membranes where two originally existed. This criterion has the further practical objection that in many cases no examination was made and so no facts are available later on.

3. When the twins are of the same sex, consider first of all their general appearance. (Do not be misled by clothing.) If it is easy for a stranger to tell them apart they are probably fraternal. If even close friends or members of their own family frequently confuse them, they are likely to be identical.

4. If a lock of hair from the head of one is brought close to and mingled with that of the other, can you see any difference in color or texture? If so, it is counted as evidence against identity.

5. When the eyes of both are viewed side by side in good daylight, can you see any difference in the color of the iris or in the folds of skin around the lids? Are the eyebrows of approximately the same color, shape and thickness?

6. Examine the ears. Are the convolutions of the same shape? Are the lobes of the same size and form of attachment?

7. Identical twins, apart from some special factor of illness or accident, usually do not differ in height by more than an inch or in weight during childhood by more than two or three pounds. Compare these measurements for your cases.

8. Finger, palm, and sole prints of identical twins show close agreement with each other, though not absolute identity. A rule sometimes proposed is that if the twins are identical, the left-hand prints of one will resemble the left-hand prints of the other more closely than do the right and left hands of the same individual. The same thing will be true of the right hands. If you are able to enlist the assistance of some one who has had experience in reading finger-prints, these should be secured as additional criteria.

9. Place the corresponding hands of the subjects side by side and examine first the palms and then the backs, noting the degree of correspondence in size and shape especially of the fingers and knuckles, and the lines of the palm (this is especially important if regular finger-print reading cannot be done.) Any marked differences makes it unlikely that the twins are identical.

10. Identical twins always belong to the same blood-group, but so do many fraternal twins. This criterion, too, requires technical assistance. It cannot establish identity of genetic constitution but may rule out the possibility of it.

11. Under reasonably similar environments, the resemblance between identical twins usually tends to increase with advancing age; that between fraternal twins is likely to decrease. If re-

liable evidence in respect to changes in degree of resemblance can be obtained, this factor, too, may be taken into account, though it is less dependable than the other points that have been mentioned.

If all or practically all of these criteria are in agreement in an individual case, you may feel reasonably certain that your classification of the twins as identical or fraternal, as the case may be, is correct. If they disagree, with some of the criteria suggesting that they are identical and others that they are fraternal, you may have to suspend judgment until you can have the advantage of more expert opinion.

If you are able to locate a pair of identical and another pair of fraternal twins of the same sex and approximately the same age, you will find it interesting to compare their resemblances in mental traits, such as general and special abilities, motor skills, interests and activities and personality characteristics. Your instructor in this course or some other competent psychologist will advise you about simple tests and measurements that you yourself can give. If you are able to secure an interview with the parents it is worth while also to compare their resemblances in early developmental items such as age of walking and talking, cutting teeth, etc.

Chapter IV

PRENATAL DEVELOPMENT

Into what three periods do embryologists classify prenatal life? How long does each last? What is the chief characteristic of development during each period?

Are the separate parts of the body—the arms, legs, trunk, head, and internal organs—present in miniature from the start? If not, how do they come into existence?

Why it is so essential for the nervous system to lead the rest of the body in growth?

How does the ratio of brain weight to body weight in the new-born child compare with that in the adult?

Which part of the brain grows most rapidly during prenatal life? Why is this significant?

Is all muscular activity aroused by nerve action?

At about what age does the human heart begin to beat? Why is it necessary for it to begin so early?

What are the chief differences between idiomuscular and neuromuscular behavior?

What is meant by the law of anterior-posterior development?

At about what age will the human fetus first respond to stimulation of the skin? What are its first movements like? How do they change with advancing age?

Does the brain or the spinal cord play the greater part in controlling fetal behavior?

77

PHYSICAL DEVELOPMENT DURING THE PRENATAL PERIOD

On the basis of the type of growth most characteristic at the time, embryologists commonly divide prenatal life into three periods. The first two weeks after fertilization comprise the *period of the ovum*. During this time the ovum remains a free organism, existing within the body of the mother but not attached to it, and, so far as we know, not obtaining any sustenance from it. It does not increase in size during this time, but changes greatly in internal structure. The single fertilized cell divides into two, then each of these cells divides again to make four, and so on until a globular mass of cells has been formed. At each of these and of all subsequent cell-divisions each chromosome splits lengthwise so that every new cell formed has a complete assortment of genes.

The first indication of a change in form is the development of a small cavity in the interior of the mass. This cavity is formed by the death of some cells and a rearrangement of others. The cavity gradually increases until two parts are formed: an outer membrane and an inner mass of cells. Two further cavities then form in the inner mass. Between them is a small disk, known as the *germinal disk*. From this disk the child is ultimately formed.

At the end of about two weeks, the ovum attaches itself to the uterus. The outer layer of cells has the power of cutting away the uterine surface, and in this way the ovum becomes completely imbedded in the uterus and surrounded by the blood stream. Only the outer membrane, however, is in contact with the maternal organism. The child now exists as a parasite, taking its nourishment from the mother but living a separate life of its own and growing according to its own nature. (See Figure 14).

The period from the time the ovum attaches itself to the mother and the time when the general form and structure of the body parts have all been laid down is known as the *period of the embryo*. It lasts from about the end of the second to the end of the tenth week. During this period growth in size proceeds at a tremendous rate and differentiation of the bodily parts is brought to about 95 per cent of completion. Thus within the short period of eight weeks, the tiny disk that can be seen only under the microscope changes into an unmistakable human being. To be sure, this human being still differs greatly in appearance from the adult or even the new-born baby. Its head is enormously large in proportion to the rest of the body. (See Figure 14.) The eyes are large and far apart; the arms and legs are tiny, and the fingers and toes are not yet completely separated from each other. Nevertheless it is a baby, a human being, and not a bird or a puppy. To the trained eye it is not even a monkey, though you or I might have some difficulty in making the last distinction.

The rapid growth in size is quite as remarkable. By the end of the embryonic period the embryo has increased in mass about 2,000,000 per cent. It is then approximately two inches in length and weighs from one-half to one ounce. A waggish mathematician has figured out that if the organism were to continue to double itself in size at the embryonic rate, it would be as large as the whole solar system by the age of twenty-one years. It is just as well that this tremendous rush of growth soon begins to slow down.

The third and last period of prenatal life is known as the *period of the fetus*. It includes the last thirty weeks before birth. Fetal development is characterized chiefly by growth in size, or perhaps we had better say by growth in "absolute" size, since the time required for doubling either the weight or the length of the fetus is far greater than the corresponding time during the embryonic period. During the first part of the fetal period growth is accomplished mainly by increase in the number of cells through cell-division; during the later part of the period the rate of cell division slows down and growth takes place chiefly through increase in the size of the individual cells.

DIFFERENTIATION OF THE BODY INTO PARTS

The fertilized ovum bears little resemblance to the child into which it will develop later on. The most powerful microscope cannot enable us to distinguish within it anything resembling a human body. Nevertheless from it a human body will grow. But how?

The most plausible answer we have so far is that proposed by

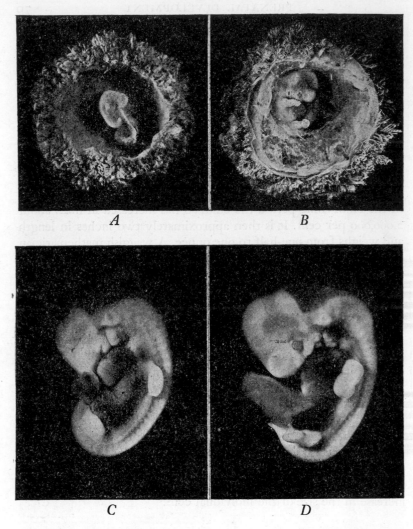

A B

C D

FIG. 14.—EMBRYOS AND FETUSES OF DIFFERENT AGES

A. Human embryo about six weeks old. Here the surrounding membranes of the placenta to which the embryo is attached by the umbilical cord are shown in cross-section. Note the many thousands of finger-like processes by which the placenta is embedded in the lining of the uterus.

B. Human embryo about nine weeks old. By this time arms and legs can be clearly distinguished as well as many other organs and structures.

C and *D*. Enlarged photographs, showing embryos about six and seven weeks old without the surrounding membranes. Note the very large size of the head and its relatively advanced state of development as compared to the lower parts of the body. At this stage the embryo is about ½ inch in sitting height.

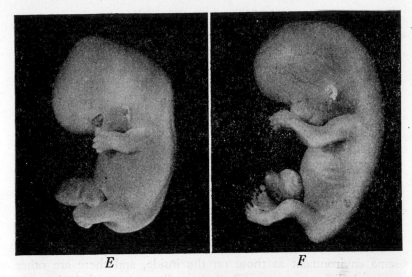

E   F

E. Embryo about eight
weeks old. Sitting height at
this age is about ¾ inch. Note
the development of the limbs,
the eyes and the opening of
the ear, which at this time is
located toward the base of the
neck. Note, too, that the "finger buds" are further ad-
vanced than the "toe buds," a
fact that provides another example of the rule that development of the upper regions
of the body is more precocious than that in the lower
regions.

F. Embryo about ten weeks
old. Sitting height about 1½
inches. The ear lobe can now
be seen, and the position of
the ear, as a result of more
rapid growth of the lower
part of the neck and face, is
more nearly that which it will
take later on. Growth of the
skeleton is shown in the out-
lining of the ribs. Both arms
and legs have increased markedly in length.

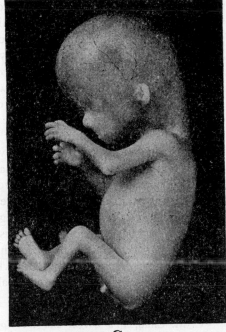

G

G. Embryo about twelve
weeks old. At this age the sitting height is about 2¾ inches, and the total
height from crown to heel is nearly 4 inches. The usual weight is a little
less than half a pound. Sex can usually be determined by external inspection.

Child.[1] Child points out that the differentiation of the body into parts cannot well be accounted for solely on the basis of the genes, since each cell contains all the genes and yet, as the body grows, the cells in different regions grow to be very unlike each other both in form and in arrangement. The brain is not like the stomach; the liver is not like the teeth; the bones are not like the muscles. Nevertheless, all these different parts develop from the single fertilized ovum. If they were not there in miniature at the start, how did they come into existence?

The answer, at least in part, is to be found in the environmental conditions under which the cells develop. At first thought it may seem to you as though the environment of all the cells is the same. But a moment's consideration will convince you that it is not. The cells on the outside of the child's body have not the same environment as those on the inside, and there are other regional differences as well. Some cells are crowded close together; others have plenty of room to grow. Some receive ample nourishment; others get relatively little. These are just a few examples of the differences in cell environment that are found from one region of the growing body to another.

Experiments carried on with lower animals during the very early stages of development have shown how completely the body as a whole controls the development of its parts. By transplanting certain cells to other regions of the growing body, that is, by changing their environment, almost any cells can be made to transform into almost any part, provided only that this is done early enough, before the transformation into a particular kind of cell is too far advanced. Primitive cells that would normally have become skin cells can be made to develop into the spinal cord if placed in the appropriate region; those that would have become eyes can be made to give rise to brain and so on. Thus we see that the cells which make up the body are never independent units. The single cell from which the child develops need not, in any physical sense, "contain" all the parts that later appear. All that it need contain is a single kind of protoplasm that is

---

[1] C. M. Child, *The Origin and Development of the Nervous System* (Chicago, University of Chicago Press, 1921); *Physiological Foundations of Behavior* (New York, Henry Holt and Co., 1924).

capable of developing in various ways according to the influences or "environment" in which it is placed. As the cells multiply, those in certain regions become unlike those in other regions because they are not subject to the same influences from without the organism or from within it. Certain cells are compressed more than others; some receive a more abundant food supply; in others waste matter accumulates in greater amounts, and so on. Thus the growth and development of one part of the body directly affects the growth and development of other parts. The body, not the individual cells of which it consists, is the fundamental living unit.

Such a highly organized system as the human body can work effectively only if there is communication from one region to another. The hand must work in coöperation with the eye; the internal organs must coördinate their activities if the organism is to survive. This highly important function of supplying a means of communication from one region of the body to another so that all parts may work together harmoniously is supplied by the nervous system. The development of the nervous system is therefore of particular interest to the psychologist in his studies of behavior. In this chapter we shall not attempt to give more than a very brief account of its growth but will merely call attention to some of the main features.

DEVELOPMENT OF THE NERVOUS SYSTEM AS A WHOLE

In the development of the child from the germinal disk, the first marked differentiation that can be seen is the formation of a ridge or thickening on the surface. This fixes the axis of the body. Gradually this thickened portion lifts itself above the germinal disk, carrying with it part of the surrounding surface. Eventually the whole thing pinches off except for a small attachment that later becomes the umbilical cord. Along the center of the original ridge the outer layer of cells now begins to proliferate more rapidly than the remainder, thus forming a thickened row of cells running down the center of the back of the developing embryo. This *neural plate*, as it is called, marks the beginning of the nervous system. A little later on, the center of the neural plate begins to fold in, as shown in Figure 15. The groove thus formed is called the *neural groove;* the edges of the groove, where the developing nervous tissue joins the non-nervous surface layer of cells, is called the *neural crest* or the *neural fold.* The infolding continues until in about a week's time the edges of the groove meet and join to form a tube. Successive stages in this process are seen in Figure 15.

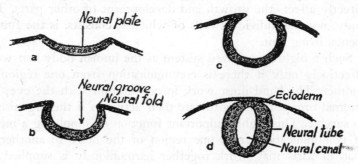

FIG. 15.—SUCCESSIVE STAGES IN THE INFOLDING OF THE
NEURAL GROOVE

(From *A Textbook of Embryology* by H. E. Jordan and J. E. Kindred. D. Appleton-Century Co.)

The *neural tube* formed by the closure of the sides of the infolded neural groove is the starting point of the spinal cord and brain. Very soon the head end of the embryo can be distinguished from the caudal end [2] by the faster growth of this part of the neural tube. The spinal cord develops from the caudal portion of the tube by a gradual and regular thickening of its walls. The brain results from a much more rapid but uneven thickening of the forward end of the neural tube.

In the course of this uneven growth of the part of the tube that will later become the brain, two bulges soon appear, one on each side of its foremost portion. These mark the beginning of the *cerebral hemispheres.* Their growth is the most conspicuous feature of brain development during the embryonic period, though all the other main divisions of the brain are also laid down

[2] From the Latin word meaning "tail."

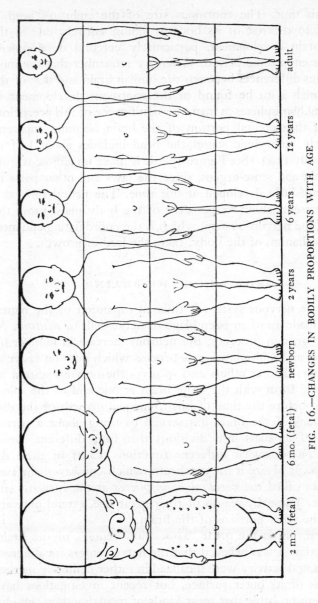

FIG. 16.—CHANGES IN BODILY PROPORTIONS WITH AGE

(From chapter on "Developmental Anatomy," by R. E. Scammon in Morris's *Human Anatomy*, Sixth Edition. Courtesy P. Blakiston's Son & Co.)

during this time. The enormous size of the embryo's head as compared to the rest of its body is almost entirely due to the rush of brain development, particularly cerebral development, during the embryonic period. When we remember that the most conspicuous differences between the human brain and that of the lower animals is to be found in the enormous development of the cerebral hemispheres in man, the significance of this precocious growth of the cerebral portion of the brain becomes apparent. In the early embryonic stages the head includes about half of the total body mass. (See Figure 16.) It is made up almost wholly of the brain and sense-organs, since the jaws and other parts of the head are little developed at this time. The neural tube as a whole represents about 75 per cent of the body mass. From the very start, the nervous system, which is the coördinating and integrating mechanism of the body, takes the lead in growth.

GROWTH OF THE BRAIN

The entire nervous system is thus an expansion of the neural tube. It is made up of an assemblage of nerve-cells or *neurons*. As embryonic growth proceeds, the neurons increase in number by cell-division and multiplication, a process which goes on faster at certain points than at others and so gives the nervous system its characteristic form with the large brain at one end of the spinal cord. Long before the time of birth, unequal growth of the different regions of the brain has served to bring about a partial separation of its mass into divisions that bear different names and carry on somewhat different functions. Chief of these divisions in point of size is the cerebrum, which consists of the two large masses called the *cerebral hemispheres* at the forward end of the tube. These, by reason of their great size, extend outward and over the other portions of the brain.

The cerebrum is the great "association center" of the brain. For a long time it was believed that the nerve centers for different kinds of mental activity were localized in rather definitely marked out regions of its outer surface, but recent investigations have made it seem probable that most kinds of mental activity involve large rather than small areas, and that when parts of the brain which ordinarily are active in certain connections are disabled,

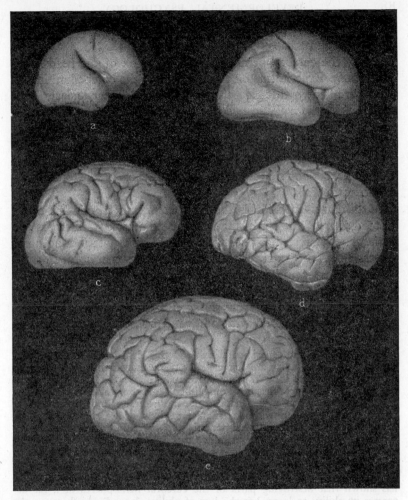

FIG. 17.—CHANGES IN THE EXTERNAL APPEARANCE OF THE CEREBRAL
HEMISPHERES FROM THE SIXTH TO THE TENTH LUNAR MONTH OF
PRENATAL LIFE

Anatomists commonly reckon ages during the prenatal period in terms
of lunar months of four weeks (28 days) each in order to avoid the irregularities resulting from the unequal length of the different calendar months.
The figures show the developmental changes at monthly intervals from the
sixth to the tenth lunar month (168 to 280 days of age) which is the usual
age at birth. Except for the increase in size, little further change in the
appearance of the cerebral hemispheres takes place between birth and maturity, but microscopic examination shows that at birth many areas are
still unmyelineated and other differences in cell structure exist. (Courtesy
of Dr. R. E. Scammon.)

in many cases at least their work can be taken over by other parts, though perhaps not as effectively.[3]

Below the cerebral hemispheres at the back of the head is the *cerebellum*. Experiments on the removal of the cerebellum in animals have shown that this part of the brain is particularly concerned with the maintenance of posture. When the cerebellum is removed from a pigeon, for example, the bird can no longer stand. It falls to one side or the other, and though by fluttering its wings and moving its legs it may make a little progress, it cannot keep right side up if it tries to fly or keep from falling if it tries to walk.

A third main division is the *brain stem*, which consists of an enlargement of the spinal cord at the point where it enters the brain. The brain stem is a sort of way-station or distributing point for the fibers that connect the brain and the spinal cord. In addition the brain stem has certain nerve centers of its own. Among these the *thalamus* is of particular interest because it is there that the nerve fibers leading from the eye, ear, and most other sense-organs make connection with other fibers leading to the cerebral

---

[3] Since most of the experimental work in this field has been carried out on animals whose brains are less elaborately organized than is the human brain, generalizations about the specialized functions of the latter are hazardous. One rule, however, has been established with reasonable certainty. The further we go up the phylogenetic scale, the greater is the degree of specialization of function within particular regions of the brain. Complete equivalence of function or "equi-potentiality," is found only in the nervous systems of animals of a very primitive type, such as the jelly-fish, which has no brain, properly speaking, but only a system of connected nerve-cells that spread out in a network over its entire body. Lashley in *Brain Mechanisms and Intelligence* (Chicago, University of Chicago Press, 1929) has shown that destroying parts of the cerebral hemispheres of a rat decreases its ability to learn, but the loss of ability depends chiefly upon the *amount* of brain tissue that is destroyed; its *location* makes little difference. But when we come to an animal such as the chimpanzee with a brain more nearly like that of man, an injury to one part of the cerebrum may have quite a different effect from that resulting from an injury of equal extent to another part. Generally speaking, therefore, we may say that increasing complexity of brain structure from one animal species to another is accompanied by increasing specialization of the different parts of the brain for particular kinds of mental work. Even in man, however, there is evidence that such specialization is rarely absolute and there is no foundation at all for the idea that minor variations in the shape of the head—the "bumps" of the phrenologist's fancy—tell us anything at all about the abilities or character of the individual.

hemispheres. Within the brain stem, too, appear to be located certain nerve centers that are actively concerned with emotional behavior, a point that will be discussed further in another chapter.

No new cells form in the cerebrum or in the brain stem after birth. Increase in size in these parts of the brain after birth is brought about wholly by increase in the size of the individual cells and by the outgrowth of fibers and the addition of the protective sheath described in a later section. In the cerebellum about 95 per cent of all the cells are formed before birth; in the spinal cord some new cells continue to be formed for about two or three years after birth.

At the time of birth, the brain of an average child weighs from ten to twelve ounces, or nearly 10 per cent of the body weight. In the adult the brain weighs about two and three-quarter pounds on the average, though there is much variation from one person to another. In other words, the brain alone constitutes about one-tenth of the weight of the new-born infant but only about one-fiftieth of the weight of the adult. And just as the brain as a whole leads the rest of the body in growth, so the cerebrum, which is the part of the brain that shows the greatest difference both in size and in complexity of structure between men and animals, takes the lead over the more primitive, less uniquely human portions of the brain. At birth the brain is about 90 per cent cerebrum, about 7 per cent cerebellum, and about 3 per cent brain stem. The corresponding proportions in the adult are 87 per cent cerebrum, 11 per cent cerebellum, and 2 per cent brain stem.

THE NERVE-CELLS

For the first three months of prenatal life the nervous system grows almost entirely by increase in the number of cells through cell-division. At first these cells are all very much alike; but, as they continue to multiply, differences between them increase until eventually many different forms can be distinguished. Each mature cell, however, includes a cell body with its nucleus and one or more fibers by which it maintains its connection with other cells. Some neurons have many fibers growing out from them; others have only one or two. Some of the fibers are of microscopic length; others, such as those making up the nerves that run from the lower part of the spinal cord to the feet, may be as much as three or four feet long. A number of different forms of neurons are shown in Figure 18.

The neurons are divided on the basis of their function into three

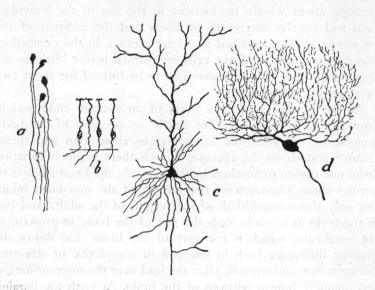

FIG. 18.—DIFFERENT FORMS OF NEURONS

a, unipolar cell; *b,* bipolar cell; *c,* pyramidal cell; *d,* Purkinje cell. (From *Brain and Spinal Cord,* by Emil Villiger. Courtesy J. B. Lippincott Co.)

classes, the *sensory neurons,* the *motor neurons,* and the *central or associative neurons.* The sensory neurons, as the name implies, are those which conduct impulses [4] from the organs of special sense in which they terminate to the brain or to the spinal cord. In the motor neurons the *nerve impulse* takes the opposite direction,

[4] We do not know exactly how the nervous system works. We do know that by its action "communication" is made from one part of the body to another and thus bodily organization is maintained. Most physiologists now regard the activity within the nerve as a wave of some form of electrochemical energy, but later discoveries may necessitate a restatement. The true nature of nerve action has not been ascertained with certainty. The term *nerve impulse* (or *nervous impulse*) thus refers merely to some form of energy propagated along the nerve fibers, the exact nature of which is unknown.

passing from the brain or cord outward to the muscles and glands. The associative neurons are located within the central nervous system, where they form a complicated system of interconnections with the sensory and motor neurons and with each other. All neurons are distinct units in the sense that they never fuse with each other, their fibers simply meeting in such a way that the wave of energy can pass from one to another, much as an

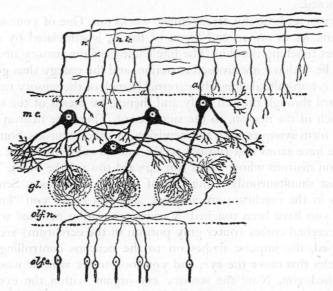

FIG. 19.—DIAGRAM SHOWING SYNAPSES BETWEEN THE OLFACTORY NERVE CELLS LOCATED IN THE NASAL MUCOSA AND NERVE CELLS IN THE OLFACTORY BULB (AN ENLARGEMENT OF THE OLFACTORY NERVE AT THE POINT WHERE IT ENTERS THE BRAIN)

(From *A Textbook of Histology* by H. E. Jordan. D. Appleton-Century Co.)

electrical current passes from one wire to another when the wires are in contact. The fibers that receive the impulse from another neuron are called *dendrites;* those along which the impulse passes from one neuron to another or to its terminus within a muscle or gland are called *axons.* The point at which the dendrite of one neuron comes into functional contact with the axon or cell body of another is called a *synapse.* (See Figure 19.) The synapse is like a one-way turnstile; the nerve impulse can pass through it in only one direction. The impulse comes to the synapse over the axon of one neuron and, as a rule, is taken up on the other side by the dendrites of another. In some cases the synapse is made directly on the cell body of the second neuron. A given mental act may involve few or many neurons, but there is reason to think that the number involved is far greater, as a rule, than was formerly supposed.

Let us see how this arrangement works out. One of your sense-organs, let us say an end-organ of touch, is stimulated by some object touching the skin. The fine endings of the sensory neurons that lie within it are aroused to action, and the energy thus generated is transmitted along the external branch of the sensory neuron inward through the cell body and thence, by means of the spinal branch of the neuron, to the spinal cord. There the neuron endings form synapses with the dendrites of other neurons. Some of these have axons that run out to the muscle cells; others are association neurons whose axons run upward toward the brain. Thus almost simultaneously a number of things can happen. Sensory areas in the cerebrum are aroused, and as a result you "know" that you have been touched. Various association neurons within the cerebral cortex (outer gray portion of the cerebrum) are also aroused, the impulse flashes on to the neurons controlling the muscles that move the eye, and you look to see what it was that touched you. Now the sensory end-organs within the eye are set in action, and the impulse is flashed back by way of the optic nerve to the optical centers in the brain stem. But in order not merely to see but to understand what you see, associations of many kinds must be made; and in order that these may be made, neurons in the cerebrum are again aroused to action. As a result of their action you "recognize" that you have been nudged by a friend, and at the same time realize that he has probably done so for a reason. A fresh set of neurons is now brought into action and by means of a complicated interplay of motor, sensory, and association centers you are enabled to ask him, "What do you want?" Even before this, and probably before you had time to realize that anything had happened, a synaptic connection was made with the motor neurons in direct communication with the part of the body that was originally touched. These neurons at

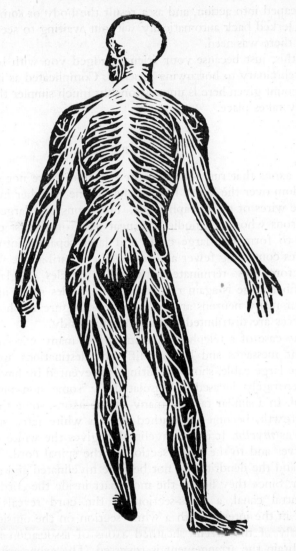

FIG. 20.—DIAGRAM ILLUSTRATING THE GENERAL ARRANGEMENT OF THE NERVOUS SYSTEM

(From Martin's *Human Body*. Courtesy Henry Holt and Co.)

once leaped into action, and as a result the body or some part of it was jerked back automatically without waiting to see whether or not there was need.

All this, just because your friend nudged you with his elbow as a preliminary to borrowing a pencil. Complicated as it sounds, the account given here is unquestionably much simpler than what actually takes place.

THE NERVES

The axons that run out from the cell bodies are not scattered at random over the body. Instead they come together in bundles like the wires of a telegraph cable. The axons of a large number of neurons whose cell bodies are near each other first come together to form one large cable and later separate into smaller branches containing fewer and fewer fibers until at the very end, just before they terminate within the muscles or glands, the single-fiber stage is again reached. These cables made up of the axons of many neurons are called *nerves*. Figure 20 shows how the nerves are distributed throughout the body.

In the case of a telephone system, when many wires carrying different messages and having different destinations are bound into one large cable, short-circuiting is prevented by having each wire separately incased or insulated by some non-conducting material. In a similar fashion many of the axons, some time after their growth, become ensheathed with a white fatty substance known as *myelin*. It is the myelin that gives the white color to the nerves and to the outer section of the spinal cord. The cell bodies and the dendrites do not become myelinated and are gray in color. Since they lie for the most part inside the cord next to the central canal, a cross-section of the cord reveals a gray portion in the interior with a white section on the outside made up chiefly of the myelin-sheathed axons of association neurons. In the brain the arrangement is reversed. The axons are for the most part found in the interior, the cell bodies and dendrites on the surface. In the brain, therefore, the outside is gray and the inside white, just the opposite of the arrangement seen in the cord. The outer gray surface of the brain is known as the *cortex*.

The axons do not become myelinized until some time after they are formed. Although the process of myelinization begins during the fetal period, it is far from complete at the time of birth. In man, more than half of the axons acquire their myelin sheath after birth. In some animals myelinization is further advanced at birth than in man and is completed at a much earlier age. In general there is a fair agreement between the amount of myelinization that has been completed at birth and the animal's developmental level at birth. In animals such as the chick or guinea-pig that can stand and run at birth, prenatal myelinization is further advanced than it is in babies or in white rats that are comparatively helpless at birth. However, there is still much controversy over the exact function of the myelin sheath, and while there is evidence that those neurons which eventually become myelinized do not attain complete functioning until the sheath has been laid down, it is by no means certain that there can be no activity at all in a nerve fiber before myelinization has taken place. As a matter of fact, there are indications that the relation between nerve action and the laying down of the sheath is a reciprocal one in which the growth of the sheath which facilitates the activity of the neurons is itself directly stimulated by nerve action.[5] The question is of

[5] The theory that myelinization of nerve fibers is a necessary antecedent to their functioning was first propounded by Flechzig toward the end of the nineteenth century. The idea seemed so plausible in view of its analogy to a telephone system that it was at first rather generally accepted. However, contradictory facts were soon reported. Watson, in 1903, showed that in the white rat, coördinated reflex behavior is present from birth, although no myelinization whatever has taken place at that time. Moreover, he showed that the animal is capable of learning and retaining certain motor skills before any myelinization has occurred in the cortex. The question was again brought to the fore when, in 1924 Tilney and Casamajor published their classical study on the relationship between the development of certain behavior patterns in kittens and the growth of the myelin sheath. Their procedure was to make careful observations of the kind of behavior shown by the kittens at successive ages, after which, by means of postmortem examination of the nervous structure, they compared the course of myelinization with the course of behavior development. They were able to demonstrate beyond reasonable doubt that in this species, at least, the two are related. Again it was taken for granted by some that this could only be interpreted to mean that myelinization must precede nerve action. Once more, contrary data were not long in appearing. Angulo, in 1929, verified Watson's earlier findings for white rats and at about the same time Langworthy, working with fetal and young kittens and with opposums still living in the mother's pouch, demonstrated that, in spite of a fairly close general relationship between the onset of behavioral patterns and

interest to us because of the rather unqualified assertions made
by some present-day psychologists that since so many of the
cortical neurons of the human infant are still unmyelinized at
the time of birth, its behavior is of necessity governed by the
subcortical rather than the cortical centers, which, if true, would
mean that it would not be able to "learn" [6] in the ordinary sense
of the word, until some time after birth. Without going into
details, we need only say that there is as yet no sound neurological
evidence that the cortex of the new-born infant is wholly non-
functional or that its learning is fundamentally different in kind
from that of the older infant or adult. The latter have developed
certain aids to learning that the new-born infant lacks, of which
the most important is unquestionably speech. Nevertheless, in
spite of the incomplete myelinization of his cortical centers, there
is warrant for believing that the infant begins to learn as soon
as he is born.

---

the myelinization of nerve-tracts presumably concerned with those activities, a considerable amount of reflex activity can and does take place
previous to the formation of the sheath. Further evidence that activity in
the nerve stimulates, if it does not actually give rise to the process of myelinization, is to be found in a study by Held who found that premature opening of one eye of young animals such as kittens and puppies, whose eyes
normally remain sealed for several days after birth, caused the optic nerve
of that eye to become myelinized more rapidly than that of the unopened
eye. It has also been demonstrated that the process of myelinization shows
very marked acceleration at the time of birth. This has been demonstrated
for human infants as well as for animals. That this increase in the rate of
myelin formation is not simply a matter of maturation of the organism but
is definitely related to the environmental changes that come with birth is
evidenced by the fact that it occurs in infants prematurely born as well
as in those born at full term. All in all, the weight of evidence seems to
favor the hypothesis of a reciprocal relation between myelinization of the
nerve fibers and the establishment of behavior, rather than absolute dependence of either one upon the other.

[6] This does not mean that the infant's behavior would be completely unmodifiable, since it has been shown that some learning or "conditioning"
of a very simple and primitive kind can take place in animals that have
been completely deprived of the cerebral hemispheres. Such learning, however, is very specific and unstable, not carrying over at all to conditions
only slightly different from those under which the reaction has been acquired.

IDIO-EXCITABILITY OF MUSCLES

The first detectable movement either in the human or the animal embryo is the beating of the heart. In the chick this has been observed as early as the second day of incubation, before anything that looks like a chicken can be seen in the egg. In the human embryo the heart begins to beat at about the third prenatal week. You can easily see why this is necessary, for the fetus has its own circulatory system from the beginning, and if food and oxygen were not carried by the blood to all parts of the growing organism, the processes of growth and of waste and repair of tissues could not go on.

There is fairly good evidence that the beating of the heart begins independently of neuron action; probably it starts before the outgrowing axons have reached the heart. Even during the early stages of development, it has been found possible to stimulate muscle tissue directly and so to cause it to contract without nerve action. Hooker,[7] for example, found that when frog embryos were operated on in such a way that all connection between the neural tube and the muscles was severed at a very early stage of development when the axons had not yet begun to form, the muscles would continue to develop, but except for the heart there was no spontaneous movement. The heart, however, began to beat at about the same time in the frogs without nerves as in normal animals. Mechanical stimulation of the skin with the point of a stiff hair would induce movement in the voluntary muscles [8] of the normal animals but not in those without nerves. If, however, a very fine needle that would penetrate the skin was used, the muscles would contract; but the contraction was limited to a much smaller area in the operated animals than in the normal ones.

[7] Davenport Hooker, "The Development and Function of Voluntary and Cardiac Muscle in Embryos without Nerves," *J. Exper. Zoöl.*, 1911, 11: 159-186.

[8] The *voluntary muscles* are those that we are able to move at will, such as the muscles of the arm and legs, as opposed to the *involuntary muscles* of the viscera, which are not under our control. The voluntary muscles are made up of fibers that run parallel to each other, giving them a striped appearance; hence they are known as *striate muscles*. Most of the involuntary muscles are made up of extremely fine fibers that run in all directions like a fine web. They are known as *smooth muscles*. The heart, however, is modified striate muscle.

Electrical stimulation of the muscles also brought about contraction. Hooker sums up his findings as follows: "Cardiac muscle, which we have reason to believe is the most primitive, will function spontaneously and rhythmically without nervous control. The axial muscles, on the other hand, will not function spontaneously in the absence of the nervous system, though they will respond to direct stimulation."

In this primitive excitability of the muscles we have a device, not so much for organizing and coördinating the different parts of the body with each other as for providing a certain crude protective mechanism for local parts at a stage of development when neuron action is as yet imperfectly organized. The contraction of the muscles in the operated animals was always confined to the part stimulated, and it always resulted in withdrawal of the stimulated part a little further away from the point of stimulation. But the body as a whole did not move, showing that the idio-excitability of the muscles does not serve to keep the parts of the body in communication with each other. It is not an integrating device like the nervous system but serves only a local function. Moreover, although this capacity of muscle tissue to respond to direct stimulation does not disappear even in adult life, its chief usefulness is temporary. Even heart action is soon brought under the control of the nervous system.[9]

MUSCULAR ACTIVITY ARISING FROM NERVE ACTIVITY

In normal animals a form of behavior soon appears that is in many ways very different from the simple localized contractions of small groups of muscle cells that can be aroused by direct stimulation of the muscles. This later behavior is aroused and controlled by the nervous system and is therefore known as neuromuscular activity. Practically all postnatal activity is neuromuscular.

[9] This is true at least to the extent that the heart will be made to beat more rapidly by direct action of the nervous system. Whether the normal heart rhythm is *neurogenic* (having its origin in the nervous system) or *myogenic* (having its origin in the muscle tissue) is still a matter of controversy, though the weight of evidence appears to favor the myogenic theory.

In the early behavior of the fetus, whether it be animal or human, generalized rather than local responses are characteristic of neuromuscular activity. It was formerly supposed that complex forms of behavior came into being by little bits which developed separately and later became chained together to form the whole act. But recent studies have shown that this "chain reflex theory," as it was called, has little to support it. Instead of the independent development of the separate parts of an act which are later linked together into a whole, the mass movements appear first and the finer movements develop out of them. We may liken it to the growth of a tree. First there is the main shoot. As it grows, offshoots or branches arise; as these grow, smaller branches proceed from them. So in the development of behavior during the fetal period, movements of the trunk precede movements of the limbs; movements of the arms and legs precede independent movements of the fingers and toes, and so on. There seems, moreover, to be a tendency for movements of the upper parts of the body to precede those of the lower parts, just as in physical growth the head portions of the body are precocious in development as compared to the legs.

Coghill,[10] who has made very extensive studies of the development of *Amblystoma* (the common salamander), has shown that the progressive development of behavior is paralleled to a remarkable degree by the growth and development of the neural mechanisms that keep the parts of the body subordinate to the whole. By the use of motion-pictures he was able to make permanent records of the behavior shown by an animal at any given stage of development and then, by means of post-mortem examination, to determine the degree of neurological development corresponding to that stage. He found that the first spontaneous movement that can be detected is a simple coil of the trunk, which later develops into a double coiling movement something like the letter *S*, from which the swimming movements are derived. (See Figure 21.) Later still the limbs participate, the fore limbs first and later the hind limbs. In the case of salamanders that become able to live either in water or on land, the walking movements develop directly out of the swimming movements that were displayed at

[10] G. E. Coghill, *Anatomy and the Problems of Behavior* (Cambridge, Mass., Harvard University Press, 1929).

an earlier stage of development. Walking is a more advanced stage in the sequence than swimming, however, because in walking the leg movements, which represent a comparatively advanced stage in development, play a much more important part than they do

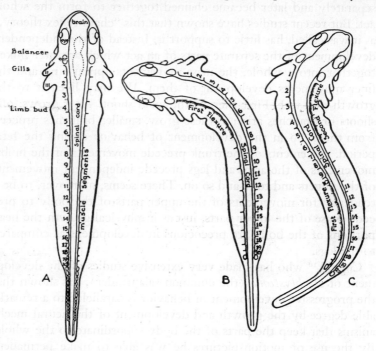

FIG. 21.—DEVELOPMENT OF SWIMMING MOVEMENTS IN AMBLYSTOMA

From the resting position (A) a flexure (B) begins in the head region and proceeds tailward as if, according to its earlier habits, the animal were going to throw itself into a tight coil but instead of doing this it reverses the flexure in the anterior part before the first flexure has passed through the entire length of the animal. There are now two flexures in progress at the same time, one to the right and the other to the left, both of them progressing from the head tailward (C). (From *Anatomy and the Problems of Behavior*, by G. E. Coghill. Courtesy Cambridge University Press.)

in swimming, which is performed in large measure by the alternating double flexion of the trunk. Coghill has shown that the growth of these behavior patterns is always a matter of the total organism, that they are tied together from the start and do not develop as small units that later become coördinated with each other. The whole is not built up from its parts, but the parts develop out of the whole.

The explanation for this, in Coghill's opinion, is to be found in the precocious growth of the neural structure. By studying the nerve development of animals at different stages of behavior, he was able to show that the growth of the nerve-fibers outward to the muscles or, more exactly speaking, to the region where the muscles are being formed, precedes the actual differentiation of the tissues into true muscle-cells. The growth and differentiation of nerve and muscle proceed simultaneously, but the neural growth keeps safely in advance of the muscle growth. "As a result of this precocious invasion of limb-forming tissue by branches of nerve-cells that are already integrating the trunk, the earliest movements of the limbs are of necessity totally integrated with trunk action." [11]

Working with cats, Windle and Griffin[12] found that much the same type of sequence holds. The earliest movement that could be seen was a flexion of the head and upper trunk. At later stages the movements had progressed to include first the lower trunk, then the limbs, the tail, and the toes, and still later the finer muscles of the face, throat, and tongue. Here again we see that the earliest movements are mass movements and not movements of local parts, and that the order of functional development, like the order of physical growth, proceeds from the head downward and outward to the limbs.

THE BEHAVIOR OF THE HUMAN FETUS

By the middle of the prenatal period, the human fetus begins to make movements that are of sufficient magnitude to be felt by the mother. The popular idea that there is no movement previous to this time is, however, a mistaken one. Study of fetuses that have been artificially delivered during the early stages of pregnancy[13] has shown that as early as the end of the second month the human fetus will move in response to stimulation by the point

[11] Coghill, op. cit., p. 22.

[12] W. F. Windle and A. N. Griffin, "Observations on Embryonic and Fetal Movements of the Cat," J. Comp. Neurol., 1930, 52: 149-188.

[13] Cases in which some physical malformation or other abnormal condition of the mother made it unsafe to allow the pregnancy to continue.

of a fine hair. The fact that under normal conditions the mother is unable to "feel" any movement at this early stage of development is in all probability due to the extremely small size of the fetus which, at the end of the eighth week, is still only about one and a fourth inches in length. At this age, too, movements are slow and of very small magnitude.

The earliest extensive study of the behavior of the human fetus was made by Minkowski.[14] As in the case of animals, he found that mass activity appears first and local activity second, and that the development of behavior is closely paralleled by the growth and development of the nervous system. But the nervous development is primary, the behavior secondary. The one closely follows the other.

The fetuses studied by Minkowski were all artificially delivered by Cæsarian section because of some special condition in the mother which made it unsafe to allow the pregnancy to continue. Their ages ranged from two to five months. Because of the way they were delivered, there was no question of birth injury, which often makes it hard to interpret the earliest forms of behavior shown by infants born in the usual way, as we shall see in the following chapter.

The tiniest ones, those only about three inches in length, whose age was estimated at about two to three months, made only slow, uncoördinated, and non-rhythmical movements which were not confined to the part of the body that was stimulated but might affect almost any part. For example,

a light pressure on one foot or often merely a stroke of the foot with a small camel's hair brush would cause not only a withdrawal or some other movement of the stimulated leg but also various reactions in the opposite leg (bending, stretching, etc.) and in both arms (as for example, bending and afterward stretching or twisting or bringing both arms forward). Movements of the head and body might also occur. ... *One might say, therefore, that every section of the skin can serve as a reflex zone for extremely variable reactions which have a tendency to spread out, more or less, over the entire fetal organism.*[15]

---

[14] M. Minkowski, "Über frühezeitige Bewegungen, Reflexe, und muskulare Reactionen bei menschlichen Foetus, und ihre Beziehungen zum foetalen Nerven und Muskelsystem," *Schweiz. med. Woch.*, 1922, 3: 721-724, 751-755.

[15] Italics are Minkowski's.

With the older fetuses, however, especially those from seven to ten inches long whose age was estimated at four to five months, the responses to stimulation were sometimes confined to the part of the body that was stimulated, "yet there remained a tendency for the movement to spread to the other extremities and to the whole body in most instances. In one fetus of 19 cm. [about seven and a half inches] a diagonal reflex was observed in which a stimulation of one foot in the same constant manner always aroused a movement in the opposite hand.... In a few fetuses of 11 to 21 cm. [about four and a half to eight and a quarter inches] a touch on the upper lip or on the tongue produced movements of opening and closing the mouth as in the beginning of suckling."

Minkowski also found evidence of idiomuscular activity which differed from neuromuscular activity in the same way as was shown by Hooker's frog embryos. Separation of the brain from the rest of the body made very little difference in behavior, showing that most of these early reflexes are under the control of the spinal cord rather than the brain.

In a more recent study by Hooker[16] moving pictures were employed to make permanent records of the responses of the fetuses. Since the respiratory apparatus is not yet functional in these very young organisms, they do not survive for more than a very brief period after delivery, and the advantage of securing durable records that can be examined repeatedly and at leisure is very great. Hooker also exercised exceptional care in his experimental technique. Many investigators of fetal activity have employed relatively coarse instruments such as a horse-hair, a cactus thorn, or a fine needle, any of which, unless handled with extreme care, is likely to penetrate the very delicate skin of the young fetus and induce idiomuscular activity which may be mistaken for true reflex activity. Minkowski used a fine hair but did not attempt to determine its exact stiffness. Hooker used a human hair, mounted in a handle. The degree of resistance of this hair was determined by finding how many milligrams of pressure had to be exerted against its end to cause it to bend. He found that many human hairs were too coarse and stiff to be safe, especially when experimenting with the smaller fetuses.

[16] Davenport Hooker, "Early Fetal Activities in Mammals," *Yale J. Biol. and Med.*, 1936, 8: 579-602.

All of the fetuses examined by Hooker that were under eight weeks of age proved to be non-motile. The first response was obtained in a fetus 1.18 inches in length, whose estimated age was just over eight weeks. When the neck of this fetus was stimulated with the point of a hair, there was a slow bending of the body toward the side away from the stimulus. Two other fetuses, estimated to be about nine and one half weeks old, exhibited a kind of movement that Minkowski had previously described as "worm-like." The body was bent away from the stimulus with rotation of the hips, a downward movement of both arms, and rotation of the head. At eleven and one half weeks the movements were elaborated and more rapid. The arms were first separated and then brought forward "as if to clap the hands." By the age of fourteen weeks many new responses had appeared. Even mimetic facial grimaces occurred if the lips or cheeks were touched. Hooker states that at this age "except for respiration, almost all the specific reflexes of the new-born are represented."

Almost every one has observed that if a finger is placed in the hand of a young infant, the baby's fingers will close about it. This is known as the *palmar or grasping reflex*. (See Figures 23 and 24.) Minkowski reports the beginning of this reflex at ten and one half weeks; Hooker observed it at eleven and one half weeks at which time "a light stimulation of the palm, if repeated,[17] induced a barely perceptible flexion movement of the fingers accompanying a slight flexion of the wrist. At thirteen weeks the flexion was more pronounced. At fourteen weeks a fairly respectable 'fist' was made, but it was not of a closed type, nor did the thumb play much of a rôle in the flexion. The grasp does not hold an object placed within it until twenty-two weeks, and then but feebly."

Hooker's work is of great importance both because it is the only large-scale study of the early reactions of the human fetus since the classic study by Minkowski that appeared in 1922, and also because it affords so nice an example of experimental technique. The close agreement of his findings with the general prin-

[17] This is an example of a neuro-psychological principle known as the *summation of stimuli*. When a stimulus is too weak to evoke an overt response, it nevertheless has some effect. If a series of such *sublimenal stimuli*, as they are called, is given at the proper rate of speed, the effect is cumulative, and after a time the response may occur.

ciples laid down by Coghill may perhaps be traced, in part at least, to the facts that they used much the same procedures in stimulating their subjects (both used a human hair as the instrument) and that both were extremely careful to control other factors that might confuse the results. However, it is but fair to note that the theory of development by the differentiation of fine patterns of response from an initially generalized or "mass" reaction is not uniformly supported by the evidence from all sources. Bridgman and Carmichael,[18] for example, have reported that the very earliest responses that could be elicited from the fetal guinea-pig were as often movements of the foreleg as of the neck and that movements of the trunk did not appear until at least a day later. Hooker, however, points out that the leg movements did not occur unless pressure had previously been applied to the amniotic sac in such a way as to change the position of the fetus. He suggested that the responses observed by Carmichael may have been due, not to stimulation of the touch receptors in the skin but to responses of the proprioceptors (see p. 120) in the muscles and joints as the fetus returned to its original position. After comparing all the available findings from his own and other studies, Hooker states that "all the evidence points to the conclusion that the responses of human fetuses to tactile stimulation follow a Coghillian sequence, first the expanding total pattern; then the rapid individuation of specific reflexes from that pattern."

GENERAL SUMMARY OF PRENATAL DEVELOPMENT

The development of behavior in the unborn child or animal, like the development of the body itself, follows an orderly course. The mass movements of the young fetus, in which the body moves as a whole and there are few or no independent movements of local parts, become gradually differentiated into movements that show the beginnings of adaptation to the particular stimulus employed or to the part of the body that is stimulated. At first only generalized movements can be made. This is true of

[18] C. S. Bridgman and Leonard Carmichael, "An Experimental Study of the Onset of Behavior in the Fetal Guinea-pig," *Ped. Sem. and J. Genet. Psychol.*, 1935, 47: 247-267.

the human fetus as well as of animals. The very young fetus of the salamander can do nothing but coil when he is touched; if he moves at all, that will be his reaction. The unborn kitten at a corresponding level of development will make a squirming movement chiefly of the head and upper part of the trunk. The first reactions of the human fetus are much like those of the cat, and as with the cat and the salamander, the child's behavior at the beginning is not well adapted to the stimulus that calls it forth. A touch on any part of the body may arouse movement in almost

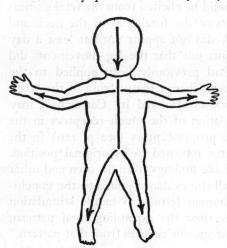

any other part. Fairly early in the fetal period, however, the movements of the local parts begin to acquire some degree of independence. Local reflexes appear in which stimulation of one part of the body no longer brings about a movement of the whole, or, at least, in which the mass movements are much reduced. A touch on the lips brings out the suckling reaction as the major response, usually accompanied, it is true, by some general bodily squirming which shows that the act of suckling is not yet completely freed

FIG. 22.—DIAGRAMMATIC REPRESENTATION OF THE DIRECTIONAL TENDENCY IN PHYSICAL AND MOTOR DEVELOPMENT

from the mass movements out of which it developed. Stimulation of one part of the body becomes increasingly likely to elicit more pronounced movements of that part than of others, and thus behavior becomes adapted to particular needs and excess movements are eliminated.

Behavior patterns thus appear to follow the same general course of development as the development of the physical organism in that the course of growth is from the general to the specific, from the whole to the parts. Moreover, just as the head regions of the animal and particularly of man are more precocious in their growth than the other parts of the body (see Figure 16, p. 85), so there appears to be a tendency for body movements to appear first in the upper regions of the trunk and from there to spread downward and outward to the limbs. (See Figure 22.) In physical growth, this is known as the *law of anterior-posterior development*. In its general aspect at least, it seems to hold good for certain kinds of behavior as well.

This gradual spread of reaction with its accompaniment of increasing independence of local parts has been shown to follow upon corresponding changes in the nervous system. The major nervous pathways are laid down first, the local pathways later. And from the very beginning, the growth of the brain, and particularly of the cerebral part of the brain, keeps far in advance of the growth of the remainder of the body. This tendency for brain growth to run ahead of general bodily growth is far greater in man than in other animals. In general it may be said that the greater the intelligence of the animal the more precocious is the growth of the brain and particularly of the cerebral hemispheres. It is not only that in the more intelligent animals the cerebrum tends to be larger (in proportion to body weight) than it is in the less intelligent, but the excess growth occurs at an earlier stage of development. Coghill,[19] after citing certain examples, makes the following comment:

In man at a stage of development when bodily movements are of the simplest order, that part of the mechanism of association which deals particularly with the highest mental and moral processes not only is relatively massive but has definitely begun to organize itself into the mechanical pattern that characterizes it in the adult. . . . The greater the possibility of behavior in the animal, the more the cerebral conditioning mechanisms run ahead of the motor or effector mechanisms in development.

We have stressed the importance of the prenatal period in development because it is important for the student to realize from the start that from the earliest to the latest stage of development both mental and physical growth follow an orderly course which is determined by the interaction of the inborn qualities of the cell tissue and the environment in which the cells find themselves. As a result of this interaction the parts of the body are

[19] *Op. cit.*, p. 99.

differentiated from each other, and in this differentiation the nervous system takes the lead. By the time of birth all the main parts of the nervous system have been laid down, the sense-organs are able to function, and the child, who has until then lived a protected life within the body of the mother, is ready to adapt itself to a new world of ever-changing conditions. Up to then he has had little to do but grow. Food and oxygen have come to him regularly from his mother; he has not been bothered with indigestion because he has had nothing to digest for himself; he has not known cold or excessive heat, or the restraint of clothing. At birth all this is changed. For the first time he begins to breathe, eat, digest for himself; for the first time he is subjected to a varying temperature to which his body must adjust as his sense-organs begin to react to outside stimulation. He tastes, smells, perhaps hears a little, sees but without understanding. A tremendous change, this, yet the preparation for it has been so perfectly made that both physical growth and mental development continue their normal course with only a brief period of adjustment. Before going on with an account of his growth and development after birth, it is well to pause long enough to examine the new-born baby with some care, to try out a few experiments with him, to look into the matter of his abilities and talents, his weaknesses and defects, his ability to learn. In the next chapter we shall make a brief survey of the mental traits of the new-born child, of his equipment for meeting the demands of the new and varied environment into which he has so suddenly been thrust.

VISIT TO AN ANATOMICAL MUSEUM

If your college or university has a medical school connected with it, see if you can make arrangements to visit its anatomical museum for the purpose of seeing some actual specimens of human fetuses and fetal skeletons at various stages of development. Ask also to see specimens or models of fetal brains. Note the comparative shallowness of the *convolutions*—the folds and wrinkles on the surface—and note also that as you pass down the age scale to earlier levels of development, many of these convolutions have not yet put in their appearance at all. Since the cell bodies of the neurons are found chiefly on the outer surface of the brain, it is evident that the development of the convolutions is a means of increasing the relative amount of space available for them as the brain increases in mass.

Chapter V

THE CHILD AT BIRTH

Can we tell whether a particular baby is going to be bright or dull by watching his behavior during the first few weeks of life?

Are all babies really the same age at birth?

What three general classes of body-mechanisms enable us to make adjustments to conditions in the outside world? Which of these is least developed at birth? Which seems to be most highly developed?

What is meant by the term "stimulus error"?

Would it be an advantage to us if each of the sense-organs could respond to a good many different kinds of external conditions, if, for example, the eye could respond to sound as well as to light, and so on? Give reasons for your answer.

Into what three general groups are the sense-organs classified?

What is the physiological basis for hunger sensations? for thirst sensations? for sensations of posture?

Does a given temperature as registered by a thermometer always feel the same to us? What conditions are necessary to arouse a sensation of warmth or cold?

In what ways does the structure of the eye correspond to that of a camera?

Why can a very faint star often be seen better if you look a little to one side of it rather than directly at it?

What special apparatus have we to help in keeping our balance? In what way does it work?

By what means are we able to tell the direction from which a sound comes?

Can the new-born baby see form? color? Can he hear? smell? taste? Can he feel cold? warmth? touch? pain? Is there any difference between the kind of information the infant receives through his sense-organs and that which an adult would get from the same situation?

Into what classes may the motor activities of the new-born infant be divided? What kind of motor activity, prominent in later life, is largely or wholly absent at birth?

What two main classes of glands are found in the body? Name some of the most important in each class.

THE ORDEAL OF BIRTH

The first two weeks after birth are best considered somewhat apart from the general course of development because of the unusual difficulties which must be met at that time. Not only must the child adjust to a change of environment greater than it will ever again meet, but it also has to recover from one of the most difficult and dangerous events of life. Although being born is not only a natural but a necessary part of every child's experience, it is not an easy one. For hours he is subjected to dragging and pushing, to strong compression—particularly of the head, which at this age is the widest and most resistant part of the body. A fairly large percentage of all infants are artificially delivered. This means that in addition to the usual severe pressure, the child is forcibly dragged through the narrow passages of the mother's body by forceps clamped about its head. Even in modern civilized communities, mortality statistics show that the hazards of the neonatal period are almost twice as great as those undergone by soldiers during World War I.

Considering the severity of the birth process, it is surprising how few children show any permanent effects of it. Although children's hospitals always include a few cases of paralysis or other difficulties attributed to birth injuries, the percentage is very small when compared to the number of infants whose heads are pressed out of shape or who suffer marked contusions, indentations of the skull, or other noticeable injuries at birth. Fortunately, even injuries that to the novice appear very severe rarely seem to exert any lasting damage upon the child's mental or physical growth.[1] The infant's remarkable power of recuperation from head injuries at birth is in part due to the softness of the skull bones at this age and to the leeway provided by the open fontanelles (popularly known as the "soft spots") at the top and sides of the head where calcification has not yet proceeded far enough to unite the bones of the skull completely.

Temporary effects of the birth experience are probably greater than most psychologists realize. It is likely that for some hours at least, the general mental and physical condition of the new-born child is analogous to that of an older person who has just undergone a major operation, and when labor is unduly difficult or prolonged or when forceps have been used, several days may elapse before recovery is complete. However normal may be the fact of birth, the new-born child is nevertheless not in a normal condition for some time thereafter.

For this reason it is unsafe to judge the abilities of an infant on the basis of his behavior immediately after birth. The length of time that must elapse before complete recovery from the minor injuries of a so-called "normal" birth will vary from child to child, but it is safe to say that for the first two or three days at least, and for a longer period when delivery has been unusually difficult, the fact that a child fails to show a given form of behavior must not be taken to mean that he would not be able to do so if his physical condition were normal. Accordingly, the fact

---

[1] This does not mean that birth injuries never leave permanent effects. Paralysis of different parts of the body as well as lasting mental defects sometimes result. One of our leading institutions for the feeble-minded reports that approximately 5 to 10 per cent of all its cases are attributable wholly or in part to injuries at birth. E. A. Doll, W. M. Phelps, and R. T. Melcher, *Mental Deficiency Due to Birth Injuries* (New York, Macmillan Co., 1932).

that some babies, shortly after birth, are able to yawn, sneeze, bring their hands to their mouths and suck their fingers, raise their heads, and so on, is probably more significant than the fact that not all do so. Success means that the ability has been established; failure may be due to any one of a number of causes. It may be due to more than usually severe birth injury, to premature birth,[2] or to genuine backwardness. It is probable that the hope expressed by some psychologists that the time may come when the intelligence of the new-born may be tested as accurately as we are now able to test the ability of older children will not be realized for many years to come, if at all. Certainly, until more accurate methods for determining the real age [3] of the new-born child and for measuring the extent of birth injury have been worked out, it is very unsafe to attempt to predict from his behavior during the first few days of life how a given child is likely to develop later on.

ADJUSTING TO THE NEW ENVIRONMENT

The first thing the child does upon entering the world is to cry. The significance of the "birth cry," as it is called, has been the subject of much solemn speculation on the part of certain philosophers. Kant interpreted it as a sign of wrath; Adler, as an indication of the child's sudden and overwhelming feeling of inferiority at being placed in so new and complex an environment. Unsympathetic bachelors have been heard to express the belief that the baby is merely giving the parents an early sample of what he can and will do later on! Physiologists, however, tell us that the birth cry is merely a reflex accompaniment of the first

---

[2] Gesell, who has followed the early development of a number of premature infants, has been able to show that in most respects at least the behavior of the child who is prematurely born is retarded during infancy by about the extent of his prematurity. For example, the baby born two months ahead of schedule shows about the same level of mental and physical development at four months after birth as he would have reached at two months had he been born at the usual time. In reality, the child born two months early is a seven-months fetus and should be looked upon as a fetus rather than as a full-grown baby. Cf. Gesell's *Infancy and Human Growth*, Ch. XV.

[3] By present methods, age at birth can be determined only within rough limits. The error of estimate may be two weeks or even more unless the date of conception is known.

entrance of air into the lungs. It probably has no emotional significance whatever.

The physiological adjustment that the infant has to make during the first few days of extra-uterine life is very complicated. Evaporation of water from the tissues, together with imperfect nutrition while the new process of digestion is being established, results in a loss of weight during the first few days after birth. This loss usually amounts to several ounces, and it may be ten days or two weeks before the birth weight[4] is regained. With the taking-on of such new functions as breathing, eating, digesting, and assimilating, numerous changes occur in the internal organs and glands. Still other adjustments are required by the sudden change from a constant temperature of approximately 100° F. to one that is not only much lower on the average but varies within comparatively wide limits, and from uniform protection of all parts of the body to exposure of certain parts while the remainder is kept covered. There are also the new postures and the comparatively rigid means of support in place of resting in a fluid medium and shifting position only at the dictates of its own needs. All this has its psychological as well as its purely physiological aspect, and the adjustments required are not the less important because as yet their exact nature is uncertain.

For all these reasons, much caution must be observed in interpreting the results of experiments carried out with very young infants. Nevertheless, if the points that have been mentioned in the foregoing paragraphs are kept in mind, much that is of great importance may be learned from the study of the abilities shown by the infant as soon as the grosser effects of birth have worn off. Although growth and development have their beginning long before birth, most of the infant's learning may fairly be said to start at birth, since, no matter what his abilities may be, his opportunities for learning before birth are very limited. If we are to understand his later development, we must therefore try to get as clear an idea as possible of the initial equipment with which the new-born baby sets out to discover and explore the world about him.

[4] Weight at birth averages about seven pounds for girls and seven and a half pounds for boys. The usual length of the new-born infant is about nineteen inches.

THE BEHAVIOR OF THE NEW-BORN[5]

Helpless as the new-born baby seems, he is nevertheless able to perform a rather large number of complicated acts. He breathes, suckles, sneezes, coughs, and moves his whole body. He starts at

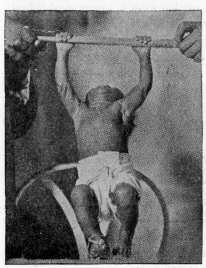

A   B

FIG. 23.—THE GRASPING REFLEX

A. Month-old baby supporting weight by both hands. Many babies are able to do this at birth, and frequently by the use of only one hand, but as a rule the weight cannot be sustained in this way for more than a minute or two. The reflex reaches its maximum strength about the fourth month, then wanes and later reappears as a voluntary act. The voluntary grasp is, however, different from the reflex grasp of the new-born. In the voluntary grasp the thumb plays an important part, while the reflex grasp is performed entirely by the fingers. (See Figure 24.) (Courtesy *Journal of Heredity*.)

B. New-born monkey supporting weight by one arm. This position was maintained for thirty-three minutes. (From "The Grasping Reflex in the New-born Monkey" by C. P. Richter, *Arch. Neurol. and Psychiat.*, 1931, 26: 784-790. Courtesy of the publishers.)

a sudden noise, cries if he is hurt, turns his head freely from side to side when lying on his back, and if placed face downward on a bed or table he promptly turns his head so as to free his nose

[5] The term *new-born* as used here includes the first two weeks after birth unless exact ages are stated.

for breathing, or he may even lift his head clear of the table for an instant. If an object is placed in his hand, the fingers close about it, and so strong is this reflex grasp that many new-born infants can support their entire weight by their hands. (See Figure 23.) When at rest, the prenatal posture (Figure 14) is usually maintained by most infants during the first three or four weeks. In premature infants this posture is retained somewhat longer than is the case with children born at full term, but not as much longer as might be expected if age alone were to be considered. Not only maturity but opportunity and learning play a part in determining the posture patterns of the young infant.

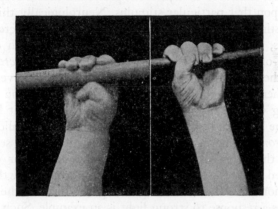

FIG. 24.—DIFFERENCE BETWEEN THE REFLEX GRASP OF THE NEW-BORN
AND THE VOLUNTARY GRASP OF THE OLDER INFANT

(From *Growth: A Study of Johnny and Jimmy*, by Myrtle B. McGraw.
D. Appleton-Century Co.)

These acts must not be thought of as "random" activities, even though they may not seem to accomplish any useful purpose. Always they are responses to stimuli, and they play their part in the difficult task of learning to adjust to the complex and varying conditions of the outside world which the child must master if he is to survive.

In order that an individual may adjust to its environment two things are necessary. First, it must have some equipment by which external conditions can affect the organism ("receptor" or sensory apparatus) and secondly it must have some means of bringing about a change in its own relationship to these conditions ("effector" or motor apparatus). Deficiency in either may be equally serious, just as it makes little difference whether the motorist approaching a grade crossing fails to see the oncoming train or whether he is unable to get his foot on the brake quickly enough. The first act (seeing the train) begins with the stimulation of the visual apparatus in the eye by the particular pattern of light rays reflected from the train. The second is a response of the muscles in the foot, leg, and trunk. But there is obviously something more than this. There must be a central or adjustive process by means of which it is insured that just that particular motor response shall follow upon that particular stimulus. Neurologically this requires three distinct though closely organized and connected sets of apparatus, commonly known as the *receptors*, which consist of the sense-organs and their associated neurons; the *effectors*, which include the muscles and glands, together with the nerves that run out to them from the brain and spinal cord; and the *adjustors*, consisting of the complicated system of neurons that lie mainly within the brain and spinal cord. The latter are also called *association neurons*. Some of the connections leading from sense-organ through the brain or spinal cord to the muscle or gland are established before birth as a part of the normal growth process. Contraction of the muscles regulating the size of the pupil of the eye as a response to strong light is an example. Such responses are commonly called *reflexes*.[6]

It is chiefly because of the relative fewness and uncertainty of the adjustor or associative mechanisms (other than reflex) that the behavior of the new-born baby differs from that of the older child or the adult. As far as we are able to determine, his sensory equipment is reasonably well perfected before birth, although it is likely that some further development of the more delicate parts of the apparatus continues during infancy. Likewise his motor equipment, apart from obvious differences in size and strength of the muscles, is in fair working order at birth. He is born, then, with a good set of tools but with little knowledge of how to use them.

[6] See pp. 140-141.

THE SENSORY APPARATUS

The essential quality of a sense-organ is that it must have the property of "receiving" some special form of energy outside itself and transforming it into nervous energy which can be propagated in the form of nerve impulses along the nerves connected with the sense-organ and thence, by means of synaptic connections with other nerves, to various parts of the body. Anatomically, each sense-organ consists of the finely branched endings of a sensory or *afferent* nerve [7] together with the specialized cells in which these nerves usually terminate. Each sense-organ can be aroused by one, and as a rule by only one kind of physical event. We cannot see with our ears or hear with our eyes or smell with the taste-buds in the mouth. Since each sense-organ has its own particular set of afferent neurons which run to a particular part of the brain or spinal cord and there make synaptic connections with association neurons and with the motor or efferent nerves that run to other parts of the body, a system is at once provided for making a kind of preliminary classification of neural activity in terms of the particular sense-organ in which it originated. For example, if the nerve impulse comes in to the central nervous system over the afferent nerves that run from the touch receptors [8] in the skin on the back of the left hand, the only thing that can have happened to produce that effect is a touch on the skin at the point in question. But if those sense-organs could be stimulated by any one of half a dozen different things, if they were sensitive alike to touch, to light, to sound waves, to pin prick, to cold or to heat, the organism could not make useful adaptations to changes in the world about it because it would have no way of distinguishing them. The limitation of sensitiveness in a given sense-organ to a particular kind of external condition is thus a very great advantage to the organism as a whole because it provides a means by which appropriate responses can be made in terms of the particular afferent nerves over which

[7] From the Latin *ad ferre* meaning "to carry to," hence "to carry inward or toward." The term *efferent nerve*, which refers to those leading outward from the central nervous system to the muscles or glands, is similarly derived from *ex ferre*, meaning "to carry outward or away from."

[8] The sense-organs are called "receptors" because they are the receiving instruments for the nervous system.

the stimulus was received. The sensory apparatus as a whole may thus be looked upon as a very elaborate and delicate sorting machine by means of which events going on both without and within the body [9] are classified.

In addition to the sensitive tissue and the neuron endings within it, many of the sense-organs are also equipped with special parts or accessories that serve to bring them into better contact with the environmental conditions to which they respond. The eye, with its eyelid to protect it from injury, its muscles for turning it about, and its many other special parts which will be described later, is an outstanding example. The amount of accessory apparatus varies greatly from one organ to another. Moreover, the whole organism may respond to a faint or confusing sensation by doing certain things that bring a particular sense-organ into better relationship to the outside stimulus. We walk toward the source of a faint sound, we pick up a small object and hold it at the distance at which it can be seen most clearly, we move our fingers over objects in order to intensify and clarify the touch sensations. Almost any part of the body may be temporarily drafted into the service of one or more of the sense-organs.

Sensations are aroused by *changes* or *differences* rather than by constant conditions. As long as the oxygen supply in the air does not vary beyond a certain limit, we are not conscious of its existence. But reduce it below this limit, and sensation definitely begins. We do not feel the circulation of the blood as long as it proceeds in a normal fashion, but let some local area be constricted, so that there is interference with the circulation in that area, and the resultant pressure of the accumulating fluid upon the surrounding tissues is immediately perceived. If all light waves were of the same length [10] we should not know color.

The fact that a change in the stimulating condition is necessary for the arousal of sensation is demonstrated in many phenomena with which we are all familiar. There is, for example, the principle of *adaptation* whereby we become so used to a condition that we no longer notice it or make overt reactions to it. There is also the principle of *contrast* whereby a given sensation seems to be much stronger or more noticeable if it occurs in close

---

[9] See pp. 119-120.
[10] See pp. 129-130.

proximity to another that is very different. The change from prenatal to postnatal life is essentially a change from an environment of great constancy and few demands for sensory and motor adjustments to one of great variability with many demands for adjustment.

THE INTERNAL SENSE-ORGANS

There are sense-organs that are stimulated by conditions within the body as well as those that are sensitive to conditions in the external world. If this were not so, we should not have aches and pains to warn us of indigestion or fatigue; we could not tell when our jaws were moving or whether our elbows were straight or bent without looking to see or touching them with our fingers.

We do not know as much about the internal senses as we do about those with sense-organs on the surface of the body. We know that we have a number of internal sensations such as hunger, fatigue, internal pain. But these senses have no elaborate apparatus like the eye or ear. Hunger has been shown to be directly occasioned by the contractions of the stomach and the alimentary canal which normally occur when certain chemical changes associated with lack of nutriment take place in the blood. This probably means that there are very minute sense-organs within the stomach walls that are stimulated by such movements. Thirst results from dryness of the throat. In normal or true thirst, the dryness comes from a reduced action of the salivary glands. These glands respond very quickly to a loss of water from the body by lowering their output. Thirst may also arise from factors unrelated to the supply of liquid in the body. This is the so-called "false thirst" that comes from prolonged speaking or other conditions that dry the mucous membrane of the throat. Internal pain is probably more easily aroused by chemical changes in the body than by mechanical injuries, since physiologists have shown that the viscera may be burned, cut, or crushed without causing pain. Fatigue is a general sensation, which is felt in the muscles and joints all over the body. It is believed to be due to the accumulation of waste products in the blood.

All these organic senses—hunger, internal pain, and so on— seem to function actively from the time of birth, and we may infer from this that their sense-organs reach complete or nearly complete functional development before birth. The receptors for these senses are sometimes grouped together under the name of *interoceptors*. They consist chiefly of sensitive nerve-endings located in the internal membranes. They require little accessory apparatus. If we may judge from his behavior, the new-born baby feels stomach-ache as keenly as we do, the chief difference being that he has not learned to know what is the matter with him.

A second group of internal receptors are known as the *proprioceptors*. These consist of nerve-endings located within the muscles, tendons, and joints. They are stimulated by movements of these parts. Through them we have what is commonly known as the "muscle sense" by which we know the position of the different parts of the body without having to look. These, too, probably reach complete or nearly complete development before birth, but, as with other sensations, the baby has to learn to interpret them. He probably gets much the same sensation from crooking his elbow that we do, but he does not know what it means or from what part of his body it comes.

THE EXTERNAL SENSE-ORGANS

The third group of sense-organs, known as the *exteroceptors*, are sensitive to environmental conditions outside the body. They include a series of "skin senses" located within the skin all over the surface of the body, the senses of smell, taste, hearing, and sight, and the less well-recognized sense of head-position through which we are able to maintain bodily balance.

1. *The Cutaneous Senses*

Until the latter part of the nineteenth century, scientists as well as laymen used to speak of the "five senses" as making up all the sense-equipment of the body. Under the "sense of touch" they grouped all four of the cutaneous senses—cold, warmth, pain, and touch—as well as the organic and muscular sensations. We now know that the four cutaneous senses are just as distinct as sight and hearing. They have different sense-organs whose activity is transmitted to the central nervous system over different nerve fibers, and they do not feel the same to us. A cool breeze yields a very different kind of sensation from a pin-prick; a feather touching the skin does not feel like a hot iron. There are two reasons why the skin senses were formerly confused. Their sense-organs are not conspicuous like the eye and are so near together in the skin that they are often stimulated simultaneously, which makes the separate sensations hard to distinguish. That the skin senses really are separate from each other can be shown by exploring the skin with instruments so small that they are not likely to come into contact with more than one sense-organ at a time. The blunt end of a cold needle or the point of a lead pencil can be used to locate the "cold spots" or sense-organs of cold in a small section of the skin. The inside of the wrist is a good place. Touch the skin gently here and there and it will be found that in some places the needle, as we say, "feels cold." But a touch of the same instrument at other points fails to elicit any sensation of cold whatever. Why? Because the sense-organs that are stimuuated by cold—the "cold spots," as they are often called—do not occur everywhere in the skin but only at certain definite points. Moreover, if one of these sense-organs is aroused at all, the resulting sensation is one of cold, no matter what the stimulating agent may have been. As a rule, the "cold spots" can be stimulated only by temperatures colder than that of the skin but a mechanical stimulus such as a quick, sharp tap at exactly the right spot may be effective, and they can always be stimulated chemically by the application of menthol. A menthol pencil always "feels cold," no matter what its temperature, because it stimulates the sense-organs of cold.[11]

In a similar way, the sense-organs of touch ("touch spots") can

[11] So commonly do we fail to realize that the character of a sensation depends upon the particular sense-organ stimulated, that the untrained person finds it very difficult to realize that there is any difference between the qualities of an object and the sensations these qualities arouse in him. Only when the sensation is aroused by some out-of-the-ordinary stimulus, as when a menthol pencil that has previously been "warmed" before the fire nevertheless induces a sensation of cold, is it clear that the kind of sensation experienced is a matter of the particular receptors that have been stimulated. To say that an object is "cold" means only that it possesses some physical quality that stimulates the specialized receptors in the skin from which nerve impulses pass to the brain which are "interpreted" (because of their source) as "coldness." Failure to grasp this principle, thinking that a sensation is directly caused by the physical qualities of the objects around us is known as the *stimulus error*.

be stimulated separately by touching the skin at different points with a stiff hair or bristle; those for warmth, by using a small, blunt object heated until it is a little warmer than the skin; and the pain spots may be found by exploring with the point of a pin or needle. Very hot or very cold objects may also stimulate the pain spots. The sensations they arouse are likely to be so strong that the feeling of warmth or cold is almost blotted out.

The temperature senses, both for warmth and for cold, have variable thresholds (points at which sensation begins to be aroused) dependent on the temperature of the skin.

Hold your right hand for a few minutes in a basin of very cold water, your left in a basin of hot water. Then plunge both into a basin of tepid water. To the right hand the water will feel warm; to the left hand, cold. "Cold," as we experience it, really means "colder than the skin"; "warm" means "warmer than the skin." The usual skin-temperature in regions exposed to the air is from 85° to 90° Fahrenheit. If the skin is cooled below this point, the temperature senses adapt themselves to the changed conditions. In order to stimulate the cold spots, the temperature must then be lowered below the usual point at which cold is felt, while temperatures that would not usually seem warm will then be felt as warm. If the skin is warmer than usual, the opposite condition arises. Temperatures that normally would seem warm fail to arouse the temperature senses at all, or, if the difference in skin-temperature is marked, they may even be felt as cold. The condition that stimulates the temperature senses is not absolute warmth or cold as shown by a thermometer but a difference between the skin-temperature of the moment and the temperature of the air or the object that comes into contact with the skin. In most parts of the body, a difference of as little as 1° Fahrenheit will arouse one or the other of the temperature senses. If the skin is the warmer of the two, the sense-organs of cold will be stimulated; if the skin is cooler, the warm spots will be aroused to action.

For the most part, the organs of the cutaneous senses consist of finely branching nerve-endings in the layer of the skin just below the cuticle or outer skin. However, if a section of the skin be examined under a microscope, it is seen that many of the sensory nerves end in little corpuscles or bodies of specialized tissue. These are of several kinds and are believed by some physiologists to be receptors for the cutaneous senses.[12] Sensory nerve-endings also tend to cluster about the roots of the short, fine hairs that are found on nearly all parts of the body. When the hair is moved, the nerve-endings are stimulated. The surface hairs may be therefore looked upon as accessory organs for the purpose of increasing the body's sensitivity to touch.

Although we speak of the four senses of warmth, cold, pain, and touch as the cutaneous senses, their distribution is not confined to the skin alone but extends to the mucous membrane and to some extent into the subcutaneous tissue; this is particularly true of the sense of pain. The organs for these four senses are not distributed evenly over the surface of the body but vary in density from place to place. We all know, for example, that the finger-tips are far more sensitive to touch than is the middle of the back and that the outer coat of the eye is extraordinarily sensitive to pain. A grain of dust which on the skin would not be noticed at all or at most would arouse a faint tactile sensation, will cause intense pain if it happens to get into the eye. This again illustrates the principle that what is felt in sensation is the response of the sense-organ and not the thing that arouses it.

2. Smell

The receptors for smell are located in a small cavity far back in the nose. They are stimulated by tiny gaseous particles of certain substances dissolved in the air. The older person learns to intensify faint scents by sniffing the air through the nose so as to bring larger quantities of these substances into contact with the olfactory apparatus. The infant does not do this, and for this reason he has sometimes been thought less responsive to odors. However, Disher[13] has shown that when the olfactory receptors are stimulated by forcing a puff of air laden with an odorous substance such as a violet perfume, turpentine, or asafoetida into

[12] There is not complete agreement among physiologists about the nature of tne receptors for the cutaneous senses. Some take the position that cutaneous sensitivity is a direct function of the nerve endings, independent of any specialized accessory cells.

[13] D. R. Disher, "The Reactions of Newborn Infants to Chemical Stimuli Administered Nasally," Ohio University Studies; Contributions to Education No. 12, 1934, pp. 82-93.

the nostrils of a new-born baby, an increase in bodily activity results. For every one of seven different odors tried, the increase in activity was greater than that found when a puff of air alone was used. The greater the intensity of the odor, the greater was the amount of activity aroused by it. Other investigators have obtained similar results. It seems reasonably certain, therefore, that the new-born infant is sensitive to odors, but it is very doubtful that different odors affect him as they do us. Even among adults there is much disagreement about what odors should be classed as pleasant or unpleasant, fragrant or malodorous, and so on. It is worthy of note that in spite of long effort, no psychologist has yet succeeded in working out a wholly satisfactory system for classifying odors, although Henning's grouping into six main classes—*fragrant, etherial, resinous, spicy, putrid,* and *burned*—has attracted most attention. Undoubtedly, a large share of our adult liking or disliking for certain odors is based mainly upon experience, and in our attempts to classify olfactory sensations we are hampered by an unconscious effort to associate the odor with the the thing to which it usually belongs and to make our classification conform to what we know about odors, rather than just the qualities of the odor itself.

3. Taste

The organs of taste are called *taste-buds.* They lie near the bottom of little pits extending down from the surface of the tongue. In the adult and in the older child the taste-buds are chiefly confined to the extreme tip, the edges and the rear part of the tongue, though there are a few on the soft palate and in the back of the throat. The early distribution of taste-buds is very different. At birth and during the latter part of fetal life they are found on the inner surface of the cheeks, all over the tongue, in the throat, on the lips, and even in the larynx. Later on they become localized and increase in number within the areas in which they occur. Thus a much larger area of the infant's mouth is sensitive to taste stimuli than is that of the adult. Whether or not the infant's taste is more acute we cannot say, but experiment has shown that the taste-buds are sensitive at birth.

Taste sensations are much fewer in kind than most people suppose. Most of what we regard as taste is really smell. Blocking the nasal passages so that no air can pass through them causes most of the characteristic flavors of food to disappear. Every one has noticed that a bad cold in the head which produces partial obstruction of the nasal passages makes all food taste very much alike. This is not a direct effect of the cold, but occurs because the cold interferes with the sense of smell. Careful investigation has shown that there are only four distinct taste sensations: sweet, sour, salty, and bitter. In the adult or older child sweet tastes come chiefly from the tip of the tongue, sour from the sides, salty from the tip and from the sides, and bitter from the upper surface of the back part of the tongue. These regions have not been mapped out in the infant, however, and because of the very different distribution of the taste-buds, the distribution of the areas for the separate taste sensations is probably not the same.

4. *Sight*

The senses that have the most elaborate apparatus are sight, hearing, and the apparatus in the inner ear by which we maintain balance. All these are very precocious; their development is well-nigh completed at birth.

The eye, which, as we all know, is the organ of sight, is constructed much like a camera. The sensitive nerve-endings in the *retina* correspond to the sensitized plate or film on which the image is projected. In the front of the eye are two strong lenses, the *cornea* and (back of this) the *crystalline lens*, which bend the rays of light as they enter the eye and bring them to a focus on the retina. In the ordinary camera it is necessary to adjust the focus for near and distant objects by changing the distance between the lens and the sensitive plate; in the eye this is done automatically by means of a little muscle, called the *ciliary* muscle, that changes the curvature of the lens as needed.

On the outside, the eyeball is covered with a strong white membrane called the *sclerotic coat* or *sclera;* it is this that we ordinarily speak of as the "white of the eye." The sclerotic coat is lined with a second membrane whose purpose is to absorb any stray light rays that may happen to penetrate the eye except through the pupil. This coat is black in color and is known as the *choroid coat.* The sclerotic and the choroid coats extend all the way around the eye except for the region in the front that is occupied by the transparent cornea, underneath which the choroid coat is replaced by the *iris*, or colored portion of the eye. The iris is like a colored curtain with a circular hole in the middle, known as the pupil of the eye, through which light is admitted. The cornea in front of the pupil and the crystalline

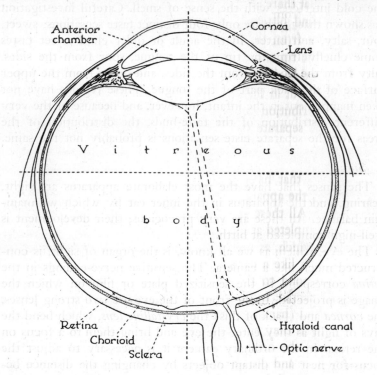

FIG. 25.—TRANSVERSE SECTION THROUGH THE EQUATOR OF THE LEFT EYE SEEN FROM ABOVE

lens behind it together focus the rays of light so that an image of the object from which they are reflected is formed on the retina. Without the lenses we could distinguish light from darkness, but we could not see the forms of objects. It would be like exposing a photographic plate outside the camera. The whole thing would be darkened but there would be no picture.

The eyeball is filled, both before and behind the lens, with a transparent semi-fluid substance that keeps it in shape. The part that lies in front of the lens is known as the *aqueous humor*, that which lies back of it the *vitreous humor*, or *vitreous body*.

The iris is equipped with a series of little muscles that regulate the size of the pupil and hence control the amount of light that enters the eye. They correspond to the diaphragm of a camera. You have all noticed how the size of the pupil enlarges after having been in the dark for some time and how it contracts on exposure to strong light.

In the retina are the sensitive cells that react to light. These cells are of two kinds, called from their shape the *rods* and the *cones*. (See Figure 26.) They lie at the back of the retina. The layer of retinal cells which is just beyond the rods and cones, next to the choroid coat, contains pigment, and it is thought that the incoming light produces some chemical change in the pigment which stimulates the rods and cones. The endings of the sensory nerve fibers (the optic nerve) enter the bases of both the rod cells and the cone cells.

You know that you see an object most clearly when you look directly at it, although you also see the objects near it fairly well. This is because the part of the retina that lies directly back of the pupil of the eye and is called the *fovea* contains very many cones and no rods at all. The cones are the most sensitive cells; they respond best both to form and color. As you go out from the fovea an increasingly greater number of the cones are replaced by rods. The rods are entirely insensitive to color; however, they respond to changes in light and shade (that is, to form), though not as well as the cones. They have one great advantage over the cones, which is that they become adapted to very dim lights better than the cones do. In deep twilight we cannot distinguish colors at all, because the rods and not the cones are functioning at that time. Color-vision is purely a function of the cones.

The physical basis of visual sensation is the activity incited in the visual apparatus by light-waves. Generally speaking, differences in the apparent brightness of light correspond to differences in the energy of these waves as they strike the eye, but other factors, both in the character of the waves and in the organism itself, also affect brightness sensations. Not all the waves known to exist but only those falling within the range of 390 to 760 millionths of a millimeter [14] in length are seen by us as light. The human organism has no sense-organs that respond directly

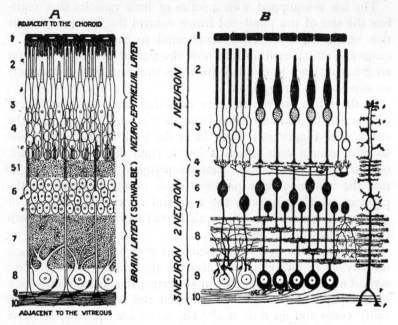

FIG. 26.—DIAGRAM OF THE HUMAN RETINA, SHOWING THE RELATION-
SHIPS TO EACH OTHER OF THE RETINAL NEURONS AND THEIR DIS-
POSITION IN THE DIFFERENT LAYERS OF THE RETINA

The retina may be said to be formed by an expansion of the fibers of the optic nerve which enters the eye from the back, pierces the sclerotic and the choroid coats and spreads out over the inner surface of the eyeball. Ten separate layers can be distinguished under the microscope. These layers are composed of three neurons which form synapses with each other as shown above. The inner layer of the first neuron is the pigmented layer mentioned on p. 127. The second layer is the layer of rods and cones. Synapses between the neurons are made at the fourth and the eighth layers. The tenth layer consists of the fibers of the optic nerve which pass back to the brain. These layers are numbered from the back of the retina inward toward the center of the eyeball. (After Fox's *Ophthalmology*.)

to the waves immediately outside this range, but man's ingenuity has nevertheless turned some of them to practical use and in so doing has greatly extended the effective range of our sensory

[14] Commonly written as 390 $\mu\mu$. to 760 $\mu\mu$.

powers. An outstanding example of this is seen in radio broad-casting, which makes use of waves too long to affect the visual organs or to be felt as heat but far shorter than the atmospheric waves that constitute the physical basis for hearing. At the other extreme we have the ultra-violet waves that we neither see nor feel but which affect the pigmentation of the skin, causing it to tan and produce other changes in the organism which are as yet only partially understood but are tied up with matters of general health and resistance to infections. Still shorter than these are the X-rays that have been made to serve so many valuable purposes in physical and medical science. In spite of the fact that all these waves fall outside the range of our unaided per-ception, they may nevertheless be reckoned among the most valu-able of our "natural resources," although their very existence would forever have remained unknown to us were it not for that greatest of all resources, the mind of man.

Ordinary uncolored light (as daylight) consists of a mixture of waves of all lengths within the visible spectrum. When this mixture is broken up into groups of more nearly uniform length, we see color. The longest visible rays (760 $\mu\mu$.) give a sensation of red; the shortest (390 $\mu\mu$.) a sensation of violet. The other colors are spread out between them in the order in which they appear in the rainbow or *spectrum*.

In all studies of color sensations it is important to distinguish between the color of objects, which is due to reflected light, and the color of radiant light itself. Object-color results from the absorption of light rays of certain lengths by the surface of the objects so that only those *not* absorbed are reflected back to the eye. It is therefore a subtractive process, while the direct mix-ture of light rays of different lengths is an additive process. It is possible to take light waves of known length and, by combining them in the proper proportion, make white light out of a number of colored lights. One cannot do this by mixing the corresponding pigments because the two processes, although at first thought they may seem the same, are actually very different.

Wave-length as well as energy affects the apparent brightness of light. Other things being equal, some colors appear brighter—nearer to the white end of the brightness scale—than others. It is interesting to note that in twilight the relative brightness of the various colors appears to change. Reds and yellows look darker, blues and greens lighter than they do under full illumination. This change, which is believed to be the result of greater participation of the rods in the process of seeing, has been named, for its discoverer, the *Purkinje shift*.

Peiper [15] made use of this shift in an attempt to ascertain whether or not new-born infants see colors. That they do respond to differences in the brightness of light (whether colored or uncolored) had previously been determined. According to Peiper, the response of the infant to a change in the brightness of uncolored light is a sudden throwing back of the head called the *eye-neck reflex*. Since the apparent brightness of colors for the normal adult eye changes when the eye has been adapted to darkness, Peiper reasoned that if the same change (the Purkinje shift) occurs in infants, the eye-neck reflex should appear in response to color as a result of dark-adaptation, even though the color itself remains unchanged. Experiments with four new-born infants yielded, so Peiper thought, evidence for his hypothesis, but his results have been criticized on technical grounds, and since not all colors were tried with all the infants and the possibility of error in judging whether or not the reflex really occurred is rather large, it is by no means certain that his conclusions are valid. In contradiction to Peiper's findings are those of Smith [16] who studied the responses of twenty new-born infants to three colors—blue, red, and green—using as a criterion of response the inhibition of crying and of general bodily activity. She concluded that at birth boys are totally color-blind and girls partly color-blind. However her results are not very clear-cut. Another experiment, by Chase, [17] is likewise somewhat questionable since its validity rests on the accuracy of Peiper's findings. The infants used in this study were slightly older (fifteen to seventy-four days) and the procedure was to see whether or not the child's eyes would follow a colored spot moving back and forth over a

[15] A. Peiper, Über die Helligskeits und Farbenemfindungen der Frühgeburten, *Archiven für Kinderheilkunde*, 1926, 80: 1-20.

[16] Josephine M. Smith, "The Relative Brightness Values of Three Hues for Newborn Infants," *University of Iowa Studies in Child Welfare*, 1936, 12: 91-140.

[17] Wilton P. Chase, "Color Vision in Infants," *J. Exper. Psychol.*, 1937, 20: 203-222.

background of another color but (for the adult light-adapted eye) of the same brightness. Since nearly all the infants studied did follow the moving color it would appear that they were at least not completely color-blind, provided that the brightness value of the different colors was, as Peiper thought, the same for them as for adults. However a totally color-blind person [18] who was tested by Chase was also able to see the moving spot, and this is just what might be expected, since for color-blind persons the relative brightness of colors seen in full daylight is like that of normal persons under dark-adaptation. Staples [19] found that by the age of three months, infants would look at a colored disc about twice as long, on the average, as they would look at a gray disc of the same brightness, which seems to indicate that at that age, at least, color was seen as something different and more "interesting" than gray.

We may sum up all these investigations by saying that while it is practically certain that at birth the infant responds to differences in the brightness of light, the question of his ability to respond to color is still not entirely settled, though the weight of evidence suggests that at least the beginnings of color vision are present. The question is of interest to psychologists because it may eventually help us to a better understanding of the nature of the process by which the eye responds to color.[20]

[18] Defective ability to distinguish colors is a well-known sex-linked trait. The mechanism of its inheritance is described on p. 55 ff. Color-blindness is of several types, ranging all the way from total color-blindness, in which the individual is unable to distinguish any colors at all, to the milder cases of red-green blindness in which red cannot be told from green. Total color-blindness is comparatively rare, but partial color-blindness is found, on the average, in about 6 per cent of men and in less than 1 per cent of women.

[19] Ruth Staples, "The Responses of Infants to Color," *J. Exper. Psychol.*, 1932, 15: 119-142.

[20] Many theories of color vision have been proposed in the course of the century and more during which the problem has been studied. Of these, the oldest was propounded by Thomas Young early in the last century and was later somewhat modified by Helmholz. It is commonly known as the Young-Helmholz theory. This theory is based primarily upon the fact that all the colors in the spectrum can be produced by mixing in various proportions lights of only three colors—red, green, and blue. It was therefore natural enough to assume that the retinal cones were of three different kinds, each of which was especially sensitive to the wave-lengths for one of these colors, though it was believed that all three were to

5. The senses of hearing and bodily equilibrium

Sound is caused by waves or vibrations in the external air (or other mediums such as water). Roughly, we perceive as sounds vibrations that occur at the rate of 20 to 20,000 per second, the slower vibrations with longer wave-lengths producing sounds that are low in pitch and the faster, shorter vibrations producing the high pitches.

The difference between musical tones and noises is due to differences in the character of the sound waves. Musical tones come from waves that are regular and even; noises, from waves that are broken and irregular in sequence. Pure tones result from waves that have a simple and uniform pattern, with each wave like the preceding one; complex tones from waves that have a more complicated though rhythmic pattern, with little waves superimposed upon or interspersed between the larger ones. But strictly

---

some extent responsive to waves of all lengths within the visible spectrum.

For a time this theory was almost completely overshadowed in popularity by a later one proposed by Hering which assumed the existence within the retina of certain photochemical substances which were differentially acted upon by light of various wave-lengths. Each of these substances, according to Hering, would undergo a catabolic (destructive) process when acted upon by waves of a certain length and an anabolic (constructive) process when acted upon by waves of another length. Hering's theory was especially designed to account for the fact that whereas certain colored lights such as red and yellow fuse when mixed and give rise to an intermediate color sensation, others, such as yellow and blue, do not give an intermediate sensation when mixed, but one of white or light gray. According to the Hering theory, the reason why some color sensations blend while others do not is because the latter result from opposed processes in the same retinal substance. When both these processes are aroused simultaneously and in equal degree, they cancel each other and neither of the corresponding color sensations can occur. Since it has been found by experiment that there are two pairs of colors—yellow-blue and red-green—which show this non-blendable characteristic, it was assumed that there must be two different kinds of substances to correspond. In addition, Hering posited a third substance, capable of responding to waves of any length but of varying degrees of brightness. Lights of an intensity lower than that to which the eye was adapted would induce an anabolic process and give a sensation of dark gray or black; those of a higher intensity would induce the opposite process and give a sensation of light gray or white. However this part of the Hering theory had to be discarded when von Kries showed that black-white sensations are due to rod-vision. A further obstacle to the unqualified acceptance of the Hering theory is the discovery that among those persons whose color vision is defective there are some who can distinguish green but not red and a still larger number who can distinguish

pure tones are rarely heard because any material substance tends to vibrate not only as a whole but in parts. Careful observation of a violin string when it is lightly bowed will reveal this tendency to vibrate in halves or thirds in addition to the fundamental vibration of the whole string. These partial vibrations produce faint complementary sounds which are higher in pitch than the fundamental and hence are known as overtones. The differences in tonal quality, in timbre, by which we are able to distinguish one musical instrument from another are the result of the variations in the form of the sound waves caused by the number and character of the overtones.

The ability to localize sounds depends in part upon the relative intensity of the sounds at the two ears and in part upon differences in phase, that is, the fact that the crests of the sound waves entering the two ears will not exactly coincide in time, hence

---

red but not green. It is hard to see how this could be true if both sensations were due to opposed processes in the same receptors.

A third attempt to explain color vision was proposed by Ladd-Franklin. The Ladd-Franklin theory is of particular interest to us because it is based upon a concept of development by differentiation and is thus in line with a principle that we have found to hold good in many other areas of growth and behavior. According to this theory the retina goes through three stages of development. In the first stage it responds to differences in the energy of light but not to differences in wave-length; hence the only possible sensations are those of white, black, and the various shades of gray. Total color blindness is said to result from permanent arrest at this level of development. A little later, the receptors become capable of making a differential response to light-waves of various lengths. At first the differentiation is only between the long waves at one end of the spectrum, which at this stage are believed to give a sensation of yellow, and the very short waves at the other end from which there is a sensation of blue. Some individuals remain at this stage. They can distinguish blue from yellow but not red from green; they are the partially color-blind. Still later a third stage develops in which the eye becomes able to make a distinction between the longest waves and those of medium length. The primitive yellow sensation then breaks up into two, as a result of which we have sensations of red and green. When red and green lights are mixed so that the eye cannot respond to them separately it reverts to the more primitive stage and we have a sensation of yellow. When blue and yellow are mixed, the original white sensation is given because this is equivalent to a blend of light rays of all lengths within the visible range.

Which, if any, of these three theories is the correct one is still a matter of controversy, but recent investigations suggest that some further modification of the Young-Helmholz theory may come nearest to accounting for the facts as they are known to us thus far.

the successive stimulations of the auditory sense-organs will occur at different intervals. We learn to translate these differences in intensity and in phase into terms of localization at the right or left of the body. If our own positions in space were fixed, if we could not turn our heads or move our bodies, we should only be able to tell when a sound was at the right or at the left. We could get no information about whether it came from above or below, from the front or from the rear. But by moving our heads in various ways we are able to vary the sound effects so as to receive a very complex system of cues by which the direction of the sound waves can be judged. Children learn to do this very early in life. Before the end of the first year the infant will promptly turn toward the unseen source of a sound or cock his head this way and that in attention to a faint or unusual sound. Through repeated experiences of this kind the art of localizing sounds is learned.

Like the eye, the ear accomplishes most of its growth before birth. This is particularly true of the parts of the ear that lie inside the head. The shell-like structure on the outside is not an essential part of the ear but only an accessory that in many animals is useful for collecting and directing the sound waves inward toward the real hearing apparatus. In man the external ear has lost most of its usefulness except as a partial protection from dirt and insects.

Within the head are the real organs of hearing. Extending inward from the external ear is the canal leading to them. In the adult, this canal is a little more than one inch in length. Across the inner boundary of the canal is stretched a membrane known as the *tympanic membrane* or ear-drum. When the sound waves reach this membrane, they cause it to vibrate, and this vibration is passed on to the nerve-cells in the inner ear by means of a chain of three little bones known as the *ossicles* that are hung across the middle ear in such a way that the vibration is concentrated upon a small opening between the middle and inner ears. (See Figure 27.) The inner ear is filled with a salty fluid, and this fluid is set in vibration by the vibration of the ossicles. Besides the special apparatus for hearing, the inner ear contains the apparatus for the sense of static equilibrium or, as it is sometimes called, the sense of head-position. This apparatus consists of three semi-

circular canals lying nearer the outside of the head and somewhat higher up than the part of the inner ear in which the
sense-cells for hearing are located. As can be seen in Figure 28,
these canals lie in three different planes, corresponding to the
three plane surfaces that make up a solid right angle like that
on the corner of a cube. In addition to the canals there is a

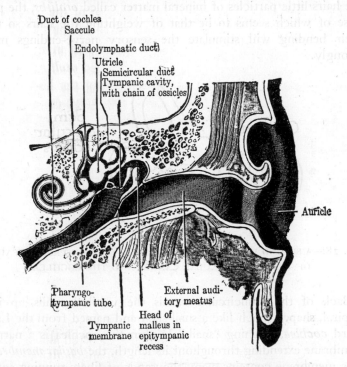

Duct of cochlea
Saccule
Endolymphatic duct)
Utricle
Semicircular duct
Tympanic cavity,
with chain of ossicles

Auricle

Pharyngo-
tympanic tube

External audi-
tory meatus

Head of
Tympanic malleus in
membrane epitympanic
recess

FIG. 27.—DIAGRAM OF PARTS OF THE HUMAN EAR

(Reproduced in Olof Larsell, *Anatomy of the Nervous System* (New
York, D. Appleton-Century Co., Inc., 1942), from Cunningham, *Textbook
of Anatomy*, London, Oxford University Press.)

rounded cavity called the *vestibule* from which the canals open.
Both the vestibule and the canals are filled with fluid and are
equipped with receptor cells that end in fine hairs sticking up
into the fluid. When the head is turned in any direction the hairs
bend and the fine sensory nerve-endings that lie at their bases
are stimulated. The fact that the canals lie in three different

planes means that it is impossible to move the head even slightly in any direction without setting up a flow of liquid in one canal or another, and thus stimulating the nerve-cells. Sensations of this kind are rendered even more acute by reason of the fact that in the vestibule, which is really a part of each of the canals since all open into it at each end, there are entangled in the ends of the hairs little particles of mineral matter called *otoliths*, the purpose of which seems to be that of weighting the hairs so that their bending will stimulate the sensory nerve-endings more strongly.

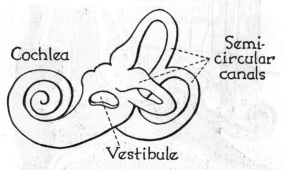

Cochlea

Semi-circular canals

Vestibule

FIG. 28.—A SECOND VIEW OF THE INNER EAR, SHOWING ARRANGEMENT OF THE SEMI-CIRCULAR CANALS AND THE COCHLEA

Back of the semicircular canals the vestibule rolls up into a spiral, shaped much like a snail-shell and named from the Latin word *cochlea*, meaning "snail." Within the cochlea is a narrow membrane extending throughout its length, the *basilar membrane*. The membrane contains many thousands of fibers running across it. At one end the membrane is comparatively narrow and the fibers are short and very tightly stretched; at the other end, where the membrane widens out, they are longer and less taut, thus making a structure something like a harp. On the basilar membrane the receptors for hearing are located. These receptors consist of hair-cells with the sensory nerve-endings twined about their bases.

Although both the physical properties of sound and the general structure of the inner ear which is the receiving instrument for the sound waves have long been known, the exact manner in which the auditory mechanism works is still uncertain. It is reasonably sure that the loudness of sound depends upon the number of sense-cells and their associated nerve-fibers that are stimulated at one time and that the differing length of the fibers in the basilar membrane (also known as the *organ of Corti*) has something to do with sensations of pitch. You know that when a tone of constant pitch is sounded near a piano, the strings that are tuned to that particular pitch will vibrate, while the other strings will not. The physical structure of the organ of Corti with its long slack fibers at one end and its short, taut fibers at the other might well operate in a similar fashion, and as a matter of fact, both post-mortem examination of the ears of human beings who were known to have been deaf to certain pitches and experiments carried out with animals in which certain parts of the membrane were destroyed while leaving the remainder intact indicate that something of this kind does in reality take place. However the matter is probably not quite so simple as Helmholz,[21] who first proposed this *resonance theory*, as it is called, supposed. It was originally thought that pitch sensations could be adequately accounted for in terms of the particular sensory end-organs and associated neurons that were activated, but an ingenious experiment carried out by Wever and Bray [22] shows that the principle is more complex than that. In this experiment, a fine wire was attached to the auditory nerve of a cat which had first been anesthetized so that the nerve could be laid bare. The electrical potentials from the nerve were amplified and then led off to a telephone receiver in another room. It was found that an observer listening at this receiver could hear very distinctly every sound made before the cat's ear. Pitch, loudness, and tonal quality were reproduced exactly. Even speech could be heard and understood with ease. This means that in some way the exact vibration pattern of the sound waves must be reproduced in the electrical phenomena of the nerve itself. Thus something more is needed than just the simple resonance theory which assumed that differences

[21] H. Helmholz, *Sensations of Tone*, tr. by Ellis (London, Longmans, Green and Co., 1875).
[22] E. G. Wever and C. W. Bray, "Action Currents in the Auditory Nerve in Response to Acoustical Stimulation," *Proc. Nat. Acad. Sci.*, 1930, 16: 344-350; "Present Possibilities for Auditory Theory," *Psychol. Rev.*, 1930, 37: 365-380.

in pitch sensations resulted directly from the fact that the nerve-impulses came to the brain over different neurons.

It should be noted, however, that the new experiments do not make it necessary to discard the theory but only to add something to it. Although there is difference of opinion as to just how these results are brought about, the weight of evidence seems to indicate that the physical properties of the sound waves induce sympathetic vibration in the organ of Corti from which the wave pattern is passed on directly to the neurons that together constitute the auditory nerve. Since the frequency of sound waves corresponding to the highest audible pitch is about 20,000 per second, which greatly exceeds the upper limit of frequency of nerve impulses, Wever and Bray have suggested that different neurons within the nerve may work in alternation with each other, just as a drummer increases the rate of his drum-beats by using the two hands in alternation. This is equivalent to saying that the reproduction of the pattern of the sound wave within the nerve may be accomplished through the coördinated action of many neurons, rather than by each singly.

Testing the ability of a new-born baby to hear sounds is not as easy as one who has never tried it might suppose. Failure to make overt response does not necessarily mean that the child has not "heard" a sound, and since he does not have to move his ears in order to hear as he must move or fixate his eyes in order to see, an observer has no sure criterion by which he may judge whether or not hearing is present. Some babies appear to be partially or totally deafened for a few days after birth because the middle ear is filled with amniotic fluid, but this usually drains off within the first week. Thereafter, sounds of fair intensity, particularly if they occur suddenly and are of a different character from those that the child is accustomed to hearing in the nursery, are likely to elicit some response that can be observed, usually a start or a blink. According to Pratt, Nelson and Sun,[23] mixed tones or noises, such as those made by striking a tin can were more likely to elicit a response from the infants than pure tones of equal intensity, such as those made by ringing a wooden

[23] K. C. Pratt, A. K. Nelson, and K. H. Sun, "The Behavior of the New-born Infant," *Ohio State University Studies, Contributions in Psychology*, No. 10, 1930.

THE CHILD AT BIRTH

bell. However, differences in pitch may also have played a part. Moreover, in few if any of the investigations that have been carried on so far has there been adequate control of such complicating factors as (1) loudness or intensity of the sound, (2) its duration, (3) pitch, (4) pureness, (5) suddenness of onset, (6) condition of the child with reference to such factors as hunger, fatigue, and habituation to sounds similar to those used in the experiment. In a good experiment only one of these factors should be varied at a time with all the others held constant. Unless this is done, it is impossible to be sure which of the many attributes of sound are most important in determining a child's response or, indeed, whether or not infants are at all able to differentiate sounds on the basis of pitch, intensity, and so on. About all we are sure of at present is that new-born infants hear. Just how well they hear or what kind of sounds they hear best is something for future investigators to determine.

MOTOR AND GLANDULAR EQUIPMENT OF THE NEW-BORN

The stimulation of the sense-organs is the first link in a series of reactions that may be relatively simple, prompt, and highly localized, as when the pupil of the eye contracts on being exposed to more intense light; or may be a complicated, time-consuming series of affairs that involves the entire organism, as when the trained automobile mechanic catches the sound of a faint "knocking" in the engine of a car and proceeds to overhaul it in order to discover the cause. The strength or intensity of the stimulus is not necessarily related to the intensity of the internal and motor response. Rather we should think of the stimulus as something like the spark that ignites a fuse leading to some stored-up source of energy. The reaction thus set off depends upon the organism and upon the particular train of responses within its repertoire. The same external conditions may and do set off very different trains of reaction in different organisms or in the same organism at different times.

The motor equipment of an individual consists of the motor neurons and their end-organs, together with the skeletal and muscular systems and the glands of internal secretion. Unlike those of the sensory neurons, the outer termini of the motor neurons have no very elaborate structure. At the final point of contact with the muscles, each neuron ends in a tuft of finely branched neuro-fibrils known as an *end-brush* from which the nerve impulse is communicated directly to the muscle fibers.

Movement is produced by the alternate contraction and relaxation of the muscles. The latter are of two kinds, the *striped muscles* which are attached to the bones and are made up of fibers all of which run in the same general direction and give the muscles their well-known fibrous appearance, and the *smooth muscles* of the internal organs and blood-vessels which are made up of much smaller fibers that form a compact network capable of a more elaborate pattern of contraction than that of the striped muscles. You can see that an organ like the stomach which carries on its job of reducing food to a semiliquid condition by means of a combination of chemical and mechanical action would be greatly handicapped if it were equipped only with muscles like the biceps in the upper arm where all the fibers run the same way so that the muscle as a whole can contract only in one direction. The muscles in the wall of the stomach and other organs, on the contrary, have their fibers so arranged as to enable those organs to contract in a circular fashion as well as in other directions in order to carry on their special work.[24]

The motor activities of the new-born infant may be divided roughly into two classes; so-called *spontaneous activity*, which consists in the main of responses to organic and proprioceptive stimuli such as internal pain or discomfort, fatigue from remaining too long in a single position, and so on; and *reflex activity*, which consists of more highly localized reactions, occurring as a rule in response to stimulation of the exteroceptors. The distinction between the two forms is, however, more apparent than real. At one time, reflexes were thought to be neurologically simple acts in which the cerebral cortex took little or no part and only a few neurons were involved. More recent study has shown that even

[24] The muscles of the heart do not fall within either class. They look like striped muscles, but they function like smooth muscles. Moreover, while the rate of the heart-beat may be quickened or slowed by stimulation from the nervous system, the beating itself is self-stimulated. It begins before the outgrowing neurons of the very young embryo have reached the heart and continues until death.

such an apparently automatic and mechanical response as the jerk of the leg in response to a tap on the patellar tendon is influenced by so many other factors that to speak of it as a "simple" reflex is to understate the fact. The knee jerk varies, for example, with the momentary state of bodily and emotional tension, becoming more pronounced when the subject is irritated or excited, while during states of relaxation it is so weakened that it may be hard to elicit at all. It is usually abolished in sleep. Other reflexes vary in a similar fashion. For these and similar reasons the modern psychologist no longer regards the reflex as a kind of activity that differs from other forms of motor behavior in any truly fundamental way. Instead, he uses the term as a convenient name for certain forms of behavior that have a comparatively invariant pattern which appears with little or no previous practice in response to a particular kind of stimulus. As a rule, a reflex act involves only a circumscribed area of the body. Examples are the knee jerk previously mentioned, the wink that occurs in response to some threat to the eye, and the salivary reflex or mouth-watering which is the normal response of the salivary glands of a hungry individual to the taste or odor of food.

A fairly large number of reflexes are well developed in the newborn infant, although, as the Shermans [25] have shown, many of these do not appear consistently for some hours after birth. In view of the fact that most of the reflexes studied by the Shermans emerge gradually within the first two or three days of life, their non-appearance at first may best be ascribed to the effects of birth trauma. Their study is a nice illustration of the hazards of attempting to ascertain the abilities of the infant before the effects of temporary birth injuries have disappeared.

In addition to the comparatively circumscribed and patterned forms of behavior that we call reflexes, the infant from the time of birth displays an increasing amount of the kind of activity that we call "spontaneous" because we cannot directly observe the stimuli which arouse it. That such stimuli exist we may be very sure, but in all probability they are for the most part internal in origin. Besides these, external events of a more diffuse or generalized character such as draughts of air that affect a fairly

[25] Mandel Sherman and Irene C. Sherman, "Sensori-motor Responses in Infants," *J. Comp. Psychol.*, 1925, 5: 53-68.

large portion of the child's body at one time, or other matters that the observer fails to notice, may arouse activity in the infant. "Spontaneous activity," is therefore nothing more than a name that we give to behavior arising from stimuli the exact nature of which is not known to the observer.

Older children and adults show still a third type of behavior that is largely or wholly absent in the new-born baby. This is the kind of behavior that we call "voluntary" because we are able to control it at will. The process of acquiring control over an act which is one of the most important types of learning, will demand a large share of our attention in the chapters that follow. Voluntary acts range in complexity all the way from such relatively simple skills as picking up a pencil to learning how to perform the complicated evolutions of writing with it and at a still higher level, of utilizing the mechanical art of writing in the composition of a poem or the report of a scientific experiment.

No account of the mechanism by which the organism responds to its environment is complete without mention of the glandular component. In addition to the skeletal and muscular systems by which gross bodily movements are accomplished, the body also contains a large number of little organs called *glands*. One of the important functions of these organs is to regulate body chemistry by means of the special secretions which they prepare. Glands are of two kinds, the *duct glands* that have special outlets and serve a comparatively local function and the *ductless* or *endocrine glands* that discharge secretions called *hormones* directly into the blood stream, by which they are carried all over the body, where they exercise a widespread effect upon growth and behavior.

Among the most familiar of the duct glands are the *sweat glands*, with their outlets leading to the surface of the skin; the *salivary glands*, with ducts opening into the mouth; the *tear glands* that provide moisture for the eye; the *kidneys*; and the *sex glands*, as well as many glands in the stomach and intestines by the action of which the chemistry of digestion is carried on. Since each of these glands has a highly specialized work that is carried on in a circumscribed area of the body they are, by comparison, easy to study and their functions are fairly well understood.

But the ductless glands which make up what is often called the *endocrine system* are in a very different category. Only during

recent years has science begun to grope its way toward some
fragmentary and not-too-certain knowledge of the part played
by these glands in the regulation of growth and behavior. That
their rôle is both extensive and profound is evident when something happens to interfere with or change their normal function-

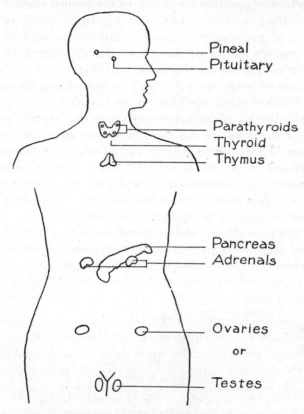

Pineal
Pituitary

Parathyroids
Thyroid
Thymus

Pancreas
Adrenals

Ovaries
or
Testes

FIG. 29.—DIAGRAM SHOWING THE LOCATION OF THE MOST IMPORTANT
ENDOCRINE GLANDS

ing. The results of such a defect may be so dramatic or so bizarre
that it is not surprising to find writers of sensational fiction developing fantastic plots of the Dr. Jekell and Mr. Hyde variety by
unwarrantably exaggerating some new development in glandular
therapy. Nevertheless in this case the truth may be even stranger
than fiction. Let us consider just a few of the physical anomalies

resulting from malfunction of these glands. There is the midget who at maturity may be no taller than the normal infant of six months, or the giant who may reach a height of well over eight feet. Both these conditions are believed to be mainly due to malfunctioning of the anterior lobe of the *pituitary gland* (see Figure 29), the former resulting from lack of the normal amount of the secretion, the latter from an excess.[26] The bearded lady of circus fame is in all probability suffering from excessive activity of the *cortex* or outer surface of the *adrenal glands* situated, as shown in Figure 29, just above the kidneys. The fat lady in the next booth likewise owes her pay check to her glands. In her case, several different glands are likely to be involved.

Occasionally an infant is born in whom the *thyroid gland* at the top of the larynx in the throat is largely or wholly inactive. If nothing is done about it, such a child will develop into what is known as a *cretin*. Its mental level will be that of an idiot, its body stunted and malformed. (See Figure 30.) But if thyroid extract, which is now available commercially, is administered in the proper dosage an amazing transformation [27] may be brought about. The pot-bellied, helpless dwarf becomes a normal, active child and remains so as long as the treatment is continued. But deprive him of his daily allotment of thyroid and in a very short time the magic will have departed and the child will again become a misshapen idiot.

Even more interesting to the psychologist than their effects upon the body are the influences exerted by the endocrines upon behavior, and more especially upon those patterned and more or less persisting forms of behavior that we call "personality." That

[26] Probably in none of these cases is the difficulty to be ascribed solely to the influence of a single gland. The entire endocrine system works together in a complicated interlinkage of checks and balances, the relationships of which we are only just beginning to grasp.

[27] The treatment of cretinism by means of thyroid has not been equally successful in all cases. Some degree of improvement is almost universal, and when the treatment is begun in infancy and continued without intermission under competent medical supervision, a complete return to normality has sometimes been brought about. Regulation of the dosage is not an easy matter, however, and in many cases the most that can be done is to ameliorate the condition without effecting a complete cure. The probability of success is in part a matter of the age at which treatment is begun. Other things being equal, the younger the child, the better is the prospect of success through treatment.

personality characteristics are modified by, and thus to some extent, at least, are dependent upon hormones secreted by the glands of the endocrine system is a generally accepted fact. Nevertheless we must be extremely cautious about accepting the pronouncements of those enthusiasts who, on the basis of a small amount of questionable evidence, are ready to tell the world just

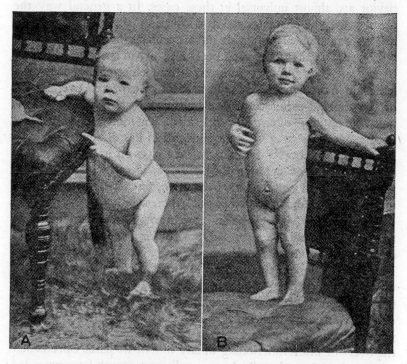

FIG. 30.—A CRETIN BEFORE AND AFTER FOUR MONTHS' TREATMENT WITH THYROID POWDER

(From H. O. Nicholson, *Archives of Pediatrics*, Vol. 17, 1900.)

what kind of behavioral trends result from any particular pattern of hormone balance or inbalance. Investigation in this field is still in its neonatal stage, and while the infant science is a lusty one, we must wait for it to grow considerably beyond its present level of development before we can be safe in stating the exact nature of the relationships between endocrine function and personality traits, even though we may now feel reasonably sure that such relations exist. A few have been established with a reasonable degree of certainty. Deficient thyroid activity, for example, when occurring in an adult whose growth was completed before the onset of the condition, produces a state known as *myxedema*. In addition to certain structural changes such as excessive dryness and roughening of the skin, alterations of personality and behavior are almost universal in these cases. In a general way the changes may be characterized as a lowering of all forms of physical and mental energy with an accompanying loss in rate of response. The affected person becomes slow in speech, indifferent to matters that formerly interested him, emotionally depressed, lethargic in movement. As might perhaps be expected, overactivity of the thyroid seems to induce behavior that in many ways is quite the opposite of that just described. The individual so affected becomes "high-strung" and nervous, often has difficulty in sleeping, and all his bodily functions tend to go on at an accelerated rate. He becomes emotionally excitable, is easily elated or depressed by small causes. He is overactive, finds it difficult to relax, must always be doing something or other.

Relationships between behavior patterns and other endocrine functions have also been studied, but the results are not so certain or clear-cut as those found for the thyroid. Moreover, there is increasing reason to think that the effect of glandular secretions upon such individual differences in personality and conduct as may be observed among the rank and file of people can be better described in terms of what we may call the "balance of power" within the endocrine system as a whole, rather than in terms of the over- or underfunctioning of any one of its parts. Spectacular cases such as those described in an earlier paragraph have provided many cues as to the types of relationship that may perhaps be found to hold for man in general, but much further study is needed before we can hope to make much practical use of endocrine treatment in the improvement or modification of the personality traits of the average person.

Little is known specifically about the functioning of the endocrines at the time of birth other than the fact that (since in the absence of the essential hormones no child could survive) the glands must of necessity be active at birth. It is interesting to speculate on the possibility that the pattern of endocrine balance in early life may not only play a part in determining the child's personality at the time, but may also give rise to modes of reaction that persist as habits even though the glandular condition that gave rise to them may be modified with the passage of time. Such speculation precedes scientific investigation; we can but hope that in the not too distant future, scientific research will provide the answers to some, at least, of our questions about the physical basis of personality differences.

SUMMARY

At the time of birth the infant's sense-organs have reached a stage of development at which they function with fair effectiveness. Careful experiments have shown that within a few days after birth the normal child will respond to changes in temperature, to differences in the brightness of light, to odors, to taste qualities, to pain from such stimuli as light pricking with a needle or (presumably) internal discomfort arising from colic or hunger, and to sounds, though some infants remain insensitive to sound for a few days after birth, a fact that is thought to be due to the presence of amniotic fluid in the auditory canal. Whether or not the new-born infant responds to differences in the color of light or the pitch of sounds has not yet been established with certainty.

On the motor side, the infant at birth also shows a wide variety of reactions. Most of the basic reflexes such as the knee jerk, the plantar response, the pupillary reaction to light, and many others appear in almost adult form as soon as the effects of birth trauma have disappeared.

In addition to the reflexes that persist throughout life, there are a few that appear only in infancy. The reflex clasp which disappears around the age of four months and is later replaced by the voluntary grasp is an example.

Besides the reflexes that appear in response to known stimuli and that as a rule involve a limited area of the body, the new-born infant displays many other forms of reaction that are believed to arise, for the most part, from internal sensations, though it is likely that in some instances these movements are responses to stimulation of the external sense-organs that the observer fails to notice. Although activity of this kind is commonly called "spontaneous," it is, in reality, quite as much a response to stimuli as are the reflexes that occur when the appropriate stimuli are intentionally administered in the course of a scientific experiment. "Spontaneous activity" is therefore just a name that we give to reactions of unknown origin. However, because much of the spontaneous activity displayed by the infant is presumably aroused by internal sensations that are diffused rather than highly localized, activity of this kind is, as a rule, less definitely patterned, less predictable either as to the time or manner of its occurrence, and is likely to involve larger segments of the body at one time than do the simple reflexes.

The new-born infant shows little or no indication of the "voluntary" activity that makes up so large a share of the reactions of the older person. This is not surprising when we recall that "voluntary" activity is learned activity and that up to the time of birth the child has had little or no opportunity for learning such skills, whatever his capacity for acquiring them may be. For the most part the infant's abilities are nascent rather than actual, and the differences between one infant and another in respect to their *potentialities* for later achievement are far greater and more significant than any that may already be manifested.

It is not true that all infants are alike, even at birth. Some are relatively alert; others are sluggish. Some are irritable, crying frequently from causes that appear slight; others are "good babies" who make little trouble. Some take their food eagerly from the beginning; others have to be "fussed with" in order to get them to eat at all. Their physical characteristics differ. Some are large, others small; some are blond in coloring, while others are dark; some are fat, some thin. But the differences that can be seen at birth are trivial indeed compared to those that will develop later as latent capacities and characteristics gradually ripen into actualities.

The all-important business confronting the infant is to learn. In the next two chapters, therefore, we shall take up some of the major principles that have to do with learning and with the retention of things learned.

THE NEW BABY: A BOOK OF PICTURES

Louise Zabriskie, *Mother and Baby Care in Pictures*
(Philadelphia, J. B. Lippincott Co., 1935), pp. x + 196.

Most normal young people look forward to becoming parents.
Many, even before the time of their own marriage and parenthood,
are called upon to help or advise friends or relatives at the time a baby
is born. Yet the majority of college students have never seen a birth,
even of an animal, and know very little about everyday matters of
prenatal and early postnatal care of mother and child.

This is a book prepared for the layman by a trained nurse who was
formerly the head supervisor of a large maternity hospital. For the
most part it consists of photographs with just enough text to explain
the pictures. It shows how the fetus is carried in the body of the
mother, how the birth takes place, and how the new-born baby is
cared for. Although this is not a book on psychology in the ordinary
sense of the word, a little time spent in looking through the pictures
will give you a much clearer idea than you are now likely to have of
the nature of the birth process and the care and behavior of the very
young baby.

Chapter VI

HOW ACTIVITY IS AROUSED

What is the literal meaning of the word motive?

In what respect do motives differ from other stimuli?

Are all the motives experienced by a given person present at birth? If not, how do new motives come into existence?

What is meant by the term conditioned response? *How does the process of conditioning take place? In what way does conditioning affect the arousal of activity in the individual?*

What can you say about the relationship of motives to personality?

SOME EXAMPLES

A baby lies asleep in his crib. Presently he stirs, begins to squirm about and kick. He wrinkles up his face and whimpers a little. He tosses his arms about, and in so doing chances to bring his fist into contact with his mouth, whereupon he thrusts in as many fingers as possible and sucks them vigorously. In a moment or two, however, he pulls the fingers out of his mouth and begins to cry loudly. Just then his nurse comes with his bottle. "No wonder he cries," she observes. "It's almost half an hour past his feeding time."

A child of five is playing on the floor with his blocks. He is not hungry; he had a hearty lunch only a short time ago. But his brother has just come into the room, blissfully licking an ice cream cone. The younger child jumps up and demands a share but is refused. He reaches for the cone, grasps his brother's arm and pulls hard. This failing, he begins to kick and scream, call

150

names, perhaps goes so far as to pelt his brother with blocks or break some of his toys.

A boy of eighteen has just finished high school. He has no money and his parents are poor. But the lad wants to become a doctor. He spends the summer working as a farm laborer—the only job he is able to get. The hours are long and the pay small, but by saving every cent of his wages he is able to put enough by to pay his entrance fees at the state university. There he manages to support himself after a fashion by doing all sorts of odd jobs. His room is cramped and without heat, his food scanty and of the cheapest quality he can find. Nevertheless, in spite of hardships he keeps on working until, after eight long years of privation and struggle he holds the coveted medical diploma in his hands.

Viewed in one way the three episodes just described may seem very different. Actually, however, they have many features in common. In the first place, each consists of a more or less completely organized series of activities that are set off from other activities of the individual by the fact that each has its own unique starting point and its own individual goal. Just as we define a journey in terms of its point of departure and its terminus, so we define an activity in terms of the factor or group of factors that gave rise to it and the goal at which it is aimed. That which gives rise to activity is known as the *stimulus*, and it is the intimate association between the stimulus and the goal that gives to an activity its cyclic character. In a very real sense, each stimulus defines its own goal, for the activity that it arouses cannot, as a rule, be satisfactorily brought to a close except by the attainment of some particular end.[1] In the case of the hungry baby who, by accident, got its fist into its mouth, the response aroused by the tactile stimulus did not lead to satisfaction of the bodily need and was therefore soon discontinued.

The three instances have another common factor. In each case the stimulus that set off the activity was the presence of some condition that was unsatisfactory to the organism. In the first

---

[1] It is of course true that a new goal is sometimes substituted for the original one before the latter has been attained. In such cases, however, we are really dealing with a new series of activities that usually involves not only a substitution of goals but a substitution of stimuli as well.

example, the unsatisfied state was due to the relatively simple physiological need known as hunger. In the two remaining instances, as in most of the activities of older children and adults, we have to do with far more complicated sets of conditions in which the memory of past experiences, the ideas aroused by the observation and interpretation of the behavior of others, and a host of other factors are involved. Some of these, like the five-year-old's fondness for sweets, are well-nigh universal among normal human beings, while others, like the older boy's desire to become a doctor, may be highly individualized, their specific character determined in very large part by the particular kind of experiences through which that person has passed. All, however, have this in common. The organism has in some way undergone a disturbance of its "normal" equilibrium and is thereby thrown into a *state of striving*. We must not assume that either the goal toward which the striving is directed or the nature of the disturbance that set the activity going, is always or of necessity understood by the subject, although it is true that the existence of a partial or complete awareness of his needs and aims is likely to change the pattern of the activity that follows, rendering it more directly adapted to accomplishing those ends. The young infant certainly does not "know" that he is hungry. We can only speculate as to whether or not anything even remotely resembling our own internal feelings under similar conditions is present at so early an age. For no matter how real his hunger contractions may be, the adult's knowledge of what is the matter with him unquestionably plays a major rôle in determining the subjective character of his hunger experiences. But the infant's bodily need is just as sure a stimulus for the arousal of activity as a similar need in the older person, and once aroused, the activity is likely to be quite as intense.

WHAT IS MEANT BY "MOTIVATION"

Any kind of stimulus that arouses activity which seems to be *goal-directed*, is known as a motive, and the process by which such stimulation is brought about is known as *motivation*. A motivated activity is to be distinguished from the simpler sensory experiences of which the individual may be aware but that do not, as far as can be determined, lead to any kind of response beyond the sensory experience itself.[2]

To motivate means to induce activity. A motive is something that arouses an organism to action. Of course by "action" we do not mean just the movements of the muscles, which, as we have pointed out before, are only the later stages in activity. All actions begin with some kind of intraorganic change, which the outsider is unable to observe. Motivating an individual means getting him to do something. This "something" may involve muscular activity; it may be just sitting still and thinking. People are motivated to do a great many different things—to read, to study their lessons, to play football, to go to parties, to make love, to write novels, to hoe corn, or to dig ditches. But the motives which lie back of all these diverse activities are, in one sense, alike. People are motivated—that is, they are induced to do things—because they are not entirely satisfied with their present condition. If this state of dissatisfaction becomes strong enough to overcome their inertia, they do something to bring about a change. The particular thing that they may do depends first of all upon their abilities and accomplishments and secondly upon what experience has taught them is most likely to relieve their dissatisfaction or to bring about a state of greater satisfaction. The first step in motivation is, then, the arousal of an organic state that is not entirely satisfying. Such a state in itself, if it is sufficiently pronounced, will induce a kind of general activity or restlessness, but in order to change this undirected activity into a definitely organized

[2] Evidently this distinction is one of degree rather than kind. It may plausibly be argued that even such a simple and automatic reaction as the pupillary reflex which is the normal response when the eye is exposed to a strong light is in a sense goal-directed, since it unquestionably serves a useful purpose for the individual. Nevertheless, we do not commonly think of the reaction to light as a motive. Unquestionably, the fleeting visual impressions gained from aimless looking about frequently take on the rôle of motives when, suddenly and without warning, they crystallize into a reminder of something or other that should be done. Very probably there are other instances of which even the adult is unaware in which casual and unnoticed sensations and perceptions, each too small to arouse a reaction by itself, gradually become organized into a motive strong enough to induce action, thus following the principle of *summation of stimuli* that has been described before.

pattern that will lead to useful accomplishment it has to be directed toward an end or goal. The real goal, of course, is a return to a state of satisfaction; but the immediate goal toward which the individual directs his striving is something that nature and experience, acting together, have taught him is likely to bring about such a state.

Consider a few examples: A healthy young cat has been given no food for several hours. At the end of that time he is put into a cage, the door of which is closed by a simple contrivance such as a button that he can turn with his paw or a loose strap that he can pull off its fastening. A piece of fish is put outside the door where the cat can see and smell it.

Before we observe the cat's behavior let us look at the conditions. First of all, the cat's organic state is not one of complete satisfaction. He is hungry. This, alone, is enough to make him restless, as every one knows who has observed a hungry animal. But just outside the cage is something that would satisfy his hunger, something, moreover that is particularly pleasing to a cat's appetite. So, naturally enough, he tries to get it. He claws at the bars of the cage, scrambles about more or less, but always directs most of his struggles against the part of the cage that lies directly between himself and the fish. This is not purely random activity; from the beginning it is aimed at attaining a given end and so takes on a particular direction and a pattern that varies only within certain limits. The cat jumps, claws, perhaps bites at the bars, occasionally stops and runs about the cage, but for the most part he keeps his head and body turned toward the fish. He may mew, but he does not purr; neither is he likely to chase his tail, to sit down quietly and wash his face, or to show a good many other forms of behavior that young cats often do exhibit under other circumstances.

Put the same cat, in the same state of hunger, into the cage on another occasion, but this time put no food outside. Again the cat runs about and claws at the cage but less violently. He does not select any one part of the cage toward which to direct his efforts, but roams about restlessly, now here, now there, stopping sometimes to stand with his paws against the bars, watching the experimenter, or to lick his fur for a minute or two, after which he resumes his restless wandering. His behavior is more varied, less predictable, and far less vigorous than it was on the first occasion. Most of all, the animal's behavior now lacks apparent direction.

Now give the cat all the fish he will eat. Then put him in the cage again with another piece of fish outside the door as before. The chances are he will pay no attention to it. Probably he will lie down and go to sleep.

Try one more experiment. Put the cat into the cage but instead of a piece of fish, place a piece of apple outside the door. What will the cat do this time?

If he is hungry, he will probably act much as he did on the second occasion. He will roam around, perhaps claw at the bars occasionally, but he will not pay any particular attention to the apple, which for him is not food. His state of hunger keeps him moving around, but his activity is undirected. If he is not hungry, he will probably be less restless, but he will still pay no special attention to the apple.

These experiments illustrate a number of factors in human and animal behavior. The hungry cat, because of its unsatisfied organic state, behaves differently from the cat that has just had all it can eat. And the hungry cat that sees a means of satisfying its hunger behaves differently from the hungry cat when no food is in sight. Furthermore, the cat that not only perceives the goal but has learned by experience how to get to it—that has learned, for example, how to turn the button or to pull the strap by which the door may be opened—behaves differently from the one that is equally hungry, and that sees the fish equally well but for whom the button or the strap has as yet no meaning. All along the road leading to the final goal—satisfaction—are objects that eventually, as the route is learned, take on the character of semaphores or guide-boards, showing the individual that he is on the right track. In this instance as in many others, learning to read these semaphores and to respond to them proceeds for the most part in a backward direction from the goal. First the goal itself is perceived as such; later the button or the strap comes to be singled out and responded to in a fumbling, haphazard fashion; still later the particular movements—turning the button or pulling the strap—are learned with more or less exactness. Once these signals have been learned, they may arouse almost or even quite as consistent and intense reactions in the subject as the original objective which they have come to signify.[3]

INCREASING THE RANGE OF THE STIMULUS

The young infant at first makes no response to the mere sight of his bottle, no matter how hungry he may be. But with repeated experiences in which the sight of the bottle *directly preceded and overlapped with* the satisfaction of hunger, there comes a time when the mere visual appearance of the bottle—at first inadequate to arouse directed activity—comes to be almost, if not quite as potent a stimulus for eliciting the behavior patterns associated with the act of feeding as is the direct contact of the milk from the nipple with the taste-buds in the mouth. (See Figure 2, p. 14). Just what is the nature of the neurological process by which this type of associative learning, commonly spoken of as *conditioning*, takes place is not known, but we do know a good deal about the factors that facilitate or interfere with its occurrence or that make for the extinction of such "conditioned" responses after they have been established. Of this we shall have more to say in the next chapter. For the present it is

[3] For example, to many people the obtaining and accumulation of money becomes an end in itself, almost completely divorced from its use as a means of obtaining goods and services. The sign has for them become equal to or even greater in value than the thing signified. Chimpanzees that have learned to use poker chips as a means of getting food from a specially constructed slot machine will work about as hard and as persistently to secure the chips as they will work in order to obtain the food directly, and they show a good many of the same traits which human beings exhibit in their use of this "money." In times of plenty they may hoard the excess, or they may "spend" all that they have and make themselves ill from overeating or scatter food recklessly about the cage. It has even been found possible to train white rats to use tokens for securing food. In the case of one rat who had been trained to secure his tokens by pulling a string to which was attached a weight, sufficiently heavy to constitute rather hard labor for the rat, the slot machine from which he secured his food was intentionally put out of order although he was still able to get his tokens in the usual manner. When the rat found that no food was forthcoming, he carefully stored his tokens in a corner of the cage and continued to work as before until the machine was readjusted. He then made use of his stored tokens before returning to the job of securing new ones.

sufficient to note that an essential feature of the infant's learning consists in the acquisition of an increasingly elaborate and effective system of signals for the arousal and direction of his activity. These signals, moreover, have the all-important property of being self-multiplying. Because no two concrete events are ever exactly alike, new associations involving different and more finely differentiated sets of signals are constantly being formed.

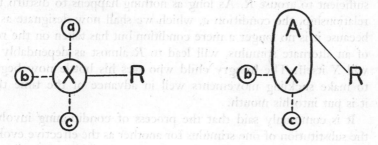

Situation 1   Situation 2

FIG. 31.—DIAGRAM ILLUSTRATING THE FORMATION OF A CONDITIONED
RESPONSE

This principle is shown graphically in Figure 31. The letter X represents a "biologically adequate" stimulus which is capable of eliciting the response, R, without previous experience or training. An example is the suckling reflex that occurs when the tactile and the taste receptors in the infant's mouth are stimulated by the pressure of a nipple from which milk is secured. The small letters, a, b, and c stand for other conditions simultaneously present (such as the sight of the breast or bottle, the voice of the nurse, or the posture in which the child is usually placed for nursing) to each of which he is potentially capable of reacting in some way but that do not at first evoke suckling as a specific response. But all are in *temporal association with* X, and this association is nearly if not quite the same from one occasion to another. Moreover, because of their association with X, all will likewise be associated with the *satisfying effects of the response R,* though not necessarily to the same extent. Such differentials as unequal overlapping in time, priority of occurrence, comparative biological intensity or any of a number of other factors may operate to bring about a closer effective relationship between a as a potential stimulus and the response R than exists for either b or c. Because of this intimate association of a with both X and R the condition illustrated in Part 2 of Figure 33 is likely to arise. There comes a time when, even before the occurrence of X, (the biologically adequate stimulus), the appearance of a becomes sufficient to arouse R. As long as nothing happens to disturb the relationship, the condition a, which we shall now designate as A because it is no longer a mere condition but has taken on the rôle of an alternate stimulus, will lead to R almost as dependably as will X itself. The hungry child who sees his bottle now begins to make suckling movements well in advance of the time that it is put into his mouth.

It is commonly said that the process of conditioning involves the substitution of one stimulus for another as the effective evoker of a given kind of response. In order that this "substitution" may occur, however, the two stimuli—the "adequate" and the "inadequate"—must first be combined in such a way as to form a unified stimulus-pattern. The "substitution" is then seen to correspond more nearly to a process of extension than to one of substitution in the ordinary sense of the word. When the first part of the pattern occurs, the response follows immediately without waiting for the stimulus to be completed. But this will not occur unless the series of events normally making up the total pattern has become a functional unit, the only purpose of which is to point the course from the felt need to the goal by which it can be satisfied. "Conditioning" is nothing more than a process of short-cutting, whereby the response occurs at an earlier stage in the total course of events than was formerly possible. The original stimulus, X, has become expanded to include A as one of its integral parts. A is no longer a separate event; it is the beginning of X and so arouses the response that is appropriate to X.

The conditioned response is subject to many variations, since children are constantly responding to many stimuli besides the particular ones that may chance to have caught the attention of an observer. Conditioning occurs with reference to the former as readily as to the latter. So it may come about that a child in whom a conditioned response to A has been built up may consistently fail to show this response when *b* is also present. This means, of course, that *b* elicits a reaction of its own which is sufficiently potent to take command of the organism. For example, a child who has learned to fear a particular person may start to cry instead of making his usual suckling movements on seeing his bottle offered to him by that person. In like manner, the suckling response may be replaced by laughter and crowing if, simultaneously with the bottle, he catches sight of an older brother or sister with whom he is accustomed to engage in lively play.

HOW NEW MOTIVES ARE ACQUIRED

Consider the rôle of the hunger motive in each of the three examples cited at the beginning of this chapter. In the case of the young infant, this motive is relatively simple and uncomplicated. In the five-year-old, matters have taken a very different turn. Hunger, in the strict sense of the word, plays a very minor rôle in determining the behavior shown, yet his struggle to secure the ice-cream cone is even more violent than that of the truly hungry infant. Experience in eating different kinds of food with all the associated factors that arise from seeing others eat, hearing them describe this food as delicious and that as unpalatable or nauseating, together with personal associations of certain foods with pleasant or unpleasant circumstances, soon overlays the simple hunger-motive. A heavy veneer of associated ideas, attitudes and emotions usually prevents it from appearing again in precisely its original pattern. The kernel remains in the form of the bodily need, but even by the age of five, this need must be great indeed to force the child who has been daintily reared to satisfy his hunger by eating a raw snake or toad, or an apple that has been smeared with filth. On the other hand, certain kinds of food, as we have just seen, have by this time taken on for him such highly desirable qualities that appetite is awakened at the mere sight of them, even when hunger is at a minimum.

Experience thus serves as a differentiating agent. For the young and healthy infant, food is food. Unless the differences in taste are marked, a hungry baby, literally speaking, will eat almost anything he can swallow. But before many months have passed, this early generalized attitude splits up into many specific ones.

At least for the ordinary person, who rarely experiences extreme states of hunger, food, as such, has lost most of its usefulness as a concept to be employed in discussions of human motivation. To be at all accurate we must now speak not of food in general but of foods. The matter is made even more complicated by the fact that the same food will have different motivating value for different individuals. Popeye is supposed to be most highly motivated by spinach, but many parents would tell a different story.[4] New and more specific motives thus arise through the differentiation of earlier and more generalized motives as a combined result of personal experience and social conditioning. As a result of conditioning, a stimulus may be either expanded to include elements not formerly a part of it, or it may be refined through the elimination from it of parts not previously differentiated from the total.

Nor is this all. The world is so constituted that motives of different kinds frequently conflict with each other in such a way that one can be gratified only at the expense of the other. We shall have more to say about this later on,[5] but for the present we may note that such conflicts sometimes result in compromises that are very different from either of the originals. They may nevertheless lead to such satisfying goals that the new motives thus established come to take preference over those originally favored. Because of this ever-present necessity of choosing among the many motives that are competing for control of his activity at any given moment, every normal individual, whether knowingly or not, is forced to arrange his motives in some kind of hierarchy of importance. In the case of the high school lad who wanted to become a doctor, we see that this desire had so gained the ascendency over other more primitive motives arising from bodily discomfort and physical appetites that the latter became inconspicuous by contrast.

Motives take on new forms through alliance with each other as well as by differentiation. The five-year-old and the ice-cream cone is an example. The child's original motive was in all probability just what it seemed to be—a special fondness for ice-cream.

---

[4] This provides us with one more illustration of the principle that the stimulus is within the individual and not outside him. The spinach is the same but Popeye and Billy Smith are not.

[5] See Chapter XIX.

But almost immediately we see another factor entering it. This is what Woodworth has called the *mastery* or *self-assertive* motive, here shown by the shift from the child's direct attempt to secure the sweet to an effort to overpower his brother. The desire for mastery, if only to enter adequately into any present situation, seems to play some part in nearly all human activities. It has been suggested that even such primitive reactions as the increased strength of the reflex grasp when an object placed in the palm of a new-born child is withdrawn before the grasp has started to relax, or the stiffening of the muscles of the child's leg when pressure is applied to the sole of his foot, may perhaps be looked upon as blind, early manifestations of this motive.

Not only desire for mastery but almost any other motive known in human behavior may work in combination with other motives toward a goal that is different, in some respects at least, from those toward which the activity would be directed in the absence of any one of the motivating forces leading up to it. Jealousy is a nice example. Every one knows that a feeling of jealousy may be a very powerful spur to action. Jealousy is not a simple motive but one involving many components, differing somewhat from instance to instance. Generally speaking, however, we can single out of the complex such elements as the urge for personal prestige, together with a special attitude that is often hard to identify as either love or hate but that certainly is not indifference toward the person of whom one is jealous. With this there are combined certain very specific attitudes with reference to the objective toward which the jealousy is displayed. Better clothes, better grades in school, the love of another person, wealth, or professional success are examples of such objectives. It is safe to say that unmixed motives are rarely if ever found in any individual after the period of early childhood has passed. A careful analysis would in all probability show that no two motives are absolutely identical.

Motives, then, are not independent of the individual by whom they are felt but are intimately tied up with every aspect of his personality. The external circumstances that motivate one person to fight may put another to flight and start a third to laughing. As a matter of fact, if we could get a complete and truthful account of all the motives by which an individual's behavior is influenced during the course of a single day or week, we should have a more accurate picture of that elusive thing we call "personality" than could be gained in any other way. For motives are the starting points of activity which set the goals toward which activity is directed. Motivation may therefore be thought of as personality-at-work, the very essence of character. The emergence of new motives is as essential a feature of growth and development as is the eruption of teeth or the addition of new words to the vocabulary. Both maturation and experience play a part in determining the appearance and character of these new urges that with the passage of time will gradually crystallize into the unique hierarchy of personal values by which each of our lives is shaped.

In Chapter I we asked, Why do people behave so differently? We now see that their behavior differs because they are striving for different goals, because that which seems good and desirable to one person leaves another indifferent and arouses a feeling of aversion in a third. But the arousal of activity and its direction toward a desired end is only part of the story. There is also the question of the means by which that end is to be accomplished. Not only do people differ in the goals for which they strive. They forge different tools for accomplishing their purposes, and they select different routes for arriving at their chosen destinations. The tools that they contrive are not equally effective nor durable. Some are but clumsy contrivances having only a limited purpose which must soon be discarded; others are like well-tempered steel that may serve its owner for a lifetime. Neither are the routes to accomplishment or satisfaction always direct and easy to follow. Nevertheless the tools must be forged, the routes must be chosen, and every individual must be his own workman and guide. As aids to the task he has only the raw materials provided by his sensory and motor equipment and his mental potentialities. He is at once the work and the workman; the structure that he builds is himself.

When we look at a new-born baby we have no way of knowing what the design of his life is to be nor how well the pattern will be developed. We see only that he is actively at work upon it, and we do not have to wait long to find that the structure is beginning to take form. In the next chapter we shall consider some of the factors that influence the selection of the goals toward which activity is directed and the varying means by which these ends are sought.

WHAT WOULD YOU CHOOSE?

Suppose that, like Admiral Byrd, you were to spend a winter alone in Antarctica. In addition to necessities you may take with you fifty units selected from the following list. Which would you choose?

	Units
Books	1 each
Camera	10
Film	5 rolls = 1 unit
Chemicals and equipment for developing and printing, including paper	Reasonable supply, 15 units
Gramophone	10
Records	1 each
Violin or other portable instrument	10
Sheet music	5 sheets = 1 unit
Paints (choice of medium)	5 colors = 1 unit
Brushes, paper, canvas, etc.	Reasonable supply, 15 units
Modeling clay	5
Cards for solitaire	1 per deck
Chess set	3
Dominoes	1
Games of motor skill as darts, ten-pins, quoits, table croquet	3 units each
Wood carving tools with supply of wood	8
Knitting or other handwork materials	2 units per pound
Typewriter	10
Typewriting paper	2 per ream
Candy	2 units per pound
Chewing gum	10 pkg. = 1 unit
Small personal "keep-sakes" valued only for their associations, such as photographs of friends or relatives, souvenirs of special places or events, etc.	1 each

When you have made your list, compare with other members of the class until you have found (*a*) four other people who agree fairly closely with you in regard to their pattern of choice, and (*b*) five persons whose preferences are very different from yours. How do the two groups compare with respect to general similarity or difference in such factors as sex, age, home background, childhood experiences and interests, present vocational plans, etc.? Do the members of your own group appear to resemble each other in these matters more closely than they resemble those of the opposite group?

Suppose you could take exactly ten books with you. What would those books be? Compare your list with that of other members of the class until you find (a) the person whose list has the greatest number of titles in common with yours, and (b) the one who has the fewest, or perhaps none, that are the same as yours. Which of these persons seems more like yourself, especially in regard to early experiences and family background?

Chapter VII

HOW ACTIVITY IS PATTERNED

*Is the activity of a child ever completely lacking in
pattern? Why?*

*If you ask a new-born baby to spell the word "cat," he
will not be able to do so. But some years later, the
same request will promptly elicit the response,
"c-a-t." Is this a completely new behavior pattern,
unrelated in any way to the behavior repertoire of
the infant? If not, can you trace the course of the
successive modifications in behavior by which the
later pattern was developed out of the earlier ones?*

*What are some of the external conditions that facilitate
learning?*

*What conditions within the organism are favorable for
learning?*

*Is anything once thoroughly learned likely to be com-
pletely forgotten? Can you cite some well-authen-
ticated instance in which a behavioral response was
retained over a long interval without intervening
practice?*

THE CONTINUITY OF BEHAVIOR

From the very beginning of life, the course of behavior is not
unorganized and chaotic but conforms to certain basic rhythms
induced by the necessities which attend all living and growing.
Periods of activity alternate with periods of rest and recuperation; food-taking is followed by digestion and assimilation and
by excretion of waste materials, after which the hunger contractions recur, to signal the need for more food. Posture is changed

as the muscles involved in its maintenance become fatigued, and is changed again as new needs arise. Even before birth, while the child is still carried in the mother's body, careful study of the fetal movements have shown that they are somewhat rhythmic in character, with periods of activity followed by periods of quiet as if the fetus alternately slept and wakened. Whether or not this is the case we have no way of knowing, but the hypothesis is plausible enough in view of the fact that the habit of sleep is well established at birth, although it requires adjustment to the new environment.

The patterns of behavior that distinguish one adult from another do not, then, arise from a formless nucleus of unorganized activity but develop by means of a series of progressive changes from earlier patterns that are imposed upon the organism by its own life processes. These simple patterns serve the needs of the organism during the early stages of life in the protective and unexacting environment of the uterus. With birth new necessities appear which the infant must satisfy for himself. The processes by which the child adjusts to these new demands are often grouped together under the general name, *learning*.

Learning is not, as we sometimes naïvely think of it, the simple acquisition of new skills or items of information without reference to what was there before. We do not see the first stages in any act of learning. All that we can observe is the modification of some behavior pattern already present into a new and somewhat different form. If no original pattern exists, learning is impossible, and if the change in behavior demanded by any particular act of learning is too great, learning may likewise be impossible; at all events it will be slow and laborious. It is unlikely that the child who has not yet learned to distinguish between three and four could be taught decimals, let alone the calculus; the difference between the two levels of accomplishment is too great to be spanned at a single stride. Few adults accustomed to sleeping at night and working during the day can reverse this habit without an intervening period of adjustment to the new régime, in spite of the facilitating effects of bodily fatigue. In order that modification of behavior may progress smoothly and easily, not only must there be a felt need for change that sets the activity going, but the organism must also be in a state of "readiness" for the particular kind of modification that is to occur. This means that while the order of acquiring new skills is not absolutely fixed and invariant from one individual to another, there are nevertheless certain general hierarchies inherent in the nature of these skills as well as in the nature of the organism that set the general pattern for their acquisition. The very fact that an individual grows and develops in an orderly way means that he also learns in an orderly way.

SOME BASIC PRINCIPLES OF LEARNING

1. *The first stage in any act of learning is the arousal of a goal-seeking state in the individual.* It is not essential that the striving individual understand the urge by which he is driven or that he know beforehand what will satisfy it, though it has been shown that such knowledge facilitates learning.

2. *This increased state of neuro-muscular activity tends to spread or diffuse itself in such a way that other reaction systems, simultaneously in operation but not previously directed toward the goal in question, become involved in the main response that for the moment is the chief concern of the organism.* This process which was briefly described in the last chapter and is known as *associative learning* or *conditioning* [1] has been carefully studied by many psychologists. The first important work in this field was carried out about the beginning of the present century by Pavlov, a Russian physiologist who at that time was conducting certain experiments on the rôle of the salivary glands in digestion, using dogs as subjects. Pavlov inserted a little tube into the duct by which the saliva from one of the glands finds its way into the

---

[1] The two terms are used interchangeably by most writers, but others prefer to reserve the term *conditioning* for (1) those situations in which the response to the originally inadequate stimulus is not under the control of the subject (as in the case of the reaction of the pupil of the eye to a change in the intensity of light) or only partially so, or (2) instances of learning in which the subjects are animals or young children who have not learned to speak and who therefore cannot facilitate the process of learning by the use of verbal symbols. "Associative learning," as the term is used by these writers, refers to those instances in which the possibility of learning by the aid of verbal symbolization is not excluded.

mouth and brought the other end out through the dog's cheek so that the saliva would pass out through the tube into a vessel where the amount could be measured.

FIG. 32.—IVAN PETROVITCH PAVLOV

(Reproduced from I. Pavlov, *Lectures on Conditioned Reflexes*, by courtesy of International Publishers, New York City.)

Every one knows that the flow of saliva is directly stimulated by the presence of food in the mouth. But Pavlov noticed that not only the actual taste of food but all sorts of other conditions usually associated with the dog's feeding-time would increase the amount of the flow. The sight of the attendant who usually fed him or the sound of footsteps coming down the row of kennels at feeding-time would do so. Pavlov's interest in this phenomenon became so great that he decided to study it under conditions that could be more completely controlled. He therefore arranged a special laboratory, light-proof and sound-proof, with a separate compartment for the dog and another for the experimenter.[2] By means of a system of levers extending into his own compartment the experimenter was able to work the various parts of the apparatus while he observed the dog's general behavior by eye through a clever arrangement of mirrors and periscopes. (See Figure 33.)

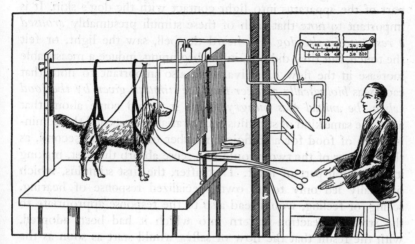

FIG. 33.—PAVLOV'S ARRANGEMENT FOR STUDYING THE PROCESS OF SALIVARY CONDITIONING IN THE DOG

(Reproduced from I. Pavlov, *Lectures on Conditioned Reflexes*, by courtesy of International Publishers, New York City.)

The dog was first trained to stand quietly within the experimental cabinet by accustoming him to receive food there. The dish containing the food was swung around in front of the animal by means of a moving arm of the apparatus which the experimenter controlled from his own room. We may note that this

[2] This was done in order to be sure that every change in the external conditions of stimulation would be under the control of the experimenter. If the latter had remained in the same room with the dog, he would himself have constituted an "uncontrolled" stimulus.

training in itself involved a process of conditioning, for the dog's original tendency would have been to struggle against the harness by which he was confined. By seizing upon the brief intervals when he was comparatively quiet and then administering food, the dog was soon brought to a point where he no longer objected to being placed in the cabinet but stood quietly with eyes and body oriented to the point where the food usually appeared. When this stage had been reached, the experimenter (after first making sure that the dog was alert and watchful) would present some extraneous stimulus immediately before giving the food. He would ring a bell, flash a light, sound a buzzer, or bring some part of the apparatus into light contact with the dog's skin. It is important to note that each of these stimuli presumably aroused *a response in the dog.* He heard the bell, saw the light, or felt the touch. But they did not, in the beginning, induce a measurable increase in the flow of saliva. It is also important to note that each was *biologically weaker than the stimulus given by the food when the animal was hungry.* Thus it would come about that after the same kind of stimulus had invariably preceded the administration of food for a sufficient number of times, the second, as the stronger of the two, would in a sense absorb the first, making it an integral part of itself. Thereafter, the first stimulus, which originally led only to its own specialized response of hearing, seeing, or feeling, would lead also to the response appropriate to the stronger reaction-pattern into which it had been adopted, with the result that the flow of saliva would start as soon as the first stimulus took place. But it should be noted that such a flow of saliva is not a response to the bell or the light as such, but a response to an *earlier point* in the food-getting situation. It is still a response to food. (See Figure 31, p. 157.)

3. *The conditioned response, like other learned reactions, tends to disappear after a period of disuse, but that some effect of the earlier learning lingers is shown by the fact that the response can be reëstablished with fewer trials than were at first necessary.* It will disappear more rapidly if the conditioned stimulus is given frequently during the interval without being followed by the natural stimulus, e.g., if the bell is often rung in the dog's hearing without giving any food. This process of negative condi-

tioning seems to be essentially similar to that of the original conditioning with this difference, that where the conditioned stimulus was first a signal for the dog to respond by behavior suitable to the receiving of food, it has now become a signal for him not to respond or to respond in other ways. This is not at all the same state of affairs as existed previous to training when the bell was an indifferent occurrence, not a signal of any kind. It is an active, not a passive state. If the animal is distracted by some other stimulus just after the original conditioned stimulus is given, the old response is likely to occur again just as if the habit had never been broken up. Or if an animal who has been conditioned to wait for a time before responding is distracted during the waiting period, the response is likely to occur at once. Most of us are familiar with similar occurrences in our own lives. Perhaps we have learned or "become conditioned" to waking at a particular time under a daylight-saving schedule. The first of October arrives; we go back to standard time and rejoice in the extra hour of morning sleep. (At least this was the case before the present war.) But for some time, although we may sleep out the allotted time if everything remains quiet, a slight noise occurring near the former rising hour will be enough to waken us. The Middle Westerner who, as the result of a prolonged residence in New England, has acquired a Boston accent is more than likely to revert to the broad *r* of his childhood under conditions of unusual strain or excitement. The force of earlier habit is never so strong as when something happens that throws us off our guard.

Many elaborations of Pavlov's methods have been worked out, using as subjects animals of many different species and human beings of all ages from early infancy to maturity. The reaction patterns that have been experimentally attached to new stimuli range all the way from such apparently automatic and "uncontrollable" responses as the pupillary reflex (which has been trained to occur in response to a spoken word or to the sound of a bell) to the most complex actions of which the mature human being is capable. Whether or not the principles of simple conditioning can be extended to explain all aspects of learning, especially in human beings, is a controversal issue that it would not be profitable to discuss at this point. Certainly these principles play a part in most if not all types of behavior modification, even though they may not suffice for a complete account of what takes place in the highly elaborated changes that are observed at the more advanced stages of development.

4. *Once a stimulus has been integrated with a response pattern to which it did not originally lead, it becomes potentially capable of adding other stimuli to the series.* Under proper conditions, this process may be extended through an undetermined number of stages, though with increasing difficulty as the distance from the biologically adequate stimulus increases. In the language of conditioned-reflex psychology, response patterns that have been built up in this way are known as *conditioned reactions of the second order, third order,* and so on. Just how far the process can be extended depends on a variety of factors. In organisms with highly developed nervous systems such as man, it can be carried further than is possible with less intelligent animals such as the cow or goat. Occasional reinforcement by association with the original stimulus makes the establishment of higher order responses easier to accomplish and more stable after they have been built up. Invariability of the associations between the various links in the chain also facilitates the process of extension, as does the existence of just the proper degree of intensity of the various stimuli with reference to each other. Within limits, the more intense the stimulus, the more likely it is to bring others into the chain. But this statement can be made only with great caution, for too intense a stimulus is likely to disorganize behavior instead of organizing it. It should also be noted that the stimulus which is to be tied into the system must always be weaker (biologically speaking) than the associated stimulus that is already integrated with the response. Otherwise the "balance of power" will be such that if any conditioning at all takes place it will be in the wrong direction.

The formation of conditioned responses of a higher order provides at least a working hypothesis to account for the existence of the vast host of specific prejudices, attitudes, likes and dislikes, attractions and repulsions displayed by each of us. You see a stranger in a crowded restaurant or meet him on the street. A momentary glance is all you have, yet in that brief instant you think, "I should like to know that person," or "I'm surely glad I don't need to have *him* around me." Why? If asked, the chances are that you cannot say. You know only that the response occurred. To trace it back to its origin would require a long and elaborate process of analysis that in most cases would not be worth the effort. Sometimes, however, it happens that reactions built up in this way take on a pattern that is very troublesome to the individual, interfering with his other activities by causing him unreasonable fears or anxieties, or impelling him to perform actions that he knows to be foolish or undesirable. He cannot explain these tendencies any more readily than you can explain your attitude toward the stranger so casually encountered. But if, as occasionally happens, a reaction of this kind becomes so intense and engrossing as to constitute a real handicap, it is sometimes possible to follow its course of development backward and thus uncover the original association that started all the trouble. If this is done the difficulty will often disappear, because it then becomes clear to the subject that his fear or anxiety is not really a fear of the particular object or situation toward which it is now displayed but occurs because, by means of a longer or shorter series of conditioning processes, it has become psychologically a part of some terrifying experience of the past. Just as the occurrence of the conditioned salivary reflex in the hungry dog was shown to be not a response to the bell, properly speaking, but to the total feeding situation which had become expanded to include the sound of the bell as its first component, so the "unreasonable" fear is shown to be essentially a response to the earlier situation (to which it was appropriate) rather than a response to the present stimulus for which it is inappropriate.

5. *An important function of the conditioned response in everyday life is that of establishing short-cuts that lead directly to the goal without the necessity of completing all the steps that lie between.* The dog who responds to the call of his master at feeding time gets his dinner much more quickly and surely than if he were obliged to hunt about until by happy chance he located his feeding pan. The student who has learned to waken at the sound of an alarm clock or in response to some other dependable

signal is less likely to miss his first-hour class than is the one who has formed no consistent habits [3] of waking.

It is probable that much of our "time sense" is built up through a process of learning ("becoming conditioned") to respond to a complex system of signals from the internal and external sense-organs. Typically we have at best only a partial knowledge of the exact nature of these signals. The adult who, without consulting a timepiece says, "Well, it must be around four o'clock now," is making his estimate on the basis of a very complex system of cues, some of which are known to him, while of others, equally or perhaps even more important, he may be quite unaware. If asked, he is likely to point out such matters as the position of the sun or the character of the light, the amount of work he has accomplished since he last looked at the clock, the observation of certain events that characteristically take place at some fixed hour, and so on. That matters such as these do serve as partial cues by which the passage of time is judged has been experimentally verified. A change in any one of them is likely to bring about some change in one's estimate of the passage of time.

That the beginning of adjustment to routine, which may be looked upon as a rudimentary type of becoming conditioned to respond after a given temporal interval and not before, takes place at a very early age has been neatly demonstrated by Marquis.[4] The amount of bodily activity of two groups of healthy new-born infants was measured by means of stabilimeters,[5] attached to their cribs. One group of infants was fed at three-hour intervals for the first eight days of life; the other group was fed

---

[3] It is hardly necessary to point out that conditioned responses to bodily signals of a nature not precisely determined may also be formed. Some people can be depended upon to waken at approximately the same hour without external aids.

[4] Dorothy P. Marquis, "Learning in the Neonate: The Modification of Behavior under Three Feeding Schedules," *J. Exper. Psychol.*, 1941, 29: 263-282.

[5] A stabilimeter consists of a spring balance on which the support (bed, bassinet, chair, etc.) in which the individual rests is attached. The balance is made sufficiently delicate so that each movement of the subject is conveyed to a writing attachment which traces a record on a kymograph. A simultaneous time record is made by a separate instrument. By this means the amount of activity occurring within any specified period of time can be measured very exactly.

at four-hour intervals. Throughout this time, the average amount of activity was greater for the group less frequently fed than for those whose hunger was satisfied at more frequent intervals. But on the ninth day, the three-hour group was changed to a four-hour schedule. After their usual feeding hour had passed, these babies showed a much greater increase in activity than did

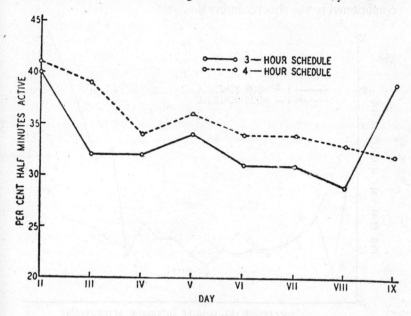

FIG. 34.—RELATIVE ACTIVITY OF INFANTS FED AT LONGER AND SHORTER INTERVALS

Comparison of three- and four-hour groups in total amount of activity per day. Average of all subjects. (Reproduced from "Learning in the Neonate: The Modification of Behavior under Three Feeding Schedules," by Dorothy P. Marquis, *J. Exper. Psychol.*, 1941, 29: 263-282, by permission of the author and the publisher.)

the group who had been accustomed to wait an additional hour. Before the four hours were up, this activity had reached a point at which it actually surpassed that of the other group who had previously been the more active of the two. Figure 34 shows the differences between the two groups in total amount of active time per day over the period from the second to the ninth day, while Figure 35 shows the data for the ninth day in terms of each successive ten-minute interval after the last feeding. Note that practically all of the change in activity of the three-hour group took place during the last hour. The group previously accustomed to the longer interval also showed some increased activity during the final hour, presumably as a result of the onset of hunger, but the change is small in comparison with that of the group previously conditioned to the shorter interval.

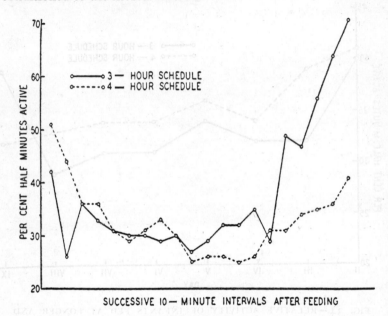

FIG. 35.—EFFECT OF A CHANGE FROM A THREE-HOUR TO A FOUR-HOUR INTERVAL BETWEEN FEEDINGS UPON THE ACTIVITY OF INFANTS

Comparison of three- and four-hour groups on Day IX when the three-hour group changed to a four-hour schedule. Average of morning and afternoon periods for all subjects. (Reproduced from "Learning in the Neonate: The Modification of Behavior under Three Feeding Schedules," by Dorothy P. Marquis, *J. Exper. Psychol.*, 1941, 29: 263-282, by permission of the author and the publisher.)

6. *The conditioned response involves a choice among stimuli or (what really amounts to the same thing) a differentiation among part-stimuli.* The dog in whom the salivary reflex appears when the bell is sounded is at the same time stimulated by a number of other factors—the sight of the apparatus, the "feel" of

the harness, and so on. But these do not become tied in with the salivary reflex as does the sound of the bell because the latter is the only one that consistently leads to the satisfaction of the bodily need by eating, of which the salivary reflex is an essential element. Now it is apparent that by adding to the number of extraneous stimuli that are present, the choice can be made more difficult and more discriminating. The animal can be trained to respond to a bell but not to a buzzer, to a bell of a certain tone but not to one of a different tone, to a bell and a flash of light occurring simultaneously but not to either one singly and so on. There is practically no limit to the possible elaboration of problems that can be set in this way, but there are definite limits to the kind and the degree of difficulty of the learning tasks that a given subject can master. It is scarcely necessary to add that more difficult tasks require a longer time for their accomplishment or that some subjects can be trained much more readily than others when the external conditions of the task remain the same. But it may be well to point out that "difficulty" is not entirely a matter of the task. It depends also upon the subject, upon the potentialities with which he has been endowed by nature and upon the entire course of behavioral modifications of his original reaction patterns that have made him what he is to-day. Every animal trainer knows that it is possible to "spoil" the best-endowed animal by mishandling him in such a way that his reactions diverge further and further from the desired pattern. Eventually this condition may become so extreme that no ordinary course of reëducation can overcome the effect of the earlier experiences. In a preceding paragraph it was noted that even after the apparent extinction of a well-established conditioned response, it may appear again spontaneously after a period of disuse. In any case its reëstablishment through renewal of the original conditions under which it was laid down is rendered much easier. It is doubtful whether anything once learned is ever completely forgotten, though the process of forgetting ("extinction") may have proceeded so far that the response cannot be brought back without external aid. The trouble with the animal that has become untrainable, or practically so, is not that his behavior was unmodifiable, but that the modification has proceeded too far in the wrong direction.

One of the most beautifully controlled examples of the facilitating effect of previous experience upon the later acquisition of an act is to be found in an experiment carried out by Burtt [6] with his little son. Beginning when the child was fifteen months old, Burtt read aloud to him daily a twenty-line selection of Greek drama. The child had no knowledge of Greek and therefore, of course, could not understand the meaning of the poem at all. But even as early as fifteen months, most bright babies respond to the rhythm of poetry, a fact that has led many of the makers of nursery-rhymes to embellish them with meaningless lines and nonsense-syllables that are nevertheless highly attractive to children.[7] The same selection was read every day for a period of three months, and then a new one of the same length was begun which also was read daily for a three-month period. The procedure was continued until the child was three years old, a new selection being used every three months. No further practice was given until the age of eight and one half years. Then the child was taught to repeat from memory the selections that had been read to him in early childhood as well as an equal number of other selections of the same length not previously heard. The new selections required an average of 435 repetitions per selection before they could be repeated without error, whereas those heard in early childhood required, on the average, only 317 repetitions. The effect of maturation and of elaboration of response patterns that goes along with it is shown by the fact that the selections read later in childhood, that is, shortly before the age of three years, were learned more readily than those originally heard before the age of two, but even the latter were learned more easily than the new ones that had never before been heard.

Not all of the selections heard in childhood were memorized at the age of eight and one half. Some were reserved for a

[6] H. E. Burtt, "An Experimental Study of Early Childhood Memory," *J. Genet. Psychol.*, 1932, 40: 287-295.

[7] "Hey-diddle-diddle, the cat and the fiddle,
The cow jumped over the moon."

or

"A frog he would a-wooing go
Whether his mother would let him or no,
Sing heigh, ho, gammon and spinach
Heigh-o says Anthony Rolly."

later experiment which was carried out when the boy had reached the age of fourteen.[8] Again the comparison was made between the number of repetitions necessary for the learning of completely new selections with that needed for material heard during very early childhood. Some advantage of the latter over the former was still apparent except for the very earliest read of the selections, but the effect of the early childhood experience had become much less apparent as a result of the longer interval.

7. *Differentiation among part-stimuli often occurs spontaneously, with the result that the conditioned response will appear whenever any stimulus involving the differentiated element occurs. The result of this differentiating process is an apparent generalization or spread of the conditioned reaction to include other stimuli that in their totality may appear to an outsider to be very different from the one to which the response was originally set up.*

A classical example of this is found in a study by J. B. Watson [9] which describes how a conditioned fear response was built up in a healthy child less than one year of age. The child was first shown a white rat. He reached for it repeatedly, showing no signs of fear. Evidently the rat itself, in the absence of any unpleasant associations with it, was not a fear-provoking object. Now the rat was shown again, but this time, just as the baby reached for it, an iron bar just behind him was struck, making a loud bang. Even the new-born baby will frequently start and begin to cry when such a stimulus is given, and by the time the child is a few months old this response is likely to be accompanied by more finely differentiated reactions of the kind that we call fear. He starts more violently, draws back, perhaps tries to escape or clings to some one for protection, and his crying takes on a sharper and shriller note. In part these reactions are learned by experience, but it is likely that further maturation also has something to do with it.

When the bar was struck, the child reacted in much the way described above. The hand with which he was reaching for the rat

[8] H. E. Burtt, "A Further Study of Early Childhood Memory," *J. Genet. Psychol.*, 1937 50: 187-192.

[9] J. B. Watson and R. R. Watson, "Studies in Infant Psychology," *Scient. Mo.*, 1921, 13: 493-515.

was jerked suddenly back, he started violently, screamed, and tried to crawl away. A week later when the rat was shown again, mild evidences of fear or at least of avoidance appeared, and after two or three reinforcements by repeating the original combination of rat—loud sound, the mere sight of the rat was enough to provoke very marked evidences of fear. Shortly afterward it was found that the fear reaction had spread to include all sorts of furry or fuzzy objects—a piece of cotton wool, a fur coat, a Santa Claus mask.

This tendency for the conditioned response to be generalized rather than highly specific is particularly characteristic of the early stages of learning and accordingly is seen most frequently in the responses of infants and young children. The process of learning is thus seen to accord with other aspects of development. The typical course of the behavior patterning is from the general to the more specific. At first, any kind of bell, any kind of furry or fuzzy objects, a touch on any part of the body will bring about the same response. To the subject at this stage of learning, they all seem alike. But with repeated experiences it is found that only certain conditions, that is, only certain parts or combinations of part-stimuli lead to the completion of the pattern and thus belong with it. Not all bells but just this one bell belongs to the feeding situation; not all furry objects but only those possessing certain other characteristics evoke fear.

We see, therefore, that not only by progress through a series of higher order conditionings are behavior patterns not common to the generality of people built up. Unusual forms of behavior also appear when conditions are such that the discriminating reactions which are forced upon most people as a result of experience fail to occur. This may happen either because the person in question is incapable of learning them or because he has never been exposed to the conditions that would bring about the discrimination. When we say of an adult that "he acts like a child" we usually have just this sort of thing in mind. He has not learned to make the finer adjustments in his behavior that most adults make. Perhaps he is too impulsive, never having become conditioned to delaying his responses until certain essential cues appear. One of the most important parts of the growing-up process consists in the acquisition of inhibitions, of becoming conditioned *not to react* in the simple and direct fashion immediately prompted by one's bodily needs as the child does, but to wait for something else. This, it may be repeated, is just as active a state for the individual as any other. The outsider may not be able to observe the response of the trained poker-player who sees four aces in his hand but this fact does not mean that the player is not responding. He has learned a different pattern of response. The untrained child or animal when hungry will snatch instantly at any food in sight; the civilized adult delays his eating until certain rituals have been completed. He does not take his place at the table until his companions are ready; he unfolds his napkin at the start of the meal, though he will probably not make active use of it until later. He does not spring at the waitress and snatch the food from her, even though he may know that he is physically capable of getting it a little sooner by such means. If he has been reared in a religious household he may wait for grace to be said; in any case he will probably pass food to others before helping himself. Any of us can testify that inhibitions of this kind are as positive forms of behavior as any other, and that under some circumstances, at least, they involve a distinct effort of will.

Since the days of Rousseau [10] and perhaps even earlier there has existed a fairly widespread idea that the ordinary customs of society are of necessity "artificial" and that the "natural man" is he who fails to conform to society's rules. Enough has perhaps been said to show the fallacy in such a point of view. Nothing in the nature of man is more fundamental than his ability to learn.

[10] Rousseau, a French philosopher who was much interested in social theory, published in 1762 a book called *Émile* which outlined what he regarded as an ideal system of education. The hero, a fictitious child called Émile, was said to have been brought up under the most primitive conditions possible and with a minimal amount of formal training and restraint. He was wholly a "child of nature," guided only by nature's rules. This state of complete freedom was continued until the age of ten or eleven years, after which he was returned to society, unspoiled by the artificialities of ordinary childhood education, ready, after a short period of acquiring some of the more formal arts of civilization, to take his place as a leader of men and a reformer of society. Rousseau's theories were dictated largely by rebellion against what he correctly regarded as a decadent social condition in which, at least among the upper classes, attention to form had taken precedence over almost everything else and children of tender years were expected to show all the social graces so prized by their elders. It is perhaps unnecessary to add that Rousseau had no children of his own and had little or no association with those of others.

Societies differ, and the man reared under the influences of one form of culture will not develop the same patterns of behavior as one brought up under other circumstances. Each learns according to the conditions provided for his learning, and their differing manners and morals furnish the best possible evidence that each is a "natural man." The scholar or the man-about-town is in the final sense no less a product of nature than is the savage. Within the limitations set by his endowment, each mirrors the specialized conditions of his own particular rearing.

MORE ABOUT HOW WE LEARN

E. R. Guthrie. *The Psychology of Learning* (New York, Harper and Bros., 1935), pp. 258.

The chapter you have just read tells only a very small part of the story of the learning process. Many of the things that psychologists have found out about it are not even mentioned. As a matter of fact, the literature on this topic is so extensive that even a moderately complete summary of it would fill a fair-sized encyclopedia. To some extent this is due to a fact of which even the beginning student should be aware, namely that there is as yet no general agreement among psychologists as to the precise mechanisms by which behavior is modified. This does not mean that there is serious question about the facts of learning as these can be objectively seen; the disagreements have to do with the more theoretical explanations of these facts. The advanced student will want to learn more about these differing opinions and points of view, but before this task can be profitably undertaken, the principles of learning as shown in actual behavior must be known.

The little book named above provides a clearly written and far more detailed account of the process of behavior-modification through associative learning (conditioning) than has been given in this chapter. It takes up such questions as the time factor in learning, which is a matter of much importance to all busy people. It tells how responses become more generalized or more specific and the effect of repetition and of the reinforcement of responses through emotional association. It describes the conditions that make for quick forgetting or long retention and the effects of reward and punishment. It compares the progress of a learner who knows what it is that he is trying to master with that of one who is working in ignorance of his goal. It shows how one's perception of the stimulus and his train of ideas associated with both the stimulus and the response change as learning progresses.

Your university library can probably provide you with a copy of this book. You will find it well worth reading.

PART III

The Normal Course of Human Development

Chapter VIII

THE PERIOD BEFORE SPEECH:
I.   BASIC DRIVES AND EMOTIONAL
REACTIONS

Since development is a continuous process, is there any justification for dividing it into separate stages for purpose of study? Explain.

What are some of the main features that characterize the reactions of young infants to internal and external stimuli?

What three types of reaction are of particular importance in the genesis of emotional responses in the infant?

What are the main points of difference between the Moro reflex and the startle pattern? Should either of these be identified with the emotion of fear as the child experiences it after infancy? Explain.

What general conditions facilitate the onset of sleep?

Why is it usually hard to identify the emotions of the young infant? Of the adult? What would you regard as the approximate age-period at which the interpretation of the signs of emotion in others is likely to be most successful?

What is meant by the "evolutionary theory of emotional behavior," and what two men were largely responsible for its formulation?

How does the child learn to identify and name his own emotions?

What is the James-Lange theory of emotion? To what extent does this theory conform to the developmental view of emotions as "conditioned cortical-thalamic responses" set forth in this chapter? In what respects does it seem inadequate?

What is the autonomic nervous system? How does it function in emotion? What is its relation to the central nervous system?

What are the three main divisions of the autonomic nervous system? Which of these divisions is especially active during the more violent emotional reactions. What pair of endocrine glands has a similar function?

Describe the interaction of the optic thalamus and the cerebral hemispheres in emotion and give an example from your own experience of behavior resulting when one or the other temporarily assumes the dominant rôle.

Do you agree with Kant that the "man of pure reason" is the ideal toward which humanity should strive? Give reasons for your answer.

What are some of the main principles to be observed in guiding the emotional development of children?

PHASES OF HUMAN DEVELOPMENT

Within two or three days after birth the grosser effects of birth trauma have usually disappeared, and by the end of ten days or two weeks physiological adjustment to the new life has been pretty well accomplished. In most cases the birth weight has been regained by this time, the processes of digestion and assimilation of food are fairly well established, and if the child has been well managed the beginning of adjustment to the daily routines of life can already be seen. He sleeps for longer periods during the night and stays awake for longer periods during the day. He is more likely to awaken when it is nearly time for him to be fed. So early in life does habit begin to operate!

Under normal conditions, therefore, we may safely look upon the first two weeks as marking the end of the neonatal period of recovery from birth injury and of physical adjustment to the new conditions of life. From this time on the child's mental and physical growth will proceed along lines that in many respects are continuations of the course laid down before birth, but that also reflect the new conditions under which he is now living. Although this growth is steady and continuous, without marked changes or sudden advances from one well-defined stage to another, there are nevertheless a few landmarks along its course that we may use as convenient reference points for dividing our account of human development into periods that make it easier to study. The division used here is arbitrary. No attempt has been made to keep the periods of equal length or to adhere to any one principle in deciding when a division should be made. In some cases a physical or physiological factor serves as the dividing line, in others a mental or intellectual factor; in still others common educational practice or social custom has determined the division. Practical justification for this seemingly haphazard system of classification is found in the fact that the individual functions as a whole and that a change in any factor which affects his growth and behavior along one line will also affect him along many other lines. Children do not grow physically one day and mentally the next, while the third day is reserved for education and social contacts. Growth of all kinds takes place simultaneously. Behavior is determined by the interaction of the basic laws of growth with the particular combination of circumstances under which growth takes place. So, whether we divide the life of an individual on the basis of such internal factors as physical growth, mental development, and social traits or upon external factors such as education or social experience makes less difference than might at first be expected, for all these processes are going on together and each affects all the rest.

However, if one is studying a particular aspect of development, its salient points can be brought out most clearly if the division into stages is based upon events that are particularly conspicuous or important for the field studied. For this reason the anatomist is likely to divide life into periods of slow or rapid physical growth, while the educator finds it more useful to employ school grades. The psychologist who is interested in total behavior finds that major changes are sometimes introduced by things that are *done to* the child, such as sending him to school for the first time; sometimes by growth changes that *occur in* the child, such as the acquisition of walking or speech, or the onset of puberty. There is no real inconsistency, therefore, in using such apparently diverse facts as these for marking off the course of development into stages that have certain aspects more or less peculiar to themselves, for both internal and external events have psychological importance for the behavior of the individual. We may note, however, that the internal changes which come with growth and development are most conspicuous during childhood and youth, while phases of adult life are most readily set off by such events as the completion of college, choosing a career, marriage, and parenthood.

Development during infancy proceeds at so rapid a rate and involves so many fundamental changes in abilities and behavior that any one of a number of conspicuous events might be chosen as a dividing point. But it is doubtful whether any other single event in the lifetime of the individual involves so many vitally important reorganizations of behavior and attitude and opens up such a host of new possibilities for learning and achieving as does the acquisition of speech. Before speech begins the child is confined by the barriers of his own inarticulateness. He is, to be sure, not wholly without means of communication. By his posture and facial expression, by vocalizations, gestures, and gross bodily movements he is able to indicate, though crudely and imperfectly, his attitude toward persons and things immediately present. He shows desire, affection, aversion, rejection. Some comprehension of the language of others also begins before the actual use of speech by the child himself.[1] He obeys simple commands, looks and waves his hand in the proper direction when asked to point out familiar persons or objects, squeals with joy when asked if he would like to "go bye-bye." But all these quasi-linguistic per-

[1] The precocious appearance of language comprehension as compared to language usage is not confined to the period of infancy. At all ages, the former runs considerably in advance of the latter. Particularly in reading, all of us recognize and understand many words that we rarely if ever employ in conversation.

formances of infancy are clumsy and ineffective when compared
to the ease and fluency of true speech in which the use of symbols
takes the place of physical dealings with unwieldy reality. Because of the widespread importance of speech in the development
of the individual, its appearance may be said to mark the end of
the period of infancy, properly speaking. Although children
differ, on the average about eighteen months of postnatal life will
elapse before speech becomes a really useful tool, even though
the majority of infants begin to use a few words slightly before
that age.

SOME BASIC REACTIONS OF THE YOUNG INFANT

It was shown in Chapter V that the sensory equipment of the
infant functions in a wide variety of different ways from the
time of birth. Our basis for assuming that a particular kind of
stimulation acting upon his sense-organs really affects the child
is usually not anything that can be observed directly in the sense-
organ or its accessory apparatus properly speaking [2] but a response
in the child himself, an increase or decrease in the amount of his
activity or an alteration in its pattern. These changes sometimes
take the form of an *increase and gradual extension or diffusion
of the bodily activity* as when the hunger contractions of the
child's stomach lead at first to increased restlessness, then to wailing which, if satisfaction is not attained, gradually increases to
screaming accompanied by violent kicking and thrashing of the
arms with occasional thrusting the fingers into the mouth and
vigorous sucking. Excitation of the interoceptors by noxious
stimuli leading to sensations that the adult would classify as
"unpleasant" (such as pain, hunger, thirst, or under certain conditions, fatigue [3]) typically lead to such increase and diffusion of
bodily activity.

[2] That is to say, in the accessory apparatus peculiar to the sense-organ
itself. Many of the sense-organs have little accessory apparatus. An exception
to the rule is seen in the muscles that move the eye or that cause the pupil
to contract.

[3] A moderate amount of fatigue that is unassociated with marked activity
of the ductless or endocrine glands normally leads to muscular relaxation
and sleep. But every one is familiar with the well-nigh uncontrollable and

Sometimes the change in activity takes the form of a sudden and temporary *inhibition of bodily movement* as a response to a change in the quality of a stimulus. This is not at all the same as the relaxation or cessation of movement next to be described. It is an active, not a passive state. In its external form, at least, it is not unlike the condition that in the adult we call *set* or *attention*. The muscles do not relax but remain tense; as a matter of fact they may even become more strongly contracted. As a rule this condition is not long maintained. In the infant its duration does not usually exceed a few seconds, but it is easily perceptible to an observer. In most cases such a response is occasioned by some event in the outside world like an unusual sound, a change in the color or intensity of a light, or almost any similar occurrence that is not so intense as to be startling. Occasional instances of response by inhibition of bodily movements can be seen even in the new-born infant. As children grow older the number of responses of this type increases rapidly.

Satisfaction of a bodily need results in temporary *cessation of stimulation* from the group of interoceptors that are sensitive to that particular bodily condition with consequent *reduction in the total number of stimuli that are acting upon the organism*. Since activity is a response to stimulation it is but logical to expect that a reduction in stimulation should lead to a reduction in activity, and this is just what actually happens. If the reduction in stimulation is sufficient, the individual drops quietly off to sleep. The healthy infant almost invariably falls asleep after he is fed. In the normal person of any age, the satisfaction of hunger usually brings about a feeling of muscular relaxation, not infrequently accompanied by a tendency to drowsiness. In older persons, however, stimulation through other avenues is likely to prevent the relaxation from passing over into actual sleep. In the infant, exteroceptive stimulation, unless fairly intense, is less likely to touch off activity than is interoceptive stimulation, because so many of the connections leading from the external source of

---

"prickly" restlessness that sometimes comes as a result of extreme fatigue or excessive emotional strain. All who have much to do with the care of children know how hard it is for the overtired child to fall asleep and how he tosses about even in sleep. Infants seem particularly prone to extreme fatigue which literally makes them "too tired to sleep."

stimulation that affects the exteroceptors to the release of energy in the muscles must be formed by experiences that have not yet taken place.[4] Accordingly, stimulation that has its roots in the basic physiological needs of the organism and for which the neurological connections leading to energy release are established by the growth process itself predominate for a time over those that do not attain full effectiveness without the integration that comes with meaningful experience.

SPECIFIC VS. GENERALIZED FORMS OF RESPONSE

Most persons who have studied the early responses of infants to external stimulation have noted two things. When a stimulus of moderate intensity is experimentally applied, the response tends to be most pronounced and to appear most consistently

---

[4] This is another example of the fact that the intensity of the external stimulus does not determine the strength of the response. The latter depends upon the amount and pattern of the energy-release in the individual. Any stimulus that is capable of arousing a particular response pattern at all, arouses it in full, just as a small spark, if it ignites a fuse leading to a train of gun-powder produces just as big an explosion as a larger spark could set off. The difference lies in the relative probability of arousing the response, not in its magnitude if aroused. However, there is some association, though far from invariable, between magnitude of response and intensity of stimuli. More intense stimuli may, and under some circumstances do, set off *additional* forms of reaction or release stores of energy that less intense stimulation would be powerless to set free. This is not at all the same thing as intensifying the reaction already aroused. It does not mean an increase in the original energy but the addition of new energies not previously released.

The chief factor that determined whether or not a given stimulus will arouse a response is thus the condition of the organism at the time. Just as a "hair-trigger" mechanism is released by a touch that would be powerless to affect an apparatus in a less delicate state of adjustment, so an organism that is in a state of readiness or "set" for responding in a particular way is likely to react, (and sometimes very intensely) to stimuli that would normally be disregarded. If the organic set is sufficiently intense, the response may even be set off by stimulation that would normally be wholly inappropriate. And the strength of the response will be proportionate to the organic state—to the need or desire which the response is designed to satisfy—rather than to the strength of the stimulus. If the need is great or the desire strong, the *threshold of stimulation* will ordinarily be lowered, that is, a weaker stimulus will be sufficient to induce the response than is the case when the need or desire is slight.

in the part of the body that was stimulated. Secondly, there is usually a tendency for this response to spread or diffuse itself over adjacent areas.[5] A light that is not too bright is more likely to elicit movements of the eyes than of any other part of the body, and movements of adjacent parts such as the head or mouth are more likely to accompany the eye-movements than are movements of the limbs. A light "flick" of the finger on the palm of the hand or the sole of the foot of a new-born infant is about twice as likely to elicit movement of the limb stimulated as of the other limb on the same side, while the likelihood that movement will occur in either one of the limbs on the opposite side of the body is even smaller.[6] Repeated stimulation, however, will in many cases cause the response to appear in other limbs, thus affording one more example of the rule of "summation of stimuli."

Increased intensity of the stimulus, as is pointed out in the footnote on p. 191, is likely to bring a number of responses not otherwise observed into play, and thus the apparent association between the part stimulated and the part responding disappears. A very intense stimulus is likely to bring about a response of the entire organism, and although this response may have so consistent a pattern that we speak of it as a "reflex," it is by no means a local response.[7]

Place the infant of a few weeks on a firm but moderately resilient surface such as a hard mattress. Strike the mattress a fairly sharp blow with the fist. The infant's response will be immediate and fairly uniform. There will be a slight arching of the back, frequently accompanied by a twisting movement of the body, the head will be thrown back, and the arms extended sharply on either side and then brought together more slowly

[5] See especially K. C. Pratt, A. K. Nelson, and K. H. Sun, "The Behavior of the Newborn Infant," *Ohio State University Studies, Contributions in Psychology,* No. 10, 1930.

[6] L. Delman, "The Order of Participation of the Limbs in Responses to Tactual Stimulation of the Newborn Infant," *Child Development,* 1935, 6: 98-109.

[7] It is necessary to distinguish between those generalized responses such as the Moro reflex or the "startle pattern" in which the form of the response is so nearly invariable from one case to another that we must regard it as a single unitary affair, and the more irregular though widespread movements of the child's body that appear to be made up of many independent reactions occurring more or less simultaneously.

as in an embrace. This is the so-called "Moro reflex." It is frequently, though not invariably, accompanied by crying and sometimes by a spontaneous appearance of the plantar reflex in

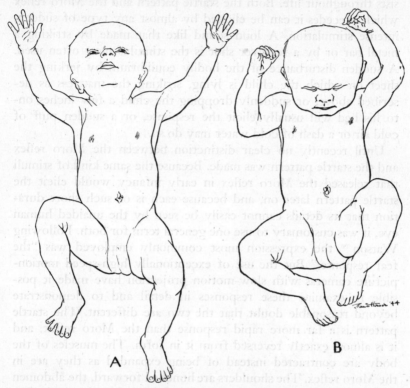

FIG. 36.—DIFFERENCE BETWEEN THE MORO REFLEX (*A*) AND THE STARTLE PATTERN (*B*) IN INFANCY

which the toes are first spread out fan-wise and then curled inward.[8] The Moro reflex has attracted the attention during recent years of a number of psychologists and neurologists who regard

[8] A very complete description of the Moro reflex is given by Myrtle McGraw in *Amer. J. Dis. of Child.*, 1937, 54: 240-251. The difference between the Moro reflex and the "startle pattern" that appears at a later age have been summarized by William A. Hunt and Carney Landis in *Psychol. Rev.*, 1938, 45: 267-269. A number of behavioral responses that frequently accompany each of these responses have been described by F. M. Clarke, W. A. Hunt and E. B. Hunt in *J. General Psychol.*, 1937, 17: 398-402.

it as a sign of cerebral immaturity. It normally disappears at about
the age of four months, after which it is replaced by a different
form of response known as the "startle pattern," [9] which persists throughout life. Both the startle pattern and the Moro reflex
which precedes it can be elicited by almost any type of sudden,
intense stimulation. A loud sound like that made by striking a
metal bar or by a revolver shot is the stimulus most often used.
A sudden disturbance of the bodily equilibrium by jerking the
sheet on which the child is lying, striking the mattress as described above, or suddenly dropping the child a few inches on-
to his bed will usually elicit the response, or a sudden puff of
cold air or a dash of cold water may do so.

Until recently no clear distinction between the Moro reflex
and the startle pattern was made. Because the same kind of stimuli
that released the Moro reflex in early infancy would elicit the
startle pattern later on, and because each is of such short duration that its details cannot easily be seen by the unaided human
eye, it was customary to use one general term for both. Following
Watson [10] the expression most commonly employed was "the
fear response." But the use of exceptionally high-speed motion-
picture cameras with slow-motion projection have made it possible to examine these responses in detail and to demonstrate
beyond reasonable doubt that the two are different. The startle
pattern is a far more rapid response than the Moro reflex, and
it is almost exactly reversed from it in form. The muscles of the
body are contracted instead of being expanded as they are in
the Moro reflex. The shoulders are hunched forward, the abdomen
drawn in, the knees and elbows bent and the fists clenched. (See
Figure 36.)

The study of these two forms of reaction to the same stimuli
are of interest to us for at least two reasons. From the standpoint
of experimental technique it shows once more how the inventive-
ness of the scientist can overcome the limitations of his perceptive
faculties. The student of behavioral mechanics is impressed by the
discovery of a complex reaction that passes through two such
clearly defined stages as those here described and that, once in its

[9] Carney Landis and William A. Hunt, *The Startle Pattern* (New York,
Farrar and Rinehart, 1939), pp. x-168.
[10] See pp. 179 and 197.

final form, remains apparently unchanged by any of the vicissitudes of human life.[11] Experience may modify the conditions under which it appears, for it is subject to the usual principles of conditioning, but its pattern follows the all-or-none rule.

Another question that has aroused much interest among present-day psychologists has to do with responses to frustration. What happens when activity is interfered with? And what light, if any, can the behavior of the infant throw upon the responses of the older person to frustrating conditions?

Once set off, energy must find some kind of outlet. The stimulation of the interocepters by a single hunger contraction releases a given store of muscular activity in the child. He kicks, cries, and waves his arms about. If the state of hunger is well established, further contractions will occur at sufficiently frequent intervals to keep the activity going either until the intake of food puts a stop to further stimulation or until the stored-up energy is so depleted that activity can no longer be maintained at its former level. The baby, we say, becomes too tired to cry any longer.

We now see why restriction of a child's activity produces the effect that so often appears. What we have is an overflow of the released energy into behavior systems that were formerly not involved or involved to a much smaller extent. The child whose leg movements are restrained expends the energy that formerly went into kicking by more violent movements of other parts of the body. He cries more loudly, twists and squirms, and thrashes with his arms. Moreover, the restraint itself, particularly as he grows older, acts as a new stimulus that can arouse activity in its own right. The child fights against restriction of his movements even though his activity before the constraint was imposed was so slight that the interference is just barely great enough to be felt. And this reaction is not confined to the striped muscles but extends to the internal organs and glands. The heart beats more rapidly, and the pattern of breathing is changed. There is increased flow of blood to the surface of the body, especially to the head and face, which take on an "angry" flush.

[11] It has been shown that the form of the startle pattern, once it has become established, is practically unrelated to sex, age, race, home background, etc., and is the same among uncivilized as among civilized persons.

Thus we note that either by direct observation or by the supplementation of observation through the use of appropriate instruments, a number of rather clearly differentiated responses can be observed, even in the young infant. First of all there is sleep, which is a recuperative mechanism apparently occurring whenever the combined effect of internal and external stimuli becomes too weak to arouse fully coördinated activity.[12] Sleep is facilitated by both internal and external factors which make, on the one hand, for a reduction in the number and intensity of the stimulating conditions and on the other hand for the reduction of sensitivity to stimulation on the part of the organism. The infant who is untroubled either by hunger or colic, and the older child or adult who can add an undisturbed mind to the blessings of food and good digestion fall asleep more readily because of the comparative absence of internal stimulation. For similar reasons, sleep comes more quickly if exteroceptive stimuli are reduced. A quiet, darkened room is more conducive to sleep than a noisy, lighted room. Within limits, fatigue is also conducive to sleep, apparently because the accumulation of waste products in the blood has the effect of reducing the organism's sensitivity to stimulation.

Awake, the most characteristic behavior of the infant is commonly described as generalized physical activity. Actually, this is nothing more than a blanket term under which we include all the manifold squirming and kicking, crying and burbling, turning of head and eyes and waving of arms that occur without specified order as responses to the varied incidental stimuli to which the child is constantly exposed. Against this background of alternating periods of sleep and activity, a number of specialized reactions appear that serve as a matrix from which more elaborated patterns will later develop. Of these, three deserve special mention: (1) inhibition of activity as a response to changes in quality of stimuli, (2) resistance to interference with activity that is already under way, and (3) the Moro reflex, followed at a later age by the startle pattern as a generalized, patterned response

[12] Neither cerebral nor somatic activity is completely suppressed during sleep. We dream, and we also toss about to a greater or smaller extent. But the movements of our bodies are not adapted to the content of our dreams; even in the sleep-walker the adaptation is not complete.

to any stimulus that is sudden and intense. In the first of these we may trace the nucleus of the phenomena that at a later age we call "set" or "attention"; the second holds the germs of anger; the third is allied to fear. Less clear in early infancy but becoming very evident later on are indications of pleasure on the part of the child when the sensitive or "erogenous" zones in the skin are stimulated by stroking or patting or by "cuddling" the child in the arms. These responses, however, are less uniform from child to child and are rather later in appearing than those previously mentioned. They are assumed by many to constitute the basis for the "love" response.

Viewed from the heights of adult achievement, these blind, feeble responses of the young child may seem trivial, unworthy of the careful study they have received or of the space that has here been devoted to their description. Neither of these verdicts is sound. They are important, not only because they lie so near the beginning of the stream of responses that constitutes the personality, but because they serve as indicators of the direction of its flow. But we may well ask whether there is warrant for speaking of them as "emotions" in the sense that we are accustomed to use this term, even though a majority of the psychologists of twenty years ago would have had little hesitation in doing so.[13] Evidently the question hinges, at least in part, upon what

[13] J. B. Watson, an American psychologist whose most important work was done at Johns Hopkins University and who is famous as the founder of the system of psychological thought known as "behaviorism" (see p. 28) believed that the first emotional responses of the infant come into existence just as his arms and legs do, because it is the nature of the human organism to grow and develop in that way. Their existence in the young child is a necessary consequence of the fact that he developed from a fertilized human ovum within a human uterus under at least approximately normal conditions. Watson's experiments with infants led to the rather dogmatic assertion that there are three—and only three—"basic emotions," which he called "fear," "rage," and "love." All three, so he asserted, are present in the normal infant at birth and can be readily distinguished from each other by a competent observer. Actually, however, as we have seen, the distinctions are not so easy to make as Watson thought and his own accounts of the reactions do not agree with those secured by the more refined methods of the modern experimenter. Watson's account of the "fear" response is a mixture of the components of the Moro reflex and the startle pattern, which is understandable enough, since he did not distinguish between the two. His description of the "anger" response is far more specific than that which most modern investigators have been able to elicit as a response

we are to include under this term. But since definition implies description, other and more specific questions at once arise. By what means do we identify emotion in ourselves and in others? How are the different emotions distinguished from each other? And by what processes do the relatively uncomplicated emotional responses of young children become elaborated into the highly complex forms that appear later on? As we saw in an earlier chapter, the principles of conditioning provide a partial answer to the final question, though we shall have to amplify this concept to some extent in order to account for some of the later developments. But what of the earlier questions?

HOW WELL CAN WE INTERPRET THE EMOTIONAL RESPONSES OF OTHER PEOPLE?

The experiments of the Shermans [14] and others have demonstrated that it is not easy to interpret the behavior and facial expression of the young infant. Without the aid of special record-

---

to restriction of bodily movement in the very young infant. Moreover, Watson does not sufficiently stress the point that unless movement is actually in progress, holding the child's arms or legs is not likely to have any effect at all. Watson's third "emotion" which he called "love" is hard to demonstrate in the young infant, because it is almost impossible to separate the stimulus itself from temperature changes, simple tactile effects, and so on. Moreover, many of the responses enumerated by Watson (such as smiling, gurgling and cooing) do not fall within the repertoire of the very young infant.

That the three forms of "emotional" reaction described by Watson are not so easy to recognize as he claimed has been neatly demonstrated by Sherman (*J. Comp. Psychol.*, 1927, 7: 265-284) who showed motion pictures to some observers in their complete and normal sequence, to others in incomplete form with the parts showing the administration of the stimuli removed so that only the responses of the subjects remained, and to still other groups in wrongly assembled form with each set of stimuli followed by the responses to some other set. He found that under these conditions neither trained nor untrained observers showed better than chance agreement in their attempts to name the "emotions" indicated by the behavior of an infant a few hours old who had just been pricked by a needle, one who had been dropped a few inches on to a pillow, one whose feeding had been delayed, and one whose bodily movements had been restrained by holding the arms at the side. The "emotions" named were those judged appropriate to the stimulus (if one had been shown). The behavior of the infants seemed to have little to do with the judgment of the "emotions" they were presumed to be experiencing.

[14] See footnote above.

ing instruments, even such relatively fixed and uniform reactions as the Moro reflex or the startle pattern may escape recognition. Nevertheless, though it may be well-nigh impossible to tell from the behavior of a crying baby two weeks old whether he is afraid or angry, hungry or suffering from stomach-ache, as he grows older his emotional behavior soon begins to take on definite patterns that enable us to classify his reactions with a fair degree of assurance. (See Figure 37.) It is unnecessary here to give

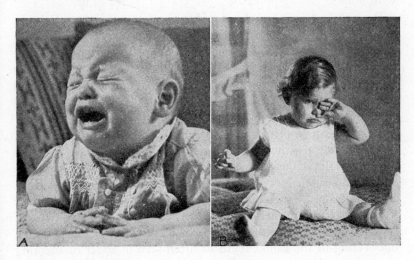

FIG. 37.—DIFFERENTIATION OF EMOTIONAL BEHAVIOR WITH
ADVANCING AGE

A. The baby is certainly unhappy, but it is hard to say whether he is hurt, angry, or afraid. *B.* The child of two shows a more distinct pattern of emotional behavior. Even from the single photograph one can be fairly sure that anger, resentment, or disappointment is present. (Photographs by Roy Goin and Doris E. Wright.)

elaborate descriptions of the differences between the way children or older people behave when they are angry and the way they behave when frightened, jealous, happy, sad, expectant, resentful, or disappointed. Every one has observed these reactions. It is true that the behavior shown under such conditions is not so fixed and invariable that no one can mistake it. Many experiments have been carried out which show that people often disagree when they attempt to decide just what emotion some one else is experiencing, particularly when they are asked to make their judgments on the basis of some limited part of the whole behavior pattern such as a single photograph—a method that has been used in a number of experiments. Moreover, as people grow older they learn to be fairly clever at concealing their feelings and feigning others when social custom makes it desirable for them to do so. Little children display their emotions more openly, and for this reason it is often easier to judge their real feelings than is the case with adults.

Even though we sometimes make mistakes, upon the whole we are able to tell what emotions our friends are experiencing with a great deal better than chance success. Although people have their own individual ways of showing their feelings which differ somewhat from one person to another, there is still a good deal of similarity in the emotional patterns shown by people of all ages and races.

This general similarity of emotional pattern has aroused much discussion during the past half-century. In 1872 Darwin [15] and Spencer [16] simultaneously expressed the point of view that the emotional behavior of human beings has an evolutionary origin, and that many of the apparently unserviceable acts shown under strong emotion are merely survivals of actions that had a useful function in a more primitive state of existence. For example, the uncovering of the canine teeth so often seen in anger or sneering was said to be a survival from the time when our prehuman ancestors did much of their fighting with their teeth. Frowning is explained as a residual effect of an action originally useful in shielding the eyes from the direct rays of the sun during fighting when clear vision is most essential. Certain other forms of emotional expression Darwin was inclined to trace back to the infancy of the individual rather than the infancy of the race. Shaking the head as a sign of denial or unwillingness is an act that appears early in most children and is continued throughout life. Darwin ascribed this to the survival of a habit formed during the nursing

---

[15] Charles Darwin, *The Expression of the Emotions in Man and Animals* (London, John Murray, 1872).

[16] Herbert Spencer, *Principles of Psychology*, Second Edition, Vol II, (New York, D. Appleton-Century Co., 1872).

period when turning the head to the side was the natural way
of rejecting unwanted food.

Many other examples might be cited, but the above will serve
as illustrations. They are not always convincing. While the relationship to infantile experience seems more in keeping with
known facts than the arguments from the history of the race,
neither explanation seems adequate to account for all that takes
place.

In opposition to the point of view which stresses the *similarities*
in the emotional behavior of different persons and considers that
these reactions are for the most part native and unlearned, without, however, denying that they may be to some extent modified
by experience and inhibited or feigned at the will of the individual, is a more modern idea that emphasizes the *differences* in
the way the same emotions are shown by people of widely different social experience and ascribes the origin of these behavior
patterns chiefly to early imitation by children of the behavior
of others, together with their tendency to repeat actions that
bring them approval or indulgence and to refrain from those of
which the results are unpleasant. Emotional behavior, according
to this point of view, is almost wholly learned during the lifetime
of the individual. The particular patterns by which fear, anger,
jealousy, and so on are expressed are not the native results of
continuing maturation but are acquired by experience.

As in many similar points of controversy, the truth probably
lies somewhere between the two extremes. It is a considerable
strain upon one's credulity to accept the idea that the crying
which appears as an accompaniment of pain or discomfort within
the first hour of life has been learned either by imitation or
through reward and punishment, though most of us are agreed
that the child who finds that crying is a means of getting attention
under almost any circumstances soon learns to resort to crying
in situations in which the one who has found it a less effective
weapon would remain quiet. And if crying as a form of emotional behavior can occur without training, there seems to be
no logical reason why frowning, kicking, striking, running away,
smiling, sneering, stamping, and so on throughout the long list
of reactions that appear one after another may not also be the

unlearned results of maturation,[17] although, as we have seen in the discussion of conditioning, their occurrence under particular circumstances may be determined by experience. As age advances, imitation and social custom undoubtedly play an increasingly important part in fixing their exact pattern. An important sign of emotional maturation is to be found in the bringing of these unlearned emotional reactions under voluntary control.

We are able to identify emotions in others, then, on the basis of certain patterns of behavior which are their normal accompaniments and which differ somewhat from one emotion to another. Like most of the other basic behavior patterns, the major features of emotional reaction are the unlearned products of maturation. At birth only the broad outlines of these patterns are present, but as age advances finer details emerge. Long before the end of childhood, the external evidences of most, if not all, of the emotions experienced by the adult appear in recognizable form. With increasing maturity these external signs are brought more and more under the control of the individual, and as a result many of the more primitive forms of emotional behavior are likely to be inhibited or modified, which makes them harder to identify.

As a result of very intensive observation of about 60 infants over a period of several months, Bridges [18] came to the conclusion that during the first two years, at least, there is so much similarity from one child to another in respect to the order in which the behavioral signs by which we judge the kind of emotion that a child is experiencing put in an appearance, that it becomes possible to draw up a kind of general chart, or schema, showing the ages at which they most commonly appear. (See

[17] Further evidence of the unlearned character of many of the physical signs by which emotions are recognized in others is to be found in the behavior of children who are cut off from many of the ordinary opportunities of learning by reason of sensory defects. I have described the behavior of one such child, a little girl of ten who had been totally blind and deaf from birth. Although imitation of the behavior of others was out of the question in her case, nevertheless her reactions under conditions that would be expected to arouse such emotions as fear, anger, or pleasure showed amazing fidelity to the classic descriptions of emotional behavior. Cf. "Expression of the Emotions in a Deaf-blind Child," *J. Abnorm. and Soc. Psychol.*, 1932, 27: 328-333.

[18] K. M. B. Bridges, "Emotional Development in Early Infancy," *Child Dev.*, 1932, 3: 324-341.

Figure 38.) It will be noted that Bridges has named the responses from the standpoint of the child who is (presumably) experiencing them, rather than from the standpoint of what the observer actually sees. This is less hazardous at the older than at the

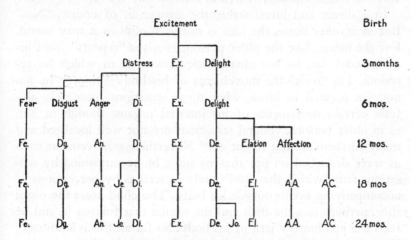

FIG. 38.—BRIDGES' SCHEME OF EMOTIONAL DEVELOPMENT
DURING INFANCY

By the age of three months, the primitive excitement which is observable at birth has differentiated into the two contrasted states of distress and delight. The distress pattern later differentiates further into fear, disgust, and anger, along with the more primitive pattern of simple distress. By the age of twelve months, elation and affection as well as simple delight can be distinguished on the positive side of the emotional picture, and in another half year a distinction can be observed between affection for adults (A.A.) and affection for children (A.C.) At the same time a further division of the distress pattern can be seen with jealousy (Je.) coming in as something distinct from ordinary distress. By the age of twenty-four months, a distinction can be made between the high-pitched emotional fervor of delight and the more stable emotion known as joy. (Reproduced by permission of the author and the publishers from "Emotional Development in Early Infancy," by K. M. B. Bridges, *Child Dev.*, 1932, 3: 324-341.)

younger ages, but it may have something to do with the fact that the only emotion (regarded as a personal experience) that she is able to impute to the new-born infant is that of a generalized excitement. Yet, as we have seen, even at birth the behavioral repertoire of the child is fairly extensive.

HOW WE LEARN TO IDENTIFY OUR OWN
EMOTIONS

Can the mechanisms of simple conditioning account for the way we feel in emotion as well as for the way we act?

In a direct and literal sense, the answer is, of course, "No." But in another sense, the idea is not as foolish as it may sound. For the infant, like the older person, receives "reports" from his own body, i.e., he has kinaesthetic sensations to which he responds. He "feels" the movements of his body although he has not yet learned to know what these sensations mean. He also feels certain movements of his internal organs, though in him as in older persons, visceral sensations are not well localized and many of them are not felt at all.[19] Nevertheless, movements such as were described on pp. 192-195 must be accompanied by sensations from within the child's body as well as by perceptions of accompanying events outside his body. The child hears the pistol shot, perhaps sees the flash and the smoke that follows it, and he feels the involuntary jerk of his body. So far all this is automatic. We can scarcely call it "fear," for such a term implies more than we dare suppose exists at this stage. It is a reflex, occurring because of neural connections that are as essential and basic a part of the child's equipment for living as is the contraction of the pupil of the eye when exposed to strong light. And the important thing about it is this. *The sensations from stimuli without and within the child's body are occurring simultaneously*, and so in

[19] Contrary to popular opinion, which assumes that the inside of the body is more keenly sensitive than the outside, the viscera have relatively few sensory nerve-endings. "We are unaware," says Cannon, "of the contractions and relaxations of the stomach and intestines during digestion, of the rubbing of the stomach against the diaphragm, of the squeezing motions of the spleen, of the processes in the liver—only after long search have we learned what is occurring in these organs. Surgeons have found that the alimentary tract can be cut, torn, crushed, or burned in operations on the unanesthetized human subject without evoking any feeling of discomfort. We can feel the thumping of the heart because it presses against the chest wall, we can also feel the throbbing of blood vessels because they pass through tissues well supplied with sensory nerves, and we may have abdominal pains, but apparently because there are pulls on the parietal peritoneum. Normally the visceral processes are extraordinarily undemonstrative." From W. B. Cannon, *Bodily Changes in Pain, Hunger, Fear and Rage*, Second Edition, Revised (New York, D. Appleton-Century Co., 1929).

the course of time not only the *essential* aspects of the external stimulus—in this case the loud sound—but other commonly associated features become tied in with it. There is the sight of the pistol, perhaps of the person who fired it. And finally, as the child grows older, there is the word that stands for all these increasingly complicated feelings and experiences. *Fear!* Now he knows it for what it is. He can call it by its name.

Conditioning, associative learning, thus not only provides us with an explanation of the way by which emotional reactions become attached to new stimuli but also tells us how we learn to identify and to name the emotions we experience. Of course the sensations involved are very complicated, and the older the child grows, the more he learns about the world and its workings, the more complex and varied do his reactions become. All sorts of sensations, not originally present, enter into the total and become an integral part of it. There is the tingling of the muscles in anger that he has learned not to carry over into blows; the feeling of great effort, as if against an actual backward pull upon the body, when moving toward something of which he is afraid. All these and a vast number of other associated feelings, taken in connection with the associated processes of knowing and understanding which change the nature of the stimulus from something alarming to something interesting, from something to be loved and petted to something to be destroyed or avoided, together constitute the basis for the conversion of the reflex response of the infant into the emotional experience of the adult.

THE JAMES-LANGE THEORY OF EMOTIONS

During the last quarter of the nineteenth century, William James in America and Carl Lange in Denmark independently formulated a theory of emotion that will seem far less audacious to the modern reader than it did to the psychologists of that date. Actually the theory is not so very different from the account given above. It differs from it only in that it *identifies* the emotion with the bodily sensations, whereas the point of view taken here is that this conception of emotion is too limited. We learn to *name* our emotions, it is true, by associating such sensations with the stimuli that led up to them and with the verbal sounds made by others when these conditions were experienced.[20] But the sensations alone do not "make" the emotion. The startle pattern, with its accompanying sensations from the muscles and viscera is not the same as real fear, even though it is its frequent accompaniment. Many persons will continue to start every time a pistol is fired, even though they know quite well that it is only their best friend shooting at a mark. Real fear is more complicated than that.

Although the theory that emotion is nothing more than the perception of organic sensations is commonly accredited to James and Lange, since they were the first of the modern psychologists to formulate it clearly, its origin goes back much further. The idea is suggested in the writing of Aristotle and Plato; St. Thomas Aquinas states that the bodily feelings are an essential part of emotion, though he is not, apparently, willing to assign them the entire rôle; Descartes [21] in 1646 and Malebranche [22] in 1672 stated the theory almost, if not quite, as explicitly as either James or Lange, and it is given in more or less detail in the writings of many of the earlier philosophers and physiologists. It is a theory with which every student of psychology should be familiar, not only because of its importance in the history of scientific thought but because of the many brilliant experiments that have been stimulated by it and the thought-provoking discussion and criticism that it has awakened. As a result of all this, another link has been welded in the chain that unites psychology to physiology, a union from which much of our future knowledge seems likely to come.

BODILY MECHANISMS CONTRIBUTING TO EMOTIONAL RESPONSES

In Chapter IV a brief account of the development and structure of the central nervous system was given. This system, it will be recalled, is made up of the brain, the spinal cord, the brain stem and the nerves that are connected with them. Many people think that this system includes the entire nervous mechanism

[20] See the discussion of the acquisition of speech in Chapter XI.
[21] *Sur les passions de l'âme.*
[22] *De la recherche de la vérité.*

of the body, but that is not the case. There is another set of nerves, called the *autonomic* nerves, that originate for the most part in a series of *ganglia* (that is, clusters of cell bodies) that run alongside the spinal column. However, in some cases the cell bodies are found within the organ whose function they activate or inhibit; this is the case in the heart and in the stomach. In the head and in the lower pelvic region, the ganglia are placed near the organs which the nerves supply.

The autonomic [23] nervous system is so called because it controls the actions of the smooth muscle fibers of the internal organs over which we have but little voluntary control. Its nerves run to the stomach, the intestines, the heart, the lungs, the walls of the blood-vessels, the ciliary muscles that dilate or contract the pupils of the eyes, the sweat-glands, the liver and other viscera, and the ductless glands themselves. It maintains its connection with the central nervous system by means of a series of neurons with cell bodies in the cord and in the brain stem that send their axons out to the autonomic ganglia and make synaptic connection with them. Thus, although it is able to carry on its everyday functions of regulating the vital processes of the body without the direction of the brain, the autonomic system is nevertheless capable of being influenced by brain action, by thoughts, ideas, associations. The student at the start of an important examination may turn pale and perspire; his breath may come quickly and his heart beat faster. All these physical symptoms are the direct result of the action of the autonomic nervous system which comprises the motor channel through which events in the brain arouse activity in the smooth muscles and glands. So the autonomic nervous system is connected at all points with the central nervous system and works along with it. It should not be thought of as an independent organization of neurons.

The fibers that connect the autonomic ganglia with the central nervous system do not leave the cord in a regular unbroken series but are divided into three distinct groups: (1) an upper group that has its origin in the brain stem and is known as the

---

[23] *Autonomic* means "self-governing" or "(relatively) independent," but as will be seen the term is only partially appropriate; for although the autonomic nervous system sometimes works independently of the central nervous system, it does not always do so.

cranial division, (2) a middle group that runs out from the thoracic and the upper lumbar regions of the cord and is known as the *sympathetic division*, and (3) a lower group that emerges from the sacral part of the cord and is called the *sacral division*.

The cranial division of the autonomic system is particularly concerned with the process of digestion, the movements of the stomach, the secretion of saliva and of gastric juice. By its action, too, the pupil of the eye contracts and the heart rate is slowed. All this goes along with a calm, relaxed, organic state. The baby who has just been fed drops peacefully off to sleep. When the child who is "hungry and cross" is given food, the crossness usually disappears along with the hunger. It is a stupid wife who has not learned to take advantage of her husband's after-dinner mood.

The fibers of the sacral division run out to the organs that have to do with the removal of waste material from the body. Like the cranial division, they are concerned with processes that make for greater comfort. They also innervate the contractile tissues of the external genitals and thus are actively concerned in sex emotion.

Unlike the fibers of the two foregoing divisions, which run to only a small group of specific organs and in general make for organic states of calmness, peace, relaxation, and pleasure, the nerves from the sympathetic division are widely distributed over the entire body. Wherever they are found, their relationship to the action of the cranial and sacral divisions is antagonistic. The cranial supply to the eye contracts the pupil, the sympathetic dilates it; the cranial slows the heart, the sympathetic accelerates it; the sacral contracts the large intestine and relaxes the exit from the bladder, the sympathetic relaxes the intestine and contracts the exit from the bladder.[24] And the organic states that accompany the action of the sympathetic division are, as might be expected, the opposite of those that go with the activities of the cranial and sacral divisions. Instead of peacefulness, calm, contentment, relaxation, we have excitement, anxiety, restlessness. Moreover the entire sympathetic system is connected up by fibers that run from one ganglion to another (see Figure 39) in such

---

[24] In coöperation with the action of the central nervous system. Elimination is partially automatic, partially voluntary.

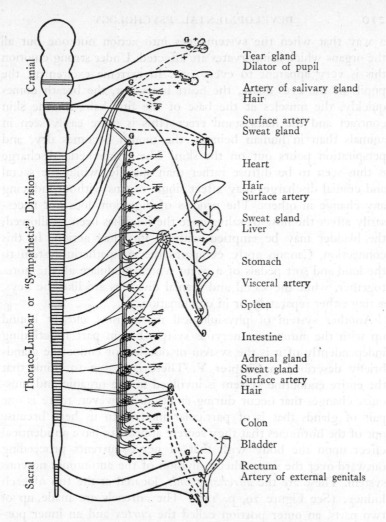

Cranial

Thoraco-Lumbar or "Sympathetic" Division

Sacral

Tear gland
Dilator of pupil

Artery of salivary gland
Hair

Surface artery
Sweat gland

Heart

Hair
Surface artery

Sweat gland
Liver

Stomach

Visceral artery

Spleen

Intestine

Adrenal gland
Sweat gland
Surface artery
Hair

Colon

Bladder

Rectum
Artery of external genitals

FIG. 39.—DIAGRAM OF THE MORE IMPORTANT DISTRIBUTIONS OF THE
AUTONOMIC NERVOUS SYSTEM

The brain and spinal cord are represented at the left. The nerves to skeletal muscles are not represented. The preganglionic fibers of the autonomic
system are in solid lines, the postganglionic in dash-lines. The nerves of the
cranial and sacral divisions are distinguished from those of the thoraco-
lumbar or "sympathetic" division by broader lines. A + mark indicates an
augmenting effect on the activity of the organ; a — mark, a depressive or
inhibitory effect. (From *Bodily Changes in Pain, Hunger, Fear, and Rage*,
by W. B. Cannon. D. Appleton-Century Co.)

a way that when the system goes into action not one but all the organs which it innervates are affected. Under strong emotion this is very apparent to every one. In extreme excitement the pupils of the eyes dilate, the heart beats fast, the breath comes quickly, the muscles at the base of the fine hairs on the skin contract and the hairs stand erect (this is more easily seen in animals than in human beings), the mouth becomes dry, and perspiration pours out on the skin. The sympathetic discharge is thus seen to be diffuse rather than specific, while the sacral and cranial discharges may affect single organs without inducing any change in others. The process of digestion does not necessarily affect the flow of saliva once the food has been swallowed; the bladder may be emptied without intestinal action. In this connection, Cannon aptly compares the sympathetic system to the loud and soft pedals of a piano which modulate all the notes together, while the sacral and cranial divisions are like the keys, acting either separately or in combination.

Another system of physiological mechanisms, closely bound up with the autonomic nervous system but in part functioning independently of it is the system of ductless or endocrine glands briefly described in Chapter V. There is reason to think that the entire endocrine system is involved in the organic and muscular changes that occur during emotion. However, there is one pair of glands that is of particular interest to us here because one of the hormones that they secrete appears to have an identical effect upon the body with that of nerve currents proceeding outward over the sympathetic division of the autonomic nervous system. These are the *adrenal glands*, located at the top of each kidney. (See Figure 29, p. 143.) The adrenals are made up of two parts, an outer portion called the *cortex* and an inner portion called the *medulla*, each of which discharges its own hormone into the blood stream. The hormone secreted by the *adrenal medulla* is called *adrenin* (or, in the form prepared for commerical use, *adrenalin*). One of the chief functions of adrenin is that of helping to maintain a normal state of muscular tonus. It effects this by its control over the amount of blood sugar that is released from the liver. Blood sugar is the chief source of muscular energy; it is stored in the liver and muscles and delivered to the muscles through the blood stream as it is needed. Now in conditions of strong emotion, particularly fear or rage, the adrenal glands are stimulated to increased activity; more adrenin is poured into the blood; and the effect of this increased supply upon the body is marked and widespread. Exactly as when the sympathetic division of the autonomic nervous system goes into action, the pupils of the eye dilate, the fine hairs on the surface of the body stand erect, and the muscles are made ready for vigorous action. At the same time the activity of certain organs is inhibited. Digestion is stopped; the secretion of saliva is diminished, causing the mouth to feel dry. The fine capillaries of the skin contract, thus diminishing the supply of blood to the surface of the body and causing the face to become pale.

Some further evidence that emotion, experienced after the period of early infancy has passed, is more complex than just the bodily sensations alone, has been derived from experiments in which adrenalin has been administered artificially. When this is done the same organic changes occur as would take place as a result of a discharge of adrenin from the subject's own adrenal glands or under the action of the sympathetic nerves. Subjects to whom adrenalin is given often report that they feel keyed up, "as if" something were going to happen, or even "as if" they were going to be angry or afraid. But giving adrenalin rarely, if ever, makes them angry or afraid or produces any of the other emotions that are normally associated with the physiological states induced by a natural secretion of the hormone itself. All that commonly occurs is recognition that their physiological sensations resemble those felt previously under different conditions. Except for one thing, the situation is much the same as when we say, "That man makes me think of Mr. Jones" or "These cookies taste like the ones mother used to make."

MOODS

The exception noted in the last sentence is this: Many subjects who have been given adrenalin do appear to be thrown into a state which predisposes them toward a display of anger, fear, or other emotions of the excitatory group on relatively small provocation. Such a state of predisposition toward one kind of emotional reaction rather than another we call a *mood*. Moods are of many kinds. We have joyful moods, irritable moods, contented moods. As we have just seen, a physiological condition may be responsible for a mood. Everyday life provides us with many similar examples. Hunger, as we all know, is likely to make one irritable. Goodenough,[25] working with children, and Gates,[26] working with college students, have shown that the frequency of anger increases steadily with the length of time since the last meal. (See Figure 40.) Likewise indigestion, constipation, or other bodily disturbances predispose to anger, i.e., create an irritable mood, while good digestion promotes cheerfulness and content.

Not only do moods sway the balance in favor of certain types of emotion, but the arousal of emotion, particularly if it occurs repeatedly, frequently leaves an after-effect in the form of a mood. You get up in the morning feeling particularly cheerful. At breakfast some one spills coffee on your suit, necessitating a trip to the cleaners. You arrive at the corner just in time to see the street-car leave and have to wait fifteen minutes for the next one. As you are entering it, you collide with a fat man who first steps heavily on your toe and then wants to know why you can't look where you are going. The chances are that by the time you reach the office your original good temper will have been entirely dissipated and your happy mood changed to one of irritability in which even a slight annoyance will precipitate a storm.

A mood, then, is not an emotion but a state of readiness, a "set" toward some particular kind of emotional reaction. Since moods may be induced either by physiological factors or remain as aftermaths of emotional episodes (in which physiological factors are involved), it is very possible that if all were known it would be found that moods always have a physiological basis of some kind, even though we are not at present always able to determine in what this factor consists.

All this tells us a number of things. First we note that the mechanism for responding to conditions that might conceivably affect the well-being of the organism is exceedingly complex; more so, perhaps, than any other part of the bodily arrangements.

[25] F. L. Goodenough, *Anger in Young Children* (Minneapolis, University of Minnesota Press, 1931).

[26] G. S. Gates, "An Observational Study of Anger," *J. Exper. Psychol.*, 1926, 9: 325-336.

Secondly we note that the arrangement is such that this mechanism can be set off in either of two ways, instantly and automatically as in the case of the startle pattern or more slowly when the stimulation is of cerebral origin, arising through more complicated mental processes, as when we learn of the death of a dearly loved friend or hear that an impending flood threatens to destroy the house in which we live, or receive a letter from

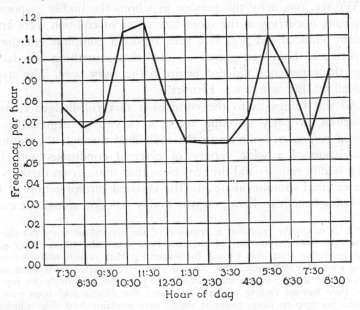

FIG. 40.—DIURNAL VARIATIONS IN FREQUENCY OF OUTBURSTS OF ANGER AMONG YOUNG CHILDREN

(From *Anger in Young Children*, by F. L. Goodenough. Courtesy University of Minnesota Press.)

our sweetheart. The two situations differ, not only from the neurological point of view but to at least an equal degree in the quality of the individual experience. In the first instance the neural pathway is, as it were, short-circuited. The nervous impulse passes directly to the muscles and glands from the centers in the brain stem that are the terminal points for the axons of the sensory nerves without involving the cerebral association centers at all. These may come in later, when the sensations resulting from the bodily movements are relayed back to the brain. But in the second instance, no gross reaction of the body occurs until *after* cerebral action has interpreted the impulses from the sense-organs as something that has personal reference to the individual. It is in this latter instance only that we regard the reaction as "emotional." Those of the former type may better be classed as generalized bodily reflexes.[27]

We see, too, why the persons in whom the bodily responses typically occurring in the secondary phase of emotion were artificially induced did not, as a rule, report a complete emotional experience. They recognized at once that something was lacking; the experience did not begin in the right way. The stage was all set. But where was Hamlet? [28]

All this brings us to the conclusion that full-fledged human emotions, properly speaking are to a very large degree *conditioned responses*, built up in the individual through the gradual association of a wide variety of external conditions with his own bodily reflexes and the sensations that result from them. Not the external stimulus alone nor the cerebral interpretation of its probable benefit or harm, not the bodily reaction alone, not even

[27] It is of course true that a response of the second or truly emotional type may follow upon one of the first type when the subject later sees that his reflex start was caused by something that reason tells him was dangerous. It is not unusual for persons who have escaped from some sudden danger during which they acted promptly and effectively to report that they had no feeling of fear until after the danger had been passed. "I had no time to think about it then," they explain. And this "thinking about it" is much more than the perception of bodily sensations which James noted. One does not experience such delayed fear after the occasion has passed unless there is recognition that the danger existed. A mere startle reaction, if marked, may be followed by clear perception of internal sensations, but these alone do not induce fear.

[28] We must remember, too, that internal as well as external sensations may serve as the starting points for true emotional experiences with their initial cerebral involvement. Perhaps all of us have known times when some new and unexplained gyration of our viscera has aroused concern in our minds. Since the muscular tremors, the change in the heart rate, and other physical symptoms that follow the administration of adrenalin are very apparent to the subject, they are quite capable of arousing fear in their own right. Thus it is entirely possible that the very small number of persons who reported genuine fear after the administration of adrenalin were truly alarmed by the unfamiliar bodily sensations that they were experiencing. This is a possibility that seems not to have occurred to the experimenters nor to most of the people who have interpreted their reports.

the sensations resulting from the reaction constitute the emotion. Emotion involves all three components, no one of which can be omitted without destroying the form and character of the whole. The body jerk of the neonate is not fear but the seed from which fear may develop. The bodily sensations of the adrenalized subject may suggest fear through association with previous experiences in which similar feelings occurred, but they do not constitute fear. The engine is not the automobile, though it is an essential part of it.

THE RECIPROCAL ACTION OF THE OPTIC THALAMUS AND THE CEREBRAL CORTEX IN STIMULATING AND CONTROLLING HUMAN BEHAVIOR

The startle pattern, even in the adult, is little if at all subject to voluntary control, nor is it the result of any process of reasoning or judgment. There is not time; the reflex start occurs before you know what gave rise to it. In contrast to this are instances in which immediate sensory stimuli play no part at all in arousing reaction. Lying in bed, you remember a remark made by an acquaintance some days ago. At the time you thought nothing of it. It was just a casual remark without special significance. But to-day other facts of which you were then ignorant have come to your knowledge, and in thinking of them the earlier remark takes on a new meaning. Your face grows hot, your fists clench, and your jaw sets in anger as for the first time the veiled implication becomes clear. You think of retorts that you might have made or of vengeance that you may still be able to inflict. But then, on further reflection, you become more reasonable. Common sense comes to your aid, telling you that such action on your part would defeat its own object, since it would be tantamount to an admission that the insult might have some basis in fact. Better to ignore it, better to keep up the appearance of not understanding as a more subtle type of retort than any other could possibly be.

In this episode three rather distinct phases of the emotional response can be noted. First there is the element of understanding; the mental processes of remembering, associating, and comprehending that give rise to the second stage in which nascent muscular reactions of a violently impulsive character together with internal reactions and sensations are the dominant features. About all you are conscious of is the urgent need to act. You do not think much about the results of your action; you only know that you *must* do something. Finally there comes the third stage in which reason again assumes command, the bodily tension relaxes, and a saner course of action is projected which leaves you with a comfortable sense of having devised a plan for discomfiting your enemy more completely than you could possibly have done by direct bodily attack. Even though there may remain a few lingering prickles of disappointment ("I sure would have liked to get in one good swing at that guy!") the dictates of common sense still held your muscles in check.

Brief consideration will show that these prompt and vigorous reflex acts are of vast importance for the safety of the individual and have played a significant part in the preservation of the race. If you *always* had to think before you could act, the chances are that your life would soon be blotted out under the wheels of an oncoming car or that you would be blinded before you could figure out which way to move your head to avoid some object threatening the eye. But the autonomic nervous system is not in itself an adaptive mechanism. In its evolution, vigor and speed have been emphasized at the expense of wisdom. Under its influence, man cannot choose; he can only act. It is in the cerebral hemispheres of the central nervous system that the mechanisms reside by which inhibition of activity takes place, giving time for reasoned judgment, for intelligent choice among possible courses.

If only one of the two controlling mechanisms could act at a given time, if the autonomic system were to cease to function whenever the cortical mechanism took hold and vice versa, we should indeed be in a sad way. Of course this is not the case. There are very few occasions in life when both mechanisms are not operating, but the "balance of power" varies greatly from time to time. There are on the one hand the blind panics, the insane rages, the "brain-storms" with which reason has little to do, and on the other hand there are moments of such rapt and concentrated thought that neither pain nor terror, neither anger nor grief can interrupt its flow.

During recent years, physiologists have been much interested in ascertaining whether or not there is any particular region in the brain from which the stimuli that set off the more violent emotional or quasi-emotional reactions such as intense fear or rage are relayed. This interest was stimulated by a number of observed facts. When the cerebral cortex is temporarily thrown out of action as in the delirium of a high fever, in the earlier stages of ether anaesthesia, or under "laughing gas," many of the reactions commonly shown during true emotion take place spontaneously. The patient laughs or cries without apparent cause; he throws himself about, shouts, and sometimes tries to attack those about him as if in rage. Animals from whose brains the cerebral hemispheres have been experimentally removed frequently behave in much the same way. Tumors located in certain parts of the brain have been found to produce characteristic effects both upon the emotional experiences and the emotional behavior of the persons so affected. In their attempts to account for these facts, physiologists removed not only the cerebral hemispheres but successive layers of the brain stem in cats to see when the behavior known as "sham rage" would cease to appear. The name "sham rage" was applied to behavior similar to that shown by cats under conditions that might normally be expected to arouse true rage in the intact animal, but which, in the cats whose cerebral hemispheres had been removed, appeared spontaneously or at least without adequate external stimuli. It was found that such operations had no effect upon the behavior until they reached a part of the brain stem known as the *optic thalamus* or *diencephalon*, an ancient portion of the brain in which the difference between man and animal is far smaller than in the case of the cerebrum. After this region, shown in Figure 39, is removed, sham rage is promptly abolished and the animal cannot be made to show strong excitement even by violent stimulation.

These experiments provide a neat demonstration of the reciprocal action of the two functional divisions of the central nervous system in the stimulation and control of behavior. The energizing drive to action comes through the stimulation of the autonomic nerves by impulses relayed by way of the thalamus. But emotion, as it occurs in the life of the normal person, is not the untrammeled aimless raving of delirium, not the sham rage of the decorticated cat that occurs without reason and strikes without object. The part played by the cortex in the emotional life of the normal human being in full possession of all his senses is that of control and direction of the forces set free by thalamic action. And emotion, to be experienced and realized to the full, demands some measure of cortical guidance, without which it wastes itself in a fruitless display of physical energy that lacks both depth of feeling and strength of purpose. The thing that gives emotion its peculiar character is its feeling of drive, its insistent demand that

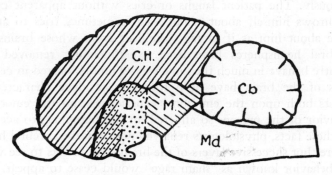

FIG. 41.—MEDIAN SECTION OF THE BRAIN, SHOWING THE LOCATION IN THE THALAMUS OF THE REGION BELIEVED TO BE MOST ACTIVE IN STRONG EMOTION

CH, cerebral hemispheres; *D*, diencephalon or thalamus; *M*, mesencephalon; *Md*, medulla. The cross-hatching from right downward to left marks the portion of the brain which can be removed without interfering with the emotional expression of rage. The posterior half of the diencephalon (indicated by dots without cross-hatching) is therefore assumed to be the part of the brain most concerned in the violent emotions, since with its removal rage responses are abolished. (From *Bodily Changes in Pain, Hunger, Fear and Rage*, by W. B. Cannon. Courtesy D. Appleton-Century Co.)

you *must do* something about this at once. So long as the "something" remains vague and uncrystallized, so long as the impulse is undirected, and the energy left to expend itself in a thousand useless activities that give no satisfaction, the emotional experience is incomplete. But when reason takes hold, when the cortical processes assume control of the thalamic discharge, the picture is changed. The primitive impulse to activity, the need to do something, remains, but instead of being dissipated in all directions without useful accomplishment, the forces are unified and directed toward a definite goal. You no longer flee blindly, any-where, anyhow, just so it is away from the bear, but you see a spot that promises safety and make for that. As soon as this occurs, as soon as the activity takes on form and purpose, the feeling changes. It is no longer, "I must do something, I don't know what," but instead, "I must and will do this."

It is just here, in the directing of the primitive forces released by thalamic action into useful channels, that the emotional beha-vior of the normal civilized human being differs from that of the decorticated cat, or the man suffering from delirium tremens. Emotion does not lose in strength by being brought under con-trol but gains immensely in form and vividness. The ravings of the person in the first stages of anaesthesia, or the "sham rage" of the decorticated animal, cannot be looked upon as true emo-tion. They represent nothing more than the disorganized activity resulting when the cortex is thrown out of action, leaving the thalamus to be stimulated directly by the diffuse mass of uninter-preted sensations coming in from the sense-organs. The responses· aroused are primitive and unadaptive; the person has no later memory of them; and they have no effect upon his later behav-ior. "Conditioning" does not normally occur.[29] In real emotion there is this difference, that the thalamic activity is aroused, not vaguely and indefinitely by sensations without cortical interpre-tation, but by sensations that cortical action has interpreted, that have taken on a meaning more or less clear. The cortex as well as the thalamus is then taking an active part in the arousal of the reaction that we call emotion, but it has temporarily delegated to the thalamus a part of its task of stimulating the body to action. As long as the cortex remains in command of the situation—as long, we say, as the individual keeps his wits about him—the coöperation of the thalamus lends to the whole experience a force, vividness, color, and warmth that it would not otherwise have. But when cortical control is relaxed, when the primitive nerve centers are left to work their will with the organism, then we have the blind, unreasoning terrors, the rages, the "brain-storms" that exhaust without profit and that have none of the

---

[29] This statement is only approximately correct. It has been shown that very simple and unstable conditioned responses can be established in de-corticated dogs, but only with great difficulty and after many trials.

return glow, the feeling of satisfaction, the "thrill" that comes when a strong emotion drives to accomplishment along a course made clear by reason and judgment.

This return glow, this feeling of satisfaction, is an integral part of normal human emotion. Without it no experience is complete, for every experience has its emotional component that needs to be satisfied. It is when this need is left unsatisfied, when the thalamic excitement exhausts itself without useful result or when cortical control is directed only toward repressing the outward signs of emotion with no attempt to divert the energy into suitable channels, that harm results. Emotion is the great driving force of life. Properly controlled and directed into useful courses it adds richness and depth to all experience, gives strength to our efforts, joy to our accomplishments. Allowed to run wild or dammed up without suitable outlet, it may wreak untold harm.

Only the coward seeks to avoid emotional experience. Only the weak allow emotion to become their master. Emotion is not to be feared but sought, met squarely, ruled, utilized, and enjoyed. This is living.

GUIDING EMOTIONAL DEVELOPMENT DURING INFANCY

In the conditioning of emotional reactions we have a mechanism that in all probability furnishes the chief explanation for the modification of behavior in infancy and early childhood. It is a mistake to think that the results of emotional conditioning are seen only in the manifestation of emotional reactions under new conditions, in the attachment of the emotional response to a new stimulus. That is only the beginning. Emotional reactions, whether they be natural or acquired, are the forces that determine the child's relations to the universe about him, that decide what aspects of it he shall seek to explore and what he will avoid; what things he will actively try to change either by direct attack or by diplomacy, and what he will try to preserve and to bring into closer relation to himself. From the comparatively purpose-less and undiscriminating reactions of infancy come the emotional experiences that give to the world its meaning and to the individual his purpose. And these meanings and purposes are highly personal affairs. It is not what an object or a situation *is* that matters, but what it can do to me and what I can do with it.

In this growth of meaning through maturation and experience lies the basis of the finer differentiation of emotional patterns that takes place with advancing age. Just as growth in motor behavior is characterized by increasing adaptation to the particular situation in which it occurs, so the diffuse, massive emotional reactions of the young infant gradually assume forms that are more appropriate to the exciting conditions. The baby cannot talk to tell us how he feels about things, but we can see very definite changes in his behavior from which we infer that his feelings, too, have gained exactness and clearness of outline. When his attempts to do something are thwarted, he struggles more violently to accomplish his ends and at the same time shows his displeasure by loud screams, kicking, and holding his breath. At first there is no direct attack on the person or object who is interfering with his activities, but about the end of the first year striking, slapping, biting, or kicking at the offender begin to occur.

This kind of emotional resistance, which is often (though not always) accompanied by emotional attack, we call anger. As the infant grows older, his desires and purposes become more clear-cut and varied because of the increased meaning that his surroundings have taken on for him and his consequent greater understanding of their possibilities for his personal exploitation and enjoyment. At first the infant has but few desires, and we cannot suppose that he realizes very clearly what these desires are. "Bodily needs" is probably a better name for them. But before very long he shows us pretty clearly that he is beginning to know quite definitely what he wants, and when he fails to get it anger ensues. There is probably no well-defined point at which the diffuse emotional reaction and generalized bodily struggle against interference with the gratification of some felt but not understood bodily need—which is the forerunner of anger in the young infant—passes over into the sudden and violent struggle, the direct attack upon the offender, the discharge of energy through such motor channels as stamping, jumping up and down, and dashing objects to the floor that we see in children somewhat older and even, at times, among adults who are lacking in self-control. The change takes place gradually.

As age advances, other emotional patterns emerge. We see the beginnings of jealousy, coquettishness, affection, joy, surprise, shyness, and resentment all before the end of the first year. Not only does the list of emotional patterns lengthen with age, but the number of different situations that are capable of arousing a given emotion increases rapidly.

This increase takes place in several ways. First and most important is the increased number of possible occasions for the arousal of emotional states that inevitably comes about as the environment takes on meaning for the child. With the growth of meaning come more definite and stronger desires, and the more frequent the desire, the stronger the impulse, the greater will be the likelihood of interference or thwarting and the more frequent will be the occasions for anger. Likewise, only a relatively strong stimulus can emerge from the unorganized environ-

---

FIG. 42.—EXPRESSION OF EMOTION IN AN INFANT OF TEN MONTHS

The situations (note that this list includes four additional situations not corresponding to any of the pictures):

1. Astonishment. I counted loudly and emphatically as I walked toward him—"twenty, twenty-one, twenty-two." He looked me uncomprehendingly in the face.
2. Grimacing. The rogue is trying to wink.
3. Satisfaction and affection. He was looking at his mother, who talked to him in a friendly manner.
4. He was tired of sitting and wanted to come out of the high-chair into my arms. (This is a later stage in the situation described under 3, above.)
5. Roguish smiling (with affection and tense expectation). His mother was teasing him. "Only wait, now, I'm going to catch you!"
6. Pleasure. I rolled a shining tin can on the tray. He said softly, "Dai."
7. Anger and displeasure. A toy had been taken away from him.
8. Astonishment (with auditory attention). He is listening to the ticking of a watch.
9. Dissatisfaction (with slight obstinacy). I had taken him up in my arms and then put him back into the chair. He wanted to come to my arms again.
10. Astonishment (with ocular attention). A bright-colored new toy clown was shown to him.

The pictures and the accompanying descriptions are reproduced by permission of the publishers from "Die Entwicklung der Gemütsbewegungen im ersten Lebensjahre," by Martin Buchner, *Beiträge zur Kinderforschung und Heilerziehung*, 1909, 60, 19 pp.

The correct matchings are listed at the end of Chapter IX.

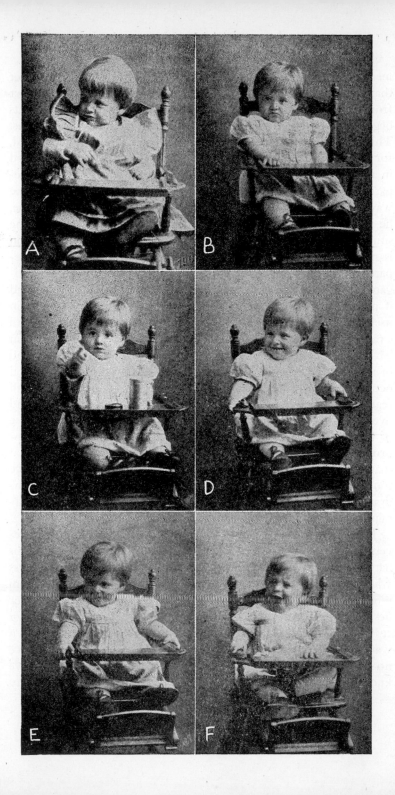

ment of the young infant with the sudden and disturbing effect that we call fear, but as the child begins to know what to expect from the people and things about him, events, persons, and objects begin to stand out from each other and to take on new qualities. This is familiar, that is strange; for this happening he is prepared, for that one he is unprepared. Now whenever the child is placed in a situation that seems to require a response which he is unprepared to make, when he feels the need for responding in some way but does not know what response will best serve his purpose, he is most likely to try to solve the problem by avoiding the situation or escaping from it. To be sure, the unfamiliar situation is not always or necessarily the one which the child is unprepared to meet. Most children have a natural tendency to investigate an unknown object, to manipulate it in various ways; and if nothing has happened to interfere with this tendency, it is in itself an adequate preparation for responding to the new and strange. But if, on previous occasions, his attempts at investigation have been unsuccessful and unpleasant, so that some *new* method of meeting the situation is clearly called for and no such method occurs to him, the avoiding or escaping response that we call fear is very likely to appear. And if it so happens that over and over again his experiences in new and untried situations are those of failure, embarrassment, discomfort, or pain, the confident approach which is the child's natural response to any new situation that does not appear too overwhelming or that does not induce too general a bodily disturbance is likely to be replaced by withdrawal, retreat, flight; his interest and self-confidence by uncertainty, by feelings of inadequacy, insecurity, and inferiority.

The secret of maintaining a child's self-confidence and of preventing undue timidity or fearfulness lies in seeing to it that his natural exploratory tendencies meet with pleasantness and success whenever this is possible; and that, when these tendencies lead him into ways which he must be taught to avoid because real danger lies in that direction, in making sure that he is taught *the right way to respond* and is not simply left to find out that his own way leads to unpleasant consequences. Fear comes when we have no satisfactory way of meeting a situation; it disappears when we know exactly what to do and are able to do it. This explains why flight from a situation is not always accompanied by fear. If we recognize that the situation is one to be avoided, and if we know exactly which way to run, and are certain that our legs can be depended upon, flight from danger may become an exciting sport, as every country boy who has teased an irate gander knows.

So with anger. If we wish to train children to be even-tempered on most occasions and to reserve their anger for circumstances under which anger seems to be justified, we shall be most successful if we direct our attention to the impulses and attitudes from which behavior springs. Anger comes when a strong impulse or desire is thwarted. In a world made up of many people, the child who does not early learn the necessity for reasonable conformance to the rights and wishes of others but who must have his own way at all cost is likely to meet with many difficulties that the more coöperative child will escape. The inflexibility of purpose on which some people pride themselves is not always a virtue. It is much more likely to be plain bull-headedness. Leadership has no greater asset than the ability to see the other person's point of view.

HOW WELL CAN YOU INTERPRET BEHAVIOR?

Shown on p. 223 are six pictures illustrating the responses of an infant of ten months to different situations that might reasonably be expected to arouse some kind of emotional reaction. Descriptions of the situations are given in irregular order in the paragraphs at the bottom of the second page. Each description is prefaced by a word or phrase indicating what emotion the father of the child thought the child was experiencing when the picture was taken. Descriptions of four additional situations not here shown have been added in order that the matching of the last picture may not be automatically determined by elimination of all other possibilities.

Begin by examining each picture carefully and reading through all the descriptions. Then go back to the picture marked *A* and compare each of the descriptions with it in turn till you decide which situation would have been most likely to elicit the posture and facial expression there shown. On a sheet of paper write the number of this situation opposite the letter *A*. Continue in the same manner until all have been matched. Then turn to the key at the end of Chapter IX and check your responses against the correct ones to see how many were right.

1. With six pictures and ten descriptions, how many correct matchings are to be expected by chance? How much better (or poorer) than this was your performance?
2. If results for the entire class are pooled, how much better than chance is the percentage of success for each picture?
3. In the class results, is there any picture that is more often matched with some one incorrect description than is to be expected by chance? If so, can you give some reasonable explanation for the confusion?

Chapter IX

THE PERIOD BEFORE SPEECH:
II. PHYSICAL GROWTH AND SENSORI-MOTOR
DEVELOPMENT

*For what reasons is the psychologist interested in the
physical as well as in the behavioral development
of children? In what ways does his interest differ
from that of the anatomist?*

*What part of the brain grows most rapidly during the
first year of postnatal life? Why is this significant?*

*Do all the bodily tissues follow the same pattern of
physical growth? Is there any difference between
the prenatal and the postnatal periods in respect to
differentiation of growth patterns? Describe.*

*Should the seemingly aimless movements of the young
infant be described as "random activity"? Explain.*

*Why do little children sometimes continue an activity
that results in mildly painful sensations instead of
becoming "conditioned" against it?*

Do children have to be taught to walk?

*If a child's body is kept in a horizontal position
throughout the first year of life so that he is unable
to practice sitting or walking at all, but without
interfering with his physical development, will he
be able to carry out these acts the first time he is
allowed to try them? Is he likely to require as long
practice in order to learn how to sit and stand as
the child who begins his practice at an earlier age?
Explain.*

227

*At about what age do children, on the average, begin
to show some signs of hand preference?*

*What are some of the other developmental changes
that occur in connection with the child's acquisition of motor skill?*

WHY THE PSYCHOLOGIST IS INTERESTED IN THE STUDY OF PHYSICAL GROWTH

The notion that the mental characteristics of an individual can be inferred from his bodily form and size, the contour of his features, the shape of his head, or the lines of his palm is as old as psychology. As long ago as the fourth century before Christ, Aristotle in his *Physiognomonica*,[1] set forth a rather elaborate outline of this theory. Apparently the idea did not originate even with him, since he began his discussion with an account of previous writings on the subject which shows that even at that early date the literature in the field must have been fairly voluminous. More than two thousand years have passed since that time, yet even now, as we approach the midpoint of the twentieth century, many people still believe that it is possible to foretell the future or ascertain the character of an individual by means of bodily signs. Palmists, phrenologists, and others of their kind still do a flourishing business in spite of the fact that careful study has repeatedly shown that their character analysis and their predictions of future events are alike worthless.

Other more recent attempts at finding bodily correlates of mental traits have been equally unsuccessful as far as the estab-lishment of universal laws or simple relationships is concerned. These studies have been chiefly of a statistical nature. They have sought to answer such questions as these: Do children who are taller than the average also tend to be brighter than the average? Is there any relationship between intelligence and such indices of body form as the ratio of sitting height to standing height or

---

[1] Although the *Physiognomonica* is included in the collected works of Aristotle, modern scholars believe it to have been written by one of his followers rather than by the master himself. There is, however, little doubt that it was prepared under his influence at a time shortly after if not dur-ing his lifetime, though its exact date is not known.

the ratio of the circumference of the head to its length measured from the crown to the point of the chin? Does the short, stocky individual show characteristic differences in his personality make-up from the one who is tall and slender?

Over and over again relationships of this kind have been painstakingly sought and from time to time some one has thought that a key to the solution of this age-old problem had been found. But with discouraging regularity, further study with better control of conditions and more careful selection of subjects has proved that the new formulae, like those previously tried, are of little value. As far as averages alone are concerned, relationships between body type and certain traits of personality or types of ability unquestionably exist, but the apparent rules have so many exceptions that diagnoses of mental traits from physical signs are almost as likely to mislead as to inform. Even the small relationship between mental and physical traits that has commonly been found is susceptible to more than one type of explanation. We cannot remind ourselves too often that the mere fact that two things are related (in the sense that they are more likely to be found in agreement than in opposition to each other) does not necessarily mean that one is the cause and the other the effect,[2]

[2] The whole concept of cause and effect is a popular rather than a scientific one. Strictly speaking, the scientist does not recognize the principle of causation as the layman conceives it. He is concerned only with ascertaining which of two events characteristically comes first in time. As a matter of fact, that is all the layman knows about it. We speak of causes merely because we have learned by experience that a certain kind of event is likely to bear a certain temporal relationship to another. When such an association between events is observed with more than chance frequency, we are likely to think of the one that usually comes first as being the "cause" of the other. Because the concept has practical convenience, especially since we have as yet no short and easily understood terminology to substitute for it, we shall continue to use it in this book as it will doubtless be used in everyday speech for many years to come. No confusion need result from this practice if the student is careful to remember that all we mean when we use such terms as "cause," "effect," "result," and the like is that we are dealing with events that are, as a rule, of a somewhat different nature from each other (we do not think of a plant as "causing" its buds) but that nevertheless occur in a given order more often than is to be expected by chance. So, in the inexact language of everyday life, we sometimes say that rain and sunshine "cause" the rose to bloom. In making such a statement we are obviously leaving out a good many other equally necessary antecedents, but in this case little confusion is likely to result, because any intelligent hearer will supply them. What we really

or that even if a "causal" relationship exists, we can tell which is the cause.

Consider, for example, the fact (and it is a fact) that on the average bright children tend to be slightly taller, age for age, than backward children. With equal plausibility we might argue that (a) superior physical status makes for superior mental development, (b) individuals of superior mental level are more likely to observe the rules of health and so develop better physique, (c) the factors making for greater height on the one hand and superior mentality on the other hand show some kind of genetic linkage whereby the two characteristics tend to vary together, or (d) both superior height and superior mentality are at least in part the result of having been reared in a superior environment. A fifth explanation is also possible. It is known that parents of superior mentality are likely to have children who are mentally superior. Accordingly, the better physical care that intelligent parents are likely to provide may account for the children's superior physique.

On the basis of data collected in connection with the Harvard Growth Study [3] Cabot [4] suggests still another explanation for the small relationships usually found between physical types and personality differences. Cabot was interested in testing Kretschmer's theory that persons who are short and stocky in build (in Kretschmer's system of classification such persons are said to be of the

---

mean is that, provided certain other necessary conditions are present, the addition to the total of rain and sunshine will facilitate the blooming. A plant that would not bloom at all if kept in a dark cellar may do so when brought out into the garden if it is a plant that normally blossoms, if it is sufficiently mature, if it is the proper season for it to bloom, and if the soil and other conditions are right. The rules of science have no exceptions, but few of these rules are simple. When a scientific "law" fails to work out, it means only that a complete understanding of the relationships between events has not been reached or that some of the conditions essential to its working have been overlooked.

[3] A very extensive study of the physical and mental growth of several hundred school children by means of repeated measurements at annual intervals throughout the school period.

[4] P. S. deQ. Cabot, "The Relationship Between Characteristics of Personality and Physique in Adolescents," *Genet. Psychol. Monog.,* 1938, 20: 3-120.

"pyknic" type) show more than usually pronounced swings of mood from elation to depression, while those who are tall and slender (the "aesthenic" type) are inclined to be somewhat reflective and introvertive in personality. From a very thoroughgoing study of sixty-two adolescent boys Cabot was unable to confirm Kretschmer's theory, but he did find that the stronger and larger boys whose bodies were more athletic in type tended to *develop* traits of leadership more readily than those with less physical prowess. Thus Cabot is inclined to the view that the social advantages which accrue from the possession of a strong and handsome body contribute to the establishment of "good" social and personal traits, but he is doubtful of the existence of any inherent or necessary relation between the two.

The psychologist's interest in the physical growth of children does not arise from a hope that he may be able to substitute some kind of physical measurement for intelligence tests or other more direct methods of studying their mental development or personality characteristics. He is interested in physical growth for its own sake, because it is an important element in the intricate pattern of developmental processes that have combined to make the individual person what he is. He regards the body as a highly essential part of one's whole personality make-up, its growth as something that is worthy of study in its own right, and not merely as a possible sign of something else. But because his main interest is in the individual as a whole, he is not content to study physical growth from the same point of view as does the anatomist whose interest does not extend beyond the measurement of bodily size and structure. Slight and undependable as the relationships between physique and behavior have been shown to be [5] when single traits are considered without reference to other conditions that play a part in determining this relationship, nevertheless when we turn our attention from the abstract trait to the concrete and very human child, we need not seek long to find instances in which we can scarcely doubt that physique has played a very important rôle in the total complex of factors that have formed his personality. One reason why these relationships do not always

[5] See D. G. Paterson, *Physique and Intellect* (New York, D. Appleton-Century Co., 1930), pp. xxviii + 304.

show up in group statistics is because they work out in so many different ways under different conditions. Consider, for example, the boy who is so much smaller than his schoolmates that he cannot compete with them successfully in games or sports where size and strength are important. This fact will almost inevitably influence his behavior but not all children will respond in the same way. Some will find companionship among children younger than themselves, among whom, because of their greater experience, they frequently assume the rôle of leaders and sometimes of dictators. Others turn to solitary activities such as reading or various intellectual hobbies. Still others develop some form of compensatory behavior which they sometimes carry to such an extreme degree that we speak of it as "overcompensation." They attempt to make up for their short stature by carrying themselves very erect, usually with the chin held as high as possible. They adopt an attitude of cock-sureness, are frequently very talkative and fond of argument. Thereby they demonstrate to themselves if not to others that their other gifts more than make up for their physical inferiority. Still others show behavior that is quite the opposite. They become fearful, timid, and if they are unable to find satisfaction in pursuits of their own, they cling to their earlier relations with adults, maintaining a position of childlike dependence until long past the usual age.

None of these reactions is a necessary result of the child's small size taken by itself, but no one can deny that the retarded physical growth has played its part in shaping the child's behavior. Just as no amount of sunshine will cause a fern to bloom, and as sunshine alone, in the absence of moisture and soil will not bring the rose to flowering, so the effect of variations in physical size and body build upon the personality of children will differ according to the relative strength of the drives by which they are motivated and with the conditions under which they are reared.

Another reason for the interest of psychologists in the laws of physical growth arises from the fact that these laws often suggest new problems or ways of attacking them that apply to behavior as well as to structure. The principle of development by differentiation, first noted in the study of physical growth, has been found to apply to most aspects of mental growth as well. The rules of cephalocaudal and proximo-distal progression [6] hold, within limits, for motor skills as well as for the development of body structure. (See Figure 22, p. 106.) Many other similar examples might be cited.

GROWTH OF THE BODY AND ITS PARTS

Like the prenatal period which preceded it, the period of infancy is characterized by extraordinarily rapid growth in body and mind. During the first five months the birth weight is doubled; it is trebled by the end of the first year. The brain as a whole more than doubles in size. The gain in the first year is about 130 per cent, as compared with a gain of 25 per cent the second year and about 10 per cent the third year. Growth, however, is not equally divided among the parts of the brain. The cerebrum, which was so precocious in growth during the prenatal period, is already beginning to slow down. Its gain in the first year is only about 115 per cent, while the cerebellum shows the enormous increase of 300 per cent. Since, as we pointed out before, the cerebellum is particularly concerned with the control of posture, its rapid growth at the time when the child is first gaining the ability to sit and stand is significant.

Scammon [7] has shown that at about the time of normal birth a marked change in the growth patterns of the different bodily tissues can be noted. If their prenatal growth is measured in terms of the percentage of their birth weight that has been attained at each prenatal age and the results are plotted to form a growth curve, it is found that each of the different bodily tissues grows at a uniform rate throughout the prenatal period. But if a similar procedure is followed for postnatal growth and the results are expressed in terms of the percentage of the total amount gained between birth and maturity that has been attained at each suc-

[6] That is, the rule that development proceeds from the head downward and from the trunk outward to the limbs with the large muscles of the arm and shoulder attaining independent and well-controlled movement at an earlier age than do the smaller muscles of the hand and fingers that are more remote from the mid-line of the body.

[7] R. E. Scammon, "The Measurement of the Body in Childhood," in *The Measurement of Man* (Minneapolis, University of Minnesota Press, 1930).

ceeding year of postnatal age, it is found that the rate of growth is no longer uniform and that the forms of the growth curves for the different bodily tissues after birth differ greatly from each other. (See Figure 43.) The nervous system grows very rapidly at first and more slowly thereafter; it has attained 90 per cent of its adult size by the age of six years. The lymphoid tissues (tonsils, lymph glands, etc.) increase in size up to about the time of puberty and decrease thereafter. The genitals grow very slowly

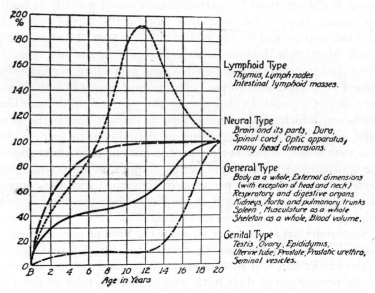

FIG. 43.—FOUR MAIN TYPES OF POSTNATAL GROWTH

(From "The Growth of the Body in Childhood," by R. E. Scammon in *The Measurement of Man.* Courtesy University of Minnesota Press.)

until shortly before the time of puberty and then with extreme rapidity. The postnatal growth curve of the general body tissues, including bones and muscles, blood, and most of the internal organs, shows a double flexure, with rapid growth at first, then a period of slow growth that lasts until about two years before the onset of puberty, when a second period of rapid growth known as the "preadolescent spurt" takes place, after which the growth rate again becomes slower and continues to slow down until adult size has been attained.

THE RÔLE OF AUTOGENOUS PRACTICE IN THE ACQUISITION OF EARLY MOTOR SKILLS

Perhaps the first thing that strikes the eye of the naïve observer of infants and young children is their seemingly constant activity. Even in sleep, little children move much more frequently than does the average adult,[8] as any one who has ever shared a bed with a young child can testify. When awake, the healthy baby will soon exhaust even the trained athlete who tries to duplicate his movements. An acquaintance of mine, a young man of nineteen who rather prides himself upon his physical prowess, ruefully describes an afternoon when he was left in charge of his sister's ten-months-old infant. It was a warm day and the child, clad only in a diaper, had been placed on a blanket on the floor. His gleeful kicking and squirming caused the young man to wonder how much energy in proportion to his size the infant was actually expending. The only criterion he could think of was an endurance test. Which would hold out longer, himself or the baby, if their activities were as nearly identical as they could be made? So he stretched his own six-foot frame beside that of the child and the race began. Although the youth assures me that he "did his darndest" to keep up, the baby had the best of it from the start. Not only could he kick and squirm and wave his arms more rapidly than his competitor but he seemed able to keep it up almost indefinitely with no sign of weakening, whereas the youth was, so he says, "out for the count" in well under an hour.

All this self-stimulated, or, as it is sometimes called, "autogenous" activity is more than just random movement. It furnishes the means by which the child eventually learns to make the parts of his body serve the needs and desires of the whole.

One of the earliest needs that can be noted in the young child, secondary only to those arising from such organic drives as hunger and thirst, is the need for stimulation of the external sense-organs. We noted in the last chapter that even in the young infant, almost any stimulation of the exteroceptors that is not

[8] C. R. Garvey, *The Activity of Young Children During Sleep*, University of Minnesota Institute of Child Welfare Monograph Series, No. 18 (Minneapolis, University of Minnesota Press, 1939), pp. x + 102.

too intense is likely to be followed by a brief inhibition of physical activity that the naïve observer is likely to call "attentiveness." This period of comparative immobility is brief and as a rule is followed immediately by an increase in the speed and vigor of the child's bodily movements that to the observer has all the appearance of "striving." Like the quasi-emotional responses described in the last chapter, both the "attention" and the "striving" are as yet nascent rather than actual. They are analogous to the blind movements of the very young pouch-dwelling oppossum who, immediately after birth (which may occur as early as eleven days after conception) clambers up the mother's abdomen through thick hair until it finds the nipple without which it could not survive. Also analogous is the diurnal bending of the stem that turns the face of the sunflower from east to west as it follows the course of the sun.[9] But the movements of the child arouse sensations from the proprioceptors in his muscles and joints. These sensations are not all alike; neither are the accompanying results. This wave of the arm, with its associated "feel," may produce nothing new, but that one brings the fist into contact with something that induces an interesting tactile sensation and likewise varies and intensifies the visual sensation as a new and moving object enters briefly into the visual field. It will be some time before the infant learns that this object which moves in so fascinating a manner is his own fist, but the time will come when this discovery will bring him many hours of happy preoccupation as he waves his hand before his face and watches the intercepted pattern of light and shade; or as he experiments with pulling the fingers of one hand by means of the other.

This need for sensory stimulation which some one has aptly called the "itching of the child's sense-organs" provides the impetus for much of the motor activity that is so characteristic of the young child. And this activity, which is sometimes followed by more varied and "interesting" sensations, sometimes by sensations so intense as to be startling or painful, and sometimes by nothing at all provides the raw material for gaining control of the motor mechanisms of the body. Through the processes of

[9] Such a relatively invariant reaction of the organism as a whole involving movement toward or away from a source of stimulation is called a *tropism.*

positive and negative conditioning the child learns to repeat movements of the former type, and to avoid or inhibit those of the second type while those of the third type gradually become "extinguished" because of the absence of the sensory stimulation which satisfies the need.[10] (See Chapter VII.)

THE RÔLE OF MATURATIONAL FACTORS IN THE ACQUISITION OF EARLY MOTOR SKILLS

There is evidence that motor control is not wholly a matter of practice but maturational factors also play a part. We have seen that well-organized patterns of behavior which cannot possibly have been practised before birth appear immediately afterward. The pupils of the child's eyes cannot react to light where there is no light, yet they do so on the second day or earlier. The child cannot breathe where there is no air, yet breathing occurs immediately after birth. It is well that this is so, for if the newborn baby had to go through all the slow and toilsome stages of learning as we know it in order to be able to perform such necessary acts as breathing, eating, digesting, assimilating, and excreting, his chances of survival would be small. Fortunately this is not the case. At birth, or even before, all the neural mechanisms needed for performing these and other motor acts are completed. As soon as the occasion arises and the stimulus is given, the appropriate behavior pattern follows, complete in all its necessary details the first time it is tried. To be sure, the activity may not be quite as perfect, quite as efficiently performed on the first trial as it will be later on. Careful studies of the first eating reactions both of human beings and of animals have shown that, although from the very beginning the behavior is well enough coördinated to enable the baby to secure the food it needs, there is some improvement in efficiency with practice. According to Breed [11] and to Bird,[12] when baby chicks are forcibly fed by hand

[10] Because the sense stimulation seems to be a goal in itself, even sensations of a mildly painful nature often seem to induce repetition rather than avoidance of an act in young children.

[11] F. S. Breed, "Development of Certain Instincts aud Habits in Chicks," *Behavior Monog.*, 1911, 1: 1-78.

[12] Charles Bird, "The Relative Importance of Maturation and Habit in the Development of an Instinct," *J. Genet. Psychol.*, 1925, 32: 68-91.

and not allowed to peck for several days after hatching, their first performance on being allowed to peck at their food is little better than that of newly hatched chicks. The aim of one of these chicks is so inaccurate that he often misses the grain completely, and even if he succeeds in picking it up he may drop it again before he has succeeded in shifting it to the back of his mouth in order to swallow it. In the beginning, only about 15 per cent of the pecks are completely successful, but the percentage improves rapidly with practice.

Practice, however, is not the only factor determining success. As the chicks grow older, their pecking, even without practice, becomes somewhat more accurate; and when normal feeding is permitted the older chicks improve more rapidly than the younger ones, so that within a few days those for whom pecking was experimentally delayed reach the same level of efficiency as the ones who were fed naturally from the start. It looks as if maturation processes alone without any practice whatever were sufficient to bring the behavior pattern up to a degree of perfection that is sufficient to sustain life, but that after this point (which is normally attained before the time of hatching) has been reached, practice is needed in order to bring about the high degree of skilled coördination in aiming, striking, seizing, and swallowing the grain that is displayed by older chickens.

It is known that in animals a number of rather complicated acts appear without previous practice. Avery [13] for example, was able, by means of X-ray photographs, to show that unborn guinea-pigs shortly before the time of normal delivery make no attempt to right themselves when the body of the mother is placed in such a position that the fetuses are upside down, but that they do so immediately and without difficulty if placed on their backs after artificial delivery a few hours later. Even more convincing are the experiments of Carmichael,[14] who divided a mass of frog's eggs into two parts, one of which was kept in plain water and

[13] George T. Avery, "Responses of Fetal Guinea Pigs Prematurely Delivered," *Genet. Psychol. Monog.*, 1928, 3: 245-331.

[14] L. Carmichael, "The Development of Behavior in Vertebrates Experimentally Removed from the Influence of External Stimulation," *Psychol. Rev.*, 1926, 33: 51-58.

————, "A Further Experimental Study of the Development of Behavior," *Psychol. Rev.*, 1928, 35: 253-260.

the other in water containing chloretone, a drug which anesthe-
tizes the developing animals so that they do not move within the
egg but which has no effect upon their physical growth. After
a time the eggs in both groups hatched as usual into tadpoles.
Those in the plain water shortly began to swim, but the anesthetized group remained motionless. After the normal animals
were swimming well, the others were removed to fresh water
that did not contain any drug. Within a short time all began to
swim, and in a few minutes they were swimming just as well as
those that had been practising the art for some time. As soon as
the effect of the anesthetic had worn off, the behavior appeared;
it did not have to be learned. Salamander's eggs, treated in the
same way, gave the same results.

While it is obviously impossible to keep babies anesthetized
throughout the early stages of their development in order to see
whether or not similar results would be obtained, a few experiments have been performed that throw some light on the question.
All of you have seen pictures of Indian babies bound to a kind of
wicker framework known as a "cradle board." In the tribes
among which the cradle board is used, the infant is bound to it
shortly after birth and is kept upon it almost continuously, being
removed only for the brief periods necessary for his physical
care. Obviously this practice provides us with an excellent opportunity for studying the effects of restricted practice upon the
development of such motor skills as sitting and walking, even
though the position on the cradle board does not completely
abolish all activity.

Dennis [15] undertook to investigate this question, using as subjects the infants of Hopi Indian tribes which had come sufficiently
under the influence of white civilization to induce some of the
Hopi mothers to discontinue the use of the cradle board, while
others still kept their infants bound as their ancestors had done.
This situation was most fortunate in preventing the occurrence
of a scientific error that might easily have arisen if all members
of the tribe had been using the board, for it was found that the
Indian children were, on the average, about one or two months
later in learning to walk than American white children. But that

[15] W. Dennis and M. G. Dennis, "The Effect of Cradling Practices upon
the Onset of Walking in Hopi Children," *J. Genet. Psychol.*, 1940, 56: 77-86.

this is a racial characteristic and not the result of the cradling practice was apparent when it was found that the children who had spent the greater part of their first year bound to the cradle board learned to walk just as early, on the average, as those who had been allowed to move freely from the time of birth.[16] Another study by Dennis [17] provides further evidence on this question. A pair of twin babies were kept in a special observation room from the end of their first month until the age of nine months. During this time each child was kept on his back in his own crib from which he was removed only for necessary physical care. Even then they were kept in the horizontal position as much as possible. While in their cribs they were prevented from using their hands to reach for objects by keeping the bedclothes drawn around their hands and bodies so tightly that the hands could not be withdrawn.[18] In feeding, the hands were so restrained that they could not touch the bottle or spoon. They had no opportunity to practice sitting or standing or many of the other common activities of infancy until the experiment was discontinued.

The most striking result of this experiment is the exceedingly small effect of the restriction upon activities that, in the normal child, usually appear before the age of nine months, and that were not rendered impossible for these children by very reason of the restriction. Even the latter, however, in a number of instances appeared spontaneously during the brief periods of freedom necessitated by bathing, dressing and so on. Although lack of opportunity for practice brought about some degree of retardation in such skills as sitting and walking, the retardation was not great. One of the twins was able to sit unsupported for

[16] When bound to the board the infant can move only the head. There is wide variation in the age at which the board is completely discarded, but after the age of three months most infants are given short daily periods of freedom. Typically, however, the child is kept bound to the board for the greater part of the day until toward the end of the first year.

[17] W. Dennis, "The Effect of Restricted Practice upon the Reaching, Sitting and Standing of Two Infants," *J. Genet. Psychol.*, 1935, 47: 17-32.

[18] Of course the restriction of activity was not so great as to run any risk of injury to the child's health or general bodily development. The children were able to turn and wriggle around under the bedclothes but they were unable to withdraw their hands or to sit or stand. Throughout the experiment they remained in good health and maintained a normal rate of physical growth.

a full minute by the 298th day; the other not until the 326th day. The first twin was able to walk alone at 17 months which, while later than the average, is still within the range shown by perfectly normal children. The second twin did not walk until after the age of two years but this cannot fairly be attributed to the restriction of practice but rather to the fact, later discovered, that a mild injury at the time of birth had produced a slight paralysis of the left arm and leg.[19]

As a result of his experiments Dennis came to the conclusion that, once a given level of maturation has been reached, children will develop most of the basic skills in a relatively short time and with only such stimulation as is given by their own organic needs and by the stimulation of their sense-organs through the sights and sounds, the odors and tactile contacts of an ordinary environment. Except for a few reflexes, specific forms of motor reaction are not acquired without practice, but if the child is normal and is given freedom to initiate such practice he will do so himself as soon as he is sufficiently mature to learn the act. The little child does not need to be taught his motor skills, nor does he have to be urged or reminded to practice them. Only give him a chance; he will take care of all the rest by himself.

Just as is true with older persons, the amount of practice needed to perfect a given skill differs from child to child. A number of carefully controlled experiments have demonstrated that at least during the early years a child who is physiologically more mature will usually be able to learn many of the ordinary motor acts with a smaller amount of practice than a younger child. The favorite method for studying questions of this kind has been the procedure known as *co-twin control*, first used by Gesell and later adopted by a number of other investigators. The procedure is a neat one because it makes it possible to vary experimental procedures while keeping the subjects in the experiments essentially the same; a thing that is impossible by any other known method. The secret lies in the use of identical twins [20] as subjects.

[19] See note on pp. 217-218 of Norman L. Munn, *Psychological Development* (Boston, Houghton Mifflin Co., 1938), in which a personal communication from Dennis is cited.

[20] See pp. 69-73.

One of the twins is put on a particular kind of training regimen,[21] the other on a different kind, or is simply kept in an ordinary environment. Because identical twins can for practical purposes be regarded as almost exact duplicates of each other, any differences in their behavior that appears at the end of the period of special training can be ascribed to the training with more assurance than is warranted when the possibility of differences in the ability of the children themselves is not ruled out.

Gesell and his co-workers have employed this method in studying the acquisition of a number of motor skills and other developmental traits such as block-building, stair-climbing and the acquisition of language.[22] Their results have been fairly uniform in showing that when one twin is given a specified amount of daily practice in these skills while the other is prevented from practicing them at all, the trained twin will acquire some proficiency[23] while the other will fail to make noticeable headway. But if, at the end of the period, the untrained twin who now has the advantage of some additional weeks of age is subjected to the same kind of training as was given to the other, he will acquire a comparable amount of skill in a shorter length of time. This is, of course, about what one would expect because of the extraordinarily rapid rate at which development proceeds during the period of infancy. Since ability as well as practice affects the rate of learning among people of all ages the twin who is older when training is started should, of course, learn more easily. McGraw, in her widely known study of Jimmy and Johnny,[24] obtained results that do not differ essentially from those just described.

[21] Note that although Dennis used twins as subjects in the experiment last described, he did not employ the method of co-twin control. Although of the same sex, the twins were fraternal, not identical, and both were submitted to the same experimental regimen.

[22] Arnold Gesell and Helen Thompson, "Learning and Growth in Identical Infant Twins," *Genet. Psychol. Monog.*, 1929, Vol. 6, No. 1, p. 123.

[23] Provided, of course, that at the time training is begun the child has reached a maturational level at which real "practice" is possible. There would be little use in trying to teach stair-climbing to an infant two weeks old.

[24] Myrtle B. McGraw, *Growth: a Study of Johnny and Jimmy* (New York, D. Appleton-Century Co., 1935), p. 319.

THE NORMAL COURSE OF MOTOR DEVELOPMENT IN INFANCY

At birth, as we have seen, the child's activity consists chiefly of mass movements, with a few specialized responses that are fairly well coördinated. Show the month-old baby a toy, say a rattle, shake it about, and what are the results? He may not respond at all; if he does, the most we can expect is some increase in general activity, perhaps momentary fixation of the eyes on the object, a little harder kicking, a few extra waves of the arms, or mouth movements as in suckling.

Return six months later. The baby who formerly lay helpless on his back is now sitting in his high-chair with only such support as it affords; perhaps he may even be able to sit alone on the floor for a minute or two without toppling over. Show him the rattle. The baby watches with interest as you take it from your bag; his gaze, formerly so uncertain and wavering, now follows your every movement. As you extend the toy toward him he reaches for it without hesitation. The forward thrust of the hand may not be perfectly aimed, but any error in direction is promptly corrected and the extended fingers close about the toy as soon as it is touched. Once in his hand the rattle is manipulated in a dozen different ways. It is waved about, hammered, chewed, sucked, rubbed against his face, passed from one hand to the other, laid down and picked up again, scratched and patted, all with an intentness of expression which rivals that of the scientist engaged in investigating the possibilities of a new laboratory instrument. The remarkable advance in motor abilities that has taken place in the short space of six months is seen in every movement; in his posture with erect neck and shoulders and well-coördinated head movements, in the dexterity of his hand movements and his ability to direct the movements of his hands by the use of sight, in the readiness with which he is able to follow a moving object with his eyes, and most of all in the decrease in non-specific mass activity and its replacement by adaptive movements of local parts. Although he is still inclined to "wriggle all over" when he tries to do something, particularly if it is something new, his wriggling is more likely to produce the desired

FIG. 44.—THE MOTOR SEQUENCE

(From *The First Two Years: A Study of Twenty-Five Babies*, by Mary Shirley. Courtesy University of Minnesota Press.)

result, even though a good many unnecessary movements are involved.

Try the same experiments six months later. We now find the year-old baby creeping about with considerable agility, sitting alone with perfect balance and changing from the sitting position to the creeping position without hesitation or difficulty. He pulls himself to a stand by the help of a piece of furniture, walks with the aid of a supporting hand or the rails of his crib. At six months he could manipulate fairly good-sized objects, using his entire hands without very much independent finger movement; by nine or ten months, finger movements have advanced to the stage at which he can pick up tiny objects between his thumb and finger. (See Figure 45.) Before the end of the first year the index finger is used alone for pointing, touching, and exploring objects in many ways. By this time, too, most children show some tendency to use one hand in preference to the other, though the difference is not very marked. Hand preference at this stage is, in fact, so slight that nearly all babies will be likely to grasp an object with the hand nearest it whenever there is a definite advantage of position; but if care is taken to offer an object exactly in the median line of the child's body so that neither hand is given any advantage over the other, it is found that as age advances more and more children come to reach with the right hand rather than with the left. (See Figure 46.) We have no way of knowing, at present, whether this general preference for the right hand is determined by some native process of maturation or whether it is the result of training. Undoubtedly most mothers tend to encourage children to use the right hand whether or not they are aware of doing so. Objects are put into the right hand more often than into the left; the right hand is more likely to be picked up and patted or stroked (as a result of the hand-shaking habits formed in ordinary adult intercourse). Some mothers from the beginning make a definite effort to train the child to be right-handed. They feel that since this is a right-handed world, with its machinery and its social customs adapted to right-handed people, the child who is right-handed has a distinct advantage over the one who is left-handed. It is possible, therefore, that hand preference is entirely a matter of early training, but the fact that right-handedness is the rule among practically all races of mankind

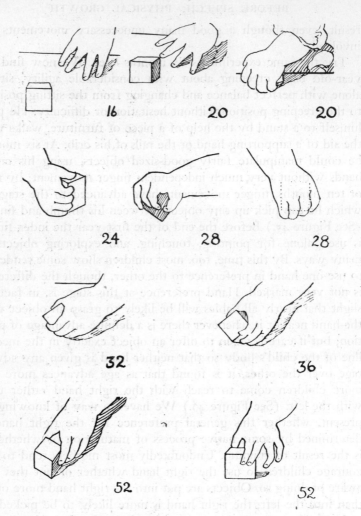

FIG. 45.—DEVELOPMENT OF MANUAL PREHENSION IN INFANCY

The ten stages in the development of the ability to seize and hold a one-inch cube have been named by Halverson as follows: (1) reach but no contact, (2) contact but no grasp, (3) the primitive squeeze, (4) the squeeze grasp, (5) the hand grasp, (6) the palm grasp, (7) the superior palm grasp, (8) the inferior forefinger grasp, (9) the forefinger grasp, and (10) the superior forefinger grasp. The numbers below the drawings show the ages at which each of the above stages is likely to appear. (Reproduced by permission of the author and the publisher from H. M. Halverson. "An Experimental Study of Prehension in Infants by Means of Systematic Cinema Records." *Genet. Psychol. Monog.*, 1931, 10: 107-286.)

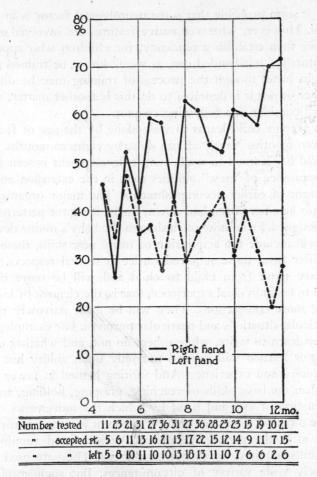

80
%

70

60

50

40

30

20

10

0

—— Right hand
--- Left hand

4   6   8   10   12 mo.

Number tested	11 23 21 31 27 36 31 27 36 28 23 23 15 19 10 21
" accepted rt.	5 6 11 13 16 21 13 17 22 15 12 14 9 11 7 15
" " left	5 8 10 11 10 10 13 18 13 11 10 7 6 6 2 6

FIG. 46.—DEVELOPMENT OF RIGHT-HANDEDNESS IN INFANTS
(From H. S. Lippman, "Certain Behavior Responses in Early Infancy,"
J. Genet. Psychol., 1927, 34: 424-440. Courtesy Clark University Press.)

makes it seem probable that some neurological factor is involved as well. However, whatever native features are involved cannot do more than establish a tendency, for children who appear to be "naturally" left-handed can, as we all know, be trained to use the right hand, though the process of training may be difficult. Whether or not it is desirable to do this is another matter, which we shall consider in a following chapter.

The average child learns to walk alone by the age of fourteen or fifteen months. Nearly all can do so by eighteen months. After the child has learned to walk, motor development is seen less in the appearance of "new" abilities than in the extension and improvement of earlier accomplishments. The major organizations of motor acts have been laid down, the basic motor patterns have been designed. From now on, although the baby's motor development will include the acquisition of many new skills, these skills will differ from those acquired earlier in several respects. They will vary more from child to child and will be more closely related to his individual experience, that is, the element of learning will be more conspicuous. They will be more narrowly related to particular situations and particular purposes. For example, some children learn to write, while others do not, and whether or not writing is learned will depend not only upon ability but upon opportunity and experience. And writing is used in fewer situations than the basic skills of reaching, grasping, holding, and the coördination of eye and hand by which the movements of the pen are directed. The same thing is apparent in other motor skills gained after the period of infancy. Walking and running are basic skills acquired by all normal persons. They are used in an extremely wide variety of circumstances. But such specialized adaptations of these acts as dancing, walking a tight-rope, and skating are not universally learned and have a much narrower range of usefulness.

In summary, then, we may note that the acquisition of motor skill by the infant is not, as some have thought it to be, merely the result of "accidental" conditioning through experiences gained in "random" activity. In the first place the child's activities are not "random" at all. They are, as we have seen, the direct result of an organic craving for sensory stimulation—a craving that is secondary only to the primary organic drives of hunger and thirst.

FIG. 47.—SOME EARLY MOTOR SKILLS

(Photographs by Harold M. Lambert.)

This craving alone, in the normal child, is sufficiently pronounced to insure that in any ordinary type of environment that the child is free to exploit, enough self-initiated practice will be had to give reasonable proficiency in such basic motor skills as sitting, standing, walking, running, and handling objects. Few people realize the enormous amount of practice in these arts that every child gains in the course of his everyday activities. From morning to night he is busily exploring the world about him. Every new object he sees is exploited in a dozen different ways and by the aid of as many senses as he can bring to bear on it. It is felt, tasted, hammered, pushed about, dropped and picked up again, turned over and over, looked at from every angle, listened to, dragged about, and stuck into every available crevice, and its possibilities as a noise-maker, a scratching or engraving tool, a lever, and a poker are tried out on as many different objects as possible, not forgetting the parlor furniture. Not only does this incessant practice bring about rapid improvement in motor skills, but it also provides the personal experience that gives form and meaning to the sensory impressions that accompany all the child's activities. Objects lose their impersonal character, if, indeed, they existed as objects for the child before experience had brought them into some kind of personal relationship to him, which seems rather doubtful. The cup from which he drinks his morning milk is no longer merely a visual pattern of lights and shades or something that stimulates his organs of touch but is also a *desired object*, a giver of pleasure, a satisfier of his bodily needs. It is not a thing completely external to himself but something that has a very intimate relationship to himself. Thus we see once more how the intimate connection between the varying aspects of the developing personality makes it impossible to consider one of these aspects without reference to all the rest. The infant acquires control of his motor processes through the conditioning of his movements in such a way as to gain greater satisfaction of his need for sensory experiences. And all the time that he is acquiring these experiences and gaining these skills he is learning many other things. He is beginning to grasp some of the routine habits of things, the everyday laws of the physical world, so that he knows more exactly what to expect from his actions. When an object with which he has been playing slips from his grasp, he no longer gazes helplessly in all directions but he leans from his high-chair to look and gesture toward the floor. Moreover he demonstrates that he has acquired some knowledge of human psychology as well, for if help is not immediately forthcoming, the chances are that he will scream until he gets it. He is becoming more discriminating in his reactions both to persons and objects. He has learned that this thing hurts, that this person will always yield to his demands if he is sufficiently insistent, while that one is likely to remain obdurate. He learns that certain objects are adapted to particular uses, while others will not serve. Thus his behavior becomes better suited to the gratification of his needs and desires.

Learning how to control his own body is of the utmost importance to the infant for its own sake. But the child does not acquire his motor skill just for the sake of becoming skillful. That which he aims at is the mastery of his world to which end the mastery of his body is merely a necessary means. In the course of his incessant practice and experimentation he gains quite as much in the way of intellectual experience as in motor skill, and his patterns of personality and social reactions undergo quite as marked changes as does his motor ability. We shall turn to some of these matters in the next chapter.

THE BIOGRAPHY OF A BABY

Jessie Chase Fenton, *A Practical Psychology of Babyhood* (Boston, Houghton Mifflin Co., 1925), pp. xiv + 348.

In this chapter and in the ones immediately preceding and following it you have been told something about the typical course of development during the period of infancy. But no two babies are alike, and in order to see how all these manifold aspects of ability and experience work together in producing the highly individual personality of a living child we must deal not merely with averages but with individuals.

Many accounts of the growth and development of individual children have appeared since Tiedemann, in 1787, published a report of the early responses of his little son. The book by Mrs. Fenton is not new, but it is one of the best of its kind that has appeared. It has the merit of being written by a psychologist who was at the same time alert to the fact that many of her readers were likely to be interested in practical questions of child care and training as well as in the more strictly scientific questions of the manner and order in which new forms of behavior emerge. Based as it is upon painstaking records of the development of the author's little son, it is replete with interesting and illuminative anecdotal accounts of actual episodes that lend vividness and meaning to the factual material.

Young people sometimes think that books of this kind are suitable only for those who are already parents. This is not true. Parenthood, like other major concerns of life, demands preparation in advance if its responsibilities are to be adequately met and its joys fully realized. Young men as well as young women will profit by gaining a more concrete acquaintance with babies and their development. To many young fathers as well as young mothers their first child with his constant exhibition of "ways that are dark and tricks that are vain" is indeed an alien creature. Reading about the growth and behavior of a baby is by no means equivalent to raising one, but it may be the best available substitute.

KEY FOR MATCHING PHOTOGRAPHS AND DESCRIPTIONS AT END OF CHAPTER VIII

Picture	A	B	C	D	E	F
Situation	7	9	1	3	5	4

Chapter X

*When we speak of "adaptive behavior" are we neces-
sarily referring to a special kind of reaction that
differs from all others? Explain.*

*Through which sensory avenues are stimuli leading to
adaptive responses on the part of the infant most
commonly received?*

*How do Bühler's three "types" of social behavior as
seen in the infant compare with your observations
of older children and adults?*

*What do we mean by "insight," and how do human
beings differ from the lower animals in the use
that they make of insight in learning?*

*Is it equally easy for all children to gain insight into
social situations? Why not?*

THE UNITARY CHARACTER OF ADAPTIVE BEHAVIOR

The distinction between "motor behavior," which was considered in the last chapter, and "adaptive behavior," which is our
present concern, is largely arbitrary, determined for the most
part by the interest of the observer. Adaptive behavior itself is
not necessarily different from that previously discussed. Behavior
as such cannot be divided into classes, for no form of behavior
ever stands alone. But the interest and attention of the observer
may so shift from time to time that for the moment he is willing
to ignore all aspects of a given bit of behavior except the one
that temporarily interests him. So whereas we were formerly

concerned with the increasing complexity of the child's movements with advancing age and with the accuracy of his bodily coördinations, we shall now turn our attention from the form of the movements to their success or failure in attaining the goals at which they appear to be directed and to the changes in the stimulus-value of these goals with changes in maturity and experience. In so doing we shall often find ourselves impelled to depart from pure description and pass over into the more debatable area of interpretation and inference. The hazards are obvious; yet they must sometimes be risked if we are to avoid the sterility of mere enumeration of observed fact. But if we are careful to note the points at which observation leaves off and interpretation begins, many of the most serious pitfalls can be avoided.

The child's early adaptive responses are directed toward the outside world and are initiated almost entirely through stimulation of the exteroceptors.[1] They are termed *adaptive* because they are not merely repetitive activities but their patterns change with each new performance in a more or less systematic fashion and with relation to a goal. The idiot who sits on the floor and rocks himself forward and backward all day long is not exhibiting adaptive behavior. Neither is the child who sits aimlessly at his desk cover-

---

[1] Internal sensations can sometimes be intensified or abolished, but they do not greatly change in quality. But an article of food, for example, can give rise to a wide variety of sensations. It can be seen, smelled, and in the mouth of an unskillful eater it may even be heard! It stimulates the organs of touch in the mouth, lips and throat, perhaps those of the fingers as well, and it stimulates the temperature senses. Under some conditions it may give rise to cutaneous pain. And all these sensations can be varied within rather wide limits by changing the relationship of the body to the source of the stimulation. Manipulating the stimulus object in various ways will greatly alter the visual sensations; the taste sensations can be modified by masticating food for longer or shorter periods or by shifting it to different parts of the mouth. It may be approached or avoided. The duration of the association with it may in most cases be increased or shortened at will. But a stomach-ache is a different matter. Only indirectly does it give rise to adaptive behavior. It may so change the child's mood that his adaptations to external conditions are very different from those that would have been made in a good state of digestion, and it may serve as a warning to the adult that a change in diet would be desirable. But one cannot run away from a stomach-ache that is already present nor change its form or intensity through any simple kind of behavioral adaptation such as lies within the capacity of the infant.

ing sheet after sheet of paper with meaningless scribbles.[2] But if the idiot begins to vary his rocking by additional movements of his body so as to intensify the bodily sensations or when he shifts his position away from the wall or furniture so as to gain greater freedom or if the child presently turns his attention to what he is doing and begins to draw a picture or write a story, then we classify the behavior as adaptive because its form has been modified in at least a quasi-purposive way. Adaptive behavior is behavior that is directed toward a goal, to the satisfaction of a need or desire. It is therefore characterized by attentiveness or bodily set and by changes in the form of the behavior pattern that show a systematic trend, though this trend may be and often is broken by interruptions and retrogressions. In everyday language we say that in order to show adaptive behavior the individual must be able to utilize the experiences of the past as directional cues by which he steers his behavioral course in order to reach his goal. At least in a rudimentary way he must make discriminations, classifications, judgments. He must remember, and he must also be able to forget.

All this sounds very much beyond the infantile level. Actually, however, we have ample evidence that the beginnings of these processes are under way long before speech has become sufficiently advanced to enable the child to provide us with evidence of a more direct type.[3] In a sense we may speak of these adaptive reactions as indicators of the infant's growing intelligence; but as we shall see later, no one has yet managed to select from the manifold responses of the infant the particular ones which give unequivocal indications of the results to be expected from standard intelligence tests at a later age.

[2] Of course it is likely that even in these cases small adjustive movements that, if pressed, we should be forced to call "adaptive" are taking place, but they are so slight that for practical purposes we may ignore them.

[3] Some persons question whether verbal reports of these processes are more dependable than the evidences provided by observable motor actions. This is a moot question, but there can be no doubt that the verbal reports can be more conveniently handled and that there will be fewer disagreements in interpreting them.

ADAPTIVE RESPONSES OF THE INFANT TO
OTHER PEOPLE

In all forms of conditioned behavior, the process of learning is circular. The stimulus that arouses the organism is followed by a response that induces return sensations which in their turn act as new stimuli. Behavior is not a succession of isolated acts but a continuous series in which each element is at once a response to the preceding event and a stimulus for that which is to follow. It is therefore not surprising to find that those responses which induce intense and widespread stimulation of the organism bring about more rapid and clearly patterned modification of the child's responses than those which are faint and poorly localized.

For the young infant, nothing else in his environment fulfills these conditions so uniformly and completely as the human beings who minister to his daily needs. Spatially they are large objects upon which his uncertain gaze can focus without undue strain. They move about, intercepting the light and providing points of fixation for the eyes to follow. They make sounds of varying pitch and intensity. And most important of all, their presence is associated with most of the child's sensations of comfort and relief. They provide food when he is hungry, give warmth when he is cold. They ease his tired muscles, soothe his chafed skin, and quiet his wailing by tender caresses. Small wonder that his earliest adaptive responses are usually directed toward people rather than inanimate objects; that his earliest indications of "memory" have to do with people, that his eyes follow their movements so insistently that in experiments carried out with infants between the ages of two and six months [4] it is often found necessary to screen the experimenter from the infant's sight before any other stimulus can be made effective.

The baby's first reactions to human beings are positive. He watches them, smiles when they speak to him. It makes no difference, in the beginning, whether the voice is kindly or threatening,

---

[4] These ages are approximate. However very young infants have not yet had time to build up very distinct social reactions, and at a later age their developing ability to manipulate objects and consequent interest in them brings about a partial displacement of the early and all-consuming interest in persons.

whether the face smiles or frowns. All his associations with human beings are pleasant; he expects, we may say, nothing but kindness from them. But at about the age of five months his response to frowns and a threatening voice or gesture begins to be somewhat different from that shown to a smiling face and a friendly voice.[5] To the latter he continues to respond by smiling and approaching movements; but the threat or the frown is likely to cause withdrawal and in many cases crying. A little later, many children begin to reinterpret the threat as a form of play, and after a moment's hesitation respond once more by smiling and laughing.

Awareness of strangers appears at about the same time that the differentiated response to friendly and unfriendly voices can be observed. The baby is less responsive when a stranger appears; he sits quietly and stares without smiling. If the stranger approaches too near him or tries to take him in his arms, the baby draws back and perhaps begins to cry. In all this there are great differences between children, differences that it is often hard to account for purely on the basis of experience. It is very probable that hereditary tendencies are involved as well; tendencies that do not fix the behavior irrevocably, but that predispose some children to be unduly disturbed by unfamiliar and perhaps unskilled methods of handling and hence, all other things being equal, to be more easily "conditioned" against unfamiliar social contacts thereafter.

The very young infant is less likely to respond to other children than to adults, but this is probably because adults are larger and more active, because they are likely to make stronger attempts to attract his attention, and—perhaps most of all—because adults rather than children have ministered to his daily wants and have therefore become objects that have special and personal meaning for him. Bühler,[6] in a study of the social reactions of infants toward each other, reports that when two babies less than six months old are placed in the same crib facing each other they are likely to pay little attention to each other. If an infant

[5] C. H. Bühler and H. Hetzer, "Das erste Verständnis von Ausdruck im ersten Lebensjahr," Zsch. f. Psychol., 1928, 107: 50-61.

[6] C. Bühler, "Die ersten sozialen Verhaltungsweisen des Kindes," in Sociologische und psychologische Studien über das erste Lebensjahr (Jena, Gustav Fischer, 1925).

happens to meet another's look, he may smile as he would at an adult, but at this age babies do not make active advances toward each other. In the second half-year, however, the baby begins to make definite attempts to attract the other child's attention. He touches him, makes cooing sounds, and interferes with his activities. If the other baby does not respond he may go further. He squeals, pulls the other child's feet or clothing, snatches at his toys. Before the end of the first year, practically all the forms of social behavior seen in later life can be observed in embryonic form. There is domination of one child by another, leadership, rivalry, bullying, and submission. There is imitation, coöperation, generosity, and selfishness. There is the dog-in-the-manger child, who snatches all the other baby's toys but makes little attempt to play with them. There is the overgenerous child who proffers all that he has to the other.

Elsewhere Bühler describes three general types of social behavior that can be observed in children between the ages of six and eighteen months, as follows: [7]

(a) The *socially blind* infant behaves in the presence of another child as if nobody were present; he looks at the other without any emotion, he takes toys, plays and moves without any regard for the other child; he does not pay any attention to the other's movements; he is neither impressed nor interested in the other's presence or activities. (b) The *socially dependent*, on the contrary, is deeply impressed by the other's presence and activities; he can either be inhibited or else be stimulated by the other's presence. In the first case he will not move, will watch the other or copy him, will obey him, and sometimes even give signs of fear in front of him; in the second case, he will display in front of the other, will demonstrate objects and gestures, will try to rouse the other, and sometimes will even get enthusiastic and excited. In both cases all his movements are dependent on the presence of the other child; he observes the effect of his behavior on the other and carefully watches the other's reactions. (c) The third type is still different. The *socially independent* child is one who—though aware of the other's presence and responsive to his behavior—yet does not seem dependent on him, is neither intimidated nor inspired. He reacts to the other, wards him off when necessary, yet never becomes aggressive himself. He may or may not join the other in play, is not inconsiderate, but sometimes even consoles the

[7] Charlotte Bühler, "The Social Behavior of the Child," in *Handbook of Child Psychology*, Carl Murchison, ed. (Worcester, Clark University Press, 1931).

other, encourages him, takes part in his activities; yet, with all that, he remains independent in his movements; for instance, he may suddenly turn away and do something for himself.

All these types may be seen among older children and adults as well as in babies. Just how persistent they may be we do not know. Whether or not the baby who pays little attention to the people around him is more likely than others to develop into the "socially blind" adult who keeps to himself, lives for himself, and when thrown into the society of others makes all kinds of social blunders because of his insensitivity to the way his associates are reacting; whether or not the gregarious baby becomes the highly socialized man or woman, and the child who is socially independent in infancy continues to be able to get along with his companions or without them as circumstances seem to require are questions that the future must answer. Bühler tells us that the babies whom she studied behaved, on the whole, in much the same way on repeated trials at intervals of a few weeks or months, but that is not long enough to tell the whole story. Common sense as well as everyday observation, however, would lead us to think that in social matters as well as in other things such as health and physical development, the child who gets a good start early in life has an advantage over the one who does not.

Social training, then, does not begin when a child enters dancing-school or when he goes to kindergarten, or even when he begins to speak and is taught to say "thank you" and "if you please." Social habits have their starting point much further back. Their basic patterns are laid down in early infancy, before formal training begins, in the unremembered period before speech when impulses and attitudes are translated directly into action. The social behavior of the infant differs from that of the adult in many of its details, but its broad outlines foreshadow the form that it may later assume.

ADAPTATION TO THE PHYSICAL WORLD:
DISCRIMINATIVE BEHAVIOR IN THE INFANT

The child's preoccupation with sensory stimulation leads him to constant exploration of objects and their properties. Although the normal baby repeats the same sensori-motor activity over and over again, he soon begins to introduce variations into his play. He scratches the surface of objects with his nails and then shifts to patting them with his open hand or trying to get them into his mouth. He manipulates his own toes, hands, and ears, pulls at his clothing, drags himself to a stand by the aid of the bars of his crib. From the results of these manifold operations he soon begins to learn the laws by which his physical world as well as his social world is governed. The infant of six months at first reacts to practically every new object in much the same way. He reaches for it and if he succeeds in getting hold of it he manipulates it in various ways, fingering it, scratching it, hammering it, waving it in the air, dropping it, and picking it up again. The mouth as well as the fingers participate in this activity, regardless of whether or not the object actually goes into the mouth, for the lips and tongue are in almost constant movement and the increased flow of saliva often dribbles from the lips. The seemingly undiscriminating character of this behavior in which a shoe, a rattle, a wooden block, and an apple are received with equal apparent enthusiasm and are handled in as nearly identical fashion as the structure of the objects permits might lead one to wonder whether the infant, at this age, responds to the external characteristics of objects enough to make it possible for him to classify or assort them at all.

Ling [8] has provided us with a little information on this point. In her experiments, babies between the ages of six and twelve months were seated before a table on which were two (or more) bright yellow wooden blocks of different shape or size. The apparatus was so constructed that either of the blocks, regardless of its position, could be fastened to the table, thus making it impossible for the child to secure it. The other block could readily be picked up and handled. To make the stimulus of the "correct" block even stronger, before each trial it was first carefully sterilized and then dipped into a saccharine solution which made it taste sweet if put into the mouth. The purpose of the experiment was to find out whether infants as young as six months of age could learn to discriminate between two blocks of different

[8] Bing-chung Ling, "Form Discrimination as a Learning Cue in Infants," *Comp. Psychol. Monog.*, 1941, 17, Serial Number 86, p. 66.

shape, say a cross and a triangle or a circle and a square. After he had had time to find out that one of these blocks could not be budged from its place no matter how much tugging was applied, while the other could be easily secured and was pleasantly flavored as well, would a time come when the child would reach directly for the correct block and pay no attention to the wrong one, no matter what the relative position of the two might be?

This proved to be the case. The number of trials needed to establish the association varied greatly from child to child, as might be expected in view of what we know about individual differences. When the forms used were very different from each other, as a circle and a cross, fewer trials were required for the infants to make the discrimination; when they were more nearly similar, as a circle and an ellipse, more time was needed. (See Figure 48.)

There was evidence that the process of learning involved something more than just making the discrimination required at the moment. The *first* discrimination was always harder to learn than those that came later in the series, a fact which suggests that the babies were not merely learning particular discriminations but were learning to discriminate. Moreover, there were several children who showed evidence of a still higher type of generalizing process. These infants were first trained to select a circle and ignore a square. After this reaction had been thoroughly built up, the principle was suddenly reversed. Now it was the circle that could not be dislodged and the square that had become the motivating stimulus. For the greater number of the children, this was indeed bewildering. They continued to tug at the circle and frequently cried or became angry. Even after lucky accident had demonstrated that the despised square now had acquired all the virtues formedly possessed by the circle, they were slow to respond to the cue and would revert to the circle at frequent intervals long after the shift had been made But there were four of the eighteen infants with whom this experiment was tried who behaved very differently from the others. After a few preliminary assaults on the circle, the discovery would be made that the square could be easily dislodged. Unlike the other members of the group, these babies showed signs of surprise and interest in this fact. Whereas the other babies had handled the square only briefly and then renewed their attacks upon the circle, these children immediately shifted their attention to the square. They examined it at length, turning it over and over, occasionally bringing it to their mouths as if to verify the flavor. "From that time on," so says the author, "the facial expression relaxed, the fretful, bewildered vocalization was

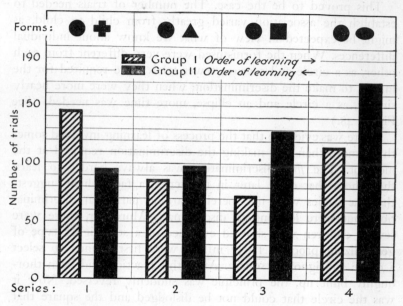

FIG. 48.—THE COMPARATIVE EFFECT OF INTRINSIC DIFFICULTY OF THE TASK AND THE AMOUNT OF PREVIOUS PRACTICE UPON PERCEPTUAL DISCRIMINATION BY INFANTS

(After Bing-chung Ling. The children in Group I learned to discriminate the forms in the order from easiest to most difficult. Those in Group II began with the most difficult and then progressed to the easier ones.)

promptly replaced by a cheerful and contented one and the infant seldom or never returned to the once highly motivated circle." The author regards this as affording some indication of the early stages of what the Gestalt psychologists call "insight" which means that the subject reacts to a new situation on the basis of some general principle (as "squareness" or "roundness") that enables him to make the correct response almost immediately without going through the slow and laborious process of learning by conditioning or by "trial and error." [9]

THE BEGINNINGS OF ''INSIGHT'' IN INFANCY

The ability to use tools is one of the marks that distinguishes man and to a lesser extent the monkey from animals below the level of the primates. Köhler, in his fascinating book on the behavior of apes,[10] describes many instances of tool-using and even of a primitive kind of tool construction in chimpanzees. When a banana was hung just beyond the reach of a hungry chimpanzee, he would bring boxes, pile them one upon another, and climb upon them in order to reach it, or he would get a stick and knock it down. Babies early learn to use pieces of furniture in the same way. Babies and apes alike find that sticks, spoons, or other objects can be used to pull objects toward them or to poke things out of crevices. (See Figure 49.) In using objects in this way they show, by their mistakes as well as by their successes, that they are responding to ideas about objects and not to objects as such. The ape who uses a stick to knock down a suspended banana may try to do so with a bit of straw if no stick is handy; the baby gets many a bump from his attempts to use a rocking-chair or other unstable object as a highway to the cookie-jar.

These are simple matters, yet they signify an enormous advance in power of thought over that indicated by the direct bodily attack which is the only method of problem-solving that animals below the level of the primates are likely to display. The dog, the horse, and the rat will starve with food hanging within their sight, no matter how many objects are available that could be used as stepping-stones and that are quite within their power to move. To be sure, the development of the hand as an instrument

[9] Learning by "trial and error" is not greatly different from learning by conditioning except that the former term is usually confined to learning some kind of means-end relationship, whereas in the latter instance the substitute stimulus that becomes sufficient to evoke the response may and sometimes is basically unrelated to the unconditioned stimulus that serves as the goal. Usually, too, the term "trial and error" is used only with respect to behavior carried on at a higher level than that of a simple reflex.

[10] W. Köhler, *The Mentality of Apes* (New York, Harcourt, Brace and Co., 1925).

for grasping and holding makes it simpler for the child or the monkey to use tools than it is for the horse or the dog to do so, but this cannot entirely account for the difference.

FIG. 49.—CHIMPANZEE FITTING TWO STICKS TOGETHER TO MAKE A LONGER ONE WHICH HE CAN USE TO OBTAIN FOOD

(After Köhler from *Great Experiments in Psychology* by H. E. Garrett. D. Appleton-Century Co.)

Evidence that "insight" is a more advanced type of mental performance than is simple associative learning comes not only from the fact that its manifestations are almost wholly confined to man and a few of the higher animals. Insight depends on the ability to make abstractions [11] and this, in its turn depends upon memory, discrimination, judgment—in short upon all the various mental processes that we often lump together under the heading of "general intelligence." It would appear from the evidence thus

[11] See pp. 358-359.

far given that even before he has learned to express his ideas in words, the infant shows clear signs of at least a simple level of abstract thinking. And there is further evidence that babies differ in respect to their ability to think and reason quite as markedly as they do in the size of their bodies or the quality of their motor performances. All this has led to a continued effort to develop some means by which infant intelligence can be measured in objective terms as we are now able to do with older children and adults. How far these efforts have succeeded will be shown in the next section.

THE MEASUREMENT OF INTELLIGENCE IN INFANCY

The first formal series of intelligence tests for infants was devised by Kuhlmann in 1922.[12] In 1925, as the result of long and very careful study of the behavior of infants and young children, Gesell [13] published a series of developmental norms for successive age levels beginning with the age of four months. This was followed by a second and revised series [14] for the earlier ages in which the developmental standards were carried downward to the one-month level. A third version of these tests has recently been published.[15] Bayley [16] developed a series of tests for the first year of life in connection with a long-term study of a group of California children, and at the Catholic University of America Linfert and Hierholzer [17] worked out a somewhat

---

[12] F. Kuhlmann, *A Handbook of Mental Tests* (Baltimore, Warwick and York, 1922), pp. vi + 208.

[13] Anold Gesell, *The Mental Growth of the Preschool Child; A Psychological Outline of Normal Development from Birth to the Sixth Year, Including a System of Developmental Diagnosis* (New York, Macmillan Co., 1925), pp. x + 447.

[14] Arnold Gesell, *Infancy and Human Growth* (New York, Macmillan Co., 1928), pp. xvii + 418.

[15] Arnold Gesell, H. M. Halverson, *et al., The First Five Years of Life: The Preschool Years* (New York, Harper and Bros., 1940), pp. xii + 393.

[16] Nancy Bayley, *The California First-Year Mental Scale* (Berkeley, Calif., University of California Press, 1933), pp. 24

[17] Harriette-Elsie Linfert and Helen H. Hierholzer, "A Scale for Measuring the Mental Development of Infants During the First Year of Life," *Studies in Psychology and Psychiatry from the Catholic University of America*, 1928, Vol. 1, No. 4, pp. 33.

similar device for the same age-range. In Vienna, Bühler [18] made up a scale for use with Viennese children which has been translated into English and used in a number of studies of infant development in this country. A few of the items from this scale are reproduced below in order to give you a more concrete idea of the kind of acts that psychologists have thought to be diagnostic of "intelligence" in the young infant. The age given for each is that at which the average child will usually pass the item. Bright children will pass many of the items at an earlier age than that indicated; backward children may not be able to do so until a later age.

Age in Months	Test Item
1	Turns head when touched (feeding reaction)
2	Turns head and eyes to look around when being carried
6	Distinguishes between bottle and rubber doll
9	Uncovers a hidden toy
12	Pulls self to a standing position with support
15	Obeys simple commands
18	Inhibits action in response to "No, no."

The most recently devised test for infants was developed by Psyche Cattell.[19] It is intended as a downward extension of the 1937 Revision of the Stanford Binet Scale [20] which will be described in a later chapter. In many ways this test "looks" more promising than many of its predecessors but so far no reports as to its value for predicting the mental level of children at later ages have appeared in the literature.

Much time and thought has been spent in these attempts to develop a useful measuring instrument that would enable us to go beyond the level of description in our attempts to study mental progress during the period of infancy. Such a measuring device (if we had it) would be of great practical service as well as an important tool for scientific research. Even as matters now stand, the time spent in developing these tests has by no means

[18] Charlotte Bühler, *Testing Children's Development from Birth to School Age*, tr. by Henry Beaumont (New York, Farrar and Rinehart, 1935), pp. 191.

[19] Psyche Cattell, *The Measurement of the Intelligence of Infants and Young Children* (New York, Psychological Corp., 1940), pp. 274.

[20] See pp. 376-378.

been wasted, for they have provided us with a far more exact account of the course of behavioral development in infancy than we should otherwise be likely to have secured. And by the application of these tests we can make much more precise statements about the present developmental level of an individual baby than would be possible by any other means. But the infant tests have thus far failed to justify one important assumption that we commonly associate with intelligence tests as they are used with older

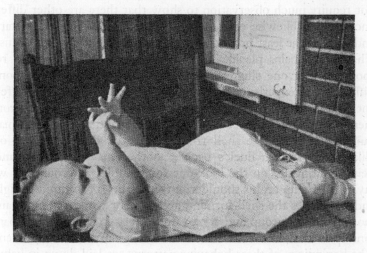

FIG. 50.—AN INFANT OF THREE MONTHS DISCOVERS HIS FINGERS

This is one of the items in the Cattell series of infant intelligence tests. (Reproduced by courtesy of Dr. Psyche Cattell.)

children. *We cannot predict a child's later intellectual standing on the basis of tests given in infancy.* The relationship between the mental test scores earned before the beginning of speech and those earned by the same children during the nursery-school and elementary-school periods have been studied by a number of investigators, all of whom have obtained closely similar results. The "bright" infant who does exceptionally well on these tests is no more likely to do well on the tests given later than is the one whose performace when a baby is poor, nor is he any more likely to be thought to be exceptionally bright by his teachers. Tests for infants tell us a good deal about what an individual child is like now; but nothing of what he may be.

INDIVIDUAL DIFFERENCES AMONG INFANTS

Thus far we have emphasized the points of similarity among children rather than the differences between them. But children differ even at birth; and as age advances these differences become more easily seen. With their differences in size, features, and coloring we are all familiar. We know, too, that some babies are strong and healthy from the start and that others are sickly. But it does not require much observation to show that there are other differences which likewise exist from the beginning. This baby starts and cries at the least provocation or even without apparent cause. That one remains placid. This one is active, energetic, and responsive, that one sluggish. And as babies grow, they respond differently to experience and training. If several children of different emotional and personality make-ups are placed in an environment where annoyances are unusually frequent, one of them may build up a protective shell from which the difficulties roll off "like water from a duck's back"; another may fight back and, being continually on the look-out for trouble, go around, as we say, with a chip on his shoulder; a third who is too timid to fight and who lacks the shell-forming ability may withdraw more and more from the group and try to find safety in solitude, companionship in day-dreams, satisfaction in imaginary accomplishment. The beginnings of these behavior patterns are laid down in babyhood, but too often they remain unrecognized until the habits have been so well formed that it is hard to change them. Or if a child, no matter what his original disposition may be, is reared in a situation where he is overprotected, overindulged, where the give-and-take of normal childhood intercourse is denied him, his behavior will tend to conform to the kind of education that is given it. As long as the pattern of education remains the same, as long as new kinds of demands do not occur, all seems to go on well, but changes must come as the child grows older. They will be met more easily if they are not too great, if even in babyhood the child has begun to learn the habits of social conformity and social coöperation that he will be called upon to practise later on.

Babies differ. They differ in abilities of all kinds—in intelligence, in social adaptability, in tenacity of purpose, in emotional control.

Their experiences differ. One is indulged, another is unduly repressed; one is permitted and encouraged to find out all that he safely can concerning the things about him. He investigates the qualities of sand, the anatomy of grass and flowers, the behavior of bugs and beetles. He learns to go up and down stairs without being carried and rightly considers that the knowledge has been cheaply gained at the price of a tumble or two. Another is surrounded by a barrier of "don't's" and "mustn't's." One child finds the adults about him behaving in a consistent fashion that gives him the beginning of insight into social relationships and lays the foundation for a feeling of confidence in the reactions of others. He knows what is likely to happen and is able to adjust to it. His social world as well as the world of nature seems to behave in a reasonable fashion that he can learn to understand, that he is not afraid to grapple with and try to control. Another is unexpectedly kissed, slapped, laughed at, played with, indulged, repressed, praised, and scolded according to no apparent principle or rule.

Out of all these differing abilities and experiences, behavior is shaped.

CAN AN APE BE MADE TO BEHAVE LIKE A HUMAN BEING?

W. N. Kellogg and L. A. Kellogg. *The Ape and the Child: a Study of Environmental Influence upon Early Behavior* (New York, Whittlesey House, 1933), pp. 341.

In common with many other people you may sometimes have wondered how far the behavior of the higher animals could be modified if they were reared as human babies are reared. Here you have an account of an actual experiment of this kind. A psychologist and his wife temporarily "adopted" a young chimpazee, seven and one half months old, as a companion to their little son who was then ten months old. During the nine months that the experiment was continued, the two infants were constant playmates and received exactly the same kind of treatment. They were dressed alike, ate at the same table with similar utensils, and as far as was deemed advisable they were given the same food. They slept in the same room in similar cribs, were bathed in the same manner and each was petted and caressed, punished and rewarded according to the same rules. A certain amount of time each week was devoted by the authors to a series of formal tests and experiments which were carried out with both children, in order that their performances might be compared. In addition, careful records of their everyday behavior were made and many photographs were secured, a number of which are reproduced in this book.

It is unfortunate that the experiment had to be brought to a close so soon, because of the strong attachment that developed between the two children, for the results as they stand are less conclusive than they might otherwise have been. Nevertheless the study is an important one which you will find both interesting and instructive. It is suggested that in reading it you maintain a critical point of view and when you have finished, ask yourself these questions: (1) In what respects might the procedure have been improved? (2) What facts and principles that the study was potentially capable of yielding remain undetermined? (3) What are its main contributions?

Chapter XI

THE BEGINNINGS OF SPEECH

What is the difference between vocal sound and speech? What organs are chiefly concerned in the production of vocal sound? What additional organs are brought into play in the production of speech?

Does a child when first learning to talk make use of the same mental processes which an older person employs when learning a foreign language? If not, in what respects does their manner of learning differ?

What is meant by the "period of the single-word sentence" and why is it so called? What is meant by the term trick *vocabulary?*

What part does the jargon of infancy play in facilitating the development of true speech?

What are some of the theories proposed to account for the acquisition of speech by primitive man?

How does the study of the language of twins help us to understand the social factors in language development?

What are some of the factors likely to cause retardation in language development?

If you wished to stimulate a child's progress in language as much as possible, at what age would you begin and what methods would you employ?

271

THE SPEECH MECHANISMS

Among the parts of the body chiefly involved in the production of vocal sounds we refer first to the diaphragm, the lungs, and the muscles of the thorax that coöperate in the act of breathing whereby air is forced up the windpipe and over the vocal cords in the *larynx* or "Adam's apple." The larynx is the prominent movable lump which can easily be seen about the middle of the front part of the neck in men and in boys who have attained maturity. In women and children the larynx is less prominent but can still be felt by passing the fingers over the corresponding part of the neck. The vocal cords are two membranes stretched across the inside of the larynx in such a manner that air must pass between them in the process of breathing. They are separated by an opening called the *glottis*. The membrane of which the vocal cords are composed is highly resilient. Their state of contraction or expansion is controlled by means of a complex series of muscles which likewise regulate the size of the glottis. When the muscles are relaxed and the glottis is consequently wide open, air passes through the glottis without producing sound. When the muscles are contracted, the vocal cords more tightly stretched, the glottis is reduced to a narrower slit, and the passage of air forces the cords to vibrate, giving rise to waves or vibrations in the air as it passes out of the mouth. Thus vocal sounds are produced. The quality, intensity, and pitch of the tones vary with a number of factors such as the degree of tension of the vocal cords, the size of the opening between them, the length of the cords, and the condition of the resonators provided by the cavities in the chest, throat, nose, mouth, and the bones of the head. Because the larynx is relatively small and the vocal cords short in women and children, their voices are typically high in pitch. The change of voice so noticeable in boys after they arrive at puberty results from the rapid increase in the size of the larynx and the consequent lengthening of the vocal cords that occurs at that time.

Speech consists of interrupting and otherwise modifying the sound waves as they pass through the nose and mouth by intricate movements of the tongue, lips, teeth, and soft palate. The movements necessary for the production of comprehensible speech involve such extraordinarily fine coördination of these muscles, such precise timing [1] and delicate adaptation of the extent and force of the muscular movements, that the wonder is not that disturbances of speech sometimes occur but rather that they are not more frequent. Nor is it remarkable that the infant must spend a year or more of intensive practice in gaining enough control of the speech mechanisms to permit the utterance of even a few imperfectly articulated words. The marvel is that he begins so soon.

THE VOCALIZATIONS OF INFANCY

The first vocal reaction of the new-born infant is the "birth cry" which accompanies the passage of air over the vocal cords in the larynx as the lungs are expanded for the first time. Crying, as a spontaneous response to physical discomfort of any kind, occurs from birth onward. Even during the first week of life, individual differences can be observed among babies both in respect to the amount of time spent in crying and in the volume and timbre of their cries.

The cries of the very young infant are almost wholly laryngeal, slightly if at all modified by the organs of speech. During the first few days of life vocalization other than crying is rare, but by the age of two weeks or even earlier, occasional low grunts and cooing sounds are uttered. These increase very rapidly in number and variety. The first sounds have been described by

[1] A fluent speaker will utter, on the average, from 300 to 350 words per minute; an exceptionally rapid speaker may run as high as 500 words per minute. The number of movements involved in the production of these sounds cannot easily be calculated, but a conservative estimate would put the figure at not fewer than 1,000 per minute. Let the reader repeat to himself the time-honored sentence "The big black fox jumped over the lazy dog," observing the number and kind of motor coördinations that must be made both successively and in combination with each other and how careful the timing must be if the sentence is to run off smoothly and easily, and he will gain a limited appreciation of the complexity of the speech process. There is also the adjustment of the voice-producing mechanism to be considered, the changes in pitch, intensity, resonance, and rhythm that lend expressive quality to what is said.

Shirley [2] as "vocal grunts" frequently with some nasal involvement resulting in sounds that may be indicated phonetically as *ug, ng,* or *ungh.* Soon afterward, vowel sounds appear, at first as single syllables often long drawn out such as *ah-h-h, oo-o-o,* and later as reduplicated syllables, *ah-ah-ah.* Consonants are soon added to the child's repertoire. There is not entire agreement among observers as to which consonants usually appear first, a fact that is in all probability as much due to the difficulty of distinguishing and recording the sounds phonetically as to differences in the true order of the appearance of these sounds in different children. For the young child is polyglot. There is good evidence that during the period before true speech occurs, the normal infant at one time or another utters all the sounds used in human language. The French nasals, the German gutturals, the Hottentot "click"—all the linguistic peculiarities of primitive and civilized nations alike can be distinguished in the untutored babblings of the growing infant.

Although there is not complete agreement as to the details, certain broad features in the developmental sequence of infant vocalization have been fairly well delimited. The single syllables of the young infant are followed at first by reduplication of the same syllable. The syllables uttered rapidly take on variety both by the addition of a greater number of consonantal and vowel sounds and by uniting these sounds into new combinations. This ushers in a period during which the normal child spends a large share of his waking hours in a kind of vocal play that the Germans call "Lallung." Lying in his crib, the infant repeats over and over again, "da-da-da-da" or "ngee-ngee-ngee," occasionally varying his performance by changes in tonal inflection or volume of sounds, or by suddenly shifting to some other type of oral activity such as forcible expulsion of frothy saliva from his lips— "blowing bubbles"—or shifting to a new sound-pattern. At first the child seems to carry on these vocal experiments purely for his own amusement, and if we can imagine the case of a child brought up by some kind of totally unresponsive machine, it is

[2] Mary Shirley, *The First Two Years: A Study of Twenty-five Babies,* Vol. II, *Intellectual Development,* Institute of Child Welfare Monograph Series, No. 7 (Minneapolis, University of Minnesota Press, 1933), pp. xvi + 513.

unlikely that they would ever serve any other purpose. But children are not reared by machines but by human beings who respond to their activities in ways that are highly satisfying to the infant. Before long, therefore, the child's vocalizations are no longer wholly self-centered. They become socialized. Shirley has designated this as the third stage in the infant's progress toward speech. The infant now begins to squeal or shout at the approach of a familiar person and to utter responsive gurglings and coos when played with or talked to by some one accustomed to doing so. (See Figure 51.)

The fourth stage begins when the simple reduplication of the same syllable is elaborated by the combination of two or more different syllables to form a more highly organized "word." From his simple "da-da-da," the child progresses to "daddle-daddle-daddle" and to "daddle-ee-oog-ee-ug-ug-uggle," with increasingly varied syllabification and such "expressive" tonal inflection that it often sounds amusingly like true speech.

FIG. 51.—A FOUR-MONTHS-OLD BABY GREETS HIS FATHER

This "expressive jargon," as Gesell, who has given the most complete account of its development, has christened it, usually begins during the second half of the first year and reaches its height early in the second year, when it overlaps with and is gradually replaced by actual speech. Children differ greatly both in the length of time for which this jargon-period persists and in the extent to which the sounds and their inflection are elaborated. A little girl of my acquaintance chattered away so incessantly with so natural an inflection and such a wide variety of different sounds that her hearers almost invariably remarked, "She sounds exactly as if she were speaking a foreign language." In her "conversations" some syllables were stressed, others slurred over; there were rising inflections as in questioning, and falling inflections that sounded like a response. There were pauses as if concluding a sentence, staccato phrases like commands, and short, strongly emphasized sounds indicative of emotional stress that her father insisted were "swear-words."

THE ORIGIN OF SPEECH IN THE INDIVIDUAL

The question arises, By what process does this jargon of sounds develop into comprehensible and meaningful speech? Up to this point, progress seems to have been largely due to the increased neuromuscular motility that goes along with the maturation of the organism, and the consequent increasing variety of sounds brought about more or less fortuitously as vocalization happens to coincide with differing positions of the lips, tongue and soft palate. Add to this the fact that the child hears and is apparently interested in the sounds that he makes, and learns to reproduce them and to vary them by a gradual association of kinaesthetic sensations in the vocal organs with the sounds heard, and we have one side of the mechanism by which progress from the babblings of the infant to fully developed speech may be accomplished. It shows, that is, how the child's repertoire of speech sounds becomes elaborated, but it does not show how these sounds are brought into conformity with the language patterns of other people. It shows how the child learns to "jabber," but it does not show how he learns to speak.

People formerly thought that formal speech is acquired by a more or less conscious process of imitation. It was taken for granted that children learn to talk in much the same manner as older persons learn a new language, by listening to the sounds made by others and trying to imitate them. But few psychologists now believe that imitation, in this sense, plays a very important rôle in the early stages of speech. According to modern theory, the elements of speech, the vowels and consonants and short syllables, are not learned by imitation at all. They develop spontaneously in the course of the child's vocal play. What is learned by imitation is not the mechanical formation of sounds but the *selection* of certain sound-combinations from the rich variety of elementary sound-forms that the child has "taught himself" to pronounce and the *application* of these sound-combinations to the particular situations in which he has heard them used by others. So the incomprehensible babbling of the younger child passes over into true speech, not so much by a process of extension as by one of limitation.

Formerly the sight of his well-loved kitty called forth an unassorted jumble of vowels and consonants in all sorts of combinations. One day, perhaps quite by chance, the *k* sound is made. His mother hears it and exclaims in delight. "Just hear him! He's trying to call his kitty!" She repeats the word, "Kitty, kitty!" perhaps picking up the kitten and carrying it to the child as she does so. Now the child does not have to *learn* how to pronounce the sound of *k*. He knows that already; he has been doing it in play for some time. What he has to learn is to use the *k* sound in connection with the "kitty" situation and refrain from using the *g*'s and *s*'s and *m*'s and *p*'s that were a part of his former response. So when the mother selects this sound out of all the rest and holds it up, as it were, for admiration, repeats it, and praises and caresses him for having said it, perhaps crowns the occasion by capturing and presenting him with the elusive kitten that he has been vainly pursuing for some time, all these pleasant experiences operate to bring about a closer connection between the sight of the flesh-and-blood kitty and the utterance of the *k* or, as it soon becomes, the *kee-ee* sound.[3] This may have to be repeated many times, but sooner or later, as a result of repeated experience in this and similar situations, the great idea dawns. *There is some kind of sound that is the key to every situation. When one utters the right sound, other people obey one's will.* We cannot suppose that the child of sixteen or eighteen months formulates the idea as clearly as this, yet that some sort of generalizing process has

---

[3] In the beginning the child commonly uses initial consonants only. Later on final consonants are added, and still later consonants in the middle of words appear. The first words are usually monosyllables, reduplicated monosyllables such as "pa-pa" or "bow-wow," or monosyllables with a single vowel syllable appended, such as "dog-ee," "ta-ah" (tail), "tab-oo" (table).

taken place in his mind and that this idea has come to him rather suddenly seems evident from the marked change in his behavior that takes place within the short space of a few days.

This association of word with object which marks the beginning of true language is a very different matter from the mere repetition of words to win social approval—an art that most babies acquire to some extent at an earlier stage of development. As was pointed out in an earlier chapter, infants begin to respond to social stimuli, on the average, by the time they are a few weeks old, and it is not long before they begin to make definite attempts to secure the attention of others for the sake of social satisfaction alone, even when there is no bodily need that requires attention. Before the end of the first half-year, the normal baby has become a definitely socialized creature. Most babies, by that time, have learned the important lesson that by the exercise of various little tricks and wiles they can often gain adult attention and fondling that is not to be had so readily by any other means. So when by chance, in the course of his babbling, the reduplicated syllable *ma-ma* happens to be made, and the mother responds by praising and fondling the child and by repeatedly urging him on this and other occasions to "say ma-ma" the child eventually connects the request with the motor performance and becomes able to repeat the sound on demand. The process of acquiring new words in this way is a slow one because the discrimination demanded is fine and the child's learning is still at an early stage. The stimuli to which he must respond are simply vocal sounds— "ma-ma," "daddy," "bow-wow"—and the response serves no other purpose than that of winning social approval which can often be gained by other and less arduous means. This stage in the development of speech overlaps with the later stages of the "jargon period." Early in the second year, most children learn to say a few words of this kind, which, because they serve no purpose beyond that of a social trick which the child uses to win the approval of adults, are often referred to as the child's "trick vocabulary." A period of at least two or three months commonly elapses between the acquisition of the first "word-trick" and the beginning of active speech. During this time new words are acquired slowly and the child's attitude toward their acquisition is one of distinct indifference. Since the pronunciation of any word in his small repertoire is received with acclaim, why should he go to the bother of learning new ones? But with the discovery that speech is not merely a parlor trick but can be used to control the world in hitherto unsuspected ways, the picture changes. Now he has become the active seeker after words. He learns that everything has a name. "What's that?" "Who's that?" is his constant demand. No longer need he be urged to show off his verbal accomplishments. He practises them on all occasions. "Baby!" "Doggie!" "Car!" he calls out in delighted recognition when he is taken out for a walk or as he turns the pages of his picture book. Now his vocabulary grows apace, and as it grows his sentences expand in length and complexity. In his first use of language the single word is made to serve the purpose of an entire sentence; it is at once subject, predicate, and object—a question, a command, or a statement. "Milk!" calls the baby as he hammers the table with his cup. This is the infantile equivalent of "I want some milk" or "Give me some milk." "Milk," he announces with satisfaction as he sees the arrival of the milkman. This time he is giving information. "Milk?" he inquires with rising inflection as he points to the picture of a bottle in the morning paper. So characteristic is this stage in the development of language that many writers have referred to it as the "period of the single-word sentence."

LINGUISTIC PROGRESS IN EARLY CHILDHOOD

Figure 52 shows the average number of words in fifty consecutive remarks recorded by McCarthy [4] for twenty children at each of the following ages: eighteen, twenty-four, thirty, thirty-six, forty-two, forty-eight, and fifty-four months. Table I shows the average size of vocabulary at successive ages from eight months (at which age few children can say any words) up to six years as reported by Smith. [5] The sudden and marked change in the average number of new words added to the vocabulary in the course of a single month that occurs at about the age of eighteen

[4] Dorothea McCarthy, *The Language Development of the Preschool Child* (Minneapolis, University of Minnesota Press, 1930).

[5] Madorah Smith, "An Investigation of the Development of the Sentence and the Extent of Vocabulary in Young Children," *University of Iowa Studies in Child Welfare*, 1926, Vol. 3, No. 5.

TABLE I

AVERAGE SIZE OF VOCABULARIES OF 273 CHILDREN FROM EIGHT MONTHS
TO SIX YEARS OF AGE *

Age in Years and Months	Number of Children	Average Vocabulary	
		Number of Words	Average Gain per Month
0-8	13	0	—
0-10	17	1	0.5
1-0	52	3	1.0
1-3	19	19	5.3
1-6	14	22	1.0
1-9	14	118	32.0
2-0	25	272	51.3
2-6	14	446	29.0
3-0	20	896	75.0
3-6	26	1,222	54.3
4-0	26	1,540	53.0
4-6	32	1,870	55.0
5-0	20	2,072	33.7
5-6	27	2,289	36.2
6-0	9	2,562	45.5

* Adapted from Smith.

months is a striking illustration of the effect of the shift from the
passive attitude toward words that is characteristic of babies who
are still in the period of the "trick vocabulary" to the active interest in word-learning that suddenly appears when language becomes a tool.

As children grow older their language changes in other ways.
Nouns and interjections form a smaller proportion of the total.
Pronouns, verbs, adjectives, conjunctions, and prepositions in-
crease in frequency. Table II shows the proportion of the differ-

TABLE II

PERCENTAGES OF THE DIFFERENT PARTS OF SPEECH USED BY YOUNG
CHILDREN

Age in Months	Nouns	Verbs	Adjectives	Adverbs	Pronouns	Conjunctions	Prepositions	Interjections	Unclassified
18	50.0	13.9	9.6	7.9	10.3	0.5	0.0	7.6	0.0
36	23.4	23.0	16.1	7.0	19.2	2.4	6.9	1.5	0.5
54	19.3	25.1	15.2	7.0	20.5	3.8	7.1	1.2	0.8

ent parts of speech at three different ages as found by McCarthy.[6] However, the conventional classification of words into parts of speech which is based upon the language usage of adults is not entirely appropriate to the speech of children who have as yet not developed far beyond the stage of the single-word sentence.

Moreover, the relative frequency with which certain parts of speech are used by children at play with other children differs markedly from that observed in conversation with an adult. McCarthy[7] has shown that many more interjections are used in the former situation than in the latter, while Goodenough[8] finds that the proportionate use of pronouns of the first person singular during play with other children is almost twice as great as it is when engaged in conversation with an adult. This is understandable enough when one stops to

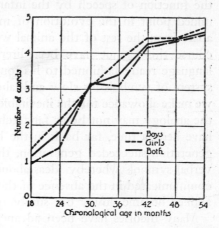

FIG. 52.—CHANGES IN AVERAGE LENGTH OF SENTENCE WITH AGE

(From *Language Development of the Preschool Child*, by Dorothea Mc-Carthy. Courtesy University of Minnesota Press.)

think that it is in the former rather than the latter situation that the child finds the greater need to assert himself as an individual.

THEORIES ABOUT THE ORIGIN OF LANGUAGE IN THE RACE

The question of how man first acquired a language has awakened the curiosity of scientists for generations. In no other aspect of his behavior is the difference between man and animal so

[6] *Op. cit.*

[7] Dorothea McCarthy, "A Comparison of Children's Language in Different Situations and Its Relation to Personality Traits," *J. Genet. Psychol.*, 1929, 36: 583-591.

[8] Florence L. Goodenough, "The Use of Pronouns by Young Children: A Note on the Development of Self-Awareness," *J. Genet. Psychol.*, 1938, 52: 333-346.

apparent, for while it is true that animals have certain crude methods of communicating with each other,[9] even the most primitive of the races of man known to us to-day have advanced far beyond the most highly developed animal in command of speech. It almost seems as if something analogous to the "discovery" of the function of speech by the infant occurred at some undetermined point in the evolution of man, a discovery that set him apart from the rest of the animal world for all time to come. Of course this cannot have been literally true. The child finds a language ready fashioned to his tongue; man had to build up his system of symbols by slow and laborious stages. Nevertheless, if we make allowance for the inevitable difference in the time factor, the analogy may not be as far-fetched as it seems for there must have been a time, far back in the history of mankind, when, as generation succeeded generation, the advantages of a system of verbal symbols whereby ideas about objects and events could be communicated in the absence of the material facts to which they applied became slowly but surely apparent.

Many theories have been advanced to account for the origin of language in the human race. Because among the lower animals the chief purpose of vocalization seems to be the expression and communication of emotional states, as well as because interjections constitute a much greater percentage of the total number of words used by young children than of the number used by older children or adults, some anthropologists have taken the interjection to be the most primitive type of word form and have ascribed the origin of language to a gradual differentiation among vocal symbols in order to convey more exact shades of meaning in the expression of emotion. This is known as the "interjectional theory" of the origin of language.

Another theory, known as the "onomatopoeic theory" is concerned particularly with the question of how words acquired their particular forms. Those who advocate this theory point to the fact that even in the languages of groups of widely sepa-

[9] In his *Pilgrim's Progress*, Bunyan gives the following quaint description of the "language" of the hen:
"So they gave heed and perceived that the Hen did walk in a fourfold Method toward her Chickens. 1. She had a *common call* and that she hath all day long. 2. She had a *special call* and that she had but sometimes. 3. She had a *brooding note* and 4. She had an *outcry*."

rated geographic and ethnic background, there is greater than chance resemblance in the form of certain words, particularly those having to do with natural phenomena. "Thunder," "tonnerre," and "Donner" are all quite similar in sound, and all carry a certain quality of resonance that by the exercise of a moderate degree of imagination may be thought to suggest the sound of thunder. The fact that what seems like the same idea is in other instances expressed by very dissimilar words in different languages is explained by saying that few of the facts of nature are simple and that the particular words selected to convey a particular meaning may owe their origin to quite different aspects of the thing each has been chosen to symbolize. Moreover, inasmuch as languages have changed so greatly, even within the brief period over which our written history extends, it is not to be expected that its present form should show more than occasional faint traces of the seeds from which it grew. The onomatopoeic theory thus assumes that language arose through the playful attempts of primitive man to imitate the sounds of natural phenomena as children often do to-day. As one member of the tribe began to imitate a particular sound, others joined in and in so doing were influenced, not only by the sound originally heard, but also by the attempts at reproducing it made by each other. Thus the sounds made would, in the course of time, crystallize into a comparatively uniform pattern that by common consent would be accepted as the "right" way to make the sound of thunder, of running water, of wind in the trees, of the hum of bees or the cry of a particular animal. From this simple beginning, two things would almost inevitably follow. First, people would begin to make these sounds on occasions when the thing imitated was not actually present and when this occurred, others who had learned to make the same kind of reproduction would know what the sound made by his neighbor represented. Thus a new kind of communication would be established between them. Various uses for this verbal relationship would soon become apparent. It could convey a warning or serve as a reminder. The cave-woman could make the "bear sound" when her husband started out for his daily hunt to remind him of what he was expected to bring home for dinner; the "thunder sound" would convey warning of an approaching storm. Secondly, the word forms thus established would be passed on to succeeding generations as children learned to copy the "speech" of their elders. Each new generation would add new forms to the list. Once the process of symbolization has begun, its continuance is well-nigh assured. The weak point in the onomatopoeic theory is its basic premise. We have no evidence that before his development of speech, primitive man felt any more urge to imitate the sounds of nature than is now evinced by the most intelligent of our domestic animals or by the anthropoid apes.

Whatever may have been the mode by which speech first came into being, every situation carries within itself the soil from which the growth of language is nourished. Each new situation demands a new word or phrase by which it may be fixed in memory; and the more apt the phraseology, the more completely the experience can be exploited to the advantage of the individual and of society. If two persons with equally acute hearing attempt to describe a tone that both have heard, the one who has had musical training can do so better than the other who has no knowledge of musical terms. The physician can give a better description of the symptoms shown by a sick person than can the layman, not only because he knows what to look for but also because he has acquired a vocabulary that enables him to express the results of his observations in precise rather than general terms. So the child, as he grows older and is subjected to an ever-widening range of experiences, is continually forced to revise and improve the symbols of these experiences that he carries with him as guides for the future. Whether, as many believe, thought is nothing more than subvocal speech [10] is uncertain, but no one can seriously ques-

---

[10] The identification of thought with suppressed language is often attributed to J. B. Watson. However, the idea did not originate with him. Many of the older philosophers—J. S. Mill, Max Müller, Hegel, Leibnitz, Bain, and others—had expressed a similar belief. Dashiell, in his *Fundamentals of General Psychology* (p. 569) points out that all of these men belonged to the learned professions, had been stimulated in large part by reading, and found their outlet in writing. That is to say, they were all highly verbalistic in type. He raises the question whether their modes of thought are identical with those of manual workers such as the skilled cabinet maker or pipe-fitter; with the deaf-mute, or with the professional boxer. He points out that symbolism may be carried out through the agency of any part of the body. Gestures are often quite as symbolic as speech, and to the person whose daily activities are largely of a manual or motor character, "thinking" may perhaps be accomplished as readily, by a nascent movement of the part of the body accustomed to carry out an act of skill

tion the fact that most, if not all, of our thinking is carried on in verbal terms, and that the use of language greatly increases the precision and clarity of thought.

FACTORS INFLUENCING THE DEVELOPMENT OF LANGUAGE IN CHILDREN

The talkativeness of the female sex has formed one of the chief stand-bys of the comic papers for generations. Like many other stock jokes, it has some foundation in fact. Nearly all investigators have found that on the average girl babies begin to talk a little earlier than do boys, that their vocabularies at any age are a little larger, and that they use longer sentences. McCarthy found that at the age of eighteen months 14 per cent of the boys' remarks and 38 per cent of those made by the girls were comprehensible to a stranger. At twenty-four months the proportions of comprehensible responses were 49 per cent for the boys and 78 per cent for the girls. In every aspect of language development that has been studied, girls seem on the average to be a little more precocious than boys. (See Figure 52.)

Language development is closely related to general intelligence or "brightness." Studies of bright, average, and dull children have universally shown that the brighter children begin to talk at an earlier age than those who are backward; their vocabularies increase faster; as a rule their articulation is better; and they use longer and more correct sentences. Indeed, the quality of a child's speech is one of the chief things by which we are guided in judging his intelligence.

Social class is also related to language development. Not only do children from cultured homes speak more correctly than those from the lower social classes but their speech is more advanced in other ways. As will be shown later, they also rank higher on intelligence tests, but the intellectual difference between social classes is smaller than the difference in language development. Environment as well as intelligence probably has something to do with it. Figure 53 shows the extent to which children from different

---

as by subvocal speech. Nevertheless Dashiell agrees that for most people at least, "the speech mechanisms are the thinking mechanisms *par excellence*."

social classes differ in respect to average length of sentence. In this figure, Group I represents children whose fathers belong to the professional classes—doctors, lawyers, college professors, and so on. Group II is made up of the children of business men. Group

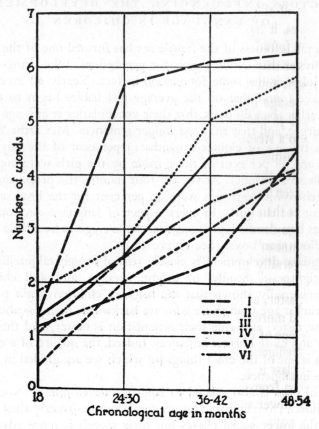

FIG. 53.—RELATIONSHIP BETWEEN PATERNAL OCCUPATION AND AVERAGE LENGTH OF SENTENCE USED BY CHILDREN OF PRESCHOOL AGE

(From *Language Development in the Preschool Child,* by Dorothea McCarthy. Courtesy University of Minnesota Press.)

III is composed of the children of clerical workers and skilled tradesmen, and Group IV of the children of semiskilled workers, chiefly factory hands. Group V includes children whose fathers are icemen, drivers of milk-wagons, junkmen, and men following other trades which require little skill. Group VI is made up of the children of day-laborers. At the age of three, the children of Group I use, on the average, more than twice as many words to the sentence as the children in Groups V and VI.

Another example of the way social stimulation affects language development is seen in the development of language in twins. Most children learn their language from persons older than themselves. If there are younger children in the family, the difference in age is great enough for the older child to feel his own linguistic superiority to the baby so that he is unlikely to copy the latter's mode of speech. But twins are in a different category. Because of their similarity of age and interests they spend much more of their time together than brothers and sisters of different ages are likely to do, and for the same reason they are less dependent upon adults for companionship. Twins play together; they talk together; and they imitate each other's speech. There are a number of instances on record in which a pair of twins have developed a language of their own, comprehensible to each other but to no one else. Sometimes this secret language is continued into adult life, but as a rule it is discarded as soon as normal speech is learned. The learning of normal speech, however, is likely to be considerably delayed in these cases. In one such case that I was able to observe, a pair of twin girls four and a half years old used no words at all that could be understood by others. They were unquestionably of normal intelligence. In some ways they were distinctly in advance of their age. To each other they chattered continually, and their behavior gave clear evidence that they understood each other. Yet their language was entirely incomprehensible, even to their parents.

Although the development of an independent language is unusual, Day [11] has shown that twins, on the average, make slower progress in speech than single children. This retardation is shown in practically all aspects of speech development—in vocabulary, in average length of sentence, and in articulation. Figure 54 shows the extent of this retardation in respect to average length of sentence.

That the language retardation of twins is a social rather than

[11] Ella J. Day, "The Development of Language in Twins. I. A. Comparison of Twins and Single Children," *Child Development*, 1932, 3: 179-199.

a biological phenomenon is neatly shown in a follow-up of Day's study by Davis,[12] who compared the language development of twins with that of single children after they had been subjected to the wider social experience of school life. Davis used as subjects children of five and one-half to nine and one-half years of age and followed the procedure used by McCarthy and by Day

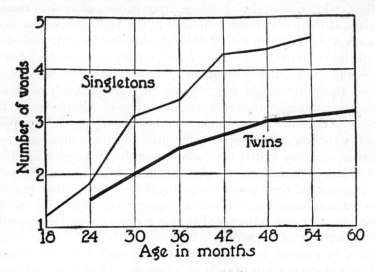

FIG. 54.—LANGUAGE RETARDATION IN TWINS

(From Ella J. Day, "Development of Language in Twins," *Child Development*, 1932, 3: 179-199. Courtesy Dr. Buford Johnson.)

exactly except for the substitution of different toys and picture books more suited to the interests of older children. Her findings indicate that even a half-year of kindergarten is sufficient to erase most, if not all, of the difference between the groups as far as average length of sentence is concerned. Apparently the wider social contact with children of normal speech development was having its effect. The greatest residual effect of the early handicap was noted in respect to articulation. Even at the age of nine and one-half, the number of twins with faulty articulation was

[12] Edith A. Davis, *The Development of Linguistic Skill in Twins, Singletons with Siblings, and Only Children from Age Five to Ten Years*, University of Minnesota Institute of Child Welfare Monograph Series, No. 14 (Minneapolis, Minn., University of Minnesota Press, 1937), pp. x + 165.

distinctly greater than the number of single children with such defects.

Davis also compared the speech development of "only" children with that of twins and of singly born children from families of more than one child. Her assumption was that if the imperfect language of twins is the result of hearing and imitating each other's faulty speech, then "only" children, whose early association is almost exclusively with adults should, on the average, be more advanced in speech than the general run of children from larger families. That this hypothesis was amply substantiated by her results [13] is shown by Figure 55.

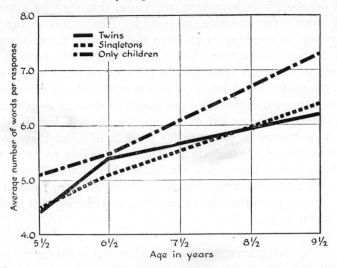

FIG. 55.—LANGUAGE DEVELOPMENT OF ONLY CHILDREN COMPARED WITH THAT OF SINGLY-BORN CHILDREN IN FAMILIES OF MORE THAN ONE CHILD AND OF TWINS
(After Davis.)

This brings us back to a further consideration of the rôle of imitation in the acquisition of language. Evidently we cannot discard the concept entirely. Common sense alone would show the

[13] It may be well to note that Davis, Day, and McCarthy were all careful to guard against errors resulting from unequal sampling of cases from the various socio-economic levels by matching each of the groups which they studied to the occupational distribution of employed males for the cities of Minneapolis and St. Paul as reported in the U.S. Census.

fallacy in doing so. Imitation of the speech of others sets the pattern for speech and provides the necessary basis for acquiring new words, once the linguistic process is under way. Thus the progress in speech made by any child is determined to a great extent by the kind and quality of the language that he hears. Not only does a child learn to speak a particular language—English, German, French, or Chinese—according to the language of the home in which he is reared, but an English-speaking child who hears only good English will himself speak better English than another whose early training has been less fortunate. Children imitate the speech of those about them, whether this speech be good or poor. It is important, therefore, that they be given as good models for imitation as possible. Adults should not use "baby-talk" in speaking to children if they wish the children to learn correct articulation. And when children are unavoidably exposed to imperfect speech, as in the case of twins where each hears the undeveloped language of the other, special care should be taken to see that they also get their full share of conversation with older persons and that any specific speech defects which arise be corrected as promptly as possible in order that mutual imitation may not cause these defects to persist to an age at which they would become a serious handicap. Not all twins are backward in language development. Whether or not they shall be so depends upon the kind of attention and training that is given them in the home.

LANGUAGE AS AN INDEX TO OTHER MENTAL TRAITS

Before the beginning of speech we are very often at a loss to interpret the baby's behavior. "If he could only *tell* me what ails him," laments the mother as she tries to quiet her baby's wails, and again, "I simply cannot understand what he wants," as he squeals and tugs at her skirts. But once speech has developed, the relationship of the child to others changes in many ways. It becomes more intimate; its outlines are more clear-cut. Now the child can do more than show that he wants something. He can make requests, ask questions, give commands. He can understand and respond to the requests of others. With the beginning of speech the entire pattern of social intercourse clarifies. Its details as well as its broad outlines can now be seen.

We therefore study and record what the child says in various situations not only as an index to his language development but in order that we may better understand the child himself. When we do this, we find that children differ quite as greatly in the uses to which they put their new accomplishment as in respect to the accomplishment itself. Johnny is continually asking questions. Mary's speech is a succession of commands. Polly uses six *I*'s to every *you*. Billy has little to say about himself but much about the other children.

All these differences have a meaning. When properly understood they throw much light on the total personality of the child. More than anything else in his behavior, the child's language provides us with a key to his character. Through his answers to our questions and his own spontaneous remarks and questions we are also able to find out something of his thought processes, how he reasons, what he believes. We cannot see the world through the child's eyes without danger of distortion, but after he is able to talk he can give us some idea, imperfect though it may be, of how the world appears to him.

DISCUSSION

Putting together the material presented in this and preceding chapters, we note first of all that like all other forms of behavior, the ability to communicate with others by means of language does not come into being all at once but has a history of its own. Its development conforms to the same general principles of learning that were set down in Chapter VII. It is motivated by organic drives and acquires its special form by a process of associative learning or "conditioning." It is subject to loss through disuse [14]

[14] Helen Keller, who lost both sight and hearing at about the age of nineteen months, had begun to learn to speak before the illness that destroyed her sensory apparatus. Except for the retention of a single word, "water," the language ability previously gained gradually disappeared. Even so, it is probable that, as she herself points out, the retraining which was begun shortly before the age of seven was facilitated to some extent by the skill acquired earlier of which practically all observable traces had disappeared. Many studies have shown that deaf-mutes who lost their hearing after

but can be reëstablished more easily than if it had never been acquired, and it is probably the most effective of all learned reactions for extending the chain of responses through "higher-order" conditioning. Its usefulness as a mechanism for short-cutting, for substituting symbols that can be quickly and easily handled for time-consuming and laborious muscular acts can hardly be overestimated. As facility with the speech mechanisms and their uses is gained, finer distinctions appear. To the very little child, all feathered bipeds are "chickies" or "birdies"; to the non-mechanically minded adult, almost any complex arrangement of metal parts is a "machine" or a "gadget." To be sure, the application of special names to particular classes of objects involves much more than the mere development of a new verbal response. But the distinctions noted are not easy to hold in mind without the integrative aid of particularized verbal symbols.

In this chapter, only one aspect of the development of the art of communicating with others has been considered. It is necessary to remember, however, that communication is carried on by other devices as well. Even before speech is established, the use of gesture by the infant is well under way. Indeed, if "gesture-language" is so thoroughly established that the child finds it sufficient for most if not all of his needs, he may be slow in acquiring speech. But gesture is too crude and too much an affair of the moment to be effective for all purposes. Sooner or later, even the child who has been able to get what he wants by the primitive methods of crying, pointing, and snatching will feel the need of other devices for controlling his expanding universe.

HOW A BLIND AND DEAF CHILD
ACQUIRED A LANGUAGE

Helen Keller, *The Story of My Life* (New York, Doubleday, Page and Co., 1905), pp. xviii + 441.

In this book, written in her early twenties, Helen Keller tells of her childhood and youth. The difference in age and experience as well as the fact of her remarkable intellectual brilliance necessarily

---

some facility in speech had been gained are usually easier to train than those whose loss goes back to early infancy and that the difference is more apparent in respect to the acquisition of oral speech than in learning the manual alphabet.

makes her story of the way she first acquired the ability to communicate with others somewhat different from the process by which the normal child gains this accomplishment. The difference is further accentuated by her sensory limitations which for many years reduced her associations with the language of others to that maintained with her teacher. Despite these differences, the points of similarity between her experiences and reactions and those of the normal infant are both striking and informative. Her discovery, so vividly described, that everything has a name, and the almost phenomenal advance in her vocabulary that immediately followed this discovery provides one of the most dramatic descriptions in biographical literature. Even the account of her temper tantrums that resulted from her inability to make herself understood, find their parallels in miniature in the history of most normal babies.

Miss Keller tells her story so skillfully as to hold the reader fascinated to the very end. The appended letters by her famous teacher, Miss Elizabeth Sullivan, which tell the story of the same events as they were observed by her at the time, make a valuable and instructive supplement to Miss Keller's own account of the experiences through which she lived and the responses they aroused in her.

Chapter XII

PHYSICAL GROWTH AND MOTOR DEVELOP-
MENT DURING EARLY CHILDHOOD

What deveolpmental features set off the period of early childhood from those that precede and follow it?

What are the most conspicuous changes in motor abilities that take place during early childhood? What are some of the changes that occur toward the end of this period in respect to the child's utilization of his motor skill?

Which plays the greater part in the perfection of a skilled motor act—addition of new movements, or the loss of some movements formerly present? Explain.

How does the efficiency of each of the two hands become modified in the establishment of hand preference?

What is meant by ocular dominance? About how early in life is it established? Are there more cases of left-eyed or of left-handed people in the general population?

DURATION OF THE PERIOD

As used here, the term *early childhood* includes the period from the beginning of speech, which in most children occurs at about eighteen months, to the age of five years. Two general considerations have led to this division, namely, developmental change on the one hand and educational and social practice on the other. As will be shown in the next section, the changes in abilities and conduct that take place during this time are very marked. More-

294

over, at about the age of five a large proportion of children, particularly in the cities, enter kindergartens.[1] They are thus brought for the first time under regulations other than those of the home and are faced with the need of adjusting to the demands of a large social group made up of other children. Before entering kindergarten the majority of children have relatively few contacts with companions of their own age. Save for the infrequent twin, brothers and sisters are usually too much older or younger to play together on entirely equal terms, for at these early periods a difference in age of as little as two years counts for a good deal in physical size and strength and mental ability and interests. In many ways the preschool child is a somewhat different type of human being from the baby that he was or the school child that he will presently become.

CHARACTERISTIC FEATURES OF GROWTH DURING EARLY CHILDHOOD

The rapid physical and mental growth that was characteristic of the period of infancy described in the last chapters is continued with only a small decrease in rate throughout early childhood. By the age of five, most of the basic motor skills have been well perfected. The child walks, runs, handles objects, jumps, and climbs almost as well as he will ever be able to do. As his legs grow longer he will be able to run faster, and there will be further gain in speed of movement and in motor control, particularly of the fine muscles of the hand and fingers, but the motor development that takes place after the age of five is very small when compared to that occurring earlier.

Even more sharply than by the changes in motor development, this period is set off from those that precede and follow it by the acquisition of speech. Before the age of fifteen to eighteen months the average child makes small use of speech. By the age of five he has commonly acquired all the basic speech forms used among adults. He asks questions, makes long and involved statements, uses phrases, clauses, adjectives and adverbs, pronouns,

---

[1] According to the report of the United States Commissioner of Education, in 1940 there were 594,647 children attending public school kindergartens in the United States, with an additional 57,341 in private kindergartens.

and interjections. His grammatical construction is well-nigh as good as that of the adults with whom he associates and from whom his language has been learned. As he grows older his vocabulary will become larger and his sentences show some further increase in average length, but the basic language forms are all acquired during the preschool period. Articulation, too, is well perfected during this time. In the average child "baby-talk" has become pretty much a thing of the past by the age of five years.

Physical growth is likewise rapid. Up to the age of five years children gain rapidly in height and weight. Their bodily proportions are changing; the arms and legs are lengthening out, the lower part of the face is growing rapidly, while the forehead and cranium are making but small gain (see Figure 56), and the features are taking on clearer outlines. After the age of five, growth is less rapid, and it continues at a comparatively slow pace until the prepubertal spurt begins at eleven or twelve years.

MOTOR DEVELOPMENT

Although walking is begun by most children toward the end of the prelinguistic period, few children become really skilful walkers before the latter part of the second year. The child's first steps are likely to be unsteady, performed with the feet widely separated in an apparent attempt to secure better balance by widening the base of support. Even so it does not take much to upset him, and for some time after walking begins he is likely to revert to the rôle of quadruped whenever the surface of the ground is irregular. However, his interest in walking is so great and he practises it so incessantly that the period of early childhood is often referred to as "the run-about age."

A conspicuous result of the child's rapid gain in motor control is seen in his growing ability and desire to do things for himself. Over and over again comes the insistent demand "Let me do it. *I* want to do that! Let me carry it! I can open it myself! No, don't help me! Let me wash my own face!" At this age the normal child's interest in *doing* is almost unbelievable. Again and again he repeats the same simple action, apparently for the sheer pleasure of producing a result that he can see. Scupin reports that his young son once opened and closed the hinged cover of a box seventy-nine times in immediate succession, and it is probable that careful observation of any normal baby would reveal many similar instances. It is a pity that instead of cultivating and encouraging this worth-while tendency in young children, many parents are

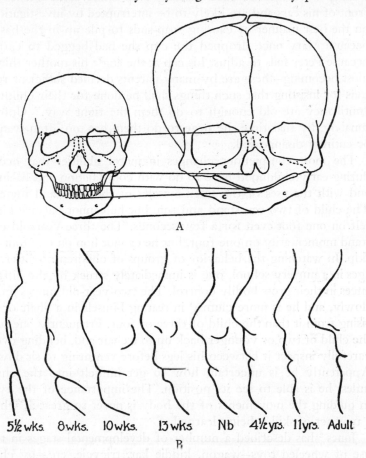

A

5½ wks. 8 wks. 10 wks. 13 wks. Nb 4½ yrs. 11 yrs. Adult

B

FIG. 56.—CHANGES IN FACIAL PROPORTIONS WITH AGE

A. Skulls of the adult and the new-born drawn to the same face height to illustrate changes in the relative proportions of the neural and facial portions at birth and in maturity.

B. Changes in facial profile from the middle of the embryonic period to maturity.

(After Holl, from chapter on "Developmental Anatomy" by R. E. Scammon in Morris's *Human Anatomy*, Sixth Edition. Courtesy P. Blakiston's Son and Co.)

led by thoughtlessness and hurry or by overconcern about the material result to curb the child's attempts to do for himself at the very age when this natural tendency is at its height. Because Johnny's attempts at face-washing stop short some inches in front of his ears and are likely to be interrupted by investigations on the best manner of causing soap-suds to pile up in the basin; because Mary once dropped the cup she had begged to carry; because Peter fails to adjust his cap at the angle his mother thinks most becoming—these are by many parents deemed sufficient reasons for insisting that such things shall be done for their children "until they are old enough to do them the right way." Unfortunately, by that time the urge to do them has too often waned or entirely disappeared.

The most conspicuous changes in motor abilities that occur during early childhood have to do with coördination and balance and with the uses of the finer muscles of the hand and fingers. The child of two can stand and run, but he cannot balance himself on one foot even for a few seconds. The three-year-old can stand momentarily on one foot, but he cannot hop on one foot or skip. In watching the behavior of groups of children of different ages in a nursery school, one is immediately struck by the differences in their gross bodily control. The two-year-old moves more slowly, and he is more clumsy in seating himself in a chair or in rising from it than the child of three or four. Frequently one sees the child of two or younger back up to a chair and, bending over, carefully inspect it between his legs before venturing to sit down. Apparently he is uncertain how to get himself into the chair unless he is able to see its position. The importance of the eyes in guiding the movements of the body is never so great as when a new act of skill is being learned.

Jones [2] has described a number of developmental stages in the use of wheeled toys—wagon, kiddie kar, tricycle, etc.—by children between the ages of twenty-one and forty-eight months. He found that the children under two years spent most of their time in simple manipulative activities involving pushing and pulling,

[2] T. D. Jones, *The Development of Certain Motor Skills and Play Activities in Young Children*, Child Development Monographs, No. 26 (New York, Teachers College, Columbia University, Bureau of Publications, 1939), pp. xi + 180.

with very few attempts at propelling themselves about. Beginning at or about the age of two, attempts at riding the kiddie kar and, later on, the tricycle became more frequent. Once this had begun, the amount of time spent in practice rapidly increased. At first the child's movements had the appearance of a series of separate activities. They were jerky, uncertain, and so poorly coördinated that progression would often be momentarily halted or even reversed in direction. However, as soon as learning had reached a stage at which the child's whole attention no longer had to be fixed on the motor performance itself, a merging of the separate parts of the activity began to take place and continued until the whole thing eventually ran off as a unitary pattern. By the age of forty-eight months most children had succeeded in perfecting these skills to a point where they were no longer the child's primary concern but had become adjuncts to a more complex form of imaginative and dramatic activity. The child became a cowboy or a mounted policeman, the tricycle his horse. The wagon became a fire-engine or an automobile or a "choo-choo train." Among the younger children there was little evidence of deliberation or, as Jones phrases it, of "thought before action." They plunged ahead. If things went right, well and good; if wrong, they depended upon muscular struggle or upon adult aid to extricate themselves from their difficulty. But the older children gave evidence both by behavior and conversation that they were beginning to substitute thought for action. After the age of three years, such remarks as "I better not ride my kiddie kar over here, I might get hurt," or "If I make my feet go like this I go that way; when I make them go like *this*, I go the other way" became increasingly frequent.

Dexterity of hand improves rapidly. Before the age of five the average child has learned to feed himself, using spoon and fork, to put on his own shoes, stockings, and other clothing that is not too complicated, to fasten buttons and snaps that he can see. Shoe-laces are likely to baffle him for another year or two, especially when it comes to tying them, and the simultaneous use of knife and fork in cutting meat or the nice adjustment of movement and pressure involved in spreading butter on bread continue to present difficulties.

This improvement in the use of the hands is shown in another

way, which illustrates the fact that differentiation of local movements from movements of the body as a whole is not yet completed. As age advances and manual dexterity improves, the child
becomes less likely to engage in general bodily contortions along
with his hand movements. The little child who is just beginning
to draw or write usually goes through all sorts of unrelated movements along with it. He hangs out his tongue and twists it up
and down with each movement of his pencil. He moves his body
from side to side, contorts his neck, twists his feet around the
legs of his chair, breathes hard. As he grows older these accessory
movements drop out one by one, and the movements of the hands
become more nearly independent of the rest of the body. Age,
however, is not the only factor. Practice has something to do
with it. Even you and I, when we try to learn a new motor skill,
will find some difficulty at first in refraining from useless accompanying activities of other parts of the body One of the most
conspicuous features of the acquisition of skill consists in the dropping out of unnecessary acts that interfere with the speed and
smoothness of the motor performance. Motor learning consists
quite as much in learning what not to do as of learning what to do.

THE ESTABLISHMENT OF LATERAL DOMINANCE

Hand preference, which began to be apparent during infancy,
is well established before the age of five. There is, however, a
distinct relationship between the complexity of the task and the
extent to which the hand preference is shown. The right-handed
child or adult will commonly use the right hand in preference
to the left in reaching and grasping if the object is equally convenient to both hands, but a slight advantage of position will cause
him to change to the left. However, if the task is one requiring
considerable dexterity, say the manipulation of a difficult fastening, he will use the right hand even at the cost of considerable
awkwardness and inconvenience. The development of handedness
is most clearly shown in tasks involving complex movements
rather than in the simpler ones. The difference between the performance of the two hands is brought about by a steady improvement in the skill of the right hand, while the left shows little
change. This is strikingly shown in Figure 57, which is based

upon Wellman's[3] study of the ability of young children to trace
a path through an alley decreasing in width from 5 mm. at the
start to 1 mm. at the end without coming in contact with the
sides.

At the age of three years, the difference in skill shown by the
two hands is slight. As age advances, however, the improvement
in the performance of the right hand is rapid, in that of the left

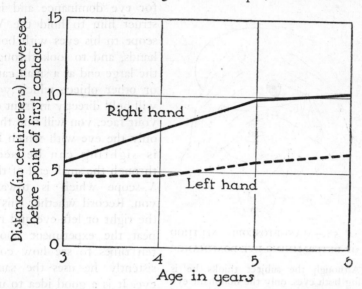

FIG. 57.—COMPARATIVE IMPROVEMENT IN CONTROL OF THE RIGHT AND
LEFT HANDS FROM THE THIRD TO THE SIXTH YEAR

(Adapted from Beth Wellman, "The Development of Motor Coördination in Young Children," *University of Iowa Studies: Studies in Child Welfare,* 1926, Vol. 3, No. 4, pp. 93.)

hand, slow. The right hand gains more in the fourth year of life
alone than the left hand gains in the entire three years covered
by the study.

Handedness is not the only way in which the dominance of
one side of the body is shown. Not only do we use one hand in
preference to the other, but in ordinary near vision we "sight"

[3] Beth Wellman, "The Development of Motor Coördination in Young
Children; an Experimental Study of Arm and Hand Movements," *University of Iowa Studies in Child Welfare,* 1926, Vol. 3, No. 4.

with one eye in preference to the other. This can be demonstrated in a number of ways, but one of the simplest and most convenient methods is by use of a little device called a *manopter* (also known as a *manoptoscope* or *V-scope*), devised by W. R. Miles. You can easily make one by following the instructions given at the end of this chapter. Now if you stand at a distance of about ten feet from the person whom you are going to test

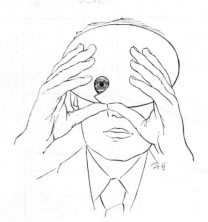

for eye dominance and instruct him to hold the V-scope to his eyes with both hands, and to look through the large end at a small card or other object which you will hold directly in front of your face, you will find that only the eye with which he is sighting can be seen through the small end of the V-scope which is toward you. Record whether this is the right or left eye and repeat the experiment about ten times to see how consistently he uses the same eye. It is a good idea to use different cards or objects and ask him to tell you what they are, not only to make certain that he is looking in the right direction but also to keep him from suspecting the real object of the test. (See Fig. 58.)

FIG. 58.—MANOPTOSCOPE METHOD OF DETERMINING EYE DOMINANCE

Although the subject thinks he is using both eyes, only the dominant eye can be seen through the small end of the manoptoscope. The subject should be instructed to look directly at the examiner's eyes.

How early in life does eye dominance appear? Updegraff [4] has reported the results of a study of 190 children between the ages of two and six years. These children were given repeated tests at intervals varying from two months to two years. In this way, not only could eye dominance at a given time be studied, but also the persistence of the trait over a period of time could be observed.

[4] Ruth Updegraff, "Ocular Dominance in Young Children," *J. Exper. Psychol.*, 1932, 15: 758-766.

It was found that only a small percentage of the two-year-olds showed definite eye dominance. However, by the age of three not only did over 75 per cent of the children use the same eye very consistently throughout a single series of ten trials, but on a second test given two months later no change in "eyedness" had taken place. They continued to sight with the same eye they had used before. Of the children who showed no definite eye dominance at the age of three, about 75 per cent had become definitely right-eyed or left-eyed by the age of five or six. Studies of older persons have shown that a small percentage of cases (most investigators have found fewer than 5 per cent) remain "indefinite-eyed" throughout life, that is, they sight sometimes with the right eye and sometimes with the left.

Eye dominance then seems to be established in most children somewhere between the age of two and three years. In some cases it occurs earlier and in some not until several years later, while a few people remain indefinite-eyed throughout life. Updegraff found not only that the percentage of indefinite-eyedness decreases with age but that changes in eye dominance occur somewhat more frequently in young children than in older ones or in adults.

Right-eyedness, like right-handedness, is more common than left-eyedness, but the difference is less marked than in the case of the hands. At all ages after three years, from 60 to 70 per cent of all people are right-eyed, but more than 90 per cent are right-handed.

It is difficult to explain the facts of eye dominance on any other basis than that of some inborn tendency. The fact that it is relatively late in showing itself proves nothing, for many inborn traits, e.g., the growth of whiskers in the male, do not appear until some time after birth. The fact that most people are entirely unaware of eye dominance either in themselves or others affords some evidence that the condition is not likely to have been brought about by training. In one sense, eyedness and handedness may be said to go together, since the right side is commonly superior in both traits, but whether left-handed people also tend to be left-eyed is still open to question. At least the relationship is not invariable, either in children or adults.

"Footedness" has also been studied, but the findings are less clear. The two feet are not often used independently of each other, and when both participate in an act, even though they play somewhat different rôles, it is often hard to say which is taking the chief part. Such investigations as have been made seem to indicate that foot dominance is not as clearly marked as either eye or hand dominance, and that it varies more from one activity to another in the same person. However, this may be because our techniques for studying it are poor.

A CLASS EXPERIMENT ON THE CONSISTENCY OF LATERALITY PREFERENCE IN THE INDIVIDUAL

W. R. Miles, "Ocular Dominance in Human Adults," *J. General Psychol.*, 1930, 3: 412-430.

Wendell Johnson and Dorothy M. Davis, "Dextrality Quotients of Seven-Year-Olds in Terms of Hand Usage," *J. Educ. Psychol.*, 1937, 28: 346-354.

The object of this experiment is to determine the extent to which eye dominance and hand dominance correspond, that is, whether the left-eyed person is more likely to be left-handed than is the person whose right eye is dominant.

In Figure 59 you will find specifications for constructing a manoptoscope similar to that shown in Figure 58. The following pages give instructions for administering and scoring the Iowa Scale for measuring hand preference and for the test of eye dominance. For the use of the Iowa Scale only such materials are required as any one can easily secure. Before beginning the experiment, mimeographed copies of the scale and record forms for the test of eye dominance should be prepared for the use of the class, or, if this is impractical, each member of the class can prepare his own by copying the form given on p. 308. Inasmuch as only one copy will be needed by each person, the task of copying is not too laborious. The two references given above should also be read, either by the members of the class separately or by selected individuals who will later make a report to the group.

The class should then divide into pairs for individual testing of each other. This testing can best be done outside the regular class period. After it has been completed, results for the entire group should be assembled in such a way as to answer the following questions and any others that may suggest themselves:

1. What is the form of the distribution of dextrality quotients? If ocular dominance quotients (computed on the basis of twenty trials) are determined by the same method as was used in

finding the dextrality quotients, and the two curves for the same group of individuals are superimposed one upon the other, what are the main differences between them?

2. Classify the laterality quotients made on each of the two tests (eye dominance and hand dominance) by each student separately according to the scheme shown below:

A = Decidedly dextral (right hand or eye dominant):
   DQ or ODQ = 85-100 per cent
B = Somewhat dextral: DQ or ODQ = 60-84 per cent
C = Ambidextral or ambiocular:
   DQ or ODQ = 41-59 per cent
D = Somewhat sinistral (left hand or eye dominant):
   DQ or ODQ = 16-40 per cent
E = Decidedly sinistral: DQ or ODQ = 0-15 per cent

3. In what per cent of the cases do the two quotients fall into the same general class? In what per cent do the two measurements correspond in direction though not necessarily in degree? In what per cent of all the cases is definite laterality shown in respect to only one of the two measurements with near or complete ambivalence (Group C above) in the other? In what per cent of the cases is there (a) moderate or (b) extreme divergence in the laterality preference of eye and hand?

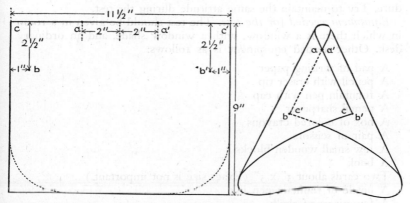

FIG. 59.—DIAGRAM ILLUSTRATING METHOD OF CONSTRUCTING THE MANOPTOSCOPE ILLUSTRATED IN FIGURE 58

4. If your class includes both men and women, is there any sex difference in the percentage of individuals who are (a) left-handed? (b) left-eyed? (c) divergent in the laterality tendencies of eye and hand?

5. By referring to the Subject Index of the *Psychological Abstracts* which you will find in your university library, ascertain what previous investigators have found out about these problems. Compare their results with yours.

INSTRUCTIONS FOR GIVING THE IOWA HAND-PREFERENCE TEST

For best results with this or any other test designed to measure hand preference the subjects should be unaware of the purpose of the test. Otherwise there is likely to be some feeling of self-consciousness, a tendency to stop to consider which hand is to be used that may render the test less valid as an indicator of real hand preference. In carrying out the experiments described here, knowledge of the purpose of the test is inevitable, but reasonably satisfactory results may still be obtained if each subject is careful to follow these rules.

(1) *Put out of your mind* just as completely as possible *all thoughts of what the test is about.*

(2) *Keep your attention centered on the instructions.* Try to follow them just as quickly as you can. Act as you would if this were a test of speed.

(3) Above all, *do not look at or think of your hands,* or of *how* you are performing the tasks. They are all so simple that normally you would carry them out automatically with no thought to procedure. Try to maintain the same attitude during the test.

Equipment needed for the test. The test should be given in a room in which there is a window, with a window shade, and an ordinary desk. Other needed equipment is as follows:

A pad of writing paper
A pencil with eraser tip
A fountain pen with cap
A pencil sharpener
A box of colored crayons
A pair of scissors
A few small wooden blocks
A book
Two cards about 3" x 5" (Exact size is not important.)
A bottle of fountain-pen ink
A few pieces of chalk

For the procedure to be used in giving the test, students should, if possible, consult the article by Johnson and Davis cited at the top of p. 304. However, the instructions are very simple and if the original article is not available the following will serve.

Say to the subject: "I have a number of things that I would like you to do. First, will you please pull down the shade just a little?" Record which hand is used and wait, if necessary, for the subject to remove his hand from the shade. Then say, "Thank you, Just a little further, please." Again record which hand is used.

Then say, "Please take the ———— (naming some object) from the desk and give it to me. Thank you. Now give me the ————." Record as before.

The same general procedure is followed throughout the list of sixty-four items.

As each item is performed, write in the space before it on the record blank the appropriate letter to indicate the hand used; R for the right hand, L for the left. If both hands participate but one is clearly taking the major rôle, record R or L as if that were the sole hand used. When the two hands perform rôles that seem of about equal importance, mark the item B.

After the test has been completed compute the subject's dextrality quotient (DQ) according to the formula given at the bottom of p. 308. A high DQ (.85 or higher) indicates strong right-handedness, a very low DQ (.15 or less) marked left-handedness, while quotients around the 50 per cent level indicate that the subject has no marked tendencies in either direction. According to Johnson, most people use the hand that is ordinarily not the preferred one rather consistently for certain activities.

TESTING EYE DOMINANCE WITH THE MANOPTOSCOPE

Prepare a series of small cards with a single good-sized letter or numeral on each. Place the subject at a distance from you of about ten feet, facing a window or other good light. Hold one of the small cards at the bridge of your nose and ask the subject to place the large opening of the manoptoscope held with the short side downward over his eyes and look through it at the small card so that he can read the number. (See Figure 58.) Repeat for twenty trials, having the subject lower the manoptoscope and replace it in position after each trial. Record each time whether the left or the right eye was visible through the small aperture. Ocular dominance quotients (ODQ's) can then be computed in the same way as was done for the dextrality quotients in the previous experiment.

Iowa Scale for Measuring Hand Preference *

NAME _____ SEX _____ DATE _____ DQ _____

TESTED BY _____

Hand Used

<table>
<tr><td>————</td><td>1. Pull down curtain.</td></tr>
<tr><td>————</td><td>2. Pull down curtain.</td></tr>
<tr><td>————</td><td>3. Take article from desk.</td></tr>
<tr><td>————</td><td>4. Take article from desk.</td></tr>
<tr><td>————</td><td>5. Tear paper from tablet.</td></tr>
<tr><td>————</td><td>6. Turn over paper.</td></tr>
<tr><td>————</td><td>7. Sharpen pencil.</td></tr>
<tr><td>————</td><td>8. Write with pencil.</td></tr>
<tr><td>————</td><td>9. Erase with pencil-tip eraser.</td></tr>
<tr><td>————</td><td>10. Write with pencil.</td></tr>
<tr><td>————</td><td>11. Draw a picture.</td></tr>
<tr><td>————</td><td>12. Put pencil in desk.</td></tr>
<tr><td>————</td><td>13. Take crayon from box.</td></tr>
<tr><td>————</td><td>14. Take crayon from box.</td></tr>
<tr><td>————</td><td>15. Color with crayon.</td></tr>
<tr><td>————</td><td>16. Color with crayon.</td></tr>
<tr><td>————</td><td>17. Put crayon in box.</td></tr>
<tr><td>————</td><td>18. Put crayon in box.</td></tr>
<tr><td>————</td><td>19. Close crayon box.</td></tr>
<tr><td>————</td><td>20. Close crayon box.</td></tr>
<tr><td>————</td><td>21. Pick up scissors.</td></tr>
<tr><td>————</td><td>22. Put scissors in desk.</td></tr>
<tr><td>————</td><td>23. Point to block.</td></tr>
<tr><td>————</td><td>24. Point to block.</td></tr>
<tr><td>————</td><td>25. Pick up block to pile.</td></tr>
<tr><td>————</td><td>26. Place block on pile.</td></tr>
<tr><td>————</td><td>27. Pick up block to pile.</td></tr>
<tr><td>————</td><td>28. Place block on pile.</td></tr>
<tr><td>————</td><td>29. Pick up block to carry.</td></tr>
<tr><td>————</td><td>30. Pick up block to carry.</td></tr>
<tr><td>————</td><td>31. Point to card.</td></tr>
<tr><td>————</td><td>32. Point to card.</td></tr>
</table>

Hand Used

<table>
<tr><td>————</td><td>33. Pick up card.</td></tr>
<tr><td>————</td><td>34. Pick up card.</td></tr>
<tr><td>————</td><td>35. Lay down card.</td></tr>
<tr><td>————</td><td>36. Lay down card.</td></tr>
<tr><td>————</td><td>37. Tear paper from tablet.</td></tr>
<tr><td>————</td><td>38. Turn over paper.</td></tr>
<tr><td>————</td><td>39. Fold paper.</td></tr>
<tr><td>————</td><td>40. Sharpen pencil.</td></tr>
<tr><td>————</td><td>41. Turn page of book.</td></tr>
<tr><td>————</td><td>42. Turn page of book.</td></tr>
<tr><td>————</td><td>43. Draw a picture.</td></tr>
<tr><td>————</td><td>44. Put pencil in desk.</td></tr>
<tr><td>————</td><td>45. Pick up scissors.</td></tr>
<tr><td>————</td><td>46. Put scissors in desk.</td></tr>
<tr><td>————</td><td>47. Pick up pen.</td></tr>
<tr><td>————</td><td>48. Take top off pen.</td></tr>
<tr><td>————</td><td>49. Take top off ink bottle.</td></tr>
<tr><td>————</td><td>50. Fill pen.</td></tr>
<tr><td>————</td><td>51. Write with pen.</td></tr>
<tr><td>————</td><td>52. Put top on pen.</td></tr>
<tr><td>————</td><td>53. Erase with pencil-tip eraser.</td></tr>
<tr><td>————</td><td>54. Fold paper.</td></tr>
<tr><td>————</td><td>55. Pick up pen.</td></tr>
<tr><td>————</td><td>56. Take top off pen.</td></tr>
<tr><td>————</td><td>57. Take top off ink bottle.</td></tr>
<tr><td>————</td><td>58. Fill pen.</td></tr>
<tr><td>————</td><td>59. Write with pen.</td></tr>
<tr><td>————</td><td>60. Put top on pen.</td></tr>
<tr><td>————</td><td>61. Pick up chalk.</td></tr>
<tr><td>————</td><td>62. Write with chalk.</td></tr>
<tr><td>————</td><td>63. Pick up chalk.</td></tr>
<tr><td>————</td><td>64. Write with chalk.</td></tr>
</table>

Score: Total R ————. Total L ————. Total B ————.

$$\text{Dextrality Quotient} = \frac{\text{Total R} + \dfrac{\text{Total B}}{2}}{\text{No. test items tried}}$$

* Reproduced by permission of the author and the publisher from *J. Educ. Psychol.*, 1940, 31: 46.

Chapter XIII

SOCIAL AND EMOTIONAL BEHAVIOR OF
YOUNG CHILDREN

*In what ways do the development of walking and
speech affect the child's social relationships?*

*What are the chief factors that make for leadership?
Are leaders "born" or "made"?*

*Does the saying, "Opposites attract," apparently hold
for the establishment of friendships among children? Illustrate.*

*Are quarrels among children usually a sign of "malad-
justment"?*

*What important change can be noted in respect to the
relation between emotional and social behavior as
childhood succeeds infancy? What new sources
for the establshment of emotional responses appear
in childhood that were not present in infancy?*

THE TOOLS OF SOCIAL INTERCOURSE

Before the child is able to walk, his avenues for communication
with others are limited. He cannot approach the people of his
choice or join effectively in their activities. But once he becomes
able to move about at will, his social horizon as well as his physical
horizon is greatly broadened. As his motor skill increases with
age, we find him making increased use of his newly acquired
abilities in furthering his social relationships. He runs, climbs,
jumps, and dances with other children. He coöperates in the
building of block houses, and he uses his fists to enforce his
authority. In almost every area of social behavior, the motor

skills that children have developed play an important rôle in determining the reactions shown.

Equally or perhaps even more important as a tool of social intercourse for the child is his newly developed speech. By the use of speech he is able to influence the behavior of others in a host of direct ways, in comparison with which his earlier language of gesture and facial expression seems pitifully inadequate and clumsy. He does not learn the possibilities of his new tool all at once, but as he grows older we find that an increasingly greater proportion of his conversations with children of his own age is directed toward modifying their behavior in some way. He gives more commands, offers more suggestions, makes very many more criticisms, asks more questions. Physical strength, motor skill, intelligence, range of information, linguistic ability— every asset that the child possesses is enlisted in the service of his social desires.

METHODS OF APPRAISING THE SOCIAL REACTIONS OF CHILDREN

Many attempts have been made to classify behavior on the basis of the degree or intensity of the social participation displayed. None of these attempts have been highly successful because there is no general agreement about what criterion should be employed for determining whether this bit of behavior is "more social" or "less social" than that. Broad distinctions can of course be readily made. We shall all agree that the child who sits by himself in a corner, paying no apparent attention to those around him, is at the moment behaving in a less social manner than the one who is "the life of the party." But except for the simple dichotomy of participation or non-participation, social distinctions of the "more" or "less" type are not easy to make.

Parten [1] proposed a scheme of classifying the social behavior of young children according to amount of apparent participation without reference to its desirability or undesirability. Her six categories were as follows: (1) solitary without apparent occupation, (2) solitary but occupied, (3) physically solitary but

[1] Mildred B. Parten, "Social Participation Among Preschool Children," *J. Abnorm. and Soc. Psychol.*, 1932, 27: 243-269.

engaged in watching the activity of other children with apparent interest, (4) "parallel" activity in which a child plays *beside* other children but not *with* them,[2] (5) associative group play in which children work at the same kind of project jointly but without differential assignment of rôles, or join in play of a kind where all do the same thing either simultaneously or in succession, and (6) coöperative group play in which there is not only association but each makes his own specialized contribution to the success of the enterprise as a whole, as in "playing house."

Parten's six categories unquestionably form a rough hierarchy indicating successive levels of complexity of social influence and interaction. There are, however, many other aspects of social behavior that are equally worthy of study. One that has attracted particular attention in recent years is that of social ascendance or submission. This behavior has many nuances that bear different names. There is, for example, a difference between leading a group and dominating over an individual. There is a difference between compliance and submission. There is a difference between commanding and requesting. Our interest in each of these may center around the manner by which social ascendance is attained or in the characteristics of the child who attains it; or, on the other hand, it may shift to the conditions that contribute to the display of ascendant behavior on a given occasion or that induce a particular child to maintain a dominant or a submissive rôle in most of his social relationships.

ASCENDANT BEHAVIOR IN YOUNG CHILDREN

Parten's study of social participation included a special investigation of leadership.[3] Even among the preschool children who

---

[2] This is a form of social relation that is particularly characteristic of two-year-olds. It is seen at the sand table in a nursery school where half a dozen young children may work away together with little or no indication of social interaction. There is little conversation and no attempt at coöperative play. Each child has his own sand toys which he uses by himself and keeps for himself. Yet all are aware of each other in a gregarious sort of way. When one child leaves the group, others are likely to follow; if one child pours sand from cup to pail, an epidemic of sand-pouring may start. But each child pours for himself and not for his neighbor.

[3] Mildred B. Parten, "Leadership Among Preschool Children," *J. Abnorm. and Soc. Psychol.*, 1933, 27: 430-440.

were her subjects, it was apparent that some children were exerting a much greater influence than others upon the behavior of the entire group, and that in the relationships of individual children with each other, one child commonly assumed the dominant rôle. Moreover two definite classes of ascendant children could be distinguished, the "diplomat" and the "bully." The former worked by indirect suggestion and by so doing maintained control over large groups; the latter depended upon brute force in bossing the small number of children in his own "gang." The first type is admirably illustrated by the following episode.

A group of four-year-olds were playing house in a large packing-box. They had built a number of crude pieces of furniture out of their blocks, but as space within the box was limited, it was necessary to move about with extreme caution in order to avoid knocking things over. Clumsy and excitable Jimmy found this well-nigh impossible. After half a dozen accidents, the "father" of the family announced in the tones of one who has just made a thrilling discovery, "We gotta have a dog, too! Jimmy, you be the dog! You have to stay outside and bark whenever anybody comes by the house. Bark *loud!*" A place had been found for Jimmy, and he entered into his new rôle with energy and enthusiasm.

In this little incident is exemplified what is perhaps the most important attribute of the successful leader of any age or level of development: ability to recognize the special abilities and limitations of others, together with versatility in devising rôles into which these characteristics will fit. Too, the able leader usually shows a knack for depicting these rôles in such glowing colors that the person for whom they are designed will not merely agree but will actively desire to accept them. The "Bark loud" in this case was a stroke of genius. It provided Jimmy with just the outlet for his overflowing energy that he needed. So in later years the person who is full of ideas that meet the needs of his associates and who can present his ideas in attractive terms is more likely to be sought for and to have his plans accepted than is another whose ideas, though equally good in the abstract, are not so well suited to the individual interests of the members of his group, or a third whose ideas may be both good and suitable but who is unable to present them in vivid and forceful terms.

The story of Jimmy illustrates still another point. All other things being equal, the successful leader is the one who is able to foresee and forestall dissension among the members of the group without losing any one from the ranks. One way of disposing of Jimmy would have been to put him out of the group. Indeed, a number of the children had already begun to demand his expulsion. But the little "father's" solution of the difficulty not only retained Jimmy among his followers but also, it is safe to assume, increased the solidarity of the group, for any one is likely to be loyal to a leader who assigns him an important position. Surely no one can deny that the presence of a loudly barking watchdog lends stability and importance to any household!

Whether or not some children are "born leaders" or whether social dominance is wholly the result of experience we do not know, but it is probable that here as elsewhere the truth lies somewhere between the two extremes. Undoubtedly, physique has something to do with it, for it is easier for the child who is larger and stronger than his mates to maintain an ascendant rôle than it is for the one who is weak and puny to do so.[4] Nevertheless it is not at all unusual to find that it is the small child, forced to substitute resourcefulness for brawn, who has become the real leader of a group. Early experience in the home may have something to do with it. Before they enter school, some children find that their most effective way of controlling the people about them is by temper tantrums or teasing or whining. But later on, after entering a nursery school or kindergarten, they find that their previous methods do not work. Of course they can learn other ways, but by the time they have done so it may well happen that the social patterns of the group have become so well established that it is difficult to overcome their early handicap. So the child who learns in his own home the patterns of social behavior that make him popular with his mates enters school with an initial advantage that is likely to gain in strength with the passage of time. The repercussive effect of behavior upon the behaving organism is nowhere more clearly seen than in the field of social interaction.

Can anything be done for the child who is so lacking in self-assertiveness that he almost always assumes the non-ascendant

[4] See reference to study by Cabot on p. 230.

rôle, allowing himself to be bullied about or imposed upon by almost any one so inclined? According to Jack [5] and to Page [6] this is quite possible if the usual principles of learning that have been found to apply in other fields are kept in mind. That is to say, the child must have an incentive to learn, he must be given opportunity for practice under such conditions that success is not beyond his power to achieve and as his skill increases the difficulty of the task must be proportionately advanced. So the non-ascendant children in the groups they studied were placed in experimental situations where some degree of competition existed, with children so much smaller and weaker than themselves that domination was both natural and easy. As their self-confidence increased they were given opponents who were not so easy to control. At least in the experimental situations and in the nursery school where the experiment was conducted, the behavior of these non-ascendant children is said to have changed rather markedly in the direction of greater self-assertiveness.

Rather less attention has been paid to the question of too great assertiveness in the child's relation to other children than to that of too little. However, a number of studies have been made of factors influencing the child's readiness to comply with the rules and requests of adults. These will be considered elsewhere but we may note in passing that one's judgment as to the desirability or non-desirability of ascendant behavior appears to vary according to the position of the judge. [7]

[5] L. M. Jack, "An Experimental Study of Ascendant Behavior in Preschool Children," *University of Iowa Studies in Child Welfare*, 1934, Vol. 9, No. 3, pp. 7-65.

[6] M. L. Page, "The Modification of Ascendant Behavior in Preschool Children," *University of Iowa Studies in Child Welfare*, 1936, Vol. 12, No. 3, pp. 69.

[7] Even the language used in the two situations is different. In the child-adult situation we hear of "resistance," "compliance," "obedience," "negativism." Rarely if ever are such terms as "leadership" or even "ascendance" heard in this connection. But it is almost, if not equally, uncommon for adults to make such statements as "he is a good follower" with unqualified approval in speaking of a child's social relations with his companions.

CHILDREN'S FRIENDSHIPS

As early as the age of two years, children begin to show distinct preferences for the society of certain playmates. That elusive but highly important characteristic which we call "popularity" can be observed even among the youngest children in a nursery-school group. (See Figure 60.) But apart from this matter of general personality, individual friendships also show up. The bases that determine these friendships are exceedingly complex, but just as with adults [8] they are more often based upon similarities between the friends than upon the possession of opposite characteristics which the popular saying about the "attraction of opposites" would lead us to expect. For example, in a very carefully conducted study of the number of times any two members of a nursery school group were found playing together, Challman [9] found no clear-cut indication of the "attraction of opposites" but clear evidence of the "attraction of likes." Girls form friendships with girls; boys with boys. Similarity in age, in physical activity and in play interests are also important. But little children apparently hold different standards of personality values from those of adults. Little relationship was found between the popularity of a given child with his playmates and his average rating by adults on a scale for judging "attractiveness of personality."

Friendship is not simply the opposite of enmity. It is a positive matter where agreement or disagreement between the friends is of relatively little consequence. A number of carefully conducted studies have shown that, at least in early childhood, quarrels between friends are much more common than they are between those members of a nursery-school group who rarely seek each other's society.[10] In like manner, Murphy [11] reports that children who were most aggressive were also the most sympathetic members of the groups studied by her. The same child who at one

[8] See Chapter XX.

[9] Robert C. Challman, "Factors Influencing Friendships Among Preschool Children," *Child Development*, 1932, 3: 146-158.

[10] E. H. Green, "Friendships and Quarrels among Preschool Children," *Child Development*, 1933, 4: 237-252.

[11] Lois B. Murphy, *Social Behavior and Child Personality: An Exploratory Study of the Roots of Sympathy* (New York, Columbia University Press, 1937), pp. x + 333.

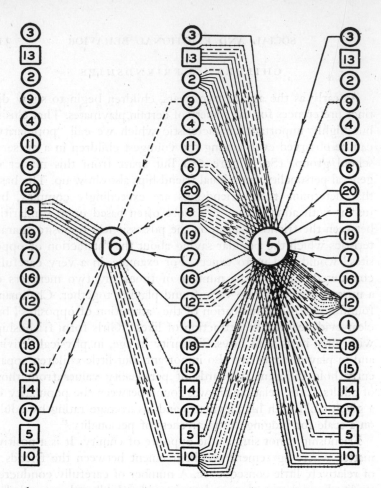

FIG. 60—DIFFERENCES IN THE NUMBER OF SYMPATHETIC SOCIAL CON-
TACTS MADE AND RECEIVED BY TWO NURSERY-SCHOOL CHILDREN:
DIAGRAM OF INDIVIDUAL RÔLES IN THE GROUP

The columns of squares and circles at right, center and left represent the
different members of a nursery-school group. Circles indicate boys; squares,
girls. The lines running from the two central characters of this study show
the number of times each of these children approached, or was approached
by, each of the other children with apparent intent to give help or comfort
(sympathetic behavior) or the reverse (unsympathetic behavior.) The direction of the arrow heads indicates the direction of the contact. The solid
lines indicate some form of active attempts to help or comfort; the dash
lines represent verbal sympathy or desire to help; the cross-hatched lines
represent instances of unsympathetic behavior or attempts to increase another child's distress, while the dotted lines represent other responses to the
unhappiness of a playmate, not clearly belonging under any of the three
heads just mentioned. (Reproduced from Murphy, *Social Behavior and
Child Personality* by permission of the author and of Columbia University
Press.)

moment pulled a playmate off his kiddie kar in order that he might ride it himself would run to comfort another in distress. As a matter of fact, it not infrequently happened that the aggressor himself would be the first to attempt to console his victim. Do we not see the same thing happening at a later age?

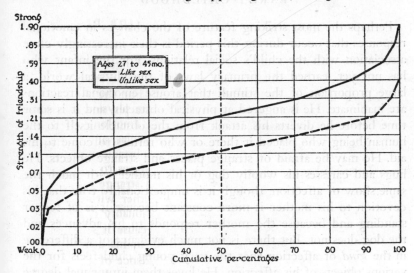

FIG. 61.—SHOWING THE PROPORTIONATE NUMBER OF TIMES NURSERY-SCHOOL CHILDREN WERE FOUND PLAYING WITH MEMBERS OF THEIR OWN AND OF THE OPPOSITE SEX

(Reproduced by permission of the author and the publisher from "Factors Influencing Friendships among Preschool Children," by Robert C. Challman. *Child Dev.*, 1932, 3: 146-158.)

All this seems to point to one conclusion. The particular pattern of social relationship is less important than the fact that social relations exist. The primary cleavage is between those who do and those who do not seek the companionship of others or those who seek it less urgently and less frequently. The amenities of social behavior must be learned, just as is true of other skills, and the process of learning them is not basically different from that seen in other areas of acquired behavior. Here, as elsewhere, practice is necessary. Quarrels and disagreements are normal features of the pattern of social life among children, and unless they become excessive they need cause no concern. Learning rarely if ever proceeds without error, and the learning of social relations is so complex that few adults completely perfect their social skills.

CHANGES IN EMOTIONAL BEHAVIOR DURING EARLY CHILDHOOD

Perhaps the most striking feature of the changes in emotional responses that occur during this period is their increasingly close association with the child's social relations. For the infant who has not yet learned the primary laws of the physical world, a large proportion of the stimuli that arouse emotional reactions are inanimate. He is angered at physical obstacles, and it is some time before he diverts his attack from the obstacle itself to the human being who placed it there or who refuses to come to his aid. He may be afraid of strange places and strange objects. He hugs and caresses his woolly dog or his mother with much the same show of affection, though it is unquestionably true that his devotion to his mother is more constant because it is of longer standing and because the mother responds to his advances and the dog does not. But there is not much evidence of a difference in the *kind* of affection that the very young child feels for the various objects of his affection. He loves them in unequal degree but in the same manner. Somewhere around the age of two, however, a distinct difference begins to be shown in the child's emotionally toned responses to other people and those shown toward things or situations not involving people. Both in his anger and in his fear one can note an element of expectancy when people are concerned that is less apparent in their absence. His screams will be momentarily interrupted as he assumes a "listening" attitude to see if they are taking effect. Social stimuli either directly or indirectly become the chief sources of the child's emotional reactions as he grows older and his responses to these stimuli are likewise directed toward human beings in increasing degree.

Like other forms of social behavior, emotional episodes become easier to describe and classify after the child begins to talk. Moreover, now that he is able to understand the speech of others, a new and very important basis for emotional reactions is provided. During infancy his emotions could be aroused only by means of things done to him or in his presence. Now he can be made angry or afraid or sympathetic or jealous through things that are said. From now on, emotional responses will often appear that seem quite inexplicable to his elders who have not followed through the course of his childish reasoning.

A little boy, not quite three, was very fond of being taken to a near-by lake to bathe. He showed not the slightest fear of the water and delighted in being taken far out from shore by his father, who was an expert swimmer. One day he was taken fishing in the same lake and this too he appeared to enjoy greatly. He sat in the boat, "fished" with a light rod, and shrieked with glee when he succeeded in catching a small fish. A few days later he was again taken swimming. To the amazement of every one he refused, with every sign of fear, to go near the water. His father finally undressed him by force and attempted to carry him in, but no sooner had his feet touched the water than he began screaming in such extreme terror that it was thought best not to force or urge him further. He could give no explanation of his fear at the time, but a few days later he confided, "Mummy, do you know why I couldn't go in ze water one day? I was apraid ze pish would bite my peet [afraid the fish would bite my feet]."

His reasoning was simple enough. On the fishing trip there had been much talk of the way the fish were "biting." At the time this did not trouble him, for he was safe in the boat and the fish were in the water. But the next time he was called upon to go into the water with nothing to protect his "peet" from the biting fish, the situation was entirely different. Fear appeared, and not, it should be noted, through the mechanism of simple "conditioning" but through a more complicated intellectual process. So as understanding grows, emotional reactions also grow and change. New information may give an entirely new meaning to any object or situation, making fearful that which was formerly enjoyed, turning annoyance into pleasure, likes into dislikes, admiration into disgust.

The increasing importance of abstract ideas occurring through the medium of language as emotional stimuli for children is nicely shown in a study by Jersild and Holmes.[12] (See Figure 62.) This

[12] A. T. Jersild and F. B. Holmes, *Children's Fears*, Child Development Monographs, No. 20 (New York, Teachers College, Columbia University Bureau of Publications, 1935), pp. ix + 358.

figure is based upon the reports of parents of children between the ages of two and five years who reported every instance of fear shown by their children during a period of three weeks.

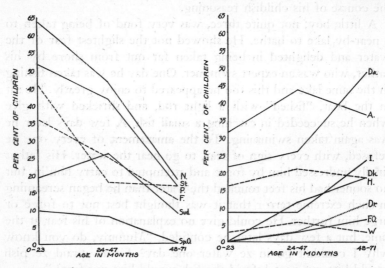

FIG. 62.—AGE CHANGES IN THE STIMULI INDUCING FEAR

The left-hand chart shows the proportionate number of children who, in the course of a twenty-one day period of observation, showed fear at least once in response to certain stimuli that in general are less likely to arouse fear as age advances. The right-hand chart shows the corresponding data for stimuli that become increasingly likely to cause fear (at least in childhood) as children grow older. The interpretation of the symbols is given below:

N—Noise
St—Strange events, objects or per-
    sons
P—Pain
F—Falling
Sud—Sudden or unexpected events,
    shadows or flashes of light
Sp. O.—Special objects or things,
    also fears of which the cause
    could not be determined

Da—Being alone in the dark
A—Animals
I—Imaginary creatures or objects
Dk—Darkness
H—Real or imagined bodily harm
Dr—Fears experienced when dream-
    ing: night terrors
F. O.—Signs of fear in other persons
W—Fears aroused by warnings of
    adults

(Adapted from *Children's Fears*, by A. T. Jersild and Frances B. Holmes. Bureau of Publications, Teachers College, Columbia University.)

There was a steady decrease with age in the proportionate number of fears caused by immediate concrete factors and a corresponding increase in those having to do with imaginary terrors or the anticipation of future events. This is another example of the rule we have so often emphasized. The unit of behavior is the child and not the ability or trait. Every developmental change that occurs, every new skill that he acquires, every new bit of information or experience changes his behavior in ways that may at first thought seem only remotely associated with the area immediately involved. No aspect of the child's personality can be changed without affecting all the rest.

METHODS OF STUDYING THE CHILD'S EMOTIONS

As with infants, direct observation with occasional supplementation by moving pictures or still photographs is still the favorite method of studying emotional behavior during childhood. However a few attempts have been made to utilize instrumental records of bodily changes as indices of emotional conditions that are presumably "felt" but that do not clearly manifest themselves in overt behavior. It was pointed out in Chapter VIII that when the sympathetic division of the autonomic nervous system goes into action, numerous responses occur in the smooth muscles and glands. Among these, the action of the sweat glands in the skin is noticeable. Presumably as a result of their action, perhaps also of contractions in the surface musculature, the electrical resistance of the skin is changed.[13] For many years it has been known that if the electrodes of a sensitive *galvanometer* (which is an instrument for measuring the strength of an electric current) are placed at two different points on the skin, a deflection of the galvanometer needle will indicate the passage of an electric current. It has been found that under emotional stimulation the deflections of the needle will usually increase (see Figure 63), and the amount of the increase has by some been regarded as an indication of the strength of the emotion. Most people, however, mindful of the fact that the experiment is an exceedingly delicate one and that the apparatus itself is likely to get out of order and give misleading results, have felt that at most the galvanometric method can

[13] There is not complete agreement among authorities as to the precise nature of the bodily changes involved in the psychogalvanic reflex, but it is generally believed to originate in the sweat glands and the tissues surrounding them.

only be used to indicate the existence of bodily changes typically occurring in emotion and not of the extent of these changes.

Jones [14] made simultaneous records of the galvanic skin reflex and of behavior as directly noted by a concealed observer in pre-school children who were subjected to a number of stimuli that might be expected to arouse fear, such as a loud sound, a white rat suddenly released in their presence, and so on. He found that

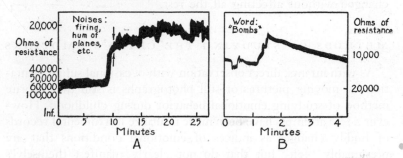

FIG. 63.—CHANGES IN THE ELECTRICAL RESPONSES OF THE SKIN DURING EMOTIONAL STIMULI

The left-hand chart (*A*) shows the changes recorded for a woman sub-ject during an air raid over London in World War I. At about the be-ginning of the tenth minute she heard the sirens indicating the approach of enemy planes, then the humming of the planes and the sound of anti-aircraft fire, which continued for some time. The right-hand chart shows the response of the same subject on another occasion to the mere pro-nouncement of the word "bombs" when no air raid was in progress. It shows how effectively a word can function for the thing which it sym-bolizes.

(These charts are based upon a study by A. D. Waller published in *Nature*, 1921, 107, p. 185 and in the *Proceedings of the Royal Society of London*, B, 1917, 90, 217, and have been reproduced here from *Fundamentals of General Psychology*, by J. F. Dashiell. Houghton Mifflin Co.)

there was not much relation between the two forms of response. This, he thought, suggested that even in childhood some indi-viduals express their emotions by outward signs that any one can see, while in others the bodily response is largely covert, a matter of the internal organs and glands. Whether or not his inter-pretation of this particular finding was correct we have no means of knowing, but there can be no doubt that both children and

[14] H. E. Jones, "The Galvanic Skin Reflex as Related to Overt Emo-tional Expression," *Amer. J. Psychol.*, 1935, 47: 241-251.

adults differ greatly in their bodily responses to emotional stimuli. A very extreme fright may cause one child to scream and another to vomit. In anger some people flush, and others grow pale; still others flush and pale alternately. Social training leads to the suppression of certain forms of emotional responses, and even at the nursery-school ages the effect of such training has begun to appear.

Many other forms of bodily change have been and still are used as indicators of emotional responses. Changes in the systolic blood pressure rank as a close second to the galvanic reflex in popularity, while other devices that may be mentioned are the *plethysmograph* for measuring changes in the distribution of blood to different parts of the body,[15] as well as various devices for measuring changes in heart rate or in the rate of breathing. All of these have been used much more extensively with adults than with children.

SOCIAL-EMOTIONAL ASPECTS OF CHILDREN'S PLAY

Jersild and Markey [16] report greater differences in the frequency of quarrels between children attending different nursery schools than between children of different sex, age, or intelligence in the same nursery school. This seems to indicate that within the age-range studied, external factors such as differences in play space and play materials, and probably most of all in the personality of the various teachers and their aptitude for handling childhood disagreements count for more than differences in the children themselves. However we cannot leave the last factor out of account, for we are dealing not with the independent action of single children but with the interaction of groups where the behavior of each child affects that of all the rest. One quarrelsome child can spread conflict throughout an entire group. These authors note, as others have done, that the pattern of conflict differs with age and sex. When angry, boys are more likely to hit and

---

[15] During strong emotion there is withdrawal of blood from the surface of the body to the internal organs, causing paling of the skin; or, conversely, the capillaries of the skin may dilate, causing the skin to flush.

[16] A. T. Jersild and F. V. Markey, *Conflicts Between Preschool Children*, Child Development Monographs, No. 21 (New York, Teachers College, Columbia University Bureau of Publications, 1936), pp. ix + 181.

kick; girls to call names and cry. As children grow older, their quarrels are less frequent but they are not so quickly brought to a close.

With advancing age, dramatization and make-believe become increasingly important aspects of children's play. This fact caused much speculation about the inner meaning of play in childhood among psychologists of the generation just past, and it has aroused equal interest among modern clinicians. But the modern interest is very different from that of the older group. Formerly, psychologists were chiefly concerned with the question, Why do children play? To this, Spencer replied by saying that play is simply an outlet for superfluous energy—a letting off of steam. Groos, in his well-known book *The Play of Man* emphasized the utility of the child's play as a preparation for life. The little girl who plays with her dolls is unconsciously fitting herself for the care of a baby later on; the little boy who hammers nails into a board for fun is getting ready for the serious constructive work of the man. G. Stanley Hall, along with many others of his time, rejected both these ideas in favor of what is called the *recapitulation theory* of children's play. This theory is of some importance because it furnished such an impetus for the earlier studies of child development. Briefly stated, the theory is this. *The child, in his development, repeats the history of the race.* So in his play the child was supposed to go through the same general stages as primitive man followed in his progress toward civilization. Those who accepted this theory studied the play of children not so much as an index to the characteristics of the children themselves but as a possible key to the behavior of their primitive ancestors.

The modern student of child development is less concerned with the question of why children play than with that of how they play. He sees in the changing patterns of play and its associated social and emotional reactions a reflection of the child's whole personality. In his play the little child displays his abilities, his interests and attitudes, his assets and his handicaps. Had we but the wisdom to read the signs, we should find in the child's play the surest index to his character.

Some modern clinical psychologists, especially those most strongly influenced by the teachings of the psychoanalytic school (about which we shall have more to say later on) are attempting to do that very thing. The procedures employed are grouped together under the general heading of "play analysis" or "play therapy," depending on whether the worker's aim is mainly diagnostic or whether attempts at improving the child's emotional and social adjustments are made. The experimental procedures and the manner of handling the results vary according to the purpose of the investigation, but one of the problems for which their use is especially popular is the study of the child's relations with his parents and the other members of his family. We all know that such personal relationships play an exceedingly important part in the development of the child's personality, yet there is perhaps no other field about which information is quite so difficult to secure. The theory underlying the method of play analysis is that the child in his dramatic play recapitulates not the history of the race but his own experiences reorganized into the form given by the particular meaning that these experiences have taken on for him. And while he does not anticipate his own future activities, as Groos would have it, he may and often does dramatize the fulfillment of his present unsatisfied wishes.

So in the play interview the child is provided with dolls which are named for the members of his family. Their sizes and clothing are roughly appropriate to the ages and sex of the persons they are to represent, and as they are handed to the child, one by one, the experimenter in a playful manner names them for him. "You have a daddy at home, haven't you? Then we'll play this doll is daddy. See, he has a coat and trousers and a shirt, just like daddy. And this one we'll call Mother, and this is sister Mary, and this is baby Dick. And *this* one," with smiling emphasis as he points from doll to child, "is Caroline" (or whatever the child's name may be). "And here are some things to put in their house," giving the child some pieces of toy furniture. "Now I have some writing to do so you may take all these things to play with for a while. You may do whatever you like with them. You needn't worry about hurting them." And later on, if the child does not appear to be playing freely, the experimenter repeats, "You may play with the things just as you wish. I don't care what you do to them."

As the child plays, notes are made of his behavior with each of the dolls. The number of times he caresses or spanks each one, his remarks to and about each, the special favors he bestows upon them together with many other aspects of his behavior in the play situation are looked upon as diagnostic signs of the child's attitude toward the real members of his family. The method holds promise, but a good deal of further work needs to be done before we can know just what to expect from it. Particularly is it dangerous when used, as many zealous but poorly trained clinicians are using it to-day, as a device for verifying some of the more extreme psychoanalytic theories of the emotional development of children. In their zeal for fitting facts to theory, these persons frequently commit the error of reading into very simple and ordinary activities of the child the psychosexual meanings that arise through adult experience.

THE PSYCHOANALYTIC VIEW OF CHILDREN'S EMOTIONS

The old saying, "Just as the twig is bent, the tree's inclined" unquestionably holds much truth. There can be no reasonable doubt that most of us carry about with us a store of likes and dislikes, dreads and anxieties, superstitions and phantasies that have their roots in the unremembered experiences of early childhood. Recognition of this fact led Dr. Sigmund Freud, a Viennese physician specializing in mental disorders, to formulate the principles of what is now known as psychoanalysis. It would be out of place to attempt to outline these principles in detail, especially since they were greatly extended and elaborated in the course of Freud's long life. We shall merely mention a few of the leading points that have bearing on our discussion.

One of the important contributions of psychoanalysis to the study of human development and behavior consists in its recognition of the fact that sex impulses do not spring into being all at once at the time of puberty but have their origin in early childhood. True, they are neither well localized nor (as a rule) very strong at that time, and it is probable that Freud and his followers, most of whose work has been done with pathological cases rather than with normal children or adults, have grossly exaggerated the rôle of sex in their theories of emotional development. But it is equally likely that too little attention was paid to this aspect of child behavior in the past. According to the psychoanalysts, most of the mental disorders that have no ascertainable organic base, as well as most of the persistent worries, fears, and anxieties to which the majority of us are subject in greater or less degree, are traceable to certain suppressed desires. At the outset these desires are suppressed by the direct action of father, mother, and others in authority, but very soon they are suppressed by the child himself, by the ideas of what is and what is not socially acceptable that develop in the course of his experience. Freud contends that there are only two really strong impulses by which all people are dominated, the impulse for self-preservation and the sex impulse. Now the impulse for self-preservation is generally recognized as something respectable and even desirable, so that no one interferes very much with its free expression. But sex is different. Very early in life the child is taught that sex, the sex organs, the parts surrounding them, and all things relating thereto are tabooed subjects of conversation in polite society.

A theory much stressed by the psychoanalysts is that during early childhood each little boy falls in love with his mother and is highly jealous of, perhaps even comes to hate his father, while each little girl loves her father and resents having to share his love with her mother. Here we have the much-talked-of Œdipus complex (named from the Greek tragedy *Œdipus Rex*) in the case of the boy, while its feminine counterpart is known as the Electra complex.

Because sex and all things associated with it are represented to the child as something wrong and shameful, he is forced to relegate them to a rather mysterious part of the mind known as the "Unconscious," a mental domain which, because of its vast importance in psychoanalytic theory, deserves to be capitalized. There sex ideas are held down by the "Censor," a name applied to the attitudes toward these matters that social pressure has forced the child to take. But the Censor has only limited power. It may consign sex and all its devilish works to the realm of the Unconscious, but they don't stay put. Instead they merely don enough of a disguise to deceive the Censor (who seems to be rather easily fooled) and thereupon break loose in all sorts of ways. Nail-biting, thumb-sucking, even lying and stealing, according to this point of view, are likely to be nothing more than manifestations of the sex urge that have chosen this way of evading the Censor.

Like many another promising train of ideas, the theories of psychoanalysis have lost much of their significance by being shunted off on a single track. It is not necessary to postulate any special mental compartment such as the Unconscious to understand that meanings may persist and continue to determine behavior long after one has forgotten how these meanings came into existence. Your own memory does not tell you how you learned that a chair is something to be sat upon, that it is pleasant to eat an apple and unpleasant to eat pepper. Nevertheless you react to these present meanings without hesitation. So all sorts of early experiences may give special meanings to particular situations, and if nothing happens to change these meanings they may continue to dominate one's behavior throughout life. In all this there is nothing mysterious, nothing that requires a special explanation outside the general laws of human behavior. According to this point of view, the Unconscious is nothing more than the forgotten emotional experiences that originally gave rise to the meanings by which our present behavior is governed.

Let us now have a closer look at the Censor. The first thing that strikes us is that he is not so stupid as he has been represented. So far from being fooled by the pestiferous tricks of the illicit impulses he has penned up, he connives with them in devising forms by which they can appear in decent society. But Freud was mistaken in supposing that sex impulses are the only ones that must don false mustaches and checkered suits in order to conceal their identities. Years ago, G. Stanley Hall [17] pointed out that few if any of the primitive emotions are permitted free expression under modern conditions of civilized life. Take anger as an example. You do not as a rule give the waitress a black eye because she puts her thumb in the soup, but you may refrain from giving her a tip. When one of your classmates offends you, you are not likely to attack him with your fists, but you may make a sarcastic retort. In like manner, fear, jealousy, or other

[17] G. Stanley Hall, "Anger as a Primary Emotion and the Application of the Freudian Mechanisms to Its Phenomena," *J. Abnorm. Psychol.*, 1915, 10: 81-87; "The Freudian Methods Applied to Anger," *Amer. J. Psychol.*, 1915, 26: 438-443.

emotions when experienced under such conditions that the primitive response would fall under the social taboo are likely to find some kind of substitute expression. The process of substitution begins very early. A little boy not yet two when restrained from investigating the contents of his father's pockets ran screaming to the floor lamp, jerked at the cord and pretended he was going to tip the lamp over. A little girl of about the same age when punished for some small misdemeanor pulled all the cushions off the davenport. Somewhat later the day-dream comes in as a form of substitution for emotions that are denied more active expression. In the day-dream you are exalted, while the rival who has made you angry or jealous or afraid is made to suffer all the punishment that you were unable to inflict at the time.

The lesson that we may learn from the psychoanalysts is not the limited idea that we must always look for some underlying sex factor in connection with any unexplained fear, worry, or other symptom of maladjusted behavior in a child or an adult, but rather that we should try to ascertain what meaning the situation giving immediate rise to the behavior over which we are concerned has taken on for him. Since, as we have seen, the most vivid and persistent meanings arise in connection with situations of marked emotional content, we may expect to find that in the majority of cases the origin of the difficulty may be traced back to an emotional episode of some kind. It may be a sexual event; it may be something quite different. Moreover, we shall find that such conflicts usually have their roots in something that interferes or threatens to interfere with some strongly developed impulse or desire. This desire may be related to sex, to the craving for self-assertion, to material wants such as money or professional success, or to the desire for social companionship or for the love or friendship of some one person. And the particular symptoms that develop as a result of the conflict will depend on the meaning that the original situation had for the individual in question and the method by which he attained satisfaction at the time. If the meaning was, so to speak, "correct," that is if the nature and causes of the interference were clearly understood, the resultant behavior is likely to be simple and direct. We have plenty of examples of children who, instead of developing strange fears and anxieties over the birth of a baby brother or sister, recognize him at once for the interloper that he is and vent their displeasure by attacking him, trying to tip him out of his cradle, or perhaps refusing to look at him and denying his existence when asked about him. Behavior of this kind is, by comparison, easy to deal with because its motive is evident. But when, either through direct conditioning, through incomplete understanding of the situation, or as a result of conflicting motives, some extrinsic and often trivial object or circumstance becomes capable of arousing an unusual form of response, the condition is harder to correct because its origin is so obscure and the resulting behavior may appear so inappropriate to the motives from which it sprang.

WHAT IS A "MENTAL CONFLICT"?

Suppose that a child who dearly loves both his parents but who also wants to stand first in their affections is continually made jealous by the signs of their fondness for each other. He feels that he *must* do something about it. This feeling of "must," as we have seen, is an essential component of emotion. Yet what can he do? His jealousy prompts him to do injury, but his love for both parents makes this impossible. Something *must* be done. In the course of his restless groping for an outlet that will satisfy both his love and his jealousy, chance often provides a solution. Perhaps he is startled by some unexpected noise after he is put to bed. He cries out, his mother comes to him and soothes him. The original fright was slight, and ordinarily would have had no permanent effect. Note, however, that the result of the fright is something which satisfies the deeper emotion that was there all the time, the jealousy, the unsatisfied desire to be the center of affection. So, by a process closely resembling that of ordinary conditioning, the situation "being alone in bed" takes on a terrifying meaning for him. It becomes identified with a state of jealousy culminating in terror. He cannot tell what he is afraid of, for he does not know. But his night terrors persist, sometimes for years or even into adult life.

The blocking of emotional behavior, the state of anxiety and indecision that comes when emotions leading to opposite courses of actions are simultaneously aroused, constitutes what is commonly known as a mental conflict. Because the drive to action is as strong as ever but its usual pathways are blocked off, a mental conflict often results in the setting up of some unusual form of behavior that seems quite unreasonable to an outsider. The feelings of anxiety, uncertainty, and worry that result from the conflict become attached to some outside fact, perhaps very trivial in nature, but which thereafter takes on a meaning that is far from trivial to the person concerned. To him it has become an object of worry, of fear, anxiety, and dread. He does not know why, because the original emotion had no clear pattern. It was not a case of "I *must* get away from that bear" but rather of "I *must* do something, but I don't know what."

Unusual fears, worries, and anxieties are not the only obscure forms of behavior that mental conflicts may engender. It some-times happens that the child who is the victim of conflicting motives discovers a method whereby his difficulties may for the time be reconciled. He loves his parents and wants their undivided attention; he would like to punish them for diverting to each other some of the love that he feels to be rightfully his. He finds that both these desires can be satisfied by some form of misbe-havior. So he takes to nail-biting or perhaps to swearing or steal-ing. In this way he gets both revenge and a larger share of attention. Thus he finds a kind of pleasure in his misdemeanors. They have become for him a way out of his difficulties. And so the emotional drive, the feeling that "I *must* do something but I don't know what" changes to "I *must* bite my nails," or steal, or swear, or whatever other act it may be that has provided satisfaction for the emotional conflict.

Mental conflicts may then lead either to a transfer of fears and anxieties aroused by the conflict to some other factor in the situa-tion (as in ordinary conditioning) or to certain compulsive acts, things that one feels obliged to do whenever the feeling of con-flict becomes acute. In either case the reason lies in the attach-ment of a new and ofttimes very unusual meaning to a situation or an activity. On the one hand we have, "This object or situation is something that (through conditioning) I have grown to fear"; on the other hand, "This act is something I must do to relieve my distress."

Mental conflicts, like other emotional states, vary in duration and intensity. Many are trivial and soon over; some persist for many years. But the meanings to which they give rise often far outlive the conflicts themselves. Because early childhood is of all periods in life the time when new meanings are being formed most rapidly, it is not surprising to find that a large proportion of adult worries and anxieties, particularly those which seem to others to be unwarranted, have their origin in the unremembered experiences of childhood.

THE RECONDITIONING OF EMOTIONS

The best way to ensure healthy emotional development would be to see to it that no unfortunate experiences leading to the attachment of emotional behavior to inappropriate events should occur in the child's life. Like many other ideals, however, this is one not likely to be completely possible of fulfillment, though intelligent understanding of the mechanisms by which undesirable emotional behavior may arise sometimes makes it possible to avoid difficulties that would otherwise ensue. But is prevention the only answer? Can't we do something for the emotional conflicts or other difficulties that already exist in ourselves and in others?

Yes. If we can find out how the difficulty started, we can attack the matter directly by pointing the way to a new and more suitable emotional outlet, if the disturbing condition still exists, either by correcting the cause of the disturbance or by explaining facts that may have been misunderstood; thus a new and more desirable meaning may be substituted for the former undesirable or inappropriate one, and so the difficulty may be overcome. In the case of the little boy who became afraid to go in swimming, once the origin of the fear was discovered its correction became an easy matter. It was explained to him that fish do not bite little boys but only fish-worms and that when little boys come into the water all the fish swim away fast (and this was verified by taking him to a pool where there were a number of minnows and encouraging him to put his hands into the water). Further assistance was given by buying him a bowl of goldfish in order that pleasant associations with fish might take the place of the unpleasant ones. In this case the fear disappeared within a few days and never returned.

If the fear or anxiety has arisen through simple conditioning and there is no longer any active cause for it, it is often possible to correct matters by "reconditioning," even though the origin of the trouble may remain unknown. Reconditioning means that you attach a new and pleasant meaning to the fear-producing object or situation by associating it repeatedly with pleasant events. Jones [18] found, for example, that children who were much afraid of rabbits or other small animals could be trained to accept them with no signs of fear by bringing the animals gradually nearer and nearer when the child was eating food that he liked. So an initial dislike of some one who has never offended us and which was probably caused by the fact that he happened to remind us of some unpleasant experience soon disappears if later associations are pleasant. Even better is the method employed by Jersild and Holmes,[19] who successfully overcame various kinds of fear by teaching children *what to do in the fear-arousing situation*. For example, children who were afraid of high places were taught to walk a plank that was at first placed flat on the floor and then raised a few inches at a time as skill was gained. In the course of a few weeks of practice, children who at first had been afraid to venture upon the plank when it was just barely above the floor, would dash gleefully across it at a height of several feet.

But suppose we are dealing with a mental conflict that is still present and that, through one or another of the mechanisms we have described, is expressing itself in some undesirable or bizarre form. In such cases it is not likely to do much good to recondition the particular behavior that happens to be shown, for the underlying cause is still there and is likely to break out again in some other form. If careful study fails to reveal the true nature of the difficulty, it may be best to consult a psychiatrist whose training and experience in such matters will often enable him to unravel mental snarls that to the layman seem hopelessly puzzling.

[18] Mary Cover Jones, "A Study of the Emotions of Preschool Children," *School and Soc.*, 1925, 21: 755-758.
[19] A. T. Jersild and F. B. Holmes, "Methods of Overcoming Children's Fears," *J. Psychol.*, 1935-36, 1: 75-104.

THE STORY OF PSYCHOANALYSIS

Edna Heidbreder, "Freud and the Psychoanalytic Movement," Chapter X in *Seven Psychologies* (New York, D. Appleton-Century Co., 1933), pp. x + 450.

Psychoanalysis is something almost everybody talks about but few people understand. For many people it has all the hidden fascination of the sex difficulties with which it is so largely concerned. Some think of it as a magic cure for all mental ills; others reject it with an emotionally toned vehemence that its protagonists regard as the best possible evidence that they need its therapy.

It is not necessary to accept the doctrines of psychoanalysis *in toto* in order to appreciate the positive contribution that psychoanalytic studies have made to our understanding of human behavior. It is doubtful whether any other school of thought has affected quite such revolutionary changes in our ideas of how the mind works and how personalities become warped as those arising through the gradual infiltration of psychoanalytic concepts into modern psychological theory. To be sure, these ideas have often become so modified that their origin is scarcely recognizable. But trace them back and you will find whence they sprang.

So it is not just because everybody has something to say about it and because so many jokes are made about it that you should know what psychoanalysis is really about, how it originated, and what it teaches. You should know about it because it is worth knowing.

In thirty-seven interesting pages, Dr. Heidbreder, who is now Chairman of the Department of Psychology at Wellesley College, tells this story. You will enjoy reading it, and when you have finished you should have a much clearer appreciation than you are now likely to have both of the debt that science owes to the psychoanalytic movement and of the weaknesses inherent in its underlying theory.

Chapter XIV

THE GROWTH OF PERCEPTION, JUDGMENT, AND UNDERSTANDING IN CHILDHOOD

How does perception differ from sensation?

How does the study of perceptual illusions contribute to our knowledge of the development of perception in the child and the factors influencing perception in the adult?

Do we perceive in wholes or in parts that are later pieced together to form wholes? Cite evidence in support of your answer and if possible give an illustration from your own experience.

What are some of the external factors affecting attention? The internal factors? What is the relative importance of external and internal factors in determining the attention-getting value of an object or situation at the age of three months? At the age of twenty?

What are some of the factors affecting the length of time that can be interposed between stimulus and response in childhood?

What appear to be some of the main characteristics of child logic? Do adults ever reason in a similar manner?

THE CHILD'S PERCEPTUAL WORLD

As far as we can judge from his behavior, before the end of the first year the child's sense-organs are functioning as well as they ever will. As a result of his growing experience he soon learns to interpret most of the simple impressions he receives through his senses with a high degree of accuracy. Careful experiments have shown that by the age of four or five years, children will react to distance by reaching to the correct point, will match lines of different length, and will choose the heavier of two weights almost if not quite as exactly as adults.

But we must not fall into the error of supposing that, because simple perceptual skills such as these have approached the adult level of development, the world as a whole looks to the child the same as it does to the adult. A simple experiment will illustrate. When children of different ages are shown, one at a time, a series of colored geometrical forms—stars, circles, squares, and the like —and are asked in each case to choose between matching the figure with another similar in form and size but differing in color, or with one of the same color but differing in form, it has been found [1] that children under two and a half years usually match on the basis of form. At about the age of two and a half or three years a swing toward color appears. Thereafter an increasingly greater percentage of the matchings are made in terms of color, ignoring differences in form, until a maximum preference for color is reached at about the age of four and a half. Then the tide of interest again turns. Form and not color decides the issue in more and more of the choices until the adult level is reached, at which time about 90 per cent of the matchings are made in terms of form and only 10 per cent in terms of color. (See Figure 64.)

Just how the elementary attributes of perception that enable us to respond correctly to differences in distance, depth, form, and so on are built up is not completely known for any of the senses. We do know something about the cues by which such qualities may be judged, and we know, furthermore, that a change in the usual cues may at first be so deceptive that very erroneous responses may occur. Persons reared on the eastern seaboard who are accustomed to estimate distance in terms of the atmospheric conditions of that climate find it almost impossible to believe that a peak in the Rockies seen for the first time can be as much as fifty miles away. "I'm sure I could walk to it in less than an hour," says the tenderfoot. More than one life has been

[1] C. R. Brian and F. L. Goodenough, "The Relative Potency of Color and Form Perception at Different Ages," *J. Exper. Psychol.*, 1929, 12: 197-213.

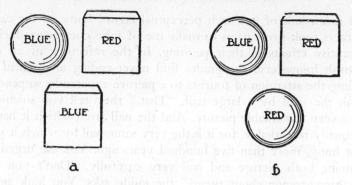

ILLUSTRATING PLACEMENT OF FORMS BEFORE CHILD

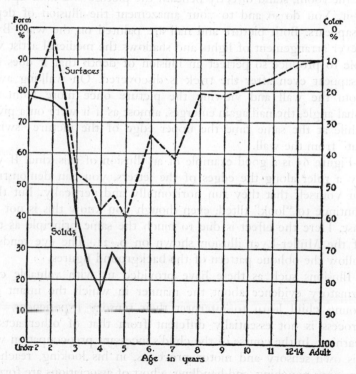

FIG. 64.—AGE CHANGES IN COLOR-FORM PERCEPTION

(From C. R. Brian and F. L. Goodenough, "The Relative Potency of Color and Form Perception at Different Ages," *J. Exper. Psychol.*, 1929, 12: 197-213. Courtesy Psychological Review Co.)

lost as a result of just such perceptual errors. Some of the early painters took great pains to make use of false cues in producing deceptive effects in their painting. In the refectory of an old Spanish monastery, the guides find never-ending amusement in calling the attention of tourists to a picture apparently suspended from the wall by a large nail. "That," they tell you solemnly "is a very remarkable picture. And the nail from which it hangs is equally remarkable, for it is the very same nail by which it was first hung, more than five hundred years ago. You are urged to examine both picture and nail very carefully. "Don't you see anything strange about them?" the guide asks. You look again but see nothing unusual. Then you are told to walk to the end of the room, stand directly beneath the picture and look upward at it. You do so and to your amazement the illusion of depth disappears. Both picture and nail are painted on the wall! By a clever arrangement of lights and shadows the medieval artist was able to produce so perfect an illusion of depth that it does not disappear even after the trick is discovered. On walking away from the wall and viewing the picture once more from the usual angle, the nail again emerges, almost as if it were on a pivot, while at the same time the upper edge of the picture "swings out" from the wall.

Figure 65 is a good example of an illusion of this kind. If you lay a ruler along the edges of the letters, you can demonstrate for yourself that they run horizontally and vertically. But they continue to "look" tilted, even though you know this is not the case. Here the effect is due to much the same principle as that of the Müller-Lyer illusion shown on p. 21. The eye tends to follow the oblique pattern of the background figures.

Illusions such as these have provided us with valuable confirmatory evidence about the manner in which the infant and young child learn to interpret their sensory experiences. The process is not essentially different from that of other acts of learning. In the course of the child's incessant preoccupation with his own sensory and motor processes, in his looking, reaching, grasping, touching, and handling, a host of associations are formed between visual, auditory, and motor performances at a very early age. Most of these associations remain unverbalized throughout life unless some special experience (such as taking a course in elementary psychology) calls attention to them. Even then, you determine the nature of the cues by which you are able to say that this book is further away than that one, or that a given sound comes from the right, not from the left, more by a process of reasoning and inference than by direct attention to your own perceptual processes. And your only way of finding out whether your inference is sound is by altering or removing, one by one, the cues to which you attributed the perceptual judgment and noting whether or not the perception itself is altered thereby.

FIG. 65.—THE TWISTED CORD ILLUSION

(After Fraser.)

Many experiments have been conducted with view to ascertaining whether or not the perceptual judgments that we make quite automatically and constantly throughout all our waking hours were learned by experience or result from neurological organizations inherent in the growth of the organism. For instance it is known that the rays of light reflected from seen objects are inverted as they pass through the optic lens and thus fall upon the retina "upside down." The question is, How does it come about that we see them right side up? In an attempt to answer this question, Stratton [2] had a system of lenses made that artifically reversed and inverted the images of all objects seen through them. These lenses were fastened over his eyes in such a way that no

[2] G. M. Stratton, "Some Preliminary Experiments Without Inversion of the Retinal Image," Psychol. Rev., 1896, 3: 611-617.

light could enter except through the lenses, which he wore for twenty-four hours distributed over three days in his first experiment and for eighty-seven hours distributed over eight days in a second experiment. He reports that at first he felt very helpless and confused, and had great difficulty in locating objects by the use of sight. But experience helped. In the course of a few hours localization of objects had become easier, and by the fourth day the process was on the way to becoming so automatic that he frequently reached directly for an object with no feeling of confusion. Stratton [3] also reports that by the end of the experiment, his visual world no longer seemed grossly out of harmony with the impressions gained through other senses. He *felt* that his legs were where they looked to be, and that the sound of a bird's song came from the direction where the bird was seen. Other experimenters, however, have not completely verified Stratton's reported experience. Like him, they found that learning to make the proper motor adjustments to the changed visual cues took place rapidly, but they failed to confirm Stratton's claimed "feeling of normalcy" in their subjective visual experience. The world still "looked" upside down.

Inasmuch as none of the later persons who repeated Stratton's experiment (and there have been several who wore the lenses continuously for two weeks or longer) succeeded in relearning their visual cues well enough to make the world seen through the reversing lenses appear to them as it had under normal vision, some people have taken the position that for the most part, at least, perception is as much a matter of the child's native equipment as sight or hearing. According to this point of view, the ability to perceive form, size, depth, distance, position, and so on is chiefly a matter of innate neurological organization. They believe that we do not learn to *perceive* these qualities but merely learn to react correctly to them. But when it is recalled that the adults who carried out these experiments had been practicing their perceptual skills for many years, the two or three weeks over which their experimental period lasted seems too short to provide crucial evidence. Moreover, if we remember what we have already learned about the principles of conditioning, the reason

[3] G. M. Stratton, "Vision Without Inversion of the Retinal Image, *Psychol. Rev.*, 1897, 4: 341-360; 463-481.

why the new motor adjustments took place more rapidly than the perceptual adjustments becomes readily apparent. For we know that learning proceeds most rapidly if every trial brings an unequivocal result. A conditioned salivary response in the dog will be established slowly and with great difficulty (if at all) if food is sometimes given when the bell is sounded, but more often not given. Now when the wearer of reversing lenses *reaches* for an object where his vision erroneously indicates that it is located, his mistake is immediately apparent. But when he merely *looks about him*—as he inevitably will be doing much of the time—there is no necessary correction of the perceptual relationships. Thus while his motor errors are invariably made known to him, the greater number of his perceptual errors remain unobserved and uncorrected. Accordingly the perceptual habits previously established are less readily changed.

All in all it seems probable that we learn to perceive in much the same manner as we learn to walk. In both cases the physical and neurological mechanisms that make the learning possible are inherent in the organism; in both cases the basic drive, the urge to put these mechanisms to work, is equally a part of the basic equipment with which nature has endowed us. Our tools are the combined experiences derived from the simultaneous operation of many sense-organs in a world where the physical laws are stable. Light rays do not pass through opaque solids; hence when we see all of one member of a pair of juxtaposed objects and only part of the other, we have a cue that in connection with many others enables us to learn to "see" that the second object is more distant than the first. Of course this is only part of the story. Sensations of eye convergence play a part. The fact that since the eyes are differently situated in the head the two images come in at different angles and are therefore not identical with each other, aids in giving an impression of depth. (See Figure 107, p. 611. This figure is discussed on p. 610.) Atmospheric effects, lights and shadows, and the integration of all these with the simultaneously experienced proprioceptive and tactile sensations associated with the movements involved in reaching, grasping and manipulating objects, in approaching, passing and going away from them, all serve as cues by which perception is learned. When the cues are changed, perception changes accordingly.

And the change is a *total* change, for perception is unitary. We do not merely see, but we see something; we not only hear, but we hear something.[4] We may not know what the "something" is.

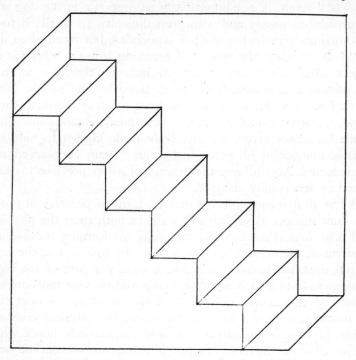

FIG. 66.—THE ALTERNATING FIGURE ILLUSION

If you look intently at this figure for some minutes you will find that the apparent perspective shifts from time to time so that the staircase is seen sometimes from the front, sometimes from the rear. (From *Great Experiments in Psychology*, by H. E. Garrett. D. Appleton-Century Co.)

Its form and structure may be so weak that it changes continually, but it always maintains some kind of internal unity and coherence.

The most significant phases of the development of perception normally take place in early infancy, long before children can

[4] If this is true, we may ask what the new-born baby sees whose opportunities for learning to perceive have only just begun. In all probability he perceives nothing at all until integration of his sensory experiences has begun to give form and structure to the amorphous raw material provided by his sensory and motor activities.

describe them. However, the first visual experiences of persons blind from birth whose sight has been restored by operations performed after they were grown up have been reported in a few instances. In the beginning few details of objects are seen. Objects and persons appear like lumpy indefinite shapes whose contour changes with changing visual regard. But they are always totalities; not mosaics made up of little bits. With practice in seeing, more details emerge and the outlines of the seen objects become more definite and stable.

Previous knowledge about a thing has a great deal to do with perception. We perceive things as we know they are or as we think they should be, and we overlook much that is there but that does not fit into our preconceived pattern. Persons inexperienced in proof-reading find it difficult to see typographical errors unless they are very glaring. Careful experiments have shown that even persons with excellent hearing actually *hear* only about 75 per cent of the sounds in an ordinary conversation. The gaps are filled in by means of the context, and the listener is so unaware of the process that he cannot tell which parts he actually hears and which he supplies. He thinks he hears it all. This tendency to fill in gaps, to complete every experience and make it into a perceptual whole, shows itself in many ways. Little children just learning the alphabet frequently confuse the letter C with the letter O. The C to them is a broken O; they fill in the gap without knowing it, and the C becomes an O. But once they learn to identify the C as a C, the broken circumference becomes an integral part of the thing perceived. It is no longer an accident to be overlooked but an important part of the new picture. When this stage is reached, the letters are no longer confused.

Whatever else perception may be, it is always an act of integration, of the construction of meaningful wholes. When elements that seem necessary to complete a perceptual unit are lacking, they will be supplied if the gap is not too great; when discordant elements are present, they will be overlooked or pushed out of the picture into the background or the whole scheme may be remodeled to fit them into it.

Perception varies with the phenomenon known as attention. Probably all of you, when sitting in a train and looking more or less idly at another train on an adjacent track, have suddenly "felt" your own train begin to move backward. The illusion is complete; you even make postural adjustment to it. You receive an actual physical jolt when the last coach of the other train passes out of your view and your eyes and body readjust to the fact that you have remained in the same place all the time. But if, instead of keeping your attention fixed on the other train, your gaze had shifted back and forth from the train to the people on the platform or to other objects unconnected with the moving train, no such illusion would have occurred. Perception is so largely governed by attention that at times the two seem merely different aspects of the same thing. Yet attention is not its sole determinant, for two people may pay equally close heed to the same object, and yet their perception of it may differ greatly. Perception varies, not only according to set or attention, but also according to one's subjective and objective points of regard. A cup viewed from above does not look the same as when viewed from the side, nor, in effect, does the cup look the same to two people, regardless of the angle from which it is seen. To the child or the savage, a gaudily painted cup from a cheap variety store may be far more beautiful than one of fine old Sèvres china.

THE PHENOMENON OF PERCEPTUAL CONSTANCY

One of the striking things about perception which has attracted a good deal of attention during recent years is the fact that the subjective point of regard so soon gains ascendancy over the objective impressions brought in by the senses that the latter seem to be almost, though not completely, disregarded.[5] Actually, of course, they are not disregarded at all but are reorganized in conformity with the subjective features of the perceptual experi-

[5] The most complete and careful studies of perceptual constancy that have so far appeared have been made by Egon Brunswik and his associates. Brunswik has shown that in controlled laboratory experiments when subjects are requested to select from a series of geometrical solids the one that best matches another placed some distance away on the basis of "real" size, there is a tendency to choose one somewhat smaller, but by no means as small as that which would be selected on the basis of the actual visual angle subtended. This tendency to intermediate judgment rather than to absolute constancy of perceptual qualities is referred to by Brunswik as "Zwischengestand," or intermediate judgment. The judgment, however, is normally not at the half-way position but much nearer to the "real" size than to the size as projected on the retina.

ence. Seated at the dinner table, you do not "see" the plate belonging to your friend at the other end of the table as something very much smaller than your own. You may even look enviously at his piece of apple pie and think that the waitress has treated him more generously than you. Yet the visual angle subtended by your own plate may be several times as great as that of your

FIG. 67.—THE CAMERA RECORDS THE ACTUAL PROJECTION OF
THE IMAGE

Note the comparative size of head and feet as "seen" by the camera.

friend's plate. A camera, which has an "eye" but no central nervous system, records the light rays as they actually strike the lens with no subsequent reorganization. Figure 67 illustrates the difference between what the eye sees and what the total organism perceives.

Not only size but practically all other aspects of our perceptual experience exhibit this characteristic feature of experiential constancy to a greater or less extent. A piece of anthracite coal viewed in bright sunlight reflects far more light into the eyes than does a dull white object seen in shadow. Again the camera would reveal this fact, but to the eye the coal is still black and the white object remains white. A melody transposed to a different key is still the same melody. However, we do not completely lose sight of the objective factors in perception. We say, "Bring that nearer, so I can see it better," or "Take those two colors into a better light; I can't tell which is darker." At times we may be caught unaware, and then the facts given by sensation are reorganized into a very deceptive but equally clear perception. An irregularly shaped spot on the wind-shield of your car may be momentarily seen as a far-off airplane, or conversely, the faint scream of a distant siren on a hot night may be "heard" as a mosquito close to your ear.[6]

As with other perceptual phenomena, there is not complete agreement among authorities as to the relative importance of neural preorganization and subsequent life experience in the establishment of attribute constancy. Particularly the more elementary aspects, such as size constancy, have been shown to exist in well-developed form at a fairly early age.[7] By the time a child's vocabulary has advanced to a stage at which he knows the meaning of "bigger" or "smaller," he has no difficulty in selecting the larger of two blocks so placed that the visual angle subtended by the smaller block is greater than that of the larger block. Nevertheless when we recall his enormous amount of previous experience in the manipulating of objects seen at varying distances, it is evident that there is plenty of time for such perceptual learning to occur long before the beginning of speech. Attempts have been made to conduct similar experiments with infants, using reaching as a criterion, but these have not been very successful [8] because

[6] Poe's story *The Sphinx* gives an amusing illustration of the effect of such a perceptual illusion.

[7] This does not mean that the tendency to perceptual constancy is completely developed in early childhood. Brunswik and others have shown that although clearly present at the age of two years, constancy in the perception of size continues to improve at least up to the age of ten.

[8] An excellent English summary of the classic work of Brunswik and his associates on perceptual constancy (Egon Brunswik and others, *Wahrnehmung und Gegenstandswelt: Grundlagen einer Psychologie von Gegenstand her* (Leipzig und Wien, Dentick, 1934), pp. xi + 244) is to be found in a review by E. C. Tolman, *Psychol. Bul.*, 1935, 32: 608-614.

of the difficulty of knowing whether the infant who reaches for the small object nearer at hand really "sees" it as larger or merely grasps it because it is more conveniently placed.

ATTENTION

We have seen that perception, the way objects and events are apprehended, varies with many factors, one of which is the behavioral "set" of the individual at the moment. We may ask, then, what factors affect attention. As with perception itself, these may be divided into two classes: the external features of the object or situation and the internal predispositions and activities of the subject. Among the former are such attributes as size, intensity, duration,[9] movement, and so on. Internal predispositions vary both in intensity and in duration. On the one hand we have the shifting and more or less recurrent physiological drives. Every restaurant window catches the attention of the hungry man, but after lunch he passes them without a look. Circumstantial factors of many kinds temporarily induce shifts in attitudinal set. You inspect the windows of the clothing stores more closely than usual when you are in need of a new suit, and you scan the headlines of the morning paper with more eagerness at times of an international crisis. But more important than all of these are the comparatively habitual "sets" or attitudinal predispositions that each of us builds up in the course of his everyday living.

Nowhere in the study of human behavior is the circular effect of action and reaction more clearly shown than in the matter of attention. All sorts of factors, both external and internal, affect the child's momentary reactions to passing events. But through these reactions attitudes are built up that later on will determine much of his perceptual experience. Two children walking along

[9] The effect of the duration of a stimulus upon attention varies in an exceedingly complex way. Under certain conditions, longer duration makes for attention, as when the automobile driver engaged in lively conversation gradually becomes aware of a slight "knocking" in his engine and turns his attention to it. Under other conditions it may make for negative adaptation —you become "used" to a sound that originally annoyed you and no longer notice it. The effect of duration or repetition of a stimulus appears to be chiefly a matter of the predisposition of the subject. This shows that the internal and external factors that affect attention are not truly distinct, though for practical convenience they may be so regarded.

the same street see and hear very different things. To the one, the trip is an exciting adventure. He reaches home eager to tell of what he saw and heard. His parents discuss it with him and provide information that directs and intensifies his original predisposition to give heed to the world about him. The second child takes little note of his surroundings. He is preoccupied with thoughts of the report card in his pocket and of the scolding he is almost certain to get when his father sees it. Because his attention is differently directed, he fails to gain a number of things that his companion obtained from that half-hour of life. Not only did he miss the particular bits of information acquired by the other lad, but he lost what is of infinitely more importance from the standpoint of his developmental progress. He failed to gain the disposition, the attitudinal set that would lead to further observation and the acquisition of further information. With repeated experiences of this kind we get the man who travels around the world and at the end of his trip can tell you little beyond the cost of his ticket and the fact that he encountered bedbugs in Naples. Paraphrasing Anita Loos's epitomized account of her party, "So one thing led to another and then the police came," we may say, "So one thing leads to another and thence attention grows."

FACTORS AFFECTING MEMORY IN YOUNG CHILDREN

Psychologists are accustomed to classify acts of memory under three heads: *recognition, recall,* and *reproduction.* Each of these presupposes two things, that the fact or skill has been *acquired* at some time in the past and that it has been *retained* up to the time of the test. Although in an academic sense we speak of the act of acquisition as "learning" and that of retention as "memory," we have no means of knowing whether or not either has taken place except by noting whether or not it can be recalled, reproduced, or recognized. It is customary, however, to classify investigations centering about the effect of changing the conditions under which the facts or skill is acquired as studies in *learning.* Experiments in which a comparison is made between different methods of demonstrating retention or of different conditions during the period of retention are considered studies of *memory*. Thus a study of the relative effectiveness of longer or shorter periods of study would be classed as an investigation of learning, while one dealing with the comparative amounts retained after a specified number of hours spent in sleep or in ordinary daytime activity would be called a study of memory. The term "memory" is also used to denote studies of the ability to reproduce material seen or heard but a single time.

It is evident that infants remember, for we know that they learn, but because they do not coöperate actively in the testing situation (that is, they do not respond to verbal instructions), it is not always easy to study the matter directly. Many of the tests for infants described in an early chapter have to do with indications of recognition of something previously shown or of surprise at some experimentally introduced change in it, but the scoring of these responses is for the most part based upon the child's vocalization, facial expression, or similar matters that are often hard to interpret. For example, in one of the Bühler-Hetzer baby tests, the child of twelve to fifteen months is given a small rubber ball. When the ball is squeezed a chicken or rabbit comes out. The child is allowed to play with the ball for a minute, making the animal come in and out with the examiner's help. Then the ball is taken away and the child is given other toys for a period of three minutes, after which he is given another ball, like the first except that the chicken has been removed. The test is passed if the child shows indications of surprise or distress at its absence.

The most satisfactory method so far devised for studying the retention of previous experience in children whose speech is not yet well advanced is the "delayed reaction technique." In experiments of this type the aim is to find out how long a time can be allowed to intervene between the presentation of a stimulus and the making of a correct response.

The subject is first taught to respond to a signal. He is placed before a box that has two or more doors, exactly alike except for the one thing that is to serve as the signal. Perhaps one of the doors has a lighted electric bulb behind it. This light is changed irregularly from one door to the other but always marks the one behind which food or some other lure is to be found.

Both animals and children will soon learn to respond to such a signal. When it is given, they will run promptly to the correct door and pay no attention to the other. The question then arises, Suppose the light is shown only for a moment and then turned off. If the subject is restrained from responding at the time, how long a delay can be interposed without interfering with his ability to choose the correct door? How long, that is, can he "remember" the position of the signal, and what factors other than time affect his ability to do so?

Hunter, who conducted the pioneer experiment in this field,[10] found that most animals that are able to learn to respond to a signal will continue to respond correctly after a brief delay. With rats the maximum is about five seconds. Unless the act can be carried out within that time it cannot be done at all. Cats can wait a little longer, perhaps a quarter of a minute; raccoons and dogs still longer and children longer still, the exact time depending on the age of the child. Hunter's figures for children are not very reliable because of his few cases, but Skalet,[11] who conducted a similar experiment with larger groups, found that even after several days had passed, children of two to four years could select the one of three plates under which they had previously seen the experimenter put an animal cracker. She also found that the length of delay after which a correct response could be made varied with the kind of stimulus used. The more concrete and meaningful the situation, the longer was the possible delay. Children would respond to the animal cracker situation after a longer delay than was possible when the task was to select the right one of three pictures of common objects; and the picture situation, in its turn, permitted a longer delay than was possible when meaningless geometrical figures were used. Tinklepaugh,[12] with monkeys as subjects, used a plan similar to Skalet's first experiment. He would put lettuce or banana under one or the other of two inverted cups while the monkey looked on. The monkeys, like the children, were able to respond correctly after a considerable delay, in some

[10] W. S. Hunter, "The Delayed Reaction in Animals and Children," *Behavior Monog.*, 1913, 2: 1-86.

[11] Magda Skalet, "The Significance of Delayed Reactions in Young Children," *Comp. Psychol. Monog.*, 1931, 7, 82 pp.

[12] O. L. Tinklepaugh, "An Experimental Study of Representative Factors in Monkeys," *J. Comp. Psychol.*, 1928, 8: 197-236.

cases after several hours. This is not equal to the performance of the children, but it is far better than any of the other animals that have been studied were able to do.

In addition to the time over which the reaction could be delayed without interfering with the response, Hunter noticed [13] another point. The less intelligent animals usually have to keep their eyes, heads, and bodies turned in the right direction all through the period of the delay. If the bodily orientation is lost the response cannot take place. But with the children, the monkeys, and some of the dogs and raccoons, a change of position during the period of delay makes little or no difference. The children and the monkeys can even leave the room, go on with their regular occupations, and still respond correctly on their return, provided the interval is not too long.

Although a change in bodily orientation does not make it impossible for a child or an adult to respond correctly after a delay, it does increase the likelihood of error, and there is evidence that some persons are more disturbed by such a change than others are. Many of you have probably noticed this in yourselves. You enter a large building by one door and after wandering about for some time you leave by a different door. You may then find that you have become "turned around" so you can no longer find your way without reorientation, or you may even walk off confidently in the wrong direction. By way of testing Hunter's observation more carefully, Emerson [14] studied the ability of children between the ages of two and five years to reproduce the position of a large wooden ring on the second of two easels fitted with a number of wooden pegs on which the ring could be hung. In successive trials the easels were so placed in reference to each other and to the child as to provide a graded series of tasks ranging all the way from that in which the child was merely required to replace the ring on the same peg after it had been momentarily removed, through varying levels of reorientation up to one in which the two easels were placed back to back, thus forcing the

[13] More recent experiments suggest that bodily orientation toward the goal is not an absolute requirement for success, even in the case of rats, but if bodily orientation is lost the reaction cannot be delayed for as long a time.

[14] L. L. Emerson, "The Effect of Bodily Orientation upon the Young Child's Memory for the Position of Objects," *Child Dev.*, 1931, 2: 125-142.

child to walk all the way around and face in the opposite direction in order to place his ring. It was found that even among children of similar age and mentality, there were marked individual differences in the extent to which success was affected by the change in orientation, though all children made more errors when the amount of such change was increased. For the group as a whole, the average number of successful placements for each of nine positions arranged in order of the amount of ocular and bodily reorientation demanded were as follows: 17.8, 6.5, 6.8, 5.5, 5.0, 5.4, 4.6, 3.7, and 1.8. It will be noted that the largest change in the number of successes occurs between the first and second positions. In the first position no change in orientation at all was involved. Only one easel was used. The child was merely required to replace the ring on the same peg from which the examiner had just removed it. In the second position the child had to make a complete shift in ocular orientation but only a slight shift in muscular adjustment. Here the two easels were placed side by side within the child's easy reach, and the child was required to place his ring on the second easel in a position corresponding to that selected by the examiner on the first easel. The next largest difference is found at the end of the series, where actual rotation of the child's body is involved. The two easels were placed back to back, so that the child had to walk around and face in the opposite direction in order to place his ring. Although on the average the older children were more successful than the younger ones, there were great differences between children at all ages. We see the same thing among older persons. Some find their way about a strange city with little difficulty, while others become "lost" after the first few turnings.

Many experiments, both with children and adults, have shown that the ability to apprehend and remember the individual items of a series varies according to the extent to which they can be grouped into meaningful wholes. A child of three has less difficulty in reproducing such a sentence as "I have a little dog" than in repeating three digits like 5-2-8 after a single hearing. The older person who has learned to read will be able to reproduce about as many short words as single letters after a brief exposure, and many more of the words are arranged to form a sentence. We shall have more to say about these matters in a later chapter.

THE FORMATION OF CONCEPTS

It has been shown that simple processes of generalization and comparison are present even among animals. For example, cats, raccoons, and apes can be trained to discriminate among simple forms (as a triangle, a circle, and a square), and they will continue to make the correct choice even when the size of the figures is changed or the shape of the triangle is altered. Infants as young as six months have been similarly trained. But until speech has appeared, only very simple generalizations seem possible. Language appears to lie very close to the base of truly symbolic processes. Without its aid the child particularizes, but as far as we are able to discover, his generalizations are few and simple, not permitting much change from the particular object or situation in connection with which his reactions have been built up. Even among children of nursery-school age, only relatively simple concepts of a generalized nature have been established. And when a young child has learned to respond correctly to some general principle, he often has difficulty in stating the principle by which he is reacting. He cannot easily put ideas of relationship into words. This is well shown in an experiment reported by Heidbreder.[15] In this experiment it was found that children of three and four years had little difficulty in learning to react correctly to a general feature in a simple situation but that they could not, as a rule, describe the principle to which they were reacting. When the problem consisted of choosing the one of two boxes which contained a small doll and the solution lay in always taking the nearer box, regardless of its markings or of whether it was placed on the right or left of the subject, children who had learned to choose the correct box without hesitation could not formulate the reason for their choice. When urged to tell why they chose that particular box, they could not, as a rule, get beyond such vague statements as "Because I took it," or "I just knew it." Often the time sequence of ideas was reversed, that is, the reasons given were in terms of events occurring after the choice had been made, such as "Because I opened it and saw her."

Piaget, who has made some of the most extensive studies of

[15] Edna Heidbreder, "Reasons Used in Solving Problems," *J. Exper. Psychol.*, 1927, 10: 397-414.

the development of conceptual thinking in children, is of the opinion that true conceptualization is rarely present in early childhood. He describes the child's thinking as characterized by *egocentricity, syncretism,* and *transduction.* By *egocentricity,* Piaget means that the young child rarely questions whether his ideas about objects are understood by others (unless, of course, their failure to understand interferes with the gratification of his wishes). The child's language and his thought are self-centered; he does not attempt to place himself in another's position, and he does not trouble about the latter's point of view. Of course this tendency is not confined to childhood. Many who have attempted to reproduce his experiments have failed to confirm Piaget's statement that egocentricity is more characteristic of early than of later childhood. Differences in interpretation may be responsible for this, at least in part.

The second of Piaget's characterizations of child thought seems to rest on safer ground. When Piaget says that a child thinks *syncretically* he means that the child's ideas of objects and events are rarely based on an analysis of their qualities. He thinks of concrete objects, persons, and events rather than of the characteristics that they have in common or by which they are differentiated from each other. He thinks of individuals rather than of classes. And in such simple generalizations as he does form, the influence of the particular is still seen in his tendency to base his generalizations on a single instance. This is what Piaget calls *transduction.*

Although there is little doubt that Piaget has been somewhat overzealous in his efforts to show developmental stages that make childish thought qualitatively different from adult thought, nevertheless his studies have done much to clarify our ideas about the nature of thinking and of the formation of concepts at all levels of development. Certainly the three types of thinking mentioned above occur in adults as well as in children, and it is equally sure that their presence interferes with the clearness and the logical character of thought. By comparison, they are primitive types of mental response, not making for highly efficient levels of reaction. That upon the whole they are more common in children than in adults is probably true, but it is also true that the thinking of many adults does not progress far beyond this level.

Both children and adults think more effectively in some areas than in others, and every one is less likely to regress to primitive types of thinking along lines where he is well informed than in matters of which he is more ignorant. Nevertheless, all of us are probably guilty of many more examples of both transduction and syncretism than we should care to admit. Mr. Brown was once cheated by a Jew; since then he believes firmly that all Jews are dishonest. "I don't like to shop at Blank's store," says his wife. "Why not?" you ask. "I don't know why. I Just don't," is all she can tell you. Mr. Brown is thinking transductively, his wife syncretically, and in so doing both are reacting unjustly to others and are unnecessarily limiting their own opportunities for personal and social advancement. The moral is obvious.

HOW IDEAS ARE BUILT UP

Jean Piaget, "Children's Philosophies," Chapter 12 in *A Handbook of Child Psychology*, Second Edition, Revised, ed. Carl Murchison (Worcester, Mass., Clark University Press, 1933), pp. 534-550.

In this short chapter, Piaget describes some of his studies dealing with children's ideas of natural phenomena. He reports the answers of children to such questions as "With what do we think?" or "Where do dreams come from? With what do you dream?" and notes the changes in their ideas with advancing age. For example he asked, "What makes the sun move?" or "How can you tell whether something is alive?" After the child had given his ideas on the nature of life, he was questioned further, "Is the sun alive?", "Is an automobile alive?", "How do you know?"

Piaget cites many examples of children's answers to these questions. These answers are both amusing and illuminating because they show the type of logic characteristic of the untutored mind. Although later investigation has indicated that many of the explanations that Piaget ascribed to the immaturity of the child's ways of thinking are in all probability the result of lack of information rather than of a fundamental difference in mode of thought, it is unquestionably true that in childhood the two are associated. Knowledge provides the tools of thought. In its absence no one can think efficiently.

Chapter XV

GENERAL INTELLIGENCE AND ITS MEASURE-
MENT IN EARLY CHILDHOOD

*How well can we judge from a child's everyday be-
havior whether he is bright or dull?*

*Why is casual observation not always a safe guide in
estimating the intelligence of others?*

*What do we mean by an intelligent action? By an in-
telligent person?*

*What are some of the advantages of an "intelligence
test" as compared to casual observation? Who devised the first useful intelligence test?*

What is the meaning of the term mental age? *Intelligence quotient? Percentile rank?*

*What, approximately speaking, is the highest IQ
known to have been earned on the best of the individual intelligence tests in present use?*

*Does the IQ always remain the same for a given indi-
vidual? What are some of the chief factors making
for large changes upon retest?*

*What are some of the practical uses of intelligence test-
ing in early childhood?*

*Are there sex differences in intelligence? What factors
other than sex show a relationship to intelligence?*

*How do Spearman and Thorndike differ in their views
of the organization of mental abilities? What general fact are both theories designed to explain?*

What is meant by the "null hypothesis"? By whom was it proposed as a clarifying principle in scientific experiment? Upon what principle of elementary logic is it based?

WHAT IS MEANT BY "GENERAL INTELLIGENCE"

"My, isn't he smart!" exclaims the cordial visitor, as she watches the antics of her friend's baby. "You would think he was a year old instead of six months!"

"Helen is the brightest child I ever saw," says a teacher. "She learns a thing almost before you have told it to her and never forgets it afterward."

"I never saw anything like the way George will figure things out," says another. "He found an old alarm clock that his father had thrown away, took it all apart, and fixed it so that it runs as well as ever again."

We hear judgments such as these almost daily. Brightness, smartness, cleverness, brains—whatever this quality may be called, it is universally recognized as one of the most important attributes of any individual at any age. Probably as far back as the times of our cave-dwelling ancestors, intelligence, particularly that aspect of intelligence which we call "mental alertness," was recognized as important, and those who were most alert mentally had some advantage in the struggle for existence over those who were more dull and sluggish.

But although we may talk about it glibly enough, when it comes to stating clearly just what we mean by *intelligence* we find ourselves in some difficulty. What causes us to classify this child as bright, that one as stupid?

Before we can answer this question, we must first of all rid ourselves of the idea that intelligence is any kind of quality or substance that exists in man apart from his actions. Just as we may say that John runs or dances gracefully or speaks eloquently or writes fluently, so we may say that he acts intelligently or unintelligently. Too, just as we may on occasion use any of the foregoing terms to describe a single action, an individual bit of behavior, so we may also use them in a more general sense to characterize the most usual or typical quality of the actions of any person. We may say, "How fast John is running!" Here we refer only to the action of the moment. There is nothing in the statement that indicates John's usual speed. But if we say, "John is a swift runner" then we have reference not to a single perform-ance but to the average of many. "Intelligence," like "speed," "grace," "eloquence," is nothing more than a term used to charac-terize certain qualities of human action. Like them it is manifested in varying degrees by different persons or by the same person on different occasions.

What qualities of action are included under the term *intelli gence*? To answer this question we shall do best to think first of a single act. Instead of trying to say what a person must be like in order to be intelligent, we shall first ask, What is an intelligent action?

Most of us will agree that an act which is well adapted to achieving its object, a plan that works quickly and easily, should be classed as more "intelligent" than one that fails to work at all or that accomplishes its results only at the expense of much waste motion and after many false starts. Now if we go a bit further and ask what it is that makes for well-adapted action, for "intelli-gent" action as opposed to stupid bungling, we are likely to come to the conclusion that we act most intelligently when we respond to relationships between things, to abstract ideas and general prin-ciples, and not when we respond only to single items that are only a part of the situation. Terman, who is the author of our most widely used "intelligence test," is of the opinion that *we are able to act intelligently in proportion as we are able to think in abstract terms.*

Consider a few examples. If you put a hungry hen on one side of a fifteen-foot length of wire fence and scatter corn on the other side, the hen will dash at the fence, beat her wings against it, rush back and forth for short distances, but it will be a long time before she finds her way around it. If you continue to do this every day, using the same fence in the same place, after a time the hen will learn to run around the fence very quickly when she sees the corn. But now if you take her to a new place and substitute a wooden picket fence for the wire fence, her previous experience will not help her much. She will go through the same old round of fluttering her wings against the fence, dashing against it, running back and forth along it until finally she happens to find her way around. Each new fence in a new place is a completely new experience to her because she is responding only to the individual items—the particular fence, the particular place. But to a human being, even to a child, the two situations would have so much in common with each other and with other previous experiences of a like nature that they would present but few difficulties. A child of three years or an ape will pile boxes one on another in order to secure an object that is beyond his reach, but a goat sees no relationship between a box that he could easily push into position and food that is too high for him to secure.

Responding to relationships, to abstract ideas rather than to single concrete facts, has another consequence which we also associate with intelligent action. This is *adaptability*. An abstraction embraces many facts to all of which the same rules will apply. The baby whose cart is caught by the rocker of a chair pulls and jerks at it and perhaps screams for help, but he does not look to see what is holding the wheel or how it may be loosened. The child of five looks for the cause of the difficulty and tries out one plan after another until he succeeds in freeing it. Each of these plans is based on some idea of relationship, not clearly thought out, perhaps, but nevertheless distinctly more than just random fumbling.

As a first step toward our definition we may then say that intelligent action is action that is governed by broad rather than narrow meanings. It is response to relationships, to likenesses and differences, to principles rather than to isolated facts. If the principle is right, then the action will meet our first practical criterion of effectiveness. It will "work." But even when the principle selected is wrong, the action that is based upon a general idea differs from that determined by single isolated facts that have not been brought into relationship to each other. The former action is organized. Its parts follow each other in a patterned order. The latter has no very clear-cut pattern, or at most its pattern consists of the repetition of a single act that may or may not be appropriate to the situation.

A child is playing on the floor with his blocks. At first he piles the blocks aimlessly, putting two or three together, then knocking them down, stopping now and then to hammer one against another or to toss them about the room. Suddenly he stops, pushes all the blocks to one side so as to leave a clear space, then selects certain ones and begins to arrange them in a definite order. You say, "He has an idea." You do not see the idea. You may not even be able to guess what it is. But the change in his behavior is so marked that you cannot help but notice it. Now his plan may not work. Judged from an adult standpoint it may even seem foolish, unintelligent. But here is the important thing. By making a plan, even a bad plan, and actually putting it to the test, he has given himself a kind of experience that is highly charged with meaning. And the next time he tries, he will be far more likely to devise a plan that does work than he would be if he had spent the same amount of time in the random activity with which he began.

We often hear it said that the intelligent person is the one who profits most by his experience. It would be more correct to say that the experiences of the intelligent person are more likely to be of a kind that facilitate learning. Experiences with carrying out a plan, with testing an idea, with seeing a relationship carry more meaning and so leave a more lasting impression than experiences that deal only with isolated concrete facts.

In summary, then, it may be said that intelligent action is planned action, action that is determined by the organization of many simple meanings into a complex and relatively complete whole. A practical test of intelligent action is the extent to which it "works," how effectively it achieves the desired result. For we all know that when our plans fail to work it is usually because they are incomplete, because we have failed to take account of something that has an important bearing on the result. Now the only practical way of handling many facts at once is to pack them up into a series of mental bundles, being careful to put into the same bundle only those things that have a like relationship to our problem. Instead of having to handle each little fact separately, we can then deal with a multitude of facts at once because we can think in terms of the various bundles, that is in terms of rules, relationships, principles, instead of the isolated concrete facts on which they are based. And still greater efficiency is gained when we cease to work even with these more conveniently handled bundles of facts, and substitute for each a symbol that is to the bundle what a luggage check is to the heavy and clumsy trunk that it represents. The modern engineer would be hard put to it if he had to plan his bridges, his tunnels, his skyscrapers in terms only of such miscellaneous unmeasured blocks of stone as might be available, hunks of metal, spadefuls of cement, as does the African native in building his hut of mud and reeds. Even weights and measures, strains and stresses, velocities, and forces are clumsy material for thought in comparison with the compact mathematical signs that stand for them. Mental activity is classed as intelligent activity in proportion as it substitutes broad abstract meanings that can be efficiently manipulated in many situations for the narrow concrete meanings that are applicable to but few situations. But to meet our additional criterion that intelligent action is action that "works," that brings results, these abstractions must be built up on a sound basis of facts as they exist in nature. The visionary whose head is always in the clouds is not necessarily a man of high intelligence. Abstraction is not an end in itself. It is a tool which, if properly forged and efficiently manipulated, enormously extends man's control over his concrete environment.

JUDGING INTELLIGENCE FROM BEHAVIOR

Observation of the everyday behavior of children or older people gives us some basis for judging how intelligently they usually act. This one shows planfulness, resourcefulness, judgment. He can do many things. He has a large fund of information on many subjects. He talks well, and this is a fact that it is important to note, for words are symbols, and facility in their use is good evidence of the ability to think in abstract terms. Another has a small vocabulary which he uses inexactly; he is inept, attacks problems in a random, fumbling manner, and rarely succeeds in solving them. Even the most casual observation leaves little doubt that a real difference in ability is to be seen here. But how great is this difference? Observation alone does not tell us.

Observation, moreover, is not always a safe guide. Everyday behavior tells us something, but chance circumstances rarely provide the best possible conditions for judging ability of any kind.

Not all of a child's conduct provides a fair picture of his intelligence any more than his everyday play always gives evidence of his physical strength. The child who is sitting quietly on the floor looking at a picture book is not using enough of his physical strength and energy at the moment to give us much idea of what he could do in a pinch; nor is the one who is sitting at the window aimlessly looking out into the street using enough of his mental ability, just then, to provide much basis for judging his real intelligence. Of course if we watch children or older persons for a long period of time, enough situations will naturally arise that challenge either their physical strength or their mental powers to tell us something about their ability along those lines. But these situations vary so greatly from one person to another that even long acquaintance will not provide more than a rough basis for judgment.

If you take a group of children of the same age and ask two persons, both of whom have known them intimately, to arrange them in order of intelligence, complete agreement between the judges will rarely be found. Here, for example, is the way two nursery-school teachers working with the same group of fifteen children estimated their relative intellectual abilities. All the children were between the ages of three and four years.

Teacher A	Teacher B
1. Polly	1. Polly
2. James	2. Peter
3. William	3. Mary
4. Mary	4. Emily
5. Harry	5. James
6. Stanley	6. Catherine
7. Peter	7. William
8. Thomas	8. Harry
9. Betty	9. Frank
10. Frank	10. Stanley
11. Emily	11. Thomas
12. Joan	12. Joan
13. Catherine	13. Betty
14. George	14. Sidney
15. Sidney	15. George

Both teachers agree in placing Polly at the head of the list and in regarding George and Sidney as the most backward. But Peter, whom Teacher *B* ranks next to the top, is placed near the middle of the group by Teacher *A*. William, Emily, and Catherine are also judged very differently. Of the fifteen children, only Polly and Joan are given exactly the same rank by both teachers. Yet there is some tendency to agreement. Children placed near the top of one list are not found at the bottom of the other, though they may have moved downward a few places. The agreement is better than chance, though it is by no means perfect.

People disagree when they attempt to rate the intelligence of others on the basis of casual observation, not only because so many of the situations they have observed offer no effective challenge to ability but also because, often without being aware of it, they are influenced in their judgments by many things that are not intelligence at all. Rare indeed is the person who can successfully disentangle a child's everyday manifestations of intelligence from his dirt, dimples, curls, and cuddliness. Mary is regarded as bright because she has big dark eyes and pretty manners; Tommy is looked upon as stupid because he is physically clumsy and is subject to colds in the head that force him to breathe through his mouth. Peter is so large for his age that every one judges him by the standards of children two years older than he is. Because he does not always meet these standards, he is thought to be mentally backward. Really he is of average mental ability for his age, though not for his size. Doris is so shy that few people ever get a glimpse of her real ability, while Edward displays himself and his ideas without stint before any one who will pay him a moment's attention.

EARLY ATTEMPTS AT "MEASURING" INTELLIGENCE

Early in the present century Alfred Binet, a French psychologist who for many years had been studying differences in ability as shown by school children, was entrusted by the school authorities of Paris with a difficult and important task. "How," said the school people, "are we to know what causes children to fail in school? Some children fail because they are lazy and mischievous. Others fail because they cannot learn as easily as the average even when they try. Is there no way of telling which children cannot profit by the ordinary kind of teaching so that we can pick them out and put them in special schools where they will no longer hamper the progress of the others but can be given work that they can learn to do?"

Binet undertook to answer this question. First he tried to see how well teachers could judge the ability of children. He found, just as we saw in the last section, that there was a good deal of disagreement among them even when the children were well known to them. When he asked the teachers what they took into account in making their judgments they gave various answers. Some relied mainly on the child's appearance—the shape of his head, the "glance of the eye." Others mentioned such things as his powers of observation, his memory for things seen and heard, his range of information. But none of them had more than a vague and general idea about what store of information it is fair to expect of a child at any age, how good should be his memory or what his ability to observe.

This was in 1904-1905. The idea of devising tests of mental ability was not a new one at that time; for more than a decade psychologists in England and America had been experimenting with simple tasks that they called "mental tests." But to Binet belongs the credit of first devising tests that really worked, that did to a fair extent serve to differentiate the dull from the bright. Binet succeeded where others failed because of two important differences between his method and those of his predecessors. Earlier workers had thought it not feasible to try to test anything but the "simpler" abilities. They had hoped to find out how fast a person could think by seeing how rapidly he could move his fingers in a tapping test; how soundly he could reason and draw conclusions by finding out how well he could judge the length of lines or distinguish small differences in weight. Furthermore, they had hoped that a person's "general" ability could be determined by means of only a small variety of tests. Binet's plan was very different. In his tests he emphasized difficulty rather than speed, complexity of performance rather than simplicity. He aimed to set for his subjects tasks that would really serve as a challenge to their mental powers. So he tried to test their ability to solve difficult and complex problems by setting them problems of increasingly greater complexity until a level of difficulty was reached at which they could no longer succeed. Binet, moreover, did not confine himself to a few kinds of test. Children, in his opinion, differ so greatly in special aptitudes, in individual experiences, and in home training that to rely exclusively upon a small number of measures is likely to mean that some children who have had unusual advantages along those particular lines will be unduly favored, while others with a different background of experience will be handicapped. His selection was therefore made with the idea of including as great a variety of performances as possible. Although to an inexperienced person his tests seem rather like a hotchpotch, actually no test was included in the series that had not been shown by actual trial to differentiate between children whom their teachers thought to be dull and those who were adjudged bright.

Binet's first series, known as the "1905 scale," included thirty tests arranged in order of difficulty. In giving it, the easier tests were first tried, then the harder ones, until it became evident that the child could go no further. The number of tests he could pass was then taken as an index of his level of ability. The method was crude, but it worked better than any that had been tried before.

Still Binet was not satisfied. He had devised a method of testing, to be sure, but there was no very meaningful way of expressing the results. He could say that Mary had passed seventeen of his tests while Johnny could only pass twelve, but what of it? Did that mean that both were backward, but Johnny more so than Mary; or that both were bright, but Mary was the brighter? And what about ages? If Mary were older than Johnny, we should expect her to do better. Perhaps in proportion to age the two were equally bright.

Then Binet had a happy thought. Since ability increases with age throughout the period of childhood, why not make use of this fact in interpreting test performance? Why not find out just what children of different ages can do on tests of this kind and make up a series of tests for each age? Then when other children are to be tested, we can first try them with the tests at their own age level. If they cannot do these, the tests for the age next lower can be tried and so on until a level is reached at which the child can just barely succeed. In this way his performance takes on a more definite meaning, for if he is ten years old and yet can only do the tests that the average five-year-old can pass, we have gained a much clearer picture of his ability than is given by finding out that he can only pass nine out of a series of thirty tests. It is like saying that at ten years a child is so small that he only takes a five-year size in suits. We not only know that he is retarded in growth, but we have a fair idea of the amount of his retardation.

In 1908, Binet published his first "year scale" in which the tests were arranged in groups according to the age at which they could ordinarily be passed. There were four or five tests for each age. Scores earned on this scale were no longer to be expressed simply in terms of the number of test items passed but as "mental ages," a new expression destined to become very popular. A child who can pass the six-year-old tests but not those designed for seven-year-olds is said to have a mental age of six, no matter what his actual chronological age may be. If he is only four but can nevertheless pass the six-year-old tests, then he is much brighter than the average. If he is nine years old but has still not advanced beyond the six-year test level, he is backward; perhaps he should be classed as feeble-minded.

Binet died in 1911, just after revising his scale of tests a second time. But although his methods were then far from having been perfected, their possibilities had been glimpsed by many persons. In America both the 1908 scale and the 1911 revision had been translated into English by Goddard and were already gaining extensive use. Later on Terman, Kuhlmann, and others worked out further modifications in the scale as it was left by Binet and succeeded in correcting a number of its weak points. They also extended it at each end. As left by Binet, the scale included tests for the ages from three to thirteen years. Terman extended it upward to the adult level; Kuhlmann added tests for very young children and infants down to the age of three months.

A further step of great importance in interpreting the results of tests was taken when, in 1912, William Stern of the University of Hamburg proposed the use of the intelligence quotient, now generally known as the IQ,[1] to show the relationship between a child's mental age and his chronological age. It obviously is much

[1] In writing the IQ it is customary to omit the decimal point.

more significant for a child of four years to be mentally two years in advance of his age than it is for a child of twelve to be accelerated two years, for the former has had only four years in which to gain his advanced standing while the latter has taken twelve years to do so. The intelligence quotient, which is obtained by dividing the child's mental age by his chronological age, is designed to reduce the amount of acceleration or retardation to a uniform standard for all ages by expressing the one as a percentage of the other. A child of six with a mental age of eight would thus be said to have an IQ of 8/6 or 133. One whose chronological age is six and whose mental age is only four would have an IQ of 4/6 or 67. The IQ was first made popular by Terman and is now the most widely used method of expressing the results of intelligence tests when given to children. For older persons other methods of specifying test results, such as those mentioned on p. 369 and 378, are preferable, because after mental maturity has been reached, the age comparison ceases to have meaning, just as it would be foolish to say that a man of thirty years is only as tall as the average man of twenty-five.

THE DISTRIBUTION OF INTELLIGENCE

Common observation shows that not all people are equally gifted in mentality. The differences among them range all the way from the level of the vegetative idiot who can neither walk nor talk to the genius of an Aristotle, a Leibnitz, a Goethe, or an Einstein. The number of cases at either of these extremes is, however, small in comparison to the great mass of ordinary people who are neither geniuses nor idiots but range about midway between the two.

If you were to select a thousand people by some unbiased method[2] upon which we can base safe generalizations and ap-

[2] Because of the tendency of people in general to congregate in groups that have some important characteristic in common (see Chapter XX), it is usually necessary to make use of some special method for selecting the cases to be used in any study that is to have more than limited significance. Otherwise one is likely to include too many from certain groups and not enough from others. For example, most of the earlier studies of the decline of abilities in old age gave an exaggerated impression of the age-handicap because they were based almost entirely upon the study of persons in homes for the aged. The use of groups of this kind was, of course, dictated

praise their general intelligence by the best methods now available, you would probably find that a graphic representation of the comparative number falling at the various intellectual levels would look something like the curve shown in Figure 68. Because so many of the measurable characteristics of living organisms are distributed in a manner that conforms at least roughly to this curve, it is often called the *normal curve*. It is also known as the *probability curve* because, if one knows certain of its properties, it becomes possible to calculate from it the probability of occurrence of any stated event with the smallest likelihood of error that is possible under the circumstances.[3] For this reason it forms the chief basis for the statistics of probability.

Figures 69 and 70 which are based upon the actual testing of fairly representative groups [4] show how closely the distribution

---

by convenience because large numbers of old people could thus be located quickly and easily. But the investigators failed to take account of the fact that the necessity of spending one's declining years in an institution indicates, in most instances, that one has been unable to make suitable provision for his old age at an earlier date. Accordingly, the fact that these older persons showed a relatively low level of ability, on the average, could not be taken as *prima facie* evidence that their ability had shown a great decline. In all probability many of them had never been very bright.

[3] Needless to say, this does not mean that from the use of this curve one gains any magical means of foretelling the future. All that one gains is a more precise estimate of the likelihood that a prediction will be in error by some stated amount. Thus, on the basis of certain evidence, one may find that the chances are ten to one that the cattle of a certain breed will yield, on the average, a higher percentage of butter-fat than those of another breed, or that children of similar mentality will make more rapid progress when taught to read by Method *A* than when taught by Method *B*. The probability distribution does not enable one to make predictions that are sure to be right but merely indicates about how much risk you are taking in acting on a given premise.

[4] That is, reasonably representative of the populations named. There is no such thing as abstract representativeness. When we speak of a group as being representative of a given population, we mean only that care has been taken to give every member of that group an equal chance of being included in the sample. A very common error in the statistical study of group characteristics is that of imputing the findings from a particular sample studied to groups of which the sample is not a representative part. The inmates of the homes for the aged mentioned in the footnote above were in all probability fairly representative of the institutional population but not of aged people in general, of whom the institutionalized members constitute only a single group and one that differs in various ways from other groups not included in the study.

of measured intelligence conforms to the theoretical curve that has been imposed upon it for comparison.

From the standpoint of the *form* of the distribution, it makes little difference whether the classification is based upon the judgment of persons who know all the subjects well enough to form an estimate of their relative intelligence or upon the results obtained by the use of a good intelligence test. There will be a good many disagreements between the test results and the judges'

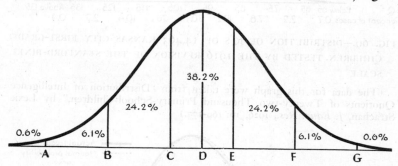

38.2%

24.2%   24.2%

0.6%   6.1%   6.1%   0.6%

A   B   C   D   E   F   G

FIG. 68.—THE NORMAL PROBABILITY CURVE

In modern statistics the extent to which any individual differs from the average of the group to which he belongs is usually expressed in terms of the so called *standard deviation*, which is the square root of the average of the squares of all the individual deviations from the group average or *mean*. In Figure 68, D shows the position of the average or mean in a normally distributed population. C and E are at points located ½ of a standard deviation (S.D.) below and above the mean; B and F at 1½ S.D. and A and G at 2½ S.D. from the group mean. The percentages of the total number of cases falling within each of these divisions is shown above.

One of the many advantages of expressing a person's standing in terms of the number of standard deviations by which he exceeds or falls short of the average attained by his group lies in the possibility thereby afforded of comparing his scores on many different measures which were originally expressed in such different units that no comparison between them was possible. For example, if you find that your score as expressed in terms of the number of items correctly answered on a psychology test was 48; on a mathematics test, 87; and on a history test, 164, you have no way of knowing on which of these subjects you made the best grade. But if the class average on the psychology test was 30 with a standard deviation of 12; on the mathematics test 100, S.D. 13; and on the history test 150, S.D. 28 it becomes possible to answer the question by reducing your scores on the three subjects to standard units. To do this you first find the difference between your score and the group average and then divide the difference by the standard deviation of the scores for that test. If you do this you will find that in the example given the best grade was not earned on the test with the highest original score.

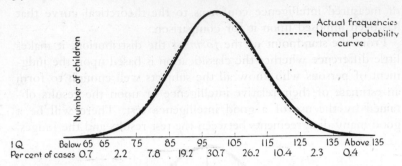

FIG. 69.—DISTRIBUTION OF IQ'S OF 14,463 KANSAS CITY FIRST-GRADE CHILDREN TESTED BY THE 1916 REVISION OF THE STANFORD-BINET SCALE

(The data for this graph were taken from "Distribution of Intelligence Quotients of Twenty-two Thousand Primary-School-Children," by Lexie Strachan, *J. Educ. Res.*, 1926, 16: 169-177.)

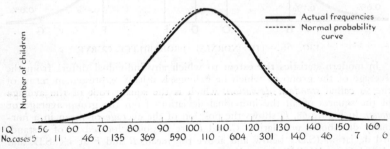

FIG. 70.—DISTRIBUTION OF IQ'S OF 2,970 CHILDREN TESTED BY THE 1937 REVISION OF THE STANFORD-BINET SCALE (ORIGINAL STANDARDIZATION GROUP)

It will be noted that this curve is decidedly flatter than that shown in Figure 69, with more cases having very high and very low IQ's and fewer in the middle ranges. A part of this difference may be due to a difference in the populations tested, but in the main it may be accounted for by a difference in the tests used. The significance of an IQ varies to some extent with the test from which it is derived.

estimates for individual persons, but some will be pushed up and others down (when the latter is compared to the former) so that the total frequency at each level of ability will not be greatly altered. Both methods of appraisal will show a comparatively small proportion of the total at the extremes and a large number in the middle ranges.

THE INTERPRETATION OF MENTAL TESTS

An important application of the statistics of probability to the study of intellectual differences consists in making more exact estimates than would be possible without their use of the amount of confidence that can be placed in the results of a single test. All persons having anything to do with tests or with the results of testing—and that, nowadays, means practically everybody—should realize that no test is infallible. If the same child be tested on two consecutive days under the best possible conditions and by the most competent examiners, the chances are that the results will not be precisely identical, though it is unlikely that they will differ enough to affect any practical recommendations that might be made. Momentary fluctuations of the child's attention, small differences in the precise wording of a response, slight changes in the inflection of the examiner's voice when asking a question, and a host of other small matters that are difficult to bring under close control may be enough to shift the balance of success or failure on a particular item for which the chances of success or failure were almost equal at the start. The number of such shifts will be small in most cases, and their effect upon the total score will for practical purposes be negligible; yet the fact that small changes in standing upon retest are the rule rather than the exception is sufficient evidence of the fallacy in saying, as people often do say, "John has an IQ of 125." A correct statement would be, "On such-and-such an occasion John earned an IQ of 125 on the ――― test." And in order to make such a statement really meaningful, two things must be known. First, we may ask what proportion of children in the population at large do as well as this. In the second place, we wish to know the likelihood that John's standing will be maintained. In more precise language, we may say, What are the chances that if retested tomorrow or after some other stated interval, the IQ obtained would be as low as 100 or, on the other hand, as high as 150?

This is not the place to explain the procedures by which answers to questions such as this can be obtained. For this, the interested reader should consult any of the standard texts on statistical method. The important thing is for all to realize that information of this kind is not only essential but is also available, and that any person who gives a mental test should be able to provide it. Inability to do so should be looked upon as *prima facie* evidence that the examiner is incompetent.[5]

It is impossible to make any statement whatever about the probable variation of IQ's upon retest unless these things are known: (1) the particular test used on each occasion, (2) the age of the child at the time of first testing, and (3) the length of the interval between the testings. A few general principles can be laid down as follows:

(1) As a rule, when the same test is used on both occasions, the variation in the child's standing will be smaller than will be the case when the test used on the second occasion is a different one. This results from the fact that no test can include more than a small sample of the tasks that a child is able to perform, and there is greater chance of a shift in the character of the sample when changing to a different test, even though the child has developed so much in the interval between testings that his ability is measured by a quite different level on the scale. The differences in content of two different scales is usually greater than the difference between two different levels of the same scale.

(2) The younger the child at the time of first testing or the longer the interval between tests, the greater is the change in standing likely to be.

(3) Test results may be and frequently are unfavorably affected by lack of interest, shyness, or similar non-intellectual factors that affect a child's effort and coöperation. This is particularly likely to occur if the child is young and unaccustomed to strange places and strange people.

(4) No test worth giving has ever been devised that is not susceptible to the influence of direct or indirect coaching on the particular items of which it is made up. This point must always be kept in mind in trying to evaluate the statements frequently put forth about the effects of some special system of teaching that is said to improve the intelligence of children. One must always

---

[5] Assuming, of course, that the test was given for the practical purpose of comparing the child's standing with that of others and that a standardized measuring instrument was therefore used.

ask, Has the *general* intelligence of the children been improved, or have they merely received a kind of indirect coaching that enables them to make a better showing on the particular items included in the test?

(5) Mere experience in taking a test introduces a certain opportunity to learn the art of test-taking. While this "practice effect," as it is called, is usually greatest when the same test is repeated after a short interval and the subject therefore is given the same tasks to perform on both occasions, it is to be seen even when the two tests used include no duplicate items. It is usually most apparent when the subjects are young children who had no experience in taking tests previous to the first occasion. Better adjustment to the whole situation undoubtedly accounts for some of the apparent gain that commonly appears when the results of a second examination are compared with those of a first. But even at the college level, experience still counts. Students who have become well accustomed to taking the modern "objective" types of examination have a measurable advantage over those of equal competence whose previous acquaintance was limited to tests of the "essay" or "question and answer" variety. Something is gained by merely "learning the trick."

(6) Because of a statistical principle known as "regression toward the mean" children initially testing high are more likely to lose in standing on later tests than they are to gain. Conversely, those initially testing low are more likely to gain than they are to lose. Neither loss nor gain in these cases necessarily represents a real change in the child's ability. It means only that because every test involves some degree of error in measurement, when the IQ obtained is high, there is greater probability that the error of measurement has been added to the child's true score than that it has been subtracted from it. In like manner, when the IQ is low, there is greater probability that it has been spuriously reduced below its true magnitude by subtracting the error of measurement from the true score than that the opposite has occurred. In both cases it must be remembered that we are dealing with *probabilities* and not with facts that invariably occur. A child initially testing high may gain in standing upon retest; one initially testing low may rank still lower.

(7) The probable error of measurement[6] differs considerably from one test to another. For this reason it is always necessary to specify what test was used as well as the child's standing on the test, if the results obtained are to be interpreted meaningfully.

(8) The method of deriving the IQ carries with it the statistical necessity that, other factors remaining equal, high IQ's will vary more from test to test than low ones do. The reason for this, while perfectly straightforward to the mathematician, is rather too complicated to be explained here.[7] The reader is therefore asked to take the statement "on faith" and in doing so to remember that this, as well as the principle of "regression toward the mean" which was discussed in a preceding paragraph, is a mathematical and not a psychological phenomenon. Bright children do not actually vary more in ability from one occasion to another than backward ones do, but the way the IQ is derived makes it appear as if this were the case.

The reader who keeps all these qualifying conditions in mind may not be led astray by the presentation at this point of a few cautious figures.

The distribution of IQ's for the total population on either of the two Stanford Revisions[8] of the Binet Scale which, by most authorities, are regarded as the most adequate of the tests at present available, covers a range of approximately two hundred IQ points, from very close to zero in the case of the profound idiot to approximately 200 IQ which represents the highest level thus far reported by any competent examiner.[9] There is nothing

[6] By the "probable error of measurement" is meant an amount of change that will be equalled or exceeded by 50 per cent of the cases; whereas the remaining 50 per cent will not change their standing by an amount greater than the probable error.

[7] Those interested will find a clear exposition of the principle together with the necessary formulas for determining the relationship involved in an article by Quinn McNemar entitled "The Expected Average Difference between Individuals Paired at Random," *J. Genet. Psychol.*, 1933, 43: 438-439. A further discussion of this principle together with a table showing its application to the 1937 Revision of the Stanford Binet test is to be found in *Measuring Intelligence*, by Terman and Merrill, pp. 44-47.

[8] To be described in a later section.

[9] Newspaper accounts have occasionally exploited cases said to test above this level but when investigated it has been found either that the tests had been incorrectly given or that the child had been specially coached. I do not personally know of any instance of a "genuine" Stanford-Binet IQ higher than 200, and I know of but one child who reached that level. How-

in the evidence thus far to indicate that this range of ability changes with age, although the test itself is inadequate for measuring the highest levels of ability among subjects over the age of fifteen or the lowest levels among the younger subjects.

When given this test, about 1 school child in 150 will earn an initial IQ of 140 or higher. About the same number will test at or below 60 IQ.[10] About a third of all cases tested will fall within the range of 90 IQ to 110 IQ.

When school children are retested by the same scale after an interval not greater than one or two years, in about 50 per cent of the cases the differences in the results of the two testings will not be greater than five I Q points in either direction. In 1 or 2 per cent of the cases retested the differences may be as great as fifteen or twenty IQ points; in rare cases they may be as great as thirty IQ points or even more.[11] For children below school age, shifts in standing are far more frequent and of much greater magnitude.[12] Under the conditions named above, the best evidence

---

ever, certain other tests, notably the upper ranges of the 1922 Kuhlmann-Binet, yield a fair number of instances of IQ's of 200 and over. This affords another example of the hazards of speaking of an IQ as if it were an absolute index of ability not dependent upon the test from which it is derived. Actually an intelligence test is like a medical examination in that it requires the insight of a highly trained expert for its interpretation.

[10] These figures are only approximate. They will vary slightly with the revision used, the 1937 Revision having a slightly higher variability than the 1916 Revision and thus tending to spread the cases over a wider range so that more will be found at the extremes. There is also a possibility that because of slight irregularities in the standardization of the test, the proportions found at either extreme may vary somewhat with age. In neither case, however, are the differences great, and it should hardly be necessary to point out that those which appear are the result of irregularities in the scales and not in the persons measured by the scales.

[11] Sometimes these differences may indicate real shifts in the child's position among his mates. More often, however, they reflect circumstantial factors unrelated to the child's real ability, such as differences in the kind of tasks included in the test at different age levels or differences in the child's interest and effort.

[12] See Florence L. Goodenough, *The Kuhlmann-Binet Tests for Children of Preschool Age* (Minneapolis, University of Minnesota Press, 1928), pp. x + 146; Florence L. Goodenough and Katharine M. Maurer, *The Mental Growth of Children from Two to Fourteen Years* (Minneapolis, University of Minnesota Press, 1940), pp. xvi + 130; also reviews and experimental studies from the *Thirty-Ninth Yearbook* of the National Society for the Study of Education (Bloomington, Ill., Public School Publishing Co., 1940), 2 vols., and reviews in *The 1940 Mental Measurements Yearbook* edited by O. K. Buros and published by the editor at Highlands Park, N. J.

now available indicates that when children are under the age of
four at the time the first test is administered, the odds are about
even that the later IQ will differ from the first by as much as
ten IQ points. While changes as great as twenty-five or thirty
points are exceptional, they still occur often enough to make it
necessary to consider the possibility of their occurrence in any
individual case. But even changes as great as this cover but a
small proportion of the total range of intellectual differences
found among civilized men.[13]

MODERN INTELLIGENCE TESTS FOR YOUNG CHILDREN

Up to a few years ago, the various revisions of the Binet scale
were almost the only kinds of tests suitable for studying mental
differences in young children. Although these tests were decidedly
better than none at all, they were nevertheless less useful for children of preschool age than for school children. As a matter of
fact, in devising tests for the ages under five, backward children
of school age had been kept in mind far more than the younger
normal children who, before the days of nursery schools, were
not often tested. The Kuhlmann 1922 revision of the Binet scale
included tests for the ages under three years and for infants, but
these tests were standardized on fewer cases than were his tests
for children of school age, and the items were probably not so
well chosen.

More recently several new tests for preschool children have

[13] If you will now reread the general principles given on pp. 371-374 and
consider each in reference to the numerical facts just presented, you will see
that they are of such a nature as to make the practical significance of the
probable error of measurement even less than it might at first appear. For,
other things being equal, errors in testing are less likely to have serious consequence if the subject is a young child, since the chances are that no immediate action will be taken as a consequence of the test, and a retest after
the child is older will usually reveal the true state of affairs. A similar
error in the case of a school child might conceivably result in his being sent
to a special class or even to an institution. Likewise, the law of regression
toward the mean and the fact that high IQ's are more variable than low
IQ's also diminish the likelihood that the practical application of mental
tests will result in unfortunate treatment of individual cases. That the use
of mental tests in the practical guidance of children works out to the benefit
of the majority is a well-established fact.

appeared. A few of these tests will be described rather briefly in order to give a more concrete idea of the kind of tasks that have been found useful indicators of general mental level in young children.

Both the Kuhlmann 1939 Revision of the Binet and the Stanford 1937 Revision were much more carefully and completely standardized at the early ages than were the earlier forms of these scales. Both follow Binet's practice of arranging the tests in groups according to the ages at which they are commonly passed, and in the selection of test items the authors were guided by the interests of young normal children rather than by those of older and more backward cases. A few of the tasks used with children between the ages of two and four years are listed below:

Age	Stanford (1937)	Kuhlmann (1939)
Two years	Naming a series of well-known objects such as a cup	Repeating two digits after a single hearing
	Building a tower of four or more blocks	Following simple commands involving use of prepositions such as "in" "under" etc.
Three years	Copying a circle	Naming pictures from memory
	Repeating three digits after a single hearing	Touching fingers with thumb in imitation of examiner
Four years	Matching simple geometrical forms	Tracing around a square
	Making a string of at least seven wooden beads	Repeating an easy sentence of ten words

The exact manner of presenting the material, including the wording of the instructions to the child, is carefully specified in the case of each test. The quality of the responses required for passing the test is also indicated in each manual, as well as the exact objects to be named (which are supplied as a part of the standardized material) the forms to be matched, the digits or sentences to be repeated, and so on. Small changes in matters of this kind may alter the difficulty of a test item far more than the inexperienced person is likely to realize. One of the first things that has to be impressed upon students who are learning to give tests is the necessity for adhering strictly to the standard procedure. Many find it hard to understand why small changes that enable a child to pass a test which he would otherwise have failed are not permissible. Such a procedure is comparable to shortening the length of the inches on a scale used for measuring height in order to make a subject seem taller. His real height is not increased, but the measurement is ruined.

The Merrill-Palmer Tests,[14] devised by Rachel Stutsman and her assistants at the Merrill-Palmer nursery school in Detroit, are intended for use with children between the ages of eighteen months and five years. They make only a small demand upon language, since they include chiefly tests of fitting blocks of different geometrical forms into their corresponding recesses in a board known as a "form board," tests of ability to button and unbutton, tests of the ability to put cut-up pictures together, to copy simple designs, and so on. Figure 71 shows a child of four years working at a block-building test.

The Minnesota Preschool Tests [15] are divided into a verbal scale, a non-verbal scale, and a combined scale which makes use of both verbal and non-verbal responses. The materials for these tests are shown in Figure 72.

In addition to mental ages and IQ's, most of the modern tests provide for the interpretation of scores in terms of *percentiles*. A "percentile score" or "percentile rank" shows where the child would stand among a representative group of 100 other children of his own age if all were arranged in order from dullest to brightest. A percentile rank of 50 means that he would rank in the middle of the group, that is, just average in ability for his age. A percentile rank of 75 means that he would stand midway in the upper half, or in other words that for every child who is brighter than he there are three who are less bright. A percentile rank of 10 places him tenth from the bottom, with 90 per cent of the children of his age brighter than he is.

The percentile method of interpreting scores has certain advan-

[14] Rachel Stutsman, *Mental Measurement of Preschool Children* (Yonkers-on-Hudson, N. Y., World Book Co., 1931).
[15] Published by the Educational Test Bureau, Minneapolis.

FIG. 71.—SUCCESS WITH THE BLOCK-BUILDING TEST

(From *The Mental Growth of Children from Two to Fourteen Years*, by Florence L. Goodenough and Katharine M. Maurer. Reproduced by courtesy of the University of Minnesota Press.)

FIG. 72.—SOME OF THE MATERIALS USED IN THE MINNESOTA
PRESCHOOL TEST

(Courtesy Educational Test Bureau, Minneapolis.)

tages over the mental age and intelligence quotient. Chief among these, especially for young children, is the fact that comparisons are made between children of the same age, not between those of different ages. A backward child of ten may have the same mental age, that is, he may pass the same tests as a bright child of five. But he is nevertheless not like the child of five, even intellectually. Much less is he like him in his social and emotional characteristics. The mental age concept is useful because it gives us an inkling of the level of development to which a child's ability most nearly corresponds, but we must not take the picture too literally. The bright child differs from the backward child of the same mental age in the *quality* of his intelligence. He is more alert, he has greater zest in doing and in learning new things. The backward child is inclined to wait for experiences to come to him; he is the tool of circumstance. The bright child does not wait for events. He goes in search of them. He creates them and bends them to his will. So as age advances the bright child continues his rapid mental growth, while the dull child also gains but at such a slow pace that the mental distance between the two steadily increases.

FACTORS RELATED TO MENTAL DEVELOPMENT

In Chapter XI the close agreement between language development and general intellectual development was mentioned. We now see why this should be so, for words are symbols, and the ability to use symbols in place of the more concrete facts for which they stand is one of the best evidences we have of the ability to think in abstract terms.

Differences in intelligence, like differences in language development, are associated with differences in socio-economic status. Figure 73 shows the relationship between intelligence-test scores and occupation for several groups of subjects.

The light solid line (Barr Scale Values) shows the differences in the intellectual *requirements* of the various occupations as rated by a large group of judges. The broken line shows the differences in the intelligence-test scores of American soldiers in World War I, classified according to their occupations in civil life. The heavy solid line shows the mean scores on another intelligence

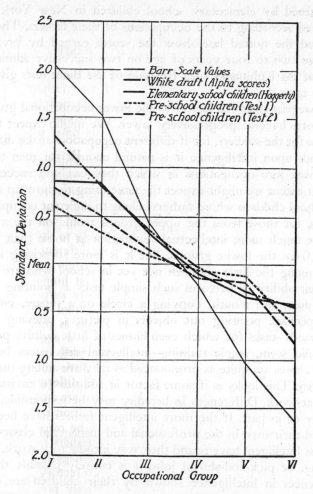

FIG. 73.—RELATIONSHIP BETWEEN INTELLIGENCE OF CHILDREN AND THE OCCUPATIONAL LEVEL OF THEIR FATHERS

(From F. L. Goodenough, "The Relation of the Intelligence of Preschool Children to the Occupation of Their Fathers," *Amer. J. Psychol.*, 1928, 40: 284-294. Courtesy Dr. Madison Bentley.)

test earned by elementary school children in New York state, classified according to the occupations of their fathers. The dash line and the dotted line show the scores earned by preschool children two to four years of age on two successive administrations of the Kuhlmann 1922 Revision of the Binet tests given six weeks apart.[16]

As we pass from the higher to the lower occupational groups,[17] the scores become progressively lower. We might expect this to be true for the soldiers, for if different occupations make differing demands upon intelligence it is natural enough for men to find their way into occupations in which they can win success. To a lesser extent we might expect the same thing to show up among the school children whose fathers belong to different occupational classes, for those from the upper groups would on the average receive much more intellectual stimulation at home than would those from the lower groups. But it is more surprising to find that among the little children not yet in school who are tested on their ability to perform such simple tasks as pointing to the eyes, nose, and mouth, copying a circle or a square, counting four pennies, pointing out objects in pictures, obeying simple commands—tasks for which even homes of little culture provide, it would seem, ample training—intellectual differences between social classes are quite as pronounced as they are among the older children. This looks as if some factor in addition to environment were at work. Differences in heredity may be responsible, either wholly or in part. If the more intelligent fathers have been able to hold their own in the professional and managerial classes while the less intelligent have found their way into factory work, truck-driving, or pick-and-shovel jobs, it is entirely possible that the differences in intelligence shown by their children are due to

[16] Because the groups differed so greatly in age, different tests were of necessity used. All the scores are therefore reduced to similar units, known as "standard scores," which makes it possible to compare them directly with each other. In this system of scoring, the unit of measurement is known as the "standard deviation" or "sigma" (σ). The zero point is set at the average score for the group. Scores higher than the average are given a $+$ sign, those lower than the average a $-$ sign. In a normal distribution about 68 per cent of all cases will earn "standard scores" that fall between the limits of one standard deviation above or below the average of the group. (See p. 369.)

[17] Occupations are classified according to the plan described on p. 286 f.

differences in native endowment rather than to differences in training. Perhaps both factors are involved.

Do boys and girls do equally well on intelligence tests? Since girls are on the average a little more advanced than boys in language development, one might expect them to stand higher on intelligence tests as well, since these scores are so closely related to language. Actually we find this to be the case, particularly among young children, when tests of the Binet type or others that make considerable demand upon language are used. But the differences are very small. When tests that are based chiefly upon certain perceptual and motor skills are employed, the difference is likely to be in favor of the boys, but here too the advantage is usually very small. Apparently there are slight differences in the *patterns* of intellectual activity most often shown by children of different sex. These differences appear very early in life. But when it comes to saying which sex is the more *intelligent* in any final or absolute sense, we are dealing with a very different question and one for which science as yet has given us no clear answer. However, we need have no hesitation in saying that, if any differences exist, they are so small that no practical account need be taken of them. Indeed it is probable that even the small sex differences shown by certain tests in regard to pattern of abilities are quite as much the result of differences in interests, in play experiences and the like that are initiated and fostered by the particular kinds of toys deemed suitable for little boys and little girls,[18] as upon any more fundamental differences relating to sex.[19]

Whether or not there are any bodily characteristics by which mental differences may be recognized is a question that has been hotly debated for decades. Many people think that the shape of the head, the features, the facial expression provide a sound basis for distinguishing the bright from the stupid. But when people have actually been set the task of making these distinctions among children who are unknown to them, so that they have nothing

[18] Magda Skalet, in an M.A. thesis written at the University of Minnesota showed that boys and girls are provided with very different assortments of toys even in babyhood.
[19] For an exceedingly fair-minded and interesting account of what scientists have been able to learn about sex differences in behavior at all ages, see *Women and Men* by Amran Scheinfeld (New York, Harcourt Brace and Co., 1944), pp. xx + 453.

but physical traits to go by, they do not as a rule have much success. Except in the case of certain types of mental deficiency which can be recognized by physical signs, neither the features, the shape of the head, nor the bodily form tell us much about the mental capacities either of children or of older persons. Not even the "bumps" or protrusions of the skull beloved of the phrenologists can give us any useful information about the mental traits of their possessor. Indeed it would be very surprising if they did, for mental traits are not correlated with the development of particular small areas in the brain. In most forms of mental activity the entire cortex is likely to be involved. Moreover, such tendencies to localization of function as exist do not follow the plan of the phrenologists' "skull maps" at all. And finally, the contour of the skull gives but slight indication of the contour of the brain within it. Unless the size or shape of the head falls completely without the limits of normal variability—and these limits are larger than most people think—we shall not find these characteristics of much help in diagnosing mental traits.

What about bodily size and form? Are tall children likely to be brighter than short ones? Is there any relationship between intelligence and weight?

Apparently there is, at least during childhood. But the relationship is very small both as regards height and weight, and there are so many individual cases that do not obey the rule that measurements of height and weight are of little help in diagnosing mental ability. If used, they would lead us astray almost (though not quite) as often as they would help us to a correct decision. Much the same thing appears to be true of most of the specific physical conditions related to health. Children of low intelligence more often than those of high intelligence are found to be suffering from diseased tonsils and adenoids, decayed teeth, rickets, and so on, but this may be only because stupid parents are more likely to have stupid children and also to give them poor physical care. The relationship of intelligence and health is a matter that opens up a number of interesting and important scientific problems, but practically speaking the question is of less significance. Good health is important enough to be sought for its own sake, no matter what relationship it may bear to the IQ.

Whether or not there are racial or national differences in

intelligence is another question that has stimulated a number of investigations during recent years. For the most part, however, these investigations have dealt only with children of school age or with adults. The work of McGraw [20] appears to show that Negro infants are more backward than whites in developing the forms of behavior included under one of the modern series of "baby tests," but although this is in accordance with what has been found for older children, further investigation is needed before we can be entirely sure of its meaning.

THE NATURE OF MENTAL ORGANIZATION

It is characteristic of human nature to hope that our inferiorities in one line may be counterbalanced by superiorities in other lines. Dozens of popular phrases attest to this: "clever but dishonest," "slow but accurate," "brilliant but emotionally unbalanced." In individual cases these combinations may be found, as we all know. But are they the rule or the exception? Is correlation or compensation more often found when the various characteristics of the same individual are compared with each other?

The fact is that it is very hard to find any two desirable traits that are not a little more likely to occur together than to run contrary to each other. Not all clever men are honest. Not all rapid workers excel in accuracy. Not all brilliant people are emotionally stable. But on the average, honesty and cleverness, speed and accuracy, intelligence and emotional stability are more likely to be found in combination with each other than with the opposites of these traits. This is true at all ages. Some traits are very closely bound together so that only occasionally will exceptions be found to the rule that a person who stands high in one will also be above average in the other. Some are more loosely connected, so that individual cases frequently break away from the rule. Sometimes the association is so slight that conformity with the rule is just barely more common than are exceptions to it and the rule itself can be discovered only by careful and unprejudiced examination of the facts for large numbers of cases. This tendency for general superiority or inferiority to show

[20] Myrtle McGraw, "A Comparitive Study of a Group of Southern White and Negro Infants," *Genet. Psychol. Monog.*, 1931, 10: 1-105.

itself in many if not most kinds of mental activity and conduct has been of great interest to psychologists concerned with questions of the organization of our mental traits. Two theories in particular have attracted widespread attention. Briefly, these theories raise the question, Have we intelligence or intelligences? Spearman, one of the greatest of British psychologists, favors the idea of a single factor that is shown in greater or less degree in all mental activity. This factor he calls g. He believes that because all behavior involves some amount of g (that is, of intelligence) the general quality of an individual's performance along any line will tend to be high or low, depending upon the amount of g he possesses. According to Spearman, the reason that people who are more than usually able along one line are likely, on the average, to show better than average ability along other lines is because these people have more than the usual amount of g. Conversely, the reason that inferiority in one line is likely to be associated with inferiority along other lines is to be found in a deficiency of g. Some kinds of performance make a strong demand upon g. These performances are closely associated with each other, since the person who ranks high in g will of necessity rank high in all of them, while the person who is low in g will do poorly in all lines that are chiefly dependent upon g. But in addition to this general factor, g, which enters to a greater or lesser extent into all performances, mental activities derive their special characteristics from various kinds of special abilities or traits known as s factors. A given s factor may be common to few or to many acts, but it always falls short of the complete generality ascribed to g. Activities that are chiefly dependent upon differing s factors and only slightly dependent upon g will have little relationship to each other. On the whole they will tend to be slightly associated, but many individual cases will be found in which superiority along one line will be accompanied by inferiority along the other and vice versa.

Thorndike, an American psychologist of equal eminence, holds a different opinion. In place of postulating a single general factor running through all mental activity, he regards different kinds of mental activity as highly specific in themselves, though having certain elements in common. These common elements are responsible for the correspondence usually found between the levels of ability along different lines shown by the same person. But the common elements do not, according to Thorndike, make up the whole of intelligence, nor is all intelligence of the same kind. Thorndike holds that there are many kinds of intelligence that can be classified, if it seems worth while to do so, into certain broad general groups of which the following three are outstanding: (1) abstract intelligence or the ability to deal effectively with ideas and symbols, (2) social intelligence or the ability to get on with people, and (3) mechanical intelligence or the ability to handle concrete things and situations. Specific abilities falling within the same general class, such as the ability to give word opposites and the ability to supply the missing word in an incomplete sentence have many elements in common and so a person who stands high in one usually stands high in the others as well. But abilities belonging to different classes have fewer elements that are common to both, and hence disagreements in standing are more frequent.

Both Spearman and Thorndike have resorted to elaborate mathematical demonstrations to support their claims, and each has his own group of adherents. No matter which idea is eventually shown to be right, the fundamental fact which each theory seeks to explain remains the same. *Correlation rather than compensation is the rule throughout all forms of mental ability.*

CAN WE STIMULATE THE COURSE OF MENTAL GROWTH?

Few questions in the entire field of psychology have been debated so hotly as this one, and few have stimulated so many investigations in the attempt to secure an incontrovertible answer. Yet in spite of all this, no answer that satisfies everybody has so far been obtained. But the situation may perhaps be clarified if the nature of the question and the limitations of the possible answers to it are clearly understood.

One of the basic principles of logic may be stated as follows: *It is impossible to prove a universal negative.* One can *disprove* such a statement, for the clear demonstration of a single positive instance is enough to show that the negative claim is not truly universal. Recently an English statistician, R. A. Fisher, has called attention to the importance of this principle in designing problems for experimental study. The *null hypothesis* as Fisher calls it, states that because of the impossibility of proving that a given principle is universally untrue, we shall avoid confusion in our thinking if we begin by positing such a general statement and then setting up our experiment to see whether any consistent exceptions to the rule can be found. That is to say, we test the invulnerability of our target by seeing whether we can demolish it. If we do not succeed, we have by no means proved that it cannot be done, but only that our own attempts have failed to do so. A clear understanding of this principle and its application to scientific investigation would do away with a good many controversies at the start, and would likewise show the underlying fallacies in some of the broad generalizations that have been too hastily drawn from insufficient data.

What of the application of the null hypothesis to the modifiability of mental growth? Evidently the question posited at the beginning of this section can never be answered in the negative, for no one can say what changes might conceivably result from methods that have not yet been tried. Moreover, it is not a very useful way of putting the question. What we want to know is not simply whether or not the course of mental growth can be experimentally accelerated. We want to know how to do it.

From time to time, rather startling claims are made about the discovery of some special method for improving the intelligence of children. These methods range all the way from some new kind of glandular treatment to a particular kind of educational régime. Much as we all wish that a method for accomplishing so important a result might truly be discovered, we should be wary of accepting these claims at their face value unless they can meet this simple test: Have the methods used been described so clearly that others can duplicate them and secure similar results? Thus far, no such method has been reported.[21]

From the discussion on pp. 371-376 it should be obvious that a change in test score does not of necessity mean that intelligence

---

[21] See the *Thirty-Ninth Yearbook* of the National Society for the Study of Education. Vol. I summarizes the literature on this topic and presents the arguments on both sides of the controversy. Vol. II is devoted to new experimental studies in the field.

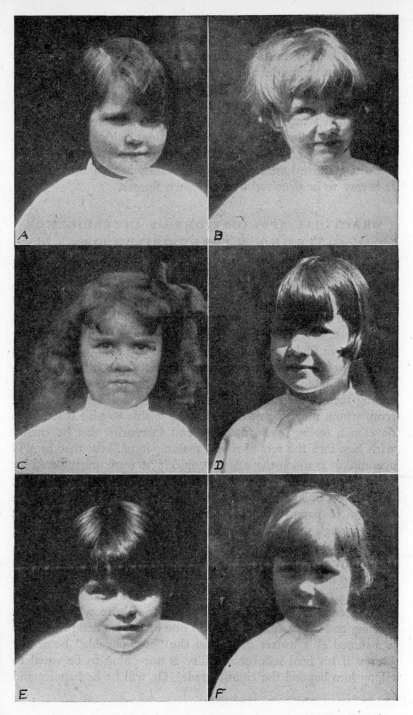

FIG. 74.—JUDGING INTELLIGENCE FROM PHOTOGRAPHS

itself has been altered. It is always possible to change the sign without modifying the thing signified. A child's IQ is not identical with his intelligence. His IQ is merely a rough index by which we are enabled to make a more adequate appraisal of his present ability than would be otherwise possible and from which we can, within limits, draw some conclusions with respect to his potentialities for future growth. But testing is a tricky business, and the statistical treatment of test results is even more tricky. It is easy to be deceived by one's own figures.

PRACTICAL APPLICATIONS OF INTELLIGENCE TESTING IN EARLY CHILDHOOD

People sometimes say, "But after all, why do we need to worry about the intelligence of children before they are old enough to go to school? Provided they are not feeble-minded, what real difference does it make whether they are bright or stupid? And in any case, why do we need to know any more about their ability than we can find out by watching them?

Long before they enter school, children form habits and attitudes that affect their later progress in many ways. Important among these are attitudes toward success and failure. The child from whom more is expected than he is able to give is likely to develop a feeling of inadequacy and insecurity that he carries with him into the school-room, making it unlikely that he will accomplish as much there as he could if he were unhampered by expectation of failure. On the other hand, the exceptionally bright child whose ability has gone unrecognized may become an active problem to parents and teachers because his alert mind is not given enough useful employment, and he is thus forced to seek it for himself. In the search he gets continually into mischief.

Even more important problems arise in individual cases. Here is a child to be placed for adoption. What kind of home should we try to find for him? "The best possible," the humanitarian will say. Agreed, but is the home of superior culture where college training and a subsequent career in one of the learned professions is assumed as a matter of course the "best possible" home for Jimmy if his final scholastic ability is not going to be equal to taking him beyond the eighth grade? Or will he be happier and stand a better chance for good emotional and social adjustment if placed in a simpler environment with foster parents who will look upon him with pride and satisfaction if he turns out to be a good carpenter and a good citizen? It is true that wrong diagnoses of ultimate capacity are sometimes made by the use of intelligence tests, particularly with very young children. But unaided human judgment is even more prone to error. Since we cannot put children into cold storage and leave them there until we have worked out infallible methods of dealing with them but must instead make decisions of both major and minor importance for their future welfare as the occasions arise, we shall do well to make use of all the evidence we can secure that will help us in making such decisions as wisely as possible. In spite of their imperfections, intelligence tests for children who are old enough to talk are nevertheless sufficiently accurate to aid materially in forecasting what a child's future development is likely to be.

AN EXPERIMENT IN JUDGING INTELLIGENCE FROM PHOTOGRAPHS

Look over the six photographs in Figure 74 and decide which child you think is the brightest. Write the corresponding letter on a sheet of paper. Then examine the remaining photographs and decide which child you think ranks next in order of intelligence. Continue until all have been ranked. Then turn to the list of IQ's at the end of Chapter XVI and see how closely your ranking agrees with the test results.

An interesting variation of this experiment consists in having the six photographs ranked independently by each member of your class and then finding the mean rank assigned to each one, in order to see how much better (if at all) is the combined judgment of all the members of a group than is that of a single person.

Chapter XVI

DEVELOPMENTAL PROGRESS DURING THE PERIOD OF MIDDLE CHILDHOOD

What characteristics of growth and experience set the limits for the period of middle childhood? What is the effect of each upon behavior?

What are the main differences between the motor accomplishments and social interests of school children and those of preschool children?

What new method of measuring intelligence not suitable for little children is widely used in the elementary school?

Do boys or girls usually have a wider range of general information? What are some of the possible reasons for this difference?

In what ways do children's drawings throw light on their intellectual processes? How do drawings made by feeble-minded children commonly differ from those made by younger normal children?

What is meant by the term "level of aspiration," and why is this aspect of personality important? At about what age can the existence of a formalized level of aspiration first be observed in children, and with what kind of goals are these early aspirations likely to be associated?

Are praise and reproof equally effective in securing maximal effort from children?

What is the difference between a "personality type" and a "personality trait"?

392

What are presumed to be the main characteristics of the "extrovert"? Of the "introvert"? Can the majority of persons be classified under one or the other of these heads?

Are such traits as cheating, untruthfulness or stealing likely to be shown to about the same degree on all occasions; for example, is a deceitful person always or nearly always deceitful? Is there any such thing as a consistently honest person?

What kind of personality difficulties in children are most likely to be overlooked by parents and teachers? Why?

How can personality be improved?

MAJOR CHARACTERISTICS OF THE PERIOD OF "MIDDLE CHILDHOOD"

If you look back at the curve of general body growth shown in Figure 43 (p. 234) you will note that there are two periods of rapid increase in body size. The first period lasts from birth until about the age of five years; the second begins from one to two years before the onset of puberty and continues until the pubertal changes have been completed. Between them is a period when physical size increases at a much slower rate and other bodily changes are less marked. This period which extends, roughly speaking, from about the age of five years up to around eleven or twelve [1] is known to students of human development as the "period of middle childhood."

Modern educational practice also sets off this period from those that precede and follow it. Most children who live in northern cities enter kindergarten at the age of five and thus make their first major break with the home. Even in places where there are no kindergartens, the average child is more likely to start school between the ages of five and six than at any other period. At the

---

[1] Not only in respect to the attainment of physical puberty but in social and emotional characteristics and even in progress through the school grades, girls go through the early stages of their developmental cycle rather earlier than boys do. The ages given above are therefore rather high for girls and lower than they should be for boys.

other extreme we have the shift from the elementary school to the junior high school [2] with its greater emphasis upon individual initiative and personal responsibility and its more highly differentiated curriculum that provides greater opportunity for the cultivation of special talent. At this time, too, marked changes in the child's social relations and in his general outlook upon life begin to be apparent. Thus the period of middle childhood is a time of slow developmental change and of rapid learning. The very fact that physical development is slowed down gives opportunity for the perfection of skills, for gaining control over motor, mental, and emotional processes which up to now have been growing and changing so rapidly that it has been hard to keep pace with them. Like the period of maturity that is to come later on, the period of middle childhood is more clearly marked by the stabilization and perfection of characteristics and skills already present than by the emergence of new traits.

THE KINDERGARTEN CHILD

The year that the child spends in kindergarten is in many respects a transitional period for him. Physically he is changing from an organism that is growing and changing very rapidly to one whose rate of growth is much slower. Mentally he is changing from the unforeseeing little child whose conduct is determined almost wholly by the needs and interests of the moment to the older child who works for more remote goals. Socially his interests are reaching out to include more persons. Formerly his preferences for certain persons were determined chiefly by the extent to which they ministered to his bodily needs. Even in his play, his interests centered largely about himself. Although, as we saw in an earlier chapter, children of three and four show the beginnings of truly socialized play, nevertheless their ideas of what play is are still, for the most part, very egocentric. The four-year-old still says, "I want some one to play *with me*." But a year or so later comes the dawn of a new social concept. Now we

[2] Although the junior high school is a comparatively recent innovation which many school systems have not yet adopted, the plan has generally been found so successful that the number of such schools is rapidly increasing, and their influence upon educational practice is felt even in places where they have not been formally established.

more often hear, "I want to go and play *with the other children.*" The child no longer sees himself purely as an individual but is beginning to identify himself with the group.

The kindergarten period is then primarily a time when the child's newly acquired abilities and skills lose something of their purely individualistic goals and begin to take on a more socialized character. Running and jumping are still fun in themselves, but they are more lively fun if done in company and as part of a game. Conversation more often takes on the character of a discussion, of an exchange of ideas and information. Emotional behavior is modified in various ways in order to conform to the ideas and customs of the group. In all his actions and attitudes the child of kindergarten age gives evidence of the dawning of a group consciousness, of a reaching out after companionship not simply for amusement but as a means of extending the range of his own personality. Vaguely but surely he is coming to see that "we" is an expression that carries more weight in the world of affairs than "I" can ever hope for.

MOTOR ACTIVITIES DURING MIDDLE CHILDHOOD

The delight in motor activity so characteristic of early childhood shows little sign of abating during the early part of this period. As age advances, however, differences between children become increasingly apparent. These differences are shown in many ways. Some children retain the clumsiness of very early childhood. They balance badly, and when they attempt to emulate the achievements of others in such matters as climbing, jumping, or doing "stunts," they are particularly prone to accident. As a result they may lose interest in motor skills and turn to more sedentary or less hazardous enterprises. Children also differ greatly in dexterity of hand. Even at an early age, some little girls learn to perform remarkable feats of needlework, and boys at the same age gain considerable skill with their jack-knives. But these cases are exceptional.[3] Upon the whole, manual dexterity of a kind that

[3] That is, exceptional under modern methods of child rearing. That they can be acquired is shown by the remarkable examples of needlework found in some of the "samplers" that every little girl was once required to make as a part of her early education. But that this skill was not acquired with ease is attested by practically all of the very old women whom I have

FIG. 75.—MOTOR SKILLS OF PRE-ADOLESCENT CHILDREN
Compare with Figures 47 and 98.

FIG. 75.—MOTOR SKILLS OF PRE-ADOLESCENT CHILDREN

Compare with Figures 47 and 98.

demands close coördination of hand and eye remains at a rather immature level until middle childhood is drawing to a close.

This is preëminently a period of large-muscle activities. Skating, swimming, diving, climbing trees, walking fences, rowing, jumping rope, spinning tops, flying kites, and a host of other active games and sports occupy every free hour. Although many of these new skills are learned and enjoyed for their own sake, as a rule the skill itself is secondary to some game of which it is a part. Baseball, marbles, jackstones, and hop-scotch are examples of the many games of motor skill that first become highly popular at these ages.

INTELLECTUAL DEVELOPMENT

Unlike the curve of growth in general bodily size, Figure 43, p. 234, shows that the growth curve of the brain does not change in form with relation to puberty. As far as we are able to determine, the same thing is true of mental growth.[4] Although the extremely rapid mental development that was characteristic of infancy and early childhood is already a thing of the past, intellectual growth continues at a rate that is still rapid enough for the annual gains to be easily perceptible throughout middle childhood.

As before, language provides one of the surest indications of the growing intelligence of the individual child as well as of intellectual differences between children. The relationship between the size of a child's vocabulary and his mental age is so high that with children from English-speaking homes who are not suffering from any marked defect of speech or of the senses, a good vocabulary test alone can serve as a rough measure of intelligence. As command of language is gained, the content of

---

questioned about the matter. Although most of them report that they accepted their daily "stints" of sewing and knitting as a matter of course because all their companions had similar tasks they did not find them pleasant, and they report many tearful hours spent in taking out irregular seams or "picking up" dropped stitches.

[4] The lack of relationship between the pubertal changes and intellectual development is clearly demonstrated in cases of precocious puberty. A fairly large number of children in whom physiological maturity of the sex organs was attained in early childhood have been studied. These children show marked acceleration in respect to growth in height and weight, but their intellectual development does not appear to be affected.

the child's speech provides many further cues by which we are able to judge the level of his conceptual thinking, and his range of comprehension and information, as well as the character of his interests and many of his personality traits. From now on, more and more of our understanding of and knowledge about children will be based upon information obtained from their speech.

Before the age of five, the average child is rarely able to define words. He knows their meaning, but his thinking, as Piaget would say, is still syncretic. He cannot distinguish the attributes of an object from the object itself, or at least he cannot do so spontaneously. He can only say, "A chair is a chair," or, if pressed, he may point to one and say, "That's a chair." But children of five or six, after a few preliminary trials in order to give them the idea, can respond to a number of the simpler abstract relationships between words. Given an action they can name the agent. That is, if asked, "What runs?" "What burns?" "What flies?" they will give appropriate answers. They can also name easy word opposites such as "yes—no"; "little—big"; "hot—cold." Giving definitions, giving word opposites, naming the agent of an action, and similar tasks all throw much light on the development of abstract thinking and so are often used as parts of intelligence tests.

The amount and kind of information possessed by children at the time of entering school is far less extensive and exact than most people suppose. Children chatter away so glibly on many topics that it is only when their actual knowledge is probed by means of careful questioning that the gaps in their information are revealed. One of the first persons to make an inquiry of this kind was G. Stanley Hall. In an article published in 1891 [5] he presented the results of a study in which five-year-old children were asked a number of specific questions such as the origin of various articles of food and clothing, the use of certain household articles, and simple facts of local geography. His results showed that children on entering school are likely to be woefully ignorant of many things that their teachers frequently take it for granted that they know. More recently, Probst,[6] working on the same

[5] G. Stanley Hall, "The Contents of Children's Minds on Entering School," *Ped. Sem.*, 1891, 1: 139-173.

[6] Catheryn A. Probst, "A General Information Test for Kindergarten Children," *Child Dev.*, 1931, 2: 81-101. Also M.A. thesis on file in University of Minnesota library.

problem with Minneapolis kindergarten children, found much the same thing to be true. In order to make sure that the hundred kindergarten children whom she studied constituted a fair sample of the Minneapolis population, she consulted the census figures to find what percentage of the adult males in the city belonged to each occupational class (see p. 286 f.). Then the occupations of the children's fathers were ascertained, and enough children from each group were selected to match these percentages exactly. In each group the number of boys and girls was also kept equal. All the children were between five and a half and six years old.

Table III shows samples of the questions asked by Probst and the percentages of children who were able to answer them correctly. In this table the column headed *U* shows the percentage of correct replies given by children whose fathers belonged to the

TABLE III

SAMPLE ITEMS FROM THE PROBST TEST OF GENERAL INFORMATION AND PER-
CENTAGE OF CORRECT RESPONSES MADE BY CHILDREN OF DIFFERENT
SOCIO-ECONOMIC STATUS AND BY THE TWO SEXES

Question	Per Cent Correct				
	U	L	B	G	Total
How many eggs in a dozen?	18	6	16	8	12
Who was the first president?	68	42	56	54	55
Of what is snow made?	80	70	78	72	75
What did Cinderella lose at the ball?	50	26	40	36	38
On what part of the violin do you play?	52	40	54	38	46
From what are little chickens hatched?	74	52	66	60	63
How many horns has a cow?	84	90	86	88	87
What is paper made from?	32	18	28	22	25
What makes a sailboat go?	60	30	58	32	45
For what is baking-powder used?	92	76	86	82	84

three upper groups of the occupational classification; *L* shows the corresponding percentage for the three lower groups; *B* gives the figures for the boys and *G* for the girls of all groups. The total percentage of correct answers is shown in the last column.

The superiority of the more favored social classes in general information is shown very clearly, not only in these samples but in almost all of the 132 items making up the list. Also there is a tendency, not quite so marked but still very consistent, for the boys to do better than the girls. The social difference is easily understood, but the sex difference is harder to explain. It is not a matter of "general intelligence" of the kind measured by the ordinary "intelligence tests," for such a test was tried, and it was found that the girls actually did a little better than the boys.

It is interesting to know that wherever tests of general knowledge or information have been tried, all the way from kindergarten to college, it has been almost the universal finding that boys and men rank superior to girls and women. We can only speculate as to the reasons for this difference. Perhaps boys have more curiosity than girls. Perhaps, even at the age of five, they are allowed to run about and investigate things for themselves more freely than girls are permitted to do. Perhaps parents, without being clearly aware of their attitude, nevertheless feel that Johnny should be taught facts, since he will some day grow into a man whose success or failure in life will be affected by the amount of knowledge he acquires, but that a knowledge of facts will be of little service to Mary in her future job of catching a husband. And it is of course possible that the explanation is to be found in heredity: that is, there may be sex-linked genes which, while not actually giving knowledge, may nevertheless predispose one sex more than the other to go in search of it. Which of these explanations is right or whether the true reason must be further sought for, no one can say at present. But the difference exists wherever the experiment has been tried. They are as well marked among children and adults who, by other criteria, are ranked as intellectually brilliant as among those who are backward or of average intelligence. They appeared in Hall's study made more than half a century ago, and there is no clear evidence that the picture is changing with the passage of time. Moreover, it appears from Terman's study of mental masculinity and femininity (see pp. 485-488) that persons whose mental characteristics resemble those of the opposite sex show, on the average, a corresponding variation in both the amount and kind of general information they have at their command. "Masculine" women on the whole are better informed than their more "feminine" sisters; "feminine" men have a narrower range as well as a different kind of knowledge than those more like the generality of their sex.

Before leaving the subject of the amount of information possessed by children, it may be well to point out that many of the unexpected and "ridiculous" things that children [7] do and say arise from incomplete knowledge or understanding due to con-

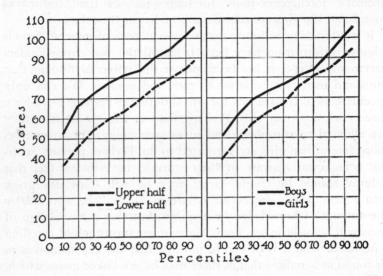

FIG. 76.—RELATIONSHIP OF THE SCORES EARNED BY 100 MINNEAPO-LIS KINDERGARTEN CHILDREN ON THE PROBST TEST OF GENERAL INFORMATION TO THE OCCUPATIONAL LEVEL OF THEIR FATHERS AND TO SEX

The curve should be read as follows: Ten per cent of the children whose fathers belonged to the lower half of the occupational classification made scores below 37; 20 per cent made scores below 46; 30 per cent below 54, etc. At every level of ability the children from the upper socio-economic levels do better than those from the lower half and the boys do better than the girls. (Drawn from data presented in "A General Information Test for Kindergarten Children," by Catheryn A. Probst, *Child Dev.*, 1931, 2: 81-101.)

fusion of a part of the stimulus with the whole. For example in Probst's study such responses as the following were common:

Butter is made by butterflies.
Baking-powder is what ladies put on their faces.
At the Ford plant they make potatoes and corn.

[7] Adults do the same things under similar circumstances. Social blunders, such as drinking from a finger-bowl are often responses to a familiar aspect of a complex situation.

The sources of confusion here are obvious, but in actual life they are not always so clear. Here is a story of an actual episode that illustrates how lack of understanding of the basic principles involved sometimes leads to behavior that to the adult may seem incomprehensible or even very "naughty" when, as a matter of fact the child was doing his best to conform.

Two small boys, aged respectively five and six years, had been brought up in a rather secluded rural district with relatively few social contacts outside their immediate family. One summer an aunt visited the farm for a few days and on a hot afternoon offered to take the boys for a swim. The children were highly delighted at the prospect, but their mother, a woman with strict Puritanical ideas, demurred on the ground that the boys had no bathing suits. The aunt pointed out that it would make no particular difference, since the lake to which they planned to go was not visible from any house or highway. Nevertheless the mother still hesitated. Finally she turned to the boys and said, "I'm sorry but I don't think it would do. I think you boys are getting too big to dress and undress before Aunt G." At this point the aunt once more intervened, this time with a compromise proposal. Some old overalls or a couple of worn suits of underwear would do exactly as well as formal bathing suits. To this the mother agreed, and in a few minutes the expedition set off, each lad carrying a small bundle.[8] On arriving at the lake shore the boys made a great ceremony about their preparations. Bush after bush was examined until at last one sufficiently dense to meet their requirements as a dressing-room was selected. Repeatedly the aunt was warned not to look or approach the bush. Her surprise and bewilderment were accordingly great when, after a few minutes, both boys dashed from their shelter and made for the lake in a state of complete and unembarrassed nudity. However, she was wise enough to ask no questions. After the swim the boys once more retreated to their bush, repeating their injunctions that the aunt must keep at a distance. The mystery was explained on the way home when the older of the two, with obvious pride in his handling of the situation remarked, "There, that was all right wasn't it? You didn't see us dress or undress at all, did you?"

[8] Later found to contain a supply of apples and doughnuts!

The person who lacks all information on a subject usually betrays his ignorance at the outset and so is less likely to be misjudged. The one with just a little information, particularly if he does not know his own limitations, is likely to act on that information with as much apparent assurance, as much evidence of intent, as the one who is fully informed. Because the period of middle childhood is a time when really adequate information about the social and ethical concomitants of many of the affairs of everyday life is likely to be lacking, while partial associations, incomplete meanings, have been built up in large numbers, misunderstanding of child behavior is very common, especially among parents and teachers. Had the mother of the two boys learned of their solution of the problem of the bathing suits, she would almost certainly have felt that they had been highly disobedient. Their failure to adhere to the spirit as well as to the letter of her instructions would, to her, have been the important thing, and it is not unlikely that she would have imputed some degree of sexual wrong-doing to their behavior. Instead she should have regarded it merely as a not unintelligent attempt to conform to their limited understanding of the peculiar social demands necessitated by their "getting big" in a way that to them seemed just as good or even better than that laid down by the mother.

THE INTELLECTUAL FACTOR IN CHILDREN'S DRAWINGS

Primitive man used picture-writing as a means of expressing his thoughts. Modern children draw for much the same reason. They do not, to be sure, make much use of drawing in order to communicate with each other as certain primitive tribes are said to have done, but this is easily understood, since long before a child is able to write for himself he knows what writing is and understands its purpose. To the young child, drawing is more nearly akin to talking to himself than to talking to others. It is a way of dramatizing his ideas through making them visible. In this sense it is a language.

Children draw what they know rather than what they see. The truth of this oft-quoted statement has been recognized for decades. The little child does not care whether or not his pictures are beautiful, but he wants them to tell what he has in mind. Details do not trouble him; he goes straight for what is to him the main fact. So if he wants to draw a man with trousers on, he draws the man first and adds the trousers afterward. The fact that the legs show through the trousers does not trouble him a bit. The man is there, so are his trousers, and who could ask for anything more complete? If he wants to draw a little girl picking flowers in a field he first draws the girl, then the flowers, then, in order to connect the two, he extends one of her arms down to the flowers at her feet in happy disregard of the laws of anatomy. Armholes may seem to be the most important parts of a coat when one is just learning to find his way into them without help, so it is not uncommon to find the armholes drawn with care on a figure that is otherwise completely nude except perhaps for a hat, which as every one should know is a far more important part of the drawing than is the hair, for hair stays on with no trouble whereas a hat must be looked after. At the age of five, approximately 35 per cent of children's drawings of the human figure include the hat, but only 13 per cent show the hair. At the age of eight the percentages have increased to 72 and 45, but baldness is still more common than hatlessness.

The changes in children's drawings that take place from age to age as well as many of the differences between the drawings of children of the same age have been shown to be far more closely related to general intelligence than to special artistic talent in children under the age of ten or eleven years. Older and brighter children less often omit essential parts of a drawing; they show a better sense of proportion; their ideas of the relationship of different parts of a drawing to each other are more definite. Children of four or five in attempting to draw the human figure make all sorts of amusing errors in assembling the different parts. Arms are frequently attached to the head or to the legs, even when the trunk is shown. Legs also are often attached to the head. This is the most logical place to put them if the trunk is omitted, but even when the trunk is added, backward children often continue to attach the legs to the head on either side of the trunk, which is then suspended between them. Sometimes the legs are attached to the arms or even to the brim of the hat.

Figure 77 shows drawings by bright, average, and dull kinder-garten children. For comparison, Figure 78 shows drawings of bright, average, and dull children of eight years. Although the drawings by five-year-olds are on the average inferior to those of the eight-year-olds, this is not true in every case. In the present case, the bright five-year-old does distinctly better than the back-ward child of eight and almost as well as the average child of that age.[9]

FIG. 77.—DRAWINGS OF A MAN BY BRIGHT, AVERAGE, AND DULL
KINDERGARTEN CHILDREN

(From *Measurement of Intelligence by Drawings,* by Florence L. Good-enough. Courtesy of World Book Co.)

The drawings of bright children are not always or necessarily more artistic than those of backward children, but they excel in such matters as the number of items shown, the correctness with which the parts have been assembled, the relative proportions of the different parts, and in the control of eye and hand move-ments as shown by the regularity of the lines and the smoothness of their joinings.

Examples of the queer errors often made in children's drawings of the human figure are shown in Figure 79. The fact that bizarre characteristics of this kind are so much more frequent in the drawings of the mentally retarded than in those made by normal children leads us to examine their nature and origin more closely. When this is done we note that in the great majority of cases the

[9] Florence L. Goodenough, *The Measurement of Intelligence by Draw-ings* (Yonkers-on-Hudson, N. Y., World Book Co., 1926).

peculiarities can be traced to a kind of mental non-adaptability, to residual features carried over from earlier drawing schemes without adjustment to the new pattern. For example, before the age of eight or nine years, most children draw the human figure in

FIG. 78.—DRAWINGS BY BRIGHT, AVERAGE, AND DULL EIGHT-YEAR-OLDS

(From *Measurement of Intelligence by Drawings,* by Florence L. Goodenough. Courtesy World Book Co.)

full face, after which the majority shift to a profile view as their preferred style. In three of the four drawings shown in Figure 79, some of the parts of the full-face drawing have been continued, along with these appropriate to the profile position. Although normal children as well as backward ones sometimes make errors of this kind, they are usually corrected after a few trials. Feebleminded children often carry along such peculiarities for years with no apparent awareness of the discrepancies. This fact is of some importance in relation to Lewin's theory, described on pp. 638-641, of the "mental rigidity" of the feeble-minded.

The methods employed for measuring the intelligence of elementary school children are much the same as those for younger children that were described in the last chapter. The chief difference consists in the supplementation of the individual tests by group tests that can be administered to an entire class of children at one time. Group tests have the further advantage that because the instructions for giving and scoring the tests are simple and highly formalized, the ordinary classroom teacher is able to handle them. They are less dependable than individual tests but serve well enough for purposes of general classification. They should always be verified by individual testing when important decisions are involved or when there is marked discrepancy between the results of the group test and other indications of a child's ability.

The following are illustrations of the kind of items used in may of the standardized group tests.

Word Opposites

Instructions: If the two words given below mean the same or nearly the same, draw a circle around the letter S. If they are opposite or nearly opposite in meaning, draw a circle around the letter O.

Examples: Slow—fast   S   Ⓞ
           Large—big   Ⓢ   O

Now try these. Work as fast as you can.

1. Little—small   S   O   20. Tidy—neat   S   O
2. Open—shut   S   O   21. Damp—moist   S   O

General Information

Instructions: Draw a line under the one word that makes each statement true, as in the following examples.

The number of cents in a dime is—5, *10*, 15, 25.

The color of a ripe lemon is—blue, red, *yellow*, pink.

1. The number of eggs in a half dozen is—6, 10, 12, 20.
2. A bird with a reddish breast is the—sparrow, crow, wren, **robin**.

For children in the primary grades whose reading ability is limited, for deaf children, and for use in schools where many of the children come from homes where a foreign language is spoken, tests like those shown in Figure 80 which make little demand upon verbal ability are often preferred. Instructions are commonly given by pantomime in which the printed sample exercises and the correct responses are reproduced on the blackboard by the examiner.[10]

[10] The first extensive use of group tests dates back to the World War of 1914-18. After America entered the war, more than a million soldiers were given tests especially developed for that purpose by a group of psychologists under the chairmanship of R. M. Yerkes.

FIG. 79.—SOME ODDITIES IN CHILDREN'S DRAWINGS

Errors of this kind are especially frequent in the drawings of backward and feeble-minded children. (From *Measurement of Intelligence by Drawings* by Florence L. Goodenough. Courtesy World Book Co.)

Although the number of separate items in a group test may be considerably greater than is usually found in an individual test of the Binet type, the variation in kind of task is commonly much smaller. A typical group test for elementary school children may include from four to eight "subtests." Each subtest is made up of ten to forty items of the same general kind, such as word-opposites, vocabulary, information, analogies, arithmetic reasoning, and so on. This plan has the merit of making for quick and easy administration because a smaller proportion of the testing time is required for giving instructions, but there is greater danger that the tasks used may be non-representative of the total pattern of abilities of a particular child. Either his talents or his defects may be disproportionately emphasized, with correspondingly distorted results. Another defect of many, though not all, of the group tests in common use is that in the process of standardizing the test to secure age norms, the authors have been more concerned about the number of cases used to compute the averages than about the representativeness of the sample. As a consequence, the mental age standards of one test may differ from those of another by as much as a full mental year or even more.[11]

THE PERSONAL-SOCIAL GOALS OF THE ELEMENTARY SCHOOL CHILD

Children of preschool age are not highly competitive. Not until around the age of five does the average child show much interest in comparing his own performance with that of other members of his group or strive to outdo his fellows for more than brief and spasmodic occasions. Little children run in company with each other, but they do not run races; they contend with each other for the possession of a toy but rarely for the sake of mastery. The four-year-old who, aping his elders, shouts joyfully, "I beat him!" frequently shows by his behavior that he has no real comprehension of the meaning of the term. Even the child leader described in an earlier chapter does not, at first, appear to be aware of or to derive special pleasure from his ascendant position. He manipulates his social world in order to effect his designs. Usually

[11] Paul V. Sangren, "The Comparative Validity of Primary Intelligence Tests, *J. App. Psychol.*, 1929, 13: 394-412.

In each line cross out the picture that does not belong there as in the two examples shown.

The large figure at the left in each line can be built up from the four small figures to the right of it. In the first two examples, lines have been drawn to show how this is done. Complete the others in the same way.

FIG. 80.—EXAMPLES OF NON-VERBAL GROUP TESTS

he is quite ready to yield his position temporarily to some one else whose plans chance to appeal to him. For the child of pre-school age, social dominance is not an end in itself but only a means toward an end.

But at about the time of school entrance the picture changes. Now the five-year-old begins to compare his possessions with those of his mates. At first the comparisons are direct and concrete. "My dress is the nicest in the whole room," said one of the kindergarten children studied by Wolf.[12] And this was satisfaction enough for her; she showed little desire to excel in other respects. Later on, children become able to differentiate between persons or objects and their attributes. They can tell what characteristics they value in others, what things they like and what they dislike. They can make comparisons that have more than immediate reference. They can set goals for themselves and recognize when and by how much they fall short of achieving them. They are beginning to develop scales of values that include more than two categories. They recognize the ameliorating factors of circumstances and motives. An unintentional offense is judged less harshly. "Did he *mean* to do it?" is heard with increasing frequency as we pass up the age-scale, and the answer to this question determines to an ever-increasing extent the appraisal of the action in question. Motives, goals, intentions—all the hidden forces that lie back of behavior—become real facts to the child long before he has reached the age of twelve.

Even before entering school, children respond to praise or reproof. But at the early ages the social incentive alone is less dependable. As a rule it must be reinforced at frequent intervals by reward or punishment of a more concrete nature. The reward may be nothing more than a caress; the punishment may be equally slight, but with the majority of young children the purely verbal type of motivation soon loses its effectiveness.

With the emergence of the competitive spirit, the influence of the group upon child behavior becomes far more apparent. From this time on one can note a clear distinction between the child's

---

[12] Theta Holmes Wolf, *The Effect of Praise and Competition on the Persisting Behavior of Kindergarten Children,* University of Minnesota Institute of Child Welfare Monograph Series, No. 15 (Minneapolis, University of Minnesota Press, 1938), pp. x + 138.

behavior toward his mates and his attitude toward adults. He senses more clearly the distinction between the generations. These are his kind. With them he must compete. By them he will be judged. So as he grows older the influence of his companions steadily increases; while the influence of adults becomes relatively weaker.

Figure 81 shows the relative effect of two kinds of social incentive upon the length of time five-year-old children would voluntarily continue to persist in a given activity.[13] In the first situation, the only incentive was the interest afforded by the activity itself. In the second a familiar adult was present who praised his performance at frequent intervals. In the third situation each child worked in competition with three of his classmates. In order to make sure that the differences obtained were not due to the particular kind of task set rather than to the incentive used, the experiment was repeated four times with each child, using a different kind of task or "game," as the children called it, on each occasion. The tasks included inserting small pins with colored heads into a peg-board, crossing out all the pictures of dolls on a series of mimeographed sheets, dropping marbles into a slot, and throwing colored rubber rings over posts attached to the backs of animals on a moving "merry-go-round." Every child performed every task three times, once under each of the three kinds of incentive previously described.[14] In each case so much material was provided that even the most persistent worker never exhausted his supply. Although it is evident that competition was on the average by far the most effective of the incentives used, examination of the records of individual children showed that this was not true of all. Several children (generally speaking, these were the younger and less mature members of the group) gave little indication of a competitive attitude in any of the activities that were tried. The following brief summaries of two of the case reports presented by Wolf will illustrate.

[13] Theta Holmes Wolf, "The Persisting Behavior of Kindergarten Children," op. cit.

[14] A fifth task, building a very complicated "Tinker Toy" model, was also used. The results obtained from this task will be mentioned elsewhere, since the principle involved proved to be quite different from that in the other four instances.

Figure 82 shows the results obtained for each of the four tasks by G.D., a little girl four years and ten months of age with an IQ of 100. Of this child Wolf says: [15]

G.D. is a very pretty child, very proud of her appearance and apparently overpetted and spoiled by her parents and other adults who have lived in her home from time to time. . . . Neither at home nor at school will she work hard at any difficult task. At home, at any rate, she can get praise and attention without doing this. The only evidence of a competitive attitude that G.D. showed during the entire experiment was when she once asked, "Who's got the prettiest dress on?" looking very pleased as she smoothed out her own dainty little dress. . . . It is significant to note that although in the experimental situation, praise was the most effective of the motivating conditions used, in no instance did it bring about a large gain over the "no-incentive" performance. . . . We may conclude either that G.D. did not understand competition or that she received so much praise at home that she was not constrained by a "need" to stay at a task that was not agreeable to her.

B.E., a boy of five years, ten months with IQ of 117, shows a very different reaction to the incentives used. For this child praise, at least from the particular adult who conducted the experiment,[16] had relatively little effect upon his performance, but he displayed a highly competitive attitude when working with other children. (See Figure 83.) Perhaps the most interesting feature of B.E.'s performance, however, is the marked contrast in his performance on the "merry-go-round" with that on the peg-board, which, in his case, was given about a month later. In spite of obvious fatigue he stuck to the "merry-go-round" for a full hour, outstaying his nearest competitor by two minutes. Toward the end of the hour, when all the others except one child had given up, in an apparent attempt to bolster up his own resolution B.E. remarked to the experimenter, "I am staying because it is fun. Other children might not stay so long." It is noteworthy that the satisfaction derived from this one complete victory

[15] *Op. cit.*, p. 81.

[16] Wolf points out that praise from some other person, possibly his kindergarten teacher, of whom he was very fond, might have produced different results and presents some evidence in support of this suggestion. Again the extremely specific nature of social interaction appears. Praise from *A* is not the same thing as praise from *B*; competition gains or loses in strength according to the interpersonal relationships among the competing individuals.

apparently carried over to subsequent occasions. Although he usually stuck to the task longer when motivated by competition than under either of the other two conditions, never again did B.E. hold out until all the other children had given up. A month

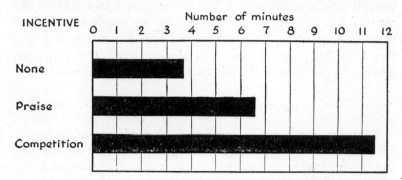

FIG 81.—MEDIAN TIME IN MINUTES FOR FOUR TASKS UNDER EACH OF THREE KINDS OF INCENTIVE

(After Wolf.)

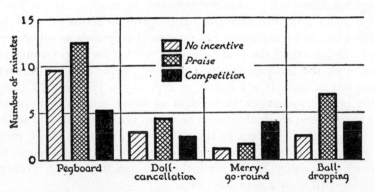

FIG. 82.—PERFORMANCE OF G.D. IN FOUR TEST SITUATIONS

(Reproduced by permission of the author and the publisher from *The Effect of Praise and Competition on the Persisting Behavior of Kindergarten Children*, by Theta Holmes Wolf. University of Minnesota Press.)

later, when competing with the peg-boards, he was the second child to leave, and as he did so he remarked to one of the other boys, "I don't care if you do get your name at the top. I got mine at the top before." Here we see the working of a principle not unlike that noted in the case of G.D. Just as the latter's drive to

excel was so thoroughly satiated by the attention paid her at
home and elsewhere [17] that she did not feel the need to demonstrate her superiority in ways that might involve special effort,
so B.E.'s one heroic effort with its resultant success brought
enough satisfaction to suffice him for at least a month. Like the
rat who has just eaten to satisfaction, he no longer felt the need
to strive mightily against fatigue and boredom to reach a goal
that from his point of view was already won. The verbal reminder, "I got mine at the top before" was quite sufficient.

THE LEVEL OF ASPIRATION

The goals that each person sets for himself are often said to
indicate his level of aspiration. These goals vary both qualitatively
and quantitatively according to the units of measurement by
which the individual judges his own achievement. One person
merely aspires to beat some particular competitor; he is satisfied
with having accomplished this end no matter how many others
may outdistance him. Another sets out to reach a certain point
at a given time. He measures his progress in terms of what he
does himself; his aspiration has no special reference to other persons. For another, the goal is marked neither by direct comparison with the accomplishments of other people nor by his own
progress as such. It is a matter of reputation. For him the thing
that chiefly matters is the opinion of other people, their praise
or their blame, their admiration or scorn. Both children and adults
differ greatly in respect to the units by which they gauge their
own achievement and with the degree of accomplishment to
which they aspire. Some "hitch their wagons to the stars"; others
are satisfied with a very low level.

Consider the academic aspirations of the college students whom
you know. Some measure their achievement by that of other
students, either particular individuals or groups. They are satisfied if their grade is as high or higher than Bill Smith's or if it
exceeds the class average. Others use a different system of meas-

[17] Visitors to the kindergarten were likely to pay special attention to
G. D. because of her personal beauty and attractive clothing. Even though
the regulations for visitors did not permit speaking to or about the children
while in the room, it was obvious from G.D.'s behavior that she was well
aware that she was receiving the lion's share of their glances and smiles.

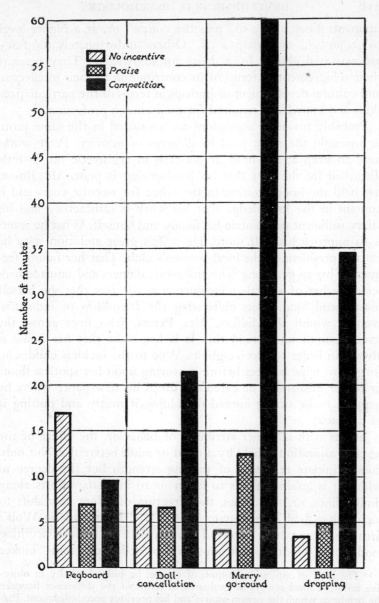

FIG. 83.—PERFORMANCE OF B.E. IN FOUR TEST SITUATIONS

(Reproduced by permission of the author and the publisher from *The Effect of Praise and Competition on the Persisting Behavior of Kindergarten Children*, by Theta Holmes Wolf. University of Minnesota Press.)

urement. They aspire to "pass the course" or, at a higher level, to get an "*A*," or perhaps a "*B*." Others—unfortunately too few—are activated chiefly by a desire for knowledge. They measure their achievement in terms of its contribution to their intellectual and cultural development or perhaps in terms of the particularized skills and knowledge required for their chosen profession.

Probably no one's aspirations are measured in the same terms or maintain the same level in all areas of activity. Peter works hard to keep at the head of his class in arithmetic but is little disturbed by the fact that his handwriting is poor. Mr. Brown has held the same position in the office for twenty years and is content in the knowledge that his work is satisfactory and his salary sufficient to maintain his family and himself. What he wants is to improve his golf score. His wife's great ambition is to be elected president of the local women's club. That her family frequently has to get along with makeshift dinners and unmade beds seems to her of as little consequence as the fact that she herself must spend long hours cultivating the friendship of influential women whom she dislikes. Mrs. Peters, who lives across the street, cannot understand this. It is her boast that her house is always in order to receive guests. Woe to the luckless child who forgets to wipe his feet before venturing upon her spotless floors or to her husband if he carelessly drops his newspaper where he happens to be sitting instead of folding it neatly and putting it in the rack!

Just as with all other attributes of behavior, the effect of the level of aspiration [18] held by a child or adult is circular. Not only does it initiate responses of varying strength but the degree to which it is attained tends to lessen or to intensify efforts along similar lines, or, sometimes, the direction of effort may shift to some other field of endeavor. This is well illustrated by Wolf's fifth situation which involved the attempt to copy a working model of a windmill, a steam-shovel or a derrick from "Tinker

[18] The level of aspiration cannot, of course, be judged wholly in objective terms. It must always be evaluated in terms of the difference between the height to which the person aspires and his previous accomplishment. Particularly among children whose understanding is limited, further account must be taken of what the child conceives the projected accomplishment to be, whether or not he knows its requirements and its rewards.

Toys." [19] The models were purposely selected to appear easy. As a matter of fact many of their elements could be constructed with tantalizingly little effort by all the children.

At the initial presentation the Tinker Toy models aroused by far the greatest interest of all the tasks used. Practically all of the children were at first very confident of their ability to reproduce the examiner's model which had been set up beforehand and left where they could use it as a copy. Actually, however, the models had been intentionally made too difficult for even the most skillful child to complete. It was found that under these circumstances the external incentive—praise or competition—was of relatively little significance in comparison with two other factors, (a) the strength of the child's apparent interest in the task and his expressed confidence in his ability to succeed with it which we may regard as the best available evidence of his "level of aspiration" and (b) the number of his previous failures. Regardless of the type of incentive used, it was found that the length of time a child would voluntarily persist in his attempts to build the model was greatest on the first trial, decreasing materially on the second, while on the third occasion many children gave up after relatively little effort.

Figure 84 shows the results obtained for B.A., a boy of six years with IQ of 116 whose initial interest in the task was unusually great and who came nearer to attaining complete success than any other child in the group.

Wolf makes the following comment on this child's reactions:

It was evident that B.A.'s level of aspiration for the first two performances was very high. He was "set" to make a complete copy of the model. He handled his work with considerable ability and in the first model, when he was working alone, he completed everything except the proper placing of the pulley belts. Once he called to the experimenter in a high voice, "Miss H., I've got into quite a problem," but he kept at the task assiduously when told that he must work by himself. . . . In the next, the competitive situation, he worked fifteen minutes longer than his nearest competitor [20] but left the task before

[19] A type of building material consisting largely of wooden pins and spools with holes drilled in them from which models of various objects can be assembled. To make the models used in this experiment, a system of belts and pulleys was included so that the completed models could be "worked" by hand. A different model was used in each of the three situations.

[20] Apparently the chief motivating factor here was not competition but

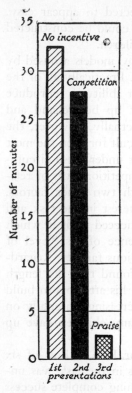

FIG. 84.—PERFORM-
ANCE OF B.A. WITH
TINKER TOY IN THREE
TEST SITUATIONS

(Reproduced by per-
mission of the author
and the publisher from
*The Effect of Praise
and Competition on the
Persisting Behavior of
Kindergarten Children*,
by Theta Holmes Wolf.
University of Minne-
sota Press.)

he had worked as long as before. On the third
occasion he stayed just long enough to put six
pieces together, although praise had been an
effective incentive in the case of the other
four tasks.

The case of B.A. raises an interesting
question of widespread import in human
behavior. What constitutes failure? Looked
at from the standpoint of objective accomplishment, B.A.'s performances on both
the first and the second trials were the best
in the entire group. But the loss in both
accomplishment and effort from the first
to the third performance was also
greater than for any other child in
the group. Although the majority of the
children showed a tendency similar to that
of B.A., the average difference in "persisting time" from initial to final performance was much smaller, and there were a
few cases in which no relation whatever to
order of presentation appeared. G.D., the
little girl previously described, is an example. The "persistence times" for G.D.
are as follows: first presentation, no incentive, 1.2 minutes; second presentation,
competition, 3.2 minutes; third presentation, praise, 5.5 minutes. It is clear that
there is no cumulative effect of "failure"
in this case. In no situation, Wolf states,
did G.D. try hard and in no situation did
she give any evidence of intending to
finish the model.

the child's own aspiration to complete the task.
Had competition been the goal, it seems unlikely
that he would have remained so much longer
than was necessary, inasmuch as it was carefully
explained at the beginning of each competitive situation that the child who
worked for the longest time would be the one to get his name and photograph at the top of the list. Note here the comments of B.E., previously
reported.

Psychologically speaking, then, failure cannot be measured in terms of overt performance. G.D. did not really fail, although her actual accomplishment was negligible in quality and quantity. Her only effort was directed toward securing praise from the experimenter and even that aspiration was not sufficiently strong to induce her to go to much trouble to secure it. B.A. did fail, in spite of his superior performance. As a matter of fact his psychological failure was the greater because he came so near to reaching his goal. Do we not all of us regret more keenly the prize that we barely fail to win? Success or failure can be defined only in relation to one's own aspiration. The emotional significance of either success or failure for the individual is likely to bear a direct relationship to the amount of effort voluntarily expended toward achieving it. A success too easily won is not likely to bring the same degree of satisfaction or to have as much effect upon later accomplishment as one achieved after long struggle. The "wounding" effect of failure is greatest when supreme effort has been put forth to no avail.

Inasmuch as social approval is a goal to which most of us aspire, though in varying degrees, and since disapproval is something that most of us seek to avoid, it is not surprising to find that both praise and reproof have generally been found to lead to increased effort on the part of children. In the greater number of the experiments on this topic, verbal incentives have been used but once. Children are first tested as to their performance of a task with no special incentive, after which one-half of the group is praised, the other half reproved for the quality of their work. On the following day the task is repeated. The second performance of the praised group is then compared with that of the reproved group and with that of other children who have merely been given a second test with no further incentive used. As a rule the results have indicated that either praise or reproof is followed by a somewhat better performance than that when there is neither, but the difference between the results under the two kinds of incentives is negligible and varies from child to child. Hurlock,[21] however, has called attention to an important factor which most of the studies have failed to reveal because they were

[21] Elizabeth B. Hurlock, "An Evaluation of Certain Incentives Used in School Work," *J. Educ. Psychol.*, 1925, 16: 145-159.

not carried far enough. Although a *single* instance of praise or reproof does not clearly differentiate the relative value of the two incentives, since the average improvement has usually proved to be about equally great in both instances, *continued* administration of either produces very different results. In Hurlock's experiment, a group of elementary school children were given arithmetic tests for five successive days. On each of the last four days they were praised for their work on the preceding day. These children continued to gain in score throughout the course of the experiment. A second group who were reproved according to the same plan, gained about as much as the praised group on the first occasion after the reproof had been administered but lost steadily thereafter. A third group who were given the tests for five days with no comment at all gained a little (but not much) on the first day of retest and thereafter lost.

This experiment may throw some further light upon the fact that the relative effect of negative and positive incentives appears to vary with the individual, for the life experience of any child extends back far beyond the classroom experiment. The child who has been continually reproved is more easily discouraged. He no longer sets as high a goal for himself because he despairs of being able to reach it. Strong effort no longer seems worth while.

One further point. Since this is a social world, the direction and intensity of the aspirations of one person have a strong effect upon those of his associates. Peoples may be stimulated to greater accomplishment, either through the desire to surpass another's achievement (for competition is actually a state in which the level of aspiration is fixed by the accomplishment of other persons) or merely by the power of social suggestion and the influence of prestige. If the accomplishments of another are obviously beyond their own powers, some persons drop out before beginning the race. Sometimes people become so irritated when another's ambitions impinge upon their own desires or personal comfort that their emotional response spreads over to the goal toward which their neighbor is striving. We not infrequently hear remarks like the following: "I vowed long ago that I'd never make my children take piano lessons because I used to get so annoyed by hearing the woman who lived across the hall perpetually nagging at her children about their practicing," or "When I was a child my mother fussed so about my always keeping my room in order that, now I have a house of my own, I get a lot of satisfaction out of just leaving things around. My rooms are always in a mess but I don't care." And in both these remarks, the effect of the social interaction between individuals is again apparent. For if the woman across the hall had been some one who was both liked and admired, the effect upon her neighbor would probably have been quite different. Instead of a negative reaction to piano practice the latter might have developed a strong aspiration to give her children as much musical training as did the woman she admired. In like manner, the orderly habits of the mother might have set a similar pattern for the aspirations of the daughter had their personal relations been different.

Nothing is more important for the child's future than the level and type of the goals he sets for himself. And because these goals are not clearly realized until after the crystallizing effect of verbal formulation has taken place and the distinction between the self and the not-self has become sufficiently advanced to give form and pattern to the child's social attitudes, the period of middle childhood takes on special importance, for it is then that the child for the first time faces his future.

THE QUESTION OF "PERSONALITY TYPES"

Pigeonholes are convenient. Classifications reduce multiplicity and thereby lessen confusion. Arrangement, to be useful, must start with a system of ordering the things to be arranged according to one or more of their attributes such as size, color, the purpose for which they are to be used or the order in which they are to be selected.

All of us, whether we stop to think about it or not, are forced to do a certain amount of human classification. The very adjectives that we use in describing the people that we know show that this is the case. We say, "William is stubborn, Peter is friendly, Amos is reserved, John is good-natured." But some people have gone much further than this. They believe that certain kinds of personality traits are linked together into such definite patterns that by identifying the pattern or "type" to which a person belongs it then becomes possible to describe most of the significant features of his personality.

The idea itself is as old as science. It is found in the writings of Aristotle and in the philosophic discussions of the seventeenth century. In modern times, hardly a decade passes without the evolution of a new system for classifying human "types." Some of these systems have been based entirely upon the individual's behavior; others have included physique as well. Of the latter, perhaps the best known is Kretschmer's system of "constitutional types," which includes three main groupings along with certain intermediate classes. The *athletic type* includes persons with broad shoulders and deep chests, of generally good proportions with rather long limbs. In personality they are alleged to be forceful and rather aggressive. The *asthenic type* includes persons with long legs, rather short trunk, and with narrow chest and shoulders, a long head with narrow face. These persons are alleged to be seclusive and withdrawing, inclined to be rather nervous and high-strung. Kretschmer named his third type the *pyknic* group. The pyknics have round heads and rounded bodies, long trunks and short arms and legs, narrow shoulders and broad hips. They are supposed to be easily stirred to emotional response, either laughter or tears, and to be fond of society.

Of the more purely behavioristic classifications, that of the Swiss psychiatrist Jung, a pupil of Freud who later rejected much of Freud's teaching, is best known. Jung's attempt to divide mankind into two general groups,[22] the *extroverts* and the *introverts* has attracted enough popular as well as scientific attention to make the terms a part of the vocabulary of most educated persons. According to Jung's descriptions, the extrovert is seen in the man of affairs, rushing from one conference to another, prominent in local politics, a member of clubs and lodges, a committee man, a high-power salesman of ideas or of goods, better at getting things started than at seeing them through under difficulties. Then there is the "introvert." The introvert is the man whose attention is more inwardly directed. He is interested in ideas, theories, philosophies. He is not gregarious, though he may have a few close

[22] The division was not supposed to be absolute. There would be a few intermediate cases, but the great majority of persons could, according to Jung, be classed under one heading or the other.

friends whom he finds intellectually stimulating. He would rather see things work than make them sell. But he is likely to brood over matters that the extrovert would soon forget in the press of new interests. He is sensitive to rebuff and because of his self-consciousness may imagine slights where none were intended.

Because people, whether they be children or adults, unquestionably differ in characteristics of this kind and because the traits said to be characteristic of each type do "hang together" rather better than those of many typologies that have been proposed, a number of devices for classifying individuals according to this scheme have been worked out. Some of these are suitable for children; others have been designed for adolescents or adults. Regardless of the age of the subjects, similar results have been obtained with each of these tests. People do not fall into two or more fairly well-separated groups as the typologists would lead us to expect. Instead, the form of the "extroversion-introversion" curve appears to be much like that of the distribution of general intelligence shown on p. 370. Although some fairly pronounced examples corresponding to the "types" are found, the great majority of people are neither introverts nor extroverts but fall midway between the two. Some of their characteristics resemble those of one type, some the other. Moreover it appears that most people behave in an introverted manner at some times and under some conditions; at other times or under different conditions they behave like extroverts. Jung seems to have been right to this extent. He has described certain patterns of behavior that have sufficient cohesion to warrant our speaking of introversion-extroversion as a continuous *trait* [23] that is displayed by all persons in varying degrees (if we think of the comparative amount of time or number of occasions on which the behavior of that person could be classified under one category or the other). But he was wrong in thinking that such a classification would result in putting the majority of people into one or the other of two distinct groups. In respect to introversion-extroversion, not consistency but inconsistency appears to be the rule for most persons.

Thus we see that in more than two thousand years of attempts

[23] A *trait* may be defined as a continuous personality variable (or dimension) with respect to which individuals may be measured with greater or less precision.

to group human beings into behavioral types, little real progress has been made. About all that has been gained is an increased realization of the complexities of human behavior and of the many factors by which it is influenced.

PERSONALITY TRAITS

The difference between the terms *personality trait* and *personality type* is not very clear-cut. Generally speaking, the second term implies a higher degree of organization than the first. It suggests the classification of individuals as the basic step from which the detailed description of their characteristics follows, while the word *trait* refers to a specific and limited aspect of behavior. By a study of *traits* we proceed inductively to a knowledge of the individual; from a classification by *types* we arrive deductively at a knowledge of the individual. Those are the theories. But in the matter of types we have seen that theory and fact fail to coincide. Let us continue our query, this time with reference to the theory of traits.

Not long ago it was rather generally supposed that such characteristics as honesty, coöperativeness, seclusiveness, perseverance, and so on were rather stable qualities of the individual; that, for example, an honest person is honest in nearly all situations, that a resourceful person will show his resourcefulness under almost any circumstances, that a persistent person can be depended upon to stick to almost any kind of task, and that an optimist goes about whistling in all weathers. But recent investigation does not bear out this idea. It is true that both grown people and children show a good deal of consistency in their conduct from one time to another, if the situation remains about the same. Because we so often observe persons repeatedly under similar conditions we become impressed with this consistency and assume that they will behave in just the same way under all circumstances. The teacher who sees Jimmie and Johnnie only in the classroom and finds that Jimmie seizes every opportunity to copy his lessons from his neighbor while Johnnie's eyes never wander from his own paper no matter how many chances for cheating are given him concludes, not unnaturally, that Jimmie is a wretched little cheat and

Johnnie is the soul of honesty. If questioned about their "personality traits," she will almost surely rate Johnnie high and Jimmie low on all aspects of honesty and trustworthiness. But she fails to take account of the fact that Johnnie has little need to cheat, for he is at the head of his class anyway and doesn't have to worry about promotion. Moreover it would be silly for him to copy from his neighbor when the chances are that his own answer is the right one. The situation for Jimmie is very different. He is on the verge of failure, and his father has promised him a "good licking" if he doesn't bring home a better report card next time. The two boys differ in classroom conduct, to be sure, for Jimmie cheats and Johnnie doesn't. And there is a real difference in "personality" besides, for Jimmie feels the need to cheat and Johnnie doesn't. But are we safe in assuming that Johnnie is consistently honest and Jimmie dishonest?

Let us follow them out to the playground. Now Jimmie, who is shaky on the multiplication table, who mixes up all the dates in his history lesson, and who spells sugar with an *h* is a "crackerjack" when it comes to marbles, but Johnnie is all thumbs. If an opportunity for cheating comes will it be Jimmie or Johnnie who yields to the temptation?

A few years ago Hartshorne and May [24] undertook to find out what the chances are that a child who is dishonest in one situation will also be dishonest in others, or, in other words, how consistently the same kind of character or personality traits will show up in all kinds of surroundings and conditions. So they invented a large number of "tests" of deceit. In all there were thirty-two different kinds. The tests were given to more than 8,000 children from all ranks of society. Some of the tests were given to children as home work, some in their school classrooms, some at parties. Some of them were made to seem like school lessons; others took the form of games. But the tests were all alike in that an opportunity for cheating or dishonesty of some kind was always given, and, although care was taken to keep the children from finding it out, some special device was always provided for finding out which children cheated and how much they cheated.

[24] H. Hartshorne and M. A. May, *Studies in Deceit* (New York, Macmillan Co., 1928).

For example, the children were given an arithmetic test similar to those they were used to having in school but too long and hard for any of them to finish within the time allowed. When the time was up, the papers were collected and taken away and a duplicate of each was prepared by a clerk. At a later time the papers were given back together with an answer sheet, and each child was told to score his own. Plenty of opportunity was allowed for changing the answers or for adding to the amount done. Afterward, by comparing the corrected papers with the copies of the originals the amount of cheating done by each child could be determined.

In other tests, athletic stunts such as measuring the strength of grip on a dynamometer or chinning a bar were used, and opportunity was given for faking a record. Others consisted of games that could easily be won by cheating, such as pinning the tail on a donkey or seeing who could carry the most beans from one box to another in a given length of time by taking only one bean at a time. Cheating in this case consisted of taking more than one bean. Tests that provided opportunity for stealing small sums of money with which the children were provided for use in working out problems in making change and which was supposed to be returned at the end of the lesson were also tried out. So also were tests of lying either to avoid disapproval or to secure approval.

When the same tests were tried twice on different occasions, but with other conditions remaining the same, it was found that the children behaved very similarly from one trial to another. Children who cheated at lessons the first time were likely to do it the second time; those who were honest the first time were honest the second time. There were some exceptions, of course, but the general tendency toward consistency was fairly marked. Likewise those who cheated on athletic contests or who lied to secure approval behaved about the same way on repeated trials. But when the performances of the same children in different situations were compared, the results were very different. There was little, if any, greater likelihood that the child who consistently cheated in the classroom type of situation would fake an athletic record or cheat in games, or steal money than that the one who was honest in classroom work would do so. Children who cheated on their home work did not necessarily cheat at school. Lying and stealing showed only a small tendency to go together. All in all, the results of these experiments seem to show that conduct is decidedly specific, depending in each case upon the particular child and the particular situation.

The same specificity of behavior was found when other so-called "traits" were studied in a variety of situations. Generosity was found to vary with the thing about which one is called upon to be generous. Some people are generous with their time, others with their money. Most of us find it quite easy to share the things we care little about. Hartshorne, May, and Maller [25] found that the children whom they studied were no more consistent in the kind of things they were willing to do for others than in the kind of situations under which they would be dishonest. This is not strange. Consider the following situation:

Each child was given a pencil box containing ten articles, a drinking cup, a pencil sharpener, a ruler, an eraser, a pen, a pen-holder, a double pencil, and three ordinary pencils. Then it was suggested that each one might give away a part of his kit to help make up kits for poor children who had none. They were scored according to the number and kind of articles they were willing to give away.

Suppose, however, that Peter's father had been out of work for two years and no one in the family had a cent to spend for anything beyond the barest necessities. For months Peter had longed for one of these pencil kits, but there seemed to be no chance of his getting one. Across the aisle from Peter sat Billy, who was an only child of parents in comfortable financial circumstances, and who had a number of devoted aunts and uncles besides. The day before the kits were given out, Billy had had a birthday and received no less than four kits of this kind, most of them of better quality than the one he had just been given. If Billy gave away all the articles in the new kit and Peter refused to part with any, can we be sure that Billy is the more generous of the two?

But the rule that behavior depends on the circumstance rather than on the child is not an absolute one. In practically all their experiments, Hartshorne and May found that although for the

[25] H. Hartshorne, M. A. May, and J. B. Maller, *Studies in Service and Self-Control* (New York, Macmillan Co., 1929).

children who sometimes cheated there was little consistency in behavior from one situation to another, there were some who were consistently *honest*, who never cheated no matter what the temptation nor how obvious the opportunity. This is a highly significant fact, for it indicates that socially desirable traits, once they have been established, may become relatively stable. So we may justifiably say of an individual that he is honest or coöperative or generous or truthful with some feeling of assurance that his subsequent behavior will bear out our statements. But this is not true at the other end of the scale. It would appear as though the comment made by Hartshorne and May that "there are no such things as honest or dishonest children but only honest or dishonest acts; no such traits as coöperativeness, service, self-control, and so on, but only people who at times act coöperatively, at times perform services for others and at times exhibit self-control," might perhaps be qualified. Concretely, of course, what they say is entirely correct; the same statement might be made with respect to all the other abstract nouns by which we describe the attributes of an individual. But it would appear that some people do set goals for themselves that make for a very high degree of stability of behavior in certain areas. In this sense we may speak of honesty, truthfulness, and so on as "character traits," because some people display them consistently. But dishonesty, untruthfulness, and similar forms of behavior are not "traits" because they are circumstantial rather than personalized forms of response. They are negative reactions, showing that the individual has *failed to develop* the positive side of his character. Resistance to temptation is a positive characteristic, depending on the establishment of definite attitudes toward the world and the self. Not-cheating is a more mature form of behavior than cheating because it is a response to a more highly organized incentive. It is a more stable, dependable form of reaction because it is a response to an attitude that has become relatively detached from the outside world and referred back to the self. I do not cheat because *I* do not cheat. The reasons for not cheating have become organized within the self; they no longer have much reference to the outside world. But for the person in whom such organization has not taken place, the conditions are very different. For him, cheating or not cheating depends upon circumstances. He cheats when he feels the need to cheat if he thinks he can get away with it; he refrains from cheating when nothing is apparently to be gained by it or if he thinks the risk of being caught is too great. Cheating is unpredictable because it depends upon circumstances that cannot be predicted in advance. But honesty can be predicted because it depends upon the individual. In this sense we may say that honesty is a character trait but dishonesty is not.[26]

Closely related to this finding are the results of a study by Rundquist and Sletto.[27] They were concerned with certain technical problems involved in the construction of attitude scales. One of these questions is this: When a statement can be expressed either in a form that conforms with or runs contrary to that generally regarded as "socially acceptable" is there any technical advantage in using one type of phraseology in preference to the other?

Consider the following examples. (In each case the subject is asked to mark the statement A if he agrees with it, D if he disagrees with it.)

———It is all right to evade the law if you do not actually break it.
———It is wrong to evade the law even though you do not actually break it.

———Most people are honest.
———Most people are dishonest.

Inasmuch as one is free either to disagree or to agree with the ideas expressed, at first thought it would seem as though it makes

[26] That is, among most social groups in a culture such as our own. Honesty is a goal for which people (in our culture) consciously strive and in which they take pride. But with the possible exception of certain delinquent or criminal gangs, dishonesty is not a trait that is openly sought for its own sake nor an attribute to be admired in others or in the self. Most people *aspire* to be honest, and this is an aspiration that can be openly cultivated and displayed. But few people in our culture aspire to be dishonest, and fewer still will openly admit such a goal. Dishonesty in most cases means that other desires have temporarily dominated over the aspiration to be (or at least to be thought) honest.

[27] Edward A. Rundquist and Raymond F. Sletto, *Personality in the Depression: A Study in the Measurement of Attitudes* (Minneapolis, University of Minnesota Press 1936), pp. xxii + 398. See especially Chapter IX.

no particular difference which one of the paired statements is used. On the basis of logic, one would expect that everybody who "agrees" with the statement that most people are honest would "disagree" when the same idea is expressed in the opposite form. But this has been found not to be the case. Just as not-cheating seems to be a more highly organized and therefore more dependable form of response than cheating, so disagreement with a statement that is disapproved by most people has been shown to be a more revealing and more dependable type of response than agreement with it. Many people who will not take the trouble to deny the statement that "most people are dishonest" will also agree with the statement that "most people are honest." [28] Apparently agreement with either statement sometimes means no more than that the subject has no pronounced feelings about it one way or the other. But disagreement means that he has previously done some thinking about the matter and as a result has formed a really positive attitude on the subject. Disagreement, in such instances, indicates a more highly organized and therefore more revealing attitudinal state than agreement, which may arise from mere passivity.

WHAT THE SCHOOL CHILD'S PERSONALITY SIGNIFIES

Even if we could measure the personality of school children with absolute precision, it is unlikely that we could tell from such measurements into what kind of an adult each individual child is going to develop. To do that we should have to know not only what a child is like now but what influences are going to come into his life from now on. But there is no doubt that we could make a guess which would be much more likely to be right than wrong. Even with the imperfect methods of studying and describing personality that have been worked out so far, we

[28] Of course both statements are not used in the same questionnaire since too many people would notice that they carry the same idea and so would see to it that their answers agreed with each other. The finding mentioned here is based upon the use of different questionnaires administered to the same subjects on different occasions separated by so short a period of time that one would not expect many real changes in attitude.

can detect in the school children of to-day many of the traits that will characterize them when they grow up. The solitary child with few friends may grow to be a man with marked social interests, but the chances are against it. The child who rebels against all authority may, as he grows older, become a docile follower of the crowd, but he is more likely to develop into an aggressive, truculent type of person who goes around with a chip on his shoulder and takes offense at the least excuse. Habits and attitudes that are so greatly "over-learned" in childhood as these are likely to be, in time become as automatic as reciting the alphabet or swimming. The same laws of learning that apply to typewriting, memorizing nonsense syllables, learning to run a maze, or becoming "conditioned" to expect food when the dinner bell rings, hold good also for learning to run away from school or home, taking other people's possessions or refraining from doing so, lying to get out of trouble or telling the truth, preferring to play alone or with other children, or preferring "boys' games" to "girls' games."

Of course these alternatives are not equally balanced in regard to ease of learning. The little child does not have to be taught to take what he wants if he can get it; it is refraining from taking what is not his own that has to be learned. Probably it is easier to teach children to lie as a way of getting out of trouble than it is to teach them to tell the truth and face the consequences. Probably, too, there are inherited differences among children of a kind that make it easier to teach some to inhibit their natural tendencies to grab whatever they want, or to train them to stick to a thing until it is accomplished, or to develop in them the kind of behavior that makes them popular with other children. The evidence for the inheritance of such behavior tendencies is not so clear as is the evidence in regard to the inheritance of either general ability or certain special talents such as musical ability. It seems fairly certain that at most what is inherited in these cases is not an absolute determining factor but only a tendency, a predisposition, that may make it more difficult to develop the right kind of social and emotional habits in some children than it is in others but does not render it impossible to do so. Some psychologists refuse to concede heredity even as minor a rôle as this in the determination of behavior but put their whole faith in the side of learning. That learning plays a tremendous part there can be no doubt.

Parents and teachers are particularly likely to overlook the personality defects that are of chief concern to the child himself. They worry about the child who disobeys or fights or steals or gets into sex difficulties because such behavior is both conspicuous and disturbing to other people, especially to those in charge of him. But the child who has troubles of his own and keeps them to himself, worrying and brooding over them in secret; or the one who finds real life so hard and unpleasant that he slips away into a dream world, shunning companionship and withdrawing further and further into his unhappy self is not likely to impress many people as being a problem because he does not bother anybody except himself. But in reality such children are quite as much in need of help as the ones who make themselves actively troublesome. Often their need is greater, for if matters are not corrected and such a child continues to spend a large part of his time and his emotional energy in brooding over his troubles when he should be doing something worth while, if he stays off by himself instead of learning how to get along with other people through the give and take of healthy play, if he forms the habit of retreating from difficulties instead of meeting them squarely, he will be poorly equipped for holding his own in the active competition of adult life. Behavior such as this is always a sign of mental ill-health. The child may get over it, to be sure, just as he may recover from physical illnesses that are allowed to run their course without proper attention. But it is foolish to trust to luck when a child's future success and happiness are at stake.

What can be done? The rule is easy to state, but to carry it out often means long and painstaking effort.

Find out the cause of the trouble.

Remove the source of difficulty if possible. If not, help the child to take an unemotional attitude toward it. This can best be done by so arranging his life that the troubling factor, whatever it may be, will interfere with it as little as possible.

Help him to form a new set of behavior patterns. Even if the actual difficulty is removed, his old habits which have been practised so long will continue to assert themselves unless new ones are acquired. Keep the principles of learning in mind. Make sure that desirable behavior brings satisfaction. See that he has plenty of opportunity for practising his new social skills, but don't overdo it. Avoid forcing him into too many new and untried situations at once.

Most important of all, find out the level and type of his aspirations. What goals has he set for himself? How valiantly is he striving to reach them? Are they realistic and practical or only day-dreams to be carried out in some improbable future?

The same principles hold good with the delinquent child who is a more active source of difficulty. Here, too, there is a reason or perhaps a whole series of reasons back of the antisocial behavior. But even after the reason has been discovered and the original difficulty corrected, the problem of retraining remains. Habits practised for years will not disappear by magic. Definite effort is necessary to get rid of them. And here, too, the child's aspirations for himself, the goals for which he strives and his confidence in his own ability to reach these goals, are of paramount importance. We have seen that much delinquent behavior arises from a low level of character organization. The child cheats or steals or commits other offenses because he has never built up a clear concept of an ideal self to which his behavior must conform. He is swayed by each passing impulse because he lacks the ballast that is provided by a major aspiration that can be openly fostered by his own efforts and strengthened by a sense of social approval.

Training should be positive. Just harping on what not to do will not take one very far, for character is positive, not negative. The thing that the child needs is to learn what to do and to get satisfaction by doing it.

Florence M. Teagarden, *Child Psychology for Professional Workers* (New York, Prentice-Hall, 1940), pp. 21 + 641.

This is a book on child psychology written for people who expect to enter professional fields other than academic psychology. It is intended for social workers, teachers, clinical psychologists, camp councillors, juvenile court workers, physicians. It is not just a "popular" book about children like many on the market that tell little more than what every intelligent person already knows. On the contrary it is based on careful study of the experimental literature by a clinical psychologist of extensive experience with real children. Theoretical principles are derived from the reports of laboratory experiments and illustrated by many accounts of the behavior of individual children in everyday life. In this way the practical significance of many psychological findings which, as ordinarily presented, seem too far removed from the life of everyday people to be worth the attention of those not primarily concerned with psychology as a science is made clear.

Although not every one may care to read the entire book, most people will find some chapters that interest them. In particular, persons who plan to enter one of the professional fields named above or others related to them not only will be interested in the book itself, but will find the well-selected bibliographies at the end of each chapter helpful in suggesting sources of further reading on the topics that particularly appeal to them.

INTELLIGENCE QUOTIENTS OF THE FOUR-YEAR-OLD CHILDREN SHOWN IN
FIGURE 74

A	B	C	D	E	F
118	92	137	105	80	127

Chapter XVII

SOME ADDITIONAL PRINCIPLES OF LEARNING
AND RETENTION

*What is the chief difference between the learning of
preschool children and that of older children and
adults?*

*Is incidental or purposeful learning usually more de-
pendable? Why?*

What kind of material is easiest to learn and remember?

What are some rules for making learning easier?

*Does learning one thing made it easier to learn other
things?*

*In what ways does a well-learned action differ from
one that is only partly learned?*

*Does continued practice always mean success in learn-
ing? Explain.*

*How does learning by "conditioning" differ from
learning by "trial and error"? By what other
methods does learning take place?*

*Do animals or children show an "instinct of imitation"?
What part does imitation play in learning? Describe.*

THE DIFFERENCE BETWEEN INCIDENTAL
LEARNING AND INTENTIONAL LEARNING

We have said that the period from six to twelve is above all
a period of learning. But this is only half the story. Children
learn from the beginning, but they learn casually, incidentally.
Things happen together and so become associated in their minds.

They learn by conditioning, by chance observation, by the random experimentation that we call "trial and error," by imitating others. But, except spasmodically and for short periods, the very little child does not learn by intention. He is not interested in his own performance as such nor does he seek to better it, though he does try to get certain material results. By the age of six or seven, however, a new element comes into his learning which will thereafter play a highly important part in modifying his behavior and extending his range of accomplishments. From then on the child not only learns. He *tries* to learn.

What difference does it make whether one learns a thing intentionally or by accident? We can say at once that it makes no difference at all provided that it is actually learned and learned with equal thoroughness. But there's the rub. What kind of things do we learn by accident, and how thoroughly do we learn them?

Several years ago, Myers [1] undertook to find out something about the precision of incidental observation when there was no particular intent to learn. He asked several hundred people, including business men, college students, high school students, and grade school children, to draw a rectangle of the same size as a dollar bill and another of the same size as the colored portion of a two-cent stamp. They were also asked to select from a number of circles those of the same size as a cent, a dime, a nickel, a quarter, and a half-dollar. Even bankers and merchants who handle money all day long were decidedly inaccurate in their guesses, though they did somewhat better than those who had had less experience with money.

The subjects were then told that they would be given a spelling test. Six very easy words were dictated as fast as they were able to write them down, but they were not told to try to remember what the words were. As soon as the list had been dictated the subjects were told to turn the papers over and write the words from memory in the order in which they had been given. Not one out of twenty was able to do this without error. On this test the grade-school children did about as well as the adults. Failure to learn was not due to the difficulty of the task but to the fact that the subjects had given their attention to spelling the words

. [1] Garry C. Myers, "A Study in Incidental Memory," *Arch. Psychol.*, 1913, No. 26, pp. iv + 108.

as separate units. They had not tried to memorize the list as a whole.

In another experiment, Myers asked his subjects to count the O's in a group of eighteen letters arranged in three rows of six letters each. There were twelve O's, with the following additional letters interspersed at irregular intervals: X, A, P, I, E, and K. Myers points out that in order to count the O's it must have been necessary for them to see the other letters at least clearly enough to recognize that they were not O's. Nevertheless when, immediately after the O's had been counted, the card was withdrawn and the subjects were asked what other letters they had seen, not one of 390 persons tested was able to recall all six letters correctly. The average number remembered was one. When they were asked how the letters had been arranged, more than half thought there had been four lines of five letters each. Many had failed to notice the color of the letters (bright red) or the color of the background (bright yellow), and few had formed more than a hazy idea of the border by which the letters were surrounded.

Many other experiments have been made with similar results. One of the most common is the "testimony" experiment. Sometimes this experiment is given the form of a mock crime. Before an unsuspecting group of students in a lecture room two or more of their associates suddenly appear and go through the form of a robbery, an assault, perhaps a murder. Immediately afterward or perhaps a day or so later the students are questioned about what took place. Sometimes in addition to answering the questions they are asked to state the degree of assurance they feel in replying, which facts they are uncertain about and to which ones they would be willing to swear. Practically always it is found that many students report that they saw all kinds of things which did not happen at all. Often they feel so sure of these false observations that they would be willing to swear to them, while many of the actions that really did take place will be found to have escaped notice entirely.

The psychological laboratory provides other evidence as to how little is learned with precision when there is no particular intention to learn. The color-naming experiment is an example. Subjects are shown a series of small disks of different colors arranged in successive rows like a page of print. They are asked to name the colors as fast as they can, beginning at the upper left corner and proceeding from left to right and downward as in ordinary reading. The time required to name all the colors is taken at each trial so as to keep the emphasis upon speed. Nothing is said about learning the order of the colors. One would think, however, that after two or three hundred repetitions, always in the same manner, the order would be learned anyway, whether the subjects tried to do so or not. Not at all. Without the intent to memorize, most students will have made hardly any progress at all toward memorizing. Their attention has been centered on naming each color as a separate unit. They have not thought of the colors as forming a connected series.

All this seems to show that we learn very little about the events taking place around us unless something about them attracts our attention. Even then, what we learn is limited almost entirely to the particular thing that we chance to notice, while other and perhaps more important features may be overlooked entirely. The trouble with incidental experience is not that it doesn't teach us anything, for it usually does, but we can't be sure just what it is going to teach.

SELECTING THE THING TO BE LEARNED

I know a woman who had great difficulty in recognizing people even after she had met them a number of times. Often she was embarrassed by her failure to recognize persons whom she should have known at once. Finally she decided to try to look into her difficulty. She found that much of her trouble was due to her habit of noticing people's clothes rather than their faces. If they happened to be dressed differently when she met them a second time, there was nothing by which she could recognize them. After she found out what was wrong and made a definite effort to see the persons themselves rather than their clothing, there was much improvement.

Children and older people as well often fail to learn because they do not center their attention on the right things. A child of ten has to learn how to spell the word *niece*. He repeats the letters over and over to himself, but he gives no more attention to one letter than to another. As a matter of fact, while his lips and tongue are moving silently and he therefore takes it for granted that he is "studying," his fingers are busy with the marbles in his pocket and his mind is rehearsing the particular kind of "shot" by which he plans to defeat all his rivals as soon as school is over. One hundred repetitions! But when he is called upon to write the word he spells it *neise*.

Now in reality, no study at all was needed for him to know that the first letter of the word in question is *n*. He could tell that by the sound. What he chiefly needed to notice was the *ie* following the *n*, and the fact that the sibilant sound is given by a *c* instead of an *s*. The final *e* would require only a moment's notice, since it follows the general rule that monosyllables containing a long vowel sound end in *e*. One minute of attentive study devoted to the parts of the word on which study was needed would have been worth far more than the hundred or more monotonous repetitions with the mind elsewhere.

In all learning, intelligent selection of the things to be learned is of utmost importance. It does not pay to spend one's time and effort in learning trivial details while the main issues are overlooked or to give as much attention to the familiar and obvious parts of a task as to those which are new or difficult. The school child who is only just beginning to learn how to study a lesson or to play a musical instrument or to perform some complicated act of skill cannot be expected to know how to direct his efforts most effectively without help. But it is easy to find grown men and women whose methods of learning are as childish and inefficient as those of the average six-year-old. Sometimes this is because they are really stupid; often it is just because they have failed to acquire good habits of learning. They read a book with the intention of remembering it, but they grasp blindly at every detail, and in their attempt to retain everything they come out with only a confused impression that has little meaning at the time and is soon lost. Or they read through it mechanically with their thoughts somewhere else and then wonder why they remember so little. Although it is never too late to correct bad habits of this kind, it is better to form good habits from the start. In the education of the school child nothing is more important than this. He should learn how to learn.

WHAT KIND OF MATERIAL IS EASIEST TO LEARN AND REMEMBER?

Here is a list of twelve nonsense syllables. Try to learn them in order. Keep count to see how many times you have to read them before you can recite them all without a mistake:

Mup, sil, fut, wal, lub, seg, yin, taz, bip, ler, ron, pij.

Now try this sentence, which contains twelve one-syllable words.

The boy tore a great big hole in his new red coat.

How many readings were required to learn the list of nonsense syllables? How many for the sentence?

To-morrow see how many of the nonsense syllables you can recall. And see if you can still remember the sentence.

Material that has meaning, that is knit together to form a connected whole, is easier to learn and is remembered much longer than the same amount of material made up of disconnected bits that have to be memorized separately. Children often have difficulty in learning because they do not comprehend the material that is given them to learn. One way of making learning easier is to try to get as much meaning into the thing to be learned as possible. Modern educators realize this principle and so try to have a large share of the child's school work revolve about actual, meaningful experience. Children learn to make change by playing at store-keeping; they learn geography by making maps for themselves which they ornament with actual samples of the products of the different regions. Mississippi gets a tuft of cotton, Pennsylvania a lump of coal and a bit of iron, Minnesota some grains of wheat. The child who has once helped to construct a map of this kind is far less likely to forget the facts he has learned in making it than the one who has spent his time studying the same facts from a printed book.

When material that has few logical connections within itself has to be learned—for example, dates, lists of persons or places, etc.—it is often helpful to build up artificial associations at the start in order to get the facts firmly anchored in the mind. Rimes and jingles may be invented. When I was a child, much of the content of our geography lessons in the primary grades consisted in the memorizing of states with their capitals, principal rivers, and so on. Since at that tender age few of us had any clear idea of what was meant by a "state," and a "capital," if it meant anything at all, was the kind of letter that must be put at the beginning of a sentence on penalty of being "kept in" at recess time to correct one's errors and repent, the whole performance was pretty much on the level of memorizing a list of nonsense syllables. But one enterprising teacher found a way to lighten the task. She set the whole thing to the tune of "Yankee Doodle," and to this day fragments of the ditty remain in my mind.

> Pennsylvania—Harrisburg
> Upon the Susquehanna;
> Oh, Pennsylvania—Harrisburg
> Upon the Susquehanna.
>
> State of Maine—Augusta
> Upon the Kennebec River

Many a person has mastered the date of the discovery of America by means of the well-known rime

> In fourteen hundred and ninety-two
> Columbus sailed the ocean blue.

Calendar reform might have been forced from sheer desperation long ago had not the present system been made endurable by the help of "Thirty days hath September."

IS IT EASIER TO LEARN IN WHOLES OR IN PARTS?

A common way of having children memorize poetry is to teach them a line or a short stanza at a time and then try to have them put the bits together into a whole. But experiments have shown that this is usually not the best method. One learns most easily when meaning is most vivid, and to break up meaningful material into parts almost always results in a loss of associations that would be helpful in learning, even though not all the thought is lost by the division. Sometimes, however, if the selection to be learned is so long that the task of learning it all at once seems overwhelming and the apparent lack of progress when the attempt is made leads to discouragement and loss of interest, better results are obtained by dividing it into sections, taking care to make the division at points where there is some break in the thought so that as little of the meaning will be lost as possible.

A common example of the wastefulness of learning in parts what should be grasped as a whole is seen in those persons who fail to make preparation for a task in advance and so have to be continually stopping their work to hunt up needed tools.

Observe two students preparing a lesson. One gets his materials ready before he starts and puts them where he can lay his hands on them as needed. The other begins to read his assignment, then decides he had better take notes and goes for his note-book. Then he must make a search for his fountain-pen. A little later he finds that the pen is going dry and what can have become of the ink bottle? Found at last, but when the pen is filled he has nothing to wipe it on and in consequence his hands become so daubed with ink that he has to stop once more in order to wash them. Ten minutes later he realizes that he is still wearing the heavy shoes he put on for hiking in the afternoon, and so another halt ensues while he changes to his slippers. Then when at last his reading is done he complains that he doesn't have any idea what the darned stuff is all about!

Of course he hasn't! The continued breaks in thought resulting from all these interruptions have so destroyed continuity that the task becomes about as difficult as learning a list of nonsense syllables. The importance of advance preparation in enabling one to carry through an entire task without interruption to the train of thought is something that the school child can hardly learn too early or too thoroughly.

THE VALUE OF RECITING TO ONESELF

After one has determined or has been shown just what it is that he needs to learn, what is the best way to set about it? Suppose that it is a passage or a poem to be learned by heart. One way to learn it is to read it over and over again, but this is not the quickest method nor the one that makes for best retention over a period of time. It is better to spend part of the time in trying to recite it to oneself. If, instead of learning by rote, the task is that of learning the general content of a history lesson or a geography lesson, the same principles hold good. First the assignment should be read through one or more times in order to get an idea of the general drift and to decide what are the important things to be remembered. Children should be taught to do this as soon as they begin to read for information. Afterward, reciting the main facts to oneself and checking up to see what has been omitted will result in much better mastery of the material than will be had from spending the same amount of time in merely reading the assignment over again and again. Not only will the lesson be learned more quickly by this method, but it will not be so soon forgotten.

Tables IV and V give you an idea of how much time and effort can be saved by following this plan. They are taken from a study by Gates.[2]

TABLE IV

SCORES EARNED IN AN EXPERIMENT ON MEMORIZING NONSENSE SYLLABLES WHEN DIFFERENT PERCENTAGES OF THE TOTAL TIME WERE DEVOTED TO SELF-RECITATION

(After Gates)

School Grade	Percentages of Time Spent in Self-Recitation				
	0%	20%	40%	60%	80%
4	9.5	12.0	16.1	17.0	20.0
6	13.2	20.2	22.6	25.2	30.5
8	16.9	23.9	25.8	27.3	35.5

TABLE V

SCORES EARNED IN AN EXPERIMENT ON LEARNING BIOGRAPHICAL DATA WHEN DIFFERENT PERCENTAGES OF LEARNING TIME WERE DEVOTED TO SELF-RECITATION

(After Gates)

School Grade	Percentages of Time Spent in Self-Recitation					
	0%	20%	40%	60%	80%	90%
4 *	14.6	16.9	16.4	18.8	17.6	17.2
6	15.1	16.6	18.0	17.7	17.8	16.6
8	20.8	22.4	24.8	25.0	25.3	23.8

* The fourth-grade children were given easier material than those in the upper grades. This accounts for the small apparent change in performance from the fourth-to the sixth-grade level.

[2] Arthur I. Gates, "Recitation as a Factor in Memorizing," *Arch. Psychol.*, 1917, No. 40, pp. 105.

In the experiment employing nonsense syllables it was found that in every grade more than twice as many syllables were learned in a given length of time when the children spent 80 per cent of their time in reciting the list to themselves as when they merely read the syllables over and over without testing out their progress. Fourth-grade children who spent 60 per cent or more of their time in reciting to themselves learned as rapidly as eighth-grade children who merely read without reciting. When meaningful material in the form of short biographies of famous men was used instead of the nonsense material, it was found better to spend a little greater proportion of the time in reading and a little less in reciting, but here, too, learning was improved by spending a part of the time in self-recitation. For the biographies, the best division of time seemed to be about 40 per cent reading and 60 per cent reciting; for the nonsense syllables, at least 80 per cent of the time might profiably be spent in reciting.

THE DISTRIBUTION OF PRACTICE

Are one or two long practice periods or several short ones with time in between more effective for learning? Many experiments have been carried out in an attempt to answer this question. The results have usually been in favor of a number of short periods spaced some time apart rather than longer periods occurring close together. The rule is usually stated as follows: Distributed practice is better than massed practice. But of course such a statement needs to be qualified, for it would be absurd to suppose that the shorter or the further apart the practice periods, the better will be the learning. Really what it means is that a proper distribution of work periods and rest periods (or periods involving a change of occupation) makes it easier to learn, and that people in general are more likely to err on the side of making their study periods too long and too close together than the reverse. This is especially likely to be the case when the learning is to be done by children and the length of the practice periods is determined by teachers or parents, for it is less bother to keep children plugging away at a single task than to be always finding a change of occupation for them.

It is impossible to lay down any single fixed rule as to the best length of the practice periods or how long a time should elapse between them, for it will vary according to the kind of thing that is being learned and the age and mental characteristics of the subjects. In general we may say that in tasks made up of many short independent units, such as learning to throw at a target or learning a spelling lesson, greater efficiency is gained by distributing the practice over a large number of very short periods than

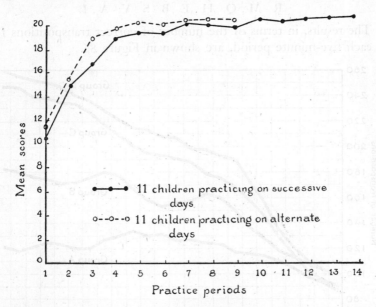

FIG. 85.—LEARNING CURVE OF CHILDREN PRACTISING ON ALTERNATE DAYS COMPARED WITH THAT OF CHILDREN PRACTISING ON SUCCESSIVE DAYS

(After Kirkwood from "Learning in Children," by Joseph Peterson in *A Handbook of Child Psychology*, edited by Carl Murchison. Courtesy Clark University Press.)

by massing it all into a few longer ones. Kirkwood,[3] in a study in which children under seven years learned to associate pictures of common objects with geometrical forms roughly resembling them (such as a diamond-shaped block to be matched with a picture of a kite), found that children who practised on alternate

[3] Julia A. Kirkwood, "The Learning Process in Young Children," *University of Iowa: Studies in Child Welfare*, 1926, Vol. 3, No. 6, pp. 107.

days required fewer trials to learn the series than those who practised daily. (See Figure 85.) The length of the practice periods was the same for both groups.

Starch [4] had four groups of subjects learn to substitute letters for numbers according to a key like the following in which each digit has its corresponding letter:

$$0 \quad 1 \quad 2 \quad 3 \quad 4 \quad 5 \quad 6 \quad 7 \quad 8 \quad 9$$
$$R \quad M \quad Q \quad H \quad E \quad B \quad S \quad V \quad A \quad L$$

The results, in terms of the number of correct transpositions for each five-minute period, are shown in Figure 86.

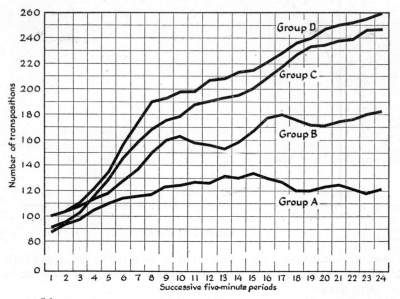

FIG. 86.—RELATION OF THE DISTRIBUTION OF PRACTICE TO RATE OF LEARNING TO SUBSTITUTE NUMERALS FOR LETTERS

All groups had 120 minutes of practice. Group A worked 120 minutes at a single sitting. Group B worked 40 minutes at a time on alternate days. Group C worked 20 minutes at a sitting on consecutive days. Group D worked 10 minutes twice a day on consecutive days. (After Starch.)

Other experiments on the learning of the so-called "drill" subjects in school have given similar results. It has been found, for

[4] Daniel Starch, "Periods of Work in Learning," *J. Educ. Psychol.*, 1912, 2: 209-213.

example, that in teaching primary number work, practice periods as short as two minutes are desirable for the youngest groups, although the time may be increased somewhat for the older ones. But when the material to be learned involves the setting-up of a train of ideas, as in literature, history, or science, it is wasteful to make the practice periods so brief that meaningful associations are cut short before they are fully developed. Interest also plays an important part. If the task to be learned is monotonous and uninteresting, the practice periods should be shorter and further apart than is necessary when enthusiasm runs high. As a matter of fact, it is very possible that most if not all of the advantages coming from distributed practice are due to the greater zest with which even a task that is intrinsically uninteresting will be attacked if practice is never carried to the point of fatigue and boredom. Learning is an active process. Just going through the motions doesn't help much.

CONTINUED PRACTICE OR "OVERLEARNING"

A list of nonsense syllables learned to the point of one correct repetition with no further practice will soon be forgotten. Ebbinghaus,[5] who conducted the first extensive study on memorizing and to whom we are indebted for the first experimentally determined "curve of forgetting" (see Figure 87), found that more than half of a list so learned would be forgotten within an hour and that by the end of a few months practically no memory of it would remain.

The twenty-six letters making up the English alphabet bear a fairly close correspondence to a list of nonsense syllables, since there is no logical connection from letter to letter. But all of us go not merely for hours but for days, weeks, perhaps even months at times when we chance to have little use for a dictionary without reciting the alphabet or thinking anything about the order of the letters. Nevertheless we do not forget it, and when the need arises we run through the letters as smoothly and with as little hesitation as if it had been recited half a dozen times daily.

[5] H. Ebbinghaus, *Über das Gedächtnis*. See also translation by Ruger (New York, Teachers College, Columbia University, Bureau of Publications, 1913).

The amount of practice after the original learning is what makes the difference. Anything that is just barely learned and never used again will soon be forgotten, particularly if it has no logical connections or personal associations to make it stick in the mind. But even a little additional practice aids retention, and material that is greatly "overlearned" or skills that are practised over and over again are retained so well that the ordinary lifetime is not long enough for them to be completely forgotten. It is said that a skilled swimmer never entirely forgets the art even though he may go for many years without practice. A student who had practised typewriting for 200 hours dropped it entirely for a year, but an hour's practice was sufficient to make up all the ground that he had lost. Four people practised ten minutes daily for seventeen weeks in reading ordinary prose in a mirror. After two years without further practice all regained their previous levels in less than a week's time by practising the same amount daily as before.

Figure 87 illustrates how much retention can be improved by even a small amount of overlearning. Here the solid line shows the rate of forgetting nonsense syllables practised to the point of one correct repetition only. The dotted line shows the rate when two correct repetitions are required before practice is discontinued.

The way to remember is to review, and to review early, for the time immediately after learning is the time when forgetting is most rapid, as you can easily see by looking at the curves. The best kind of reviewing is that which comes with putting the material that has been learned to some actual use, for use gives it more vivid and personal meaning, which, as we have seen, is one of the chief factors that make for retention. One reason why we remember the order of the letters in the alphabet so well is because we have so often made use of that order in consulting dictionaries, encyclopedias, and indexes. With plenty of additional practice to fix the newly learned accomplishment in mind and occasional reviews thereafter to renew efficiency when it has lapsed through disuse it seems safe to say that anything that has been once learned can be retained as long as it seems worth while to make the necessary effort to do so.

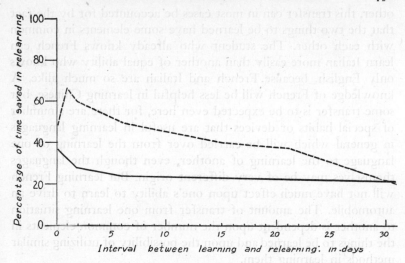

FIG. 87.—RELATION OF OVERLEARNING TO RETENTION

The solid line shows the percentage of time saved in relearning nonsense syllables originally learned to the point of one correct repetition. The broken line shows the amount of saving when the list is learned to the point of two correct repetitions. (Adapted from E. L. Thorndike's *Educational Psychology*, Vol. II. Data from Ebbinghaus and from Radossawljewistch. Courtesy of the Bureau of Publications, Teachers College, Columbia University.)

THE TRANSFER OF TRAINING

Does learning one thing make it easier to learn something else? Can the ability to learn be improved by practice?

A generation or two ago it was believed by many people that all formal studying, that is, studying with the intent to learn, had a disciplinary effect upon the mind of the student which made learning easier for him thereafter. The study of abstract subjects such as mathematics or Latin was assumed to have a marked effect upon the student's ability to learn other things, while studying the more concrete subjects such as drawing or cooking had less effect upon general learning ability.

Experiments on the effect of practising one thing upon the ability to learn other things have usually shown that, while there is often some apparent transfer from one form of learning to another, this transfer can in most cases be accounted for by the fact that the two things to be learned have some elements in common with each other. The student who already knows French can learn Italian more easily than another of equal ability who knows only English, because French and Italian are so much alike. A knowledge of French will be less helpful in learning Chinese, but some transfer is to be expected even here, for there are a number of special habits or devices that are useful in learning languages in general which will be carried over from the learning of one language to the learning of another, even though the languages themselves may be of very different origin. But learning French will not have much effect upon one's ability to learn to drive an automobile. The amount of transfer from one learning situation to another is dependent upon the number of common elements in the things to be learned and upon the possibility of utilizing similar methods in learning them.

There is, however, such a thing as the learning of habits, and of attitudes toward learning, which may transfer over a wide range of behaviors and skills which in themselves possess few elements in common. One may build up (that is, learn) an attitude of pride in one's ability to achieve, and this attitude may affect one's persistence and effort in such widely diverse skills as playing golf or learning calculus. One may form habits of giving up when a task becomes hard or of sticking it out to the end in spite of difficulty. While there is little or no reason to believe that study will improve one's ability to learn, there is good evidence that attitudes can be learned which will make for greater or less efficiency in learning.

THE OVERLAPPING OF ELEMENTS IN SERIAL LEARNING

A favorite method of studying the learning of a connected series of activities is by the use of mazes. A maze, you know, consists of a series of alleyways opening one out of another in such a way that a subject who is put into the maze at the starting point can, by taking the right turnings, find his way out at the other end. But all along the way there are blind alleys (*cul-de-sacs*) that he must learn to avoid. At the beginning the learner has no way of distinguishing between the true path and the blind alleys. Only by actual trial can he find out which is which. But by repeated trials he eventually masters the pattern. Purely empirical learning of this kind in which logic or reasoning can play no part is usually called learning by *trial and error*.

Mazes used in the psychological laboratory are of many kinds and have a wide range of complexity. With animals of very low neural organization such as the earthworm, only an exceedingly simple maze can be used; for the higher animals, including man, they may be very complicated indeed. In some of the more recent and elaborate models, an electrical recording system is used that does away with all chance of errors of observation on the part of the experimenter, but for most studies direct observation is relied upon. Those intended for use with animals are usually made large enough for the animal to run through them; with human beings smaller models to be traced by hand are often substituted. Sometimes the subject is allowed to do this with his eyes open, but more often he is blindfolded or the maze is placed under a screen where he cannot see it. Tracing is done with the tip of the finger, sometimes even with the great toe, or with the point of a stylus. Sometimes the eye alone is used. Examples are seen in Figure 88.

When a hungry white rat is put into a maze leading to a food box at the other end, he has at first no idea that food is to be found there. But his hunger makes him restless and so he explores the maze. At first he is as likely to enter the blind alleys as to follow the true path, but after repeated trials he learns the right way to go. Eventually he becomes so expert that he starts running as soon as he is put into the maze, dashes through at top speed without even pausing at the blind alleys, and reaches the food box in a short fraction of the time it took him at the beginning. He has learned just which turns to take and where they are located so well that he even makes anticipatory adjustments to them in advance. While he is dashing around one corner he is getting set to run just so far and no further before he swerves again. This has been shown by experiments in which the length of an alley has been shortened after the rats had learned to run the maze without errors. It is found that the rats in such an experiment will run full tilt up against the wall at the point where the run-

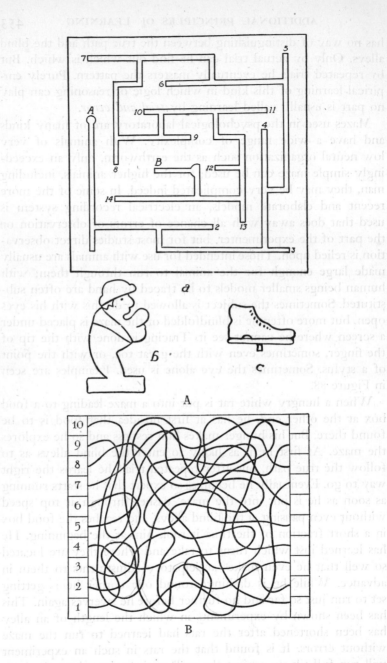

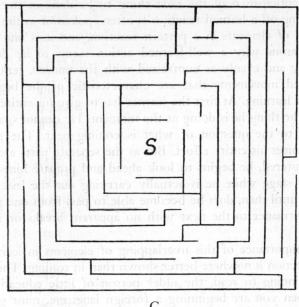

C

FIG. 88.—DIFFERENT TYPES OF MAZES

A. The Young Slot Maze (*opposite page*). The toy clown is set into the groove at *B;* the shoe is placed at *A.* The child is told to take the shoe to the man. (From Esther McGinnis. The acquisition and interference of motor habits in young children. *Genet. Psychol. Monog.,* 1929, 6: 234. Courtesy Clark University Press.)

B. An eye maze (*opposite page*). The lines must be followed with the eye only. The ending of each line is to be indicated by placing its number in the appropriate space in the column at the left.

C. One of the mazes in the series designed by Porteus. (Courtesy of the C. H. Stoelting Co.)

way has been cut off. You and I do the same thing at times and for the same reason. Have you never misjudged the height of a chair on which you were about to sit down and fallen with an embarrassing thud the last few inches after your muscles had relaxed in anticipation of a support that failed to appear? And on negotiating a moderately familiar stairway in the dark, have you never experienced the shock of having the floor seem to rise to meet you when the bottom is reached a step sooner than you expected?

This anticipation of the next thing to be done in the course of running off a learned reaction is often spoken of as the "overlapping" of elements in a pattern reaction, and it is one of the chief reasons why a well-learned action seems to be done so smoothly and evenly as contrasted with the uneven, jerky, disconnected movements that are characteristic of the beginning stages of learning. At first the learner has to give his entire attention to the thing he is doing at the moment. He cannot spare any thought to the question of what is coming next. The present task requires his entire effort. But as the separate parts are gradually mastered, he begins to look ahead and prepare himself for the next stage while he is actually carrying out the last. Then, and not until then, does he become able to pass from one part of his performance to the next with no apparent breaks or irregularities.

The importance of this overlapping of elements in learning a serial reaction is nowhere better shown than in reading. The child just beginning to read, the older person of little education, or you, when you are beginning a foreign language, must give so much attention to each separate word that the reading of a paragraph is likely to be slow, halting, jerky, and disconnected. With gain in skill, however, certain familiar or striking phrases begin to link themselves together, and when you come to these passages your reading, for the moment, runs along smoothly. Your eyes look ahead for the next words while your lips are pronouncing those seen an instant before. One of the chief things that distinguishes the good oral reader from the poor one is the extent to which his eyes and his understanding are able to keep ahead of his voice. This makes it possible for him to vary his tonal inflection as he goes along instead of having to wait until the thought of the passage is completed, when it will be too late.

In all aspects of everyday life, the factor of overlapping elements or anticipation of the second and third steps while taking the first marks off the efficient worker from the inefficient one. Watch two housewives in their kitchens. One steps briskly about her tasks without hesitation, planning for one thing while doing another, taking advantage of the moment while the dish pan is filling to get the tea towels ready, reaching for the flavoring extract with her left hand while stirring her cake with the right.

The other "putters" about, perhaps moving just as fast or faster, but everything she does requires a separate effort of mind and body. She carries in the broom, then goes back for the dust-pan; later still another trip must be made for dust cloths.

The secret of a smooth and well-organized motor performance lies in the ability to keep the attention centered on what is coming rather than on what is being done at the moment. The tennis player judges the angle at which the ball is coming and adjusts his stroke accordingly. If he waits for it to arrive before making his preparations to receive it, he will be too late. If he stops in the middle of his stroke to think how he is holding his racquet, whether or not his feet are at the right angle, the ball will escape him before he gets around to striking at it. But in order to free his attention from the activity of the moment and center it on preparing for the act that is to come he must have learned by experience to *interpret* the sensations coming in from his muscles and joints in such a way that he gets a continual check-up as to whether he is right or wrong. The skilled tennis player does not have to look where the ball has gone to know, within rough limits, whether his play has been good or bad. He knows by the "feel" of it. Learning the theoretical principles of correct playing will prevent the development of many bad motor habits that might otherwise be set up, but only actual practice and plenty of it will serve to transfer this knowledge into the world of kinesthetic meanings where it will be of real service.

But if one had to give separate attention to each tiniest part of an act, if one had to think separately about holding the racquet, moving the feet, raising the arm, bringing it forward with just so much force and no more, and then keep track of each of the kinesthetic sensations resulting from these acts in order to know whether or not the play was right, the situation would be quite as bad as that described in the well-known rime.

> The centipede did very well
> Until the ant in fun
>   Asked, "Pray, which leg goes after which?"
>   Then left him helpless in the ditch
> Considering how to run.

Evidently too much attention to the separate parts of an act can impede learning. Before a high level of efficiency can be gained, the simple and elementary units of which an act is comprised must be bound together into larger patterns that are performed as wholes. In many of the ordinary acts of life so much of this organizing process takes place at a very early age that long before the child enters school we find the patterns already laid down and operating so smoothly and efficiently that only by a careful process of analysis can we break up the act into its original units. The psychological laboratory, however, has thrown some light on how the original process of consolidation takes place. In this connection an experiment on the learning of telegraphy, carried out many years ago by Bryan and Harter,[6] has been much quoted. They studied the progress of a number of students who were learning to send and receive messages by telegraph. Learning curves were plotted for each student, showing the weekly gains in the number of letters he was able to send or receive per minute. They found that the practice curves for sending were not unlike those characteristic of maze learning. There was rapid gain at the beginning with slowing off later on, making the kind of curve that we describe as *negatively accelerated* because gains become less per unit of time as practice increases. The curves for receiving, however, were found to have a peculiar steplike form in which an initial period of gain was followed by a period when little or no advancement seemed to occur. To such a period Bryan and Harter gave the name of *plateau*. Their explanation for the plateau is this: In the beginning the student who is receiving listens to the clicks of the instrument and spells them out letter by letter. All his attention goes to the letters. He does not attempt to group them into words until after he has taken them down on paper. At first he does this very slowly, but as he becomes accustomed to the sounds his speed improves. Presently he is taking down the letters about as fast as he can hear them separately. Now it seems as though he could make no further gain, and as a matter of fact he does not gain much for a while. But sooner or later a new factor comes in. He hears the letter *t* but instead of writing it down at once he waits to see what else is coming. Yes, it is *h*, *e*, and the word is *the*. Now he begins to listen to the clicks in a new way. Instead of

---

[6] W. L. Bryan and N. Harter, "Studies in the Physiology and Psychology of the Telegraphic Language," *Psychol. Rev.*, 1897, 4: 27-53.

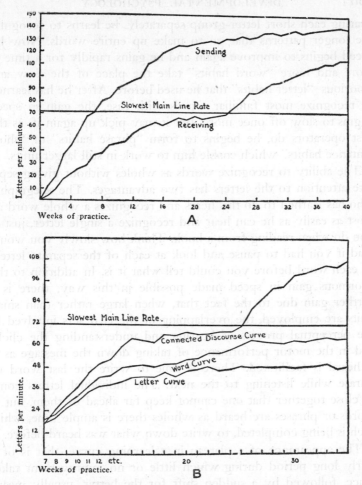

FIG. 89.—THE INTEGRATION OF SIMPLE SKILLS INTO HIGHER UNITS AS
ILLUSTRATED BY THE LEARNING OF TELEGRAPHY

A. Learning curves for sending and receiving of one subject during
forty weeks of practice.

B. Analysis of plateaus as shown by learning curves for receiving unconnected letters, unconnected words, and connected discourse. The letter
curve reaches its upper limit by about the twentieth week and shows no
further improvement thereafter. The word curve, however, makes a decided gain after letter skill has been perfected, and the curve for connected
discourse rises very sharply after the ability to receive unconnected words
has reached its limit. (From W. L. Bryan and N. Harter, "Studies in the
Physiology and Psychology of the Telegraphic Language," *Psychol. Rev.,*
1897, 4, 27-53. Courtesy Psychological Review Co.)

hearing each short letter-group separately, he learns to recognize the longer patterns that go to make up entire words. Now his speed begins to improve again and he gains rapidly for a time as more and more "word habits" take the place of the slow and laborious "letter habits" that he used before. After he has learned to recognize most familiar words with ease, the gain in speed begins to slow off once more, but it may pick up again if, as the best operators do, he begins to form "phrase habits" or "short sentence habits" which enable him to work in still larger units.

The ability to recognize words as wholes without giving separate attention to the letters has two advantages. The telegrapher who has learned to do this hears and recognizes a whole word almost as easily as he can hear and recognize a single letter, just as you do when reading from a book. Think how slowly you would read if you had to pause and look at each of the separate letters of each word before you could tell what it is. In addition to the enormous gain in speed made possible in this way, there is a further gain due to the fact that, when large rather than small units are employed, the overlapping of the two acts involved in the perceptual process of hearing and understanding the clicks and in the motor performance of taking down the message as it is heard is facilitated. There is time to write the last word or phrase while listening to the next. The individual letters come so close together that one cannot keep far ahead of them, but if words or phrases are heard as wholes there is ample time, while each is being completed, to write down what was heard before.

The appearance of a plateau in a learning curve, that is of a fairly long period during which little or no improvement takes place, followed by a sudden shift for the better, usually means that the subject has substituted a more efficient for a less efficient method of work. One way of doing this is by organizing small units into larger ones, as Bryan and Harter have shown. But any other fundamental improvement in method, coming after the limits of improvement by the old method have been reached, will bring about a similar change in the curve. A sudden increase in interest and effort, following a long period of discouragement or boredom, may also bring a plateau to an end and send the learning curve upward once more. Children who seem to have made little or no progress in their school work for some time often get a fresh start and learn with fair rapidity after a change to a more sympathetic teacher or one who makes use of methods that arouse their interest. Factory workers whose output, when they were paid by the day, remained at a dead level for months or years have been known to show a surprising spurt in production after a change to the piece-work system.

THE EFFECT OF PRACTICE UPON INDIVIDUAL DIFFERENCES

When a number of different persons take part in a learning experiment, they do not all show equal ability at the start. A part of this difference in initial ability may be due to differences in the amount of practice on similar performances before the formal experiment was begun, for it is very hard to select any kind of task that has nothing in common with the activities of everyday life. Differences in performance that are entirely due to unequal amounts of previous practice will tend to disappear in the course of time when all subjects are given the same amount and kind of training.

Even when equal opportunity for learning is given, some subjects learn more easily than others. However, if the task to be learned is so simple that even the poorest learners are able to master it when they are given sufficient time, differences in the performance of good, average, and poor learners tend to disappear as all the subjects approach the *physiological limit*, that is, as all learn to perform the act as rapidly as their bodily mechanism will permit. But if the task is very difficult, and particularly if it is one that makes a great demand upon abstract intelligence, the poorest learners will soon reach a point at which very little further improvement is possible for them, while the best learners will continue to gain. In this case, differences in the performance of the subjects will become greater with increased practice. The effect of increased practice upon the differences in the performance of individuals will therefore depend upon the difficulty of the task to be learned and the amount and kind of previous experience of the subjects. If the initial differences are chiefly due to unequal amounts of incidental practice on similar activities before the experiment was begun, these differences will become smaller when all are given equal amounts of practice in a learning experiment. If the amount of previous incidental practice has been approximately equal for all and the initial differences between the subjects are due to the fact that some have profited by this experience more than others because they learn more easily, the effect of further practice will vary according to the complexity of the task to be learned. In general, when previous experience has been equal for all subjects, with further practice the differences between individuals will be lessened if the thing to be learned is comparatively simple and concrete. In learning difficult or abstract tasks the initial differences between the subjects are likely to increase rather than decrease with practice.

GENERAL COMPARISONS OF HUMAN AND ANIMAL LEARNING AND OF THE LEARNING OF CHILDREN AND ADULTS

When we read of the experiments on learning and retention that have been carried out with animals and compare them with the findings from similar studies on human beings of different ages, the point that chiefly impresses us is the amazing similarity of the general principles that have been found to hold good for all groups. Provided the conditions of learning are the same, the laws of learning seem to apply equally well to animals, children, and adults. But conditions cannot always be made the same. Human beings learn things that animals cannot learn, and they learn them by methods that are beyond the power of animals to employ. Likewise, older children and adults learn things that babies cannot learn, and their methods of learning also show certain characteristics that differ from those typical of infancy and early childhood.

Learning by conditioning, that is, by learning to respond to stimuli that formerly produced no response or that produced a response of a different kind, is typical both of animals and of human beings of all levels of development.

Learning by trial and error may be just a special case of learning by conditioning. In ordinary usage, however, we reserve the term *trial and error* for instances of learning in which the subject is actively seeking a goal of some kind, while the term *conditioning* is used to denote those instances in which behavior is modified through conditions that the subject does not attempt to control. Learning by active trial and error, like the more passively acquired conditioned response is exhibited by animals, children, and adults alike, but animals and young children rely on it more extensively and are likely to employ it in situations where older children or adults would make more use of thinking and reasoning.

Learning by observation and imitation seems to be almost, if not quite, a uniquely human accomplishment. Even monkeys, who are popularly supposed to be such talented mimics that the expression "imitative as a monkey" has become proverbial, rarely, if ever, learn new tricks or accomplishments merely by having other monkeys go through certain performances in their presence. As far as we have been able to determine, cats, dogs, and the less intelligent animals do not learn by observation at all. One cat may have learned by trial and error how to undo the fastenings of his cage to get food. Another untrained cat is allowed to watch him do this. Over and over again the box is opened and the food secured, while the hungry companion looks on. Finally the new cat is given a turn, but all his watching has helped him not a bit. He has to learn the trick for himself by trial and error methods, just as the first cat did. Only human beings and some of the anthropoid or manlike apes such as the chimpanzee, who are nearest to man in intelligence seem able to improve their own performances by observing others. This failure to learn by observation and imitation is undoubtedly one of the main reasons why animals do not develop a language. Even apes cannot imitate well enough for that.

Although human children begin to imitate very early, their ability to learn by means of imitation increases rapidly as they grow older. Part of this gain with age comes from improvement in motor control, but much more of it comes from better directed observation and attention. Failure to imitate correctly is often due to failure to select the right thing to imitate.

Whether or not children have a natural tendency to imitate others, whether there is an "instinct of imitation" is a question that has been much debated. In the sense in which the word *instinct* is often used, that is, as a blind and unreasoning set of actions which the subject performs without previous learning when the appropriate situation arises, we may well doubt that such a tendency exists. But the normal child appears to derive a good deal of social satisfaction from being one of a group and doing what the others are doing. This tendency is particularly strong in the child of school age. To the extent that such a tendency exists, learning by imitation may be closely allied to learning by conditioning or by trial and error. If imitation itself is the goal, it may well be that what the child learns by imitation is merely a by-product of his learning to imitate. That most children try to imitate others, there can be no doubt.

Let us take a concrete example. A little child is sitting at a table beside his father who is writing. The child picks up a pencil and handles it. In the course of his manipulations he beats or rubs one end against the table where it happens that a sheet of paper is lying. The father sees this and is much pleased. "He saw me writing and is trying to write, too," he exclaims. The baby is praised and caressed. He is praised when he tries to poke his shoestrings into their holes, laughed at and petted when he holds the newspaper before his face as if reading, coaxed to drink all his milk "just like big brother does." From the beginning, social conformity, "doing what the others do," is urged upon him as the desirable way of behaving. He is praised and rewarded when he imitates successfully, punished or scolded when he insists upon following his own methods. Many of his toys are miniature tools or copies of household implements used by adults, and he is encouraged to use them as adults do. When older persons wish to teach him some new accomplishment, the usual method is to "show him how" and again he is praised or rewarded in proportion to his success in imitating their performance. Few aspects of behavior meet with such consistently pleasant social consequences as imitation of others.

The fact that children are able to grasp the abstract idea of imitation, while animals for the most part have to stick to concrete manipulation and trial and error behavior is highly significant. The fact that children do imitate as much as they do is probably more the result of their learning that imitation is likely to meet with social rewards than of any "instinctive tendency" toward imitation as such.

PROBLEM-SOLVING WITHOUT PREVIOUS TRIAL AND ERROR BEHAVIOR—"INSIGHT"

Human beings and the more intelligent animals do not always resort to pure random experimentation of the trial and error kind when faced with a problem to be solved. Instead they show evidence of what has often been called *insight* (see Chapter X), that is, they react at once to observed qualities of objects rather than to the objects themselves.

The degree of insight, as one would expect, increases with age. Apes and young children respond only to very simple relationships and to qualities of an obvious kind. Older children and adults make use of more abstract concepts.

Learning by insight does not seem to be essentially different from learning by trial and error except that it works at a higher level. Ideas are manipulated instead of objects; observation and thought replace muscular action. But although some psychologists appear to think of insight as something that comes by itself, a simpler view would regard such behavior as analogous to the building up of the "higher units" or more complex action patterns that we discussed in connection with motor learning. Through concrete experimentation by the trial and error method the child learns to work in terms of certain general principles just as the telegrapher in time learned to work in terms of "word habits" instead of "letter habits." These abstract ideas about the qualities of objects have been formed from everyday exploitation of the objects themselves. From repeated trials the child finds that objects having certain qualities—roundness, sharpness, hardness, and so on—can be made to serve purposes that other objects with different qualities will not serve. So in meeting new situations involving objects that he has not seen before, but which nevertheless possess certain familiar attributes, he does not find himself completely at a loss.

Here is a new object. He does not know its name or its purpose. But he sees that it has sharp edges and so (since earlier experience has shown him that objects with sharp edges can be used for cutting), if he wants to cut something he does not run around trying out everything in sight, but instead he picks out the unknown thing with sharp edges and uses that.

The degree of insight shown by any person depends both upon his level of intelligence and upon the amount and kind of experience he has had in similar situations. Animals below the level of monkeys show little insight because they react to objects and situations as wholes rather than to their separate qualities. But human beings of equal intelligence show varying degrees of insight according to their experience. A skilled mechanic faced with a strange piece of machinery is likely to show much more insight in dealing with it than a lawyer of equal or greater general intelligence who has had little experience with machinery will display. Although the machine as a whole is unfamiliar to both, the mechanic will see in it many familiar principles, the workings of which he understands. But the lawyer is bungling and slow because he has not built up a system of "higher units" that apply to the machine situation. Nevertheless, in dealing with legal quirks and tangles that the mechanic would find hopelessly puzzling, he may display a promptness and efficiency that would be amazing to any one who had previously watched him poking stupidly at the various parts of the machine. Insight is not independent of earlier trial and error behavior but results from it, though in varying degrees according to the intellectual level of the individual concerned.

A CLASS EXPERIMENT ON SEX DIFFERENCES IN LEARNING

It is often said that women are better than men at rote learning and that men excel in the manipulation of mechanical and numerical relations. Likewise many people believe that speed is usually gained only at the price of a loss in accuracy.

If your class is made up of both men and women, the two experiments about to be described will provide data on both these questions. If only one sex is represented, it will still be possible to ascertain whether the students who complete the greatest number of items make more or fewer errors (both absolutely and in proportion to the amount accomplished) than those who work more slowly and so accomplish less.

Experiment A. Letter-digit substitution. On a screened portion of the blackboard, write a letter-digit substitution key similar to that shown on p. 448 but using different letters so that students will not have an opportunity to learn the key in advance. Below is a series of digits arranged in random order. When the signal is given, the screen should be removed. Each student should then copy the key at the top of a sheet of blank paper, being careful to make no errors in copying. Thirty seconds should be allowed for this, after which the signal to begin work should be given. The task is to substitute the corresponding letters for the numbers listed as rapidly as possible by working directly across the page from line to line in the order in which the letters occur. "Skipping around" is not permitted. The key may be referred to as often as necessary. At the end of ten minutes the signal to stop should be given. Papers should then be exchanged and scored. Scores should include (a) number of items attempted, (b) number of errors, (c) number right.

Digits to be Used in Letter-Digit Substitution Test

2 5 8 0 3 6 4 5 9 6 1 5 9 2 1 4 0 6 3 8 5 1 2 8 4 9 0 3 7 4 0 1 8 2 1 0 4 7 9
4 6 3 0 1 4 8 2 5 9 1 2 6 8 3 1 7 0 9 1 2 8 3 6 7 5 4 0 9 8 7 6 0 5 3 1 2 4 0
1 3 5 2 4 8 9 7 5 3 1 0 6 4 2 7 9 1 0 8 6 4 2 0 7 5 3 9 1 3 6 9 4 8 0 7 5 3 1
0 1 2 9 8 4 7 5 6 2 8 0 6 3 5 7 9 4 2 1 8 3 9 2 1 5 9 0 7 2 5 9 1 6 0 4 3 4 9
8 7 0 1 9 6 5 3 4 8 1 9 2 7 3 6 4 5 1 0 7 9 5 3 1 8 4 6 2 0 7 3 6 4 9 2 5 0 1
7 2 0 1 3 9 4 5 8 6 8 3 0 2 1 5 7 8 2 1 0 3 6 0 2 9 5 8 1 2 0 3 6 9 4 2 7 1 0
6 9 5 8 4 7 0 1 9 3 1 5 6 2 9 3 7 3 8 4 2 4 9 1 3 8 7 2 0 3 9 4 8 5 7 6 1 9 7
5 0 4 9 3 7 2 6 1 8 6 4 2 6 3 9 0 4 1 3 2 7 9 0 5 4 7 3 8 2 9 1 5 6 3 1 4 8 3
3 7 2 8 4 9 1 6 0 3 5 7 2 0 9 1 8 2 7 3 6 4 5 4 8 2 1 4 0 5 9 3 7 5 2 8 4 0 6
0 4 1 3 9 7 5 4 6 2 9 3 8 1 4 9 2 0 3 7 4 0 1 6 2 9 5 1 7 0 3 9 1 4 8 2 7 4 9
6 3 8 4 6 0 9 1 2 8 3 7 4 6 5 0 2 1 3 9 0 4 8 5 6 7 1 9 0 2 8 4 6 1 3 9 5 7 2
6 3 9 0 2 8 6 4 0 1 8 3 1 7 9 5 3 7 2 1 0 6 4 1 5 7 3 9 2 8 4 6 0 1 3 5 7 9 4
0 4 9 3 8 2 7 5 1 6 0 5 9 2 3 8 4 6 8 1 2 9 3 4 8 5 6 1 7 0 3 7 1 4 7 0 3 5 8
9 1 2 8 3 4 7 5 6 0 1 3 8 2 7 6 0 2 4 9 5 0 7 4 6 8 1 5 0 5 3 9 2 0 5 1 6 8 2
8 2 4 6 0 1 9 3 7 5 1 5 7 9 0 2 8 4 0 6 4 7 5 3 9 1 3 9 6 2 8 7 1 0 3 9 2 8 5
6 8 2 4 1 9 3 0 5 6 7 2 8 3 7 1 0 2 5 4 9 7 5 2 0 1 6 8 3 0 8 2 5 4 0 7 9 1 3
5 4 9 8 2 1 0 5 8 3 6 2 1 7 0 4 3 6 5 9 2 8 3 7 5 8 1 5 9 0 3 2 8 5 2 4 1 7 9
9 4 8 2 1 5 3 8 0 1 5 2 7 3 6 5 2 1 7 4 2 4 6 8 0 1 9 7 5 3 9 1 5 0 4 8 3 7 1
2 5 3 7 4 8 5 9 6 0 1 2 8 3 9 4 8 6 0 5 1 4 0 2 6 8 1 3 5 2 7 3 8 4 0 5 7 1 8
1 2 0 3 9 4 8 5 7 6 0 4 1 7 3 8 5 7 2 9 1 6 4 0 2 8 3 8 7 5 3 1 6 0 5 9 8 3 6
2 1 3 0 4 9 5 8 6 7 1 2 0 4 3 8 6 7 4 2 1 9 5 4 0 8 3 7 1 2 5 3 9 5 6 7 2 1 5
8 0 1 7 9 2 6 4 5 1 4 9 5 0 2 1 4 7 3 8 4 9 2 5 4 1 7 0 3 8 4 7 2 0 6 1 9 5 7
6 4 2 8 0 3 1 5 9 7 2 0 4 8 6 3 1 5 0 7 9 0 3 1 6 4 9 2 6 1 7 0 5 9 3 5 8 2 4
1 3 8 6 8 4 2 9 2 4 8 1 0 7 5 9 3 1 6 0 2 5 6 9 3 4 1 7 3 9 2 8 1 5 3 0 8 8 5

Experiment B. Adding by the duodecimal system. Compared to the decimal system of notation with which we are familiar, a duodecimal system in which 12 instead of 10 is the basic unit has certain obvious advantages. Twelve can be divided into thirds or fourths as well as into halves, and these are fractions that are much more frequently used than fifths. The duodecimal system is handled exactly like the decimal system except that it requires two additional numerals, and the successive place-values represent multiples of 12 instead of

10. Thus in the duodecimal system 36 would be written as 30, since it is three 12's with no remainder. Likewise, 84 is written as 70 and 16 as 14 (one 12 and 4 over), 78 as 66, and so on. If we let $\sharp$ represent 10 and $?$ = 11 in the duodecimal system, then 35 would be written 2? and 70 would become 5$\sharp$.

Below are four examples of single column addition problems with their answers. Check through to see how these answers were obtained.

6	9	$\sharp$	3
?	2	4	8
5	$\sharp$	9	4
1$\sharp$	19	1?	13

On a screened portion of the blackboard at least twenty simple addition problems, each consisting of four rows of two-digit numbers in which the new digit symbols appear as well as the usual ten, should have been placed before the beginning of the experiment. A still better plan is to provide each student with a mimeographed sheet of problems. When the screen is removed, each student should attempt to add as many of the problems as possible within a ten-minute period. At the expiration of the time limit, papers should be exchanged and scored as in the preceding experiment. Again the scoring should indicate the number of problems attempted, the number of errors, the number right, and the number of errors per problem attempted.

I. Problems

1. Find the average number of correct substitutions (Task A) made by the men. What percentage of the women make a higher score than that of the average man?
2. Make the same kind of computation for Task B. Is the direction of the sex difference the same for both tasks?
3. Make the same kind of computations on the basis of the *number of items attempted* (without regard to the number of errors) and again compare the sexes.
4. Repeat, using the *total number of errors* made by each subject.
5. Find for each subject the *number of errors per unit of work*. To do this the total number of errors made should be divided by the total number of letters or problems attempted. Then find the average index of accuracy as determined in this way for each sex as before. Are the results similar to those obtained by the previous method?
6. Without regard to sex, divide the group into four equal subdivisions, placing the 25 per cent attempting the fewest number of items in one division, the next 25 per cent in the second division and so on. (In statistics, such divisions are called *quartiles*.) Do this for each task separately. Compare the aver-

age *index of accuracy* of the top and bottom quartiles for each kind of material. If the class is large enough, this may be done for the sexes separately in order to see whether or not a sex difference related to the type of material appears in respect to the *relation between speed and accuracy.*

II. *Interpretation and conclusions*

Summarize the findings from the above problems (including those from any additional problems that the class may devise for themselves) and draw such conclusions as appear to be warranted.

III. *Comparison with previous findings*

Consult the Subject Index of the *Psychological Abstracts* (available in practically all university and college libraries) for studies on sex differences in learning, and the relation between accuracy and speed. It is a good idea to divide the class into as many committees as there are annual volumes of the *Abstracts* (which began publication in 1927), making each committee responsible for the studies included in a single volume. Each committee can then prepare its own report to be presented to the class as a whole. Possible reasons for discrepant findings in the work of previous investigators when compared with each other or with your study should be discussed. The book by Scheinfeld mentioned on p. 383 may also be consulted.

Chapter XVIII

ADOLESCENCE

What are some of the early signs of the approach of adolescence?

What is meant by pubescence? About how long does pubescence usually last? What event marks the beginning of adolescence in girls? How is puberty determined in boys?

At about what age is puberty commonly reached in girls? In boys? How much normal variation from these averages occurs in individual cases?

What is meant by secondary sex characteristics? Give some examples.

Why are adolescents often clumsy in their movements? Is it necessary for them to be so?

In what ways do the sexes differ in motor skills and motor interests after puberty? Describe the growth changes in each sex through which these differences become increased.

Is there scientific justification for the popular idea that some men may be classified as effeminate and some women masculine in most of their personality characteristics? At about what ages are mental masculinity and femininity at their peaks in the average person?

Are sex interests and sex emotions normally present before adolescence? What causes them to become increased at puberty?

In what ways is interest in the opposite sex likely to be shown during pubescence and early adolescence?

470

*Why is this phase of sex behavior important for
the development of normal sex attitudes later on?*

*Why does the gang or clique exercise such an im-
portant influence on the attitudes and behavior of
the adolescent?*

*In what ways do the "pubic rites" practiced in many
primitive groups simplify the passage from childhood to adulthood?*

*How do the laws of habit-making and habit-breaking
apply to the relationships between the adolescent
and the adult members of his family?*

PUBERTY

The completion of the physiological changes that make one
potentially capable of producing offspring is commonly said to
mark the attainment of *puberty*. In girls, the appearance of the
first menstruation [1] is usually accepted as evidence that puberty
has been reached. In boys the attainment of puberty is not marked
off by any one sudden and conspicuous event. In practice, the
change in voice, the growth of the beard, and the appearance and
character of the pubic hair are the signs usually taken into consideration in determining when puberty has been reached in
males.[2]

In neither sex is the onset of puberty a sudden and unheralded

[1] The first menstruation is called the *menarche*, and the age at which it
occurs is called the *menarcheal age*. Recent studies have shown rather con-
clusively that more consistent results are usually obtained if studies of physical growth, motor development, and even of certain personality traits are
reckoned in terms of the number of years preceding or following the
menarche, rather than in terms of the number of years since birth (chronological age). The difficulty, of course, lies in the fact that such computations cannot be made until after the menarche has been reached, which
makes the criterion not a feasible one to use in the years preceding adolescence.

[2] Crampton makes the distinction on the basis of the development of the
kink or curl in the pubic hair which is characteristic of maturity. During
pubescence some pubic hair is present, but it is straight and scanty. Bald-
win considered the appearance of active spermatozoa in the urine to be the
most reliable single criterion for the attainment of puberty in boys, but as
this measure entails frequent examination of the urine by a trained tech-
nician, it has not often been employed.

event. It is true that during infancy and childhood, the changes in size and structure of the reproductive organs are small in comparison with those occurring in other parts of the body. (See Figure 43, p. 234.) But at about the age of eleven or twelve in girls, and from one to two years later in boys, a number of physical changes begin to appear which show that the time of puberty is approaching. This transitional period from childhood to adolescence is known as the *period of pubescence*. The period extending from the time of puberty to the attainment of complete maturity is known as the *period of adolescence*. However, the upper limit of adolescence is not very clearly marked in either sex. Generally speaking, we say that adolescence ends when the person becomes grown up, but both physical and mental growth taper off so gradually that it is not easy to say when either comes to a stop. Gain in height is the most easily measured of the growth factors, and it has practically ceased, on the average, by the age of eighteen or nineteen in girls and twenty in boys. In this as in other respects, there is much variation from one person to another.

In both sexes, age at puberty is also subject to great individual variation. Although well over half of American girls first menstruate between the twelfth and fourteenth birthdays, a few reach the menarche as early as the age of nine or ten years and in exceptional cases menstruation may be delayed until nineteen or twenty. In boys much the same range of individual differences is found, but the average age at puberty, like that of the beginning of pubescence, is from one to two years later than it is in girls.[3]

PHYSICAL CHANGES IN ADOLESCENCE

One of the first signs of pubescence in both boys and girls is a sudden and very marked spurt in physical growth, especially growth in height. The long bones of the arms and legs stretch out with such amazing rapidity that gains in height of as much as

[3] An increasing body of evidence is accumulating which indicates that in the present generation, the average age at puberty is somewhat earlier than was true of preceding generations. That the average height of college students is greater than that of their parents of the same sex has been demonstrated for both men and women in a number of universities. The reason is not entirely clear, although differences in dietary habits appears to be the most plausible explanation for both changes.

six inches in a single year have been known to occur. Trousers, skirts, and sleeves have to be continually lengthened, only to be outgrown again almost before the remodeling is completed. Gain in weight also occurs, but as a rule it fails to keep pace with gain in height, and so for a time we have the gangling long-legged boys and girls who seem to be chiefly made up of knees and elbows.

The most rapid increase in physical growth comes during pubescence. After puberty is attained, bodily growth begins to slow down, and the gain becomes less and less each year until it finally ceases completely.

The facial proportions change. The lower jaw has been growing much faster than the upper portions of the skull since birth, and it now participates in the general growth spurt with the result that in a few months much of its former childish contour is lost and the face begins to take on a definitely grown-up appearance. (See Figure 56, p. 297.) This is accompanied in boys by a decrease and in girls by an increase in the layer of fat just underneath the skin. This causes the girls' faces to become softer and more rounded in outline, while the boys' faces grow more angular and their flesh feels harder.

The fine hairs on the surface of the body become somewhat coarser and longer and more strongly pigmented. This is true in both sexes but especially in the male. In the male, too, the beard begins to grow at about the time of puberty, and within a year or so shaving becomes necessary. In both sexes the voice also changes at adolescence, becoming lower in pitch and more resonant. In girls, however, the change in voice is much less pronounced than it is in boys. In boys the larynx or "Adam's apple" becomes noticeably enlarged, and the vocal cords within it increase greatly in length. It takes a year or more for this change to be completed. During this time the voice may be noticeably harsh and discordant, often getting out of control. Sometimes there are queer and unexpected shifts in pitch, when the voice without warning jumps from a deep bass to a husky squeak.

Physical characteristics of this kind, which do not involve the primary sex organs but which nevertheless differ for the two sexes, are known as *secondary sex characteristics*. For the most part, secondary sex characteristics are small and inconspicuous during childhood, but they begin to show up clearly during pubescence, and in the adult they are very marked. Nevertheless in most cases the differences between the sexes in regard to these matters are differences of degree rather than of kind. Most men have beards and mustaches and most women do not, although in many women there is a visibly heavier growth of the surface hairs on the upper lip than on other parts of the face. In most men, the shoulders are wider than the hips, while in women the reverse is true; but the rule does not always hold good. On the average, men's voices are deeper and more resonant than women's, but this is not invariably the case. So with the other secondary sex characteristics. On the average they differ for the sexes after the age of puberty, but there are individual exceptions.

MOTOR CONTROL IN THE ADOLESCENT

There is a popular notion that the adolescent is always awkward and clumsy. Stories of adolescents usually picture them as perpetually knocking things over, stumbling over their own feet, breaking everything that they touch. The reason commonly given is that the arms and legs have grown so fast and take up so much more space than they ever did before that their owner no longer knows how to handle them. This idea is of course sheer nonsense. Even the most rapidly growing child does not increase in size so rapidly that he cannot adjust his kinesthetic perceptions to the changes as they take place.[4] Nevertheless it is easy to see why some children do show an increased motor awkwardness at this time. Changes in their appearance are so marked that people are always commenting on it, often in rather tactless fashion.

"Gracious, how John is stretching out. And look at the size of his feet!"

"My goodness, don't tell me this is little Mary! Why, she used to be such a dainty little girl. I never in the world would have known her."

Daily exposure to remarks of this kind can hardly help but

[4] Note the experiences of Stratton and others, described on pp. 339-341 on the length of time required to adjust the motor behavior to a complete reversal of the visual field. Compared to this, the motor adaptations demanded by the bodily changes of the growing child are trivial indeed.

embarrass and annoy a sensitive child, even though no unkindness is intended. Often the adolescent member of a large family is made the butt of a great deal of chaffing about his appearance. His clothes that are perpetually too short, his hands and feet which are made doubly conspicuous by protruding so far out of his outgrown garments, his voice with its unexpected growls and squeaks, all come in for their share of banter. Even though he takes it good-naturedly, some degree of self-consciousness is almost certain to be the result, and as most of us know from experience there is nothing like self-consciousness for disturbing one's motor control. It is an exceptional golfer whose drive cannot be interfered with by remarks about his personal appearance, particularly if he knows them to be true. The adolescent who is so clumsy and awkward that disaster seems to follow wherever he goes may show surprising dexterity of hand in his workshop when no one is watching him and splendid bodily control on the athletic field. His awkwardness in public is not due to lack of motor skill but is the result of embarrassment and self-consciousness.

SEX DIFFERENCES IN MOTOR ACTIVITIES

At the University of California a very complete study of development and behavior during the period of adolescence has been in progress for several years. Not all the findings from this study have been published as yet, but preliminary results on certain aspects of development during the earlier part of the adolescent period have appeared. Espenschade [5] reports the scores made on a series of tests of motor abilities at successive half-year intervals by about seventy-five children of each sex during the period extending from the thirteenth birthday to the age of sixteen and a half years. We may note in passing that developmental studies such as this in which the same children are used as subjects throughout the experimental period have certain obvious advantages over the more common procedure in which different groups of children are used at each successive age levels in order to establish age differences. Studies of the second type, known as *cross-*

---

[5] Anna Espenschade, *Motor Performance in Adolescence: Including the Study of Relationships with Measures of Physical Growth and Maturity*, Monog. Soc. Res. Child Dev., 1940, V, pp. viii + 126.

sectional investigations, are always open to the possibility that some of the differences appearing from one age to the next may be the result of differences in the composition of the groups rather than to changes that occur with age. *Longitudinal studies*, in which the same children are used throughout, are less subject to errors due to differences in sampling.[6] As a rule, more confidence can therefore be placed in the results.

Figures 90 to 93 show the results obtained by Espenschade for the sexes separately in each of four common athletic perform-ances. Figure 94 shows the findings on a composite test of motor ability devised by Brace.[7] The Brace test is made up of twenty items, of which the following are samples:

1. Walking in a straight line, heel to toe
2. Jumping into the air and making a full turn, either to the right or left as the examiner specifies, landing on the same spot
3. Jumping to the feet from a kneeling position
4. Kicking the right (or the left) foot up to a point at least level with the shoulders

Examination of Figures 90 to 94 shows that although the boys continue to improve in each of the four athletic skills that were tried, the curves for the girls show little improvement after the age of thirteen. In the case of the fifty-yard dash and the broad jump, there is even a slight loss. In the ability to jump and reach, the girls show a small continued gain, but the improvement is much smaller than that of the boys. In the distance throw the performance of the girls remains practically at a level, while that of the boys shows steady gain. The total score on the Brace test

[6] In actual practice, this statement does not always hold good. Because of the long period of time over which such studies must extend, some cases are almost inevitably lost from the original group as a result of moving from the community, death, loss of interest in the project, and so on. If, as sometimes happens, the cases that drop out differ in some systematic fashion from those that remain, and if all available cases are used at each age, the sampling error of a longitudinal study may even be greater than is likely to occur in a well-conducted cross-sectional study. If, on the other hand, only those cases retained to the end of the study are used in the age comparisons, the process of elimination may have left only a highly select group, no longer representative of the general population from which it was originally drawn.

[7] David K. Brace, *Measuring Motor Ability: A Scale of Motor Ability Tests* (New York, A. S. Barnes and Co., 1927), pp. xvi + 138.

50-YARD DASH

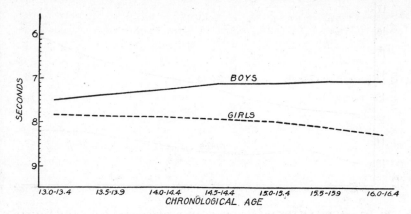

FIG. 90.—AGE AND SEX DIFFERENCES IN SPEED ON THE 50-YARD DASH

(Reproduced with slight modification from *Motor Performance in Adolescence*, by Anna Espenschade. Courtesy of the author and of the Society for Research in Child Development..)

BROAD JUMP

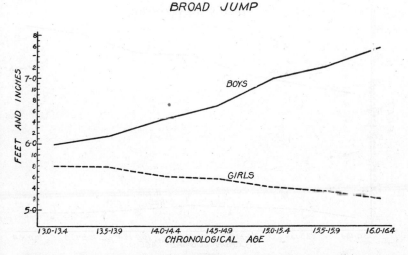

FIG. 91.—AGE AND SEX DIFFERENCES IN PERFORMANCE ON THE
BROAD JUMP

(Reproduced with slight modification from *Motor Performance in Adolescence*, by Anna Espenschade. Courtesy of the author and of the Society for Research in Child Development.)

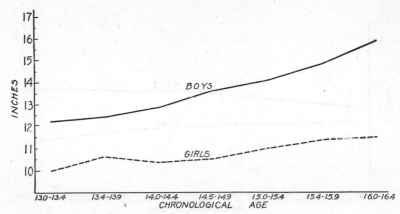

FIG. 92.—AGE AND SEX DIFFERENCES IN PERFORMANCE ON THE "JUMP AND REACH" TEST

(Reproduced with slight modification from *Motor Performance in Adolescence*, by Anna Espenschade. Courtesy of the author and of the Society for Research in Child Development.)

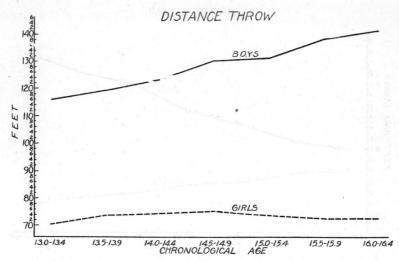

FIG. 93.—AGE AND SEX DIFFERENCES IN PERFORMANCE ON THE DISTANCE THROW

(Reproduced with slight modification from *Motor Performance in Adolescence*, by Anna Espenschade. Courtesy of the author and of the Society for Research in Child Development.)

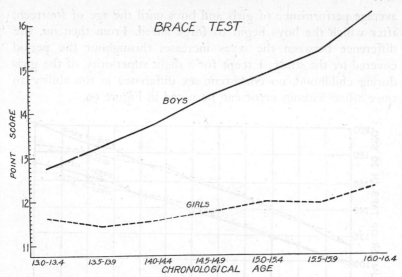

FIG. 94.—AGE AND SEX DIFFERENCES IN SCORES ON THE BRACE TEST
OF MOTOR ABILITIES

(Reproduced with slight modification from *Motor Performance in
Adolescence*, by Anna Espenschade. Courtesy of the author and of the
Society for Research in Child Development.)

is much higher for the boys than for the girls at all ages, and this
difference steadily increases throughout the period as a result of
the more rapid improvement made by the boys. However, it is
worth noting that this marked masculine superiority does not
hold for all of the items of which the Brace test is comprised.
Item 17, which consists of folding the arms, crossing the feet,
then sitting down cross-legged and rising again, is performed
more successfully by girls than by boys at every age. Likewise,
more girls than boys were able to maintain their balance for ten
seconds or longer when standing on one foot with the eyes shut.
In these two performances, not only were the girls superior to the
boys, but their scores improved with age.

Figures 95 and 96 are taken from a study conducted by Bryan
a number of years ago. The cross-sectional method was used. The
skills tested differ from those studied by Espenschade. They involve only hand movements which make little demand upon
strength. In speed of tapping there is almost no difference in the

average performance of girls and boys until the age of fourteen, after which the boys begin to forge ahead. From then on, the difference between the sexes increases throughout the period covered by the study. Except for a slight superiority of the girls during childhood, no consistent sex difference in the ability to trace a line without error can be noted in Figure 96.

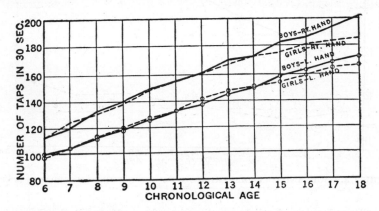

FIG. 95.—IMPROVEMENT IN SPEED OF TAPPING DURING CHILDHOOD
AND ADOLESCENCE

(After Bryan. From *The Psychology of Adolescence*, by F. D. Brooks. Houghton Mifflin Co.)

As far as large muscle activities are concerned, Espenschade's conclusion that the differences between the sexes become so great during the period of adolescence that joint participation in them serves only a social need seems well substantiated. The greater physical size of the boy, his heavier and more compact musculature, as well as other differences in body proportions and structure, give him a decided advantage over his sisters in all performances requiring strength, general bodily speed and endurance, or the quick and concentrated mobilization of energy demanded by such acts as jumping, dodging, kicking,[8] and so on. In

[8] In kicking, particularly, girls suffer a further handicap by reason of the articulation of the hip joint. In women the femur is attached to the pelvis at an oblique angle; in men this angle is more nearly straight. The mechanical disadvantages of the female type of joint for most gross motor skills have been pointed out by Carpenter. (*Res. Quart. Amer. Phys. Educ. Assoc.*, 1938, 9: 120-127.)

more delicate movements involving the coördination of hand and eye as in tracing a line, drawing or writing, or in actions depending chiefly upon bodily coördination and balance as in dancing, fancy skating, and the like, girls appear to be equal or slightly superior to boys. Probably, however, such superiority as appears is more closely related to interest and effort, resulting in a greater amount of practice in these skills than to any inherent superiority

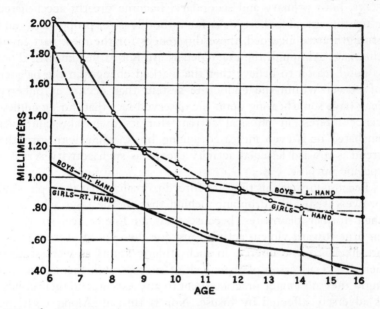

FIG. 96.—IMPROVEMENT IN PRECISION OF VOLUNTARY MOVEMENT DURING CHILDHOOD AND ADOLESCENCE

Precision is measured in terms of the number and extent of errors made in tracing a line. (After Bryan. From *The Psychology of Adolescence*, by F. D. Brooks. Houghton Mifflin Co.)

of the female sex in matters of bodily coördination or manual dexterity. Perhaps a similar explanation can be evoked for the loss in certain athletic performances by girls during later adolescence. Espenschade reports that the older girls of her group typically evinced little interest in these skills and in many instances were very reluctant to try them. A small number completely refused to do so after earlier experience had resulted in slight muscular soreness. Common observation shows that relatively few adolescent girls spend much time in practicing the broad jump or the distance throw or similar athletic tasks just for the fun of it. Boys, on the contrary, spend much of their leisure time in such sports. In all this we see once more how closely the strands of biologic aptitude, personal interests, and cultural pressures are interwoven in the pattern of individual behavior and accomplishment. Physical differences between the sexes, both primary and secondary, become greatly accentuated after the age of puberty. As far as bodily size, proportions, and strength are concerned, these differences for the most part favor the male. Although the exact details are not as yet known, there is good reason to believe that the marked changes in the balance of power within the endocrine system that occurs at puberty may have some bearing upon the observed fact that during adolescence interest in physical activity for its own sake continues unabated or is even increased among boys, while with girls the trend is toward lessened activity except as such activity serves a specific purpose.

Because girls at this time are forced to realize that their physical prowess is steadily dropping behind that of the boys who were their former playmates, because they no longer feel so strong an urge toward violent activity just for the sake of exercise, they are likely to lose interest in such athletic stunts as were studied here by very reason of their lack of success with them. Accordingly they no longer practice them to any extent, and their ability is adversely affected by disuse. Nor is this all. Along with the other changes that come with adolescence there is increased interest in members of opposite sex and a greater desire to please them. So the adolescent boy's interest in sports receives a further impetus from his desire to display his accomplishments before the girls who attract him. But the girl, if she be at all clever, soon learns that while it is an advantage for her to be able to participate in some (but not all) of the athletic sports enjoyed by boys, it is poor social policy for her to excel in them. Even in the comparative freedom of modern society, conventional ideas of the kind of behavior thought becoming for a girl are impressed upon her with increased force after adolescence has been reached. Not only from adults but even more strongly from her associates does the emphasis upon conformity to group mores arise. The girl

who is too "masculine" in her interests is likely to meet with disapproval from her companions of both sexes as well as from her
elders.

The social pressures exerted upon the boy are equally strong,
and again they make for differentiation between the sexes in certain specified areas. In most groups, interest and participation in
athletics is looked upon as almost an essential component of true
masculinity. At least moderate aggressiveness, fearlessness, social
dominance, and similar characteristics are emphasized as desirable
elements in the pattern to be cultivated by boys, while in girls
these traits are less highly prized or, if too strongly manifested,
are likely to be frowned upon.

Thus through the circular interaction of biological, social, and
cultural forces adolescence brings with it a marked increase in
the rate of change in the child's personality. Its outlines become
more clear-cut. Not only sex differences but differences among
children of the same sex become more apparent. In part, the
clearer manifestation of personality traits results from the fact
that society has established more definite standards for the adolescent than for the younger child. Behavior that would formerly
have been overlooked or condoned is now regarded with concern; idiosyncracies that would once have been thought amusing
now set the child apart as one who is "queer" or "different." Not
only by adults but even more by his contemporaries do the
child's deviations from the established pattern become a matter
for comment. Most of all, perhaps, do the pressures come from
the adolescent himself, from his own sharply visualized concepts
of what is to be sought and what avoided, what is permissible
and what not permissible, what persons are to be admired and
imitated, and who is to be looked upon with scorn or ridicule.
Against this newly emerged background of ideals and attitudes
the adolescent's own personality stands out in sharp relief.

THE MEASUREMENT OF SEX DIFFERENCES IN INTERESTS AND ATTITUDES: MENTAL MASCULINITY AND FEMININITY

That the sexes differ, on the average, in many of their typical interests and attitudes quite as markedly as they do in respect to their physical characteristics, most people will agree. Many of the terms that we use in describing people carry at least an implicit reference to this fact. We say, "James is such a manly little fellow; Mary is a perfect little lady; Mrs. Brown is a fine example of a womanly personality." Or we may comment less favorably. "Leonard is a regular sissy; Alice is a tomboy; Mrs. Ashe acts more like a man than like a woman. She should change places with her husband, who seems much more feminine than she does." Although in some instances such statements may be based largely upon single characteristics such as personal appearance, pitch of voice, or marked interest in some activity that is commonly looked upon as appropriate only for one of the sexes, in most instances the reference is to a general impression, rather than to any specific trait. Mental masculinity and femininity thus seem to be complex characteristics that have a good deal of internal consistency. Moreover, although the average man or boy is more "masculine" than the average girl or woman,[9] there is a wide range of difference among the members of either sex in the extent to which they conform to or depart from the characteristic pattern by which their own sex is most strongly differentiated from the members of the opposite sex.

In most of the earlier studies of sex differences in mental traits, the fact most strongly emphasized was the great overlapping between the sexes in respect to almost any individual characteristic that might be selected for study. Because of this overlapping, the differences found were generally regarded as of little practical importance, although enough scientific interest centered about their nature and origin to stimulate a small amount of continued investigation of the problem. But in none of the early studies was an attempt made to secure a total measure of the trait itself

[9] This is of necessity the case, because the concept itself is built up from observation of what the average man or woman is like, particularly in those areas in which the average man differs most from the average woman.

as displayed by any individual. Groups of men and boys were compared with groups of girls and women to see in what respects they differed, but the idea of studying a single individual with respect to a large number of these items to see whether or not many small differences might perhaps accumulate to form a significant total [10] is of comparatively recent origin.

In 1936, Terman and Miles published the results of a study [11] of mental masculinity and femininity that had been in progress over a period of ten years. The report includes an account of a test used to measure the extent to which the interests and attitudes of an individual conform to those usual for his sex. In spite of great overlapping between the sexes on the separate items of this test, the responses of individual persons showed enough internal consistency as to the direction of the sex trend to reduce the sex-overlap for the total score to only 8 per cent. This is shown graphically in Figure 97, from which it can be seen that although a small number of males earned a more "feminine" score than did the more "masculine" of the females, the two sex groups are on the whole very clearly separated.

The exact significance of the M-F test, as it is popularly called, is not completely known. The authors have shown that ratings of the masculinity or femininity of students by teachers and others who have known them well show only slight agreement with the test score. This is not surprising, however, in view of the fact that ratings of the same subject by different persons are often very different. Perhaps the best evidence that the test does measure a kind of psychological masculinity or femininity that in certain cases runs counter to biological sex is to be found in the

[10] This would of course only be the case if the various items were internally consistent with each other, that is, part of a larger whole. If "masculinity" in one area were as likely to be associated with "femininity" as with "masculinity" in other areas, the ratings on a large number of such items would tend to cancel each other instead of summating. The extent to which such ratings take a constant direction is at least a rough measure of the extent to which we may regard "masculinity" or "femininity" as general traits that each person displays in varying degrees, rather than a group of merely circumstantial factors without consistent association with each other.

[11] Lewis M. Terman, Catherine Cox Miles and Assistants, *Sex and Personality: Studies in Masculinity and Femininity* (New York, McGraw-Hill Book Co., 1936), pp. xii + 600.

evidence reported for one group of sex inverts [12] who, both in respect to the pattern of their physical desires and their general interests, resemble the opposite sex rather than their own sex. These persons may thus be said to represent the extremes [13] of femininity in males and masculinity in females. In a culture such as ours, sexual inversion falls strongly under the social taboo, and persons who exhibit such tendencies are therefore in constant risk of ostracism, loss of employment, or even of imprisonment.

However, our major interests in mental masculinity or femininity arises from its significance in the life of the average normal person. Terman and Miles have shown that the greatest difference between the sexes in respect to expressed interests and attitudes appears during adolescence.[14] Girls, on the average, earn their

[12] Also known as *homosexuals*.

[13] The origins of sexual inversion in the individual are not known. Many believe that it may have its starting point in some kind of glandular imbalance. This point of view receives some support from experiments carried out with animals in which more or less complete inversion of the usual pattern of sex behavior has been brought about by injecting hormones of the kind secreted by the gonads of members of the opposite sex directly into the blood stream. Young female chickens so treated will crow like cockerels, with all the accompanying ritual of arching the neck, flapping the wings, and even seeking out a high place from which to carry out the act.

On the other hand, case histories of the early development of homosexual persons appear to indicate that the early experiences of these persons also are likely to have been somewhat different from those of most children. Terman and Miles made a special study of eighteen of the group of seventy-seven male inverts whom they studied and found that in every one of these cases the mother was the preferred parent and that in fifteen of the eighteen cases the father either died during the subject's childhood, was much away from home during that time, or is described as brutal, cold, or domineering. In only one case was there close association between the boy and his father; in this case the father was an invalid. The majority showed some indication of an inverted pattern of interests in early childhood. They preferred the companionship of girls at an age when most boys play almost exclusively with other boys; they enjoyed such typically feminine activities as playing with dolls and playing house. As they grew older their interest in active games and sports decreased, and their fondness for more sedentary occupations increased. This trend is characteristic of girls but not of boys. In school they preferred languages and the arts to mathematics and science.

[14] It is possible that a test suitable for use with younger children might show slightly different results. The Terman-Miles test is not adapted for use with persons who have not a fairly extensive vocabulary and considerable skill in reading. However the fact that the eighth-grade boys ranked less masculine in their responses to this test than did those somewhat older

most highly feminine score on the M-F test when they are in the eighth grade; boys make their most masculine score during the third year of high school. Roughly, these periods correspond to the usual age at the attainment of puberty. Perhaps the explanation for the wide divergence of the sexes in psychological traits at that time is a reflection of the adolescent's intense interest in all matters that have to do with the establishment of his status as man or woman.

Scores on the M-F test show small but significant relationships to a number of factors, such as occupational choice and occupational success, education (especially among women), interests, and experiences. Although none of these relationships are high enough to make the test of much usefulness for individual guidance, the study is a beautiful demonstration of the basic consistency of the pattern of an individual personality. The sexes differ in respect to a large number of tendencies, some of which are of obvious importance, while many others appear, at first thought, to be too trivial to warrant serious consideration. The significant thing that Terman and Miles have shown is that these tendencies, both small and great, are *consistent* for normal persons as well as for the abnormal, and for the individual as well as for the averages of groups. Personality grows and develops consistently, not at random, and each individual expresses his personality in a host of ways that reveal the same fundamental tendencies in spite of their superficial differences. For example, a person whose first association with the word *trunk* is "elephant" is somewhat more likely to think a marigold is a fabric, to know that peat is used for fuel, to be angered little or not at all at having his or her political views ridiculed, to dislike study, to admire Cromwell but not Columbus, and to believe that green-eyed people are not to be trusted, than is another whose first association with *trunk* is "travel." The latter person may know that a marigold is a flower but think that peat is used for paving, be much angered at having his or her political views ridiculed, like study (or at least claim to like it), dislike Cromwell but admire Columbus, and reject the superstition that green-eyed

suggests that the changes in behavior that appear with puberty are primarily responsible for the apparent accentuation of psychological sex differences at these ages.

people are not to be trusted.[15] One of these combinations is made up of responses more often given by women than by men while the other follows the opposite pattern. Can you guess which is which?

Equally marked differences appear in the free associations to common words given by persons of opposite sex. Try these words with some of your friends of both sexes. Merely tell them that when you pronounce a word they are to respond with the very first word that pops into their minds, without stopping to think about it.

1. Pound	3. Foot	5. Lace
2. Park	4. Iron	6. Cast

Although you will find that some associations are given about as often by one sex as by the other, certain ones are much more likely to be given by males than by females and vice versa. If you try the experiment with a fairly large number of persons, the differences will almost certainly be large enough to yield rather convincing evidence that the content of the average man's mind differs somewhat from that of the average woman. Nevertheless, every normal person shares in the interests typical of *both* sexes. This fact is clearly shown both in his free associations and in his responses to such a test as that devised by Terman and Miles. Although responses in accordance with an individual's own sex usually predominate when the number of items tried is large enough to yield a reliable total, I have yet to find a single person whose responses did not also include a fair proportion of those typical of the opposite sex. It is likely that any one who, in his psychological make-up, could be regarded as either 100 per cent masculine or 100 per cent feminine would be a very abnormal person indeed.

[15] Again it becomes necessary to warn the too credulous reader that we are dealing here with a very small sampling of several hundred such items in which the sexes have been shown to differ on the average, but not in all individual cases. Probably no one who reads this, regardless of his sex, will find that his own reactions correspond to either of the above patterns in all its details. Yet each of them, considered individually, has been found to occur more often among the members of one sex than among those of the opposite sex. When the total number of "feminine" responses is subtracted from the total number of "masculine" responses made by an individual person, the result may be looked upon as representing the "balance of power" of psychological masculinity or feminity in his personality.

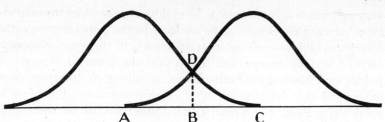

FIG. 97.—DIFFERENTIATION OF SCORES MADE BY MALE AND FEMALE
SUBJECTS ON AN INTEREST TEST

(Reproduced by permission of the author and the publishers from *Sex
and Personality*, by L. M. Terman and Catherine Cox Miles. McGraw-Hill
Book Co.)

THE GROWTH OF SEX INTERESTS

Formerly it was thought that sex interests and sex desires did
not exist before puberty. This is not the case. Even very young
children show evidence of sex feelings that appear to be similar
to, if not identical with, those appearing later. But it is unquestionably true that at adolescence sex drives become far stronger
and more definitely patterned than they are in childhood. The
little child enjoys being petted and caressed by almost any one
of whom he is fond. But his enjoyment is evidently not very
intense, as any one can determine for himself by offering a
counter-attraction such as a bit of candy or an interesting toy.
It does not take much to induce the child to wriggle away from
the fondler and become absorbed in the new interest. A much
stronger counter-interest is required to distract a boy or girl of
seventeen from the joys of a petting party.

Because the sex interests of the prepubescent child are normally
so vague and diffuse and so overshadowed for the most part by
other and more immediate drives, it is not strange that their existence was long ignored. Indeed, during the greater part of the
elementary school period most children react toward the opposite sex in a way that to the casual observer would more nearly
suggest sex aversion than sex attraction. Boys are reluctant to
permit girls to join in their play, and girls are likewise intolerant
of the behavior of the boys. But closer observation suggests that
much of this apparent antagonism is merely a cloak by which a

very real interest is concealed. As children grow older, more contacts between the sexes can be noticed. In the pubescent or early adolescent child, these contacts retain much of their earlier appearance of surface antagonism. They take the form of teasing, of pulling and hauling each other about, scuffling, or "razzing" each other, and this backhanded way of showing mutual interest is particularly likely to be resorted to if observers are present.

The sex drive is not the child of sin, as our Puritan ancestors represented it to be, but of physiology. At the time of puberty and even before, during the period of pubescence, marked changes take place in the secretions of the ductless glands, especially in those coming from the gonads or sex glands. It is to these secretions or *hormones*, as their active elements are called, that we owe the great changes in bodily form and appearance that were described at the beginning of this chapter. Remove the glands before puberty, and but few of the secondary sex characteristics will appear. Remove them after puberty and many of the characteristics will become greatly modified. If these secretions are powerful enough to change the bodily form, alter the distribution of fat cells, cause a beard to grow on the smooth face of the boy and modify the pitch of his voice, it is not surprising to find that changes also take place in the fundamental drives by which behavior is motivated, as well as in the behavior itself.

The fact that under modern social conditions the sex drive cannot be completely gratified as soon as it is felt introduces a good many complications for the adolescent. A generation or two ago, when about the only way of dealing with the matter was to try to keep the sexes apart until the proper time for courtship and marriage had arrived, the problems confronting the adolescent were somewhat different from those likely to be faced by the growing boy or girl to-day when greater freedom of association is the rule. But even now, many find it difficult to make the transition from the social life of childhood, which centers so largely around friends of their own sex, to the normal social life of the adult, which involves both sexes. Sensitive children are sometimes kept from having anything to do with companions of the opposite sex by the good-natured chaffing and ridicule of more sophisticated older brothers and sisters to whom their awkward and embarrassed flounderings in the direction of love-making are supremely funny. Sometimes, either from too much reading of romantic tales or from ideals unwisely instilled by parents in an attempt to prevent the formation of undesirable attachments, adolescents get such an exaggerated idea of the importance of any association between the sexes that they cannot take even a chance acquaintanceship casually and naturally. The rough and ready play, the pushing and tussling between boys and girls whose adolescent interests are just beginning to show themselves is the best possible preparation for building up the open, unabashed, and healthy attitudes toward persons of the opposite sex that are so necessary for happy adjustment later on.

THE SOCIAL LIFE OF THE ADOLESCENT

Not only does the adolescent, as a rule, begin to show a new interest in the opposite sex, but a new element appears in his relationships with persons of his own sex. This is the formation of clubs or gangs. It is, of course, true that long before the age of adolescence children play together in groups and form special friendships that give these groups something of a lasting character. But in most cases the social groups formed by young children lack the solidarity and the feeling of group-consciousness that characterize the adolescent gang or club.

The typical boy's gang is closely organized about a leader. The leader may earn and hold his place by force of arms—his own flesh and blood arms including the fists in which they terminate. This is likely to be the case when the gang is organized chiefly for fighting and must hold its own against other neighboring gangs. Or he may be chosen because of his athletic ability, his cleverness in planning and carrying out small pilferings, or for any other special aptitude that furthers the group interest. The leader must be a good deal of a dictator, able to down those who question his authority, else the gang will soon break up. But he must also be able to convince the other members of the group that his dictatorship is just, according to boyish standards.

Girls as well as boys form a good many special clubs and cliques during early adolescence, but with the exception of those under adult supervision, they are not likely to be as highly organized or as closely knit as the spontaneous social groups formed by boys. The boy's gang usually has a name; the girl's clique rarely has one unless an adult provides it or at least suggests the idea. The girl's group is more likely to be organized around three or four close friends who unite in deciding who shall be admitted to the group and who shall be excluded from it. For the most part their decisions are made on purely personal grounds. The boy's gang has a definite leader about whose identity there is no question, but if a girl is asked who is the leader of her group she is more likely to name two or three persons than one. The boy's gang has a fairly definite purpose. It may be athletics, it may be plundering, it may be fighting, it may be hiking. The girl's club is less likely to center around any particular activity. Its members, however, share among themselves various "secrets," bits of gossip, and so on to which they often refer mysteriously in the presence of outsiders in the hope of arousing curiosity and envy.

Both with girls and boys the club or gang gains its solidarity quite as much by excluding certain persons as by admitting others. In this respect it is very like the social cliques established by older persons. Mary objects to inviting Susan Brown to her party "because she doesn't belong to our crowd," and her mother "never sees anything" of her next-door neighbor who belongs to a different social "set." And like their elders, adolescent boys and girls look upon certain groups or cliques as superior to others and make strong efforts to be admitted to these favored circles.

Unquestionably the influence of his associates upon the way the adolescent thinks and acts is very great; greater, probably than at any previous stage of his life. For the adolescent there can be no stronger argument for having or doing a thing than the fact that "all the others are doing it." Nothing is likely to awaken so great an emotional disturbance or cause so much worry as the feeling that he is in some way different from the others. "Others" in this case, means the other members of his own particular group; he is not especially concerned about resembling those belonging to some other clan. A fashion started by the leaders of a group, even though it may happen to be uncomfortable or inconvenient, is faithfully copied by all the lesser members. Opinions, prejudices, beliefs, likes, and dislikes are likewise determined by the group, and the boy or girl who differs is made to feel the force of group ostracism unless he has sufficient force of personality to bring the others around to his point of view. Mastery, conformity, or exclusion—these are the social alternatives with which the adolescent is faced, and no half-way measures are possible. Organizations such as the Scouts, the Camp-fire Girls, the junior Y.M.C.A. and Y.W.C.A. are doing a good deal to capitalize the group interests of the adolescent and to mold the attitudes of the individual by tactful modifications of the standards of the group.

THE "HABIT-LAG" IN FAMILY RELATIONS

When a little child, the boy or girl is of necessity cared for and protected in the home. He does not have to make very many plans for himself, and he gives little thought to the future. But it will not be long, now that he has reached adolescence, before he must leave the home and look after himself. He has to grow up mentally and emotionally as well as physically. And this means a good many changes in habits and points of view. It means breaking old habits as well as learning new ones.

This often is a difficult task both for the adolescent himself and for other people. The boy who has suddenly shot up in height until he is almost as tall as his father looks in the glass and says to himself, "Now I am a man." And he expects people to treat him as a man. But his childish habits still have him in their grip. He borrows his father's neckties and fusses about the crease in his trousers, but he neglects to wash his ears. He wants to drive the family car, but he cannot remember to keep the garage door locked. He spends his allowance for ice-cream and candy and has nothing left for more important needs. He wants to be independent, to look after himself and manage his own affairs, but his old childish habits of expecting somebody else to take the real responsibility continually get him into trouble. Like Alice in Wonderland he is grown up one minute, and the next minute he is a child again.

The adolescent is not the only one who has to form new habits as a result of his growing up. His parents are faced with the same problem. All his life they have been used to watching over him, making decisions for him, demanding obedience from him in little matters as well as in greater ones. Now the time is coming when they must relax their hold in preparation for the time when it must be relinquished completely. This is not easy. It is made more difficult by the fact that there is no hard and fast rule concerning the time when parental control shall come to an end. Although legally a parent's control ceases when the boy or girl comes of age, which in most states is at twenty-one years, many young people are still in college and financially dependent upon their parents at that time, and it is perhaps not unnatural for parents to feel that personal and financial dependence should go together. Even after the child is earning his own living, the old habits of parental dominance may still hold sway. Particularly for the mother whose whole life has been given up to her children is it difficult to let them go and live lives of their own in which she will play a much smaller part.

The conflict between old habits and new requirements—represented on the part of the adolescent by his feeling that he is grown up, that he wants to be treated like a grown-up, while he still has habits of acting like a child, and on the parents' side by their recognition that the child is growing up, their feeling that he ought to act more like a grown-up, although from force of habit they continue to treat him as if he were still a child—often makes for a good deal of friction. This friction can be greatly lessened if both parties realize that they have a definite kind of adjustment to make in which old habits have to be broken up and replaced by new ones. The adolescent has to stop acting like a child and behave like a grown-up. The parent has to stop treating him as a child and permit him adult freedom, responsibilities, and privileges. If each will bear in mind that no habit is overcome all at once and that occasional lapses into the old ways must be expected, much of the irritation that is otherwise likely to result from the fact that the old ways of doing things still crop out now and then, will disappear. A good deal of tolerance is needed on both sides.

ADOLESCENCE IN OTHER CULTURE-GROUPS

In certain primitive societies the beginning of adolescence is marked by elaborate ceremonies, the "pubic rites" as they are called because they take place at puberty. After the rites have been performed the child is looked upon as an adult who is no longer subject to parental control but only to the laws of the tribe. Usually there is separation from the parents at this time. The girl is given in marriage; the boy, if he does not marry at once, goes to live with the men.

In certain respects, at least, this clear-cut separation of childhood from maturity and the public recognition and acceptance of the change in status of the youth who has fulfilled the pubic rites greatly simplifies a good many of the problems of "growing up" that adolescents in our culture are likely to experience. In these groups there is no question of the amount of responsibility that must be assumed or the degree of freedom that is permitted to any child at any time. All such matters are determined by the rules of the tribe. Moreover, special provision is made for instructing the children who are to go through the rites as to their exact part in the ceremonials and the kind of behavior that is expected from them after the rites have been completed and they have been officially recognized as adults.[16]

Authorities are not in complete agreement as to the relative difficulty of the adjustments that adolescents in primitive groups and those in more advanced societies such as our own are obliged to make. The former have the advantage of knowing more precisely just what is expected from them and of having their status in the tribe more clearly defined. In some ways they are permitted greater sexual freedom, and they usually marry at a much earlier age than is customary with us. This unquestionably reduces some of the tensions that exist among adolescents in our society, where the financial and social responsibilities incident to marriage and child-rearing are so great that they can rarely be assumed

[16] In some tribes all the ceremonies are completed at one time, and the youth passes directly from childhood to adulthood with no intermediate stage. In others there is an initial and a final ceremony, separated from each other by periods varying from a few months to three or four years. In the latter case the interval is commonly looked upon as a probationary period during which the boy or girl is expected to learn the manners and skills that will be required from him as an adult and is instructed in the tribal secrets and beliefs. In many instances the adolescents who are going through this period of initiation and training are kept in groups by themselves, the boys in one group, the girls in another. Each group is under the charge of an older person of their own sex. In other tribes, the initiates continue to live with their own families but must assume certain new responsibilities and conform to new restrictions or *taboos*.

until many years after physiological maturity has been reached. On the other hand, the primitive youth has his own problems to meet which may be equally as difficult as those of our own culture, though not of the same kind. Whiting,[17] who has given us a vivid description of the rules and restrictions governing the behavior of the children and adolescents in a New Guinea tribe with whom he lived on intimate terms for a period of several months, lays particular stress on the large number of *taboos* or tribal prohibitions, to which all members of the tribe must conform on threat of extreme punishment, for the most part believed to be of supernatural origin. Whiting disagrees with the point of view adopted by many anthropologists who, impressed by the apparent simplicity of primitive life and its freedom in respect to many matters about which our society imposes comparatively rigid rules, have assumed that problems of personal adjustment and mental health in these societies are few and easily met. By way of example he cites the case of one of the two adolescent boys in the hamlet in which he lived who became definitely neurotic. Whiting describes a number of instances in which this lad manifested extreme fear, out of proportion to that shown by other members of the group. On at least one occasion, a nightmare during which he believed that his father's ghost appeared and tried to take his soul away, precipitated an illness so severe that he was incapacitated for almost a month, although his temperature remained normal and there were no symptoms of any physiological disturbances that could account for the attack. It is not without interest to note that the boy ascribed his illness to sorcery by the father of a girl whom he was secretly courting but who fell within the incest taboo although not closely related by blood. The fact that he was officially affianced to another girl, whom he did not like, undoubtedly added to his conflict and to his sense of guilt.

All this should warn us against the easy assumption that persons living under conditions that to us seem greatly simplified when compared to our own are relatively free from problems of adjustment. Children in such groups have a different set of rules to

[17] John W. M. Whiting, *Becoming a Kwoma: Teaching and Learning in a New Guinea Tribe* (New Haven, Yale University Press, 1941), pp. xix + 226.

learn, and their behavior is governed by different concepts of good and evil, of causes and consequences. But people are human beings, regardless of the social conditions under which they live, and the problems incident to passing from childhood to maturity are not obliterated by changing their pattern. Adolescence is a time when many new ways of thinking and behaving have to be learned, and although the lessons may be interesting, exciting, and highly vital, they are not always easy. Most of you who read this will at least have passed through the greater part of this period and have acquired considerable skill in living at the adult level. Many of you have already forgotten enough of the early stages of the transition from child to adult to make it hard for you to understand and be tolerant toward the blunders of younger brothers and sisters or others who are still at the cross-roads. We should not forget that while physiological maturity comes of itself, the particular pattern of social and emotional maturity appropriate to happy and effective life in any social group has to be learned and the early stages of learning are likely to be the most difficult.

THE STORY OF AN ADOLESCENT BOY

Harold E. Jones, *Development in Adolescence* (New York, D. Appleton-Century Co., 1943), pp. xx + 166.

This is the story of John Sanders, a boy of about average ability, who grew up in an ordinary type of home in a middle-class neighborhood. Perhaps John had greater difficulty than most boys in meeting the new social requirements that come with adolescence, but certainly his problems were of a kind that many boys and girls experience. The report shows in detail the methods used by the author and his colleagues at the University of California for studying growth and behavior during the adolescent period. It is illustrated by a large number of graphs that demonstrate the many changes in skills, interests, and personality characteristics that took place in John between the ages of eleven and eighteen years. After reading it you should have a much clearer idea than you are now likely to have of the methods used by psychologists for studying children, and you will also gain a keener appreciation and understanding of the difficulties with which many adolescents have to cope.

Chapter XIX

THE COLLEGE YEARS

Why would not every school-boy be able to get into college even if he had the necessary funds?

In the elementary school, the children who come from homes of the better class do better work, on the average, than those from poor homes. Does the same rule hold good for college students? Explain.

What are some of the most important causes of failure in college?

What kind of eye movements take place during reading? Is the rate of eye movements an important factor in determining the rate of reading? About what proportion of the reading time is taken up by the movements of the eyeball?

What two factors are of chief importance in determining the average number of words that can be apprehended during a single fixation pause?

What can the slow reader do to increase his rate of reading?

What suggestions would you make to a college student who complains of his inability to remember what he reads?

How is "motivation" defined?

Does a powerful motive or drive always lead to effective action? Why not?

What is an instinct? What is the attitude of most present-day psychologists toward former theories of instinct?

*How do we judge the intensity of a motive? its clear-
ness? How do purposes differ from motives?*

*What are the chief ways in which the motives of ani-
mals and very young children differ from those
of normal adults?*

*Under what circumstances may a conflict between
motives interfere with effective action? Under
what conditions may conflicting motives be advan-
tageous?*

*What is the best way of handling conflicting motives?
To what less desirable, methods do people sometimes resort?*

What is the best sign of mature personality?

GENERAL CHARACTERISTICS OF THE
COLLEGE STUDENT

By the time the boy or girl is ready for college, both physical
and mental growth are well-nigh completed. Boys gain slowly in
height until about the age of twenty, but the total amount of this
gain is very small; while the height of girls increases little or not
at all after the age of eighteen. Recent studies have suggested that
mental growth also continues a little longer, on the average, in
boys than in girls, but of this we are less certain.[1] In both sexes
there is usually some gain in weight after growth in height has
ceased, and certain bodily measurements, such as depth of chest
in both sexes and width of hips in females, continue to increase
slightly for many years after the body as a whole has ceased to
grow.

Among males, motor abilities of all kinds reach their peak at
this age and interest in athletics and in competitive sports of all
kinds is correspondingly high. As a matter of fact, the period
from eighteen to twenty-five is the time when nearly all abilities
reach their highest level. Particularly for the college student, it
is likewise the time when serious plans for the future must be

[1] See Terman, *Genetic Studies of Genius*, Vol. III, *The Promise of Youth*
(Stanford University, Stanford University Press, 1932).

made, when childhood is finally left behind, and manhood or womanhood is begun.

If we compare the intelligence of college students with that of all the young people in the country who are of college age, we find, as we might expect, that the students are a very highly selected group. As a matter of fact, the further we go up the educational ladder the more persons we shall find whose ability is not equal to the climb and who therefore drop out, leaving only the more able ones to go on the higher levels. Idiots and low-grade imbeciles rarely get into school at all. The higher-grade imbeciles and the morons reach their limits somewhere in the lower grades of the elementary school. Most of the "dull normals" stop with the junior high school, though a few of the more industrious and ambitious struggle on a little further. Very few children whose intelligence is not at least a little above average succeed in graduating from high school (except in the vocational or trades courses), and only a highly selected few complete the college preparatory courses.

Even this repeated sifting is not enough. Most of the leading colleges, in an attempt to reduce the number of failures after entrance, make a further attempt to select for admittance only the really able members of this already select group. In doing this some colleges depend chiefly upon entrance examinations; others take only those who stood in the top half or perhaps the top third of their high-school classes, but the majority in determining admissions take into account both the high-school record and the performance on entrance examinations (which nowadays usually include an intelligence test). By careful study of the entrance records of students who afterward fail in their college work and comparison of their records with those of the students who succeed, many colleges have succeeded in locating what they call a "critical score" which serves as a dividing line between possible success and almost certain failure. For example, Johnston,[2] at the University of Minnesota, found that of 208 students who entered the freshman class with scores below the critical point, all except three had failed before the end of their first year. But of the stu-

---

[2] J. B. Johnston, "The Study of Student Aptitude for College Work as a Means of Educational Guidance," University of Minnesota *Faculty Bulletin*, 1927, Vol. I, No. 1, pp. 4.

dents whose scores were above this point, 42 per cent also failed. The critical score predicts failure very well because it selects the students who cannot do the work even though they try. But it is less accurate in predicting success because some who could succeed will not make the necessary effort to do so. However, it seems reasonably safe either to refuse outright to admit students whose scores are so low that failure seems almost certain or to advise them strongly to turn their interests in some other direction.

Another possible solution is to recommend students whose ability to complete the regular four years of college is doubtful to take their first two years at a junior college. In this way they may be enabled to continue their education up to a formal graduation and then stop with no feeling of having failed. On the other hand, if it then seems advisable they can usually transfer to a regular four-year college without loss of standing. The junior college thus serves a number of important purposes. It provides vocational preparation for certain kinds of work that require less than four years training beyond high school. It furnishes further educational and cultural training for those students whose interests or abilities do not fit into the pattern demanded by a regular four-year college course but who nevertheless desire some additional education after completing high school. It gives opportunity for many of the personal-social experiences of college life for students who would otherwise miss them. It provides students who have matured slowly some further time for "growing up."

The junior college of to-day frequently offers quite as good training as is provided by the larger colleges and universities for the first two years of college work. Upon graduation, transfer to a regular four-year curriculum may usually be made without loss of standing if the student's work has been of good quality and the college is on the accredited list.[3]

Because of successive eliminations of the less able members of the group, it comes about that the great mass of college students are recruited from the upper fourth of the intellectual distribution. Those who remain to graduate form a still more highly

[3] Students who are likely to desire such a transfer should always ascertain whether or not the school has been accredited before planning to enter a junior college. This information can be secured by writing directly to the college authorities.

FIG. 98.—MOTOR SKILLS AT THE COLLEGE LEVEL

Compare with Figures 47 and 75.

FIG. 98.—MOTOR SKILLS AT THE COLLEGE LEVEL

Compare with Figures 47 and 75.

selected group, and as a rule only the best of the graduates become candidates for higher degrees.

The greater number of college students come from better than average homes. In part this is because of the relationship between socio-economic status and intelligence. But if a college professor or a doctor has a son with an IQ of 140, the chance that this boy will be sent to college is far greater than that the equally brilliant son of a day laborer will be given the same opportunity. Although college students come from all ranks of society, the proportion coming from cultured homes is much greater than chance alone would lead one to expect. But—and this may seem strange until you stop to think about it—among those who do succeed in getting into college, there is little or no relationship between the cultural level of the home and college success. Indeed a few studies have shown a small tendency in the opposite direction, students from the poorest homes doing on the average a little better work than those from the best homes and vice versa. There are two reasons why such a reverse tendency may exist. The first is that the students from the poorer homes are more highly selected than those from the better homes. Since college is not a social tradition with these groups, parents are not likely to think of providing college training for their children unless they show very decided ability. But in the upper social classes, where going to college is pretty much the accepted thing, almost any youth who is not an absolute dunce will be entered, if family influence and special tutoring can do it. Moreover, the student whose family has made a great many sacrifices in order to send him to college is likely to make a greater effort to do his best than the one who takes his opportunity to be sent to college for granted.

FACTORS CONTRIBUTING TO SUCCESS OR FAILURE

Many studies have shown that students vary greatly in the extent to which they succeed in their college work. Some fail miserably and sooner or later drop out; some succeed by taking more than the allotted time; others make brilliant records and graduate with high honors.

In trying to account for these differences we naturally think first of the question of intelligence which we found so important in determining school success among younger children. In college, too, differences in the intelligence of the students account in part for the differences in their academic accomplishment, but non-intellectual factors likewise have a good deal to do with it.

Differences in early preparation play a part. Particularly when they first enter college, students whose high-school preparation has been poor are at a disadvantage as compared to their classmates. But if they are intelligent and industrious, this can usually be overcome. However, neither intelligence nor the kind of high school attended can account for all the differences found in the quality of the work done by college students.

Poor health accounts for some failures and for a good many cases of delayed progress. Defective sight or hearing, sometimes unrecognized by the student himself, may cause difficulty. Financial conditions that make it necessary for some students to earn all or part of their expenses impose further strain, particularly with overambitious students who insist upon carrying too heavy a load of class work along with their outside jobs and who pay the penalty in broken health or low marks.

But although all these things are significant, the fact remains that there are many students of good intelligence and excellent health, not handicapped by lack of funds, who nevertheless fail in their courses, while there are others of less ability who do good work in spite of adverse conditions. Although many factors contribute to these differences in achievement, two are of outstanding importance: differences in study habits and differences in motivation.

Even very bright students are sometimes found to have such poor habits of study or to be so poorly motivated toward their college work that they continue to fail in spite of their ability. Sometimes their difficulties are found to be very specific. Poor reading habits are among the most common of these. Reading difficulties may be classified under two broad heads; those having to do with the mechanics of reading and those having to do with the comprehension and organization for efficient retention of that which is read.

A large number of psychological studies have been made of the movements of the eye during reading. The discovery that in reading the eye does not follow the line of print with a steady sweep but moves in a series of rapid jumps interrupted by pauses during which there is fixation on some definite point is commonly attributed to E. Javal in an article published in 1878. Perception of words and phrases occurs during the fixation pauses. The actual eye movements are too rapid for anything to be perceived clearly. You can observe these eye movements for yourself by standing behind some one who is reading and holding a small mirror in such a position as to catch the reflection of his eyes. For careful study, however, a more exact and permanent record is needed which will show not only the movements of the eyeball but also the exact points at which fixation occurs as well as the length of the fixation periods. This is done by means of recording cameras with accessory apparatus especially designed for this purpose. Many thousands of such records have been made, using as subjects both rapid and slow readers, children just beginning to read and adults whose reading habits extend back over a period of many years. The effect of varying the difficulty of the material to be read, of changing the size of type or the form or spacing of the letters and many similar questions have also been studied.

As a result of all this, a number of interesting and significant points have been discovered, among the most important of which are the following:

1. Differences in speed of reading depend chiefly upon three factors, (a) the number of fixation pauses per line,[4] (b) the average duration of the pauses, and (c) the frequency of regressive (backward) movements which are usually made for the purpose of verifying what has previously been imperfectly perceived or comprehended.

2. About 90 per cent of the total reading time is taken up by these three factors. The *saccadic movements* [5] of the eye itself occupy only about 10 per cent of the reading time. The rate of these movements is not under voluntary control.

The number of fixations per line will of course vary with the number of words per line as well as with other factors. In reading ordinary prose, college students of average reading proficiency will make about four to six pauses per line on the average. This of course means that not one but several words are apprehended at each pause. And while differences in visual acuity

---

[4] Assuming, of course, that the reading material used is the same for all subjects.

[5] *Saccadic* means "quick, jerky."

undoubtedly have some bearing on the differences in the number of words perceived during a single fixation, this factor is of much less importance than the naïve person is likely to suppose, unless the visual difficulty is so extreme as to constitute a major handicap. Of much greater importance are (1) perceptual habit or over-learning [6] of the visual appearance of words through much practice in reading, and (2) extensive acquaintance with the meaning of words which enables the reader to make inferences about them on the basis of the context from relatively small perceptual cues. It can readily be shown that the clearness of perception decreases as the angular distance from the fovea or center of vision increases. Ordinary experience demonstrates this, for while you see objects in marginal vision well enough for many purposes, if you wish to examine them carefully you must look directly at them. It is understandable enough, then, that both long familiarity with the visual appearance of words and familiarity with the setting in which particular words and phrases are likely to occur will aid in the establishment of "higher-order units" [7] which can be apprehended during a single fixation pause. For it must not be thought that the fixation pause represents a period when the finer details of a word or sentence can be examined. Such examination would require additional small eye movements which the recording camera would detect. During a single glance, the eye of the experienced reader focuses upon some key point which is seen most clearly, while other parts of the field of vision are filled in, in part by less clear perceptual cues and in part by inference. Sometimes, as reading progresses, the previous perceptions do not seem to fit in smoothly with what follows so as to make a reasonable whole. In such cases the eye is likely to make a backward sweep, usually fixating on a different point, to check the accuracy of the early perception. At times the reader is aware of these backward movements, but as a rule he is not, since his attention is fixed on what he is reading and not on the means by which the reading is accomplished.

An early study by Buswell [8] shows how each of these factors

[6] See Chapter XVII.

[7] See the discussion of this principle on pp. 457-459.

[8] G. T. Buswell, "Fundamental Reading Habits: A Study of Their Development." *Supplementary Educational Monographs*, No. 21 (Chicago, University of Chicago Press, 1922).

changes with progress through school. At each grade level the eye movements of from eight to nineteen subjects whose reading ability was judged to be about average for the grade in which they were enrolled were photographed, and the results for each grade were averaged. Figure 99 shows the changes from the beginning of first grade to the college level in the average number

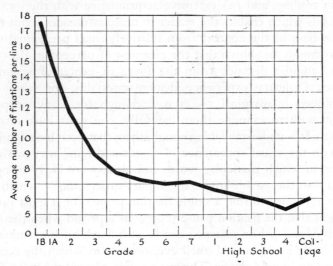

FIG. 99.—CHANGES IN THE AVERAGE NUMBER OF FIXATION PAUSES PER LINE FROM FIRST GRADE TO COLLEGE

(After Buswell.)

of fixations per line. Figure 100 shows the changes in the mean length of the fixation period, and Figure 101 the average number of regressive movements per line. In order to eliminate small irregularities presumably resulting from the fact that the averages are based upon only a small number of cases in each grade, the curves have been "smoothed" by a method known in statistics as "three-point averaging." [9]

[9] This is done by taking as the value for each successive point on the curve the average obtained by adding to the score at that point the scores for the points immediately preceding and following and dividing the sum by three. The values for the initial and final scores are found by multiplying the end score by two, adding the adjacent score, and then dividing by three.

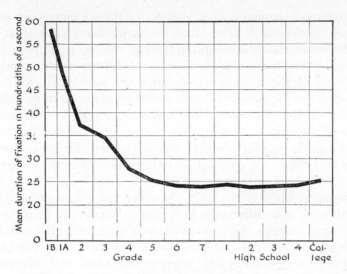

FIG. 100.—CHANGES IN THE AVERAGE DURATION OF FIXATION PAUSES FROM FIRST GRADE TO COLLEGE

(After Buswell.)

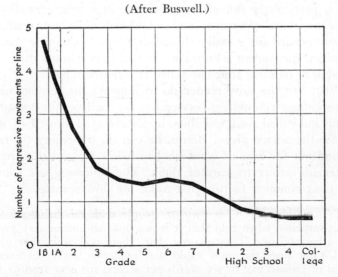

FIG. 101.—CHANGES IN THE AVERAGE NUMBER OF REGRESSIVE MOVE-MENTS PER LINE FROM FIRST GRADE TO COLLEGE

(After Buswell.)

Like most learning curves, all three of these measures are *negatively accelerated* in form, that is, the gains are greatest in the early stages and become progressively smaller as learning proceeds. There is no clear indication of further decrease in the *duration* of the fixation pauses after the sixth grade has been reached, but the *number* of such pauses continues to show a slight falling off until the end of the high-school period. The same is true of the *number of regressive movements.* The small increase shown in the number of fixation pauses by the college students is almost certainly the result of an unfortunate selection of subjects at that level.

But these are averages only. At every age and at each educational level, wide differences in reading efficiency are found when individual students are contrasted with each other. Even among college students it is not unusual to find that some individuals will require as much as four hours to read an amount of material that rapid readers will cover in a single hour. Such persons are handicapped throughout their educational career, but this handicap is particularly felt after entering college where reading requirements are extensive, and additional collateral reading is usually needed for a really thorough mastery of course material. In effect, the student who learns to read in two hours that which previously required four has added two hours to his day.

What can the slow reader do to improve his reading habits? If his college counselling service has the facilities for a diagnosis of his individual reading habits, he should avail himself of it and follow the advice given. If not, he can do something by trying to find out for himself what his bad habits are and then make a systematic effort to correct them. The following are some of the most common factors that make for slow reading.

1. *Inaudible speech movements.* People with this habit are sometimes surprised when told that it is not only an unnecessary practice but a harmful one. They protest that "there isn't any other way to read." But since the most rapid oral reader is unable to exceed a speed of around five or six words per second for easy reading material, while rapid silent reading of the same text may run as high as ten to eleven words per second, it becomes obvious that the habit of repeating the words sets definite limits to reading speed.

2. *Lack of reading experience.* The amount of reading done by many children and adults seems well-nigh unbelievable to the person

who reads slowly and laboriously. Children of high-school age not infrequently complete the reading of one or more books a day in addition to their school work. They take advantage of every free minute to snatch up a book. Thus their reading habits become greatly overlearned. But the slow reader rarely does this. He takes less pleasure in reading because he reads slowly, and so he reads less. While the rapid reader increases his speed through much practice, the slow one is likely to lag further and further behind.

3. *A "perfectionist attitude" in reading; a feeling that nothing may be overlooked. Failure to establish habits of intelligent "skipping."* Some kinds of reading material, to be sure, must be gone over completely and carefully. But much of one's incidental reading includes portions that may be dismissed with just enough rapid scanning to make sure that more careful reading is not required. The rapid reader learns to grasp the general content of a paragraph or even of an entire page by means of a few swift glances. He then proceeds to read it more carefully or passes on to the next section according to his judgment of its importance or interest value. Most slow readers have failed to learn this art. They must plod laboriously through each part before they are able to judge whether or not it was worth the effort to do so.

Thus the person who wishes to improve his rate of reading should do the following things. He should make a definite *effort* to read rapidly. A few minutes spent each day in testing to see how much of the contents of a page of easy fiction can be grasped within a space of time considerably shorter than is usually taken for reading a similar amount is a device that many people have found helpful. Some attention to suppressing any tendency to subvocal speech while reading is also desirable if such habits exist. But most of all, the thing that the great majority of slow readers need is *practice*. And this takes time. The college student who finds it necessary to spend double the time that his room-mate takes in order to read his assignments may insist that he is getting the greater amount of practice of the two. But a history of the amount of reading done previous to college entrance will in almost all cases reveal that the more rapid reader is the one who has already done most reading. Moreover, observation of the daily reading habits of the two students will usually reveal that reading for the one is a comparatively formalized affair, while for the other it is a part of his daily living. The one reads little except as he "settles down to it." The other picks up a book or magazine to occupy any odd moment. The slow reader may be instigated to read by external circumstances, by his recognition that reading is essential to securing an education, but he has not so strong an urge to read just for pleasure. The other does not need an external incentive to induce him to read and to read frequently and for long periods. The problem would be to keep him from reading.[10]

Not only slow reading but the failure to establish useful habits of taking notes or of mentally organizing what has been read in such a way as to make for systematic retention is a handicap to many students. And here the rapid reader is about as likely to be at fault as the one who reads more slowly. To gain the most information from the printed page one must seek actively for it. Many students never pass beyond an attitude of passive receptivity. They are willing to be taught but not eager to learn. They read without active curiosity; their minds do not leap ahead to wonder what is coming nor do they attempt to link that which was previously read to the new material as it is covered. They may labor diligently to memorize isolated facts, but they do not organize these facts into larger wholes. They are like the telegrapher who never progresses beyond the "letter habit" stage. They never gain the freedom and ease that come with higher-order habits of learning.

The efficient learner looks first of all for these larger units. His first reading of an assignment is likely to consist of a quick scanning of the entire article or chapter, for the purpose of ascertaining what it is about, what are the chief points that the author has attempted to bring out. From this brief survey a rough outline is then made to serve as a guide for the second more careful reading. The advantage of this method is twofold. In the first place, by providing the reader with a broad overall view of the entire topic at the beginning, it enables him to see details in their relation to each other and to the whole. As we have seen before, bit-by-bit learning is wasteful of time and effort, and, what is more important, it does not make for real understanding. In the second place, the first survey changes the attitude of the reader. Every one is familiar with the difference between incidental ob-

[10] Needless to say, the relation between speed of reading and attitude toward reading is not perfect. Some persons read slowly but with great enjoyment; others who read rapidly care little for reading. But these are the exceptions. In the majority of cases the rule that the rapid reader is the one who takes greatest pleasure in reading will be found to hold good.

scrvation and searching for specific things. If you have a fairly clear idea of what you are looking for, you are much more likely to find it.[11] In like manner, the person who reads with fairly specific questions in his mind is likely to gain more exact and meaningful information from his reading than the one who merely hopes to learn an indefinite "something" as he goes along.

Note-taking aids retention, and if notes are well organized and reasonably complete they become useful aids in reviewing the field later on.

But knowing how to study does not count for much unless the knowledge is put into practice. Arousing the desire to study, getting the studying started, and keeping it up until the work is done is the really important thing. The same principle holds good with everything else in life. It is activity that counts. The question is: How can activity be aroused and directed toward accomplishing useful results? This process, known as motivation, was discussed in some detail in Chapter VI, but because of its great importance not only in determining success in college but throughout the whole period of life, it will be worth our while to review the subject in somewhat more detail at this point.[12]

THE ORIGIN OF MOTIVES

Warren's [13] definition of a motive is as follows: "*Motive.* A conscious experience or subconscious condition which serves as a factor in determining an individual's behavior or social conduct in a given situation." To *motivate,* according to Warren, is "to serve as an incentive or to provide an incentive for an act." In the less exact language of everyday life we may say that a motive is something that induces a person to act, and to act in a particular manner.

In the process of motivating behavior effectively we may distinguish three general stages. First there is the incentive which starts

[11] The questions at the beginning of each chapter in this book were put there, rather than in the more customary position at the end in order to stimulate and facilitate an attitude of seeking instead of random reading.

[12] The student may find it desirable to reread Chapter VI before going on with this discussion.

[13] Howard C. Warren, *Dictionary of Psychology* (Boston, Houghton Mifflin Co., 1934), p. 171. Quoted by permission of Houghton Mifflin Co.

the activity, secondly the recognition of the goal, and finally the gradual emergence of intermediate goals that act as signals to mark the way. Often, though not always, these intermediate goals appear first as obstacles. But, if the individual learns that these obstacles lie on the road to successful attainment of the goal, they may come to be hailed with delight not because they are obstacles but because they have now taken on a more important meaning as signals. If you are anxious to get home, you may welcome the sight of a particularly bad bit of road ahead of you if it means that you are nearly there. People spend many unpleasant hours with doctors and dentists for the sake of the better physical condition which they hope lies beyond. They labor hard at uncongenial tasks for the sake of some later reward.

CLASSIFYING MOTIVES

If we think of motives as having their start in organic states that are not entirely satisfying, it is evident that the number of such states is legion. Some, like hunger and sex desire, are experienced at times by nearly all living creatures. Some, like the desire for mastery or the desire to explore and manipulate the things in one's environment, seem to vary greatly in strength with different individuals. Whether or not this difference is wholly due to experience we do not know. Some motives, such as fondness for reading, are restricted to human beings; others, such as the unknown urge that starts the migratory flight of birds, are confined to other species.

The difficulty in trying to classify motives according to kind lies in the fact that the nature of the organic states cannot in most cases be observed directly but has to be inferred from the activities to which they give rise and the goals toward which they tend. Sometimes the inference can be made with a good deal of assurance. If an animal that has had no food for some time goes wandering restlessly about, uttering cries and nosing about in every place where it has been accustomed to finding food, we are pretty safe in assuming that it is hungry; and, if, on being shown food, the animal makes for it with all its might, we feel that the assumption is satisfactorily verified. But the motive that causes birds to migrate is still a matter of controversy. If it is the growing scarcity of food, why do some birds migrate, while others, whose food habits are much the same, remain in the north all winter? If it is a matter of temperature, why do some species continue their flights not merely to warmer climates but across the equator?

Earlier psychologists often cited great numbers of acts which were presumed to be due to "original nature" or "instinct" and so required no further investigation. More recently the pendulum has swung in the other direction. The term *instinct* had been made to cover such an astounding multitude of scientific sins that a challenge was inevitable, and this challenge took the form of denying or at least of expressing grave doubt about the very existence of behavior that is wholly unlearned. Even the classic examples of so-called "instinctive" behavior in animals, such as the songs of birds and the mouse-catching habits of kittens, were put under the search-light of the laboratory and were found to be much less fixed and invariable, much more subject to modification through experience than had formerly been supposed.

Consider these examples: Hunger and the sex urge are such universally effective motives in all animals, including man, that we need have no hesitation in saying that to a great extent they are unlearned. But we do learn to recognize and understand them and to delay gratifying them except under certain conditions. And the particular ways in which they are gratified are determined to a great extent by social custom, by experience leading to the formation of individual likes and dislikes, and so on. So learning plays a large part in determining the kind of behavior to which even such "instinctive" drives as these are likely to lead.

Fondness for reading may seem at first thought to be wholly learned. But what about the matter of curiosity, of wanting to find out things, which seems to be one of the most dependable of human motives, if we may judge from the universality of children's questions? And what about the vicarious gratification of emotional and social urges by identifying oneself with the characters in a story, which is unquestionably one of the satisfactions that many people get by reading? Can we be sure that the desire for reading is wholly acquired?

Even if all the facts were known—and most of them are not—it would still be very difficult to decide whether to classify a given motive as *chiefly* instinctive or *chiefly* learned, admitting that both factors are operative. The difficulty lies in deciding to which of a number of conflicting lines of evidence we shall give most weight. What, for example, shall we say of the fact that most civilized persons will die of hunger before attempting to eat each other, while some savage tribes take to cannibalism even when there is no great scarcity of food? Maternal love is a powerful motive in both humans and animals, at least for a certain time after the baby is born. The ferocity of the mother bear in protecting her cubs, the vigorous attack of the mother hen when a stranger threatens to invade her nest are well known. Most of us can cite examples of greater or smaller acts of self-sacrifice and heroism on the part of human mothers in protecting their babies from harm. But what of the unmarried mother, fearful of social disgrace, who drops her baby into the rubbish can at the street corner or who leaves it unprotected in an open hallway on a winter's night?

One might go on multiplying examples indefinitely if it seemed worth while to do so, but the foregoing should be sufficient to illustrate the hazards that arise from any arbitrary method of classifying motives on the basis of their learned or unlearned elements. The important thing is that motives exist and that they incite to activity. But the same motive will not always lead to the same kind of activity in different persons or produce like activity in the same person at different times. Conversely, we cannot always tell from an individual's behavior by what motive he is activated. Even the individual himself may not know, as we shall see later. As a more profitable way of looking at the matter, let us try to see if there are any fairly general qualities, common to all or to most motives, that will help us in our descriptions. Immediately we think of three characteristics—following the fashion set by Wundt and later by Boring [14] we might even call them

---

[14] William Wundt, one of the greatest of German psychologists, under whom a large number of the early American psychologists received their training, proposed a "tri-dimensional" theory of feeling (often extended to include emotions as well), which he hoped would enable one to give a complete account of the psychological dimensions of a feeling just as we state the dimensions of a rectangular solid in terms of its height, breadth, and thickness. According to Wundt, feelings vary in one dimension along a scale running from unpleasantness at one end up to pleasantness at

"dimensions"—the intensity or force of the motive, its clearness, and the remoteness of its goal. With less certainty we might add a factor that might be called *polarity*—depending upon whether the motive is a state of discomfort from which the individual tries to obtain relief, or whether, from an already comfortable state, he catches a glimpse of something that means (so he thinks) even greater satisfaction and is thereby thrown once more into a state of activity. This last distinction is questionable, yet there does seem to be a difference between eating to satisfy hunger and continuing to eat long after the hunger is satisfied because food is offered that makes a special appeal to the palate. So also there seems to be a difference between reading a book from choice and reading the same book for fear of failing in an examination. It is unlikely that the catalogue of qualities or dimensions given here includes all that we need to know about motives, but it does provide us with a useful starting point for description and analysis.

the other, with a neutral zone in the middle. The second dimension has excitement—the greatest state of excitement imaginable—at one extreme, and numbness or depression at the other extreme, with varying degrees of excitement or its lack in between. The third dimension runs from tenseness to release or relaxation. A good many persons have objected to Wundt's scheme both on the grounds that it is incomplete, that feelings have other dimensions or qualities that are equally important (Woodworth in his *Psychology* mentions as examples, desire-aversion and familiarity-strangeness), and on the grounds that in the two dimensions last named the extremes cited are not true opposites of each other. In spite of these imperfections the scheme is an interesting one, for it suggests a method by which the qualities of feelings can be compared with each other, even though the feelings themselves lie in different classes.

Boring makes use of a similar scheme in *The Physical Dimensions of Consciousness* (New York, D. Appleton-Century Co., 1932). Proceeding upon an idea that seems to have originated with Wundt and was further developed by Titchener who, of all American psychologists, was most strongly dominated by the Wundtian tradition, Boring suggests the following as the "dimensions" of consciousness: quality, intensity, extensity, and protensity. Quality refers to such differences as color or the pitch of tones. Intensity has to do with strength or vividness. Extensity refers to differences in size or extension in space, qualities that are most easily perceived by the senses of vision and touch. Protensity refers to time qualities. Titchener added to these a fifth quality, that of clearness or attensity (from attention), but Boring regards this as unnecessary. As we have used the term, clearness of motive is not entirely a function of attention but is to a great extent dependent upon understanding.

THE FIRST DIMENSION—INTENSITY OR FORCE OF THE MOTIVE

That motives differ in the intensity of the reactions they arouse is a matter of common observation. A cat that is very hungry will respond to food much more vigorously than one that is just barely beginning to develop an appetite after its last meal, and it will be more restless and irritable when no food is in sight. A child who is badly frightened will display much more violent behavior than one who is only slightly shy or who finds himself in an unfamiliar situation to which he is not quite certain how he ought to respond. A student who is trying to make the football or the basketball team works harder over his athletics than one who takes physical education only because it is required.

We judge the intensity of the motive by the vigor and force of the activity that it arouses. Perhaps this is not always a fair criterion, but it is the only one we have. Up to a certain limit, there is likely to be a fairly close relationship between the amount of energy expended and the amount of work accomplished, but a very intense motive may arouse a frenzied, disruptive state of activity that exhausts without accomplishment. To return to our old example of the caged cat—if the animal is put into the cage when he is not hungry, he will not scratch and claw at the door when fish is put outside. The door will remain closed, and the cat will accomplish nothing in the way of learning how to open it. But if he is almost starved, the sight and odor of the fish may throw him into such a state of frenzied excitement that he claws all over the cage and does not seem to learn very much, even if he does succeed in getting the door open. He will learn most rapidly, if he is hungry enough to have the sight of the fish arouse a strong and vigorous attack on the door but not so hungry that his behavior loses all coherence and order. Likewise the student who is strongly motivated by a desire to succeed in his work will usually do better than the one who is indifferent, but if the motive becomes too intense, it may get out of hand with the result that the student becomes flustered, excited, worried, is unable to collect his thoughts or direct his attention, and says with truth that "the harder he works the less he knows."

If I were to ask a dozen college students at what point in their studies this condition is most likely to arise, it is probable that more than half of them would answer at once, "Just before examinations!" This brings us to the phenomenon of the "end spurt," which is so often noted in studies of work and fatigue. When the runner is nearing the goal, he gathers his strength for one last mighty effort, and his speed increases in spite of his growing fatigue. Factory workers employed on piece-work usually show an increase in output just before closing time. The student crams for examinations because he knows it is now or never. The sight of the goal, the awareness that the end is near, seems with many persons to have the effect of releasing a greater store of energy. The individual works harder, and in most cases he accomplishes more. But if the sight of the goal has as its chief effect the arousal of a fear of failure, then the disruptive effect described is particularly likely to occur. Fear is a powerful motive of which a very little goes a long way. A large dose is likely to be disastrous.

THE SECOND DIMENSION—CLEARNESS

The hunger motive plays as large a part in arousing a baby or an animal to activity as it does in a grown man, but it operates differently. From his past experience in similar situations a man usually knows what is the matter with him when, around lunch time, he begins to find himself growing restless and irritable. "Better get something to eat," he tells himself, and off he goes. But the baby, if no food is in sight, has no such clear understanding of his difficulty. He cries and frets, he fidgets about, but it takes the actual sight or, if he is very young, the actual taste of food to change his general restlessness and irritability into a clear-cut reaction pattern leading directly toward the goal of foot-getting.

Motives vary in clearness as well as in strength. We have said that we judge the intensity of a motive by the vigor of the reactions it arouses. We judge its clearness by the character of these reactions, by the cutting out of random movements, by the taking on of a definite pattern which runs toward a definite goal. Instead of scattering his energy aimlessly in all directions, the individual seems to converge his efforts toward a certain point.

The actual perception of the goal affects the clearness as well as the intensity of a motive. It seems to focus it, often suddenly and sharply. Contrast the behavior of the hungry cat when no food is in sight with its behavior when food it seen and smelled. Random activity ceases at once, and all its struggles are directed toward getting the food. Or compare the behavior of a white rat the first time he is put into a maze with his behavior after the maze has been learned. At first the maze means nothing to him but a strange place which the hunger motive drives him to explore in a random and undirected fashion. Later on it comes to mean a place leading to a goal where food can be found, and he makes for that goal with all his might. A motive is clear in proportion as some specific goal is perceived or foreseen.

According to their degree of clearness, motives may then lead either to activity that is formless, vague, without clear-cut pattern and relatively ineffective or to particular kinds of activity with most of the random movements eliminated. In the latter case we say with some justification that the individual knows what he wants. He may have difficulty in getting it. He may not choose the method that to you or me seems wisest. He may meet with obstructions, go through a lot of waste movements, and expend a great deal of energy fruitlessly before attaining success, or he may even fail to succeed at all. But, while his movements may be ineffective, they can hardly be described as "random." They are directed toward the goal, though they may be poor ways of getting there.

HOW PURPOSES DIFFER FROM MOTIVES[15]

A motive so clear that the individual knows what he wants to do and something, at least, about how he means to do it is often called a purpose. In human beings a purpose can usually be put into words, and this constitutes a rough way of distinguishing between motives which are vague and unanalyzed, leading to activity that is poorly adapted to accomplishing useful results, and purposes which are by comparison clear-cut, leading to effective

---

[15] For an extremely stimulating discussion of purposive action, the student should consult E. C. Tolman, *Purposive Behavior in Animals and Men* (New York, D. Appleton-Century Co., 1931).

action. Of course there is no sharp distinction between the two, for motives gradually crystallize into purposes, and purposes as well as motives vary in clearness and in the definiteness of resulting action. But the verbal test gives us some idea about where to draw the line.

Purposes differ from motives in another way. All along, in our discussions of intelligence, we have pointed out how greatly the use of symbols facilitates intelligent action. When we put our motives into words, what we have really done is to reduce them to symbols by means of which we can plan our actions in advance as an architect works out the design of his house on paper before actually building it up in brick and stone. As long as he sticks to his paper, it is an easy matter to modify his design, to compare one plan with another, to correct errors and supply omissions. Once the building is under way, it is a different matter, for mistakes made then are difficult and costly to correct. As long as we are governed solely by motives which we cannot understand or refuse to recognize, we are not likely to get full value for our labor. We may work just as hard or harder; we may stick to it as long; but we are like the builder without a plan who may toil long hours in the heat of the day, carry heavy loads, exhaust himself and his resources, without getting much of a house in the end.

Do animals show purposive action? The answer to this question obviously depends to a large extent upon our definition. If we draw the line between motives and purposes at the point of verbalization and refuse to admit the existence of a purpose that cannot be expressed in words, then we need have no hesitation in saying that animals are activated only by motives, that they have no purposes. But there is an intermediate condition. When food is placed just outside the bars of a cage, the behavior of the cat inside is certainly directed toward a very definite end, as anybody can see, even if the cat himself is not able to tell about it in words. Such behavior has in it some but not all of the characteristics of what in man we call purposive action. It resembles purposive action in its direct attack upon the end to be obtained which leaves neither the observer nor, it is safe to assume, the animal himself in much doubt as to what that end is. If a hungry human being is put into a cage with a fastening which is as hard for him to open as the one used on the cat's cage is for the cat, the human being's behavior may not differ greatly from that of the animal. Certainly it will involve a good deal of ineffective activity at the concrete trial and error level. Except for the single matter of speech, animal behavior looks to the outsider to be about as "purposeful" as human behavior when the goal or something that stands for the goal is actually in sight. But without the immediate stimulus of an objective that can be seen, smelled, felt, heard, or tasted, animal behavior gives little evidence of anything that can be regarded as purpose. The normal intelligent adult, on the contrary, forms many of his purposes when no concrete stimulus is present. He lies in bed at night, and, in spite of darkness and silence, he maps out what he is going to do the next day, the next year or, projecting his purposes still further into the future, he plans for the life and professional career of his infant son. Unknown to any one but himself, he carries these uncompleted purposes about with him, remodeling them from time to time, correcting their imperfections, always waiting for the appointed time for putting them into action.

THE THIRD DIMENSION—
NEARNESS OR REMOTENESS OF THE GOAL

The ability to act in accordance with remote rather than immediate goals constitutes one of the major differences between man and animal, between adult and child, between the successful person and the failure. The college student who puts off his preparation until examination is imminent, for whom the movie of to-day is a more powerful lure than the prospect of the future position for which he should be preparing, who is chronically "broke" because he spends his money on trivialities, who, in general, is unable to act in accordance with any considered plan because he is so completely dominated by his impulses of the moment is not likely to have a successful career in college or in life. Efficient and well-organized living requires long-range planning. It demands purposes, ideals, goals that do not shift about with every accidental circumstance. Changing conditions may and often do make it necessary to alter the means by which a goal is sought; occasionally it may happen that the goal itself must be changed. But these things are of little consequence if the changes are made deliberately and in order to conform to some major purpose in terms of which the individual is shaping his life.

In the sculptor's hands a formless lump of clay takes on meaning and beauty. The same clay, buffeted about by rain and wind or kneaded by the unskillful hands of a little child remains a useless and inchoate mass. In like manner a life without plan or one in which the only plans are the brief and fleeting impulses instigated by the events of the moment is not likely to have much value for society or to yield real satisfaction for the one who lives it. A lasting design is needed.

CONFLICTING MOTIVES

All of you have had the experience of being obliged to choose between two actions, only one of which could be carried out. What usually happens in these cases is that you hesitate for a time, comparing the advantages on each side until one becomes dominant over the other and the choice is made.

Suppose the problem is that of deciding on your life work. After a little consideration the choice usually narrows itself down to two or three alternatives for which the relative advantages and disadvantages seem so equally balanced that the decision becomes very difficult. As far as you or your vocational counselors can find out, you are about as well fitted for one as for the other. The training requires about the same length of time in each case, but, since it differs in kind, preparation for the one occupation would not fit you to enter the other. The choice has to be made in advance. You compare the probable number of openings in each field, the usual rate of advancement, the financial reward, the attractiveness of the work, and so on. Finally you make a choice. And now comes an interesting point—if you are a normal, healthy-minded person, the very fact that your choice has been made adds tremendous weight to the side on which the choice fell. In addition to all its original points of desirability, the occupation chosen is now *your* occupation. It is a part of yourself, of your own personality, and so you naturally see its good points, and the disadvantages that occurred to you in the beginning fade into insignificance. This is as it should be.

But you have all met persons whose choices rarely seem to work out that way. When forced to make a decision they have great difficulty in doing so, and no sooner do they make up their minds than the advantages of the opposite side pop up once more, and the whole question is reopened. We say of such people that "they do not know their own minds," and, like many other popular sayings, this one has much truth in it.

The trouble with people who cannot stick to a decision is, in most cases, that they do not know their own motives. Frequently this is because they refuse to know them. Some motives have more social prestige than others, and most of us like to think that all our actions begin with motives that we regard as desirable. So we refuse to recognize any others. But no matter whether our motives are unclear to us because we have not learned to know to what goal they lead or because we refuse to look them squarely in the face, the result of their lack of clearness is that, instead of giving rise to behavior that runs straight to a goal, they result in constantly shifting behavior, in changing decisions, and lack of purpose. Every one is activated by many motives, and it is inevitable that these motives should often conflict with each other. But if we know what our motives are, if we bring them out into the open where the conflict can be seen, it will sooner or later be brought to a close. It is fighting in the dark that makes the trouble.

Conflicting motives, however, are not the only causes of difficulty. There is also the danger that motives may run over into overt action before they have become organized into large enough units to accomplish much. The person who must gratify each little desire as soon as it arises; who cannot subordinate his desire for candy and movies to his need for a new suit; who is unable, in turn, to refrain from buying the suit on credit, even though he knows that he is not likely to be able to meet the payments, and who thereafter borrows from his friends as long as their good-nature holds out is likely, sooner or later, to find himself in a good deal of trouble. When every little immediate motive takes over the entire control of the organism and then leaves it to run wild until a new motive comes to the fore, not much that is worth while is likely to result.

Conflicts between the various activities of which an organism

is capable may then occur either at the intra-organic level as conflicts between motives or at the external level in the form of unorganized and conflicting actions. Conflicts between motives result
in delayed action, but if the motives are clearly understood, the
delay may be utilized in organizing them along the lines of a
major purpose. If they remain confused and unclear, the conflicts
between motives delay action without accomplishing anything
useful by the delay. Since this state of delayed action is neither
comfortable nor satisfying, the chances are that sooner or later
one or another of the motives will get its way, and some impulsive
action will be carried out.

The best way to solve the difficulties that come when motives
conflict is to try to organize them into larger units that work
together instead of separately. This process or one closely related
to it is sometimes known as *sublimation*. The idea underlying the
theory of sublimation is that it is possible to transfer the energy
or drive aroused by a certain motive to an overt activity. According to this theory, a person, unable to gratify in the normal way
such a fundamental motive as sex, may, by some method that
is not quite clear, succeed in attaching some other form of external expression to the organic state that is the normal motive
for sex activity. So the disappointed lover turns to art, poetry,
or some other form of creative work as an outlet for the sex drive.
Recent investigation, however, makes it seem very doubtful that
motives work themselves out in just that way. If they did, we
should expect the disappointed lover to write better poetry or
paint better pictures than the one whose love affairs have run
along smoothly, and there is no evidence at all that he does. Sublimation probably means nothing more than the formation of a
major purpose on a practical rather than a fantastic basis. It
comes as the result of understanding our motives, organizing as
many of them as possible to contribute to this purpose and reducing the others to a subordinate level at which they will least
interfere with its accomplishment.

There are other less desirable ways of handling conflicting motives. One is by day-dreaming. Motives that cannot be allowed
to run over into overt action may find an outlet in this way. If
the day-dream is used as a substitute for action, it becomes harmful. If it takes the form of an imaginary achievement of the goal

for which one is actually striving, it may, like the sight of the goal itself, spur one on to greater effort. Probably few great accomplishments have been brought to successful issue without anticipation of the end to help one over the hard places. But the day-dream does not dispose of a motive. Thinking about appetizing food when one is hungry does not lessen the hunger; if anything it increases it. So, when day-dreaming serves as a substitute for actions impossible or undesirable to carry out in actual life, it does not bring conflicts to an end but prolongs them instead.

Another common method is known as *rationalization*. Rationalization means that when you want to do something you know is unwise, you try to convince yourself and others that there is some good reason for doing it. Literally it means the building or constructing of reasons. You say that you feel you really should play bridge to-night instead of preparing your mathematics assignment because the other three people will be so disappointed if you fail them. Or you tell yourself that this particular necktie is such a bargain that you had better buy it even though you do not need it and do need the money for a new notebook. When the rationalization is delayed until after the act has been carried out and particularly when it is used as a way of justifying ourselves in the eyes of some one else it is popularly known as "alibiing."

Still another way of disposing of motives that hurt one's self-respect is by refusing to look at them, by denying their existence. This, too, is undesirable, largely because it does not work. If the motive is real, it cannot be got rid of by calling it a myth. Better to acknowledge it and then, having done so, to decide frankly that the satisfaction that might come from gratifying it would not be worth the price. It is a mistake to feel that every motive must work itself out in action. It is you that have to be satisfied, and you, as a total and lasting personality, count for much more than any of your temporary states. Real satisfaction does not come from yielding to every impulse but from organizing one's impulses toward a unified end.

MOTIVATION AS A FACTOR IN COLLEGE SUCCESS

In this long discussion of motivation we may seem to have wandered a long way from the college student. It is time for us to return to him.

When we say that a student is failing in his college work because he is not properly motivated, we may mean any one of a number of things. Perhaps he is so strongly motivated toward something else that his studies have little attraction for him. If we put a piece of fish on one side of the cage and an apple on the other, our hungry cat will struggle to get the fish and will disregard the apple, no matter how red and juicy it may be. As long as the fish is there, he will not even pay much attention to a bowl of bread and milk, although he would welcome it if the stronger attraction were removed. In like manner, even students who are not without interest in their class work may neglect it for the sake of other activities that interest them more strongly.

In some cases these students have a real purpose toward which they are aiming, but it is one to which their studies make no particular contribution. It may be that they have been forced by their parents into preparing for one profession when all their interests lie in another direction. More often, however, the trouble is that they lack any single dominating purpose, and so they veer about with every new interest that presents itself. They need the ballast that comes from looking beyond the little gratifications of the moment to the more important goals that lie further ahead. When one is on his way to the big game the moving-picture houses along the road have few attractions for him.

Apart from counter-attractions, however, motivation varies in degree of intensity. We all know people who seem to have little interest in anything. In college they take no part in extra-curricular activities, pay little attention to sports, and do not go out much socially. They make few friends and no enemies. They have no particular hobbies. They attend classes and prepare their assignments in a docile but unenthusiastic manner; they rarely ask questions and take no part in class discussion. They never read anything beyond the formal assignments, except, perhaps, the daily newspaper and a little light fiction. They do not always fail completely, but their accomplishments are far below their abilities.

There are a number of possible causes for this condition. Sometimes it has a physical basis. Unrecognized infections of various kinds may sap one's energy to such an extent that no attainment seems worth the effort it would cost. Sometimes it is the result of repeated frustration. Persons who have too often been prevented from doing what they set out to do are likely, sooner or later, to reach a stage at which success seems impossible. So they build up all sorts of protective mechanisms. They may take a "sour grapes" attitude, telling themselves and others that none of the purposes for which people work are worth while. Their apparent indifference may be only a pose to cover up the lack of self-confidence which keeps them from making a real effort. Or they may have learned to find satisfaction in an imaginary world where they accomplish such wonderful things with so little effort that real life seems pale and insipid by contrast. Perhaps they have become discouraged because of unfavorable comparison with some more able relative or friend. Since even their best falls short of the other person's accomplishment, they come to be ashamed of it and stop competing, perhaps with the half-formed thought that, if they take no part in the race, no one will know what poor runners they are.

Often, too, the trouble with these students is much the same as with the group previously described. They see no goal ahead of them. They see no reason for working because their work seems to lead nowhere. They have not decided on any profession, and they are content to let their parents provide for their needs. Their intellectual curiosity has never been awakened. From early childhood, information has been showered upon them faster than they have been able to use it. They have never had to fend for themselves even in little matters, and they have never been encouraged to plan for themselves. Now, though they are nearing maturity, they still wait to be told what to do.

Unrecognized motives, motives that the student is unwilling to acknowledge even to himself, sometimes wreak havoc with his accomplishment. The sex motive, particularly in girls, who, more often than boys, have been led to feel that sex desire should be immediately suppressed as something unworthy of their higher selves, is an outstanding example. Many girls, driven by motives which they are unwilling or afraid to face, rush madly from one activity to another, unable to settle down to any one steady purpose, knowing all the time that they are getting nowhere. Their lessons are poorly prepared, not because they are incapable of doing good work but because they have no purpose in studying. It is easier for boys to harness the sex motive to the goal of their life 'work, for good work in college increases their chances of securing a good position, and this, in turn, will make it possible for them to marry later on. But with the girls the connection between succeeding in college and securing a husband are not so direct. With changing social conditions in which the trend is toward joint support of the home by husband and wife, at least during the first few years after marriage, a time seems likely to come when girls, as well as boys, may find that preparation for a career is at the same time the pathway to marriage. But in the past this has not been the case. There is little doubt that much of the difference between the sexes in their achievements in the arts and science is attributable to the fact that in men the drive toward a career has been given increased strength by its integration with the sex drive, while in women the two motives have acted in opposition to each other.

CHILDHOOD MOTIVES AND ADULT PURPOSES

Children and adults differ from each other in many ways, few of which are more significant than the differences in the motives by which their activity is aroused and directed. Children work for goals that are near at hand. They sometimes make plans for the future, but their visions of distant goals are nebulous. A glimpse of something nearer at hand soon disperses them. They are deceived by perspective. The mole-hill in the immediate foreground shuts out the view of the mountains in the distance. But as maturity is approached the normal, well-balanced individual becomes more nearly able to appraise his goals on the basis of their true worth, with less attention to their nearness or remoteness.

How shall we measure maturity? Not by years or by stature, not by the franchise, the marriage certificate, or the college degree. The mark of maturity is the ability to organize one's life for a purpose and to hold steadily to the road whether it be rough or smooth. Some persons reach this stage early; others never arrive at it. The student who finds himself nearing the end of his college life without having formed any plans by which he can direct his future will do well to pause and consider the matter, for a purpose in life is something for which there is no substitute. Neither wealth nor education can take its place.

FINDING YOUR NICHE IN LIFE

Donald E. Super, *The Dynamics of Vocational Adjustment* (New York, Harper and Bros., 1942), pp. xiii + 286.

This book was written by a man who has had extensive experience in helping college students to ascertain the kinds of vocation in which they are most likely to win happiness and success, and to select the college courses necessary for training in their chosen field. Although the book will have special appeal for those who have not yet decided upon a line of work, those who have already made their choice will also find much information of interest in its fifteen compactly written chapters.

In concise but clear language the author discusses a number of the most important factors which contribute to vocational success. He shows how differing interests as well as differing abilities play a part in determining the kind of job for which one is best suited. He calls attention to a number of economic factors which the student should take into account in making his choice, such as technological changes, depletion of natural resources, the effect of business cycles, and similar matters that are too often overlooked by the inexperienced person. He describes the methods used by modern student counselors and points out the danger of too exclusive dependence upon any one line of evidence. For sound advice, it is necessary to have information from many sources. The student's health and physical vigor, his level of intelligence, his special aptitudes and abilities, his interests and personality characteristics, as well as many other factors must all be considered.

A brief but helpful chapter on how to secure a job is followed by an equally important discussion of the difficulties experienced by many persons in adjusting to their first job, and of ways of meeting these problems. The bibliographies at the end of the chapters suggest additional sources which may be consulted for more detailed information on topics of special interest to the individual student.

Chapter XX

MATURITY

How does the psychological definition of maturity differ from the legal definition? From the anatomical definition?

What differences are likely to appear between one's own judgments of his personality characteristics and those made by acquaintances?

What do you think are the most important factors in determining the kind of goals for which one strives? Why is it important to choose one's goals?

About what proportion of marriages in the United States end in divorce? What are some of the main factors leading to unhappiness in marriage?

Are short engagements usually wise?

Do people who are "opposites" usually attract each other?

Why do some people believe in fortune-telling?

How, in general, do we acquire our beliefs?

What are some of the devices employed for building up the prestige of a person or an institution? How have these been employed in Nazi Germany?

How can freedom best be safeguarded?

THE NATURE OF MATURITY

Although it is customary to think of the beginning of physical maturity in terms of the age at which physical growth ceases, the attainment of social and psychological maturity is not so easily dated. It is not the same thing as intellectual maturity which, as we have seen, is reached somewhere in the late teens, though this does not mean that you cannot learn a great deal and become much wiser as the years go by. Nor can we properly regard it as synonymous with legal maturity, which in most states is officially placed at the twenty-first birthday. Psychological maturity, in the broad sense, involves the total personality, as indicated in the familiar words of Paul to the Corinthians: "When I was a child I spake as a child, I understood as a child, I thought as a child, but when I became a man I put away childish things."

It is this "putting away of childish things," of feeling oneself to be an adult, ready to assume adult responsibilities and take one's place in the world of men and women, that marks the boundary between the youth and the man, between the girl and the woman. Some reach this point early, some not until much later. Some never really attain it. But maturity, like every other stage in the growth process, is essential for a healthy life. Without experiencing it to the full, in all its phases and aspects, many of life's chief satisfactions are irrevocably lost. For this reason it is of the highest importance that every young person, as he approaches adult years, shall have developed the kind of attitudes and habits that will enable him to make the most of the brief quarter-century or less during which his energy and abilities continue at a high level and when opportunity for success in his chosen field is at its zenith. The period between the early twenties and the middle or late forties is also the time when, for most people, personal and family life becomes stabilized into a more or less fixed pattern, when marriage takes place and children are born. Even for those who do not marry, this period is normally marked by a process of "settling down" to a more or less definite mode of life.

The physical differences between the adolescent—a term which literally means one who is in process of becoming an adult—and one who has already achieved adult status are familiar to all of us. A quarter of a century's intensive research has also provided us with detailed information about the maturation of intellectual and motor abilities. But we know less about the maturation of the personality in a broad sense. For this reason, two studies which have made use of very different methods for getting at this important question are of interest. The earlier of these, by Willoughby [1] had as its primary aim the development of a scale for measuring emotional maturity. Willoughby's concept of emotional maturity is based upon his "belief that there is an entity or group of entities in personality, closely correlated with capacity for happy, full and effective living, which consists essentially in a loosening and slipping away of attitudes and interests which are tolerable in children but fatal in adults; these attitudes appear to consist in an over-preoccupation with the self and its satisfactions, a too great absorption of the field of attention with the ego." [2]

Willoughby's method of deriving his scale values was through the use of expert opinion. More than a hundred persons, chiefly clinical psychologists, experienced social workers, and psychiatrists were asked to rate each of a long list of short paragraphs describing various ways of reacting to life situations according to the degree of personal maturity thereby suggested. For the final scale, sixty items about which there was little disagreement in rating and which, in the opinion of the judges, varied greatly in indicated maturity value were selected. Following are examples of items receiving either very high or very low scale values. [3]

Very high values were assigned to these items:

S (the subject) chooses a course of action with reference to maximum long-time satisfaction of the entire group of persons involved. (Score 8)
S welcomes opportunity for exercise of precise or realistic thinking. (Score 7)
S welcomes legitimate association with members of the opposite sex and is not ashamed, fearful, or unduly preoccupied with the topic of sex. (Score 9)
S is clear-cut in his decisions; when it is necessary to relinquish an objective he relinquishes or postpones it entirely; when retaining it he retains all of it and without regret. (Score 7)

The following items received low scores:

S chooses his courses of action with reference to his own immediate satisfaction. (Score 1)

[1] Raymond R. Willoughby, "A Scale of Emotional Maturity," *J. Soc. Psychol.*, 1932, 3: 3-36.
[2] *Op. cit.*, p. 3. Quoted by permission of The Journal Press.
[3] Slight changes in wording have been made in a few instances for the sake of brevity or clearness, but the essential meaning has not been altered.

S characteristically appeals for help in the solution of his problems. (Score 1)

S's day-dreams usually represent the reversal of situations that are humiliating in the real world. (Score 2)

S passes rapidly from one interest or attachment to another. (Score 2)

S is jealous of his spouse; feels insecure when any other interest claims spouse's attention. (Score 1)

The scale was tried out by having two or more persons make independent ratings of each of a group of subjects with whom they were acquainted. A fair amount of agreement between judges was obtained in each of several trials of this kind. Self-ratings were also secured for some subjects. Although the amount of agreement between the self-ratings and those assigned by acquaintances was greater than would be expected by chance, it was usually lower than that between two outside observers. When the point of view changes, perception also changes, and while it is true that no two people are likely to stand in exactly identical positions with reference to a third person, or to have quite the same opportunities for observing him in many different situations, nevertheless such differences between two outside reporters are likely to be considerably less than that between an outsider and a person reporting about himself. Which of the two types of information is the more dependable is a debatable question. Certainly the only person with whom one is constantly associated is oneself. No one else has direct access to his thoughts and feelings, his dreams and aspirations. But on the other hand, it may be that by no one else is he so likely to be deluded. Many people refuse to look their own faults or weakness squarely in the face; some, through mistaken ideas of modesty or as a means of gaining attention, may magnify them unduly.

The method of self-report was used by Weitzman [4] who gave a questionnaire calling for information about a good many different aspects of personal responsibility and outlook and amount of participation in various specified activities to 899 young men and women between the ages of sixteen and twenty-four years.

[4] Ellis Weitzman, "A Study of Social Maturity in Persons Sixteen through Twenty-four Years of Age," *J. Genet. Psychol.*, 1944, 64: 37-66.

Slightly more than half were college students; of the remainder, 152 were employed in various types of industry, 101 were unemployed and not in school, and 129 were enrolled in CCC camps.[5] Inasmuch as the age period covered represents, for most persons at least, the transitional period between youth and maturity, Weitzman was interested in ascertaining what differences would be found between the older and younger members of the group. Because the items included in the questionnaire deal with so wide a variety of topics, it is not easy to summarize his findings, but certain trends may be noted.

As a rule, the older and presumably more mature subjects tended to report moderate rather than extreme participation in most social activities. They go to dances, movies, and so on "occasionally" rather than "frequently" or "never." They also indicate a narrowing of interest in members of the opposite sex which suggests that they are turning to thoughts of marriage. To the question, "How many very close friends of the opposite sex have you at present?" the older subjects were more likely to reply "one or two," while the younger ones frequently reported either "none at all" or "five or more." The older persons also indicated more thought for the future. More of them were saving money systematically, and more had assumed complete charge of their own expenditures. They gave more attention to their health by means of periodic physical and dental examinations. They assumed more personal responsibility for their own affairs along with a reasonable but not excessive concern for the affairs of other people.

When the individual papers were scored on the basis of weights derived from the differences between the responses of older and younger subjects to each of the separate items, it was found that there was a wide range of difference in the "maturity" scores made by persons of the same age. Among subjects of the same chronological age, the employed persons made the highest average score, the college students next, the CCC enrollees next while the unemployed ranked much lower than any of the other groups

[5] Civilian Conservation Corps. This was a government project set up during the depression years of the early thirties to provide supervised employment for youths unable to secure positions in industry.

of corresponding age. Here we have some evidence that personality maturation is related to vocational success, and that not all persons achieve a mature personality at the same age. Some, perhaps, may never do so, in spite of physical and intellectual ability that at least falls within the normal range.

Thus, in spite of the differences in their methods, the two investigators arrive at much the same general conclusions. Maturity is not just a matter of the number of years one has lived. It depends upon the kind of personality that is developed during those years; the extent to which one is able to think and act for oneself and with others. The truly mature person is at once highly independent and highly socialized. He has built up a system of values that is internally consistent; he chooses his goals and abides by the choice.

THE VALUE-PATTERN

For the vast majority of people, the life pattern established between the ages of twenty to thirty-five years will be maintained without radical change until old age. The variety of these patterns is almost endless, for they differ in so many ways. They differ in respect to physical ease or hardship. They differ in respect to output of energy and the goals toward which that energy is directed. They differ in the amount and kind of social relationships that are involved, and they differ in respect to the range of different experiences included within the life span. For some people the pattern of life is simple and repetitive. Their entire lives are spent in the same place with the same people. They engage in the same round of daily activities and for the most part they think the same thoughts. For others, the very essence of the life pattern is its changefulness.

Why these differences? It is unquestionably true that in part they arise from differences in opportunity. But there can be no doubt that to an even greater extent they are the result of differences in the goals which people set for themselves and in the singleheartedness with which they strive to attain those goals, in their willingness to relinquish lesser ends in order to achieve a main objective. Differences in manner of living arise first of all from differences in the *values* that people place upon different kinds of objectives.

A study made by Woodruff [6] of certain systems of values held by college students is illuminating. Woodruff prepared three sets of short paragraphs having to do with three different aspects of life. The first series dealt with the kind of place in which one would choose to live and work. The second series described various kinds of fraternity groups, and the student was asked to indicate the one which he would prefer to join. The third series described various kinds of occupations, not in terms of the kind of skills required but in terms of such attributes as financial return, personal recognition, amount of time and effort demanded, and so on.

The descriptions in each class resembled real life situations in that none of them was represented as being wholly desirable or completely free from drawbacks. Thus the student was required to balance the pros and cons in each case and to make his decision in terms of those attributes that to him seemed of greatest importance. Below are two sample paragraphs from each of the three groupings.[7] Six additional paragraphs in each class were also included but are not reproduced here. Students were asked to rank the eight paragraphs in each list in order of their choice.

I. *Choice of community*

1. This place offers rather unusual opportunities both in your line of work and for additional income in other ways, and the chances of making money fast are very good. Some have even made fortunes here. There is very little society life, and scanty chance for political activity, as a powerful clique is well entrenched and does not permit interference. There is a fair school system and the townspeople are, on the whole, progressive and successful. Most people are admittedly here for the business opportunities, and many plan to move elsewhere when they have enough to retire on. Keeping up with the competition requires vigorous attention to work, and allows little time for the armchair or afternoons on the beach, golf, etc.

6. This place has an ideal climate and quiet parks and beaches where one can relax and get away from worry and strain. There are a number of good restaurants and other places which offer many of the aspects of comfortable living. Life moves at a comfortable pace.

[6] Asahel Davis Woodruff, *A Study of the Directive Factors in Individual Behavior* (Private Edition, distributed by the University of Chicago Libraries, Chicago, 1941), pp. 165.

[7] Quoted by permission of Dr. Woodruff.

You will have a decent income without becoming wealthy, and there will be a haphazard social program of a very informal nature. Political activities are looked on as a necessary nuisance. There is an attitude of satisfaction with the world as it is.

II. *Choice of fraternity* (*or sorority*) *group.* (It is presumed that the student will live in the fraternity house while he remains in college).

2. This group has a long record of successful control of student activities and campus politics. It has maintained a rather close circle with this control in mind. The members have neglected their "house," which is obviously an old and much used place. They make little effort to improve themselves in less practical ways and are content with their fraternal activities as long as they dominate the important campus positions. They are friendly toward everyone, but their real friendships are confined to their own group. They engage in social activities only incidentally.

6. This group does the exciting thing whenever possible. In their social events anything can happen. A timid soul would not be at home here. Some of their activities get them into trouble with the school officers, but the group invariably gets away with it. The members have options on some very interesting and exciting summer vacation jobs in various parts of the country which they pass along to the incoming members as the older ones graduate. Their close friends are mostly within their own organization. They are not interested in being social leaders or campus politicians. Their house is not outstanding. They want members who like to live fast and can stand excitement.

III. *Choice of vocation.*

4. This work seems to develop the "personality" of those who engage in it successfully. It involves a type of experience which cultivates self-confidence and the ability to dominate a situation when necessary. Since you cannot settle down in this vocation, your close friends will not be numerous. Few become wealthy in this work, but you will be able to live comfortably. The work usually has no particularly beneficial effect on mankind. There can be little of the ordinary type of home life for you in it.

8. In this work you will be with an organization whose record in the care of its personnel is outstanding. One's position is safe under all circumstances except dishonesty. A retirement plan provides a good life income for retired employees. Depressions have no influence; they do not cause "layoffs." The income is sufficient for decent living, but the work does not develop the individual much. It is interesting

but your schedule frequently interrupts your free time. You work with a relatively small number of people and meet few new ones. You need never worry about being out of a job.

The strong points in each of these hypothetical opportunities are underscored.[8] These have been selected in such a way that in the twenty-four situations described, each of twelve "values" is stressed in two different settings. The values considered are as follows: wealth, society, political power, social service, home life, comfort, religion, security, personal development, excitement, friends, and intellectual activity. Woodruff does not present his results in such a way as to enable us to say how college students as a group ranked these objectives, but it is clear from the data presented that each of them was given first rank by some students.

The child's sense of values shifts with his expanding horizon. But as maturity approaches, more lasting choices must be made. Upon the nature of these choices, one's later happiness and success will largely depend. How, then, is one to choose wisely and well?

Each of us must answer this question for himself. The choice is not always an easy one, but it will be simplified if we are willing to face the matter of personal values fairly and honestly. What do you truly regard as of most importance for your personal happiness? Do not be misled into thinking that there is but one pattern of living that is superior to all others. Happiness has many facets, and the highest "good" for one is not necessarily the best for all. The thing that is of major importance is to be clear as to what you most want, and to be willing to make whatever sacrifices of less important things are necessary in order to achieve your major objective. The main choice, the choice of *values*, must always be made before secondary choices, the selection of *means*, can be made wisely.

Suppose you are planning a vacation trip. You do not begin by asking, "Shall I take Highway 35 or Highway 16? Or perhaps it would be better not to drive; perhaps I might better go by train or by bus." No; your first question is, "Where shall I go?" This choice may not be easy, for there are several places that offer attractions. But you must decide on the place before you can reasonably consider routes or manner of travel.

[8] Underscoring by Woodruff.

So it is with the choices that have to do with your way of living. Unfortunately the basis for decision here is not always so obvious. Often an opportunity appears that looks enticing for the moment but that does not lead in the direction of one's main interest. Now if you know what that interest is, if your system of values is reasonably clear in your mind, you will be in a position to judge rationally as to the wisdom of taking a little excursion along a side road. Under those circumstances, you are not likely to be tempted too far because you know that you are not on the main track. The danger comes in not having planned your route, in not knowing just where you want to go, and in trusting to luck to bring you to a good ending.

MARITAL HAPPINESS: THE WISE CHOICE OF A MATE

That an appallingly large number of marriages end in divorce or separation is attested by court records. The Report of the United States Census states that during the year 1940 there were approximately 1,656,000 marriages and 264,000 divorces [9] granted in the United States as a whole. Thus approximately one marriage out of every six ends in the divorce court. Moreover, in 78.3 per cent of all divorces, the marriage was terminated in less than five years; in 33.5 per cent, in less than one year. The most common legal basis for divorce was "desertion," which was claimed in 42.6 per cent of all cases. But the legal claim obviously tells us little. Why should so many young people who, only a few short months before, had believed themselves to be passionately in love with each other become so disillusioned that they see no way out except running away? Surely no young person anticipates such a disappointing outcome of the marriage upon which he embarks so joyfully and with such high faith in the rightness of his choice. Where, then, lies the fault?

Obviously the answer to this question is not a simple one. In

[9] These figures are estimates since some districts failed to report. The latest year for which complete official records were secured for the country as a whole is 1932. In that year there were 981,903 marriages and 160,338 divorces. (Cf. *Marriage and Divorce, 1932*, Eleventh Annual Report of the Bureau of the Census (Washington, D. C., Government Printing Office, 1934), pp. 29.)

most cases of marital unhappiness not one but many factors are involved, and the most important factor in the unhappiness of one couple is not necessarily significant for all. In spite of this difficulty, a number of people have hoped that by careful study of the characteristics of happily married couples in contrast with those who, by their own admission, are unhappy in their marriage and who state that if they had it to do over again they would not remarry the same person, some facts that might be practically helpful to young adults in the selection of their future mates could be obtained. Skeptics, to be sure, have questioned whether such a guide, even if it existed, would be consulted by young people who are, or believe themselves to be, in love, inasmuch as in our culture mutual attraction—"falling in love"—has long been emphasized as the primary requisite for marriage. Romantic literature, the stage and the screen, the poet and the artist have stressed the love interest, often to the exclusion of all other factors. And there can be no doubt that love is important. But what many people fail to realize is that the correlation between falling in love and staying in love is far from perfect. And it is a measure of the likelihood that two people will *stay* in love, rather than a measure of their present attraction for each other that is needed. Probably most, if not all, of the divorced couples as well as those who, although unhappily married, have not sought relief in divorce, were once in love with each other. How, then, is the young person to distinguish between evanescent attraction and the love that will endure for a lifetime?

Let the cynics say what they will, the healthy-minded young man or woman of to-day is interested in this question. "Marriage courses" in our colleges and universities almost invariably draw a large enrollment, and the popularity of such courses, if the subject matter is well selected, is increasing as inhibitions and embarrassment which at first tended to prevent some students from registering have gradually disappeared.

The complexity of the marriage relationship is so great that it is not surprising that no simple or sure guide to the choice of a mate has been found. Yet some progress has been made, at least in the direction of noting factors that lessen or increase the probabilities of happiness in marriage even though they do not insure it. That mutual attraction before marriage is of first importance need not be stressed, for without such attraction the likelihood that marriage will be entered upon is small. What young people are less likely to remember is that mutual attraction alone is not enough, since it so often fails to survive the first few months of marriage.

Of the many studies on marital happiness and unhappiness that have appeared, two only will be considered here.[10] They have been selected because they are based upon careful study of large groups of married couples who were at least reasonably representative of the upper middle-class population of to-day. These subjects were not "abnormal." They were like the people you meet every day, and, like them, some were more happy in their marriage than others. Their degree of happiness was judged by their scores on a questionnaire [11] which was filled out separately by each person concerned. Much care was taken to insure that individual privacy was respected. Questionnaires were not signed, and husbands and wives worked independently of each other. Thus the chief barriers to frankness were removed, and the internal evidence of the reports suggested that most, at least, responded as honestly as they were able. The amount of difference in reported happiness is indicated by the fact that in Terman's study, on a scale allowing a possible "happiness" score of 87, the actual range of scores made by the 792 couples (1,584 persons) whom he studied was from 2 to 87.

In both studies it was found that the couples who reported happiness in marriage differed significantly from the unhappily married in a number of respects. Looking first into the early histories of these persons, it was found that many more of the unhappily married reported unhappy marriages on the part of their parents and stated that their own childhood had been unhappy. There is evidence that in part, at least, this may be not so much an indication of real differences in family background and early experience as a difference in outlook, reflecting a kind of embittered attitude toward life which caused these persons to

[10] Ernest W. Burgess and Leonard S. Cottrell, *Predicting Success or Failure in Marriage* (New York, Prentice Hall, 1939), pp. xxiii + 472.

Lewis M. Terman, *Psychological Factors in Marital Happiness* (New York, McGraw-Hill Book Co., 1938), pp. xvi + 474.

[11] The questionnaires used in the two studies were not identical but were very similar.

magnify small troubles into major misfortunes. Like Mrs. Gum-
midge in *David Copperfield*, they "felt smoky chimneys more
than other people." In line with this is the finding in both studies
that the unhappily married reported many more grievances of
almost all kinds than did the happily married. This does not necessarily mean that the factors about which complaint was made
were never present among the happily married, but the latter
were less likely to be disturbed by them. In Terman's study this
factor was checked by asking first whether or not the condition
in question existed and secondly whether, if present, it had been
a source of unhappiness or worry to the person reporting. There
was much less difference in the frequency with which the two
groups reported various adverse conditions as existing than in the
frequency with which they were complained about. For example,
only 3 per cent of the happy wives who reported that their husbands were addicted to swearing found this a source of unhappiness to themselves, but of the unhappily married, 62 per cent of
those who stated that their husbands swore were emotionally
upset by it. Although both the husbands and wives of the unhappily married group cited "insufficient income" as one of the
major factors in their marital difficulties, when actual incomes
were compared it was found that there was no difference between
the happily and the unhappily married in average size of income.
Not the lack of money but the attitude toward the lack was the
disturbing factor.

All in all, there seems to be a sound basis for the conclusion
reached by Terman, who after reviewing all the evidence says,[12]

Our theory is that what comes out of a marriage depends upon what
goes into it and that among the most important things going into it
are the attitudes, preferences, aversions, habit-patterns and emotional-
response patterns which give or deny to one the aptitude for com-
patibility. In other words, we believe that a large proportion of
incompatible marriages are so because of a predisposition to unhappiness in one or both of the spouses.

This, of course, does not mean that some people are born to
be unhappy. It does mean that habits of unhappiness can be so
firmly established early in life that when the time for marriage
comes they are likely to persist. It means too, that troubles do

[12] *Op. cit.*, p. 110. Quoted by permission of the McGraw-Hill Book Co.

not, as many people think, lie outside the individual. There are many people who can remain serene in the face of great disaster; there are others who find disaster in a broken tea-cup.

Practically all investigators have found that *similarity* rather than dissimilarity of interests and attitudes is favorable to happy marriage. To achieve the most from marriage, husband and wife should be comrades as well as lovers. Questions that young people contemplating marriage may well ask themselves are these: Is our pleasure in each other's company chiefly dependent upon "petting," or can we be good companions without physical contact? Is our conversation mostly about ourselves, or do we find plenty of other subjects to talk about? Do we respect each other's opinions and enjoy an exchange of opinion whether or not we agree? Is either one of us jealous of the other's friendships, feeling hurt and neglected if he seems to enjoy the companionship of any one beside ourself?

Questions such as these cannot be answered on the basis of a brief acquaintance. Both Terman and Burgess and Cottrell found that their unhappily married groups included many more than a chance proportion of couples who had known each other only a short time before their marriage, who had rushed to the altar upon the urge of immediate desire without serious thought to the life that was to follow. This, as we have repeatedly pointed out, is a childish rather than a mature kind of behavior. The old saying, "Look before you leap," is nowhere more appropriate than in its application to marriage. The fully adult personality does not stand timidly on the bank afraid to try the crossing at all, but he scans the opposite shore with care until he can make the leap gladly and with confidence that he will find sure footing on the opposite side.

THE FORMATION OF SOCIAL GROUPS

Not only in the choice of husband or wife, but in practically all social organizations, similarity rather than difference is the cohesive force that determines the grouping. Even the temporary groups that you see about you on the streets are made up of people who have certain characteristics that tend to distinguish them from others.

Here are a number of people watching the work of excavating for a new building. Few of them know each other. Most of them will never see each other again. What factors can such a group have in common with each other?

Look again. You will note that the group is composed almost entirely of men and boys. Once in a while a woman may pause for a minute or two as she passes, but she does not remain long. So the first common factor we note is that of sex.

Observe more closely. A few of the men may be well dressed, but the greater number of them are in working clothes, many of which are patched and ragged. These are usually the ones who stay longest. If you inquire, you will find that a large percentage are unemployed. That explains why they have time to loiter around. And from these characteristics alone, maleness, interest in building operations, and unemployedness a good many other resemblances may be inferred. Their economic status is probably rather low; they live for the most part in the poorer sections of the city, and it is probable that a good many of them are receiving aid from social agencies. A little investigation would be almost certain to reveal many other points of resemblance. The similarities would not hold for all of them, but they would be found in so much larger a proportion of the men in this group than among men in general that we have a right to think of them as group factors. Yet the group itself is a temporary thing, and its members are even more temporary. Individuals come and individuals go, but in spite of its shifting membership, the general character of the group does not greatly change from hour to hour or from day to day.

One of the city newspapers carries an advertisement of a sale of children's clothing at much reduced prices. Will the people who attend the sale have any characteristics in common? Indeed they will, so much so that we can be pretty certain in advance what some of these characteristics will be. We can rest assured that most of the shoppers will be women, that they will be mothers, and, if we know the size range of the clothing, we can make a fair guess as to their average age. From the character of the shop where the sale is held we can infer something about their social and economic status. Whether they are wealthy or poor, we can be sure that most of them are inclined to be thrifty or they would not be patronizing sales. Yet this group is even more temporary than the one previously described.

In spite of the old saying that people who are opposites attract each other, neither psychology nor sociology is able to find much warrant for this statement. Even temporary groupings of human beings seem to be formed on the basis of similarities rather than differences. And in more permanent organizations such as communities, clubs, societies, or professional groups the similarities that led to the original grouping become increased through mutual imitation and the development of class consciousness.

Even in childhood the feeling of group consciousness has a powerful influence upon behavior. Among adults this influence is even stronger. A large part of our behavior is determined by the fact that the other members of our group do certain things in certain ways. We are all the slaves of custom. It is largely through custom that we have learned to look upon certain acts as right or wrong, in good taste or in poor taste, moral or immoral. We wear certain clothes and not others, use certain words but not others, believe certain things and reject others, form political allegiances, join clubs and lodges, perform a thousand unnecessary and troublesome acts for no other reason than that they are customary. The Oriental makes use of signs and talismans to keep off the evil eye; the educated American, chiefly in jest but still with a little undercurrent of feeling that it is better not to take chances, knocks on wood to insure the continuance of good fortune. He omits the fatal "13" in numbering the floors of his hotels and office buildings. Clairvoyants, soothsayers, tea-cup readers, fortune-tellers of all kinds still carry on a flourishing trade in most cities. I quote the following from the "personal" column of my morning paper.

WOMAN OF MYSTERY

> Born with a remarkable power, tells you what you want to know, good or bad. No questions asked. If in trouble, unhappy, discouraged with life, you need my help. Satisfaction guaranteed. Tel. ————.

To-day's issue contains twelve advertisements of this kind; on Sundays the number is greater. And this is in an "enlightened" American city in the middle of the twentieth century! Yet, when you stop to think of it, are all your beliefs based upon logical evidence? Of course not. You believe many things merely because people in your group whose opinions you respect have told you that these things are worthy of belief. They cite evidence, it is true. But so do the astrologers and the "women of mystery." Logic plays a much smaller part in determining beliefs than most of us suppose. Actually, unless something rather drastic occurs to disturb our faith, most of us share the beliefs and opinions and follow the customs that are current within the social groups to which we belong. We change about from group to group, but each group exerts some effects upon our behavior. Much of this influence is incidental, but in some cases it is definitely planned and utilized to increase the power of some group or of an individual member of the group.

PRESTIGE IS POWER

While I write this, the nations of the earth are locked in a bloody struggle for supremacy. The opposing sides in this struggle are not determined simply by the geographical location of the nations concerned. China, Japan, England, Russia, are more than just places on a map. An Englishman is no less an Englishman when he leaves his native island; an American carries his national character and his national rights wherever he may be. Nations are people, not places.

Yet it is obviously true that the people comprising a nation do, on the average, live in closer proximity to each other than to the rest of the world. This proximity, with the more intimate associations that it entails, will have its effect. But more important than mere intimacy of acquaintance is the feeling of group consciousness, of "belonging" to this group rather than to that one. The citizen of the United States whose home is within a few yards of the Mexican border may actually see much more of his Mexican neighbors than he does of those belonging to his own nation. In spite of this he identifies himself with the United States. Although his close association with the people of another nation may have broken down some of his nationalistic prejudices, he still regards his own country, its institutions and people as in some indefinable way superior to that of his neighbors.

Identification of oneself with a group almost of necessity leads to the assignment of some prestige value to that group. Even when the group is distinguished by some uncomplimentary term, its members are likely to show a kind of sorry pride in belonging to the clan. "I'm one of the down-and-outers" has a different ring from "I'm down and out."

According to *Webster's Dictionary*, *prestige* means "ascendancy derived from general admiration or esteem." This admiration may be based on real merit or a fictitious appearance of merit. It can be earned and it may sometimes be bought. It may be derived from real performance or from deceptive promises. And unfortunately, the power that goes with it is not determined by the soundness or unsoundness of the basis for the prestige. As long as the prestige continues, so long will its power endure.

In all ages, the importance of prestige for the establishment and maintenance of ideas, institutions, special products, and positions of leadership has been recognized. The pomp of kings, the gruesome mask of the Bantu medicine man, and the flags and bells of an American political campaign are devices for its maintenance. Hand in hand with industrial progress has gone the utilization of the new products for building up the prestige of leaders and the organizations and institutions for which they stand. The radio, newspapers and magazines, the airplane which enables the prestige-builders to cover wide territories in little time, the paved highway with its advertising signs, the widespread use of the automobile and the consequent increase in attendance at public gatherings of all kinds are only a few of the modern aids to establishing prestige that are available alike to the scrupulous and the unscrupulous. To these must be added the increase in scientific knowledge of human behavior and of the factors that influence it, greater understanding of the more subtle ways by which public attitudes may be changed and public enthusiasm aroused. The perfection and widespread use of the public opinion poll [13] has provided a means whereby the seeker for power can utilize his devices to better advantage. He can ascertain in what part of the

---

[13] For an exceedingly thoroughgoing account of the public opinion poll as a scientific method the interested reader should consult *Gauging Public Opinion* by Hadley Cantril (Princeton, N. J., Princeton University Press, 1944), pp. xiv + 318.

country his prestige is most thoroughly established and where further effort is most needed. He can find out what groups of people—the old or the young, the educated or the unschooled, the wealthy or the poor—have remained least convinced by his arguments and direct his attention to the points where it is most needed.

Nowhere else in the world have the psychological methods for building prestige been so systematically employed as in Nazi Germany. If we may believe the eye-witness account of Sigrid Schultz,[14] even before the end of World War I the military and political leaders of Germany were busily at work laying the plans for a campaign that should turn defeat into ultimate victory. And these plans in their basic outline were both amazingly simple and appallingly complete and coördinated.

First, the self-esteem of the German people must not be allowed to fall because of the defeat of 1918. Instead it must be enormously inflated, and to this end the concept of the "master race" was employed. Thus the prestige effect of belonging to the group was so tremendously increased that its individual members were willing to exert almost unbelievable efforts to carry out the will of the group leaders under the impetus provided by promises of final triumph and of great individual rewards. The feeling of group solidarity was further enhanced by the campaigns against the Jews. It is impossible to have a "chosen people" unless some are left outside. The Jews also provided a useful scapegoat by which the defeat of 1918 could be explained, as well as a target against which the accumulated bitterness of four years of unsuccessful war might be expended.

Only the broader perspective of history can show the true story of Hitler's rise to power. To what extent his early success can be traced to a recognition on the part of the larger group of military and political leaders of the fact that the people must have a national hero to focus upon, and their belief that Hitler possessed many of the personal qualities that would enable him to pose as such a hero cannot now be said with certainty. There is also, as Konrad Heiden has suggested, the possibility of an "identification mechanism." A "down-and-outer" who succeeded in rais-

[14] Sigrid Schultz, *Germany Will Try It Again* (New York, Reynal and Hitchcock, 1944), pp. xvi + 238.

ing himself to a position of power might well make a greater appeal to the imagination of a defeated nation than one who had been born to affluence. Without attempting to decide whether Hitler was for the most part self-made or owed his ascendancy to others, one thing can be said with assurance. The use of the "Heil Hitler!" salute was a stroke of genius. Think what the effect upon the millions of people in the United States would be if all the formal and friendly greetings to which we have been accustomed were to be abolished by law and replaced by some stereotyped accolade such as "Hurrah for Tom Jones!" A hundred times a day this phrase would be heard on the street, a dozen or more times one would repeat it himself. This incessant reminder could not fail to have its effect. Add to this the assurances continually reiterated by press and radio that through this magic name all good fortune was to come, that in unquestioning allegiance to Tom Jones lay the road to success and prosperity, and the effect would be greatly heightened. And if, furthermore, all contrary statements were legally abolished under penalty of extreme punishment, so that the majority of the people never heard anything other than the official propaganda, a uniformity of thought and action would ensue that persons accustomed to living under conditions of free speech can hardly imagine.

But the most effective and, in view of its purpose, the most sinister of the psychological weapons utilized in this campaign was the systematic training of youth in the ideology designed to enhance the power of their rulers. Earlier in this chapter it was pointed out that the ability to think for oneself is one of the attributes of maturity. In contrast we may say that the immature person is by very reason of his immaturity more credulous, more easily influenced by alluring promises, less able to bring mature judgment to bear upon his enthusiasms.

We have seen how this systematic development of prestige has been utilized for the establishment and maintenance of control over a deluded nation and how the power thus built up has been exercised in the subjugation of other nations and in making war upon the remainder of mankind. What assurance can we have that history will not repeat itself? How may we make sure that the children of those men and women who in the years after Pearl Harbor offered their lives in defense of a manner of living that permits each person to build his own career as seems good to him, to choose his own system of values and enjoy the fruits of his own labors will not, in their turn, be called upon to give their lives to maintain the principles of freedom?

Not by imitation of the Nazi method, powerful as these devices have shown themselves to be. For the answer to tyranny does not lie in the establishment of a greater and a yet greater tyranny. To that there can be no end except ultimate destruction. Nations grow with the growth of the people that comprise them, and no national system that relies for its power upon the prevention of free thought on the part of its people can hope to attain a state of national maturity. The safeguard of a free people lies in the nurture of its youth to the end that all shall develop their powers to the full. Only those who have so cast off the shackles of their childhood and so enlarged their social horizons that the "I" of infancy is merged in the "we" of the fully developed personality can know true freedom.

TWO GOOD BOOKS ON ATTAINING HAPPINESS IN MARRIAGE

> Ernest R. Groves, *Marriage*, Revised Edition (New York, Henry Holt and Co., 1941), pp. xvi + 671.
> Norman E. Hines, *Your Marriage: A Guide to Happiness* (New York, Farrar and Rinehart, 1940), pp. 448.

Young men and women who are looking forward to marriage will find either of these books well worth the reading. Both authors stress the fact that marriage is not just a matter of mutual attraction at the start, however important this may be. Happiness in marriage depends upon many things, of which sexual love is but one. Such questions as the rôle of courtship both before and after marriage, the length of the engagement period, the honeymoon and the establishment of a new home, the management of finances and the building of a new kind of social life are considered. Both authors present simple but frank accounts of the physical aspects of married life. They discuss the birth of children and the changes in the pattern of family life that the coming of children necessarily entails. Common sources of friction between husband and wife are pointed out and illustrated by brief case reports, but neither author has aimed at the dubious popularity sometimes to be gained from the citation of spectacular or morbid examples. The marital problems described are such as are likely to be encountered, in some degree at least, by most young couples, and the solutions offered are based upon sound psychological principles and a sympathetic appreciation of the attitudes and interests of young adults.

Your university library probably has a copy of one or both of these books. *Marriage* by Groves is the longer of the two and contains a wider range of informational material, but Hines' book, as might perhaps be inferred from his choice of title, deals with the human factors of marriage in a somewhat more direct and intimate fashion. Both books are clearly written, and either should provide valuable information for the young person who is contemplating marriage.

Chapter XXI

THE INDIVIDUAL AT WORK

What are the chief factors by which "work" is distinguished from "recreation"?

What are some of the leading conditions that cause fatigue?

What can be said about the relation between the subjective feeling of fatigue and the amount of work accomplished?

Will longer hours of work always result in greater accomplishment? Explain.

How does physiology account for the fact that extreme fatigue demands a longer period of recovery than milder conditions of fatigue?

Is alcohol a stimulant? Explain why it sometimes appears to stimulate.

Can an alcoholic condition great enough to make automobile driving unsafe always be detected by the affected person himself or by his associates? What kind of tests will best reveal that a person has been drinking?

In what way do extreme temperatures affect working efficiency?

Why is occupational discontent costly both to the workman and the employer?

What are some of the main causes of dissatisfaction on the part of the worker, other than those which come from actual unfair treatment?

553

What kind of work is done by the industrial psychologist? Why is this a promising field for the young psychologist to enter?

PRODUCTIVITY AND PROGRESS

Even in primitive societies, the difference between savagery and social organization of at least a simple kind is determined largely by the margin between productivity that is just barely sufficient to support life and that in which some individuals at times amass enough of a surplus to permit leisure for thinking and planning. In modern times we are all familiar with the phenomena of the business cycle. In periods of business prosperity there is work for almost every one who is willing and competent to perform it. New projects are undertaken; new buildings go up in large numbers; there is encouragement and financial support for the fine arts, for scientific research, and for educational advancement. In times of depression all this changes. Problems of unemployment, of relief for the needy, of increased taxation become the leading topics of conversation. We hear of schools closed for lack of funds, of children shivering in bread-lines, of riots among hungry men waiting outside employment offices.

Discussion of the sociological and economic problems making for these shifts is outside the province of this book. Certain facts, however, are axiomatic. Increased productivity of the individual per unit of time makes for increased leisure, for a higher standard of living with more material comforts and luxuries, or for both.[1] Increased leisure can be employed in the advancement of the arts and sciences, for enlarging the mental and cultural horizon of the individual and providing him with the means for deeper and more lasting pleasure in living. The material comforts and conveniences of modern civilization are also worth having, and as yet the production of material goods is far below the level that it must attain if all are to have as much as they can profitably use and enjoy. Society needs increased productivity as well as a more equitable distribution of the products of industry among the producers.

---

[1] Obviously these benefits may be very unequally distributed. That is another question and one that space does not permit us to discuss.

Even under existing conditions, when the rewards of industry are not always justly apportioned, efficient work is an advantage to the individual as well as to society as a whole. In times of unemployment, on the average, the inefficient worker loses his job first, and this in spite of some instances of retention because of political or personal preferment. There is still room for individual merit to win out. The poor boy *may* become president, in spite of his unfavorable start. The pages of *Who's Who in America* are by no means filled with the names of rich men's sons.

Just as the more able and efficient worker is more likely to win advancement than the one who is inefficient and lazy, so the manager who provides his men with proper conditions of work, both physical and psychological, is likely to find their efficiency increased. A large share of our present industrial unrest can be traced directly to failure on the part of both employers and employed to realize fully the close interaction within all parts of our social and industrial machine. Lowered efficiency, no matter where it is manifested nor from what bases it arises, has a repercussive effect upon all members of society. In the long run, efficiency means social progress; inefficiency makes for social decadence.

WORK AND FATIGUE

Work is usually defined [2] as activity that is organized, persistent, and directed toward the achievement of some material object or ideal end. Random activity, like that of a small boy with a new hatchet who chops down trees here and there for fun, is usually not classed as work, though his father who is clearing the woodland to make it into a cornfield is certainly working beside him. The New York business man who goes out for a day of deep-sea fishing is not working, in spite of the fact that the same activity is work for the fisherman who takes him out. Yet both may enjoy the day. On the other hand, if the water proves to be too choppy, it may be more fun for the fisherman who is working than for his seasick passenger. The difference

[2] Warren's *Dictionary of Psychology* offers the following definition: "*Work:* (psychol.) Production, through muscular or psychological activity, of physical or psychological results: e.g. a weight lifted, a poem written."

between work and recreation is not merely the difference between pleasure and its lack, for work is often pleasant. But in work, the main incentive is the result to be accomplished regardless of the amount of fun or of fatigue occasioned by the activity itself, while recreation or sport is carried out primarily for its own sake, even though some secondary interest may attach to the result. The business man hopes to get fish, but if that were his primary aim he would do better to visit a fish market.

The term *fatigue* is not easy to define, perhaps because it is used to denote such a wide variety of different conditions within the individual and is induced by such highly varied external factors.[3] It may be the result of long-continued or intensive muscular effort or mental work. It may come from monotony or boredom or even, paradoxically enough, from long-continued inactivity of mind or body. It may be induced by physiological conditions that have little reference to work or effort. There are drugs that make for earlier appearance of fatigue and others that temporarily delay its onset. It affects and is affected by the mental states and attitudes of the individual, and yet the feeling of fatigue is not always evidenced by a change in individual output. Increased effort may offset any differences that would otherwise appear. Indeed there are persons who characteristically speed up work when they first begin to feel tired, either because the fatigue acts as an increased incentive to complete their task or because they dislike to admit weakness.

Because of all these varying uses of the term and the lack of a truly objective measure of the sensation known as fatigue, modern psychologists are disinclined to use the word *fatigue* except in a rough and very generalized sense. In experimental work, such terms as *efficiency* (usually measured in terms of the amount accomplished per unit of time), *work decrement* or *increment*, and similar references to output are commonly substituted, while the question of *feelings of fatigue*, if considered at all, is handled by methods that make no claim to be other than subjective. The individual at work is questioned from time to time about his inter-

[3] Warren's *Dictionary* offers the following: *"Fatigue:* (1) Decreased ability of performance on the part of an organism, or of some member or muscle, resulting from prolonged work; (2) a specific feeling or sensation experienced after prolonged work."

est in the task at which he is engaged, whether or not he would like to continue, and so on. Or he may be asked to indicate the beginning and progress of his feelings of fatigue at stated intervals according to a prepared form of some kind. Frequently such reports are checked against objective measures of output made at the same time but without the worker's knowledge. Studies of this kind have usually shown that people differ about as much in respect to the relation between reported feelings of fatigue and changes in output as they do in reference either to feeling or to output considered separately.

SOME TEMPORAL CONDITIONS OF EFFICIENCY

It was noted in Chapter XVII that learning is facilitated if the periods of practice are properly spaced, and that the optimal length of the periods of practice and of the intervals between them varies with the age and amount of previous practice by the learners and with the kind of material to be learned. Much the same thing may be said of the conditions of work that make for increased output. Just as we found to be true of learning, there is greater likelihood that individual working periods will be too long, with insufficient and too infrequent rest periods interspersed between them than that the contrary will be the case. Again we may note that just as teachers and parents usually determine the length of the child's periods of study and in so doing are often guided by their own personal convenience rather than by the child's responses, so employers rather than the workers themselves usually determine the hours of work. Even when the number of working hours is set by labor organizations, the practice of permitting overtime work with increased pay may do away with a large share of the increased efficiency arising from the shortened hours of regular work.

The very long working hours common in most industrial plants of a generation and more ago were not only hygienically bad but were actually inefficient from the standpoint of output. This has been demonstrated in modern times when the length of the working week has been increased because of national emergency. During the World War of 1914-1918 workers in munitions factories in England were for a time held to very long hours because

of the labor shortage and the need to produce munitions as rapidly
as possible. But it was found that fewer munitions were produced
under these long working hours and that the cost of overhead
was greatly increased. Here are a few representative figures:
When the working hours of a group of girls in one munitions
factory were decreased from seventy-five to fifty-five and a half
hours, the work ratio rose from 108 to 169; less than half as much
time, on the average, was lost through illness, and the amount of
time spent in incidental activity at starting and quitting times was
reduced by a third. A group of men employed in a similar factory
had their work week reduced from sixty-six and a half to fifty-
five and a half hours. Their work ratio rose from 100 to 119,
and the amount of time lost from illness dropped from 7 per cent
to 4 per cent. In another study, a reduction of 13 per cent in the
length of the working week increased the average hourly output
by 39 per cent and the weekly output by 21 per cent. Of course
we cannot assign all this remarkable gain to the direct effects of
decreasing the physical fatigue of the workers. A good deal of the
difference, perhaps the major part, probably came from the
psychological effect. With shorter hours the workers would have
some time free for recreation. They could look forward to the
end of the day as something more than just a time of stopping
work. They would not spend so much time thinking about their
fatigue because they would have other matters to occupy their
minds. Perhaps, too, knowing England's need as they did, there
would be some additional incentive to maintain production at a
high level by harder work during the shorter period. Fatigue is
not just a physical matter; its effect upon attitude and effort is
quite as great as its effect upon the muscles.

Not only the total amount of time spent in work but the distribution of time has an effect upon productivity. It is a well-
known fact that after a nerve or muscle fiber has contracted, a
"latent period" occurs during which no further response can be
elicited until recuperation takes place. If a new response is forced
when just barely enough of the fibers making up a muscle have
recovered to make its contraction possible, their latent time will
be increased. It thus comes about that activity too frequently
repeated without sufficient time between repetitions to permit

complete recovery of all the fibers makes for a constantly increasing load upon those that are responding, as fewer and fewer recover in time to participate in the reaction. In time the number of active fibers will be so few that contraction of the muscle as a whole is impossible, and the time necessary for complete recuperation will have been increased far beyond its usual duration. This is the physiological explanation for the fact, well known to every one, that rapid movements repeated at short intervals induce fatigue much more quickly than slower movements with pauses between them, and that the more extreme the fatigue, the longer is the time needed for recovery.

It is unnecessary to review the large number of studies that have been carried out to determine whether or not it is practically worth while to introduce definite rest pauses into the working day. There is, of course, some delay involved in stopping and starting including, for some activities, a "warming-up period" that may further interfere with work. But for most types of factory work or other activities of a routine nature, the rest period has been found worth while, especially when there is considerable demand upon muscular strength. In a classic experiment by Taylor [4] the average daily number of tons of pig-iron handled by laborers was increased from twelve and a half to forty-seven and a half by having each man sit down and rest for a few moments after loading each twenty "pigs" of ninety-two pounds each upon a freight car, and by showing them how to eliminate waste movements in working. Leahy [5] found that clerical workers engaged in entering statistical data upon cards by means of an electrically driven punch showed a small decrease in output and a marked increase in the number of errors made after fatigue had set in. The average number of errors made by trained operators during the second half of the morning period was 1.31 times as great as that made during the first half. After the noon lunch and rest period the frequency of errors was at first approximately the same as had occurred in the first half of the morning, but

---

[4] F. W. Taylor, *The Principles of Scientific Management* (New York, Harper and Bros., 1915).

[5] Alice M. Leahy, "Punching Psychological and Sociological Data on Hollerith Cards," *J. Ap. Psychol.*, 1931, 15: 199-207.

during the second half of the afternoon a marked increase in errors brought the score to a frequency 1.86 times as great as that occurring during the first afternoon period.

Just as was found true in respect to the distribution of practice in learning (which is just another kind of work), no universal rule can be laid down about either the optimal length of the working period or the most favorable distribution of rest pauses. As with learning, it is safe to state that the tendency in most cases is to make the working day too long and the rest pauses too few. It is also true that routine activities, as a rule, show greater improvement from the interposition of rest pauses than do more complex activities or those demanding the working out of a train of ideas. That writers and scientists often keep hours that to the more practical mind may seem little short of "scandalous" is well known. Flushed with a new and exciting idea, it is said that Edison frequently remained at work in the laboratory for twenty hours or more without food or rest. According to his wife, he never kept to regular hours of work, sleep, or eating. When he was seized with an idea he commonly carried it through to the crucial test without pause; after which his debauch of work would be followed by a profound sleep "as peaceful as that of a child" which would last for many hours. In spite of all this, Edison lived to the advanced age of eighty-five without marked diminution of his scientific activities. During his lifetime, 1,098 patents were issued in his name. The patent right for his final invention did not appear until after his death.

One's subjective feeling of fatigue is not always a valid indicator of the actual amount of his work decrement. However, a good many of the laboratory studies that have been conducted on this topic may be somewhat misleading because of their relatively short duration. Increased effort may make up for loss through nervous and physical fatigue over a period of hours or even for several days, but that does not necessarily mean that the same rule will hold good over a period of weeks or months. No one's reserves are inexhaustible. For shorter periods, however, the determination to keep going will carry one along without marked loss of efficiency far beyond the time when the feeling of fatigue becomes manifest. This is true of both mental and physical work.

ORGANIC STATES OTHER THAN FATIGUE THAT INFLUENCE EFFICIENCY

Generally speaking, any condition of impaired health, whether temporary or lasting, has a detrimental effect upon efficiency. Because this is true, most drugs reduce efficiency in the long run, even though their temporary effect may be stimulating. Moreover, even the subjective feeling of exhilaration that follows the taking of certain drugs (such as alcohol) is often deceptive. There is evidence that alcohol acts first and most strongly upon the controlling mechanisms of the central nervous system where its effect is that of a depressant. The resulting condition is something like that of the decorticated animals discussed in Chapter VIII. The reduced control of activity by the cerebral hemispheres shifts the "balance of power" in the direction of the thalamus. This makes for greater activity but for lowered efficiency because action is no longer tempered by good sense. There may be more movements, but this counts for little if most of them are waste movements. And the latter has always been found to be the case. In all scientific studies where suitable controls have been employed, no matter what the field of inquiry, the use of alcohol has invariably been found to reduce efficiency. Under the influence of alcohol the speed of coördinated movement is decreased and there is marked loss of steadiness in all muscles. Errors of all kinds are more frequent. The rate of learning either motor or mental tasks is lowered and memory for material previously learned is decreased. Even the popular idea that alcohol increases good fellowship and improves social relations is hazardous, for under its influence things are often said or done that may wreck friendships of long standing.

Many recent studies of the effect of alcohol have had direct reference to an activity of tremendous importance in modern life—the driving of automobiles. The annual loss of life from automobile accidents in the United States has reached such staggering proportions [6] that special commissions have been appointed to

[6] For the year 1939, official reports place the number killed at 32,100, the number injured at 1,210,200. This compares with a total of 126,000 American soldiers who were either killed or died from disease and 234,300 who were wounded during the first World War. At this rate it needs but four years' time for the death total on American highways to equal the

study the question of how the number of such accidents can be reduced and what are their chief causes. Uniformly it has been found that alcohol ranks very high in the list of contributory factors. In one study carried out in Evanston, Ill., the findings indicated that a driver with an alcohol concentration in the blood of 0.15 per cent is fifty-five times as likely to have an accident involving personal injury to himself or others as is the person who has not been drinking.[7] Examination of the data from a number of studies led to the conclusion that at least a third of the drivers and pedestrians killed or injured in traffic accidents had enough alcohol in their systems at the time to impair their judgment and their motor control. Few people realize how small an amount is needed for this to occur. One's personal "feelings" in the matter are not a safe guide. Neither is unaided observation, for it has been shown that loss of efficiency and of sound judgment great enough to cause the difference between safety and accident when an emergency occurs may exist long before the person is visibly affected by the alcohol he has taken. Both the driver and his friends may protest that he was "sober as he ever was in his life." Chemical tests will reveal the facts when observation fails to do so.

The effect of tobacco upon efficiency has not been so clearly demonstrated. As might be expected from everyday observation, habitual smokers are not affected in the same way as non-smokers. Generally speaking the use of tobacco is likely to be followed by some reduction in speed of reaction and a slight reduction in motor coördination. Excessive use, at least in some cases, appears to lead to nervous tremors and sleeplessness, but inasmuch as under unusual strain some people resort to excessive smoking as an outlet for nervous energy, it is not always easy to separate cause from effect.

College students, in particular, are often tempted to experiment with various drugs assumed to increase their mental efficiency or to enable them to do without sleep and so increase hours available for study at examination time. Some of these drugs unquestionably have the effect of prolonging wakefulness and of producing

---

number who lost their lives before German guns, while two months suffice for the number wounded in traffic to equal the total number of war-wounded.

    [7] D. S. Berry, "Alcohol as a Factor in Traffic Accidents," *Quart. J. Study of Alcohol*, 1940, 1: 413-431.

a temporary state of enhanced activity. But they do not produce energy; they merely release an increased amount of stored energy. Elementary arithmetic tells us that after more has been used up, less will remain. Certainly no such scheme should be undertaken without careful medical supervision. The sensible student will usually find less perilous ways of improving his grades. Most of the drugs used for this purpose are relatively new, and the investigations that have been made to date commonly deal only with their immediate effects. Very little is known about the results of repeated dosage. And just here lies danger, for a student who has found (as many do) that the use of the drug will enable him to spend the night before examination in study with less discomfort than he would normally experience is likely to form the habit of seeking its aid with increased frequency.

Studies of the effect upon efficiency of temperature, poor ventilation, and so on have on the whole yielded inconsistent results. There is no doubt that very hot or cold temperatures are uncomfortable, that they decrease our pleasure in work, and that they are likely to have a distractive effect in turning the attention from the job to the shivering or perspiring body. Also, unless a good deal of self-control is exercised, there is further distraction through more or less automatic attempts to relieve bodily discomfort by action. In a cold room we try repeatedly to snuggle down closer into our clothing or to wrap it more tightly about us. We wriggle our cold toes or surreptitiously tuck our feet up into the chair. We seize every opportunity to move about. When the temperature is too warm we may waste many minutes in wiping the perspiration from our faces, fanning ourselves with any available paper, or just commiserating each other on the heat. Unless the temperature and oxygen conditions become more extreme than any that we are likely to face in ordinary life, their effect upon efficiency is chiefly indirect, resulting from the natural human tendency to keep as comfortable as possible. Loss of efficiency is probably due to the diversion of a part of our activities to combat the unpleasant conditions rather than to any direct effect of the conditions as such.

EFFICIENCY AND PERSONALITY

The chronically dissatisfied worker is known in every office and industrial plant. He is found in every school system, and is known to every social service organization. He is the bane of the personnel worker, and a "pain-in-the-neck" to his acquaintances who try vainly to escape his never-ending tales of woe. He leaves one job only to find that the next is even worse. So he quits that. Studies of the unemployed provide convincing evidence that even in times of economic depression, the number of jobs previously held by unemployed men averages considerably greater, and the usual length of stay in each is decidedly shorter, than is true for an employed group of similar age in corresponding lines of industry.

The discontented worker is likely to foment trouble among his fellows, for dissatisfaction is as contagious as measles. Because discontent is not conducive to a high level of effort, the result is likely to be a falling off in the output of his associates as well as in his own.

Causes of occupational discontent are many and complex. Sometimes the difficulty lies far back in the history of the individual. It is the result of early experience for which the employer and the job have become symbols. The child who has been harshly managed carries his resentment into adult life and rebels against all rules and restrictions. He refuses to see why the company that employs him should insist that he conform to certain hours of work or take his turn at certain unpleasant jobs that fall outside the formal requirements of his position. He tells them that "he wasn't hired for that" and quits. Such a person is hard to rehabilitate because there is little correspondence between the overt occasions for his discontent and its actual cause. However, in many cases the bases for dissatisfaction are easier to uncover. Ichheiser [8] classifies these difficulties under four heads as follows:

1. *Conflicts resulting from vocational misplacement,* as when the person of active tastes is forced into a sedentary occupation or the one whose chief interests are along mechanical lines is given a salesman's job or is set to do clerical work.

[8] G. Ichheiser, "On Certain Conflicts in Occupational Life," *Occup. Psychol.* (London, 1940), 14: 107-111.

2. *Conflicts arising from disparity between enforced practice and personal or social attitudes and beliefs.* The man hired to write advertising copy finds himself called upon to extol the merits of some particular brand of whiskey in spite of the fact that he is an ardent Prohibitionist; the laborer working on the excavations for a new block of buildings discovers that the project is financed by a shoddy real estate owner who is famous for his extortionate treatment of his poverty-ridden tenants.

3. *Conflicts arising from a disparity between ambition and ability.* The level of aspiration is too high and the disappointed worker reacts by trying to put the blame on his employer, on the conditions of work, or on his fellow-workmen.

4. *Conflicts arising from dissatisfaction over the social or geographical associations of the position.* The man accustomed to living in a large city may find it difficult or impossible to accustom himself to the social and cultural limitations of a small town, or his wife may be so unhappy over the lack of congenial associates or suitable schools for the children that their home life is disturbed.

Dissatisfactions such as these are usually more easily handled, because their basis is more easily discovered. Of course there are other reasons for industrial unrest which center about actual abuses. The number and variety of these is too great to enumerate here. We shall leave them to the sociologist and the economist.

PSYCHOLOGY AS AN AID TO HUMAN EFFICIENCY

In Chapter II some of the ways in which the psychologist is able to contribute to the practical conduct of human affairs were pointed out, and from time to time other areas in which the application of psychological principles to life problems have been indicated. In this chapter, we have touched briefly upon the importance of psychology in industry. Not every one knows that many of the large industrial corporations now employ psychologists as regular members of their research and advisory staffs as well as in their personnel bureaus. The number and importance of these positions is mounting rapidly, and the kind of work done by this group of industrial psychologists is becoming increasingly more varied. They analyze the requirements of the various kinds of jobs carried out by the firm with which they are connected, and they devise tests by which the probability of success of the various applicants for these jobs can be appraised. Through elimination of unpromising applicants without the expense of actual trial, and more efficient fitting of men to the jobs for which they are best suited, they are able to effect a material reduction in the frequency and severity of conflicts of the first of the four types previously mentioned. The industrial psychologist studies the effects of different kinds of advertising and helps to plan advertising campaigns. He interviews disgruntled employees and irons out disputes. Often he works with the plant physician in unsnarling mental quirks that in their normal course might lead the patient to a mental hospital. He studies such practical matters of plant construction and management as lighting, height and position of machines, arrangement of workers, and ways of eliminating unnecessary movements. Industrial psychology is a field that is attracting many young psychologists who are ambitious to find openings for themselves that give opportunity to develop their own ideas and that offer good chances for advancement.

Even psychologists who do not classify themselves as industrial psychologists in the strict sense are not infrequently called on to give advice on industrial questions. Many of our university laboratories are carrying on valuable research on problems relating to industry. The practical importance of increased productivity in its intimate association with so many aspects of human welfare and human happiness makes it easy to see why this should be the case.

MEN, WOMEN, AND JOBS

Donald G. Paterson and John G. Darley, with the assistance of Richard M. Elliott, *Men, Women, and Jobs: A Study in Human Engineering* (Minneapolis, University of Minnesota Press, 1936), pp. vi + 145.

Would you like to know more about how psychologists study people to find out for what kind of work they are best fitted? This short volume contains an account of a project undertaken during the great industrial depression of the early thirties. The general question which the committee carrying out the study attempted to answer was this: When industrial conditions are such that many workers must be laid off, what determines who shall be retained and who dismissed? What are the chief differences, if any, between the workers who keep their jobs and those who do not?

More than 5,500 men and women were studied. Some of them had jobs and some had not; of the latter, some had been among the first to be laid off when retrenchment began, while others had been retained long after many of their fellow workers had been dismissed. All, both the employed and the unemployed, were given careful medical examinations and a large number of mental and vocational tests. Their previous employment records were examined, and a careful appraisal was made of their attitudes and personality traits.

In general and in spite of occasional instances of favoritism, it was found that the men who were first discharged were those who had proved to be of least value to the company for which they worked. However, there were many cases among these in which the poor work record was by no means an indication that the man was a poor worker but merely that he had not had the right kind of job; that he was like the proverbial square peg in a round hole. Many of these persons proved capable and efficient when set at more suitable work after having been given the necessary training for it.

The book includes pictures of many of the tests used, as well as a number of short descriptions of actual cases handled by the Institute illustrating the differences between men and women who had been able to retain their jobs and those who had not. The way in which the information obtained helped many of the persons [9] to secure and hold positions for which they were better suited is also described. An hour or so spent in reading this book should give you a reasonably clear idea of what the trained vocational psychologist is able to do in helping people to find and keep the kind of jobs which they can do well.

[9] The organization, which was known as the Employment Stabilization Research Institute of the University of Minnesota, was not intended to serve as an employment agency. Its purpose was to ascertain as many of the facts contributing to individual unemployment as possible. But it was necessary to check the accuracy of its conclusions by seeing whether persons making use of its advice were more successful in holding a job than they had been before and to compare their later records with those of men who did not follow the recommendations made. A marked difference in favor of the former group was found.

Chapter XXII

THE MATURATION AND DECLINE OF ABILITIES

Why is it harder to measure "general intelligence" in adults than in children?

Between what ages do most abilities appear to reach their peak?

Is the curve of growth and decline the same for all forms of ability?

In general, what kinds of ability appear to decline most rapidly? Most slowly?

Do all people grow old at the same rate?

Is the saying that "you cannot teach an old dog new tricks" partially or wholly true for human beings? What are some of the chief reasons why older people seldom acquire new skills? What kinds of things are hardest for older people to learn?

Have most of the "masterpieces" of famous men been produced at any one typical age? About what has been found to be the average age?

CHANGES IN ABILITY AFTER MATURITY

Everyday observation tells us that the pattern of abilities, both mental and physical, continues to undergo change even after maturity has been reached. The man of forty differs from the youth of twenty in ways that are not wholly dependent upon his greater experience. With the changes in physical appearance that commonly occur between these ages we are all familiar; so much so that although now and then we meet some one whose appearance greatly belies his age, as a rule we estimate the ages of strangers with a fair degree of accuracy. We all know, too, the gradual loss of the overflowing physical energy that sets young men to wrestling and tussling with each other with the thermometer at 100° in the shade. Although at forty the man who has always done heavy manual labor may carry on his work about as efficiently as before, he does not put so much snap into it. His muscles may still be strong, but they are less resilient. The man of forty moves more slowly, particularly if, as is often the case, he has put on weight.[1]

But although general observation tells us certain things, when we try to make exact comparisons between the abilities of younger and older adults we find that the task is not as easy as might be thought. Unless we wait until the young have grown old, we shall not be studying the same individuals at different ages, and it is not easy to make sure that factors other than age are not influencing the results. For example, in some of the earlier studies on the abilities of very old persons, the subjects were taken almost wholly from charitable institutions, poorhouses, and homes for the aged. The very fact that these persons had failed to make provision for their old age when they were younger suggests that they were probably not highly competent at any age. As people grow older they are likely to become less interested in merely trying their skill; they want to see reasons for their work. Tasks that merely test what they can do are therefore less certain to draw forth their best efforts. Differences in recent experience also play a part. Many of the older subjects will have lost interest in activities that have no relationship to their life work and so make a poor showing on certain tasks, not so much through genuine loss of ability to acquire these skills as through being out of practice in performing them. With increasing age, interests and activities become more highly specialized. Perhaps the fairest way to test the ability of an adult would be to see how well he can do his chosen kind of work.

Until recently we had no very reliable information about the

[1] The relationship between speed of movement and weight is reciprocal. The person who moves quickly burns up more fuel in that way and so is less likely to store it as fat. Moreover, since fat is inert tissue which has to be moved by muscular effort in which it does not, itself, share, the person who carries around excess fat is likely to move more slowly because he is hampered by the load.

changes in ability that occur after maturity has been reached. During recent years, however, several outstanding attempts have been made to study this problem. Miles [2] enlisted the interest of clubs and social organizations of various kinds by offering to pay the organization for the time spent by its members and their relatives in taking a series of tests. A special bonus was offered for bringing in old people. By this means he was able to be reasonably sure that his subjects were of about the same social class and presumably of about the same native intelligence, regardless of their ages. The fact that they, or rather the organization, was receiving pay for the work undoubtedly lent it additional importance in the eyes of the subjects, and so made it less likely that they would fail to put forth their best efforts.

The tests used were of many kinds. In addition to formal intelligence tests there were a number of tests of motor ability, of perceptive ability, of learning and memory, of speed of reaction. Self-estimates and questionnaires, calling for opinions and points of view on many subjects and for expressions of interest in various activities, were also employed. Not all the results have been published as yet, but the following table shows the general trend. In this table the scores for the different age groups have been expressed as percentages of the average score made at the age when the particular ability was at its peak. The peak is always counted as 100 per cent. Thus, in speed of reaching and grasping the highest average score was made by the subjects who were between eighteen and twenty-nine years, and this score is therefore counted as 100. Subjects between the ages of ten and seventeen years attained, on the average, 92 per cent of this high mark; those between the ages of thirty and forty-nine, 98 per cent; those from fifty to sixty-nine, 88 per cent; and the old people between the ages of seventy and eighty-nine averaged 70 per cent of the maximum.

In the Otis intelligence test it was found that the peak came at

[2] W. R. Miles, "Correlation of Reaction and Coördination Speed with Age in Adults," *Amer. J. Psychol.*, 1931, 43: 377-391; "Measures of Certain Human Abilities Throughout the Life Span," *Proc. Nat. Acad. Sci.*, 1931, 17: 627-633; "Age and Human Ability," *Psychol. Rev.*, 1933, 40: 99-123. Catherine C. Miles and W. R. Miles, "The Correlation of Intelligence Scores and Chronological Age from Early to Late Maturity," *Amer. J. Psychol.*, 1932, 44: 44-78.

about eighteen years of age. Since we do not know where the zero point of this test lies, it is not easy to express the results as percentages of the maximum as has been done in the foregoing table. Miles uses a number of devices to show the relationship of scores to age, but, since most of them involve the use of somewhat complicated mathematical procedures, we shall present only the simplest and most easily understood figures here.

The following table shows the average IQ's computed on the basis of the Otis norms [3] for each successive decade from the twenties to the nineties. The subjects have been divided into three groups according to education.

From Tables VI and VII it appears that older people suffer a greater handicap in the more purely physiological functions, such as visual acuity, than they do in the kind of activities we term intellectual. There is some evidence, too, that the loss in those functions that are most often practised comes about a little more slowly than it does in those that are rarely used. The ability to learn to trace a maze, for example, shows a much more rapid decrease than reaching and grasping. Although we think of the former as a more intellectual function, it is one that is little practised outside the psychological laboratory. On the Otis tests, which make use chiefly of verbal tasks, the ability of the subjects who never attended high school and who probably were for the most part engaged in manual labor shows a somewhat earlier decrement than that of other groups who were, we may assume, getting more practice in work of this kind.

Miles also points out that in general the decrement in performance with age appears most strongly in tasks in which speed is a factor. Older people do best in tasks "where diligence is more important than speed." Older people also have much difficulty in learning new material that conflicts with well-established habits, such as a series of wrong products like $4 \times 5 = 28$. It may be

---

[3] Although the use of the intelligence quotient with adults is open to question, we have presented the results in this form because it is one with which students are familiar. It should be noted, however, that whereas Otis, following the example of Terman, assumed that the ability measured by this test reaches its maximum at sixteen years, these results as well as those secured by a number of other workers show that some further growth occurs after the age of sixteen. This accounts for the fact that the average IQ of all three groups during the decade of the twenties is somewhat above 100.

noted here that some workers in the animal field have found that old rats have more difficulty than young ones in learning new mazes so planned that the habits formed earlier in learning other mazes conflict with those required by the new maze.

TABLE VI

RELATIONSHIP OF CERTAIN ABILITIES TO AGE
(Adapted from Miles)

Ability	Age Groups				
	10–17	18–29	30–49	50–69	70–89
1. Reaching and grasping......	92%	100%	98%	88%	70%
2. Speed of rotary movement (turning a crank)	90	100	97	89	72
3. Speed of finger reaction.....	87	100	98	99	71
4. Learning a maze...........	95	100	92	83	55
5. Comparison and judgment..	72	100	100	87	69
6. Visual acuity (with glasses if worn)	100	95	93	76	46

TABLE VII

RELATIONSHIP OF INTELLIGENCE QUOTIENTS TO AGE AND SCHOOLING
(After Miles)

Age	Eighth Grade or Less	One to Four Years High School	One or More Years in College
20–29	101	107	118
30–39	94	106	116
40–49	93	105	117
50–59	89	100	111
60–69	85	95	106
70–79	82	95	100
80–89	75	85	91
90–99	–	79	–

Most significant of all, perhaps, is the fact that even in those tasks where, on the average, the decrement with age is large, some of the older people continue to do better than the average of the younger ones. In this connection Miles makes the following comment:

Although younger adults tend regularly to score higher in most of the measurements made and older adults to score lower, it is by no means true that all of the high scores belong to the young, the low ones to the old.... The measurements of dispersion are consistently large from decade to decade. In reaction time, 25 per cent of the people over 70 years of age were as quick as the average for the total group. In intelligence also, even when speed is a factor, approximately a quarter of the oldest subjects equaled or exceeded the general adult average.

Miles' subjects were for the most part drawn from an urban population. For this reason it is interesting to compare his results with those obtained by Jones and Conrad [4] from a group of people living in small New England villages. In this study the Alpha intelligence test, which was given to the American soldiers during World War I, was employed.

Figure 102 shows the average decline in ability with age for the entire group. These results agree very closely with those obtained by Miles. In both studies the peak of ability is reached at about the age of eighteen. The curve remains fairly stationary throughout the early twenties and then shows a gradual drop.

Although different tests were used in the two studies, it is possible to transmute the scores earned on one into the most probable values for the other. Since the two tests are not very different from each other in content, it is not likely that this transmutation involves much error. When this is done it appears that at every age the village group (which includes some people living on near-by farms) makes an average score about half-way between that earned by Miles' subjects who had only grade school education and that earned by those who had gone to high school. This is about what we should expect.

The Alpha test is divided into eight subtests, each comprising a different kind of task. Jones was interested in seeing whether the age decrement is equally great along all the lines tested. He found that it is not. Test 4, which is an "opposites" test (see p. 408), and Test 8, which is a test of general information, show no indication of a decline with age up to age sixty. The curves remain stationary. Arithmetical reasoning and the ability to rear-

[4] H. E. Jones and H. S. Conrad, "The Growth and Decline of Intelligence; a Study of a Homogeneous Group between the Ages of Ten and Sixty Years," *Genet. Psychol. Monog.*, 1933, 13: 223-298.

range the words in "dissected" sentences show only a small loss. The ability to follow oral directions shows a fairly sharp loss from the early twenties up to about thirty-five, after which no further change takes place before the age of sixty. The greatest age decrement is seen in the tests of mathematical completion and giving analogies, and in a so-called test of "common sense" in which the subject is required to select the best one out of a list of answers to each of a number of everyday questions.

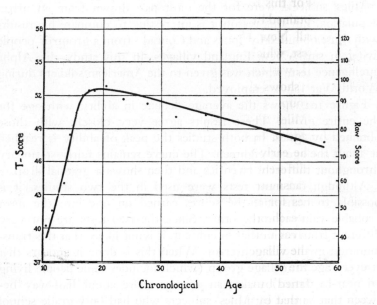

FIG. 102.—GROWTH AND DECLINE OF INTELLIGENCE AS MEASURED BY THE ARMY ALPHA TEST

(From H. E. Jones and H. S. Conrad, "The Growth and Decline of Intelligence: a Study of a Homogeneous Group between the Ages of Ten and Sixty." *Genet. Psychol. Monog.*, 1933, 13: 223-298. Courtesy Clark University Press.)

As far as test performance is concerned, therefore, there seems to be no doubt that, if we consider the average of many different kinds of intellectual performance, a small but steady decline in ability takes place after the early twenties. But this decline is not equally well marked for all tasks, nor is the maximum always reached at the same age. Some abilities reach their acme in the teens, others not until much later. Some forms of ability show no evidence of decline up to late middle age. Individuals, of course, differ greatly. Some remain intellectually "young" until after they are far advanced in years; others become old in their twenties. Individual differences in the rate of mental decline seem to be quite as marked as individual differences in rate of mental growth, but neither Jones nor Miles was able to discover any definite relationship between rate of growth and rate of decline. Those who show rapid mental development in childhood do not appear to be either more or less likely to show rapid decline in maturity and old age than those whose early growth was slower. If anything there is a slight suggestion of a negative relationship, rapid growth going with slow decline and vice versa, but a good deal more evidence is needed before we can be sure that this is the case.

So much for tests of ability. But what about learning? There is a well-known saying that it is hard to teach an old dog new tricks. If this is true, what is the matter with the dog? Is it, as we might judge from the test results given so far, because he cannot learn the tricks, because he thinks he cannot, or because he is too indifferent to try? And first of all, just how hard is it for him to learn? Let us see what the evidence is for the human animal.

ADULT LEARNING

Thorndike [5] has made one of the most careful studies of human learning during early and middle maturity that has so far appeared. In this study he canvassed a great many different fields of learning and worked with subjects of many different levels of education and intelligence. It is neither possible nor necessary for us to give all his results in detail, but the following are representative.

When university students ranging in age from twenty to fifty-seven years were given ninety practice periods of ten minutes each in learning to write with the non-preferred hand, those between the ages of twenty and twenty-five gained in speed more than those who were thirty-five or older, the averages in terms

---

[5] E. L. Thorndike, et al., *Adult Learning* (New York, Macmillan Co., 1928), pp. xii + 335.

of letters per minute being thirty-five and eighteen respectively. The greatest gain in the older group was twenty-five letters per minute; the smallest gain in the younger group was sixteen letters per minute. The ability to *increase one's motor speed* in learning a new task seems to drop off very rapidly with age. But the ability to *improve in quality* shows little relationship to age within the age limits covered. As measured on the Thorndike Scale, the older group gained, on the average, 1.16 units and the younger group 1.11 units. Another group of subjects with the same range of ages as those used in the handwriting experiment studied Esperanto, an artificial language made up according to definite rules and principles. At the beginning of the experiment all subjects were given four tests: a vocabulary test, a test of responding to directions that were given orally, another of responding to printed directions, and a test of paragraph reading. When the subjects had spent a total of twenty hours learning Esperanto, the tests were repeated. The younger students improved much more than the older ones in the test of oral directions, a fact that suggests a falling off in auditory perception,[6] but there was practically no difference between the groups in the other three tests. A comparison of the progress of these adults with that of children from eight to eighteen years of age shows that the adults were decidedly superior, a fact that is in direct opposition to the commonly accepted belief that childhood is the time when languages are learned most easily. It is probably true that correct pronunciation will be most easily acquired during the early years, but the idea that learning to read a new language is beyond the ability of intelligent adults, even after they are well along in years, seems definitely contradicted by these results.

The foregoing experiments were conducted on persons of superior ability. But a group of Sing Sing prisoners whose ability, as measured by standard tests, was distinctly below average showed the same relationship of learning to age as was found for other groups. There was a falling off after the early twenties in learning certain kinds of tasks, but the decrease was not very marked. In learning school subjects—reading, arithmetic, and the like—this drop was estimated to be about one half of 1 per cent

[6] Note the resemblance to the age changes in visual acuity found by Miles as given on p. 572.

per year during the twenty years from age twenty-one to age forty-one. In a substitution test designed to measure retentiveness over an interval of one week the older men did better than the younger ones, provided the code used was the same on both occasions; but, if it was changed in such a way that new habits had to be substituted for those previously learned, the older men were at a disadvantage as compared with the younger ones. They remembered the old habits better, but found it harder to form new ones that interfered with the old. Miles, you will remember, obtained the same results.

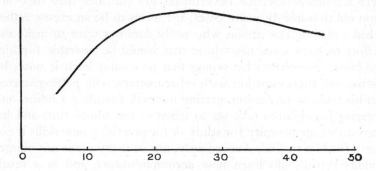

FIG. 103.—THE GENERAL FORM OF THE CURVE OF LEARNING ABILITY
WITH AGE

(From *Adult Learning*, by E. L. Thorndike. Courtesy The Macmillan Co.)

In order to obviate, as far as possible, the spurious effects of differences in experience which might enable one group to make better use of past habits of learning than the other, Thorndike conducted a number of experiments on the learning of new and meaningless tasks in which it seemed probable that differences in experience would play a very small part in determining the results. For example, he had blind-folded subjects attempt to draw lines of a specified length, with only the words "Right" or "Wrong" to aid them. In these experiments the age difference in learning ability was decidedly greater than in those involving the learning of such things as adults commonly have to learn. For all the experiments together, the general tendency was for a total drop in learning efficiency of about 15 per cent between the ages of twenty-two and forty-two years. But when one remembers the great differences in ability to learn that are shown by individuals at any one age, this decrease appears of far less consequence than it might at first seem. There are plenty of individuals well on in years who still learn more easily than the average youth. By putting in a little more time and making a determined effort they may even surpass their own earlier performances made at a time when they may have been less strongly motivated to do well.

If the actual change in learning ability from the third to the fifth decade is so small, why do so many persons who have not yet reached senescence nevertheless get the idea that they are too old to learn? In many cases, age seems to be an excuse rather than a reason. The person who really does not want to make the effort to learn some new thing that would be desirable for him to know, rationalizes by saying that he cannot learn it now; he is too old. Preoccupation with other matters, with getting started in his trade or profession, getting married, founding a home, and rearing his children take up so much of the adult's time and interest that opportunity for study or for practising new skills is not easy for him to find. Accordingly, not so many older as younger adults actually do learn new accomplishments, and as a result the popular idea has arisen that learning for older adults is much more difficult than it really is.

This difference in custom has another effect. Adults, especially if they are no longer young, often feel self-conscious and hesitant about undertaking to learn things that not many other people of their age are learning. So they either refrain from making the effort at all, or, if they begin, they learn more slowly than would be the case if they were not hampered by self-consciousness and lack of confidence in their ability to succeed. All in all, there seems to be good warrant for Thorndike's conclusion, which is that the reason many adults fail to continue learning as much or as long as they might is partly because they underestimate their powers of learning and partly because they do not care enough about learning to make the necessary effort to do so.

PRODUCTIVITY AND AGE

But laboratory tests do not tell the whole story. At what age does the average person do his best work?

A large number of studies on this topic have been made with results that are fairly similar in their general tenor. In some of these studies, the criterion used has been maximum productivity, as indicated by the number of books and scientific articles, works of art or mechanical inventions produced in a single year. In others, the age at which the single work that competent authorities regard as the person's masterpiece has been the index used. Still others have employed a financial yardstick, regarding the age at which the highest salary was earned as the best indication of the time when his ability was at its peak. But regardless of the basis of judgment, the general results are much the same. The diversity from person to person is so great that a citation of averages misleads almost as much as it informs. It has been found that in such a field as literature, for example, little can be said about the relationship of age to either quality or quantity of work without specifying the type of literature concerned. Heidler and Lehman [7] for example, found that the average age at time of writing various works of literature ranged from 27.9 for pastoral poetry to 52.5 for scientific prose. In an unpublished study by Anderson and Goodenough it was found that among psychologists, age changes in productivity vary according to whether the measurement is based upon the number of separate publications or upon their aggregate number of pages. Younger persons write more and shorter articles; older ones fewer and longer ones. Results similar to these have been obtained in a number of other fields.

Thorndike [8] reports the results of a study based upon the age at which the *opera magna* of 331 leading scientists and men of affairs were published. Only those persons were included in this study for whom an *opus magnum* could be selected with a fair degree of certainty. The ages range all the way from twenty-four (one case) to eighty-two (three cases), with the average at

[7] J. B. Heidler and H. C. Lehman, "Chronological Age and Productivity in Various Types of Literature," *Eng. J.*, 1937, 26: 294-304.
[8] *Op. cit.*

forty-seven years. The scientists on the average produced their masterpieces a little earlier than the men of affairs. A similar study by Dorland [9] agrees fairly closely with this one. According to Dorland, the average age at which 400 noted men produced their masterpieces was fifty.

The age of greatest earning capacity will obviously vary considerably with the type of work in which the person engages. For workers in occupations where muscular strength is the chief requirement and for which little or no time is spent in training, the peak comes early; for those in the learned professions it is much later. Thorndike made a study of the salaries received by Methodist clergymen at different ages. For his group of 143 cases there was a steady increase up to about age forty, followed by a plateau which lasted until about fifty-six and a fall thereafter. High-salaried men and low-salaried men showed about the same tendency to vary with age, except that the age changes were most pronounced for those earning the highest salaries.

The outstanding result of all these studies is to show that although we may compute averages, the variation from these averages in individual cases is so great that, if we except the years of early childhood and the late nineties, there is no age within the life span of man at which great accomplishment has not been recorded. Some of our great musicians published work of considerable merit as early as the age of five or six years. Sophocles wrote his *Oedipus* at ninety. Folwell, former president of the University of Minnesota, wrote his monumental *History of Minnesota* during the last years of his life, finishing it just before his death at the age of ninety-six. In his *Senescence*, Hall [10] cites many other instances of outstanding accomplishment performed long after the traditional age of "three score and ten years."

While there is no question but that the years from twenty to fifty are the ones when most people do their best work,[11] fifty

[9] W. A. N. Dorland, *The Age of Mental Virility* (New York, D. Appleton-Century Co., 1908).

[10] G. Stanley Hall, *Senescence, the Last Half of Life* (New York, D. Appleton Company, 1922), pp. xxviii + 518.

[11] The most complete and detailed studies on this topic that have appeared to date have been made by H. C. Lehman. For a summary of his findings, see "Man's Most Creative Years: Then and Now," *Science*, 1943, 98: 393-399.

is by no means a universal dividing line between excellence and mediocrity. Look at Edison! Indeed the more one studies the lives and characters of those who have continued to do creative work up to a late age or of their humbler fellows, who, although they never achieve fame, nevertheless continue to fill useful positions in the world for many years after the majority have dropped out of the race, the more strongly one comes to feel that the vast majority of individuals grow old long before there is need for them to do so. It would be foolish to claim that age is just a notion. It is a fact to which all must adjust as it comes to them. But it is equally foolish to anticipate its ravages before it has actually arrived or to use age as an excuse for failure to accomplish what a little greater effort would have enabled one to perform. Older people may not learn quite as easily as they did in youth, but most of them can still learn.

SOCIAL, PHYSIOLOGICAL, AND PSYCHO-LOGICAL PROBLEMS OF OLD AGE, WITH SUGGESTIONS FOR MEETING THEM

"Symposium on Old Age and Aging," in *American Journal of Orthopsychiatry*, 1940, 10: 27-88.

At the 1939 meeting of the American Orthopsychiatric Association, a special section meeting was devoted to problems of aging and the aged. At this meeting a number of well-known authorities read papers on various aspects of this topic and these papers, together with the discussions that followed them, were later published in the *Journal* of the association. These papers are worth reading, not only because they contain a good deal of information on a subject with which persons interested in social progress should be familiar, but also because this material is presented against a background of social theory that brings out its significance for people in general.

Chapter XXIII

OLD AGE

About how much has the average term of life increased since the sixteenth century? What have been the chief factors contributing to this increase?

Is there a greater chance now than formerly for a man of eighty to live to be one hundred?

Do the senses other than sight and hearing show changes with age? For what distances is the visual loss greatest? For what pitches is the loss of hearing most evident?

Why do the old often remember the events of their childhood better than those that occurred more recently?

What are some of the chief mental hazards of senescence?

What can young people do to improve their chances of a useful and happy old age?

HOW MANY LIVE TO BE OLD?

Obviously this is a question that does not admit of any precise answer unless we first decide at what age people become old. But if we put it in other terms and ask what are the average person's chances, under modern conditions of American life, of living to be fifty, seventy, or ninety years of age, there are statistical tables that will tell us. According to the most recent life tables published by the Bureau of the Census,[1] at birth the average

[1] These are based on the census of 1930. The figures from the 1940 census, which were not available when this was written, will almost certainly show some further increase, the extent of which can be roughly inferred from the data of those census reports that have already appeared. (See Table VIII.)

582

expectancy of life for a white boy baby is about fifty-nine years; for a girl baby it is sixty-two years. But if the hazards of infancy and early childhood are survived the chances of living to be old are better. The little boy of five may expect to live to be sixty-four; the girl of the same age is likely to live to be sixty-seven. The youth of twenty may look forward to becoming sixty-six; at the same age his sister may expect to reach the age of sixty-eight.

The average duration of life has been steadily increasing for several centuries. There are no very good figures to tell us just what was the average age at death three or four hundred years ago, but most authorities are of the opinion that in the sixteenth century at least half the population, on the average, died before the age of twenty. Since then the average age at death has moved constantly upward until, in the United States at present, more than half live to be sixty-eight or older.[2]

The very rapid change in the proportion of older individuals in the population of the United States can be readily seen by comparing the figures given in the *Population* volume of the *1940 Census Report* with those of preceding decades. Table VIII shows the comparative figures for each of the last five decades.

TABLE VIII

PERCENTAGES OF THE TOTAL POPULATION AT EACH OF THE LAST FIVE CENSUS YEARS WHO HAD REACHED THE AGE OF SIXTY OR OLDER

	Census Year				
	1900	1910	1920	1930	1940
Male	3.3%	3.5%	3.8%	4.3%	5.2%
Female	3.2	3.3	3.7	4.2	5.3
Total, both sexes	6.5	6.8	7.5	8.5	10.5

Figures 104 and 105 show about how much longer an individual who has already survived to some stated age may expect to live. These curves, which are based upon life-expectancy tables taken

[2] The average expectation of life at the time of birth is not the same thing as the average age at which half the population born are still living, because death-rates in the later years are so much more rapid than they are in the early years. (See Figure 105.)

from the census data for 1930, may be compared with those appearing in the first edition of this book, which were taken from tables based upon the 1910 census, published in 1921. During the intervening twenty years, the average life-expectancy at the age of twenty years was increased by three years for females and three-and-a-half years for males.

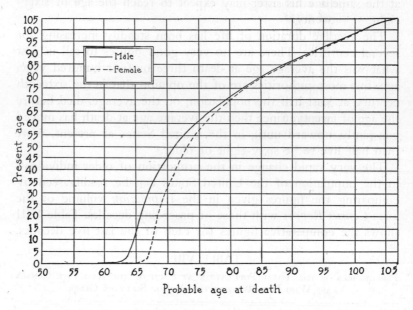

FIG. 104.—EXPECTATION OF LIFE AT ANY GIVEN AGE

To find your most probable age at death first locate your present age in the column of figures at the left. Read across to the intersection of your age line with the curve for your sex. The numbers along the abscissa show your most probable age at death. (Based upon data from Census of 1930.)

A number of people have been so much impressed by this increase in the average life span that they have built up lively hopes of continuing the increase to a point at which human life would be extended to a far greater age than we know now. But these persons have failed to take into account a very important fact. The increase in average duration of life has not been brought about by adding to the life expectancy in equal amount all along the line but instead is almost wholly due to medical discoveries and improvements in sanitary conditions which have increased our control over certain diseases from which many people formerly died. Smallpox, typhoid fever, and childbirth, which a century or two ago took the lives of vast numbers, are examples. As a result of better natal and prenatal care, the reduction in infant mortality has been very great,[3] and the death hazard has also been much reduced among children and young adults. Among the middle-aged, too, the expectation of life has somewhat in-

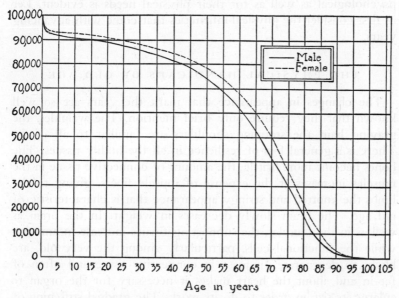

FIG. 105.—PROPORTION OF THE TOTAL NUMBER OF LIVE BIRTHS THAT SURVIVE TO ANY GIVEN AGE

(Based on Census of 1930.)

creased. But among the old, relatively little has been added to life expectancy. Apparently the man who attained his eightieth birthday in the year 1800 had almost, though not quite, as good a chance to live to the age of ninety as he would have to-day. The average span of life has increased, not so much because the

[3] During the twenty-year period previously mentioned, the increase in life expectancy at birth was approximately nine years for each sex, which is almost three times as great as the corresponding increase for those who survive to the age of twenty.

old live to be older but because a greater number of the young live to be old.

Since so many of the young people of to-day will in the course of time become old, the psychology of the declining years is an important study for them as well as for their elders who are already beginning the descent. Moreover, since the number of old people in society is on the increase (see Table VIII) the importance of understanding them and of providing for their psychological as well as for their physical needs is evident. Let us first consider the physical infirmities that come with advancing years.

THE PHYSICAL HANDICAPS OF OLD AGE

The changes in appearance that mark the years are so well known that they require only brief mention. The wrinkles, the graying hair, the stooping shoulders are familiar to all of us. There is a general loss of resilience in all the bodily tissues. The bones become more brittle; the amount of connective tissue in the muscles increases at the expense of muscle fibers, giving to the limbs the knotted and stringy appearance that is characteristic of old age. The brain slowly decreases in weight. In the brain as well as in the muscles, the supporting tissues increase in amount, while the functional cells, particularly among the very old, are likely to degenerate. Increase in connective tissue and often of fat in and about the heart makes it necessary for the organ to enlarge its size in order to do its work. The gradual stiffening of the arteries adds to the cardiac strain. Many changes also take place in the ductless glands. At about the age of forty-five in women and several years later in men the reproductive capacity ceases.

Automatic regulation of bodily functions no longer takes place so promptly. The old "feel the cold more" because heat losses are not so quickly made good. If, through unexpected exertion, they become out of breath, it takes a longer time for the breathing and heart rate to get back to normal. Other regulatory responses show a similar drag.

All the senses usually show a loss of acuity. We are familiar with the fact that the old usually suffer some impairment of sight and hearing. The visual deficiency is commonly greatest for near objects through loss of elasticity in the lens, which can no longer become sufficiently convex for adequate near vision. This causes the "far-sightedness" of old age. Loss of hearing in the old is usually greatest for the higher pitches. Drying and hardening of the skin results in loss of sensitivity to touch. Changes in the sense of taste also occur. The taste-buds on the top of the tongue gradually atrophy. Beginning at the tip of the tongue the insensitive area extends farther and farther toward the back as age advances. Taste-buds on the inner surface of the cheeks also become fewer. The old often complain that "nothing tastes as it used to." Since the olfactory senses, too, usually become less acute in old age, and since, as we have seen, foods owe much of their flavor to the sense of smell, dullness of the olfactory organs is a contributing factor here.

The breaking down of motor skills proceeds in inverse order from that in which the skills were developed. The fine coördinations which were the last to appear are the first to be lost. The same rule is very noticeable in the field of memory. Old associations persist; new ones disappear. The very old often remember the events of their childhood, while they forget those of yesterday. Undoubtedly the principle of overlearning plays a part in this selective forgetting, but it is possible that the unknown physiological changes that form the basis of learning may become less stable as age progresses, thus making for quicker forgetting of material learned during the later years.

Changes in the mental abilities of the aged were described in Chapter XXII and need not be repeated here. We shall only note, by way of summary, that if we make a rough division of activities into three classes—perceptual, motor, and intellectual—investigation seems to show that the perceptual skills which are most directly dependent on the functioning of the sense-organs are the ones that show the earliest and most rapid decline. Motor skills come next, while the intellectual functions are the last to show marked decrement.

PHYSICAL HAZARDS TO WHICH THE OLDER
INDIVIDUAL IS ESPECIALLY SUBJECT

One of the most important factors contributing to the maintenance of mental and social adjustment during the declining years is the preservation of good bodily status as long as possible. Every one, as he grows older, owes it not only to himself but even more to those with whom he is associated to subject himself to periodic physical examinations in order that the early symptoms of the diseases or degenerative conditions to which persons of his age are especially prone may be detected in their initial stages while it is still possible, in most cases, to do something about them.

Often, as persons begin to be aware of the signs of advancing age, they are unwilling to admit the facts even to themselves. To prove that they are still as young as ever, they attempt to outdo the young in respect to physical prowess. They take up strenuous exercise, engage temporarily in activities that would tax the strength of a practiced athlete. The worst of it all is, that because these activities are not undertaken "just for the fun of it" as is the case with the youth, but merely as an assurance to the aging individual that for him the years have not yet begun to make inroads upon his physical strength and vigor, they are likely to be carried out spasmodically rather than systematically. The strenuous use of muscles long unaccustomed to such demands may constitute so serious a strain upon the entire system that lasting damage results. The opposite tendency, leading to too early and too complete relinquishment of physical activity is, of course, equally undesirable. The older person should remember that a reasonable amount of regular exercise, accompanied, if necessary, by some dietary restraint, is greatly preferable to the sudden and violent spurts of effort so often exhibited by those unwilling to "be their age."

We have just said that of the three general aspects of ability—perceptual, motor, and intellectual—the first commonly shows the earliest and most rapid decline with age. One of the most important consequences of this fact under modern conditions of civilized life is the increased proneness to traffic accidents of older pedestrians. Decrease in speed and coördination of bodily movements is a further contributing factor. The older person is not only less likely to see or hear an approaching car, but less able to dodge it effectively after it has been seen. For this reason it is important for him to recognize his perceptual and motor limitations and substitute for them a greater measure of cautious judgment. Unfortunately there are many who fail to realize that as age advances the balance of probability in respect to safety steadily shifts till there comes a time when a street crossing that in youth could have been undertaken with little risk becomes far too hazardous to be ventured. Statistics of pedestrian accidents show that the number of persons injured on the streets of our large cities is definitely related to age. Both children and old people make up a far greater percentage of the victims of such accidents than their frequency in the population warrants. In both cases, heedlessness is the main factor at work. The child fails to take sufficient account of the external dangers; the old person fails to take sufficient account of his personal handicaps. Both need education.

Statistics of driver accidents show a similar trend. Both very young and the very old drivers appear to be somewhat more prone to accident, on the average, than are those of the middle ages. Older persons can, and many of them do, make up for their lowered perceptive ability and slower speed of reaction by taking fewer chances and giving closer attention to the road. The important thing is for the aging individual to recognize his limitations as facts to be compensated for by bringing other assets into play, instead of denying the existence of these handicaps and thereby bringing unnecessary danger to himself and others.

Other accidents also need to be guarded against. Along with loss of acuity of hearing there often goes some deterioration in the semicircular canals, which, as you will recall from Chapter V are responsible for our sense of balance and are closely associated with the organ of hearing. Thus falls becomes more frequent, in part as a result of some loss in the sense of equilibrium, in part because of lowered muscular control. Moreover, because of the increased brittleness of the bones, such falls are more likely to have serious consequences than was true at an earlier age. Less perfect control of the hands leads to greater danger of cuts and burns. Accordingly, along with physical aids to the sense-organs should go some attention to the provision of physical safeguards such as suitable staircase railings and the elimination from rooms much used by the aged members of the family of small rugs and similar objects likely to cause stumbling. Hazardous places such as the tops of staircases should be kept well lighted. Young persons in a household where there are elderly people should give some thought to these matters, not only on account of the old persons themselves but for the sake of the entire household.

THE MENTAL HYGIENE OF OLD AGE

As their senses grow duller, the old are more and more completely cut off from the world around them. Particularly is this true of those who suffer complete or nearly complete loss of hearing. The young often complain that old people are self-centered, that they think and talk only about themselves. One reason for this is unquestionably to be found in the increasing isolation that comes with sensory deprivation. Old people think and talk about themselves because they no longer have the means of finding out very much about what is going on around them. One of the most important aspects of the mental hygiene of old age is, therefore, to use every possible artificial aid to compensate for the increasing sensory weakness. The need for financial preparation for the years when self-support becomes difficult or impossible can hardly be overstressed. Problems relating to old-age insurance, retirement annuities, old-age pensions and the like are among the most vital social questions of to-day. But there is another hardly less important form of old-age insurance about which we hear little. In addition to financial preparation for the declining years, every young person should see to it that he acquires a store of interests, skills, friendships, and life objectives that will outlast his youth. Some people, no matter what their years, never seem to grow old in spirit. These are the ones who have laid up for themselves a store of all-engrossing occupations with which to fill the gaps that inevitably occur with the passage of time. Just as in youth we prepare for the work of maturity, so in maturity some thought should be given to the activities of old age. Most fortunate are they whose life occupations are of a kind that can be continued into old age, for they are the ones from whom the years exact least in the way of adjustment. Edison, Luther Burbank, Justice Holmes, and others who continued to do productive work for years after most people find it necessary to stop, escaped many of the most trying situations of old age. The years bear heaviest upon those to whom they bring an enforced leisure with nothing to fill it that seems worth the doing.

Many of the personality changes that so often come with age —the increased irritability, the self-centeredness, the tendency to magnify bodily ills which sometimes amounts to genuine hypochondria [4]—are less the direct result of age than of the sense of discouragement and frustration that comes from a realization of increasing inability to do the things that were formerly done. We shall see in a later chapter how conflicting impulses or continued frustration may find an abnormal outlet in behavior that in extreme cases leads to complete disintegration of the personality. But old age does not always bring frustration. To some it means increased leisure for the development of long-treasured hobbies and interests, and this is as it ideally should be. Not all forms of ability decline at an equal rate, and as was pointed out in Chapter XXII, most abilities decline slowly enough to enable the old to participate in many activities with enjoyment and profit, if they care to do so. But although the old may continue to carry on the activities of their youth with but slightly abated ardor as long as their physical and mental condition permits, they are not facile in developing new interests. They may renew old hobbies or take advantage of increasing leisure to do some of the many things for which a busy maturity left too little time. But these interests and hobbies must in the main be drawn from the reserves that were accumulated earlier. Too many old people, when confronted with the new leisure that is thrust upon them with the years, find that they have no psychological reserves from which to fill it. Morgan,[5] for example, in a study of recipients of old-age assistance in the state of New York found that a small number of factors could account for most of the differences be-

[4] The term *hypochondria* refers to an obsessive interest in one's bodily health, a tendency to magnify bodily ills out of all proportion to their true significance.

[5] C. M. Morgan, "The Attitudes and Adjustments of Recipients of Old-Age Assistance in Upstate and Metropolitan New York," *Arch. Psychol.*, No. 214 (New York, Columbia University Press, 1937), pp. 131.

tween those who seemed happy and well adjusted and those who were continually bewailing their lot. The former had kept up many more pleasant associations with friends and relatives than the latter; they had more outside interests and hobbies; and they habitually sought and found opportunity to perform some kind of useful work. They were also in better health, a fact that may perhaps be as much a result of their more wholesome way of living and behaving as a cause of it.

Senescence, which Hall so aptly calls "the youth of old age," is a time when a new kind of psychological weaning must take place if the years that follow are to be satisfying. The adolescent must free himself from emotional dependence upon his parents; the senescent in like manner must free himself from emotional dependence upon his own youth. Each age has its own satisfactions for the person who will take them. Growing old is as normal a part of life as growing up. In age, as well as in youth, the well-integrated personality lives in the present and plans for the future.

A PROBLEM IN SOCIAL RESEARCH

Consult the volume on *Population* of the *Reports of the United States Census* for the years 1900-1940 inclusive. Prepare a table similar to that on p. 583, basing the figures on the data given for the state in which you were born. Is the shift in the proportion of older individuals in the state population more or less marked than it is for the United States as a whole? If the difference between the national and state figures shows a consistent tendency either to become greater or to become less marked with the passage of time, how do you explain this?

In a similar way, compare the figures for the largest city in your state with those for the total state population and for the urban population of the United States.

List all the social consequences of the changing population trend that you can think of. Have any of these consequences become apparent in social legislation or other ways that can be objectively described?

PART IV
Personality Deviations

Chapter XXIV

COMMON HANDICAPS OF NORMAL PEOPLE

Does the ideal personality change with age?

What is meant by "frustration"? Do obstacles always frustrate? Explain.

What common ways of reacting to failure are likely to develop into habits that interfere with normal personality growth?

What is the most common basis for excessive boasting?

Under what circumstances does day-dreaming become harmful?

SOME TYPICAL CASES

Evelyn B. is a senior in high school. She is an only child, and her mother boasts that Evelyn is not silly like the other girls, that she spends all her spare time at home and does not want to go out to dances and parties with the other young people of her age. Actually Evelyn is so shy and self-conscious that she cannot feel at ease with the other boys and girls. She has never learned to dance and is afraid to try for fear she will be laughed at. Secretly she longs for "dates" and tries to make up for their lack by reading cheap fiction and by day-dreaming about all sorts of emotional scenes in which she is the heroine.

Unlike Evelyn, George S. is out for a good time, regardless of the cost. He is impatient of all restrictions, and in constant trouble with parents and teachers. After failing in his high-school work he was sent to boarding-school but ran away because the rules were too strict. Now he refuses either to enter school or to get a job. He loafs around town and is beginning to associate with undesirable companions picked up around pool halls.

Alfred M. is a college student. His two older brothers made very brilliant academic records, and Alfred feels that he is expected to equal their achievement. This he finds very difficult, if not impossible, and so he tries to account for his lower level of achievement in various

595

ways that protect his self-esteem. He feigns ill health and claims that his vision is so poor that he cannot study without difficulty. He complains that his instructors do not make things clear and that they do not always grade fairly. Once, through a stenographic error, his real grade of B was recorded as a D. Although the error was promptly corrected, he has never forgotten it but takes every opportunity to tell his friends that "the marks you get here don't mean anything. They make so many mistakes over at the registrar's office that you can't tell a thing from the grades they send out." He insists that other students obtain their high standing by cheating or through favoritism, and he greatly enjoys repeating cynical stories about members of Phi Beta Kappa and other honorary societies.

Caroline S., also a college student, is brilliant but unpopular. As a child she attracted a great deal of attention because of her precocity. Several newspaper articles were published about her achievements, and when she was ten years old a small book of her poems was printed. Now, in a college of high standards where she is for the first time meeting real intellectual competition, she cannot bear to have any one share the spotlight with her. She has developed a number of personal mannerisms to attract attention to herself, spreads ill-natured rumors about other students, and seizes every chance to tell of her own accomplishments. Her book of childish poems occupies the most prominent position on her study table.

Mrs. Gray, married ten years and childless, assumes the rôle of child in her associations with her husband. She demands constant petting and indulgence, cries when she cannot get her own way, uses baby talk and dresses in juvenile styles that are no longer becoming. She complains bitterly because her husband spends so many of his evenings at his office or at his club. She has few friends because people in general find her boring and are annoyed by her affectations. She has few resources for amusing herself and is usually very lonely and unhappy.

You have all met people like these. None of them would be classed as abnormal, but all display personality traits that interfere with their happiness and handicap them in their chances for success in life. Although their problems seem very diverse both in form and origin, one thing can be said about all of them. These persons have not grown up. Somewhere along the line their personalities have suffered from arrested development. Their bodily growth was not affected. Even in intelligence, as the term is commonly defined, they show no particular lack. But in their social and emotional characteristics, in their attitudes toward the world and toward themselves they have not advanced beyond the level of childhood. In Evelyn we see the timid child who clings to the protection and security of the home and from that safe retreat looks out longingly at the fun and adventure of the world beyond in which she has not the courage to share. George is still the spoiled baby to whom his rattle and his bottle of milk are all-important. He is even less mature than Evelyn, because she has reached a stage at which she would like to be grown up, even though her desire is not strong enough to take her over the threshold. But George is deliberately shutting his eyes upon the world where men work and achieve and reap the benefits of their labor. Instead, he clings to the privileges and immunities of babyhood.

Alfred and Caroline have advanced to a somewhat higher level, but both have stopped short of complete maturity. They have failed to develop the broader sense of social values that would enable them to view themselves and their own achievements with some detachment, to appreciate what others do and to take a sportsmanlike attitude toward honest defeat. Egocentricity is a normal attribute of early childhood, but long before a boy or girl has reached the age of entering college, this narrow preoccupation with self should have expanded into a wider conception of social aims and an appreciation of what others are doing toward fulfilling those aims. To the truly socialized person the natural disappointment over his own failure is tempered by the knowledge of another's success, but to the immature adult who has never outgrown the egocentricity of childhood, seeing another person succeed merely adds gall to the bitterness of his own defeat. We may note, too, that Alfred appears to have moved a little further along the road from egocentricity to socialization than Caroline has, for in his concern with covering up his own failures there is tacit recognition of and a covert admiration for the accomplishments of others. Caroline, on the contrary, sees only herself.

Little need be said of the case of Mrs. Gray. Like George she clings to the things of childhood, but, perhaps because of the license accorded to her sex, her behavior is more open and unabashed. George covers up his real desire to remain a child with a blustering kind of aggression that nevertheless is closely allied to the temper tantrums of infancy.

TRAITS THAT INTERFERE WITH PERSONALITY GROWTH

It would be futile to attempt to enumerate even a small portion of the almost countless ways in which people depart from an ideal pattern of personality development. All that will be attempted is to show some of the most common obstacles that lie in the way of a smooth and orderly progress from a healthy infancy to a happy and efficient maturity, and to indicate some of the pitfalls that should be avoided in attempting to overcome such obstacles.

All of us know what it is to be thwarted. There have been times when we have been unable to secure something that we greatly wanted. In spite of strong effort we have sometimes failed to accomplish what we set out to do. Ideas that to us seemed both exciting and important have been received by others with indifference or even ridicule. Planning that has occupied months or years has been disrupted in a few moments by events over which we have had no control.

Many psychologists believe that the reaction to frustration is always some form of aggressive conduct.[1] The word "conduct" is here used in its broad sense to include both overt reactions that every one can see and responses that are largely or wholly internalized, such as dreams of revenge or of compensating for the failure by some kind of stupendous accomplishment. The aggressive behavior is not always overtly directed toward the offending person or object, and on the surface it does not always look like aggression. Sometimes the thwarted individual who is unable or afraid to show aggression toward the offending agent "takes it out" on some weaker person or even an inanimate object. The business man who "bawls out" his secretary for some trifling fault when a rival firm secures the order he had been hoping to get, the teacher who gives low grades to her pupils on hearing that her request for an increase in salary has been refused,[2] or

[1] John Dollard, Leonard W. Doob, Neal E. Miller, O. H. Mowrer, and Robert R. Sears, *Frustration and Aggression* (New Haven, Conn., Yale University Press, 1939), pp. x + 209.

[2] In most cases these persons either fail to understand or refuse to admit even to themselves the basis for their acts. The business man insists that his

the little child who smashes his toys because he is denied a cookie are examples that are only too familiar to all of us. Moreover, aggression may be expressed in a wide variety of ways, many of which are not easy to recognize, or it may be so long delayed that the conditions which gave rise to it are well-nigh forgotten.

Although some may question the assertion that *all* acts of aggression have their roots in frustration, there can be no doubt that this is frequently the case. But not all obstacles, not every disappointment or failure result in a feeling of frustration. As a matter of fact, with some people and under some circumstances, encounter with an obstacle may actually incite to greater effort.[3] And among the many ways in which aggression may be shown there are some that are likely to have unfortunate consequences for society and others that interfere with the healthy development of the person who habitually resorts to them. The possible effects of aggression upon those who become its victims are too obvious to require discussion, but the effect upon the aggressor is not always so evident. Particularly likely is this to be the case when the frustration takes the form of a wound to self-esteem and the frustrated person seeks for some kind of redress that will soothe his pride and so relieve his pain without acknowledging the facts. Such devices may be compared to the application of salves to a physical wound without first cleansing it of any lurking infection. Antiseptics may cause momentary smarting, but their timely use may prevent the development of much trouble later on.

A common example of the palliative measures so often resorted to by people whose self-esteem has been wounded is the mechanism known as *rationalization* which was mentioned in an earlier chapter. Rationalization, you will recall, means the invention or construction of "reasons" for the humiliating event that will allay the hurt to one's pride. Rationalization may take any one of a wide variety of forms. It may involve the mechanism known as *projection*, in which an attempt is made to throw the blame for one's own failure on somebody else or on an inanimate object.

---

secretary thoroughly deserved the scolding; the teacher is equally sure that the low marks were entirely justified by the poor quality of the children's work.

[3] Herbert Fletcher Wright, "The Influence of Barriers upon Strength of Motivation," *Contributions to Psychological Theory*, Vol. I, No. 3 (Durham, N. C. Duke University Press, 1937), pp. 143.

"I'd have been on the green," says the golfer, "if that fellow over there hadn't yelled, 'Fore!' just as I was ready to swing." "It was all your fault," storms Mr. Brown to his wife when their house burns down the day after the insurance has lapsed. "You should have reminded me that the payment was overdue."

Because in the minds of many people no special blame is attached to a physical illness, such a condition may also be invoked as an explanation for failure or as a means of avoiding an undertaking where failure or some other unpleasant consequence is feared. "I could have passed that examination as easily as anything if I hadn't had such a splitting headache that day," says the student. "I would have been only too glad to go and help Mrs. Atkins take care of her sick baby if it weren't for my weak heart," says Mrs. Elwood. But her weak heart did not keep Mrs. Elwood from her bridge club, and the student recovered from her headache in plenty of time to go to a dance that evening.

Another way of reacting to failure is by *denial* or by the employment of various devices for *concealment*. But such devices often fail to work out satisfactorily, and so the luckless artificer is forced to add camouflage to camouflage until the whole structure seems likely to totter. Still another method by which people attempt to assuage the pain of failure is by *day-dreaming*, by making believe that success really has been attained. This is not only wasteful of time but tends to divert the attention from more constructive activities. Still others try to cover up their disappointment by adopting a *"sour grapes"* attitude, by trying to convince themselves and others that what they were after was not really worth while.

The behavior known as *overcompensation*, in which a person who feels unsure of his own abilities tries to make up for any possible lack by boasting or trying to "show off," is another familiar example of the devices for protecting self-esteem. But boasting is a weak form of defense. The man of real achievement is modest in his speech because he does not fear to be brought to test.

But the most harmful of all reactions to failure is the abandonment of effort that comes with *discouragement*. Usually this attitude is accompanied by *brooding* and by *self-pity*. Nothing is at once more futile and more disastrous for future development than dismal bewailing of one's own misfortunes. Often, too, this preoccupation with past ills is accompanied by jealous comparison with the apparent good fortune of others, by *envy* of those who have succeeded and perhaps even by ill-natured *suspicion* of the means by which their success was achieved. Such suspicion may even go so far as the spreading of unkind rumors that have little foundation apart from the festering jealousy of the person who grudges others their good fortune.

All these ways of reacting to failure are dangerous. We shall see in the following chapter how insidious is the progress from the mild and occasional lapses from which few of us are entirely free to the habitual and compulsive responses that in time may come to dominate behavior so completely that the affected person loses touch with the world of reality. In time he may even become so obsessed with maintaining his own diseased fancies that he can no longer function as a normally integrated personality but must be placed in a hospital for the mentally diseased. Mental health, like physical health, is not an all-or-none affair but exists in varying degrees. Like physical health, it is to a large extent within our own hands. Although we still have much to learn about it, nevertheless a good many basic rules that will help us to maintain it are known, and to these rules we should all endeavor to conform. Carelessness does not, of course, inevitably mean that we shall land in a mental hospital, any more than carelessness about one's bodily health always and inevitably means hospitalization or early death. But the chances in both cases are that such neglect will mean decreased efficiency and unnecessary bodily or mental discomfort. Common sense dictates that we obey the rules.

WILLIAM JAMES ON "HABIT"

William James, "Habit," Chapter IV, Vol. I, *The Principles of Psychology* (New York, Henry Holt and ⌐ ⌐., 1890), 2 vols.

We hear so much about the formation of undesirable habits that we sometimes forget the tremendous importance of good habits. If we were not able to reduce most of the routine affairs of everyday life to so automatic a level that they can be performed with little or no conscious thought or effort, we should have little leisure for anything else. Habit, as James points out, is time's great ally.

Althought the two-volume *Principles of Psychology* was written well over a half-century ago, it remains one of the great classics of psychological literature, and this in spite of the great advances in scientific knowledge and the consequent changes in psychological theory which have taken place since that time. Every student who plans to take up psychology as a profession should become thoroughly familiar with it, and all of you, regardless of your vocational aims, will, it is hoped, derive enough pleasure from the Great Pragmatist's[4] vigorous style and trenchant philosophy to stimulate you to read much more of this important work than just the single chapter mentioned here.

[4] James was called the "Great Pragmatist" because of his insistence that the facts of psychology should, as far as possible, be derived from observation of the ordinary behavior of human beings and that its principles should bear directly upon the practical affairs of everyday life. "Pragmatist" means one who emphasizes the practical application of ideas and concepts.

Chapter XXV

MENTAL DISEASE

Suppose that in a certain hospital about one hundred babies are born, on the average, each year. About how many of the hundred will at some time in their lives become patients in a hospital for mental diseases?

Are all mental disorders the result of brain injury or of physical diseases that affect the brain?

Do normal people always perceive things as they are? What is the difference between a normal illusion and a hallucination? Are there any conditions that will produce hallucinations in people who are not insane?

What is meant by "regression to childhood"? In what ways does the behavior of mentally disordered persons resemble that of normal children? In what ways does it differ?

What is means by a systematized delusion? What is the relationship between mental conflicts and delusions?

What are some of the specific devices by which the mentally ill try to solve their conflicts?

(Keep the following question in mind as you read, and try to answer it afterward.)

Do you think the different mental disorders described here are separate diseases or merely different methods or devices by which the frustrated person tries to find a way out of his difficulties? See if you can think of a series of conditions under which the same original conflict might lead to any one of the disorders mentioned.

MEETING EMERGENCIES

In the preceding chapters the essential characteristics of the fully developed personality have been described, and a number of attitudes, ways of thinking and behaving that interfere with personality growth have been pointed out. Undesirable as these characteristics are, few people manage to remain completely free from them, just as few people reach maturity with absolutely perfect physical development and with habits of living that conform in all respects to the rules for maintaining health. People differ, not only in respect to the qualitative aspects of their personality but also in a more nearly quantitative way. They differ in the *extent or degree of personality growth* that they have achieved. They differ in respect to what we may think of as the *reserve strength of personality* that they accumulate in the course of their development, a reserve that may be drawn upon when special emergencies arise.[1]

These differences among people cover a very long range. At the one extreme we have the fortunate few whose personalities

---

[1] Even in childhood the effect of this reserve or of its lack is shown in the differing responses of children to emotional strain. In a recent monograph (*Preliminary Report on Children's Reactions to the War, Including a Survey of the Literature* (New York, privately published, 1942), pp. 92 + 10 of bibliography), Louise Despert states that out of a group of sixty-three children studied intensively by herself and an additional group of seventy-one for whom the data were less complete, the only ones who showed intense states of anxiety or emotional disturbance over the war were those who had exhibited more than the usual tendency to worry and had given other evidences of emotional conflict previous to the war. They were children who, because of a feeling of insecurity, resulting in many cases from family disharmony, were failing to gain the feeling of independence and self-confidence that is one of the most essential aspects of normal personality growth. Because their emotional force was constantly being expended through unhappiness and anxiety, they were unable to lay up a reserve with which to meet the new demand. There was also the factor of the absence of an external protection upon which they could place unquestioning reliance, such as children feel who are secure in their family relationships.

approach very closely to the ideal level of development and who have accumulated such a store of reserve strength that they are able to withstand almost any blow that fate can deal them. At the other extreme we have those who have fallen by the wayside. They are grown up in body but have clung to certain aspects of their childhood personalities, either because they were unwilling to relinquish the privileges and immunities that belong to childhood or because they feared the responsibilities that come with maturity. Ostrich-like, they cherished an unconscious hope that by evading responsibility, by shutting their eyes to it and seeking refuge in some childish device for gaining temporary security, they might escape its consequences. Eventually, through continued resort to these devices the attitudes and habits became so ingrained a part of the individual personality that contact with reality was lost. The devices became more real than the situations from which the individual sought to escape. So in the course of time there was not merely arrest of personality growth but an actual retrogression to a type of personality that, while it maintains many of the characteristics of childhood is nevertheless farther removed from the goal of normal maturity than is that of even the young child. For the child remains keenly aware of the real world that he is attempting to control, even though he may be unable to express his feelings and attitudes in words, and in spite of the fact that conditioning processes,[2] of which he is probably quite unaware, are responsible for most of the particular patterns of behavior he displays. But the adult whose regression to a pseudochildhood is so complete that it has gone beyond his control, is no longer able to function effectively in the real world of men and affairs because he has ceased to see things as they are but regards them only in the mirror of his distorted fancy. Such a person, we say, is suffering from mental disease.

HOW MANY PEOPLE ARE AFFECTED?

Few people realize what tremendous social problems are created by mental diseases. Most people think of insanity as something that can safely be ignored. They assume that it affects but a few persons and that it is almost always due to bad habits or to acci-

[2] See Chapters VI and VII.

dents that affect the brain. The idea that some one near and dear to them may fall victim to it does not occur to them.

Nothing could be much farther from the truth than the assumption that mental disease is rare or that any social group is exempt from it. Pollock,[3] to whom we are indebted for some of our most careful statistical studies of mental disorders, has made a comparison of the number of first admissions to hospitals for mental disease in the state of New York with the total population of the state. He estimates that "approximately 4.5 per cent of the persons born in the state of New York may, under existing conditions, be expected to succumb to mental disease of one form or another and become patients for a longer or shorter period in hospitals for mental disease. In other words, on the average approximately one person out of 22 becomes a patient in a hospital for mental disease during the lifetime of a generation."

PROBABLE NUMBER AMONG CERTAIN SOCIAL GROUPS WHO WILL DEVELOP SERIOUS MENTAL DISEASE AND BECOME PATIENTS IN A HOSPITAL FOR MENTAL DISEASE

Among 117,000 male children born in New York State in 1927......   5,000
Among 111,000 female children born in New York State in 1927....   4,400
Among 1,030,000 boys in public schools in New York State in 1927   51,500
Among 999,000 girls in public schools in New York State in 1927.... 44,000
Among 194,000 male immigrants to the United States in year ended
    June 30, 1927...   10,000
Among 141,000 female immigrants to the United States in year ended
    June 30, 1927...   7,300
Among 3,500,000 World War I Veterans whose average age in 1927
    was 35 years.. 154,000

The estimates just quoted are based upon statistics obtained from mental hospitals in New York State in 1927. A question of much practical importance is, How do these estimates compare with those based upon more recent data? Is the frequency of mental disease increasing or decreasing? Malzberg,[4] a coworker with Pollock, has attempted to answer this question. By comparing data obtained from the census of 1940 with that of 1920 he finds that within the state of New York the rate of first admissions to mental hospitals, in proportion to the state popula-

---

[3] H. M. Pollock and B. Malzberg, "Expectation of Mental Disease," *Ment. Hygiene*, 1929, 13: 132-163.
[4] Benjamin Malzberg, "The Increase of Mental Disease," *Psych. Quart.*, 1943, 17: 488-507.

tion of corresponding ages, has increased about 25 per cent during the twenty-year period. Some of the increase in hospitalization is probably due to better diagnoses, but Malzberg is able to show that this cannot account for more than a small proportion of the increase. A major part of the change is due indirectly to the greater number of old people in the population, for, as can be seen in Figure 106, the likelihood of mental disease increases fairly rapidly during old age. Apparently, control over the degenerative diseases of age from which many formerly died has

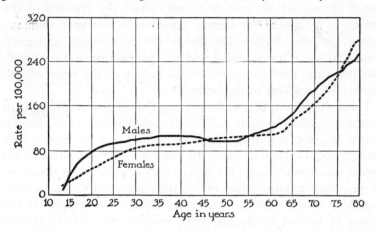

FIG. 106.—RELATIONSHIP OF THE FREQUENCY OF ONSET OF MENTAL DISEASE TO AGE

(From H. M. Pollock and B. Malzberg, "Expectation of Mental Disease," *Mental Hygiene, 1929, 18:* 132-163.)

outrun control over the organic mental diseases that often arise from them. Alcoholic psychoses also increased during this period, while those resulting from venereal infection decreased. But there is no evidence that, except for the gain brought about through better control of venereal disease, any marked headway is being made toward the reduction of mental disease in general. It still constitutes one of our major social problems.[5]

These facts are indeed startling, the more so when we remem-

[5] Detailed statistics for the United States as a whole will be found in *Patients in Mental Institutions, 1940,* U. S. Department of Commerce, Bureau of the Census (Washington, D. C., U. S. Government Printing Office, 1943), pp. viii + 184.

ber that although some persons who enter mental hospitals make sufficient improvement to be discharged after a time, a large percentage remain there for the duration of their lives. The financial burden upon the normal population of maintaining the large number of hospitals required to care for such vast numbers of the mentally ill is very great, and the loss to society through the incapacitation of so many of its members is even greater.

Although the early stages of mental ill health can be observed in childhood and some definite breakdowns occur in adolescence, mental disease serious enough to necessitate the removal of the patient to a hospital for mental disorders is not very common before maturity. Figure 106 shows the relationship of mental disease to age. During childhood the proportion is very small. The few cases that occur are for the most part the result of diseases or of accidents to the brain.[6]

The student must be careful not to confuse *mental disease* with *mental deficiency*, which will be discussed in the next chapter. There are two important distinctions between the two which must always be kept in mind. In the case of the feeble-minded person we have to do with a defect that is primarily a matter of his intelligence, rather than of his total personality. The *feeble-minded person* is unable to learn as much or as rapidly as the person of normal intellectual gifts, but in a simplified environment, where not too much is expected from him, he may be happy and well adjusted, contributing quite as much to the welfare of society as his meager endowment permits. That he rarely does so in fact is not due to the nature of his defect but to the failure of society to make suitable provision for his care and training. But the *mentally diseased person* is not truly happy, even though, by his flight into a dream world, he sometimes appears to have achieved a kind of quasi-happiness. His contribution to society is nil,[7] in spite of the fact that his potential capacity

[6] A few exceptions to this rule occur. The condition known as *schizophrenia*, which is a term applied to a rather broad class of functional mental disorders characterized by delusions, systematic phantasies, and disorganized emotional life while the strictly intellectual functions remain comparatively unimpaired until the disease is well advanced, is sometimes found in childhood, though its occurrence is rare. For further information the reader may consult *Schizophrenia in Childhood* by Charles Bradley (New York, Macmillan Co., 1941), pp. x + 152.

[7] Except in exceedingly rare instances.

may have been very high indeed. A further differentiating factor, and one that is in some ways more easily determined, is to be found in the age at the onset of the difficulty. Mental deficiency is present from birth or at least from very early childhood; mental disease is acquired during the lifetime of the individual. In the mentally defective person there is progression, but at so slow a rate that he lags further and further behind his normal associates as age advances. In the mentally diseased person there is not progression but retrogression that may proceed rapidly or slowly but that eventually takes him back to a level far below that which he had formerly achieved.[8] Later, of course, he may again show improvement, for some mental patients recover. But the course of the *disease* is always retrogressive.

CLASSIFICATION OF MENTAL DISORDERS

Mental diseases as they are known to-day fall into two broad classes. The first are the *organic disorders*, in which the behavior disturbance is directly consequent upon a known organic condition affecting the brain. Brain tumors, serious injuries that destroy parts of the brain substance, and general paresis resulting from syphilitic infection are examples. Since the origin and treatment of these conditions is primarily a medical problem, we shall not consider them here. But there are other forms of mental disorders, quite as outstanding in their symptoms and quite as disabling to the individual, for which no organic base has been discovered. They affect the way the individual thinks and acts but although we assume, just as in other forms of learned reactions, that some

[8] It is sometimes said that the mentally diseased person was entirely normal up to the time of onset. This is in all probability true when a physiological disturbance, such as a brain tumor or some disease that affects the nervous system, is the cause. But in the case of the functional mental diseases later to be discussed, it is questionable whether this is ever the case. Even though there is reason to believe that many such cases have their roots in an inherited constitutional tendency which makes the affected persons unable to withstand environmental stresses and strains that persons with more stable endowment would weather without serious difficulty, it still appears that these forms of mental disease must be considered as learned reactions, ways of thinking and behaving that were at first more or less deliberately adopted until at last, as with the drug addict, the practices first adopted for the sake of temporary relief gain such control over the individual that he is unable to do without them.

kind of change in the organism has taken place, we do not know in what this change consists. It does not involve any gross destruction of brain tissue, such as is found in paresis or other mental diseases of the so-called organic type. Because the diagnosis in these cases has to be based entirely on the way the affected person behaves, these are known as *functional mental disorders*.

NORMAL AND ABNORMAL REACTIONS

Functional disorders appear to be the result of particular experiences through which the person concerned has learned to attach wrong meanings to so many of the situations he encounters that his behavior becomes grossly inappropriate to the conditions that call it forth. Although, in this respect, the behavior of these persons is not greatly different from that of normal individuals there is, nevertheless, an important distinction to be made. The wrong meanings that the mentally diseased person assigns to the various situations that he encounters in life are not just matters of circumstantial association or casual resemblance such as occasionally throw the normal person off the track. They lie deeper than that. A few examples will make the distinction clear. All of us have at times been misled into thinking that we saw or heard something that was not there. Usually there was something there but not the thing we supposed. Mistakes of this kind are known as *illusions*. Some illusions of visual perception are experienced under the appropriate conditions by almost everybody. They are normal illusions, resulting from the way the eyes work. A number of these illusions have been described in previous chapters. Here is another one known as the "floating finger illusion" [9] that you can easily try for yourself. It is due to the fact that you have two eyes which see things from slightly different angles.

Choose a position where you can fixate the eyes on an object at some distance. Bring the tips of the two index fingers together at a distance of about eight or nine inches from the eyes and just below the line of regard. Although your finger tips are actually in contact with each other, they will appear to be separated by about two inches and to be connected by a third finger which

[9] This illusion was first described by W. L. Sharp in *Psychol. Rev.*, 1928, 35: 171-173.

completely fills the intervening space. Now if, while you continue to look at the distant object, you separate the fingers slowly, the third finger will at first appear to be floating in space between them. As the fingers draw further apart the third finger grows shorter and eventually disappears.

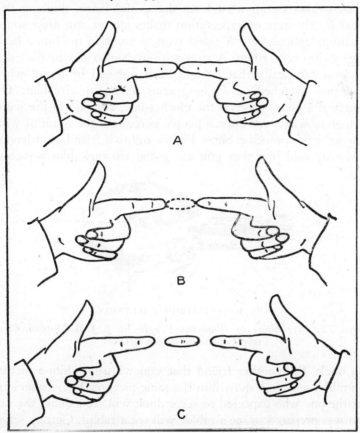

FIG. 107.—THE FLOATING FINGER ILLUSION

(From W. L. Sharp, "The Floating Finger Illusion," *Psychol. Rev.* 1928, 35, 171-173. Courtesy Psychological Review Co.)

Illusions of this kind have attracted a good deal of interest among psychologists because of the light they throw on fundamental questions of perception. But in addition to these generally experienced illusions of perception, every one occasionally has illusions that are peculiar to himself and are chiefly determined by his organic state at the moment, by what he happens to be thinking about, what he is "set" to see or hear.

I am expecting a telephone call. The telephone is in another room from which I can hear the bell but not very clearly. Half a dozen times I stop what I am doing and listen, thinking that I hear it. My state of expectation makes almost any noise sound like the telephone bell. A timid woman alone in the house hears burglars in every room. A superstitious Negro ran to his cabin shrieking frantically that he had been pursued by a tall white ghost that stretched out its long arms trying to seize him. The ghost was a pillow-case on the clothes-line, blowing in the wind.

Much of what even normal people perceive is the result of what they are set to perceive. Show Figure 108 to a friend after having previously told him that you are going to show him a picture

FIG. 108.—JASTROW'S ILLUSION

(From *The Psychology of Abnormal People*, by J. J. B. Morgan. Courtesy Longmans, Green & Co.)

of a duck. Tell another friend that you will show him a picture of a rabbit and then show him the same picture. The chances are that the one who expected to see a duck will see a duck; the one who was prepared to see a rabbit will see a rabbit. Getting set to respond in a particular way is in reality the beginning of the act of responding in that way. Unless there is a fairly sharp interference, such as would come, in this case, from being shown a picture that could not reasonably be made to conform to expectation, the activity will run on along its appointed course.

The more intense the preparatory reaction, the more likely it is to over ride the obstacles caused by discrepancies between expectation and fact and to make the external evidence conform to the pattern set by the internal drive. Emotional states such as anger, fear, jealousy, suspicion are preparatory reactions that may carry all before them. The jealous wife sees infidelity in the most ordinary acts of courtesy shown by her husband to other women. The timid pedestrian sees a bandit behind every bush. The unduly self-conscious person thinks that everybody is looking at him and talking about him.

Illusions due to strong preparatory reactions are experienced by everybody, and when these reactions are not too grossly inappropriate to the situation that touches off the response, no one pays much attention to them. The city woman walking along a leaf-strewn path in the woods starts back at the sight of a half- hidden stick exclaiming, "Gracious! I thought it was a snake!" Here as in many other cases the phenomenon which Hollingworth calls *redintegration* plays an important part. From a single feature one reconstructs a total situation. Something about the stick resembles a snake, and the woman, who in any case is prepared to see snakes, responds as suddenly and as strongly to this single feature as if the snake were there.

Illusions such as these disturb nobody as long as the "mistake" has an actual basis that other people can see. But when the intraorganic state dominates the situation so completely that the response occurs with no external conditions to justify it, we say that the person is suffering from *delusions* or *hallucinations*.[10]

---

[10] The term *hallucination* refers particularly to false perceptions that have, as far as other people can see, no basis in objective reality. Although hallucinations occur in all sensory fields, those of vision and hearing are the most common. The patient suffering from delirium tremens sees snakes, rats, mice, and other vermin; the paranoid hears voices reproaching him for his sins or urging him to crime. *Delusions* are more highly organized than hallucinations; they are *systems of belief*, usually centering about the person himself. The patient believes himself to be Napoleon, or to be incredibly rich, or to be the object of some great conspiracy.

Hallucinations may arise directly from a disturbed condition of the body, such as is produced by certain drugs or by fever. There is a plant known as *mescal* that grows in the southwestern part of the United States and which, when taken into the body, produces visual hallucinations that are remarkable for their color qualities. In delirium the fevered patient both sees and hears many things that are not there. Prolonged alcoholic poisoning seems to have a particular effect upon the visual centers in the brain, predisposing the patient to see small things in motion. Hence the hallucinations of delirium tremens are likely to take the form of small animals such as mice or insects.

When the same delusion persists for long periods of time and the individual builds up a whole series of responses that correspond to it, we say that he has *systematized delusions*. Every hospital for mental diseases has many patients belonging to this class. These delusions take many forms. Delusions of persecution and delusions of grandeur are among the most common.

A woman of about thirty-five years, a graduate student in one of the leading American universities, approached a group of her classmates one day with the remark, "I wonder whether studying psychology makes people selfish or whether selfish people are more likely to choose psychology as a major." When asked for an explanation she continued, "Never in my life have I been so unkindly treated as I have been here. I have been absent from class for the last three lectures and not one person has asked why. No one has even offered to lend me his lecture notes. But," she went on, illogically enough in view of her previous remark, "that is always the way. No one ever tries to do anything for me."

At this point some one reminded her that she could not have been absent for more than the opening lecture as she had just come from class and there had been but one previous class meeting. She was offered the use of notes on the first lecture but declined them indignantly, insisting that there had been several lectures and that the students were maliciously withholding their notes from her in order that she might be made to fail in the course.

A few days later she accosted one of the same students in the hall and began to tell a long story about her brother who had, she said, been an army officer and was murdered during his sleep by one of his brother officers because of jealousy over his more rapid promotion. In the midst of the recital she suddenly stopped, walked rapidly up the hall, stared intently for a moment at one of a group of men students, then returned and in a dramatic whisper inquired, "Do you see that man up there? That one with his back to us? He is the one. He is the man that murdered my brother!' Dropping her tone to a still more melodramatic pitch she added, *"But I'll get him yet!"*

By this time the students were convinced that here was a case of definite mental disorder. They reported it to the faculty, but before action could be taken, the woman amazed everybody by getting up in the middle of a peaceful lecture to accuse one of the students of having stolen her brief-case. (No one, it may be noted, had ever seen her carrying a brief-case.) The theft had been done, so she claimed, at the instigation of one of the professors who wanted to secure her notes on a scientific investigation she was making. She explained that, if completed, this research would undoubtedly so revolutionize psychology that no one now engaged in it would be able to hold his position.

Here we have a striking example of the type of mental disorder which is known as *paranoia*. It is characterized by systematized delusions centering around ideas of persecution. As a rule, grandiose ideas are mingled with it. The persecutions are rarely of a trivial nature but in most cases, as in this one, a reason is assigned for them that enhances the patient's importance. Auditory hallucinations are very common in paranoia. The patient "hears voices" which in some cases are referred to particular sources as angels or devils or even God, by others are simply called "voices." At first the voices are often confused, and the patient himself can distinguish very little that they say. As the disease progresses the words become clearer, and the patient often feels impelled to act in accordance with their advice.

The progress from the normal to the abnormal is well exemplified by paranoia. There is no clear boundary here between the sane and the insane; the one merges into the other by imperceptible stages.[11] Often no one realizes that anything serious is wrong until some spectacular action or remark on the part of the patient calls attention to his condition. Many true paranoiacs never find their way into hospitals but remain in society, where they not infrequently cause much trouble by casting unwarranted suspicion on others. The "poison pen" letters, filled with malicious accusations, that every now and then threaten to disrupt a community are often the work of some unrecognized paranoiac.

It is probably safe to say that at the root of every case of paranoia lies a mental conflict of some kind, a motive that cannot be carried out to its normal termination in satisfying overt action. The individual's ambition may be greater than his power to accomplish, or circumstances may combine to prevent him from fulfilling some deep-lying desire. The well-known "old maid's complex" is an example. A woman who has passed her youth

---

[11] Most paranoiacs are entirely sane on all topics that do not impinge upon their particular system of delusions. Until the condition becomes so far advanced that the delusions dominate all his thoughts and actions leaving no time free for anything else, the typical paranoiac is able to carry on his usual work, talks sensibly about everything outside the delusionary field, and shows no evidence of general mental deterioration. For this reason it is hard for friends and relatives to believe that anything is seriously wrong. The graduate student described above was doing excellent work in all her courses, was well informed on topics of the day, and had rather more than an amateur knowledge of art, especially etchings.

and realizes that her chances for matrimony are few finds herself in a difficult position. The social taboo which says that women must be the sought and not the seekers prevents her from making an open and unabashed effort to secure a husband, and she is embarrassed by the fact that men pay so little attention to her. A solution offers itself that partially satisfies her pride. She will avoid men. But avoiding men who are only too eager to be avoided does not satisfy her needs, for what she is seeking is an explanation for her lack of masculine attention in terms other than her own lack of attractiveness. So she begins to find an outlet in telling her friends about the men who from time to time have tried to force their attentions upon her. At first she probably knows, if she would permit herself to face the matter, that these tales have little foundation in fact, so she tries to lend them verisimilitude and so make them more satisfactory to herself by watching the men whom she meets and trying to find something in their behavior that might be interpreted as having special reference to herself. As time passes she finds that less and less is needed in the way of objective reality to make such an interpretation seem reasonable to her. Here again we have an example of the working out of Hollingworth's principle of redintegration. As learning progresses, smaller and smaller cues are needed to reconstruct the whole.

In the majority of cases the matter ends there. The woman's stories may grow a bit taller as time goes on; she may become a little more careless about discrepancies in their detail as the whole thing takes on reality for herself, but that is all. Occasionally, however, particularly among women who have few other interests to take up their time and attention, a more serious state of affairs develops which may pass over into genuine paranoia. The habits of make-believe are transformed into a series of systematized delusions. The woman now really believes that she is constantly being pursued by men with amatory intentions. Perhaps her delusions center around some particular man. A good many domestic complications have arisen when some unfortunate husband has been selected to play the stellar rôle in such a system of delusions. She may write him protesting notes or even denounce him to her friends and to the police.

The distinction between the occasional illusions of the normal person and the delusions of the one suffering from mental disease should now be clear. The former are casual and circumstantial; they follow no systematic pattern, and they serve no fundamental need of the individual. The latter are systematized. They are devices whereby the person derives momentary sastifaction for some unfulfilled need. And they are basically childish devices. The little girl who is not allowed to go to grown-up parties consoles herself by "make-believe." She decks herself out in fancy clothing and parades solemnly around the house in what she conceives to be the party behavior of grown people. The small boy becomes Robin Hood or Sindbad the Sailor, and he enters into his play so wholeheartedly that for the moment he may even lose sight of his own identity. The twisted stump at which he aims his home-made arrow *is* for him a grazing deer; the duck pond becomes an ocean, the bit of broken plank is a pirate's ship. *But only for the moment.* Once the game is over the magic disappears; the toys regain their prosaic character, and Sindbad becomes a hungry child dashing home to his dinner. But for the unsatisfied adult who forms the habit of consoling himself by make-believe, the return to reality is not so easily accomplished, especially when the emotional need is intense and persistent. It makes little difference what the character of his phantasy may be. It may take the form of imagined revenge, of the fulfillment of some long-established wish, of personal aggrandizement or the subjugation of a rival.

There is another difference between the child who dramatizes his desires in his play and the adult who regresses to a pseudo-childish level in which phantasy becomes real. The child is satisfied with very little in the way of objective evidence upon which to hang his fancy. Almost anything can serve his purpose. But the adult, with his more highly developed critical faculties, is not so easily contented. He must be constantly convincing himself that his phantasies are real.[12] He must proclaim their truth to the world; he must take steps to *make* them true. This need to demonstrate often takes on the nature of an internal compul-

---

[12] In the more advanced stages of mental disorder this is not always true. The extremely deteriorated patient often desires nothing more than to be left alone in his private world of delusions; he needs no assistance whatever from the external world to carry them on.

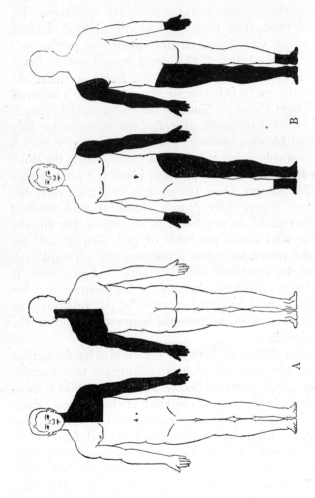

FIG. 109.—TRUE AND HYSTERICAL ANESTHESIA

A. Loss of sensitivity to pain resulting from a tumor in the cervical region of the spinal cord. (After Head and Thompson.)

B. Hysterical anesthesia of isolated parts of the body. (After illustration in Morgan's *Psychology of Abnormal People*, Longmans, Green and Co.)

sion in which foolish or even criminal acts may be carried out in order to lend verisimilitude to the phantasy.

When there is conflict between motives and objective reality, a solution is sometimes found in a physical symptom of some kind. A young woman was engaged to be married to a man who lived next door to her and whom she had known since childhood. One day the man came home, bringing with him another girl whom he introduced to his amazed family as his wife. They had been married that day. When his jilted sweetheart was told of the marriage she was greatly upset, and in the midst of her tears she exclaimed, "I will never go there to call on her. Never!" A day or so later she was taken ill, and it was soon discovered that a paralysis had developed in both legs. The relationship here is fairly obvious. She would not go, hence it was necessary for something to happen that would make it impossible for her to go. Such cases are not infrequent.

Taking refuge in a physical symptom in order to avoid a difficulty or to find a solution for a conflict, to get attention, or to secure revenge, is known as *hysteria*. At first thought it seems as if the patient were just pretending to be sick, but in true hysteria this is not the case. The patient has deluded himself so thoroughly that to all intents and purposes he is as sick as he thinks himself to be. Of course there are many cases in which the illness is pure make-believe, and it is probable that in most instances the device, which is adopted more or less intentionally in the beginning, later progresses to a stage where it takes on a character of reality to the patient. The physical symptoms assumed by the hysterical patient cover almost the entire range of human diseases. Hysterical blindness, deafness, mutism, and cardiac disturbances are very common. Hysterical disorders differ from the true illnesses which they stimulate in various ways as a result of the fact that the average person's medical and anatomical knowledge is not very exact and his symptoms follow the line of his misinformation. For example, people sometimes report complete loss of sensitivity in a hand or other local part. That this is more than just make-believe can be shown by pricking the affected region with needles, scorching the skin, or other tests that normally would cause much pain. The hysterical patient pays no attention, continuing to insist that he can feel nothing. But the hysterical nature of the symptom appears in the fact that while true anesthesia follows the course of the nerves, in the majority of cases hysterical anesthesia does not. Most people think of the body as divided up into such segments as arms, legs, hands or head, and if they seek a way out of some overwhelming difficulty by means of a bodily ailment they naturally enough locate the ailment in what, to them, constitutes a "part" of the body. So the hysterical person may exhibit complete anesthesia in a hand, but the insensitive region stops short at the wrist, and the arm above the wrist shows normal sensitivity. If the trouble were with the nerves this would not be the case. (See Figure 109.)

Hysteria, like paranoia, is not sharply marked off from less pronounced states which do not prevent the patient from passing as normal though they greatly interfere with his efficiency. Getting sick as a way out of a difficulty is a device that children learn early and that many adults continue to find useful. Note, however, that neither the child nor the adult admits the device to himself. Usually if you examine your feelings with care it is possible to locate something that with a little encouragement can be made to feel like a pain. It is not hard to imagine that you have difficulty in moving your arms and legs, and, if you do not move them for a period of days or weeks, a genuine difficulty ensues as a consequence of the prolonged inactivity. Hysterical paralysis does not become genuine paralysis, but it does, in time, lead to a state in which movement becomes increasingly difficult.

Manic-depressive insanity is a form of mental disorder which again is only an exaggerated form of behavior tendencies shown by normal persons. Everybody is subject to fluctuations in mood. Sometimes you feel happy and good-natured; all the world looks rosy and it takes a good deal to depress you. At other times you feel discouraged, depressed, and nothing seems worth doing. These changes in mood are mirrored in your behavior. When you are happy you move more quickly; you attack everything you do with zest and energy. You pass readily from one activity to another because everything seems worth doing. When you are depressed you move more slowly and you tend to plug along at the same kind of thing because nothing is worth while anyway so why bother to change?

Normally, such changes from elation to depression depend on

two things; bodily states such as indigestion or fatigue, and the external events to which the organism responds. A series of disappointments may temporarily depress the most optimistic mood; a bit of unexpected good news may do a good deal to cure an attack of the blues. But in some people these swings of mood become greatly exaggerated and dissociated from the events around them. As in paranoia, the condition is likely to develop gradually over long periods of time and only to be recognized for what it is when it reaches a very pronounced stage or when, as often happens, the person finally commits some overt act that cannot be overlooked.

Michael S. was a farmer, living in a small rural community. He was of Irish descent and had the keen sense of humor that often characterizes the Irish. At all the rural gatherings his ready wit and his high good humor were well known. As a rule, Michael was an indulgent husband and father, but there were times when his mercurial spirits failed him, when he had what his kindly wife called "black days" when his farm work was neglected and his family found it wise to keep out of his sight.

This went on for many years. Every one in the neighborhood knew of these swings of mood but took them pretty much as a matter of course. For his neighbors their chief significance lay in the series of amusing stories that grew up about his behavior, such as the time when, under the influence of one of his "black spells," he left home and went to live in the woods. Michael was not a very successful farmer because when he was "feeling fine" he found so many other interesting things to do that his farm work was neglected, and on his bad days he usually refused to work at all.

One day his nearest neighbor was attracted by the sound of repeated shots that came from the direction of Michael's home. At first he paid little attention to them, as this was the corn-planting season when most farmers were busy shooting crows. But as the shooting continued and became mingled with loud shouts, he became alarmed and decided he might better investigate. In front of the house he found Michael and his terrified wife. A rough race course had been outlined by means of small stones. Michael stood in the middle brandishing his shot-gun and shouting wildly at his wife, whom he was forcing to run at top speed around and around the course he had marked out for her. "She's too fat!" he announced excitedly to the neighbor on his arrival. "She needs exercise!" Fortunately the neighbor was an intelligent man who saw at once how matters stood. He agreed with Michael about the wife's need of exercise but called his attention to the fact that he was out of ammunition—he had been firing his shot-gun into the air as a threat to his wife whenever she slackened her speed. The neighbor then offered to stand guard over the wife while Michael went to the house to get more shells. To this Michael cheerfully agreed, handing over his shot-gun to the neighbor, who sent the almost exhausted wife for help. Michael was committed to the State hospital, where he remained for the rest of his life. There were occasional periods of improvement, but they did not last long.

Manic-depressive insanity, like other forms of mental disorder, almost certainly has an inherited base, but whether or not the inherited predisposition will develop into an actual *psychosis*— that is, into a mental disorder so grave as to incapacitate the individual from living a normal life in society—probably depends in large part upon development through experience, upon the habits one forms, and upon the kind of motives by which he is activated. Not only in the manic-depressive patient, who has passed the dim boundary by which we distinguish the "normal" from the "insane," but in normal persons, belonging to the so-called "cyclothymic" type whose swings of mood are more pronounced than those of the average person, the outstanding thing we notice is that they do not seem to be directing their activities to any major purpose. They shift about from this activity to that because there is no single direction in which they are trying to go; no one goal that is at once remote enough and possessed of sufficient drawing power to dominate their thoughts and actions for a long period of time.

Among normal persons who have frequent changes in mood the situation may be just that they have never been stimulated to integrate their motives toward a long-time purpose. In the extreme cases, those with whom the condition passes over into a real mental disorder which prevents them from carrying on in normal society, the basis for the condition is more likely to be a mental conflict in which the patient cannot work toward the purpose he desires and will not substitute another. But the result is the same except that the behavior is given more energy by the strong motive that lies back of it. The manic does not work directly toward an end, though sometimes one may see in his behavior certain trends, symbolic actions, in which his real object is not so completely concealed by his apparently trivial and aimless acts. But since he is not working toward an end, either because he does not see it or because he refuses to look at it, his behavior lacks all appearance of integration or design. It becomes flighty, unpredictable, irrational.

Take your own case. When do you find it easiest to ignore disappointments and minor annoyances, to resist the petty attractions and distractions that crop up in your way, and to keep steadily on your course without hesitation or shifting? Under what circumstances do your moods remain most stable, least affected either by your own changing physiological states or by disturbing events in the outside world? The answer is—when you are devoting all your energies to the accomplishment of some definite purpose, when you are activated by motives that are at once so intense and so strong that other matters seem, by comparison, to be of little consequence. At what times are you most subject to swings of mood? When you are at loose ends, when there is nothing to dominate your thought and action except the immediate events going on within and around you.

The manic-depressive individual has never really grown up. He has never learned to subordinate the impulses of the moment to the needs of the future. He lives in the present. He is swung about by everything and everybody, but he is little influenced in his behavior by the wishes of other people. Like the child whom he resembles, his own momentary desires are preëminent. He sings when he is happy, shouts when he is excited, has temper-tantrums when he is angry. All his impulses discharge into activity at once; they lack both coördination and integration.

One more type of mental disorder needs to be mentioned. This is a condition now generally known as *hebephrenia* [13] in which the patient solves his conflicts by refusing to accept any responsibility for them, by running away from them. Now the only persons who, by common consent, are not held responsible for their actions are children and idiots. So the hebephrenic acts like a child or an idiot. Some carry the regression further than others. It may extend only to the period of early childhood in which case the patient runs about, perhaps talks with a babyish accent, plays with childish toys and picture books and demands the privileges of childhood in the attention of other people and in the free expression of his own emotions. Sometimes the regression

[13] This is one form of the general group of mental disorders known as *schizophrenia*.

progresses to a deeper level. It may go back to early infancy. In such cases the patient becomes unable to feed himself; he may lose control of his bladder and bowels; speech is replaced by babbling and crying; the prenatal posture may be habitually assumed (and we can see now that this does not necessarily indicate any recollection of his own prenatal life but is far more likely to come about through the imitation of other babies whom he has seen and whose rôle he is now assuming).

Hebephrenia, like the other conditions we have been considering, has its milder forms within the so-called "normal" range. Here is a married woman who is unwilling to assume the duties and responsibilities of her position. She craves the indulgence, the spoiling, the petting that go with childhood. So she insists upon acting like a child. Dickens' Dora is a classic example. Often such women combine their hebephrenic tendencies with behavior of the hysteric type. When they cannot get their way by pouting and coaxing, they resort to the other device of spoiled children. They become sick.

The mental disorders we have described here do not, by any means, provide a complete picture of mental disease. They are examples only. They have been selected because they illustrate how human personality in its development may learn to adjust to its immediate difficulties at the cost of future disaster. In the paranoiac, we see how the child who learns to compensate for his disappointments through day-dreaming, who learns to project his wishes and phantasies into the external world until he sees in the behavior of others the things that actually exist only in his own mind, who learns to rationalize his failures by referring them to an imaginary system of persecution may, as his responsibilities increase with adult life, take refuge in a series of delusions where he can no longer distinguish between fact and fancy. By so doing he has protected his self-esteem, but he has lost everything else. The hysterical person adopts a different device. He makes physical disability his excuse and protects his pride by a physical handicap that is always serious (otherwise it would not fulfill its purpose) and that often means chronic invalidism. The hebephrenic escapes *in toto*. The paranoiac and the hysterical person retain certain aspects of their personality intact, but the hebephrenic sacrifices everything rather than face his difficulties.

The manic-depressive chooses another method. Like the others he has difficulties of his own, a mental conflict of some kind that he is unwilling to face. We said in a previous section that his behavior is not governed by any real purpose. This is not because he has no purpose but because the purpose that he would choose, if he could, is for some reason barred to him, and so he refuses to acknowledge it or to do anything that seems directly related to it. But while the paranoiac takes refuge in dreams, the hysterical in sickness, and the hebephrenic in childhood, the manic takes refuge in reality. He cannot work to an end, so he expends his energy on trivialities. He hails with relief anything that will help to keep his eyes away from the forbidden goal. At times the insignificance and worthlessness of all his actions overwhelm him, and then he sinks into the depressed phase. But even in his depression he must not think of his real trouble. He broods over this and that. Sometimes he seizes upon some definite thing to worry about—something that as a rule is quite trivial, but which he magnifies into terrific proportions. Having this to occupy his mind, he need not think of the other. If one has to worry, it is better to choose a subject that is not too painful.

HEREDITY VERSUS HABIT AS FACTORS IN MENTAL DISEASE

There can be no question that some persons, because of inherited predisposition, will suffer mental breakdown under conditions to which the more fortunately endowed would not succumb. The functional mental diseases occur in certain families so much more frequently than in others as to leave little doubt that a constitutional factor is involved in a large proportion of the cases. Nevertheless, as we have pointed out before, the presence of an inherited tendency is rarely, if ever, sufficient to induce a mental breakdown in persons who from the beginning have formed the kind of habits that make for mental health. Those who meet their difficulties squarely; recognize them for what they are; and, if they cannot overcome them, at least find a way of adjusting to them that does not interfere with a normal life in a world of action are in little danger of mental breakdown.

Mental disease is in large part a learned reaction. Just as we learn to seek food in particular ways and in particular places, to delay eating, though hungry, when circumstances make it seem better for us to do so, to try new methods of food-getting when our usual habits are unsuccessful, and to repeat these methods, if we find that they work, or to substitute other less palatable foods in place of those that we are either unable to get or know that we ought not to eat—just so do we learn other habits that make for sanity or insanity. Contrary to popular opinion, people do not suddenly "go crazy." What sometimes appears to be a sudden development is usually one of two things. Either it is a final yielding of the defenses to steadily accumulating mental conflicts—the proverbial "last straw"—or, more frequently, a state that has been gradually developing over a long period of time is suddenly brought to public attention when the affected person commits some overt act that can no longer be ignored.

Can mental disease be cured? Sometimes. In many cases, however, the chief difficulty lies in the fact that the patient does not want to be cured. He is unwilling to give up his beloved symptoms through which he has found a partial solution of his difficulty. Not only that, but he has learned that in these symptoms, whatever they may be, lies a way out of other difficulties that may develop later. So, even if it is possible to find out what caused the original conflict and to remove that particular trouble, when something else comes up the patient is likely to respond in the same old way. And the difficulty cannot always be removed, even if we find out where it lies. Some conditions cannot be changed, and when these conditions lie in the way of complete satisfaction of normal motives an adjustment must be made. In order to maintain the personality intact, this adjustment must involve the entire personality. The best way is to find a new purpose, one to which all one's efforts can be directed without running afoul of the obstruction, provided always that the obstruction is one that cannot be mastered by direct attack. But some persons refuse to do this. Instead, to use Bleuler's telling phrase, they succeed in "splitting off" a part of their personality by gratifying one motive at the expense of all the rest. And even this gratification is usually a poor one. Day-dreams, the protected life of an invalid, or the shallow amusements of a pseudochildhood offer but slight return for the sacrifice of a normal life of thought and action.

DO ANIMALS SHOW NEUROTIC BEHAVIOR?

Norman R. F. Maier, *Studies of Abnormal Behavior in the Rat* (New York, Harper and Bros., 1939), pp. 81 + 16 photographic plates.

In this brief volume, Professor N. R. F. Maier of the State University of Michigan reports one of the most important psychological studies of recent years. Tame laboratory rats were first trained to jump from an elevated platform to one of two doors which was marked with a black circle on a white ground, behind which food was to be found. The other door, marked with a white circle on a black ground, was fastened shut. If the wrong door was chosen the rat not only failed to secure food but bumped his nose against the locked door.

After the discrimination had been so thoroughly learned that the right door was consistently chosen, the task was made impossible of solution by mixing up the signals. If the confused rats then sensibly refused to jump at all, they were forced to do so by means of a blast of air. Under these circumstances many of the rats eventually developed symptoms that were qualitatively wholly unlike anything ordinarily found in rat behavior. They jumped to the floor and ran frantically around in circles, or they remained stiff and motionless as if paralyzed for long periods of time. Complete accounts of nine cases of this kind are presented, together with photographs illustrating various phases of the neurotic behavior described.

With commendable scientific caution, Maier warns against drawing unwarranted conclusions about abnormal reactions in human beings from the findings of this experiment. One can hardly refrain from noting, however, that in many cases of human breakdown, conditions that seem to be at least analogous to these have been present. The affected person felt himself *obliged* to strive for some goal that was beyond his power to attain. The compulsive force may have been his own pride. It may have been the demands of some other person or persons to whose wishes he felt bound to conform. It may have been a feeling of duty, or of personal responsibility too great to be borne.

When human beings become mentally deranged, we are rarely able to secure a complete history either of the course of the mental disturbance or of the conditions which led up to it. No records were kept at the time; no scientist was at hand to make observations. As a rule, not one but many trying conditions played a part in producing the final break. The thing that makes Maier's study of such great importance is the completeness of the data and its freedom from irrelevant factors that would obscure the picture. Each step in the progression from normal to abnormal behavior was carefully observed and recorded, together with the stimuli that gave rise to the change.

The daily régime of the animals was carefully regulated. They were fed on a standard diet, and every care was exercised to maintain them in good physical health.

However, in noting the apparent similarities between the conditions that induced abnormal behavior in these rats and the circumstances that appear to underlie many of the functional mental disorders in human beings we must, as Maier points out, be careful not to generalize too far. The rat is a far less complex organism than man; the nature of the experimental frustration was far more cleancut, much less complicated by the presence of other factors of unknown relevance to the problem than anything likely to occur in human life. This artificial simplification enables us to see a single relationship in clear focus, but we must not make the error of supposing that there is nothing else to be seen.

Chapter XXVI

MENTAL DEFICIENCY OR INTELLECTUAL INADEQUACY

Is it possible to set a definite level, in terms of IQ, below which all persons should be classed as feeble-minded?

What advantage has the use of the term, "intellectually inadequate" over such expressions as "mentally defective" or "feeble-minded"?

What facts other than the intellectual level of the individual must be considered in deciding whether or not he is to be looked upon as "intellectually inadequate"?

What are some of the main deviations from the usual or normal pattern of early development shown by most feeble-minded children? Do normal children ever show similar deviations?

What two important differences in the mental organization of normal and feeble-minded individuals have been pointed out by Lewin? What are the practical implications of these differences for the care and training of the feeble-minded?

On the basis of the degree of defect, into what three main classes is it customary to divide the feeble-minded? Is it always possible to say to which of these classes a given individual belongs?

Why is institutional care usually better than home care for children of the lower intellectual levels, even when the family is financially able to support the child at home?

What are the most important principles to be observed in the training of feeble-minded children?

WHO ARE MENTALLY DEFICIENT?

The fact that people differ in mental ability is well known to every one. That general intelligence is distributed within the population in a form that conforms fairly closely to the bell-shaped "normal probability curve" has also been demonstrated, at least for the populations of most American communities. The question then arises, Can we mark off any definite area of the curve (as shown in Figure 110 *A*) and say that all who fall below this point on some specified test are feeble-minded; all above it, normal?

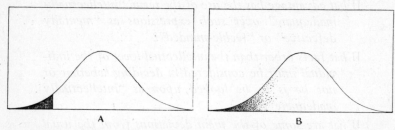

A   B

FIG. 110.—CORRECT AND INCORRECT REPRESENTATION OF THE DIS-TRIBUTION OF THE INTELLECTUALLY INADEQUATE IN RELATION TO MENTAL TEST SCORES

All who have read this book as far as the beginning of the present chapter should see at once why no such simple rule can he applied. In the first place, standing on mental tests, as has been repeatedly pointed out, is not an absolutely fixed matter but one that varies within limits that can only be described in terms of probability. The chances that on retesting after a stated interval, John Doe's IQ will not vary from that obtained on the first test by more than five, ten, or twenty points can be stated with reasonable assurance. But these are merely the "betting odds." If there is only one chance in a hundred that his IQ will vary by more than twenty points, there is still a possibility—though less than one chance in a thousand—that the change may be as great as thirty points, and an even more remote likelihood that the difference may exceed thirty points. However, it is of the utmost importance to remember that the *rare event sometimes occurs*.

The bridge player's chances of being dealt thirteen cards of the same suit are exceedingly small, yet such hands occasionally result even from unbiased dealing. If we had a complete record of all the bridge hands dealt in this country over a period of time, we should in all probability find that among those properly shuffled and dealt, the frequency of one-suit hands would correspond very closely to chance expectancy.

The existence of a probable error of measurement is not, however, the only objection to the use of the IQ as the sole criterion of mental deficiency. As the term is used in practical life, social and economic factors enter in, as well as those that we are accustomed to regard as "intellectual." The child of a day-laborer may be able to substitute brawn for brain and thus win for himself a useful place in the economic world, even though ten years in the school-room proved insufficient to take him beyond the educational requirements of the third grade. Furthermore, if he has been trained to conform to the ordinary laws of society, if he is sober, honest, and industrious, can we fairly label him as "mentally deficient," no matter what his IQ may have been found to be?

The variation in the intellectual demands of different social and vocational spheres has always been a major stumbling-block in the way of those who would like to find a single objective basis for the "all-or-none" division of society into sharply distinguished classes. Nevertheless this variation is a fact that must be admitted and one to which our practical criteria of mental deficiency must conform. Because it is true that, practically speaking, a person may be "feeble-minded" in one kind of social or vocational setting and "normal" in another, it has been suggested that in place of such terms as "mental deficiency" or "feeble-mindedness" we substitute the term "intellectual inadequacy." The advantage of the latter expression lies in the fact that it does not imply a universal condition that is wholly a matter of the individual himself. Rather, it raises the question, *Inadequate for what?* [1]

Many years ago Tredgold, an English psychologist who was particularly interested in questions of mental retardation and the social care of the intellectually inadequate, formulated a definition

[1] Leo Kanner, *Child Psychiatry* (Baltimore, Charles C. Thomas, 1935), pp. xviii + 527. See especially Chapter XXXI.

that is often quoted. "The feeble-minded," [2] said Tredgold, "are those who, by reason of imperfect or incomplete mental development, existing from birth or from an early age, are ... unable to conduct themselves and their affairs with ordinary prudence or to compete on equal terms with their normal fellows in the struggle for existence within the ranks of society to which they were born." Although American people in general have been loath to accept the final clause of this definition, the fact remains that it cannot be completely ignored. For the chances that the backward child of a successful lawyer or an important business man will form the kind of attitudes and learn the simple but necessary muscular skills needed for him to adjust successfully and happily to the life of a laborer with pick and shovel do not equal the likelihood that the child whose own father earns his living in that way will do so, even though the intellectual capacities of the two children are identical. A level of ability that is "adequate" for certain intellectual demands may be quite "inadequate" if the demands upon intelligence are increased.

Actually, then, when we speak of a given child or adult as "feeble-minded" or "mentally defective" we mean that his intellectual ability is so limited that it will in all probability be found inadequate to meet, by his own unaided efforts, the demands of any kind of environment *in which he is likely to be placed*. The profound idiot at the lowest extreme of the intellectual scale, who can neither walk nor talk, who has never learned to distinguish between food and filth but swallows indiscriminately everything on which he can lay his hands, who has never learned to control his bodily functions or to dress himself is clearly "inadequate" for the intellectual demands of even the simplest environment. It is necessary to move a considerable distance up the intellectual scale before a level is reached at which the possibility of finding a niche which the intellectually backward person can fill without supervision becomes worthy of serious consideration. Other things remaining equal, however, the likelihood of successful adjustment increases as we move from the lower to the upper ranges of the

---

[2] Tredgold, in common with other English writers, used the term *feeble-minded* in the same sense that we in America use the word *moron* to signify persons belonging to the highest, that is, most nearly normal ranks of the mentally defective group.

intellectual distribution. Eventually, a point is reached at which we are reasonably safe in saying that intellectual inadequacy can no longer be invoked as an important determinant of an individual's ability to "get along" in the world, inasmuch as there are a sufficient number of avenues open to him which he is competent to pursue if he will. True, such a person may still select an avenue for which his intellectual powers are inadequate. But in such cases we ascribe his failure to a wrong choice, rather than to intellectual inadequacy in the broad sense of the term.

The division between feeble-mindedness and normality thus corresponds more nearly to the diagram shown in Figure 110 B than to that of Figure 110 A. It is not a sharp line but a zone in which the probability that an individual will be able to "conduct himself and his own affairs with ordinary prudence" or to "compete on reasonably equal terms with his normal fellows" is limited to a smaller and smaller extent by the purely intellectual aspects of his personality make-up as we advance from the lower to the higher levels of intellectual ability. We may thus regard the proportionate number of dots at each level of intelligence shown in Figure 110 B as roughly analogous to the proportionate number of individuals at each level who, because of intellectual inadequacy, will be unable to meet Tredgold's criterion.

It follows that there must be some determinable point in the distribution of scores earned on a well-standardized intelligence test at which the probabilities of social adequacy and those of social inadequacy are evenly balanced. Below that level the odds are against the successful economic and social adjustment of the person so rated unless he is given some external supervision or other assistance. Above it the chances are in his favor. In either case, the prediction takes on increased certainty as we move further away from the point where the odds are even.

The exact point of evenly balanced probabilities has never been determined with certainty for any test, and authorities differ somewhat in their estimates of its location. Probably an approximation is all that can ever be established, for, as we have seen, social conditions as well as the characteristics of the individual cause it to vary. It will be higher in times when there is much unemployment than when there is plenty of work for all who can perform it; higher in communities where the demand is chiefly for highly skilled labor than in regions where there is more need for unskilled workers. However, with conditions as they now exist in the average American city, it appears that a Stanford-Binet IQ of somewhere in the neighborhood of 75 is at least not far removed from the point in question. It should go without saying that this is by no means equivalent to saying that all children whose IQ'S fall below 75 on this test should be classed as feeble-minded or all above that level as normal. We are not dealing with certainties but with probabilities.

Moreover, when we are faced with the need for making practical decisions about the treatment of any individual child, other facts in addition to his purely intellectual ability must be taken into account. Of two children with the same level of intelligence, one may be removed from the regular classroom and placed in a special class because he is not only learning little or nothing from the ordinary type of instruction but is such a disturbing influence that the progress of other children is interfered with. The other, who is industrious and hard-working, sensitive about his backwardness and eager to do his best on all occasions may be left where he is, inasmuch as his behavior does not handicap the other children but may even stimulate them to greater effort, while a transfer might prove definitely harmful to the child himself if it made him feel that his best efforts had resulted in failure. The nature of the special class would also have to be considered in deciding whether or not a transfer should be made in an individual case. If a useful and realistic [3] kind of vocational program has been worked out, or if successful methods for improving the personal-social adjustments of the backward child have been devised, the recommendations would differ from those made in cases where the chief purpose of the special class is to relieve the drag upon the regular classes caused by the presence of children who cannot keep up. The child's intelligence is only a part of his equipment for meeting the demands of life. Other assets and liabilities both in the child and in his environment must also be considered.

[3] Although training in manual arts is usually emphasized in these classes, this training may be of a kind so far removed from anything required in the actual world of industry that it can hardly be classed beyond the level of "busy-work."

In the past, too much emphasis has undoubtedly been placed upon the classification of individuals as an end in itself. Only recently have we begun to realize that the mere labelling of a child as "feeble-minded" is of little practical aid in guiding his future development. Better that we should ask, For what is he mentally *adequate?* The answer may be, For nothing except permanent custodial care. Or it may be, Inadequate for an unsupervised existence outside an institution but capable of at least partial self-support, as he grows older, by work within the institution. Or at a still higher level the prediction may be, Inadequate for undertaking the care and rearing of a family but capable of self-support in the outside world if given some supervision and if reproduction is guarded against by sterilization.

HOW MANY ARE INTELLECTUALLY INADEQUATE?

If we assume that a Stanford-Binet IQ of about 75 represents the approximate level at which the chances that the individual will or will not be intellectually capable of maintaining an independent life in society as it exists to-day are equally balanced, we can make a fair estimate of the proportion of the total population of the country who fall within the "inadequate" group. Although there is much variation from one community to another, when sufficiently large and representative groups have been tested it has usually been found that from 5 to 6 per cent of the total earn IQ's below 75.[4] Of course, not all of these are "feeble-minded" or "intellectually inadequate" in the sense in which we have used the term. But inasmuch as the number incorrectly classified as "inadequate" will be about balanced by the number testing somewhat above 75 who should properly have been included in the "inadequate" group, the *proportions* in each group remain about the same in spite of the incorrect placement of some individuals. It is, of course, true that the estimate of IQ 75 as the

[4] That is, on the 1937 Stanford-Binet or some equivalent scale. It cannot be too strongly emphasized that different mental tests are not always equivalent to each other. On p. 42 of *Measuring Intelligence* (Boston, Houghton Mifflin Co., 1937), pp. xi + 461, Terman and Merrill assign a "standard score" value of −1.50 to an IQ of 76. In the general population slightly over 6.5 per cent do not exceed this level. This, however, is a somewhat higher figure than most previous studies have reported.

point of balanced probabilities may not be exactly right, in which case the proportion classed as intellectually inadequate would be greater or smaller as the case may be. However enough evidence has been accumulated to justify the conclusion that any adjustment of the figures that future data may suggest is likely to be of relatively small magnitude.

THE DEVELOPMENT AND BEHAVIOR OF THE INTELLECTUALLY INADEQUATE

Because the feeble-minded [5] differ among themselves in traits other than intelligence almost as much as do normal people, it is impossible to give more than a very sketchy account of some of the ways in which the majority of the former differ from the majority of the latter. There is overlapping of the groups in practically all of the characteristics described.

1. *Development of early motor skills such as sitting, standing, walking, grasping and handling objects, especially with thumb opposition.* In practically all of these, the typical feeble-minded child shows some degree of developmental retardation. The idiot is likely never to acquire more than imperfect command over his gross bodily responses. Walking, if learned at all, may be delayed until the age of four or five years, and the gait remains shambling and awkward. Even the mental defectives of higher grade usually (though not invariably) are from one to three or four months later than the average in learning to sit and walk alone. Many never develop the "light-footedness" of normal childhood. By comparison their step is heavy and "flat-footed"; they frequently make more than normal use of the arms in maintaining balance and may always show a tendency to shuffle. Opposition of the thumb in grasping is typically slow to appear, and even after childhood is well advanced, many backward children continue to approach an object to be grasped in such a manner that the first contact is with the palm of the hand, after which the fingers close around it in a manner not unlike that of the infant.[6]

2. *Development of language.* Because language is a symbolic

---

[5] The term *feeble-minded* is here used interchangeably with the terms *mentally defective* or *intellectually inadequate.*

[6] See Chapter VIII, p. 246.

process, its development in the feeble-minded child is almost invariably slow. The idiot never acquires a vocabulary of more than a few simple words. Few of the feeble-minded begin to talk before the age of two. In many cases speech is delayed until much later. At all ages the vocabulary remains small in comparison with that of normal persons, and the articulation is likely to be imperfect and slovenly. Speech defects of all kinds are more common among the feeble-minded than among persons of normal intelligence.

3. *Emotional development and emotional control.* The chief difference in the emotional life of normal and feeble-minded persons can be roughly summarized under two heads. Emotional reactions among the feeble-minded are chiefly aroused by concrete stimuli immediately present. Except in a limited way, they take little thought for the future and soon forget the joys and sorrows of the past. Secondly, their emotional reactions are expressed more openly than those of normal people are likely to be. They are slower to learn ways either of covering up their real attitudes or of assuming the outward forms of emotions not actually experienced. In both respects their emotional behavior resembles that of children considerably younger than themselves.

4. *Learning.* From what has already been said, it may readily be inferred that in nearly, if not quite, all areas of human behavior, the patterns of reaction of the intellectually inadequate are modified more slowly and with greater difficulty than are those of normal persons. They do not adapt themselves readily to new conditions or easily acquire new ways of responding to the same conditions. Because the kind of knowledge and skill demanded by our formal system of education is of so abstract a character, the feeble-minded child is almost invariably retarded in his school work. He usually does best in those subjects that make least demand upon reasoning and judgment; in other words, in those that can be mastered by means of rote memory or, in individual instances, in those that are chiefly dependent upon special talent such as singing.

LEWIN'S THEORY OF THE DIFFERENCES IN MENTAL ORGANIZATION OF NORMAL AND FEEBLE-MINDED INDIVIDUALS

Kurt Lewin, a German psychologist who, in common with many others, came to this country in order to escape the scientific restrictions of the Nazi régime, has put forth a theory of the nature of mental defect [7] that has attracted a good deal of attention in recent years. According to Lewin the main differences between the normal and the feeble-minded can be defined in terms of *tension-systems* and the *rigidity of the boundaries* by which these systems are separated from each other. Both these concepts require explanation.

According to Lewin, a *tension system* is merely an organized system of responses all of which lead, or are designed to lead, toward some particular goal. A given tension-system may be trivial and of short duration, as when a child climbs over a fence to secure a ball on the other side of it, or significant and enduring, like the continued efforts of an ambitious man to attain success in his profession. The *strength* or *rigidity* of the *boundaries between systems* is manifested in the readiness with which the activities belonging to one can be made to overflow into another. We all know how easily, as a rule, the desires of the young child can be satisfied by the substitution of some other objective for the one initially sought. The baby who cries for the moon is quickly diverted by a shiny rattle; the older child who hopes for a clear Saturday in order that he might play baseball consoles himself by spending the rainy day in his workshop. With the adult these transfers of interest are less readily made. If necessity demands that a projected activity or one already started be discontinued for a time, there is less likelihood that the temporary substitution of some other activity will serve as a lasting distraction. The chances are that it will be only an interruption, with resumption of the unfinished act as soon as the interruption is over. There is little or no breaking down of the boundaries between the two tension-systems. Each maintains its own integrity. But in the case

[7] Kurt Lewin. *A Dynamic Theory of Personality. Selected Papers* (New York. McGraw-Hill Book Co., 1935), pp. x + 286. See especially Chapter VII, "A Dynamic Theory of the Feeble-minded."

of the infant, and to a lesser degree in the older child, there is more likelihood that the new activity or interest will displace the old either wholly or in part. The baby forgets the moon in his delight in the rattle; the boy, as a result of the day in his workshop, may transfer a part of his interest in baseball to carpentry or electricity, with the result that some of the time previously spent in the former activity is thereafter given over to the latter. As age advances, therefore, there is a gradual tendency for the boundaries between tension systems to become stronger, more clearly defined, with less tendency for energy to overflow from one system to another. The older person thus tends to become more persistent in his efforts toward a particular goal and less adaptable in the sense of being able to shift easily from one goal to another. The old saying that "you cannot teach an old dog new tricks" is evidence that this observation is neither new nor confined to the professional psychologist.

Adults differ from children in the number of their tension-systems as well as in the rigidity of the boundaries between these systems. As age advances, interests and goals become more numerous and more diversified. This point has been discussed in a number of previous chapters and requires no further consideration.

What about the mental organization of the feeble-minded? According to Lewin, feeble-minded persons resemble normal children in respect to the comparative fewness of their tension systems and are more like adults in the rigidity of the boundaries between these systems. These characteristics are illustrated diagrammatically in Figure 111.

Expressed in terms of behavior, Lewin's theory indicates that not only are the feeble-minded limited to a comparatively small number of interests and goals but, because of their mental rigidity, they have little capacity for further development. They become "set in their ways" at a very early age. They resist changes in habits or customs. They tend to do things in the same way, no matter what the circumstances.[8] There is an old story of a feeble-minded woman who was an inmate of a county poorhouse. Usually she worked in the laundry, but one day when they chanced to be short of help in the nursery, she was given a baby to wash. She did so in boiling water with disastrous consequences.

[8] See the discussion of drawings made by the feeble-minded on p. 407.

This "rigidity" of the feeble-minded is shown in another way. They have little capacity for devising artificial means of maintaining interest in a task beyond the point at which psychological

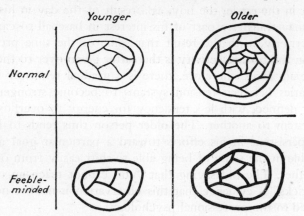

FIG. 111.—DIAGRAMMATIC REPRESENTATION OF LEWIN'S THEORY OF FEEBLE-MINDEDNESS

(Reproduced by permission of the author and publishers from *A Dynamic Theory of Personality*, by Kurt Lewin. McGraw-Hill Book Co.)

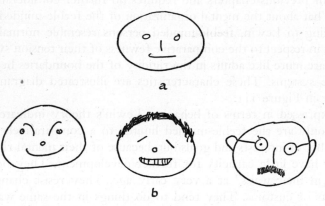

FIG. 112.—BRIGHT CHILDREN MAINTAIN THEIR INTEREST IN A MONOTONOUS TASK BY VARYING THEIR MANNER OF PERFORMING IT

"satiation" sets in, that is, beyond the point where they began to feel "fed up" with it. But the normal person can resort to various devices to whip up his flagging interest. An experiment by

Lewin [9] illustrates this. Two groups of children, one of normal intelligence and the other made up of feeble-minded children were urged to draw "moon faces" such as those shown in Figure 112 *a*. They were urged to keep on making these faces as long as they would. It was fun at first, but eventually all tired of it. However, the normal children found means to relieve their boredom by varying the task, after the fashion shown in Figure 112 *b*. Few of the feeble-minded did this. They continued drawing faces in much the same way until their patience became exhausted. Then they stopped.

Wolf [10] reports various similar devices by which the five-year-olds in her study were able to increase their "persistence time." For example, one child contrived to renew his interest in the rather monotonous task of cancelling out dolls by devising a route whereby all those on a sheet could be crossed out by a single continuous line, or by effacing the figure completely by vigorous scribbling, or by adding various appurtenances or embellishments such as drawing houses around them or adding special decorations to their clothing.

THE CAUSES OF INTELLECTUAL INADEQUACY

In many individual cases of mental deficiency, the origin of the condition can at best be only a hazardous surmise. While group statistics warrant the conclusion that a large proportion of all cases have their basis in some inherited mental defect, the exact manner of transmission is unknown. It now appears practically certain that the matter is more complicated than the early workers in the field thought it to be. Certainly their attempts to bring the observed facts under the simple Mendelian rules applicable to cases where a given type of change in the offspring can be traced to an alteration in a single one of the gene in the complex from which the trait in question derives its particular form or pattern (see pp. 45-46), were based upon far too limited an understanding of the principles involved. But even were these principles under-

---

[9] *Op. cit.*, p. 198.

[10] Theta Holmes Wolf, "The Effect of Praise and Competition on the Persisting Behavior of Kindergarten Children," University of Minnesota Institute of Child Welfare Monograph Series, No. 15 (Minneapolis, University of Minnesota Press, 1938), pp. x + 138.

stood, insufficient knowledge of the ancestral background would frequently make it impossible to apply them to individual cases. Not all cases of mental defect are genetically determined. Some result from structural damage to the brain at an early age, most commonly through injury at the time of birth. Some arise from diseases that affect the brain. Other organic conditions associated [11] with mental defect include the cases with abnormally small heads known as microcephalic idiots or imbeciles and the hydrocephalic cases whose huge bulging skulls result from a pathological accumulation of fluid within and around the brain. Still other cases include the *cretins* described on p. 144, whose condition is the result of insufficient functioning of the thyroid gland in the neck, and the *mongolians*, so called because of the fold in the inner corner of the eyelid which gives to their eyes the appearance of a downward slant like that seen in the Japanese or Chinese.[12] The condition known as mon-

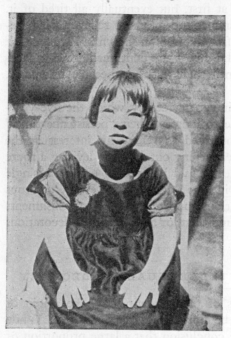

FIG. 113.—A MONGOLIAN IMBECILE

Note the slanting eyes and the square, stubby hands. (Reproduced by permission of the publishers from *Mongolism; a Study of the Physical and Mental Characteristics of Mongolian Imbeciles*, by Kate Brosseau. Williams and Wilkins Co.)

[11] The term *associated with* is used here in preference to *caused by* because in many of these conditions we do not know which is cause and which is effect. For example, it was formerly believed that microcephalic idiocy was caused by failure of the skull to grow and provide adequate space for the growth of the brain. Now most authorities believe that it is the other way around. The skull remained small because the tiny brain provided no impetus for it to increase in size.

[12] There is, of course, no racial connection here; it is just a matter of superficial resemblance.

golism is also believed to be due to glandular insufficiency of some kind, but its exact nature is unknown. Probably a number of glands are involved. (See Figure 113.)

THE CLASSIFICATION OF FEEBLE-MINDED PERSONS ACCORDING TO THEIR DEGREE OF DEFECT

Following Tredgold, most authorities define the *idiot* as the person whose intelligence is at so low a level that he cannot be taught to look after his own bodily needs, such as eating, dressing, and elimination, or to protect himself against ordinary danger. Left unguarded he is likely to wander into the path of an approaching automobile, to fall from his bed or chair, or to swallow any substance left within his reach. In terms of his performance on mental tests, such an individual does not, as a rule, exceed the level of 20 IQ. Most idiots do a little better on non-linguistic than on linguistic items.

The *imbecile* is one whose defect is not so grave as to make him incapable of protecting himself against ordinary physical danger[13] or of caring for his everyday bodily needs, but who cannot be taught the elementary skills that, under favorable conditions, might enable him to maintain an independent economic existence. The imbecile cannot, as a rule, learn to count beyond ten or to make change even for small amounts. He cannot learn to read or to write his name. His practical judgment is so poor that he cannot be trusted to perform even very simple operations without constant supervision. On standard intelligence tests his IQ usually falls within the range of 20 to 40.

The *moron*, with IQ of about 40 to 75, is the most nearly normal of the defective group. As can be seen from a brief glance at the curve of distribution of intelligence, morons are by far the most numerous of the three classes. Because, especially

---

[13] The word *incapable* is here used in a decidedly literal sense. The imbecile or the moron may be "capable," strictly speaking, of guarding themselves against ordinary physical dangers, but they cannot be depended on to exercise the same degree of judgment or caution as the normal person. Statistics show that there is a definite relation between mental backwardness and "accident proneness" even among persons well advanced beyond the level of idiocy.

at the higher levels, their behavior differs so little from that of children with better mental endowment, their handicaps frequently remain unrecognized. Because teachers and parents do not understand them, they are punished and scolded for their poor grades at school; they are held up to ridicule for blunders that could have been avoided only by the exercise of better judgment than that with which nature has endowed them. Often they become the dupes of the unscrupulous and so get into trouble with the law. The moron falls between two stools, for were he a little more stupid than he is, his condition would be recognized and allowances made for his defect; if he were a little brighter he would stand in no need of such allowances but could hold his own without help.

THE SOCIAL CONSEQUENCES OF MENTAL DEFICIENCY

The idiot is rarely a social menace. His condition is at once apparent even to the casual observer, and although if not kept under some kind of physical restraint those of the higher levels are frequently destructive and childishly "mischievous," their very lack of intelligence makes the imposition of such restraint a comparatively easy matter, for they rarely learn to manipulate a simple gate or lock. In a well-managed institution where their simple needs are provided for, and those who can walk and run are given a safe place where they can amuse themselves without disaster to themselves or others, idiots usually appear happy and content. But there is no place for the idiot in the ordinary home. Sometimes parents,[14] through a misguided sense of personal responsibility or because of parental love and pity for the child's helpless condition, insist upon keeping such a child in the household, even though his presence may impose such a burden upon those who must care for him and cause such acute embarrassment to the other children that the family life becomes completely disrupted. Properly cared for, the idiot is a social burden but one that can

[14] A far larger proportion of idiots than of those belonging to the higher levels of mental deficiency owe their condition to factors other than heredity, and are therefore as likely to be found in otherwise normal families as in families of mentally defective stock.

be borne without too great difficulty because they are comparatively few in number. But their segregation and special care is essential for the happiness and normal social development of the families from which they come.

Much the same thing may be said of the imbecile for he, too, is incapable of filling even an approximately normal place in ordinary society. While his general appearance does not always provide an immediate cue by which the outsider is made aware of his condition, his behavior may, for that very reason, be all the more embarrassing to the other members of the household. The following instance is an example.

The younger of two sisters aged respectively eighteen and fifteen years at the time of this episode was a high-grade imbecile with mental age of approximately six years. In appearance she was an attractive child with soft voice and pleasing manner. Careful training had enabled her to learn by rote most of the ordinary social formulas, and it was her special delight to open the door and receive callers. However, although the casual visitor might fail to note that anything was wrong with the child, it needed but a short acquaintance to reveal the true state of affairs. To the sensitive older sister the child's blunders were a source of constant and painful embarrassment. Her fear that the younger girl would do or say something foolish made her reluctant to invite friends to the home, and even when away from home she lived in continual dread that her sister might be mentioned. She had reached an age when it was but natural for her to become interested in boys, but her only friends were two or three girls of her own age whose knowledge of her sister's condition had ceased to trouble her. Up to this time, she had never gone out with a boy, nor had one ever called on her at home.

Then a young man entered the community who immediately showed an interest in her. Moreover this young man was regarded with special favor by all who knew him. He came of a wealthy family, was good-looking, witty, and accomplished. When he asked the girl to go out to dinner and the theater it was by far the most exciting thing that had ever happened to her.

In her concern to look her best she was slow in dressing and was still in her underwear and slippers when the young man arrived. The little sister, as was her custom, ran to open the door. Now the only visitors who had ever before asked specifically for her sister were the girls who were her intimate friends, and if you remember what has been said before about the mental rigidity of the feeble-minded, it is easy to understand what happened. To the young man's inquiry, the child replied courteously, "Margaret is upstairs, would you like to go up?" As he hesitated, some vague realization that he was not familiar with the house prompted her to add, "May I show you the way?" and with no more ado the astonished youth was ushered into her sister's bedroom.

Of course such a situation would have been disconcerting enough to any one. But to the oversensitized girl of eighteen, it was stark tragedy. The mother explained matters to her escort, who did his best to be considerate, but nothing could lessen the girl's feeling of shame and disgrace. The evening was one long agony, and the next morning she refused to leave her room, claiming an illness which, after such an emotional unheaval, was probably not wholly feigned. For months she would see no one. She believed that every one who knew her would have heard the story. Eventually the sister was sent to a school for the feeble-minded and the girl herself to a college where she and her family were unknown. Even there, although her social attitudes improved in time, she continued to be shy and reserved, avoiding the intimate discussions of close friendship lest in some way her shameful secret might be revealed. Letters from her family in which any reference, however, casual, had been made to her sister aroused uncontrollable panic. Fleeing to her room she would tear the paper into narrow strips, burn them, one by one, in the flame of a candle kept for the purpose. But this was not enough, for she had read somewhere that by special treatment ashes may be forced to give up their secrets. So after first reducing them to fine powder, she collected the charred remnants in an envelope and secretly scattered them, a little here and a little there, over the campus grounds. Not until the ashes had been distributed over a wide area could she feel safe.

Of course this is an extreme case. But the unhappiness and family disharmony that may arise in this way are facts well known to all who have had much to do with the feeble-minded in the community.

With the higher-grade imbeciles the social problems are not always confined to the family. As the imbecile girl grows older her body matures, while her mind is still that of a child. Thus there arises the danger that she may become a victim—and often an all-too-willing victim—of sexual assault. The unmarried mother and her illegitimate child are social problems to which mental deficiency makes a not inconsiderable contribution. The imbecile boy, unless carefully guarded, may also become a sexual menace, especially in rural areas. Occasionally, too, unscrupulous persons take advantage of the imbecile's lack of understanding and use him as a cat's-paw for carrying out their illicit designs.

It is the moron, however, who constitutes the greatest social problem. Both because of his numbers and his more enterprising behavior, he penetrates into many situations from which the idiot and the imbecile are barred. He slips in and out of industry, increasing the cost of employment "turn-over" as he is alternately hired and fired for incompetence. He is a prolific source of industrial accidents both to himself and others. He swells the ranks of the delinquent and criminal groups, not because of any inherent tendency to wrong-doing but because of his comparative inability to foresee consequences, to inhibit his impulses until the proper time for activity has arrived, to remember rules or understand the reason for them, and most of all because his limited understanding makes him the easy prey of the unscrupulous. His "inability to conduct himself and his own affairs with ordinary prudence" keeps him typically on the rolls of social welfare agencies whose attempts to help him to look after himself and his dependents are more often disappointing than reassuring.

This is the typical picture,[15] but it is not an invariable one. Many persons whose mental level is no higher than that of the "problem cases" described above are nevertheless able to fill useful places in society if the conditions are suited to them. They are still morons because the conditions under which they live and work must be adjusted to their limitations. They are powerless to modify those conditions or to accomplish much in the way of adapting themselves to conditions that, because of their difficulty or for other reasons are not wholly suited to them. They are not masters of their own fates, even to the limited extent that the complexities of modern civilization leave open to the majority. They are at the mercy of social chance.

The adult moron needs these things: sympathetic understanding and wisely administered advice and supervision in the management of his affairs. But this supervision must be handled in such a way as to bolster rather than break down his self-respect. He must look upon it as a favor to be sought, rather than a social imposition against which he may rebel. He needs work that is within his power to perform successfully and without the neces-

[15] It must be remembered that our classification of *moron* is not based exclusively upon mental test results, least of all upon the results of a single testing. Many persons who at some time test below 75 or even below 65 or 60 show sufficient practical judgment in the conduct of their own affairs to render such a social classification unwarranted.

sity of frequent change, once a habit has been formed. He needs suitable recreation and social life and a comfortable home in which he feels secure. But most of all and long before he becomes an adult he must have formed the kind of habits and attitudes that will enable him to adjust to his own limitations and to profit by the aid offered to him by society. For the moron as for the normal person, adult adjustment has it roots in childhood.

THE EDUCATION AND TRAINING OF MENTALLY DEFECTIVE CHILDREN

The education of backward children is a topic of such scope that an adequate discussion would require an entire book. Only the specialist in this field would be interested in so detailed an outline. But mentally defective children and adults are met with . so frequently that it is only the very exceptionally situated person who never has intimate contact with them. For this reason a few general principles to be observed in their training are not out of place here.

First, we must avoid the common attitude that all mentally defective persons of the same approximate grade of defect are alike. They are not. Like the normal child, the feeble-minded one has his special talents and defects. Because his capacities are so limited, it becomes the more important to find out what his leading assets are and capitalize upon them in his training.

Secondly, we must bear in mind the mental rigidity of the feeble-minded which Lewin has so clearly pointed out. It is harder for the defective child to unlearn a habit once formed than it is for the normal child to do so. For this reason we should be careful, even in small matters, to teach him to do things in the way that we want him to continue doing them.

The third rule should probably have been placed first. Let the feeble-minded child learn the joy of success. Let him see that he is making progress in whatever line he has undertaken. The steps by which he advances will be short; it may be that only by close scrutiny can they be seen at all. But the child has no standard by which he can judge their size. To him they can be made to appear as the long strides that, when considered in terms of his short mental stature, they truly are.

A CLASS PROJECT ON THE CARE OF THE MENTALLY DEFECTIVE

Following is a brief outline of a project to be undertaken by the class as a whole. It is suggested that the group be divided into a number of committees, each with its own chairman. Each committee should take the responsibility of gathering all the facts possible on one of the topics indicated. The library will provide most of the statistical material as well as much in the way of general discussion, opinion of authorities, and illustrative case reports. If possible, local authorities may be interviewed personally. In making such interviews it is important for the student to remember that he is dealing with busy persons whose time must be conserved. To this end he should know in advance what kind of information he wants to secure from each person that he sees. It is well to prepare a list of specific questions in advance.

After each committee has secured its information, the findings should be summarized into a series of brief reports to be presented to the class by the chairmen. Each report should be followed by a group discussion on the topic, What do you think should be done about it?

Topics for Investigation by Committee Members

I. Institutional provision for the feeble-minded in the state

   A. What is the total population of your state according to the last census? According to the figures given in this chapter, about how many should probably be classed as intellectually inadequate?

   B. How many institutions or colonies for the care of the feeble-minded does the state maintain? What is the total number of inmates?

   C. What are the laws governing admission to these institutions?

   D. Is the function of the institutions purely custodial, or is there an attempt to prepare the more promising cases for life in the outside world? Under what conditions are patients paroled?

II. Education of defective children in the public schools

   A. Under what conditions and how generally are special classes for defective and backward children provided by the public schools in the state? About what percentage of the total school population is enrolled in these classes? What are the usual requirements for admission?

   B. How does the training given in the special classes differ from that of the regular grades?

C. What, if any, are the main advantages to the backward child of placing him in a special class? Are there any other reasons for the school segregation of backward pupils?

III. Provisions for identifying and studying the feeble-minded

A. What state, county, or municipal organizations are there in your state to which a child or adult whose mentality is questioned can be taken for examination and advice? About how many cases per year are these organizations equipped to handle?

B. Examine the latest *Yearbook* of the American Psychological Association and find how many psychologists in your state are officially connected with any organization actively concerned with mental diagnosis or other clinical work. Do not include those employed on the staff of hospitals for the insane. If available, the *Yearbooks* of the various local psychological associations—the Midwestern Association, the New York Branch, the Pacific Coast Section, and so on—as well as that of the American Association for Applied Psychology should also be consulted.

C. Have any of the juvenile courts of the state a regular provision for the clinical study of the delinquent children brought before the courts? Are children who have been sentenced to juvenile reformatories examined to determine their intellectual status? Is there any provision for the regular examination of adult criminals?

D. What attempts, if any, are being made to ascertain the mental status of the recipients of public relief?

E. Is any other reasonably systematic attempt being made to locate and identify the feeble-minded in the state population?

IV. The cost of caring for the feeble-minded

A. Consult the annual report of the state division of agencies and institutions [16] and ascertain the annual expense of maintaining the various state institutions for the feeble-minded and the cost of buildings and equipment. What is the annual cost per inmate? What would be the per capita expense to each inhabitant of the state if all were assessed equally?

B. Consult the report of the state department of education to find the annual per capita cost of educating a child in the regular elementary grades. From the information on com-

[16] In some states this report may have a different name. If you have trouble in locating it, the head of the reference department in your library can tell you what to look for.

parative class size and teacher salary, make the best estimate you can of the relative cost of educating a backward child in one of the special classes.

C. Examine the sociological and psychological literature to see what you can find on the unofficial cost of mental deficiency that remains unrecognized for what it is.

V. Reducing the number of the mentally defective and simplifying the responsibilities of those not in institutions through preventing their reproduction

A. What are the present laws in your state with regard to the sterilization of those intellectually incapable of undertaking the responsibility for the maintenance and rearing of a family? To what extent are these laws carried out?

B. Is there any policy for more or less systematic parole of high-grade mental defectives from state institutions after a period of industrial training, provided that sterilization has first been done? Can you find any data on the subsequent adjustment of these cases? (If your own state has no such policy, consult the records of other states where this is done.)

VI. What is now being done in your state in the way of public education with respect to the social handling of problems arising from mental deficiency?

Chapter XXVII

JUVENILE DELINQUENCY AND ADULT CRIME

What is your estimate of the total number of serious crimes committed in the United States in the course of a single year? After you have made a guess, look on the next page and see how close you came to the facts.

Why is it hard to determine how many different criminals were concerned in these acts?

Why is the population of federal prisons so much smaller than that of state prisons?

What is meant by a "delinquency area"? In what parts of a city are delinquency areas most likely to be found? Why?

Is it possible to recognize the potential criminal by means of his physical appearance? Can you think of any reasons why this idea should have become so thoroughly established in the minds of many people? Who was the chief scientific proponent of this point of view? Have modern scientists who have investigated the matter usually supported his conclusions?

How may such characteristics as inferior intelligence or poor physique become contributing factors in the production of criminal behavior without actually causing it?

Of the types of functional mental disorders described in a previous chapter, which would you expect to be most likely to lead to criminal behavior? Why?

Would you expect to find a relation between crime and the divorce rate? When you have thought the matter over, look on p. 662 for the statistics.

About what would be your estimate of the proportion of juvenile delinquents who are convicted of crime after reaching adult life? Can you think of any way of accounting for the apparent discrepancy (actually the two figures show no necessary disagreement) between the data given in the U.S. Census Report (p. 663) and those given by Glueck and Glueck (pp. 663-664)?

Can delinquency and crime usually be traced to a single causative factor?

What can be done to lessen the amount of delinquency and crime in future generations?

EXTENT OF THE PROBLEM

According to a study carried out by the Federal Bureau of Investigation [1] the total number of major crimes committed in the United States during the year 1940 was 1,517,026. "Major crimes" include such acts as murder, rape, larceny, auto theft, robbery from the person, and aggravated assault. Minor violations of law such as infringement of traffic regulations, petty thievery, and the like have not been included. "Larceny" includes only thefts in which the value of the stolen articles or the amount of money taken amounted to $50 or more. "Aggravated assault" does not mean ordinary cases of assault and battery but includes only those cases in which deadly weapons were used in such a way as to be likely to cause permanent maiming or even death of the victim. Startling as it may seem, the figure given above is thus not padded by the inclusion of minor delinquencies. These are real crimes.

The data here given do not enable us to say how many different criminals were implicated in the million and a half criminal acts.

[1] *Uniform Crime Reports,* 1940. The data here given were taken from *Statistics on Crime and Criminals* by W. A. Lunden (Pittsburgh, Stevenson and Foster, 1942). See p. 19.

Information on this point would not be easy to obtain, because a good many of the criminals were never apprehended. We can be sure that of their number, many committed more than one crime in the course of the year. On the other hand we can be equally certain that there were many true criminals who committed no crimes during 1940, either because they were confined in penal institutions or were physically disabled or because no suitable opportunity presented itself. Moreover, a single crime is not always the work of a single individual. Some are carried out by gangs.

It is accordingly well-nigh impossible even to arrive at an estimate of the number of persons now living in the United States who either have already committed or at some time in the future will commit a major crime. The number is appallingly large; of that we can be sure.

It is possible, however, to determine the number of persons actually confined in penal institutions on any given date. Available figures on this question for the country as a whole give the number confined in the penal institutions of the United States on January 1, 1933, as 201,433.[2] Of these, 68.5 per cent were in state prisons and reformatories, 25.5 per cent were in county and municipal jails, and 6.0 per cent were in federal prisons or reformatories. Because of the rapid turnover of the prison population, especially in the jails where a large percentage of the shorter sentences are served, the number incarcerated on any single date gives a very erroneous impression of the total prison population. For example, taking the figures for the jails alone (both city and county), we find that the total number of inmates on January 1, 1933, was 46,292 but that in the course of the next six months there were 273,818 new admissions, while 269,825 were discharged. On June 30 the number of inmates was 50,285. A brief computation will show that some of those discharged must have been readmitted even during as short a period as six months. In

---

[2] Report of the United States Department of Commerce, Bureau of the Census, *County and City Jails* (Washington, D. C., Government Printing Office, 1935), pp. iv + 148. This figure is based upon actual report from about 90 per cent of all the institutions of the country, to which has been added a proportional estimate of the most probable number for those not reporting.

the state and federal prisons, where the sentences are usually longer, the turnover is less rapid but even there approximately 50 per cent of the prison population changes in the course of a single year.[3]

PSYCHOLOGY AND CRIME

One of the curious inconsistencies of modern science is to be found in the scant attention accorded to the subject of crime and the criminal in most textbooks of psychology. Examination of half a dozen of the most recent general texts reveals either no mention whatever of the topic or a few brief paragraphs dealing almost exclusively with the intelligence of the criminal. Surely this is strange negligence on the part of a profession purporting to be concerned with the study of human behavior. For the scientist does not use the word *behavior* in the limited sense in which the term is employed by the irate parent who threatens her small son with dire consequences if he fails to "behave himself." Stealing is certainly as much an act of behavior as is the packing of spools in a box (a common test of motor dexterity and speed) or the tendency to associate colors with particular sounds or abstract terms which is known as *synaesthesia*. And crime is something that intimately affects the lives of all of us. A large proportion of the money we pay for taxes goes directly into payment for the prevention and punishment of crime. The apprehension, trial, and conviction of criminals, the maintenance of jails and prisons is an expensive matter, yet this represents but a small proportion of the actual cost of crime. Not only is there the obvious matter of loss to the victim. Far more important is the loss to society of the potential services of the criminals themselves, to say nothing of the large force of men who are employed to look after them. According to Lunden, the average time actually served in state and federal prisons by 59,876 prisoners who were released during the year 1938 was nineteen months, making a total of 94,803 man-years served by this group alone. Most of these men were physically and intellectually capable of some kind of useful labor. When we think what almost 95,000 men could accomplish in a year's time if all were usefully em-

[3] Lunden, *op. cit.*, p. 224.

ployed, we begin to realize what a tremendous loss is incurred by our failure to reclaim the criminal.[4]

FACTORS ASSOCIATED WITH CRIMINAL BEHAVIOR

Volumes have been written about the external conditions that are said to "breed crime." There is no doubt whatever that far more than a chance proportion both of adult criminals and of juvenile delinquents come from those poverty-stricken and crowded areas of our large cities that we refer to collectively as "the slums." Shaw,[5] in a monograph that has been much quoted, shows that when the addresses of all the boys passing through the juvenile courts of Chicago during a given period of time were plotted on a city map and the number from the various parts of the city was in each case reduced to a ratio of the total population of that area, the proportion of delinquents in certain sections was so vastly in excess of that in other sections that these regions might properly be designated "delinquency areas." In one such area, according to Shaw, no less than 28 per cent of all the male youths between the ages of seventeen and twenty-one years of age were arrested and arraigned before the Boys' Court on charges of serious crime during the three-year period between 1924-1926. "Delinquency areas" are likely to be found near the railroad yards [6] and the manufacturing districts, in sections that are gradually being taken over by industry and where, consequently, such dwellings as remain are allowed to become run down and dilapidated. The many saloons, poolrooms and gambling-houses are

[4] Large as this figure is, it is unquestionably far too small. In the first place it is based only upon the prisoners who were released. It therefore includes a disproportionately large number of those whose sentences were relatively short and for whom the turnover is most rapid. Presumably it would include none of those serving life terms or who were under sentence of death. It does not include any of the large additional group in county and city jails or in reformatories. Neither does it include the group of unknown but certainly large size made up of criminals still at large who not only contribute nothing to society but actively prey upon it.

[5] Clifford R. Shaw, *Delinquency Areas* (Chicago, University of Chicago Press, 1929), pp. xxii + 214.

[6] Aside from the fact that proximity to railroads makes for noise and dirt and similar undesirable residential features that cause such quarters to be selected only by those who are too poor to live elsewhere, the railroad yards are usually the haunts of tramps and "transients" who go about from place to place by stealing rides on freight cars.

gathering places for undesirable characters of all kinds. In Chicago, Shaw was able to show that delinquency tended to center in the region of the "Loop" and decreased steadily toward the suburbs. Similar studies conducted in a number of other cities have confirmed Shaw's findings. These studies have also shown that many other municipal features are associated with the frequency of delinquency. It is most common in areas where there is the greatest concentration of families in receipt of public relief or who are known to social service agencies of various kinds. It is less common in parts of the city where there are public playgrounds than in those areas where there are none. The "geography of crime" is more than a catch phrase. It has become a field of serious investigation.

What of the criminal himself? Is he, as many suppose, an ignorant, stupid creature, incapable of appreciating the consequences of his acts? Are there physical characteristics that distinguish him from the rest of mankind? What of the low forehead, the "bestial countenance," the "ape-like" body on which the writers of sensational fiction love to dwell? Is there really such a thing as a recognizable "criminal type"?

ARE CRIMINALS "BORN" OR "MADE"?

Since the days of Lombroso [7] criminologists have searched for external signs by which the "criminal type" might be identified. As the result of many years' study of the physical characteristics of criminals, Lombroso came to the conclusion that in contrast to the person whose illegal acts are unpremeditated and result chiefly from circumstances over which he has no control, the true criminal is characterized by an exceptionally large number of physical anomalies to which Lombroso gave the name of "stigmata." These include such things as a peculiarly shaped skull—Lombroso noted a number of different types—an undeveloped or deformed nose, various types of dental anomalies, bodily characteristics resembling those of the opposite sex, unusual distribu-

---

[7] Lombroso was an Italian anthropologist and criminologist whose most important work was done at about the turn of the last century. A number of his books and articles are available in English translation. See especially his *Criminal Man* (New York, G. P. Putnam's Sons, 1911), pp. 322.

tions of body hair, and so on. According to Lombroso, not only could the criminal be identified by means of physical signs but even the type of crime he was most likely to commit might be predicted on this basis. Lombroso's theory was so startling that it captured the imagination of many persons and started a number of investigations designed to test it.[8] Although these studies have consistently yielded negative results, the theory is so attractive that it dies hard. It would of course be a fine thing if we could select our potential criminals just by looking at them and pop them into institutions at so early an age that they would never disturb the public. Unfortunately it is not as easy as all that. To date, no sound evidence has appeared to justify the belief that any person is *predestined* to a life of crime. It is quite possible that there are persons who, by reason of inborn personality characteristics such as a tendency to act more quickly and impulsively than the average person or because they possess less than the usual ability to foresee consequences are somewhat more *likely* than the average to drift into crime. But even this cautious hypothesis is not proved beyond question, and were it true, it would

[8] One of the most extensive and carefully controlled of these was carried out in England by Charles Goring—*The English Convict* (London, H. M. Stationery Office, 1913)—who, as a result of studying the physical characteristics of three hundred criminals, came to the conclusion that "no evidence has emerged confirming the existence of a physical type such as Lombroso and his disciples have described."

However, it should be noted that E. A. Hooton, a well-known American anthropologist, as a result of investigations of well over a hundred different measurements of very large numbers of American convicts has arrived at conclusions very similar to those of Lombroso. He finds that criminals, generally speaking, are inferior to the general populace of corresponding race and age and that there are reliably determined physical differences between persons convicted of various types of crime. Some of Hooton's findings, however, are open to more than one interpretation, even if we grant the accuracy of his data. For example he notes that a larger proportion of crimes of violence are committed by red-headed people than would be expected from the proportion of the latter in the general population. But this is as likely to be a cultural as a biological phenomenon, for if children with red hair are brought up to accept the popular tradition that people of their coloring have ungovernably hot tempers, or if other children make a point of teasing them until they fly into a rage, it is surely not unreasonable to suppose that many of them would make less than the usual effort at gaining self-control. (See E. A. Hooton, *Crime and the Man*, Cambridge, Harvard University Press, 1939). For further comments on the sources of error in studies of this kind see Donald G. Paterson, *Physique and Intellect* (New York, D. Appleton-Century Co., 1930).

by no means justify the theory of a "criminal type." Criminals are not "born," nor, strictly speaking, are they "made." Criminal behavior is learned by the individual. Its learning is subject to the same rules as learning in general. As is true with other fields of learning, there are conditions that facilitate it and others that interfere with its acquisition.

Among the personal characteristics that may predispose toward a life of crime, an inferior physique may unquestionably be mentioned. The person with poor physical endowment often feels the need to compensate for his defects in one way or another. Many do so directly and effectively. They admit frankly to themselves and others that there are certain fields of human endeavor from which they are barred by reason of their constitutional handicaps. They therefore seek some occupation where their talents can have full scope and that makes little or no demand upon those areas in which they are deficient. Others, through blundering or unwise guidance, fail to make a successful adjustment of this kind, and in the absence of true compensatory behavior they resort to one or another of the mechanisms known as "overcompensation" but for which "pseudocompensation" would probably be a better name. The boy who recognizes that he is physically inferior to others may find balm for his wounded self-esteem through playing malicious tricks on other children, bullying those weaker than himself, or excessive boasting. Or he may attempt to buy the friendship of boys with whom he is unable to compete physically by providing them with all sorts of little treats. If he lacks the money to procure these honestly, he may resort to stealing. The child who steals in order to buy friendship is a familiar figure in every child guidance clinic. But the lad who begins by stealing for his friends soon extends his activities to stealing for himself, and so the pattern grows.

Inferior intelligence is another factor that is often invoked as a major determinant of crime and delinquency. Just as with inferior physique, there can be no doubt that intellectual retardation is a handicap that makes truly successful adjustment more difficult than it would otherwise be. There is the further fact that persons of limited intellect are for that very reason less able to look far afield and understand all the likely ramifications of their own acts. They have less insight into the rules by which society is governed and so are rather more at the mercy of chance circumstances than is the person who, because of his more highly developed judgment, is able to exert more control over the persons and events by which he is surrounded. Because of his shorter range of intellectual vision, he is somewhat more likely to adopt quick and easy ways of attaining satisfaction, and these are frequently not ways of which society approves. Although there are many persons of limited intellect who are as law-abiding as you or I, it is apparently true, as many investigations have shown, that the delinquent and criminal groups include a greater proportion of mentally backward and uneducated persons than does the general population.[9] Because ignorance and stupidity are factors that block off a number of the goals to which more favorably endowed persons may aspire, it is perhaps not surprising that in their efforts to find the satisfaction that comes with success, many of those who, by lack of ability, are baffled in their efforts to accomplish the thing they set out to do may turn to some sub-

[9] In *The Prisoner's Antecedents*, U. S. Bureau of the Census (Washington, D. C., Government Printing Office, 1929), pp. 77, data are presented on the education of a sample of 19,080 persons convicted of serious crimes who were inmates of state and federal penal institutions during the first six months of 1923. This sample represents 11 per cent of the total prison population of corresponding date and is believed to be approximately representative. About 11 per cent of the group were illiterate, which, on the basis of information obtained from the U. S. Commissioner of Education, is estimated to be about twice as high as in the general population of corresponding age at that time. Conversely, the proportion who had attended high school or college was only about half as great as in the general population.

Studies of juvenile delinquents almost without exception have indicated that some degree of both educational and intellectual retardation is the rule. Nevertheless, it is a rule with many exceptions. Every juvenile reformatory and every prison can count many persons of normal and even of very superior intelligence among its inmates. R. Pintner—*Intelligence Testing*, Second Edition (New York, Henry Holt and Co., 1931), pp. xii + 555—in his chapter on the delinquent gives an excellent summary of the most important findings on this head and also points out a number of sources of error in some of the published studies. A more recent report by Sheldon Glueck and Eleanor Glueck, *One Thousand Juvenile Delinquents, Their Treatment by Court and Clinic* (Cambridge, Harvard University Press, 1934), pp. xxix + 341, compares the distribution of intelligence quotients of 979 delinquents with that of over 3,000 Massachusetts school children of similar age. Of the school children, 79 per cent were classed as normal or bright, with IQ's of 91 or higher; of the delinquents, only 41.6 per cent were in this class. Of the school children, 7.1 per cent were classed as of border-line or defective intelligence (IQ not over 80), while 30.2 per cent of the delinquents were so classified.

stitute activity of a socially undesirable kind. While it is probably true that apprehended delinquents include a greater than chance proportion of the mentally backward, since the bright are more likely to escape detection, it is unlikely that this factor alone can account for all the differences found.

The proportion of mentally diseased persons among the criminal group is not known. It is presumably higher than it is among the general population, a fact that you will not find hard to understand if you will review what was said about mental illness in Chapter XXV. But the statement sometimes made by sentimentalists of the modern school that all delinquents and criminals are "mentally sick" is neither accurate nor helpful. The personality of the criminal has been stunted in its development, particularly on the side of his attitude toward himself in relation to society. His sense of values has become distorted through having selected the wrong goals. He needs reëducation and guidance into fields where he can attain success by socially acceptable means.

Some criminals, however, are unquestionably the victims of genuine mental disease. Many states have recognized this and have provided special institutions for the detention and care of the criminal insane. The number of inmates of such institutions is, however, a poor clue to the total proportion of mentally diseased among criminals, for there are many among the regular prison inmates who belong in this group. On the other hand, there are undoubtedly some inmates of these institutions who have used the plea of "temporary insanity" as a means of escaping more severe punishment and in hope that by later claiming a cure they might gain early release.[10] Of those criminals who are diagnosed as suffering from mental disease, a large proportion are of the paranoid type. This is quite understandable when we remember the kind of systematized delusions from which the paranoid suffers. Manic-depressives make up the greater part of the remainder, and the crimes are usually committed while the patient is in the manic phase. The depressed phase is more likely to be marked by suicide than by homicide.

[10] For a brief but thought-provoking discussion of the psychological aspect of criminal jurisprudence in cases of alleged mental incompetence, see pp. 74-79 of *Law and the Lawyers* by E. S. Robinson (New York, Macmillan Co., 1935), pp. xii + 348.

It seems probable that if we were able to get at the facts, we should find that the characteristics which most clearly distinguish those who commit crimes from those who do not are not primarily matters of ability or of actual mental derangement. They are the offender's attitudes, his ways of thinking about himself and about the outside world. There is evidence, too, that the typical criminal (if there is such a person) tends to be impatient of all restraint, including self-restraint; that he is likely to act on impulse and to be willing to sacrifice any number of birds-in-the-bush in his haste to grasp at the one nearest at hand. This latter tendency may perhaps account for the extraordinarily high percentage of divorced persons among those convicted of crime. Divorce is certainly not a crime in itself, and there are unquestionably many cases in which divorce seems to be the best available way of remedying marital mistakes. Yet when we find a selected group of persons for whom the divorce rate runs far ahead of that in the population as a whole, it is reasonable to suppose that these persons have either rushed into marriage with little regard to its suitability or that they have been unduly impatient of the minor difficulties of adjustment that come to practically all married couples sooner or later. Be that as it may, the *U.S. Census Report* [11] shows that among the male convicts represented in the special study previously mentioned, the chances that a man who had been divorced would be committed to a penal institution were more than six times as great as those for married men or widowers and about three times as great as those for single men of corresponding age. Particularly among the men of forty-five or older, the most striking figure is the *low* percentage of those married and living with their wives. The chances of incarceration for this group are less than half as great as for the unmarried men and about one-eighth as great as for the divorced men of similar age. The report for women is very similar to that for men. From these figures we are probably justified in drawing the conclusion that successful adjustment within the family is highly related to successful adjustment in the community. The person who is willing to delay the immediate gratification of his impulses until he can do so on a basis that promises to be lasting, and who does not expect life to be all beer and

[11] *The Prisoner's Antecedents.*

skittles but is willing to put up with a good many minor annoyances for the sake of a larger good, is likely to make both a better husband and a better citizen than the one who is not.

THE RELATION OF JUVENILE DELINQUENCY TO ADULT CRIME

Of the 19,080 prisoners studied by the Bureau of the Census,[12] approximately 3.8 per cent were known to have served previous terms in some juvenile reformatory. This, probably, is fewer than the total number, since incomplete records of previous history would result in the omission of many cases. Glueck and Glueck, in the study previously mentioned,[13] startled their readers by the report that a follow-up of 923 boys [14] five years after they had been brought before the Juvenile Court of Boston revealed that 88.2 per cent had been arrested for further offenses one or more times during the interval. Among the 776 who continued to be delinquent, considerably over half had records of more than one arrest during the five years; 33.4 per cent had four or more arrests to their discredit. However, these boys were still young at the time of the follow-up. A later study [15] yielded a slightly more encouraging picture. Ten years after their original appearance before the Juvenile Court, 877 of the cases were investigated again, and five years later, 846 [16] were looked up once more. At the time of the ten-year follow-up, the average age of the youths was twenty-four years; at the time of the last follow-up it was twenty-nine years.

At the time of the second follow-up, 33.9 per cent of those whose behavior could be checked had not been arrested during the five years immediately preceding. This is a distinct improvement over the 11.8 per cent who had kept out of trouble during the five years immediately following their first appearance at Juvenile Court. In the next five years, the percentage not arrested

[12] Ibid.
[13] See footnote on p. 660.
[14] Out of the original group of 1,000, the later conduct of only 923 could be determined with assurance.
[15] Sheldon Glueck and Eleanor Glueck, Juvenile Delinquents Grown Up (New York, The Commonwealth Fund, 1940), pp. x + 330.
[16] The 154 cases not included in the final report were distributed as follows: dead, 60; in non-penal institutions, 2; whereabouts or conduct unknown, 92.

during that period had risen to 42.1. Although not all of those who kept out of trouble during the second period were equally successful during the third period, there was a distinct tendency toward a stabilization of behavior pattern as age progressed. Of 525 youths arrested one or more times during the second five-year period, 79.4 per cent were also arrested at least once during the next five-year period. Of the 285 who were not arrested during the second period, 86.3 per cent continued their good conduct during the final period.

It is impossible to summarize all the findings of this important study, but certain of the conclusions at which the authors arrive are worth quoting: [17]

We have ascertained that it is not so much arrival at any particular age-span . . . as the achievement of a degree of maturity, that makes for social adaptation on the part of former delinquents. Maturity is a complex concept. It embraces the development of a certain stage of physical, mental, and emotional capacity and stability, and a certain degree of integration of the personality. . . . Normally when he [the average person] reaches chronologic adulthood the development and integration of his physical and mental powers make it easier for him to achieve a capacity for self-control, foresight, planfulness; to postpone immediate desires for later ones; to profit by experience; to develop perseverance, self-respect, regard for the opinion of his law abiding fellows, and other similar attributes. These enable him to adapt successfully to the demands of society and to avoid drifting into, or persisting in, crime. However, individuals differ in their innate organization and in their early conditioning, so that development and integration of powers sufficient to be designated "maturity" are not always achieved at the expected age-span. . . .

The years from about twenty-five to thirty-five seem to be the most crucial in the lives of offenders, since during this age-zone there appears to occur the peak of a sifting-out process which differentiates those who mature normally from those who are inclined never to reach a stage of maturity sufficient to enable them to abandon criminalism, and who will either die as criminals or end their days in almshouses or on the streets. . . . With the passage of the years, a differentiation seems to occur between the offenders whose delinquency and criminality is due more to adverse environmental and educational influences than to any deep-seated organismal weaknesses, and those whose inability to conform to the demands of a complex society is more nearly related to innate (and, partly, early-conditioned) abnor-

[17] Sheldon Glueck and Eleanor Glueck, op. cit., p. 267 ff. Quoted by permission of The Commonwealth Fund.

malities of the kind that set limits to the achievement of a socially adequate degree of maturity. The former, sooner or later, acquire the requisite degree of integration of intelligence, impulse and behavior. The latter never achieve a degree of maturity requisite to lawful social adaptation. ... They continue to be criminalistic until physically and mentally "burned out." Misbehavior due to *un*-integration gives way to misbehavior due to *dis*integration, until the organism finally runs down and stops.

THE HOME BACKGROUND OF THE DELINQUENT

Without attempting to enumerate the long list of factors that have been found to be associated with juvenile delinquency, we may note by way of summary that a vast majority of our young law-breakers come from homes that afford less than usual opportunity to learn the ways of happy and honest living, where marital discord is rife and often leads to divorce or separation while the child is still too young to forego the advantages of an undivided home without serious hazard to his personality development. The following table from the original study by Glueck and Glueck, based on 966 cases for whom the data were obtainable is an example:

TABLE IX
BROKEN OR POORLY SUPERVISED HOMES
AMONG JUVENILE DELINQUENTS *

Status	No.	Per Cent
Death of one or both parents	258	26.7
Desertion, separation or divorce of parents	182	18.8
Prolonged absence of one or both parents because of illness or imprisonment	24	2.5
Criminality of one or both parents	195	20.2
Incompatibility of parents (marked)	33	3.4
Discipline poor by both parents	134	13.9
Child Welfare agencies had to intervene because of bad conditions	36	3.7
Mother working out and no substitute in the home	28	2.9
No broken home or poor supervision	76	7.9

Note: No case is tabulated more than once, although for many, more than one of the above conditions was present. Tabulation was in order of the factors given above. Thus, if a child had lost a parent, the remaining parent might be ill or criminal or exercise very poor discipline, but no further tabulation of these facts was made. Thus the table gives only an incomplete picture of the extent to which these factors were actually present in the homes of these children.

* Reproduced from p. 75 of *One Thousand Juvenile Delinquents* by Glueck and Glueck by courtesy of the Harvard University Press.

MULTIPLE CAUSATION

Many other investigators have reported somewhat similar figures. The reports vary somewhat from one study to another but it is likely that a part of the variances are due to differences in the manner of collecting the data and in the personal standards of the worker in respect to such matters as poor discipline, incompatibility of parents and so on. But it should also be noted that similar conditions exist in many homes where the children do not become delinquent. This is a fact that calls for further consideration.

Cyril Burt [18] in a study of delinquent children in England put forth a theory known as the *theory of multiple causation* which may be stated briefly as follows: People differ from each other in respect to the personal factors that enable them to withstand adverse conditions. Likewise, the surroundings under which they grow up differ in respect to the number and type of adverse characteristics which they present. Delinquency, according to Burt, varies directly in accordance with the number of adverse traits possessed by the individual plus the number of adverse conditions by which he is surrounded. A lad who has many undesirable characteristics in his personal make-up (let us say a low intelligence, plus a quick and ungoverned temper, plus poor health) may break under conditions that a better endowed boy could withstand. Of two boys with equally weak personal traits, one who is reared in a good environment may remain law-abiding, while the other who is subjected to many adverse external conditions may become delinquent. Putting all the undesirable conditions together, Burt found that the average delinquent among his cases was the victim of about nine or ten subversive factors, some of which were personal and others environmental [19] while

---

[18] Cyril Burt, *The Young Delinquent* (New York, D. Appleton-Century Co., 1925), pp. xviii + 619.

[19] This distinction is of course both arbitrary and superficial. Development, as we have repeatedly pointed out, progresses through interaction between the child and the external world. The distinction rests wholly with the observer who takes note of certain conditions lying outside the child but presumably inducing responses in him, and who also notes certain behaviors of the child himself. That the latter are at least in part the result of the former is undeniable.

the average non-delinquent of similar age counted only around three.

Burt's method of handling his results by simply counting up the number of subversive factors is of course extremely crude. A modern statistician would employ more precise methods which would enable him to arrive at some method of estimating the relative importance of the various conditions studied.[20] Burt, it is true, made some attempt to do this, but the method which he employed is not well suited to the solution of a problem of this kind. His findings on this point cannot, therefore, be accepted without further verification.

Using a somewhat more elaborate procedure than that employed by Burt, Glueck and Glueck[21] found that *recidivism*, that is, the repetition of delinquent acts after a first arrest, is also directly related to the number and kind of adverse factors in the child and in his environment. A child is far more likely to continue a delinquent career if the conditions under which he is forced to live are unfavorable than if they are favorable, and the more unfavorable conditions there are, the greater is the prospect of recidivism. In their latest study,[22] they also stress the fact that prediction of later adjustment must be related to future treatment. Factors that are favorable for good conduct within an institution are not entirely the same as those which favor independent adjustment in the outside world, nor are they identical with those most closely associated with good conduct while on parole or probation. Generally speaking, the greater the amount of personal freedom, the greater is the weight assigned to the "personal" factors. When the subject is to be kept under closer supervision, the external factors in his background are of more consequence.

THE PREVENTION OF CRIME

In the two preceding chapters, we saw how the normal course of development may be interrupted, arrested, or turned back on itself with disastrous consequences to the individual and to society.

[20] These methods, such for example as the analysis of variance and covariance, are too complicated to be described here.
[21] *Juvenile Delinquents Grown Up.*
[22] *Ibid.*

In the case of the feeble-minded person we have arrest or retardation of development that centers around the realm of abstract thinking. In the mentally diseased person we have arrested or retarded growth of the personality that takes the form of a fearful clinging on the part of the affected person to the ways of childhood. The feeble-minded person *cannot* grow up; the mentally diseased person *will not*, or perhaps we had better say, *dares not* grow up or remain grown up.

Like them, the criminal shows imperfect personality development, but in his case we have an unbalanced type of growth, with overdevelopment of the egocentric side of his personality and a deficient sense of his responsibilities to society. He is not happy, because real happiness must be shared and this he has failed to learn. So he continues to struggle vainly for satisfactions and pleasures that always elude his grasp.

It has become a truism to say that crime is less the fault of the criminal than of society. This is unquestionably true, but it is also likely to be a convenient phrase by which personal responsibility is passed on to the convenient level of a depersonalized abstraction. The delinquent and the criminal behave as they do because they have not learned to find satisfaction in more acceptable and effective ways. The road to the prevention and cure of crime is the way of education, education in the broad sense, which is not merely the acquisition of formal subject-matter. We need constantly to remind ourselves that the literal meaning of education is "drawing out," not, as so many seem to think, just "putting in."

The child reared in a "delinquency area" gains his education from his surroundings. Cut off from many of the usual opportunities for healthful play by lack of playground space, he turns to the streets where opportunities for mischief far outnumber the chances for healthy sport.[23] Defrauded as he often is of normal family affection, his emotional life is stunted and perverted. With no one to fend for him he must look out for himself as best he can and by whatever means are at hand. But this early emotional isolation is dangerous. It leads to a perverted sense of

[23] D. Harris (unpublished Ph.D. thesis, University of Minnesota) has shown that delinquent boys spend a far greater proportion of their playtime in such activities as breaking windows for fun, "hooking rides," fighting, and the like, than do boys who have never been arrested.

values. It checks the course of social development at the level of the infantile "I," which never expands into a fully developed "we." And so we get the delinquent child who, as we have seen, has more than a 50 per cent chance of growing into a criminal adult.

The answer, we have said, is through education. But this education must extend far beyond the offender himself. It must include the public. And public education, if it is to be real, cannot stop with giving information about crime and the criminal. It must fire the imagination and arouse active attempts to correct those external conditions that make for crime. The abolishment of slum areas and the provision of properly supervised playgrounds will do much to change "delinquency areas" into regions where children grow and develop normally.

Child behavior and misbehavior have their roots in the home. It has been repeatedly shown that marital disharmony, family bickering, and lack of normal parental affection are likely to leave permanent scars upon the developing personality of the child. Thus the prevention of delinquency and crime must start long before his parents become parents. It must begin with the present generation of young people, with the young man or woman in search of a mate. If all such choices were made wisely and well, the problem of delinquency and crime in future generations would be well advanced toward its solution.

THE LIFE STORY OF A YOUNG DELINQUENT

Clifford R. Shaw, *The Jack-Roller: A Delinquent Boy's Own Story* (Chicago, University of Chicago Press, 1930), pp. xvi + 205.

This is the real story of a "bad boy." Stanley, the hero, was a resident of one of Chicago's delinquency areas and had the added handicaps of a broken home, a brutal stepmother and a drunken father. From this home he repeatedly ran away and was as often returned by the well-meant but incredibly stupid action of legal authority. His life between the ages of six and eighteen years is a tale of which the locale varies from vagrancy to correctional institutions, and the action, beginning with childish delinquencies, passes on to major offenses and perversions at an ever-increasing pace.

The story told by the boy himself is given verbatim. Undoubtedly it is colored to some extent by the attitudes and the retrospective bitterness of the chronicler, but just here lies much of its interest for the student of human behavior. Although the prefatory chapters, in which the official record of the boy's delinquencies is accompanied by brief comments on the home situation by persons officially in charge of the case, show that many of the bald facts reported are unquestionably true, the critical reader will nevertheless find many instances of such defense mechanisms as rationalization, attempts to protect himself by throwing the blame on others or on circumstances, and the like. Thus the study is of particular interest in showing how circumstances beget attitudes and attitudes give rise to behavior.

For students who have had little direct contact with the life of the "submerged tenth," reading this book will be an enlightening experience that should provide a broader understanding of the factors that make for crime and delinquency, as well as a more intelligent sympathy for the offender. And this is what is needed to replace the all-too-common attitudes of the layman which are likely to veer from mawkish pity to a vindictive demand for punishment. Neither of these is likely to help the offender or protect society.

The final chapter of the book tells how Stanley was eventually helped to a more satisfactory way of life, in which, at the time of writing, he had continued for more than five years. One could wish for more detail here, but it is possible to read between the lines to some extent and infer a good deal that is not told directly. Perhaps the student will find it interesting to do a little speculating himself as to which of the factors briefly mentioned played the major part in effecting the boy's reform.

PART V

The Mental Hygiene of Development

Chapter XXVIII

BRINGING UP CHILDREN

At what age should training for parenthood begin?

*Along what lines should the training of young people
for parenthood progress?*

*Apart from the physical requirements of food, cloth-
ing, and shelter, what are the most basic requirements for healthy development?*

WHY THE COLLEGE STUDENT IS INTERESTED
IN CHILD TRAINING

Parenthood is a normal part of human life. And being a parent
is not, as some people appear to think, a state experienced only
by women and therefore of no concern to men. It is a joint enterprise and a joint responsibility. Properly realized, it is a shared
delight that becomes richer with the passing of the years. Unwisely handled, it may hold the seeds of the bitterest disappointments that human beings can experience.

Even before young men and women become parents they not
infrequently stand *in loco parentis* for short periods of time or
are able to exert an influence upon the management and training
of children for whom they are not primarily responsible. The
occasional care of younger brothers and sisters and participation
in family councils about their training, or a summer spent as
counselor in a children's camp provide valuable opportunities for
practicing the skills that will be needed later on. But just as with
any act of learning, the value of such experience will vary with
the individual. If you regard it as just a job to be got through
with as easily as possible, you will not learn much. If you look
upon it as an educational opportunity from which both you and
the child can profit, the case will be very different. Incidental

learning, as was pointed out before, cannot be depended on to yield results that are worth having. A purpose is necessary. You should know what ends you want to accomplish for the child. You should have a plan of procedure and be willing to examine the results with an open mind. If the plan doesn't work, don't blame the child. Try to find the reason for its failure.

It would be foolish to attempt to lay down here a series of rules for the rearing of children. Foolish, because children differ so greatly that no one set of rules will hold for all. Foolish, too, because for most of the readers of this book the need for specific instructions on practical matters of everyday care and training has not yet appeared. Those things can wait until the baby is nearer at hand. But the intelligent college student will do some thinking about parenthood long before he becomes a parent. He will think of it when choosing a mate and in planning a home. Most young people of the present day discuss questions relating to children before marriage, and this is as it should be. The purpose of this chapter is not to lay down set rules of parental conduct or of child management but to point out some of the things that young people who look forward to marrying at some time may well keep in mind.

TRAINING FOR THE JOB

The youth who plans to become a civil engineer or the girl who looks forward to nursing takes it for granted that preliminary training is necessary. Their preparation will ordinarily follow at least three lines. There is the gaining of factual knowledge and the integration of this knowledge into rules, principles, and ideas relating to the specialized field. There is laboratory work in which practice is gained in some of the concrete features of the work to be done. And finally there is the student's own thinking about the work and his planning for it. He visualizes himself as already on the job, thinks how he would handle this task or that, how he would respond to emergencies, what new procedures he would institute. He talks with established members of his chosen profession when opportunity arises, listens to their ideas with active interest, decides whether these ideas seem good or poor. With other students at "bull sessions" he engages in hot arguments about questions of theory, technique, and specific problems relating to his field.

From the standpoint of social progress, no other occupation in which people can engage is so important as parenthood. Had all parents of the generation just past done their jobs thoroughly and well, we should not now be engaged in a world war that threatens the very foundations of civilization. Men would not be tortured in concentration camps; children would not go hungry in a world that can produce an ample supply for all. The Jew and the Negro would no longer be the victims of stereotyped attitudes but would be judged according to their own individual merits. Labor and capital would work together and no longer at cross purposes, the gangster cease to exist, and government be cleanly administered. Utopian? Yes, but a Utopia that could be brought much nearer realization in the next generation if concerted effort were made now. If preparation for parenthood were taken as seriously as preparation for earning one's living, if young people who expect to become parents would endeavor to fit themselves for the job by the same methods that have been found useful in preparing for their profession, much could be accomplished. It is true that not everything could actually be effected in the course of a single generation, and this for two reasons. First we have not enough information. We do not always know what is best to be done either generally or in the specific instance. Secondly, we are not starting far enough back. Training for parenthood begins with the birth of the parent. By the time the boy or girl reaches an age at which formal parental or preparental education begins, attitudes, habits, ways of thinking, and ways of doing that will play a highly important part in the life of the children that are to come have already been well established. But this is no excuse for not making a start with the present generation of youth.

So the best advice that can be given to the young man or woman who is looking forward to parenthood and wants to prepare himself for it is this: Prepare for parenthood as you would prepare for any other kind of job. Get information about children and their development. Get all the advance practice in child management that you can and supplement this with directed observation. This is your laboratory training. Think over what you see, talk it over with others, just as you do with your plans for earning a living. And because this job differs from all others in the extent to which the results mirror the character of the designer, the potential parent may well ask himself, Am I a suitable model for my child to follow, or would it be well to effect some changes in my own personality and habits before he appears upon the scene?

THE CHILD'S BASIC NEEDS

The first and most basic requirement of every child is a *feeling of security*. This feeling has its roots in the personal relations of the people around him. The love of the parents for himself and for each other should be to him as immutable facts as the rising of the sun or the character of the elements. He must not be taught that this feeling has to be earned or that it can be altered by changing conditions. Under no circumstances should he be told that "Mother won't love you if you do that." Never should he have reason to question the nature of the tie that unites his parents. Family love, harmonious family relationships, provide the foundation on which the child's personality is erected. If these stand firm, the first essential is fulfilled.

The second need of the child is *opportunity for unhampered development*. This is not to say that he must not know restraint, that he be allowed to run wild without design or guidance. It means that restriction upon his acts shall not be imposed erratically or without reason, that he be allowed to make his own mistakes as far as this is at all consistent with reasonable attention to his health and safety—and these limits are much broader than many nervous parents think. It means that he shall be allowed to learn for himself, not expected to satisfy himself with the tales of other's experiences, even though they may be those of his own parents. He must be allowed to experiment widely in order that he may choose wisely. It means that he shall not be hampered by a false idea of his own place in the social world through thoughtless exploitation, by being constantly encouraged to "show off" or by unwise indulgence. It means the encouragement of initiative and independence, learning to do for himself and fend for himself. It means freedom from the hampering effects of fear by learning to meet situations that he is capable of overcoming, to avoid issues not worth a struggle, and to admit defeat honestly and courageously.

The third need is a *feeling of success*. The little child explores the world about him and tries out his abilities with a degree of zest and enthusiasm that later on is all too often lost when his self-confidence has been dampened by repeated failure and discouragement. Nothing can compensate for a loss of belief in one's own capacities. Every child faces the world with confidence at the start; the parent must see to it that that attitude is retained.

As the child grows older *his primary attachments must shift to the members of his own generation*. This shift is often hard for parents to accept. They feel that they must bind him closer to themselves. Whatever happens in these cases is unfortunate. If the parents succeed, the normal course of the child's emotional development may be stunted and deformed. He may fail to make the proper adjustments to his own group, marriage may be delayed or prevented, or, if it takes place, the parental relationship may still take precedence over the marital relationship, with unhappiness and misunderstanding as the result. When the parental efforts to hold the child fail, the consequences may be almost as unfortunate. The child resents their attitude; the parents feel that he is ungrateful; and the end is bitterness and disappointment. Wise indeed is the advice said to have been given by the oracle consulted by an anxious mother who wanted to know by what means she could retain her child's love. The answer was, "If you would hold him, you must let him go."

"Happiness first, all else follows." This is the slogan of one of our leading institutions for feeble-minded children; it may well be adopted as the first rule of every family. Happiness is the birthright of every child. As long as the child is happy he is not likely to go wrong. If unhappy, he will not make much progress that is worth while.

A PRACTICAL GUIDE FOR THE REARING
OF CHILDREN

Marion F. Faegre and John E. Anderson, *Child Care and Training*, Sixth Edition, Revised (Minneapolis, University of Minnesota Press, 1943), pp. vi + 314.

This is a book for parents that you can recommend to your friends who have children and that many of you, even now, will be interested in reading. It provides a good deal of practical information on child development and presents in simple, non-technical language, advice on the care and training of children that is concrete enough to be practical without being dogmatic. It recognizes the fact that children differ and emphasizes the necessity of studying the individual child and adapting methods to suit his personality rather than adhering blindly to rules that are unlikely to fit all cases. It discusses the aims that parents should try to achieve and describes practical methods of dealing with everyday problems of child behavior. It includes information about the common ailments of children and suggestions for the care of children during illness. Regardless of whether or not you are interested in reading the book at this time, you will find it desirable to keep it in mind as something that you may find worth looking up in the future.

Chapter XXIX

INCREASING HAPPINESS AND EFFICIENCY
IN THE ADULT

*What two major criteria may be employed in judging
personality development?*

*Why is happiness important? What can be done to
advance one's chances for personal happiness?*

*What are some of the best ways for gaining popu-
larity?*

*What things are chiefly involved in genuine service
to others?*

*What are some of the most common errors of would-
be social reformers?*

*In what ways does the leader of a democracy differ
from the dictator of a totalitarian state?*

CHARACTERISTICS OF THE MATURE PERSONALITY

Webster defines maturation as "the process of bringing or of
coming to full development." If we think of "full development"
as the utmost that is ideally possible, we must admit at the start
that few achieve it. Nevertheless we can state, at least in general
terms, by what criteria we shall judge the level of personality
development that has been attained by any individual. *Complete
maturity of personality has been reached when the individual is
able to combine the maximal degree of personal happiness with
the utmost service to humanity that for him is possible.*

This definition at once rules out a number of human types that
are sometimes admired. It rules out the martyr-like person who
sacrifices his own development for the assumed good of some one
else. It rules out those whose success in the business or profes-

679

sional world has been won at the cost of trampling ruthlessly over their subordinates or rivals. It rules out those who are hampered by timidity or by laziness and those who substitute the unreal and ephemeral delights of narcotics for the true satisfaction that comes from honest work and healthy play. But it leaves place for persons of only moderate ability who make the most of their talents and find joy in doing so.

Some of you may perhaps wonder why so much emphasis has been placed on personal happiness as a criterion of healthy maturity. It is difficult for many to escape the Puritan idea that joy, if not indeed to be looked upon with suspicion, is at least a thing of little consequence in comparison with the stern demands of duty. No idea could be more mistaken. Duty is important, surely, but just as surely there is something wrong with the individual who sees in it nothing but drudgery. Such a person is still in the childish stage where some idea of external compulsion rather than a true appreciation of the goal for which he is working is holding him in line. Perhaps he fears the ridicule and scorn of other people. Perhaps he is afraid of losing his job. Or perhaps it is sheer inertia that causes him to keep on plugging away joylessly, without enough imagination to see a way out. But none of these sources of motivation are likely to cause him to attack a piece of work with the vigor and enthusiasm that come as a matter of course when the task is enjoyed. When desire and pleasure are lacking, efficiency is almost certain to be impaired. Not only is one's own effectiveness lowered but the effect of such a joyless attitude upon one's associates is as dispiriting as it is unpleasant, and so the circle widens.

The closeness of the tie between joy and accomplishment normally increases with advancing age. For the little child who is, as yet, relatively ignorant of the world and its demands, most pleasure is egocentric. But the older person finds that joy cannot reach its ultimate height unless it is shared, and few pleasures are so keen as that which comes from the awareness of an important task well done.

Failure to achieve a completely mature personality may then arise either from a lack of successful adjustment on the personal side which has to do with one's own happiness, or on the social side which is concerned with one's attitude toward the rest of the world. But no matter in which aspect the trouble may originate, the other will inevitably be affected, for the two are as intimately related as are the concave and the convex sides of a bow.

THE PERSONAL GOAL

Finding One's Niche in Life. A large share of the adult life of most people is spent at work. We have seen that people differ greatly in the kind of thing they are best fitted by temperament and ability to do well. A good many people are unhappy because they have drifted into the wrong kind of job. The earlier in life a young man or woman is able to make the right vocational choice, the better will be his chances for future happiness and success.

It is highly unfortunate that the American tradition has tended to glorify the advantages of the learned professions and the "white-collar" types of job to such an extent that the great majority of young people hesitate to aspire openly to anything else. When questioned about their vocational plans, the number of high-school boys and girls who state that they expect to enter one or another of these fields is vastly in excess of the number of possible openings. A good deal of future disappointment could be avoided if those who are unlikely to be able to carry out such ambitions could be induced to shift their aspirations to a more realistic level.

Learning Social Skills. How many unpopular people there are in the world! How many wallflowers at every party! One of the major causes of unhappiness is the inability of many people to win friendship, to find a place for themselves in the social world which they long to enter but which seems ringed about by invisible barriers that they are unable to penetrate, however hard they try.

This lack of social skill not only means lessened happiness for the person himself but also cuts him off from some of the most important avenues of service to others. Elsewhere we have indicated a number of principles that are useful in improving human relationships. Here we shall merely enumerate a few aids to social intercourse that any one who cares enough about the matter to make the necessary effort can master.

1. Learn to play. The person who can make a competent fourth at bridge, who can dance, swim, skate, play golf or tennis, who can build a campfire and cook a steak, drive a car or ride a horse will find himself in social demand on many occasions when another of equally pleasing personality but who lacks the special skill that is in demand at the moment will be left out.

2. Keep in touch with current affairs and especially with those topics that are of particular interest to the people whom you would like to have as friends. Do not get the mistaken idea that there is something sycophantic or charlatan-like in acquiring information along lines in which you have no strong personal interest, merely for its social value. One of the most charming women I know happens not to be particularly fond of reading but enjoys the companionship of a group of people who read a great deal. This woman subscribes to one of the leading literary reviews which she reads regularly. Then when the conversation turns to books, instead of having to remain silent she can say, "No, I haven't read that, but I did read a review by So-and-so who says that . . .," and so on. Needless to say, this woman never misrepresents the facts. She does not pretend to have read the book, but her account of the review often serves the social purpose for which it was designed better than would her less expert account of her own direct impressions.

3. Be a good listener. People who are socially not quite at their ease often try to cover up their embarrassment by talking too much. Remember that the best host is not always the one who openly dominates the conversation but rather the one who is most successful in getting his guests to talk.

4. Overcome shyness by keeping your attention firmly fixed upon what is going on rather than upon yourself. Shyness and self-consciousness are almost synonymous. Don't let your thoughts wander back to yourself but give all your attention to other people.

5. Don't talk about yourself or try to force the conversation in the direction of your own interests. Find out what other people are interested in and talk about that. However, the rule does not apply to their purely professional interests, and this for two reasons. Most professional people do not enjoy talking shop during their hours of recreation, and few if any laymen are equipped to

carry on a conversation of this kind at a level that will be any-thing but an ummitigated bore to the professional man. One might add that when the layman attempts such a conversation with, let us say, a doctor or a lawyer the latter may suspect an ulterior motive, that is, that an attempt is being made to secure professional advice or information free of charge. Better to talk about the other person's hobbies, his favorite recreations and personal inter-ests. Lead him to talk about himself. Most people are only too ready to do so!

6. Have a reserve supply of good stories and jokes but don't insist upon telling them. Encourage other people to tell theirs but be ready to fill in awkward silences. Don't forget to laugh at other people's stories, even if you have heard them before.

Developing a backlog of interests and hobbies. No matter how many friends you have, there will be times when you are thrown on your own resources for enjoyment. Just as there are people who suffer from having too few friends, so there are others who are bored and unhappy whenever they are left alone. Every one, in addition to the things he enjoys doing in company, should develop additional interests and skills that will give him pleasure when he is alone. Reading is the great stand-by of many people. Some enjoy music; others painting or one of the various handi-crafts such as wood-carving, metal work, or cabinet-making. Others collect coins, stamps, or newspaper clippings on certain specified topics; still others try their hand at amateur photog-raphy. Like other personal pleasures it will be found that hob-bies of this kind have a social value as well.

Developing the kind of attitudes and mental habits that make for happiness. Not easy, you say? True, but here are a few rules that will help.

1. Learn to center your attention upon the present and the future, rather than the past. Worry over past mistakes is always useless. Plan how to avoid similar errors in the future, but don't cry over spilt milk.

2. Learn to accept inevitable facts. This includes things that have already happened and so cannot be changed. If you have made a mistake, admit it frankly, remembering that everybody does so at times and that it is chiefly by our mistakes that we learn. When conditions exist that are beyond your power to

modify, don't waste time in dreaming about a Utopia that cannot be yours or in futile complaining or resentment about things as they are. Try to adjust your life in such a way that the unpleasant conditions will interfere with it as little as possible. Fill your mind with other things.

3. Maintain a bulwark of personal pride, or if you prefer, call it self-respect. Such an attitude is not to be confused with egotism, which is bland self-admiration with little regard to the facts. Self-respect sets certain standards of conduct and achievement to which one must hold and that provide a strong anchor to leeward when things go wrong. True, personal pride can be carried to ridiculous extremes, and all of us need to check up on ourselves at times to make sure that we are not confusing pride in character with pride in reputation. But no one can be truly happy who lacks a reasonable measure of self-esteem, who is unable to say to himself with a feeling of justifiable pride, "This I have accomplished. To these standards I have held. This code I can claim as my own."

THE SOCIAL GOAL

Personal happiness is not the sole aim in life. It is true that the person who is happy in his own life is, with few exceptions, a useful and effective member of the community. Just being with a happy, jolly person is a heartening experience from which we are likely to come away in a frame of mind that enables us to attack our daily tasks with a feeling of freshness and energy. However, there are some points not covered in the preceding discussion that may be mentioned here. The fully developed personality, let us recall, is exemplified in that person who combines personal happiness with the highest level of service to humanity of which he is capable.

This does not mean just doing good to people in the limited sense that most people think of it. It does not mean merely feeding the hungry and clothing the naked, commendable as these acts are. It means something broader and bigger than this. It means so playing one's part in the world of affairs that humanity will not merely be made more comfortable at its present level of development but will be better able to raise itself to a higher level and will be stimulated to make the effort. Though the amount that any one person can accomplish toward this end is infinitesimal, the joint efforts of many can accomplish a great deal.

The task before us thus involves the stimulation of other people and the guidance of their activity into suitable channels. To accomplish this it is necessary, first of all, to form the habit of looking for their strong points and of disregarding their weaknesses beyond the point of helping them to avoid situations that would tend to magnify such faults. Remembering the importance of pride for the mental health of every one, we shall find that one of the most directly effective ways of influencing the behavior of others is by helping them to achieve a feeling of personal worth,[1] of confidence in their own ability to do something worth while. Obviously this can be best accomplished if the feeling has a solid basis in fact. A little judicious flattery by way of encouragement at the start and plenty of praise for work well done will go a long way toward stimulating others to aid in the common effort as well as increasing their satisfaction and happiness. Your contribution to the social goal cannot be fulfilled in isolation. Encouraging and helping others to do their share is an essential part of it.

Here, as elsewhere, individual differences and personal idiosyncracies must be recognized. One of the most common faults of the zealous social reformer is the tendency to want to remake every one in his own image. This is particularly the case with respect to attitudes on social or personal questions. Such a person may be quite willing to accept the fact that A likes carpentering, while B would rather be a travelling salesman, but he is disturbed to learn that A prefers jazz to symphony concerts and that B bought his wife a fur coat for Christmas instead of the washing machine that, in the social worker's opinion, she really needed. In theory he believes in religious and political freedom but he condemns Mrs. Brown for entertaining a few friends at bridge on Sunday afternoon, although he would have seen no harm in having the same people in for an afternoon of gossip. He is suspicious of the man who votes the Socialist ticket.

In many small ways, the majority of people exhibit some uncon-

---

[1] See *The Psychology of Dealing with People: Appealing to the Want for a Feeling of Personal Worth* by Wendell White (New York, Macmillan Co., 1936), pp. xvi + 256.

scious desire to remodel the world in accordance with their own tastes. Mr. J. likes his steak well done. "I don't see how you can eat that raw meat" he tells his wife with an expression of disgust. Mrs. L. is particularly fond of green, and she cannot rest content until she has persuaded her friend, Mrs. M., to purchase a green coat that the latter heartily dislikes.

Tolerance with the individual peculiarities of others, recognition of their right to hold their own opinions and to follow their own preferred way of life is, paradoxical as this may seem, an essential aspect of true leadership. It is just here that the sharp cleavage between the leader in a democratic society and the dictator in a totalitarian state is most clearly seen. The aim of the former is to help each person to the highest possible level of self-development. For him, the ideal society consists simply of a group of individuals, each of whom is working for the common good in the particular and individual way for which he is best suited. But the "common good" is merely the combined interests of the individuals concerned, and the function of the leader is not that of imposing uniformity but of creating harmony. The leader of a symphony orchestra does not attempt to make the cello sound like an oboe, nor does he demand that the tuba player sound the same note as the violinist. Without contrast there can be no melody.

One more point. We have stressed the importance of being ready to help others, but have said nothing about the equally important matter of willingness to be helped. Most people like to assume the dominant position. In the course of even the most well-meant efforts to do things for others it is easy to lose sight of the fact that these persons may likewise have something to offer you. The mature person accepts as readily as he gives and is as ready to take suggestions as to make them. The real test of leadership is not so much the ability to command as the ability to develop qualities of leadership in others.

MAKING THE MOST OF LIFE

Fred McKinney, *Psychology of Personal Adjustment: Student's Introduction to Mental Hygiene* (New York, John Wiley and Sons, 1941), pp. xii + 636.

Although this book was written primarily for the college student, it should be equally valuable for adults of all ages who are interested—as who is not?—in building a rich and happy life. The topics covered are many and varied. Not every one will wish to read all of the chapters, but most persons will find some portions of the book that deal directly with the questions in which he is interested.

The fifteen chapters deal with such practical subjects as study techniques, concentration, learning and thinking, establishing efficient habits with reference to time, money, and health, vocational planning and vocational choice, making and keeping friends, social conventions, sex attitudes and sex behavior, emotional problems, the establishment of self-confidence and the development of a mature personality.

Students will like the straightforward treatment of such questions as petting, chastity or its lack, masturbation, and similar problems that are of immediate concern to most young people but in many books receive but scant attention. The many short case histories that clarify and enliven the discussions throughout the book will also be found helpful.

Chapter XXX

A BACKWARD LOOK
WITH THOUGHTS FOR THE FUTURE

Under what circumstances would you say that a given individual has made a successful adjustment to his environment?

What factors play a part in determining whether or not a successful adjustment will be attained?

SCIENCE AND HUMAN WELFARE

Although science begins with observation and description, it is not satisfied merely with accounts of isolated phenomena as they chance to occur. It aims to coördinate its observations in such a way that from the occurrence of an event or series of events we can make valid inferences about what happened before and what is likely to happen afterward. The astronomer predicts when an eclipse of the sun will occur and on what part of the earth the shadow will fall. The engineer predicts that a certain bar of steel will break under a given strain. With less certainty the physician predicts the course of disease, prophesying how long it will take for a sickness to reach its crisis and what are the chances for recovery. He also predicts that, if certain things are done, the likelihood of recovery will be increased.

Nowhere is the question of prediction more vitally important than in the field of human behavior. We live in a world of human institutions, of human industry, of human relationships. Science has taught us to harness the forces of nature to the demands of human comfort and convenience. It has given us railroads, telephones, automobiles, electric refrigerators. It captures a ray from distant Arcturus to light the lamps at the Century of Progress Exposition; it enables the lonely Iowa farmer, by the twirling of a dial, to listen to a concert by a Boston orchestra, an address by a statesman in London, or jazz from a New York cabaret. From birth to death there is hardly a moment of our lives in which we are not making use of some product of industrial science and art. In physics, in chemistry, in engineering, in medicine, and the biological sciences tremendous progress has been made. But our knowledge of human nature has lagged far behind our knowledge of inanimate nature. The engineer who can turn rivers from their courses, who can transform the energy of the waterfall into light for a city hundreds of miles away is baffled by a child's temper-tantrum. The mathematician who attacks the most difficult prob-lems of the calculus without hesitation may be so unable to solve the riddles of his own personality that he has to be placed in a hospital for mental disease. Nations can—and do—destroy each other, largely because they do not understand each other. If our progress in the mechanical arts is to yield us its full benefit, we must develop a science of human engineering that will keep pace with it.

One reason why progress in the study of human behavior has been slower than progress in the physical sciences is the fact that crucial experiments are in so many cases forbidden to us. We cannot take a baby and operate on various parts of his brain to find out what will be the effect upon his behavior; we cannot deliberately take a group of boys from good families and put them to live in a delinquency area, while we remove another group of the same age from the delinquency area and place them in the homes from which our first group came. Even when experiments are likely to be beneficial, the difficulties do not dis-appear. We cannot, at will, take children out of the environment in which they have been reared and place them in foster homes whenever we have reason to think that the change would be to their advantage.

The chemist is free to try practically any experiment that seems desirable to him. He can vary his conditions at will. He can be sure that in the intervals between trials his chemicals are safely housed in their own bottles and jars on his laboratory shelves where nothing can happen to them. But the psychologist with human beings for his chemicals is in a very different position. Not only are many of the experiments that would add most to his knowledge completely out of the question, but he is forced to work with materials of whose individual idiosyncrasies he knows but little, whose nature is constantly changing with the passage of time, and which are being subjected to all sorts of unknown conditions during the hours when they are not with him. When we consider the complexity of the problems he is trying to solve and his very limited facilities for solving them, the wonder is not that the psychologist has made so little progress but rather that he has succeeded in finding out as much as he has.

But although we may not make certain experiments ourselves, chance and social conditions are constantly making them for us. We cannot place our subjects in any kind of environment we choose in order to see what happens, but social conditions may do this for us. We would not purposely induce sickness or accident in order to study their effects upon behavior, but sickness and accidents occur, whether we wish it or not, and as they occur we can study their psychological effects. We cannot make the same kind of breeding experiments with human beings that are made with animals, but we can study the outcome of such matings as naturally occur. The scientific progress that is made under these rather haphazard conditions is much slower than it would be if we could take matters into our own hands not only because we have to waste so much time in waiting but also because we do not know in advance when the requisite accidental conditions will occur nor whom they will affect. From lack of such advance information we are often unable to begin the study of our subjects early enough, and so, although we may find out what they are like afterward, we do not know what they may have been like before the special conditions were operative. We are in much the same position as the chemist would be if another person with little chemical training were to carry out his experiments for him in such a way that, although the chemist himself could study the outcome of the experiments at his leisure, he could find out very little about what chemicals were originally used or exactly how they had been combined.

Minor experiments, to be sure, can be carried out in the laboratory under fairly well-controlled conditions. Animal experiments, where more liberty is permitted the investigator, have taught us much about the characteristics of the higher animal we call man.

But if we wish to understand human nature from its beginnings, if we are interested in knowing not merely how people act but why they act as they do, if, in a word, we hope to make psychology contribute to human welfare and individual happiness to an extent that is comparable with other sciences, then we must cease to content ourselves with little studies of isolated bits of behavior and turn to the major problems of differential development under varying conditions over long periods of time. A single swallow does not make a summer, and a single event does not determine whether a given child will develop into a genius or a criminal or a hobo. Intelligent control of human behavior is impossible without knowing what results are likely to follow when a particular kind of organism is subjected to a given set of conditions and how lasting these results are likely to be. To answer this question we must begin early and continue long.

In our study thus far we have tried to give a simple and nontechnical account of some of the major principles of human development as they are shown under modern conditions of civilized life. In order to do this we have begun with the infant and followed his development through its rapid ascent to maturity and its slow decline to old age and death. We have seen how his behavior changes with the years and with the changing circumstances that come with the passage of time. We have noted some of the many ways in which people differ from each other and have pointed out some of the circumstances that give rise to such differences. Throughout, we have emphasized the personal and social aspects of human life and behavior rather than the sensory and perceptual reactions with which the psychologists of an earlier day were so largely concerned. We have followed this plan in the belief that the beginner will be able to see a closer and more vital relationship between these forms of behavior and the experiences of his own everyday life than he would be able to find in the more precise and carefully controlled studies of sensory perception, speed of motor reaction, and similar problems that may engage the attention of the advanced student.

Even so, we have covered a good deal of ground in a short time. Our babies have grown so fast and changed so rapidly that we may well be pardoned if we feel a little confused and uncertain about how it all happened. Now that we have come to the end of the journey it is worth while for us to spend a little time in reconstructiing the main events of the trip. One of the things that has particularly impressed us all along is the fact that our babies, who seemed so much alike at first, have grown increasingly different with the passage of time. Some have turned out to be geniuses; others have become honest and contented laborers; some have become criminals and others hoboes. Some have continued to lead useful and busy lives to the time of their death; others have broken under the strain and ended their lives in hospitals for the mentally diseased. Now that we have watched these differences as they develop, let us see if by organizing our observations we can get a clearer idea of the way in which the same principles of development and learning can yield such widely differing results.

ORGANIC LIMITATIONS TO INDIVIDUAL VARIATION

First of all, we have seen that there are certain developmental tendencies that are common to all organisms of a given class. The human being, as it develops from the fertilized human ovum, grows to have arms, legs, and other physical features that are different from those of a dog or a cat. We do not know what these developmental tendencies are. We can only describe them in terms of their results; we can only say that it is the nature of particular organisms to develop in particular ways under ordinary environmental conditions. In like manner each organism, as it develops, tends to function in particular ways, and again we cannot say why, except that it is its nature to do so.

But these tendencies that characterize the organism, the tendencies that cause men to differ from rats, and rats to differ from robins, are not exactly the same for all members of a given class. Men are not all alike; neither are all rats or all robins the same. Human beings are first of all subdivided into different races—the Negro race, the Mongolian races, the Caucasian race. The members of these races are not alike physically, and they probably differ to some extent in their mental characteristics as well. The sexes also differ from each other in a number of ways both in man and animal. And finally there are further differences, also inherent in the nature of the organism, that are the result of immediate heredity, of differences in the genes received from the parents.

None of these tendencies is absolute. Each has its own range of possible variation. Sometimes, as in the case of eye color, the range is small. The native tendencies handed down in the genes work out in about the same way under all ordinary circumstances. Sometimes the limits of variation for the individual are large, approaching the limits found for the class. Weight is an example. People inherit a tendency to be fat or thin, just as they inherit a tendency to have blue eyes or brown eyes. But weight is not so closely limited by heredity as eye-color. A person with a tendency to be overweight can do something about it by dieting, and a proper diet will likewise help to increase the weight of the person who is by nature inclined to be thin. Heredity, the original nature of the organism, fixes certain limits beyond which variation is unlikely to occur. But few characteristics are absolutely fixed by heredity. Practically all admit of some variation.

We may look at the matter in another way. The manner in which a given organism is most likely to develop depends not only upon his inherited tendencies but also upon the likelihood that the particular conditions which would give rise to variation will actually occur under ordinary conditions of life. Experimental embryology has shown that by tampering with the organism at a very early stage of development it is possible to produce monsters of many kinds. For example, by artificially changing the position of certain primitive cells it is possible to cause an animal that normally has two eyes to develop into a Cyclops with only a single eye in the middle of its forehead. Now if the particular conditions that cause the organism to develop in that manner were of common occurrence we should have many one-eyed animals. We should regard it as no more remarkable that some animals of a given species should have one eye and others two than that some human beings have blue eyes and others brown. The reason we do not often meet with this condition is not because the organism is incapable of that form of growth, but because the circumstances which would cause it to grow in that manner rarely occur.

From the very moment of conception, therefore, no two organisms are exactly alike, and as they grow they are subjected to varying conditions which further increase the differences between them. But before birth the external conditions by which development is affected are usually much more nearly the same for all organisms than those which occur after birth, and as a result newborn babies look and act much more nearly alike than do grown men.

THE LIMITS OF VARIATION IN BEHAVIOR

The behavior of the human being at any stage of his growth is also limited both by the nature of the organism and by the presence or absence of factors that modify behavior. We have no way of knowing how great might be the changes in behavior that would be produced by modifying the environment in ways that have not yet been tried, but we do have a general knowledge of the extent of the individual differences that occur under the conditions of life with which we are familiar. Some children grow faster than others but the differences in rate of growth fall within certain limits. This is as true of mental growth as it is of physical growth. A child of three may have the mental development of the average child of four or five, but there is no case on record of a three-year-old whose general mental level was equal to that of the average eight-year-old. The same is true of other aspects of behavior. There is variation from one individual to another, but only within limits.

In the case of physical structure we know that extreme changes can only be produced early, before the transformation of primitive cells into specialized tissue has progressed very far. Some people have taken the same view with respect to behavior. According to them the personality of an individual is "set" very early in life—the exact age has been put at anywhere from two to seven years—after which no further changes of importance take place. Although there is reason to think that the early years are the most important for modifying certain aspects of behavior, more recent investigations, such as those described in Chapter XXIII, indicate that maturity rather than childhood is the optimum time for learning many kinds of things. It is probably true that reactions of certain kinds, such as the tendency to yield to a difficulty, to overcome it or to run away from it, as well as many of our attitudes toward people, are formed very early in life. In the course of time through continued practice they become so greatly overlearned that the habits thus formed are hard to break. Perhaps adults would always learn more easily than children if they could start at the same point, if, in other words, they were not handicapped in learning new habits by having previously learned others that interfere with the formation of the new. If children had no more opportunity to learn habits of reacting to other people than the average child has of learning Esperanto, we might find that, even in regard to social attitudes and behavior, adults learn more easily than children. The same is true of emotional responses. The popular idea that the child is more plastic than the adult may have sprung chiefly from the fact that habits formed in childhood have a longer time ahead of them during which they may be practised. If we define the age of greatest plasticity as the time when new habits can be formed most readily and those that have already received a stated amount of practice (an amount which is made equal for all subjects regardless of their age) can be most easily broken up, the work of Thorndike, Miles, Jones, and others suggests that the end of adolescence or the beginning of maturity may be the time when real plasticity reaches its peak and that the apparently greater modifiability of the young child is only an artifact resulting from the fact that habits learned in childhood are practised for a longer time. Another factor that makes it harder for adults to learn new habits of social and emotional reactions is the fact that they have learned to find satisfaction through their old habits. To set up new devices for gaining these satisfactions, even though the new ones may be better than the old, usually means some delay and consequent annoyance in the beginning, and so many people are loath to make a start.

THE PROCESS OF LEARNING

But even though learning may be easier at certain ages than at others, there is no age at which learning does not occur. Learning begins in infancy; it continues until death. At different ages, as we have seen, the particular devices employed for learning vary somewhat, but the fundamental principles remain the same. In any act of learning we may distinguish four stages as follows: (a) a primary condition which at that time is the normal state for the organism when at rest, (b) a disturbance of this condition which may arise either from the perception of some factor outside the organism or from a physiological change resulting from its own life processes, (c) a state of activity during which the organism continually shifts its relationship to its environment until satisfaction is attained and the disturbance disappears and (d) a return, not to the original state but to a secondary condition which differs somewhat from the first as a result of the experience which has just been undergone. This secondary state now becomes the normal resting condition for the organism, and the primary state for the next act of learning. The measure of learning is the difference between the two conditions.

THE MECHANISM OF ADJUSTMENT

As Cannon has shown,[1] within the body of each individual, there are certain mechanisms for maintaining it in a constant or normal state. The internal temperature of the body varies but slightly in health, no matter what the surrounding temperature of the air may be. If anything happens to change the temperature, as in fever, the disturbance itself at once releases the trigger that sets the restorative mechanisms to work, and the bodily activities thus aroused continue until the normal condition is restored or until death intervenes. Respiration, heart rate, waste and repair of bodily tissues all obey the general rule that bodily functions must adapt themselves to the maintenance of a constant bodily condition. To this condition of the organism, in which a fixed state is maintained by means of a series of self-regulating mechanisms, Cannon gives the name of *homeostasis*.

The process of learning may be described as progress toward a special kind of homeostasis wherein the final state which the organism seeks to maintain is one of personal satisfaction. In the beginning only a few of the infant's responses lead directly to this goal. Certain of his internal bodily mechanisms, those most necessary to maintain life, have arrived at a fair degree of self-regulation previous to birth. But for most of his responses to external conditions, the self-regulation has to be acquired. Moreover, the activi-

[1] W. B. Cannon, *The Wisdom of the Body* (New York, Norton, 1932), pp. 312.

ties by which satisfaction is maintained have to be much more adjustable than those by which the physiological workings of the body are kept constant, because the conditions outside the body to which the organism has to adjust are so varied that a single method of meeting an emergency would not be enough.

The mechanism by which the organism learns to adapt its responses to these varying conditions works out somewhat as follows: First of all, something happens to disturb its placidity. This disturbance may originate within the organism, or it may come from without, that is to say, it may begin either with the interoceptors or the exteroceptors (see p. 120). Hunger is an example of the first type; a loud sound that causes one to start and catch the breath is an example of the second. At a less primitive level we have such conditions as anxiety over a coming examination for which one has not made adequate preparation or the sight of a theater sign that makes us want to see the show. We must not get the idea that the disturbance is always or even usually a profoundly uncomfortable one. Much more often it consists in the awakening of a desire, a feeling that however comfortable we may be at present, we should be more comfortable or more satisfied if we could get something we do not have or do something we are not doing or institute some other kind of change in our present condition. The organic disturbance is therefore anything that induces a change in the individual's activity. In an earlier chapter we gave it the name of *motive*.

At first the only motives that are capable of disturbing the baby's psychological equilibrium are simple physiological factors such as hunger, thirst, pain, and fatigue, and possibly very strong and sudden stimulation of the external sense-organs. For none of these conditions has a perfect self-regulating mechanism by which satisfaction can be obtained without the intervention of outside aid been established before birth. There is nothing comparable to the mechanism by which the infant replenishes his bodily supply of oxygen through breathing and distributes the supply through the action of the heart and arteries to the parts of the body where it is needed. Since this is the case, the hunger disturbance leads at first to formless, rather than patterned, activity. One after another the infant tries out about all the responses in his repertoire. He kicks, tosses about as much as he is able, waves his arms, cries, frets. Sooner or later he is given food and satisfaction arrives. But as a result of all this formless activity, leading eventually to satisfaction, certain changes have taken place in the infant himself. The next time a disturbance of the same or similar nature occurs, his behavior will not be quite so formless. He will be a little more likely to repeat certain of his former actions and to omit others. These acts and the objects or persons around him at the time are becoming bound up with the disturbance, on the one hand, and the return to a state of satisfaction, on the other. They are becoming means to an end. In the language of E. C. Tolman [2] they are becoming "sign-gestalts"; in more everyday terminology we say that they have ceased to be matters of indifference to the individual but have taken on a particular meaning with reference to a particular need. So the individual who has learned something is no longer quite the same as he was before the learning. He has gained a new readiness to perform certain acts when certain conditions arise, and he has acquired a new kind of responsiveness to certain things in his environment. As learning proceeds his activities become increasingly selective. More and more of the useless activity disappears. Moreover, in the course of time the persons, objects, and devices by which satisfaction was attained come to be identified with the return to satisfaction. They are regarded as signs that satisfaction is on the way. In time this identification becomes so complete that just the sight of these signs is enough to arouse a condition of striving. That which once satisfied a disturbed condition of the organism, which helped to allay activity, now becomes in its turn capable of arousing a new activity. The child that was lying contentedly in its crib suddenly begins to fret and coax and may even burst into tears at the sight of its mother a few feet away. The man who is in no particular need of food sees a particularly attractive dish and at once is aware of a craving for it. Through the satisfaction of organic states by means of specific actions, by the utilization of specific objects and the aid of other human beings, these actions, objects, and persons lose their impersonal character. They become goals to be striven for or things to be avoided. They are means to an end or obstacles that lie in the

[2] *Purposive Behavior in Animals and Men* (New York, D. Appleton-Century Co., 1932).

way of it. They are sign-boards that warn of danger or point the way to satisfaction.

"Sign-boards" is perhaps not the best term to use here, because it may give the impression that something new has been created and put there for the express purpose of pointing out the road. The signs with which we are dealing here are the informal kind; things that the individual chances to notice, just as you learn to find your way along an unmarked road by noting such accidental features as trees, houses, rocks, and so on. Two people may learn the same road in this incidental fashion by employing very different cues. Sometimes the two systems are equally good, sometimes one or both may be badly chosen. The cues may be impermanent, serving for a brief time but soon disappearing and so leaving the individual with nothing to guide him in the future. They may be shifting, sometimes pointing to the right way, sometimes to the wrong way. And finally the whole system may be of such a nature that immediate satisfaction is attained only at the cost of lasting damage to the whole organism. In physiology we see such a mechanism at work when a genuine bodily need is given a spurious satisfaction by means of drugs. In psychology we find that there are many people who have learned to secure a temporary and dangerous satisfaction through such mechanisms as day-dreaming, running away from difficulties that should be faced, occupying themselves with trivial things as an excuse for not attacking the big ones, or by trying to place the blame for their own failure upon other persons or upon circumstances proclaimed to be beyond their control.

These undesirable patterns of response are learned in exactly the same way as the more desirable ones that lead to real accomplishment and lasting satisfaction. Both have their starting point in something that disturbs the placidity of the organism and throws it into a state of activity that persists until some kind of solution is worked out. In both cases, the progress of learning is marked by a tendency to repeat the actions by which satisfaction was attained; in both cases the external means, the particular devices by which the goal was reached take on the character of signals, of intermediate goals that mark out the pattern to be followed. Although the final goal is satisfaction, this satisfaction may be either genuine or spurious. The particular mechanism employed may be a restorative or only a palliative which allays the disturbance for a time during which serious trouble may develop.

The differences between the normal and the abnormal, the delinquent and the well behaved, the successful and the unsuccessful are in the final analysis ascribable to the particular techniques by which each has learned to find satisfaction. The learning is not equally easy for all individuals. Some are by nature endowed with so limited a range of possible responses that their chances of achieving genuine satisfaction are small unless the demands that are made upon them are simple. For such persons a happy and satisfying life depends upon their being reared in an environment where the goals that are set for them can be attained by means of simple, uncomplicated responses. Others with a larger repertoire of behavior possibilities make use of more complicated mechanisms to achieve their results. But a more complex device is not of necessity a better one. No matter whether the behavior pattern that is finally adopted is simple or elaborate, if mental health is to be preserved and if life is to acquire its full meaning for each individual, the behavior must satisfy the particular organic need in a way that contributes to the effective working of the organism as an enduring whole.

YOU AND PSYCHOLOGY

Most people, when reading, tend to identify themselves with the hero of the book. The book you have just finished has no hero, but if you have read it thoughtfully you have undoubtedly asked yourself from time to time, Have I ever had an experience like this? Do I or any of my friends behave in this way? How closely has my own life conformed to the developmental patterns described here?

You should therefore find it both interesting and informative to complete this first excursion into the realm of developmental psychology by attempting to make a psychological analysis of your own personality as it is to-day. Of course, the ideal way of doing this would be through the study of actual records set down at the time the events in question occurred. Memory is at best a tricky guide. But if, as is true of most people, no record of your own early history was kept, your best substitute will be to begin with the present and work backward.

Your question then is, What am I like now and by what processes did I become so? In answering you will find it wise to begin with an outline of the main points to be covered, with subheadings indicating the kind of information that is desired under each category. On p. 702 you will find a few brief suggestions which may be used as a guide, but you will wish to supplement them with other matters that may be of much greater consequence for you as an individual. People differ so greatly that no single plan for writing a character sketch or a life history can be drawn up that will serve equally well for all. Your aim should be to select the most significant features in your personality and present them in such a way as to make a vivid and truthful picture. Remember that in a psychological study, more interest is attached to the subject's inner life than to such external factors as size or physical beauty. The latter are of psychological interest only in so far as they have had an effect upon one's behavior or attitudes. To be sure there are cases like that of the little girl described in Chapter XVI, in which matters such as these account for many aspects of behavior. Self-consciousness arising from a physical blemish may rank high among the determiners of social withdrawal. But for the majority of people, abilities, interests and experiences count for more than physique.

In every personality there are certain salient features which lend form and pattern to the whole. Even in the young infant some characteristics appear to dominate over others to such an extent that observers are likely to note them. Nevertheless, the personality of the infant is by comparison lacking in perspective. Its values are not clear-cut; there is no sure distinction between foreground and background. But as age advances, the personality becomes increasingly three-dimensional. Some features emerge into the foreground; others recede into the background. It is mainly for this reason that a mere analysis of the position of the individual on each of a series of separate traits is usually so unsatisfactory. For it is not merely his individual traits but the relation of each trait to all the rest within a three-dimensional universe [3] that makes every personality unique.

The following questions suggest some of the things to be considered in your analysis. The points mentioned will not be equally important for every one. In some cases, certain of the items may be of such slight consequences that they may be completely omitted. Practically every one will need to add others.

The account should begin with a personality sketch of yourself as you are to-day. After stating such things as your age and sex, natio-racial background, birthplace and any other general facts that seem

[3] Properly speaking the universe is not three-dimensional but multidimensional, since to be accurate one would have to take into account not merely the interrelations of the most typical characteristics of the individual but the changes in these relationships as they affect and are affected by other persons. When in the company of *AB*, Miss *X* may be so overcome by shyness and timidity that these traits temporarily overshadow all other features of her personality, although with other people shyness would not be regarded as one of her outstanding traits.

important in your case, give as frank and straightforward a picture of yourself as you can. Try to look at yourself in as objective a manner as if you were attempting to describe another person or an inanimate object. This is not easy. Probably no one will be able to achieve perfect objectivity, but if you really aim at frankness, avoiding as far as possible both the open egotism that claims virtues which do not exist or denies faults really present, and the (poorly) concealed egotism that expresses itself in self-depreciation, you can go a long way toward the presentation of an unbiased portrait. The following questions indicate the kind of information that is likely to be significant.

What are the major goals for the attainment of which you are ready to subordinate all lesser aims? Are these goals clear in your mind? Are there other urges incompatible with your main desire that make for conflict? What are you doing to attain your goal or resolve your conflicts?

If you could follow any vocation you wish, what would be your choice? What are your actual vocational plans?

What do you think are your chief assets in the way of abilities (physical, intellectual, special talents or skills) habits, attitudes, family background and experiences?

What are your chief handicaps?

Have you many friends? Do you like to be alone much of the time or do you usually crave companionship?

What recreations do you enjoy most?

How do you commonly react to obstacles? to ridicule? to disappointment?

Do you usually feel at ease when you are with other people who have had more social experience or who know a great deal more than you do?

Are you happy most of the time or are you often dissatisfied or "blue"?

What kind of man or woman would you like to marry?

After you have given as clear a picture of yourself as you can, try to account for the major features of your personality by tracing the course of your life and its experiences. What persons or events were most influential in deciding your choice of a vocation, or if you have not yet decided on a career, what things have contributed to your state of indecision? How were your personality assets gained, and what conditions do you think were mainly responsible for your defects? How were your social attitudes established? In what way have these characteristics affected your choice of goals?

Be specific. Cite actual events wherever possible. Describe how you felt on these occasions. Show, as far as you can, how these events and the feelings and attitudes they engendered have set the pattern for later behavior.

Index of Names

703

Subject Index

(11)